T0212043

Lecture Notes of the Institute for Computer Sciences, Social Informatics and Telecommunications Engineering 391

More information about this series at http://www.springer.com/series/8197

Mian Ahmad Jan · Fazlullah Khan (Eds.)

Application of Big Data, Blockchain, and Internet of Things for Education Informatization

First EAI International Conference, BigIoT-EDU 2021
Virtual Event, August 1–3, 2021
Proceedings, Part I

 Springer

Editors
Mian Ahmad Jan ⓘD
Abdul Wali Khan University Mardan
Mardan, Pakistan

Fazlullah Khan ⓘD
Abdul Wali Khan University Mardan
Mardan, Pakistan

ISSN 1867-8211 ISSN 1867-822X (electronic)
Lecture Notes of the Institute for Computer Sciences, Social Informatics
and Telecommunications Engineering
ISBN 978-3-030-87899-3 ISBN 978-3-030-87900-6 (eBook)
https://doi.org/10.1007/978-3-030-87900-6

This Springer imprint is published by the registered company Springer Nature Switzerland AG
The registered company address is: Gewerbestrasse 11, 6330 Cham, Switzerland

Preface

We are delighted to introduce the proceedings of the first edition of the European Alliance for Innovation (EAI) International Conference on Application of BigData, Blockchain, and Internet of Things for Education Informatization (BigIoT-EDU 2021), which was held virtually during August 1–3, 2021. The conference aims to provide an international cooperation and exchange platform for big data and information education experts, scholars, and enterprise developers to share research results, discuss existing problems and challenges, and explore cutting-edge science and technology. The conference focuses on research fields such as "big data" and "information education". The use of artificial intelligence (AI), blockchain, and network security lies at the heart of this conference as we focused on these emerging technologies to excel the progress of big data and information education.

EAI BigIoT-EDU has three tracks: the main track, a late track, and a workshop track. In total, EAI BigIoT-EDU 2021 attracted 500+ submissions. Upon rigorous review, only 144 papers were accepted. The keynote speaker was Paul A. Watters from LaTrobe University, Australia. The workshop was organized on "Information Retrieval and Algorithms in the Era of Information and Communication Technologies" by Ryan Alturki from Umm Al-Qura University, Saudi Arabia. The workshop aimed to focus on advanced techniques and algorithms to retrieve useful information from ICT and connected technologies. Coordination with the steering chair, Imrich Chlamtac, was essential for the success of the conference. We sincerely appreciate his constant support and guidance. It was also a great pleasure to work with such an excellent organizing committee team for their hard work in organizing and supporting the conference. In particular, the Technical Program Committee (TCP), led by our TPC co-chairs, Yinjun Zhang, Yar Muhammad, and Muhammad Imran Khan, who completed the peer-review process for the technical papers and put together a high-quality technical program. We are also grateful to Conference Manager Natasha Onofrei for her constant support and to all the authors who submitted their papers to the EAI BigIoT-EDU 2021 conference, late track, and workshop.

We strongly believe that BigIoT-EDU provides a good forum for all researchers, developers, and practitioners to discuss all science and technology aspects that are relevant to big data and information education. We also expect that the future BigIoT-EDU conferences will be as successful and stimulating, as indicated by the contributions presented in this volume.

October 2021

Mian Ahmad Jan
Fazlullah Khan
Mengji Chen

Organization

Steering Committee

Imrich Chlamtac   University of Trento, Italy
Mian Ahmad Jan   Abdul Wali Khan University Mardan, Pakistan
Fazlullah Khan   Abdul Wali Khan University Mardan, Pakistan

Organizing Committee

General Chairs

Mian Ahmad Jan   Abdul Wali Khan University Mardan, Pakistan
Fazlullah Khan   Abdul Wali Khan University Mardan, Pakistan
Mengji Chen   Guangxi Science and Technology Normal University, China

Technical Program Committee Chair and Co-chairs

Lu Zhengjie   Hechi University, China
Yinjun Zhang   Hechi University, China
Yar Muhammad   Abdul Wali Khan University Mardan, Pakistan

Sponsorship and Exhibit Chairs

Lan Zimian   Harbin Institute of Technology, China
Zhang Mianlin   Guangxi University, China

Local Chairs

Huang Yufei   Hechi Normal University, China
Wan Haoran   Shanghai University, China

Workshops Chair

Abid Yahya   Botswana International University of Science and Technology, Botswana

Publicity and Social Media Chairs

Wang Bo	Guangxi Science and Technology Normal University, China
Aamir Akbar	Abdul Wali Khan University Mardan, Pakistan

Publications Chairs

Fazlullah Khan	Abdul Wali Khan University Mardan, Pakistan
Mian Ahmad Jan	Abdul Wali Khan University Mardan, Pakistan

Web Chair

Shah Nazir	University of Swabi, Pakistan

Posters and PhD Track Chairs

Mengji Chen	Guangxi Science and Technology Normal University, China
Ateeq ur Rehman	University of Haripur, Pakistan

Panels Chairs

Kong Linxiang	Hefei University of Technology, China
Muhammad Usman	Federation University, Australia

Demos Chairs

Ryan Alturki	Umm Al-Qura University, Saudi Arabia
Muhammad Imran	Abdul Wali Khan University Mardan, Pakistan

Tutorials Chair

Wei Rongchang	Guangxi Science and Technology Normal University, China

Session Chairs

Ryan Alturki	Umm Al-Qura University, Saudi Arabia
Aamir Akbar	Abdul Wali Khan University Mardan, Pakistan
Mengji Chen	Hechi University, China
Vinh Troung Hoang	Ho Chi Minh City Open University, Vietnam
Muhammad Zakarya	Abdul Wali Khan University Mardan, Pakistan
Yu Uunshi	Shanxi Normal University, China

Ateeq ur Rehman	University of Haripur, Pakistan
Su Linna	Guangxi University, China
Shah Nazir	University of Swabi, Pakistan
Mohammad Dahman Alshehri	Taif University, Saudi Arabia
Chen Zhi	Shanghai University, China
Syed Roohullah Jan	Abdul Wali Khan University Mardan, Pakistan
Qin Shitian	Guangxi Normal University, China
Sara Kareem	Abdul Wali Khan University Mardan, Pakistan
Mohammad Wedyan	Al-Balqa Applied University, Jordan
Lin Hang	Beijing Forestry University, China
Arjumand Yar Khan	Abdul Wali Khan University Mardan, Pakistan
Liu Cheng	Wuxi Institute of Technology, China
Rahim Khan	Abdul Wali Khan University Mardan, Pakistan
Muhammad Tahir	Saudi Electronic University, Saudi Arabia
Tan Zhide	Anhui University, China

Technical Program Committee

Muhammad Usman	Federation University, Australia
Abid Yahya	Botswana International University of Science and Technology, Botswana
Noor Zaman Jhanjhi	Taylor's University, Malaysia
Muhammad Bilal	Hankuk University of Foreign Studies, South Korea
Muhammad Babar	Iqra University, Pakistan
Mamoun Alazab	Charles Darwin University, Australia
Tao Liao	Anhui University of Science and Technology, China
Ryan Alturki	Umm Al-Qura University, Saudi Arabia
Dinh-Thuan Do	Asia University, Taiwan
Huan Du	Shanghai University, China
Sahil Verma	Chandigarh University, India
Abusufyan Sher	Abdul Wali Khan University Mardan, Pakistan
Mohammad S. Khan	East Tennessee State University, USA
Ali Kashif Bashir	Manchester Metropolitan University, UK
Nadir Shah	COMSATS University Islamabad, Pakistan
Aamir Akbar	Abdul Wali Khan University Mardan, Pakistan
Vinh Troung Hoang	Ho Chi Minh City Open University, Vietnam
Shunxiang Zhang	Anhui University of Science and Technology, China
Guangli Zhu	Anhui University of Science and Technology, China
Kuien Liu	Pivotal Inc., USA

Kinan Sher	Abdul Wali Khan University Mardan, Pakistan
Feng Lu	Chinese Academy of Sciences, China
Ateeq ur Rehman	University of Haripur, Pakistan
Wei Xu	Renmin University of China, China
Ming Hu	Shanghai University, China
Abbas K. Zaidi	George Mason University, USA
Amine Chohra	Université Paris-Est Créteil, France
Davood Izadi	Deakin University, Australia
Sara Kareem	Abdul Wali Khan University Mardan, Pakistan
Xiaobo Yin	Anhui University of Science and Technology, China
Mohammad Dahman Alshehri	Taif University, Saudi Arabia
Filip Zavoral	Charles University in Prague, Czech Republic
Zhiguo Yan	Fudan University, China
Florin Pop	Politehnica University of Bucharest, Romania
Gustavo Rossi	Universidad Nacional de La Plata, Argentina
Habib Shah	Islamic University of Medina, Saudi Arabia
Hocine Cherifi	University of Burgundy, France
Yinjun Zhang	Guangxi Science and Technology Normal University, China
Irina Mocanu	University Politehnica of Bucharest, Romania
Jakub Yaghob	Charles University in Prague, Czech Republic
Ke Gong	Chongqing Jiaotong University, China
Roohullah Jan	Abdul Wali Khan University Mardan, Pakistan
Kun-Ming Yu	Chung Hua University, China
Laxmisha Rai	Shandong University of Science and Technology, China
Lena Wiese	University of Göttingen, Germany
Ma Xiuqin	Northwest Normal University, China
Oguz Kaynar	Sivas Republic University, Turkey
Qin Hongwu	Northwest Normal University, China
Pit Pichapan	Al-Imam Muhammad Ibn Saud Islamic University, Saudi Arabia
Prima Vitasari	National Institute of Technology, Indonesia
Simon Fong	University of Macau, China
Shah Rukh	Abdul Wali Khan University Mardan, Pakistan
Somjit Arch-int	Khon Kaen University, Thailand
Sud Sudirman	Liverpool John Moores University, UK
Tuncay Ercan	Yasar University, Turkey
Wang Bo	Hechi University, China
Ibrahim Kamel	University of Sharjah, UAE
Muhamamd Wedyan	Albalqa University, Jordan

Mohammed Elhoseny	American University in the Emirates, UAE
Muhammad Tahir	Saudi Electronic University, Saudi Arabia
Marwa Ibrahim	University of Technology Sydney, Australia
Amna Khan	Abdul Wali Khan University Mardan, Pakistan
Xiao Wei	Shanghai University, China
Zhiming Ding	Beijing University of Technology, China
Jianhui Li	Chinese Academy of Sciences, China
Yi Liu	Tsinghua University, China
Wuli Wang	SMC Guangxi Electric Power Company Limited, China
Duan Hu	Shanghai University, China
Sheng Li	Xinjiang University, China
Mahnoor Inam	Abdul Wali Khan University Mardan, Pakistan
Yuhong Chen	Inner Mongolia University of Technology, China
Mengji Chen	Guangxi Science and Technology Normal University, China
Jun Zhang	Hechi University, China
Ji Meng	Hechi University, China

Contents – Part I

Contents – Part II

Applications of Education Management and Informatization

Teaching and Evaluation of National Physical Education in Colleges and Universities Based on Data Mining Algorithm

Qing Li[✉]

Jiangxi Vocational Technical College of Industry and Trade, Jiangxi 330038, China
icelandjing@yeah.net

Abstract. Chinese national sports is one of the important ways to carry out physical education for college students. It has various forms, rich internal and external, strong cultural connotation and time value. At present, the curriculum of this major in Colleges and universities is basically martial arts, and other courses are only as elective courses. Coupled with the lack of teachers, the development of national traditional sports in Colleges and universities is not optimistic. Therefore, the teaching and evaluation of national sports in Colleges and Universities Based on data mining algorithm should strengthen the competitiveness, make national sports activities full of ornamental, select national sports items suitable for colleges and universities, and strengthen the construction of national sports talent team.

Keywords: Data mining algorithm · National sports · Physical education · Teaching evaluation

1 Introduction

Education quality is always the eternal theme of education and teaching research, and teaching effect is one of the most direct embodiment of teaching quality [1]. It is of great practical significance to build and improve the corresponding education quality evaluation system. Data mining is a professional technology that can automatically mine useful knowledge from a large number of data. It is a new field with great application value in database research. It integrates the theory and technology of database, artificial intelligence, machine learning, statistics and other fields. The data mining technology is introduced into the quality evaluation system of general education in Colleges for nationalities. This method can make a better quantitative analysis of the quality of general education in Colleges for nationalities. C4.5, K-means, SVM (support vector machine), apriori, EM (maximum expectation), PageRank, AdaBoost, KNN (k-nearest neighbor), Nb (naive Bayes) and cart (classification and regression tree) constitute the ten classic data mining algorithms. AdaBoost is a classical ensemble learning method, which has been successfully applied in other leading cities.

© ICST Institute for Computer Sciences, Social Informatics and Telecommunications Engineering 2021
Published by Springer Nature Switzerland AG 2021. All Rights Reserved
M. A. Jan and F. Khan (Eds.): BigIoT-EDU 2021, LNICST 391, pp. 3–8, 2021.
https://doi.org/10.1007/978-3-030-87900-6_1

2   The Present Situation and Problems of National Sports in Colleges and Universities

At present, there is still no complete system of national sports teaching materials published in the sports circle, and most of the teaching materials are martial arts. Although it is the backbone of this subject, the content of teaching materials for many years is mostly some boxing and some routines, which has little significance for the development of national sports. At present, the courses offered in Colleges and universities of this major are basically martial arts, and other courses are only as elective courses. Coupled with the lack of teachers, the development of national sports in Colleges and universities is not optimistic. In recent years, with the deepening of physical education reform in Colleges and universities, the importance of national sports continues to improve, from the excavation of the project to research, development has made considerable progress, but there are still many deficiencies [2].

2.1   The Development of National Traditional Physical Education in Colleges and Universities Lags Behind the Foreign Modern Physical Education

In many colleges and universities, extreme sports such as outdoor survival, orienteering, rock climbing, entertainment such as sports dance, hip-hop, roller skating, and confrontational sports such as taekwondo, karate, judo, boxing and fencing are popular with students, showing a good development trend. The traditional sports with national characteristics mainly focus on fitness, and its antagonism and challenge are not as obvious as the contemporary foreign sports. The national sports that can enter the classroom are mostly martial arts and Taijiquan, and the introduction of folk sports is extremely limited.

2.2   Some of the Contents of National Projects in Colleges and Universities are not Universal and Practical

From the current situation of national sports content selection in Colleges and universities, the selected items can basically meet the popularity, but some items lack popularity and practicality. For example, dragon dance and lion dance, the two traditional folk sports with the most national characteristics inherited by the Chinese nation for thousands of years, are not practical as the teaching content of colleges and universities. In addition, after the content of some traditional martial arts was set up, because the content was too old and not adapted, there were few students who chose courses and could not teach in class.

2.3   The Original Folk Sports Lack of Integration and Development

There are 56 ethnic groups in China, which have created hundreds of ethnic sports in their working life. Many sports focus on physical fitness, confrontation and entertainment, such as pearl ball of fireworks, shuttlecock and rattan ball, which are suitable for teenagers. They are lack of integration and development, and have not been well developed in school sports.

3   The Present Situation and Problems of National Sports in Colleges and Universities

Data mining (DM), also known as knowledge discovery in database (KDD), is a hot topic in the field of artificial intelligence and database. Data mining is a non trivial process to reveal hidden, previously unknown and potentially valuable information from a large number of data in database. A set of heuristics and calculations for creating data mining models based on data. To create a model, the algorithm first analyzes the data provided and looks for specific types of patterns and trends [3].

In order to effectively evaluate data mining algorithm, we need to understand the overall situation and characteristics of data mining technology and algorithm. The process of data mining is shown in Fig. 1.

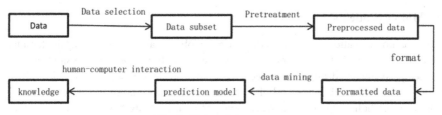

Fig. 1. Data mining process

4   Research on the Application of Data Mining in the Teaching of National Physical Education in Colleges and Universities

The application of data mining in national sports teaching and training is mainly manifested in the selection of sports teaching materials, the selection of sports teaching methods, the mining of students' characteristics and the prediction of students' physical condition.

4.1   Selection of Physical Education Teaching Materials

With the rapid development of science and technology, the trend of physical education teaching materials from paper to electronic is obvious. More and more physical education textbooks begin to show in the form of structured, dynamic and visualized graphics, images and videos in front of physical education learners, which not only enables learners to acquire knowledge in an easy and fast environment, but also makes it possible to mine useful information by using data mining technology due to the characteristics of easy storage, convenient transmission and processing of multimedia textbooks [4]; Through data mining technology, the reasonable classification, retrieval and processing of physical education teaching materials, and the establishment of knowledge system structure, provide reference for the selection of physical education teaching materials.

4.2 The Choice of Teaching Methods

Teachers can use a variety of teaching methods to complete teaching tasks, such as teaching, discussion, experiment, computer-aided teaching, visiting, investigation and practice. In general, it can be done in one or more ways. When choosing teaching methods, we can use data mining technology, use association analysis and other methods to analyze the evaluation of the course and the results obtained by students of different teaching methods, so as to find the internal relationship between the curriculum and teaching methods, and determine the teaching method to be used in a certain section of the course or course; The data mining technology of clustering and classification is used to analyze the grouping method of physical education, and to achieve reasonable teaching grouping according to the similarity of students' physical quality, and adapt to the teaching requirements of teaching according to their aptitude.

4.3 Mining Students' Characteristics

In the teaching of national physical education in Colleges and universities, Cluster analysis can be used to help teachers analyze students' initial knowledge system, current knowledge system and target knowledge system, and deeply submit students' physiological, psychological and social characteristics. The correlation is shown in Fig. 2, so as to better help students to correct their personal learning behavior, improve their learning ability, improve their personal personality, and promote the comprehensive and coordinated development of all aspects of students' quality.

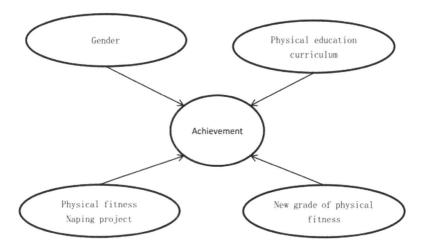

Fig. 2. Correlation network

5 The Application of Data Mining in the Evaluation of National Sports Teaching

The application of data mining technology in physical education evaluation mainly includes learning evaluation, curriculum assessment and teaching management evaluation.

5.1 Student Learning Evaluation

The evaluation of students' learning is one of the main teaching tasks of physical education teachers. To evaluate students' learning behavior scientifically and reasonably, we should not only focus on the evaluation of students' performance, but also use data mining tools to analyze and process the information of students' daily learning behavior, such as the records of rewards and punishments, so as to get an objective and fair evaluation of students, In this way, it not only plays the role of information feedback and stimulating learning motivation for students, but also is a way to examine individual differences of students, which is convenient for teaching students in accordance with their aptitude.

5.2 Course Evaluation

Under the current examination oriented education system in China, examination is not only a measure of students' learning workload and learning ability, but also an internal driving force to know students' learning and cultivate lifelong sports concept. Therefore, on the basis of collecting and sorting out students' theoretical knowledge, sports skills and sports literacy, data mining technology is used to discover and extract the knowledge and rules hidden behind the data, and to predict and timely adjust the difficulty of the examination content, the fairness of the examination methods and the rationality of the examination standards, In order to better reflect the important role of physical education examination in testing teaching effect and improving teaching quality.

5.3 Teaching Management Evaluation

Using the DEA system analysis method of data mining technology, we can evaluate the decision-making unit of physical education teaching, evaluate the effectiveness of national physical education teaching management, the scientificity of decision-making unit management policy and the effectiveness of training management, so as to guide the teaching management units to take corresponding measures to improve the level of national physical education teaching and training management.

6 Conclusion

In short, the rise of data mining brings a good opportunity for the combination of sports statistics and sports information technology. Data mining technology will become another powerful tool to promote the development of sports statistics after mathematics and computer science. However, compared with the application degree of data mining technology in other fields, the research of data mining in the field of physical education has made some achievements, but there is still a lot of work to do.

References

1. Shan, J., Liu, J., Li, J.: Research on the teaching mode of national traditional sports in colleges and universities from the perspective of traditional culture inheritance. J. Tianjin Univ. Tradit. Chin. Med. **31**(6), 107–108 (2012)
2. Meng, X.: College sports teaching should focus on absorbing the essence of ethnic minority sports. Guizhou Nat. Stud. **36**(6), 218–221 (2015)
3. Zhao, Q.: Research and design of intelligent teaching system model based on Web and data mining. Hunan Normal University (2007)
4. Li, W., Wu, S.: Ten Algorithms of Data Mining. University Press Beijing, Tsinghua (2013)

Application of Data Analysis in Mental Health Education for College Students

Ying Liu[(✉)]

Liaoning Jian Zhu Vocational College, Liaoning 111000, China

Abstract. ID3 algorithm is used to construct decision tree to predict the mental health status of college freshmen, so as to provide decision support for college students' mental health education. This paper introduces the main content of ID3 algorithm, discusses the data preprocessing, tree building algorithm, using decision tree to predict Freshmen mental health, and the application integration method of decision tree in MIS. The experimental results show that this method has a certain practical value in the construction of preventive mental health education mode for college students.

Keywords: Data mining · Decision tree · ID3 · Mental health education

1 Introduction

At present, colleges and universities in China have paid more and more attention to the mental health education of college students. Many schools have carried out a general survey on the mental health of freshmen, carried out relevant psychological tests on students one by one, and established students; personal mental health files on this basis. However, due to various reasons, the early warning mechanism and assistance system of mental health in many schools have not been established completely, so it is impossible to detect and intervene the students; psychological problems as soon as possible. However, due to the lack of early warning and intervention mechanism of psychological problems, students mental health diseases are often worsened, forming a vicious circle. How to establish a scientific and efficient early warning mechanism for students; mental health is a severe challenge for the current mental health education in Colleges and universities. Using data mining technology to find out the hidden information from the massive data of the existing college students; personal mental health archives database, and to provide decision support for college mental health education, will be the solution [1].

It is one of the effective ways to solve the above problems.

Data mining is a process of discovering potential, novel and valuable knowledge from a large amount of data. The tasks of data mining include: classification, clustering, association, regression, prediction, sequence analysis, deviation analysis, etc. There are many algorithms of data mining, such as decision tree, association analysis, Bayesian algorithm, neural network, genetic algorithm, rough set, fuzzy set and statistical analysis. Among them, decision tree algorithm is probably the most popular data mining

© ICST Institute for Computer Sciences, Social Informatics and Telecommunications Engineering 2021
Published by Springer Nature Switzerland AG 2021. All Rights Reserved
M. A. Jan and F. Khan (Eds.): BigIoT-EDU 2021, LNICST 391, pp. 9–15, 2021.
https://doi.org/10.1007/978-3-030-87900-6_2

technology. The most common data mining task solved by decision tree is classification. Compared with other algorithms, decision tree algorithm can quickly create mining model, and the created model is easy to explain. The research content of this topic is to use ID3 algorithm to build a decision tree to predict the mental health status of college freshmen, find out the most likely to have mental health problems, so that the school can achieve scientific and effective early warning, early intervention and key prevention of students; mental health problems.

2   ID3 Algorithm Principle

Decision tree is a sample based inductive learning method, which is a tree structure similar to flow chart. In the process of generating algorithm, non l eaf nodes represent attributes, while leaf nodes represent categories. The top node of the tree is the root node. A path from the root node to the leaf node forms a classification rule. Decision tree can be easily transformed into classification rules, which is a very intuitive representation of classification pattern.

There are several methods to generate decision tree. ID3 is a well-known decision tree algorithm, which was proposed by Ross Quinlan of Sydney University in 1986. ID3 algorithm uses the entropy theory to select the attribute with the maximum information gain value in the current sample set as the test attribute. The algorithm of information gain value is: let s be the set of N data samples, and divide the sample set into m different test attributes [2].

Class CI (I $=$ 1, 2,..., m), the number of samples in each class CI is Ni, then s is divided into m classes, and the information entropy or expected information is as follows:

Where Pi is the probability that the sample in S belongs to class I Ci. Suppose that the set of all different values of attribute a is values (a), and SV is the sample subset of attribute a in s whose value is v. at each branch point after selecting attribute a, the entropy of s classification for the sample set of the node is e (SV).The expected entropy caused by selection a is defined as the weighted sum of the entropy of each subset S, and the weight is the proportion of the samples belonging to SV to the original sample s:

$$E(S, A) = - \sum_{V \in Vvauws(A)} \frac{|S_V|}{|S|} E(S_V) \tag{1}$$

Where e (SV) is the information entropy that divides the samples in SV into m classes.

The information gain (s, a) of attribute a relative to sample set s is defined as:

$$E(S) = - \sum_{V \in Vvauws(A)} \frac{|S_V|}{|S|} E(S_V) \tag{2}$$

Gain (s, a) is the expected information compression of entropy caused by knowing the value of attribute The larger the gain (s, a), the more information the test attribute a can provide for classification. ID3 algorithm is to select the maximum information gain (s, a) attribute in each node as the test attribute.

3 Application of ID3 Algorithm

When freshmen enter school every year, colleges and universities will design some test questions based on the standard content of mental health test and their own specific conditions to investigate the mental health status of students. Schools with high degree of information have stored these data in the database of student management system or directly collected the data related to mental health through the network and stored them in the database, And the mental health of students in school also has tracking records stored in the database. Using ID3 algorithm in the decision tree, we can get the decision tree model from the "outdated" data in the database, that is, get the classification rules, and then use the classification rules to predict the future mental health status of the freshmen, so as to separate the freshmen who are most likely to suffer from mental diseases in the future, and list them as the key attention and assistance objects of the class teacher, student counselor, teacher, Put an end to all kinds of factors inducing mental illness, and let them grow up healthily in a harmonious and friendly campus environment. In this way, mental health education in Colleges and universities can be targeted and get twice the result with half the effort. The work of this paper is divided into the following steps.

$$E(S) = -\sum_{i=1}^{m} P_1 \log_2(P_1) + p(x_i) \qquad (3)$$

3.1 Data Conversion and Cleaning

At present, the data in the existing database in Colleges and universities can not be directly used for data mining. Only by data cleaning and data conversion, can it be suitable for ID3 algorithm and improve the prediction accuracy of the model.

The purpose of data cleaning is to remove the noise and irrelevant information in the data set. For example, there are many fields in the mental health database. According to the prior knowledge, we can see that some fields (i.e. attributes) are not related to mental health, such as gender, age, native place and so on. Therefore, these fields can not be considered in data mining. It is helpful to build a better decision tree classification model by extracting the attributes that have a key impact on students' mental health, so as to achieve better classification and prediction effect [3].

The purpose of data conversion is to convert the data type and value of data source into a unified format. For example, the "family income" field in the mental health database was originally a continuous value. When data mining, this attribute must be converted to a discrete value (the attribute name is changed to "economic difficulty", and the value is yes or no) to be suitable for classification mining tasks. After data cleaning and transformation, the sample set that can be used to train the mining model (that is, to build the decision tree) contains 1000 samples, some of which are shown in Table 1.

3.2 Constructing Decision Tree With ID3 Algorithm

Prepare the sample set for training ID3 algorithm decision tree model.The decision tree is established by the following algorithm.

Table 1. Some samples in the training sample set.

Edit number	Attribute				Category
	Introversion	Family harmony	Hereditary diseases	Economic difficulties	Mental illness
1	No	Yes	Nothing	Yes	Nothing
2	No	No	Nothing	No	Nothing
3	Yes	Yes	Nothing	No	Nothing
4	Yes	No	Yes	No	Yes
5	No	Yes	Nothing	Yes	Nothing

1. For this sample set, the information gain of each attribute is calculated, because ID3 algorithm uses the information gain as the selection criterion of classification attribute. The larger the information gain, the more important the classification will be.
2. The attribute CI with the largest information gain is selected as the root node of the tree (or subtree).
3. The samples with the same value at CI are attributed to the same subset, and the value is taken as a branch of the tree. If there are several values of Ci, there are several subsets, and each value is taken as a branch of the tree.
4. Recursively call tree building for the sample subset with both positive and negative class examples [4].
   Algorithm.
5. If the subset contains only positive or negative examples, mark P or N on the corresponding branch and return the call function. After the completion of the tree building process, because the training sample set contains noise data, the decision tree generated is more complex.

3.3   To Predict the Mental Health of Freshmen

The decision tree classification model is used to predict the mental health of the freshmen, and the students with higher probability of suffering from mental health diseases in the future are screened out. The prediction results are distributed to the head teacher and student counselors in time. The screened students are regarded as the focus of mental health education, and timely and effective mental health counseling is carried out, As an important part of the construction of preventive college students' mental health education mode.

3.4   Application Integration

Application integration is to integrate ID3 algorithm (and other commonly used data mining algorithms) into the newly developed university management information system. For example, it is embedded in the university student management system based on

B/S structure, which is programmed with C# or VC++, and becomes a functional module of the system, The formation of students' mental health data collection, data processing, mining model construction, output mining report, new data sets for prediction and other functions of the perfect MIS system, and colleges and universities no longer need to buy expensive data mining software and hire professional data mining engineers for data mining work, so as to improve the information level of school student management.

The major of applied statistics is different from the major of statistics. Statistics is a methodology subject. It mainly studies the development and utilization of statistical information in theory, and cultivates students' professional knowledge of quantitative analysis and computer operation technology. Applied statistics is an interdisciplinary, comprehensive and application-oriented major. Its course content involves mathematics, statistics, economics and other fields. It has a wide range of applications in the fields of society, population, resources, commerce, finance, economy, pharmacy, epidemiology and engineering.

There are some problems in the teaching of Applied Statistics in Local Application-oriented Universities. On the one hand, it is mainly limited by its teaching resources, which directly affects the determination of teaching mode. For example, Shanghai University of Finance and economics, Ren min University of China and Zhejiang University of technology and industry are rich in teaching resources and teachers. They apply the curriculum system of statistics to strengthen the mathematical foundation, pay attention to statistical methods, and give consideration to the basic principles of economics. They are oriented to the application of government statistics, enterprise statistics, actuarial science, financial industry data analysis, macroeconomic and epidemic law exploration However, due to the lack of teaching resources in local universities, the practice teaching mode of professional practice teaching is relatively simple.

Only in the form of experimental courses and curriculum design. Through classroom practice, students can only master how to use specific statistical methods to solve certain problems under the premise of standard examples or known data. However, statistical investigation and analysis in reality are more complex. Therefore, when students face such comprehensive statistical investigation problems, it is difficult to find appropriate and appropriate solutions. Such teaching methods can not form a systematic teaching mode Practice teaching mode is not conducive to the cultivation of students; innovative application ability.

On the other hand, limited by the experimental materials, the effect of the experimental courses of applied statistics major in quite Local Application-oriented Universities is not ideal, mainly due to the failure to analyze the actual problems with the background of practical problems or according to the time-lapse materials or virtual data; for example, the statistical analysis of a stock is not based on the current economic environment and market trend Potential and other real situation of the stock for statistical analysis, but based on historical data on the trend of the stock for a simple analysis. In other words, due to the outdated teaching materials, it can not meet the requirements of the society for the experimental course of Applied Statistics. This will directly affect the students' application of statistical knowledge to solve practical problems, and then affect the quality of personnel training of Applied Statistics.

Based on the above ideas of teaching reform, the applied statistics major in Local Application-oriented Universities can carry out "project progressive" teaching construction. The teaching process design of "project-based teaching method" is essentially different from the traditional teaching method. The whole teaching process is no longer the link that teachers transfer the theoretical knowledge of textbooks to students through classroom teaching. Instead, teachers combine the theoretical knowledge of the course with practical problems based on the professional talent training objectives and Curriculum objectives, and design the teaching process according to the actual data Some feasible projects are planned, or combined with subject competition, these projects are decomposed into multi-step teaching tasks, and task-based teaching method is combined with project-based teaching method, so that students can complete the teaching tasks and then realize the operation of the whole project, and master the practical application of theoretical knowledge in this process.

The most important thing is that the role of teachers in the whole teaching process is no longer the dominant lecturer, but the guide and supervisor of students; learning process. In the early stage of teaching activities, teachers need to select teaching materials and decompose them into multi-step teaching projects; during teaching activities, teachers need to guide students to complete projects according to their project progress; in the late stage of teaching activities, teachers need to assess, summarize and evaluate the projects. In the process of completing the project independently, students can not only master all the teaching contents, but also cultivate the comprehensive skills of solving practical problems in cooperation with each other. In order to achieve the training of knowledge and ability as well as emotional goals, teachers carefully select teaching materials according to the training objectives of professional talents, curriculum syllabus, realistic social and economic phenomena and the northern boundary of subject competition, and decompose the selected teaching materials into multi-step teaching projects combined with teaching arrangement. Each project should contain the theoretical knowledge points of statistics course, It can also mobilize the enthusiasm of students to solve problems. The decomposed projects should be practical, operational and interesting.

Teachers can design teaching ideas according to the explanation of the theoretical knowledge used to complete the tasks in the project, that is, to complete the teaching in the form of "project". It is the basis and key to realize "project progressive" teaching to select the teaching project suitable for teaching and decompose the project into multiple teaching tasks. The following principles should be followed when selecting the project: first, the difficulty of the whole teaching project should be moderate. Teaching project design is too difficult or too easy will directly affect the enthusiasm of students to solve problems. Therefore, the selection of the project should ensure that it can be completed independently within the scope of students' learning ability. At the same time, it should also control the proportion of tasks that are less related to statistical knowledge or cannot be solved by students' current statistical knowledge in the project. Second, the content of the whole teaching project should be comprehensive.

4   Concluding Remarks

This paper introduces the application of decision tree in mental health education in Colleges and universities. It uses decision tree method to predict and classify the mental health status of Freshmen in the future, and finds out the most likely to suffer from mental diseases, so as to provide decision support for mental health education in Colleges and universities. The experimental results show that this method has a certain reference and application value for the construction of preventive mental health education mode for college students. The follow-up work of this topic is to find out more attributes that are highly related to students' mental health, and use other mining algorithms (such as neural network and genetic algorithm) to further improve the prediction accuracy.

References

1. Ren, Y., Zeng, S., Huo, R., et al.: Discussion and practice of new industrial Internet identification resolution system. Inf. Commun. Technol. Policy **8** (2019)
2. Li, B.: The core of intelligent manufacturing: industrial internet research. Mod. Inf. Technol. **2**(02), 191−193 (2018)
3. XCMG: XCMG information Xrea industrial Internet platform was selected as excellent product and application solution case of MIIT in 2017. Constr. Mach. **49**(6) (2018)
4. Shi, L.: Telecom operators' industrial internet strategy selection and strategy research. Inf. Commun. Technol. Policy (2018)

An Empirical Study on Entrepreneurial Education Competency of Young College Teachers Based on K-means Clustering Algorithm

Xuemei Hu[✉]

Shandong Xiehe University, Jinan 250109, Shandong, China

Abstract. Innovation and entrepreneurship education is an important part of activating students' innovative thinking and helping them successfully implement entrepreneurial behavior. In order to implement and promote the reform of innovation and entrepreneurship education in Colleges and universities, it is necessary to study the competency of innovation and entrepreneurship education teachers. This study uses the literature research method to sort out the research status of innovation and entrepreneurship education teachers at home and abroad. This paper takes the innovative and entrepreneurial teachers in Hebei Province as the research object, analyzes the composition, current situation and existing problems of the competency of innovative and entrepreneurial teachers in Hebei Province from the theoretical and empirical levels, and puts forward some countermeasures and suggestions to improve the competitiveness of teachers. Firstly, the samples in the dataset sample space are regarded as k-nearest neighbors, and the samples in each neighborhood space are averaged to replace the original samples to form a new feature space. At the same time, after the formation of a new feature space, in order to increase the discrimination between samples, K-means clustering is used in the original feature space, the clustering center of each sample is merged into the new feature space, and the elbow method is used to determine the K value in the k-means.

Keywords: K-means · Innovation and entrepreneurship education · Teacher competency · Structural model

1 Introduction

With the progress of Internet technology and the popularization of computers, especially the rapid improvement of mobile network in recent years, the data obtained by human beings from various ways grows exponentially, and these data are often disordered. To obtain useful information from it means that the consumption of time and energy is also exponential growth. Therefore, how to retrieve effective information from big data in a short time is an important part of computer technology research and development [1]. The research of artificial intelligence provides a new way to solve problems for human

M. A. Jan and F. Khan (Eds.): BigIoT-EDU 2021, LNICST 391, pp. 16–25, 2021.
https://doi.org/10.1007/978-3-030-87900-6_3

beings. As one of the core of artificial intelligence, machine learning obtains further learning by collecting human activity data, and then uses computers to simulate the same behavior as human beings as possible, which greatly reduces the time and energy spent on some repetitive meaningless labor.

The research on Teachers' competence in innovation and entrepreneurship education is a realistic research topic in the field of teacher research and even education research. With the attention and support of the state on innovation and entrepreneurship education, innovation and entrepreneurship teachers, as the main body of teaching implementation, are highly expected. Therefore, it is of theoretical and practical significance to study the composition of teachers' competence and analyze the current situation of teachers' competence in innovation and entrepreneurship education.

2   Improved GLOCAL Algorithm Based on K-means

2.1   Global and Local Correlations

Tag relevance is the key to multi label learning framework. In order to standardize the model, label association is used. The correlation of global and local tags may coexist. In order to combine the two, the label manifold regularization term is introduced. The basic idea of global manifold regularization is obtained from the example level Manifold Regularization optimization. Specifically, the higher the positive correlation between the two tags, the closer the corresponding classifier output is, and vice versa [2–5]. In other words, the positive correlation label will make the corresponding classifier output similar, while the negative correlation label will make the corresponding output result not similar.

Similar to the example level manifold regularization term, label Manifold Regularization can be defined as:

$$\sum_{i,j} [S_0]_{i,j} \left\| f_{i,:} - f_{j,:} \right\|_2^2 \tag{1}$$

Where S_0 $l \times l$ global label correlation matrix.

2.2   Tag Relevance

The success of label Manifold Regularization depends on a good tag correlation matrix. In the correlation coefficient between tags is usually calculated by cosine distance. As shown in Fig. 1. However, there are only a few positive examples in some training sets, which results in noise in the estimation. When the label is missing, the observed label distribution is very different from the real label distribution, which will cause errors. In this algorithm, we learn the Laplacian matrix directly without specifying the correlation measure or labeling the correlation matrix.

The standard regularization formula is used:

$$R(U, V, W) = \|U\|_F^2 + \|V\|_F^2 + \|W\|_F^2 \tag{2}$$

In the original label clustering, determine the number of clusters K, the algorithm in this chapter obtains the K value by comparing the experimental results in the iterative process.

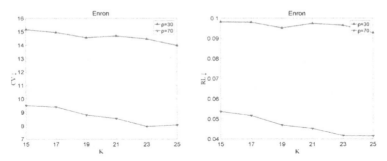

Fig. 1. Clustering number k of Enron dataset

3 Analysis on the Problems and Causes of Teachers' Competence in Innovation and Entrepreneurship Education

As a long-term systematic project, innovation and entrepreneurship education needs to continuously inject a lot of human and material resources to promote its development. In this systematic project, the construction of the capacity of the innovative and entrepreneurial teachers is very important [6]. The "basic requirements for entrepreneurship education and teaching in general undergraduate schools" issued by the Ministry of education clearly points out that colleges and universities should create conditions to set up entrepreneurship basic compulsory courses for all students, and support colleges and universities with conditions to develop and open elective courses (including practical courses) of entrepreneurship education according to the school running orientation, personnel training specifications and discipline characteristics. Referring to the ratio of innovation and entrepreneurship teachers and students in Colleges and universities, the teacher–student ratio between full-time teachers and students should not be less than 1:500. Based on the actual number of innovation and entrepreneurship education teachers participating in the questionnaire survey and the actual teaching situation mentioned by teachers, the author confirms that there is a shortage of innovation and entrepreneurship education teachers in some colleges and universities, which is difficult to meet the teaching needs. It is far from satisfying the demand of all teachers to set up the course of entrepreneurship.

3.1 The Teaching Staff Is Younger, and Most of Them Are Novice Teachers

Whether from the perspective of academic career characteristics, echelon metabolism, or compared with the structure of university teachers in developed countries, the middle-aged teachers account for the largest proportion of good university teachers, while the proportion of young teachers and old teachers is relatively small, and the two are basically symmetrical, The formation of a standard or similar normal distribution structure, innovation and entrepreneurship teachers as a part of the university teacher group is no exception [7–10]. According to the survey results of this study, the teaching team of innovation and entrepreneurship education is mainly composed of young teachers aged 40 and below, and most of the teachers have been on the job for less than five years, and novice teachers are the main teachers. Young teachers and novice teachers as a group of teachers who have just entered the new post, the sudden change of their roles makes this group have the pleasure of being a new teacher and can put most of their efforts into their work. However, teachers in this stage need to undergo a period of transformation from adaptation to stability, development and maturity. In the process of transformation, teachers' professional ideal, external factors of universities and society will play or promote or hinder the competency of teachers.

3.2 Professional Identity Is Not High, Lack of Subjective Initiative

Professional identity refers to the subjective psychological feeling that teachers can accept their profession from the bottom of their heart, and can make positive perception and positive evaluation on all aspects of teachers' occupation, so as to be willing to engage in the teacher's occupation for a long time [4]. It affects teachers' working enthusiasm and enthusiasm. Teachers' professional recognition is the basis of improving teachers' competence. Generally speaking, teachers with high professional identity can feel the pleasure of post work from the bottom of their heart and have a sense of achievement and satisfaction for the post, so as to seek help from various aspects to improve their competence. According to the results of the questionnaire, nearly 90% of the teachers think that innovation and entrepreneurship education is very important to the development of colleges and universities and the growth of students. Most of the teachers are enthusiastic and determined to strive for the cause of mass entrepreneurship and entrepreneurship education when they first enter the post of innovation and entrepreneurship education [11]. However, the score of teachers' professional identity is generally low. Some teachers even have job burnout and have the intention to change jobs. Liu Ling, a scholar, has shown that professional identity can negatively predict job burnout. The lower the level of teachers' professional identity, the greater the possibility of teachers' job burnout.

4 Simulation Analysis

We use the data obtained in the third part for simulation analysis, as shown in Fig. 2 and Fig. 3. From Fig. 2 and Fig. 3, we can know that when we use the k-means algorithm, after the set iteration, the system gradually returns to the normal level, which fully shows that the teaching and innovation level of young teachers is improving year by year. From Fig. 3, we can also see this trend, when young teachers are young teachers this trend is more obvious in old age.

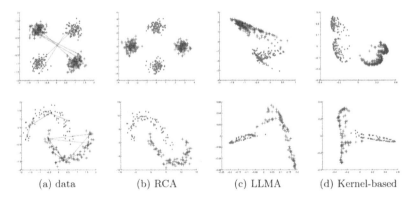

(a) data   (b) RCA   (c) LLMA   (d) Kernel-based

Fig. 2. Comparison results of several algorithms

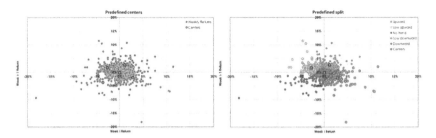

Fig. 3. Simulation results with K-means

5   Why Should We Vigorously Promote the Continuing Education of Young Teachers in Higher Vocational Colleges

5.1   It Is the Inevitable Choice to Improve the Quality of Young Teachers in Higher Vocational Colleges

Every front-line teacher hopes to become a teacher with experience, quality and ability, and get the respect and love of students. However, everyone knows that this can not be achieved in a short time, so we need to focus on our own educational ideas, In this way, the necessity of continuing education is highlighted. With the development of society, we have entered an era of information technology. Under the background of big data manipulation, the update of information is faster than before. I don't know how many times [12–14]. If we keep up with the rapid pace of development, all we can do is to constantly update our knowledge reserves and improve our professional quality. I believe that it's never too old to learn an old saying. It can be seen that vigorously promoting the continuing education of young teachers in higher vocational colleges is the inevitable choice to improve their own quality and realize their own sustainable development.

5.2 On the Development of Higher Vocational Education in the Context of Innovation and Entrepreneurship

Today, with the steady development of education, the development of higher vocational education has attracted much attention. At the time of the rising tide of the new curriculum reform, higher vocational education, as an important part of the education system, has been widely concerned. Due to the direct transportation of talents from home and abroad, the education requirements at this stage are particularly important. This concern greatly improves the requirements for young teachers in higher vocational colleges. They should not only have excellent theoretical experience, but also take into account the practical operation of skilled teaching level [15]. They should not only have a wide range of knowledge, but also have high quality and moral cultivation. This shows the development of Higher Vocational Education Based on the background of innovation and entrepreneurship the objective requirement of higher vocational education is to continuously carry out continuing education for young teachers in order to meet the needs of development.

6 How to Carry Out the Continuing Education of Young Teachers in Higher Vocational Colleges

6.1 Strengthen School Training and Improve the Continuing Education System of Young Teachers in Higher Vocational Colleges

To strengthen the training of young teachers in higher vocational colleges, this training should be carried out by the school with the goal of improving teachers' teaching ability and quality level, aiming at the further education and sublimation of teachers' knowledge level, teaching skills and moral concept. For example, it is necessary to set up a discipline based group for young teachers' continuing education, which is led by excellent old teachers to share, summarize and teach, form a good mentoring system, and pay attention to the psychological dynamics and skills improvement of young teachers anytime and anywhere. As shown in Fig. 4. We should hold a variety of professional education seminars to promote the interaction between young teachers and old teachers, and ultimately improve their own quality.

6.2 Increase the Opportunities of Off Campus Training and Make a Strong Supplement to Continuing Education

With the rapid development of the times, in order to make young teachers meet the needs of the development of knowledge education to the greatest extent, it is necessary to create opportunities to go out for further study. Only in this way can we improve the continuing education of young teachers in higher vocational colleges mo [16–18]. A model of white plan application is to select and evaluate excellent teachers regularly to work in relevant universities or higher levels for a period of time. There are two advantages in this way. First, it can form a benign competitive physique among teachers, so that teachers can pay

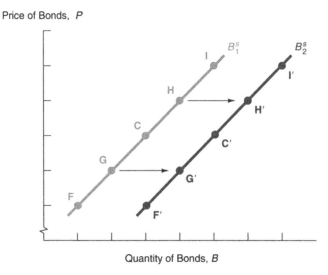

Fig. 4. Indicators of education system

more attention to their own quality and teaching skills, and get the opportunity of further study. Second, it can effectively carry out continuous education for young teachers in Higher Vocational Colleges in the process of training, so as to better help young teachers grow up.

6.3 Strengthen the Depth of Enterprise Investigation and Research

With the characteristics of education, young teachers in higher vocational colleges can conduct more in-depth investigation and Research on a related enterprise, so as to fully understand the potential development direction of the industry and the demand for talents in the direction of innovation and entrepreneurship [19]. Only in this way can we know ourselves and the other strategically, can we grasp the essence of teaching in the process of international teaching, and cultivate high-quality talents for enterprises and society, which is also an alternative way of continuing education for young teachers in higher vocational colleges.

7 Entrepreneurship Education in the Field of American Basic Education

7.1 The Origin of Entrepreneurship Education in American Basic Education

When it comes to entrepreneurship education in the field of basic education in the United States, we must talk about Horace Moses, an American businessman, and his junior achievement. Since its establishment in 1919, the youth business association has been playing an important role in American education. Horace Moses believes that high school students know very little about the actual situation of business. Business theory knowledge learned from books is only a starting point, and practical experience is much more important than book knowledge. So Moses volunteered to help curious students set up their own companies, conduct market surveys, select commodities, determine manufacturing plans, price commodities, and then sell them [20, 21]. At the same time, they set up accounts and calculate the company's profit and loss. The goods they deal in are very simple, but no matter the size of the goods, all business activities have to take certain risks. In 1919, few people could have imagined that Moses' idea of teaching business practice to students in his spare time would have such a huge repercussion in the United States. It is from the 1920s that there has been a ten-year commercial boom in the history of the United States. The education of youth business community has contributed a lot. Since then, business people throughout the United States have volunteered to organize youth business community education in schools in their communities, even during the economic crisis and war in the 1930s.

7.2 Entrepreneurship Education Program in the Field of Basic Education

In primary schools (6–11 years old), local businessmen teach basic business knowledge, such as business organization, business management, production and marketing. The total class hours are 4 h. 2. In junior high school (12–13 years old), there is a business course once a week to introduce students to more complex contents, such as supply and demand, corporate finance, global market, labor market and banking services for individuals [22]. In senior high school (14–18 years old), practical economics is taught for one semester with comprehensive contents. In addition to full-time teachers, there are also business volunteers who teach economic system once a week and help students start and run their own companies. Facing the wave of younger entrepreneurs, the United States began to implement the "financial literacy 2001 plan" in January 1998. It popularized "advanced education" in finance, investment and financing, marketing, business and other aspects to middle school students, and actively cultivated "future managers". Young business community entrepreneurship education enables children to receive free entrepreneurship education. Entrepreneurs and students share the joy of success together, It will have a profound impact on children's life.

8 One of the Fastest Growing Areas of Entrepreneurship Education in the U.S. in the Early 1980s was Entrepreneurship Education

In American colleges and universities, entrepreneurship education has been a rapidly growing field since the early 1980s.

Entrepreneurship courses are very popular in Colleges and universities. In the United States, the number of business schools offering at least one entrepreneurship course increased from 210 in 985 to 351 in 1991, with an increase of 67%. Since 2000, Harvard Business School has listed entrepreneurship as a compulsory course for MBA students in their second year. At present, 369 universities in the United States have offered at least one entrepreneurship course. Entrepreneurship courses are offered not only in business schools, but also in engineering schools, nursing schools and art schools. A study shows that 37.6% of the universities surveyed offer entrepreneurship courses in undergraduate education, 23.7% offer entrepreneurship courses in postgraduate education, and 38.7% offer at least one entrepreneurship course in both undergraduate and postgraduate education. Some universities take entrepreneurship as a minor (second major), Some universities have taken it as a major, and some even set up entrepreneurship departments. 23.7% of universities offer entrepreneurship courses in graduate education, and 38.7% of universities offer at least one entrepreneurship course in both undergraduate and graduate education. Some universities take entrepreneurship as a minor (second major), some universities have taken it as a major, and some even set up entrepreneurship departments [23–25]. The teaching methods of entrepreneurship course in Colleges and universities, case teaching and entrepreneurship plan become the center of entrepreneurship teaching. The best way to learn is to apply the knowledge to practice. Therefore, teachers organize students to carry out entrepreneurial group activities. The students in the class are divided into several groups. Each group prepares a business plan, and then evaluates it collectively. The evaluation criteria are: (1) the novelty of the entrepreneurial plan; (2) the feasibility of the entrepreneurial plan; (3) the degree of the entrepreneurial team to make the best use of their talents.

9   Conclusion

The improvement of Internet technology in the direction of mobile terminal is more powerful. People can get the information they want at any time and anywhere. The diversity of access to information and the diversity of information content means that people no longer have enough time and energy to distinguish effective information from invalid information. The emergence of artificial intelligence is a good help to solve this dilemma. Through training the existing samples, we can simulate the similar working effect according to the characteristics of human extracting information, and machine learning is an important means of its research. The competency of innovation and entrepreneurship education teachers refers to the synthesis of various abilities and qualities which are necessary for the successful implementation of innovation and entrepreneurship education teaching behavior. Clarifying the composition and development status of teachers' competence in innovation and entrepreneurship education can promote the improvement of teachers' competence, urge university administrators to carry out education and teaching reform, and select and train teachers with more pertinence.

References

1. Zhou, Z.: Machine Learning. Tsinghua University Press, Beijing (2016)
2. Zhang, M.: A new multi label lazy learning algorithm. Comput. Res. Dev. **49**(11), 2271–2282 (2012)
3. Cao, S., Lei, J.: Report on the Development of Innovation and Entrepreneurship Education in Chinese Universities. Wanjuan publishing company, Shenyang (2009)
4. Yang, X.: Research on College Students' Employment and Entrepreneurship Education. Economic Science Press, Beijing (2015)
5. Kan, Y., Zhan, T.: Research on curriculum style of higher vocational entrepreneurship education. Sci. Technol. entrepreneurship monthly **5** (2013)

6. Wu, J.: On the continuing education of young teachers. Continuing Educ. Res. **2**, 10–12 (2004)
7. Jing, W.: Problems to be solved in teachers' continuing education. China Adult Educ. **9**, 88–89 (2003)
8. Zhou, A.: On the continuing education of higher vocational teachers. Higher Educ. Res. **3**, 8–9 (2004)
9. Duan, D.: Exploring global competency training path. China Soc. Sci. J. 2021-03-17 (001)
10. Shao, W., Yu, L.: The path of improving the moral education competency of university teachers under the background of "Internet plus." J. Heilongjiang Teachers Dev. College **40**(03), 26–28 (2021)
11. Wang, Y.: Basic education teachers' competency and its promotion path under the background of smart education. Pedagogy of Teachers. Fu, H., Wang, Z.: Research on the competency promotion strategy of judicial social workers. Leg. Syst. Soc. **08**, 111–113 (2021)
12. Hong, X., Wei, Y., Ou, J.: Qualitative research on editorial literacy in the new media era. Publishing Sci. **29**(02), 32–41 (2021)
13. Wang, X., Zhang, Q., Kong, M., Zhang, Y.: Analysis on the quality of middle managers in Weihai area and discussion on the training methods. Enterp. Reform Manage. **05**, 96–97 (2021)
14. Yang, X., Xia, C., Wang, W., Zhang, J.: Research on the construction of power supply enterprise technical personnel training system based on competency model. Enterp. Reform Manage. **05**, 116–118 (2021)
15. Tian, W., Zhang, H., Geo, F., Li, J., Yu, K.: Enlightenment of civil aviation reform experience on training military pilots. Trainer **01**, 9–15 (2021)
16. Huang, S.: Research on the competency of college physical education teachers under the background of curriculum reform. Hubei Sports Sci. Technol. **40**(03), 279–282 (2021)
17. Chen, F.A.B.: The influence and enlightenment of Pisa evaluation on curriculum reform in the world. Mod. Educ. Manage. **03**, 108–113 (2021)
18. Zhu, Y.: Home school education, hand in hand. Moral Educ. Primary Secondary Schools **03**, 79 (2021)
19. Jin, J., Jiang, Y.: Analysis on the development process of enterprise internationalization talent training. Mod. Bus. Ind. **42**(10), 27–28 (2021)
20. Sun, C., Meng, X.: Global competency education for the future: review and reflection. Chongqing Higher Education Research: 1–18 [2021-04-11] http://kns.cnki.net/kcms/detail/50.1028.G4.20210310.1825.007.html
21. Lin, L., Li, Y.: Research on the application of diversified teaching evaluation methods in the practice teaching of community nursing. J. Nurs. Educ. **36**(05), 466–469 (2021)
22. Xia, Y., Wang, N., Yu, X., Che, Y.: Current situation and reform exploration of postgraduate training of obstetrics and gynecology. China Continuing Med. Educ. **13**(07), 3–6 (2021)
23. Hong, M.: The basic idea of the curriculum construction of school parent education. Chinese J. Educ. **44**(03), 14–18 (2021)
24. Cui, S., Li, W., Wang, S., Hongqing: canonical correlation analysis of thinking characteristics and implicit professional quality of preventive medicine students in Shandong province. Med. Soc. **34**(03), 60–63 (2021)
25. He, Q., Kang, Q.: The current situation, problems and Countermeasures of rural primary school teachers' teaching competence – based on the investigation and analysis of Jiangxi province. Chinese J. Educ. **03**, 82–86 (2021)

Application of Artificial Intelligence Technology in English Teaching of Drug Safety Specialty in Higher Vocational Colleges

Jin Wen[1(✉)] and Fengyang Fu[2]

[1] Chongqing Vocational instItute of Engineeing, Chongqing 402260, China
wanglei18291826361@126.com
[2] Chongqing Medical and Pharmaceutical College, Chongqing 401331, China

Abstract. Through the role of artificial intelligence technology in teaching, this paper analyzes the relationship between the technology and the teaching of drug safety English in higher vocational colleges, and makes a deep discussion on the significance of the application of artificial intelligence technology. At the same time, by listing the saiet technology, this paper makes a practical interpretation of the practical teaching application of artificial intelligence technology, and discusses the feasibility and key problems of the application of the hybrid teaching mode based on the characteristics of drug safety English.

Keywords: Artificial intelligence · Drug safety · Professional English · Blended teaching

1 Introduction

With the advent of information society and knowledge age, information is expanding at an unprecedented speed. Facing the vast amount of information resources, human natural intelligence is becoming more and more difficult to control. How to use artificial intelligence to imitate and expand the natural intelligence of human beings and realize the intelligent processing of information is a major issue faced by the information society. In order to make AI technology more suitable for practical teaching, relevant experts design products similar to expert system courses in AI tools, which is also in the process of continuous practice and innovation. It takes time to verify the importance of AI technology, and its ultimate goal is to improve teaching results and provide a more scientific teaching scheme for higher education.

The emergence of these products also marks that human language learning has entered the era of artificial intelligence. With the continuous maturity of artificial intelligence technology, more and more mobile applications have been derived, and these software are gradually connected and integrated with the field of language learning. For the language education industry, it is not only a challenge, but also an opportunity. For educators, it has a certain impact on their teaching methods and thinking, and puts forward higher requirements for teachers' own quality, On the other hand, it improves the

M. A. Jan and F. Khan (Eds.): BigIoT-EDU 2021, LNICST 391, pp. 26–32, 2021.
https://doi.org/10.1007/978-3-030-87900-6_4

interest of the classroom, expands the access to knowledge, liberates part of the burden of teachers, reduces the pressure on teaching, and realizes the innovation of teaching [1].

2   Artificial Intelligence Technology

2.1   Concept of Artificial Intelligence

Artificial intelligence is also machine intelligence, its English expression is "artificial intelligence", referred to as AI. It is a comprehensive subject which is developed from computer science, cybernetics, information theory, neurophysiology, psychology, linguistics and other disciplines. The ability of computer application system to simulate human intelligent activities, in order to extend the science of human intelligence. From a disciplinary point of view, the current artificial intelligence is a branch of computer science. Generally speaking, artificial intelligence is a challenging science, which involves computer knowledge, psychology and philosophy; It is composed of different fields, such as machine learning, computer vision and so on. The purpose of artificial intelligence research is to make the machine competent for some complex work which usually needs human intelligence to complete.

2.2   Development of Artificial Intelligence

In the mid-20th century, scientists represented by British mathematician Turing provided theoretical basis and practical objects for the birth of artificial intelligence. The artificial intelligence discipline was formally born at the Dartmouth conference in 1956. Scientists led by von Neumann and Turing are trying to implement AI through symbolic programming. Since the 1960s, with the development of technology, artificial intelligence research has experienced twists and turns in bottleneck and breakthrough. At the end of the 20th century, artificial intelligence technology developed slowly due to the lack of hardware conditions and algorithms. But since the beginning of the 21st century, big data, cloud computing and other information technologies have injected new vitality into the development of artificial intelligence. Low cost parallel computing, big data, deep learning algorithm and brain chip, these four technologies promote the rapid development of artificial intelligence. This upward trend has appeared, and the development of artificial intelligence has also provided new impetus for the penetration and integration of new generation information technology and industry. In recent years, artificial intelligence technology and industry all over the world has entered a stage of rapid development, so there are many new artificial intelligence applications and companies. International IT giants are trying to seize the commanding height of the industry and occupy a dominant position by acquiring a large number of new start-ups, recruiting top talents and increasing investment. The latest progress of artificial intelligence segmentation, such as machine learning, natural language processing and computer vision, has made great progress, and many new applications and products have been announced.

3 Significance and Development Status of English Teaching for Drug Safety Specialty in Higher Vocational Colleges

3.1 Significance of Professional English for Drug Safety in Higher Vocational Colleges

In recent years, with the continuous development of economy, the number of private pharmaceutical factories is increasing. Although there are drug trade with foreign countries, the level of China's pharmaceutical industry is still not high compared with western countries in terms of pharmaceutical technology. At present, many intellectual property rights of new drugs and special drugs need to be introduced from abroad. In this situation, we should first of all, Efforts should be made to develop new drugs and gradually close the gap of independent intellectual property rights of new drugs; Secondly, we should continue to learn foreign advanced pharmaceutical technology to supplement nutrition for our new drug research and development; Secondly, the domestic and foreign markets should be gradually opened for the domestic and newly developed pharmaceutical products. For our colleges and universities, the setting of students' majors should be in line with the market demand, which is particularly prominent in the cultivation of higher vocational students. At present, the supply of talents in pharmacy is in short supply, especially in biopharmaceutical specialty. Pharmaceutical graduates with rich practical experience and strong communication skills are very popular, and more scarce jobs are still directed to English majors with the above qualities. In this situation, the setting of drug safety English major in higher vocational colleges is very important. For the school, grasping the construction of important majors will improve the development of talent training level. For students, to grasp a good major is to get a golden key to their future life. As mentioned above, Pharmaceutical English is produced to meet the needs of social development, and its necessity is obvious [2].

3.2 The Current Situation and Problems of Drug Safety English Teaching in Higher Vocational Colleges

There will be many different problems in English Teaching in higher vocational colleges. In view of the practical needs of the society and the continuous development of pharmacy, Pharmaceutical English emerges as the times require, and many colleges and universities with pharmaceutical specialty have opened this course. However, Pharmaceutical English is a very young subject, In addition, our understanding of its importance, objectives and characteristics may not be comprehensive enough, which leads to the fact that many professional English courses for pharmaceutical majors have become a cover to cater for the enrollment of students or the investigation of higher authorities, and have not been given due attention.

From the perspective of curriculum setting of drug safety English major in higher vocational colleges, it is not reasonable. Although there are skills training courses, they are not completely aimed at the job; The syllabus is not perfect; From the perspective of textbook compilation, it is not in place. There are plenty of pharmaceutical textbooks and specialized English textbooks, but there are few practical pharmaceutical safety English textbooks; From the perspective of the orientation of drug safety English major, it is lack of innovation. At present, it seems that many colleges and universities set up this major to cater to the quality education advocated by the state. In fact, they still focus on "subject" and "reputation". In this case, pharmaceutical students still study only for credits, not for employment, How to talk about the "professionalism" of higher vocational education itself? In the long run, it is difficult for the relevant professional students trained in this state to meet the requirements of social development; In terms of teachers, there is a lack of "double qualified" teachers. At present, in terms of English, there are more pure language teachers and more Chinese language teachers with strong pharmaceutical professional knowledge. However, there are few compound teachers who are proficient in English and rich in pharmaceutical professional knowledge. Although some teachers have received different degrees of training and have double qualified certificates, most of them lack practical experience; From the perspective of pharmaceutical students, they don't pay enough attention to the English learning of drug safety major. Many higher vocational students still focus on the standard of English a or even public English Band 4, but lack of attention to this major. Taking our college as an example, most pharmaceutical students think that as long as they get the English level certificate, they should pay more attention to it, On the road of English learning, once and for all, it's over. We don't take a long-term view.

4 An Overview of Blended Teaching Mode

The development of society and information technology has changed our way of communication and learning, which will inevitably change our way of thinking. The form of communication and the management of information challenge our cognitive ability and traditional classroom teaching paradigm. The development of Internet promotes the popularity of distance education, and also brings a new form of learning online learning. People define online learning as a process in which learners use the Internet to obtain learning materials and interact with teachers and other learners. One of the most critical problems of online learning is whether students can get better learning effect compared with traditional classroom teaching. The increase in the number of students and the diversification of the population structure, as well as the development of lifelong education and information technology have brought opportunities to the emergence of new teaching mode. The president of Penn State University believes that blended learning is "the only recognized development trend in today's higher education". Blended learning combines the advantages of traditional teaching and network teaching, and can effectively make up for their shortcomings, so it has won the favor of society and education. Blended learning (BL) is a combination of traditional classroom face-to-face teaching and modern information technology, which is being more and more applied to teaching. Some scholars predict that blended learning will become the "conventional mode" in curriculum teaching [3].

The elements of blended learning can be represented by the hexagon formed by two triangles. As shown in Fig. 1, the six elements are equally important in blended learning. The six elements are divided into two systems, which support each other and integrate with each other, reflecting the characteristics of blended learning.

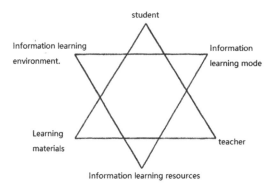

Fig. 1. Six elements of blended learning

5 Artificial Intelligence Technology and English Teaching of Drug Safety Specialty in Higher Vocational Colleges

5.1 Design of Saiets Teaching System

Artificial intelligence technology can take the professional academic perspective of modern educational technology as a foothold, under the correct guidance of information technology, complete the teaching module design with more significance of the times. As shown in the basic structure of saiets technology in Fig. 2, C/S terminal self-service system can be realized in both online and offline States, and B/s online system can also be realized in online state. The running mode of saiets includes offline mode and online mode [4]. Online connection can be realized through Internet mode. Offline mode is often called offline operation. In the process of using, users can download the system database in advance through the setting of the terminal server. Even in the offline state, they can also obtain intelligent services and knowledge provision through the artificial simulation system of the terminal server. The arrangement of the course is mainly in the form of courseware. The assistant teaching module takes the instructor as the important experiencer, while other learning modules are more oriented to English learners. Artificial intelligence technology can realize data and information mining through the courseware design of the instructor, and through the use of the instructor's teaching theory, it can give some reference and influence to the learning scheme of the students in another section. In the arrangement of the courseware, it involves the stage test and comprehensive ability evaluation of the students, Learners can choose their own courseware and video to solve the problems and realize self-learning and targeted exercise. Artificial intelligence technology divides learning content into several sections, which may include learning knowledge section, evaluation section, homework section or exercise section, so that learners can choose exercises more independently. After students complete the small section of learning, the system will automatically generate students' learning results and related maps, and give corresponding scientific guidance and suggestions, So that students can fully understand their own learning situation. And artificial intelligence technology can also be reflected in the aspect of online intelligent chat. Through the chat interface, learners can use voice to have a dialogue or ask questions directly. Artificial intelligence technology can help students deal with problems quickly through solving questions, which is also an important application in the field of drug safety professional English education.

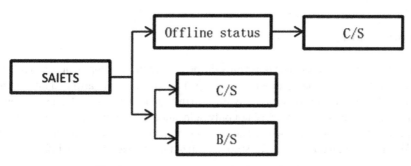

Fig. 2. The basic structure of saiets technology

5.2 Change the Traditional Teaching Quality of Colleges and Universities Through the Power of Science and Technology

Some colleges and universities are bound by traditional education mode, so it is difficult to improve the teaching quality or the innovation of teachers. Facing this dilemma, the business English Teaching in Colleges and universities needs to be separated from the old rigid by the power of modern science and technology, and artificial intelligence technology has become the best choice. It can improve the teaching effect of the teaching is not good, correct and complement the short board of the actual curriculum, so that the daily teaching is more suitable for the curriculum standard and the curriculum concept of the times. In the reform of science and technology education, AI technology can play its own unique advantages in language learning, and then make more perfect teaching plan for the teachers.

5.3 Change the Thinking Problems in Business English Teaching in Colleges and Universities

There are always problems in Chinese English teaching, which mainly shows that students have poor English thinking and lack of knowledge of history and culture in English subjects. Therefore, students can only exchange English through the complex mode transformation of "English translation and Chinese translation" and can not realize the form of "English + English", It also leads to some mistakes in English translation. The lack of oral communication ability is a typical characteristic of this problem. Artificial intelligence technology can construct a perfect English teaching system through computer language. In view of the phenomenon of lack of practical application communication ability, it can simulate the educational characteristics of human brain, which can enable students to cultivate the relative "English thinking" in daily dialogue and communication, And become the representative education achievement of modern information technology. Through computer-aided teaching, it can improve the commanding point of the reform of education mode, and make English teaching classes at all stages be able to conduct full personalized guidance, thus improving the quality of the English classroom for drug safety specialty in Colleges and universities in China.

6 Conclusion

To sum up, artificial intelligence is not only the product of the development of science and technology, but also the best partner of teaching. The application of artificial intelligence technology in the teaching of drug safety English in higher vocational colleges, combined with the hybrid teaching mode, will not only help students to optimize the skills of drug safety English, but also free teachers and students from the heavy teaching tasks, Improve the efficiency and quality of the classroom, realize the innovation of teaching.

References

1. Hua, L., Chen, L., Sun, M.: Research on College English Teaching under the background of artificial intelligence. J. Shanxi Police College **26**(03), 103–106 (2018)
2. Kan, Q., Zhao, C., Fu, S., Zou, L.: English teaching for pharmaceutical majors; my opinion. Soc. Pharm. Little Asia **1**(2) (2006)
3. Lu, Z.J: Application and practice of hybrid teaching mode in teaching reform of higher vocational education. Mod. Vocat. Educ. **11** (2018)
4. Hua, L., Chen, L., Sun, M.: Research on artificial intelligence promoting english learning reform. Mod. Distance Educ. **06**, 27–31 (2017)

Cognitive Research on the Mode of "Integration of Production and Teaching" in Colleges and Universities Based on Artificial Intelligence

Yuan Wang[✉]

Party Committee Office, Principal's Office, Changshu Institute of Technology, No. 99 South Third Ring Road (Donghu Campus), Changshu 215500, China
wangy@cslg.edu.cn

Abstract. Artificial intelligence is the science of researching and developing the theory, method and technology application system of simulating, expanding and expanding human intelligence. It is of positive significance to apply it to the College of industry. With the deep integration of artificial intelligence and classroom teaching, artificial intelligence will present a series of development trends.

Keywords: Artificial intelligence · Integration of production and education · Five link mode

1 Introduction

With the expansion of the scale of colleges and universities, improving the quality of teaching has become a consensus. According to the needs of regional economic and social development, colleges and universities should set up application-oriented undergraduate majors in close connection with the needs of industry and industry. Application oriented universities should promote curriculum teaching reform under the background of integration of production and education, so as to meet the ever-changing talent needs of regional industries and enterprises. The integration of production and teaching can improve the skills and technology of students and enhance the comprehensive quality of students. It is the need of the school to improve the quality of personnel training, the development of industry and enterprises, and the need of students to enhance the value. Foreign colleges and universities have made exploration and Research on talent cultivation from different perspectives and perspectives, and formed their own talent training modes. For example, the University of Cincinnati "work study alternation" mode of American universities, the "entrepreneurial practice" mode of bayson business school, and the "industry university research training" mode of Stanford University [1]. In October 2016, the United States promulgated the national strategic plan for research and development of artificial intelligence, which defines strategies for state funded AI research and development. This is to cope with the general trend of vigorous development of artificial intelligence, focus on the long-term impact and change on society,

M. A. Jan and F. Khan (Eds.): BigIoT-EDU 2021, LNICST 391, pp. 33–42, 2021.
https://doi.org/10.1007/978-3-030-87900-6_5

and maintain the initiative and foresight of the U.S. government on the development of human intelligence (see Fig. 1). On July 8, 2017, the State Council of China promulgated the development plan for the new generation of artificial intelligence. The rapid development of artificial intelligence promotes the construction of an innovative country and a world science and technology power.

School running mode of "combination of production and education, integration of school and enterprise".

The school running mode of "combination of production and education and integration of school and enterprise" is a new development road opened up by vocational schools, but it is just at the beginning, and because of the different actual situation of each school and the different characteristics of each specialty, the specific methods are not the same. However, as long as we are firm in thinking, persist in exploration, seriously grasp the market information, and rely on the progress of science and technology, the development of vocational education will be able to embark on the road of healthy development tomorrow.

1.1 Advantage

It is conducive to stimulate students' creativity and innovation, and create conditions for students to combine work with study and work study.

Vocational schools set up professional industry and combine it with teaching, which provides students with necessary practice conditions and rare exercise opportunities. In the production practice and management practice, students will apply the learned book knowledge to practice under the guidance of teachers, so as to deepen the understanding of knowledge and enhance the ability of applying knowledge and solving practical problems. Not only that, the combination of production and education will also stimulate students' desire and enthusiasm for creation and innovation, and encourage them to continuously explore and innovate in practice. The cultivation of innovative consciousness, innovative ability and innovative talents is the direction of our vocational education. The school set up professional industry, let students participate in production or business, get a certain reward, which objectively also created conditions for students to work study combination, work study program.

It is helpful to improve the professional level of teachers.

Now, most of the teachers in vocational schools are directly allocated from colleges and universities, they have high professional level and rich theoretical knowledge, but the disadvantage is that their knowledge application ability is not strong, and their practical operation level is not high, which also greatly affects the improvement of the teaching quality of vocational schools. The establishment of practice base and the establishment of professional industry provide conditions and opportunities for the majority of teachers, especially the teachers of professional courses, to participate in practice and improve the ability of practical work. In practical work, teachers combine theoretical knowledge with production practice and teaching with scientific research, which is conducive to improving their professional quality and teaching quality, It is of great significance for vocational schools to establish an excellent teaching staff.

It is conducive to promoting the prosperity and development of local economy.

Vocational education is the most direct service for the local economic construction. It has a close relationship with the local economic construction and has a wide range of contacts. The specialties set up by vocational schools are closely related to the local economic construction. Because of their rich professional knowledge and flexible mind, they rely on science and technology to set up their own industries, so they have a certain degree of demonstration in the local area. At the same time, vocational schools have trained a large number of talents who understand technology and management. When they enter the society, they will inevitably become experts in this field, which is conducive to driving the adjustment of the local economic structure, Promote the prosperity and development of local economy.

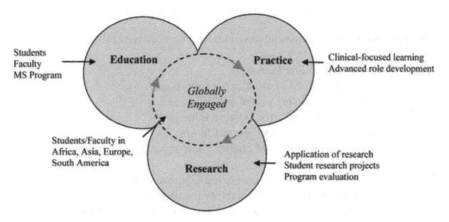

Fig. 1. Education integration

2 Artificial Intelligence

Artificial intelligence (AI) is the full name of artificial intelligence in English. In essence, it is a simulation of human consciousness and thinking, which is expected to think like human beings and even surpass human intelligence. At present, the development of new generation of artificial intelligence related disciplines, theoretical modeling, technological innovation, software and hardware upgrading, etc., is leading to chain breakthrough, and accelerating the leap from digitization, networking to intelligence in all fields of economy and society. After the deep combination of artificial intelligence and education, it will become the main force of classroom teaching, and it will also bring unprecedented challenges to education. At present, artificial intelligence is promoting the rapid development of education and teaching with the guidance of fairness, efficiency and personalization [2, 3].

3 Artificial Intelligence Control Algorithm

Feature identification is a process in which intelligent control processes the sampled information online according to the feature model, and pattern recognition determines what kind of characteristic state the system is currently in. In the whole control process, the controller will receive a lot of information and record it to judge the control effect, determine the control strategy, correct the control parameters and affect the control output. However, the memory of the controller is limited and cannot be memorized completely. In fact, for control and decision-making, most of these information are redundant, and only some characteristic information needs to be memorized. Feature memory refers to the memory of intelligent control to some characteristic quantities which reflect the prophase decision-making and control effect, and the characteristic quantities reflecting the control task requirements and the nature of the controlled object. The set of characteristic memory is as follows:

$$\Lambda = \{ \lambda_1, \lambda_2, \cdots, \lambda_p \}, \lambda_i \in \sum \tag{1}$$

Among them, the most commonly used feature memory is as follows:

$\lambda_1 : e_{mi}$——The i-th extremum of error;
$\lambda_2 : u_H$——The holding value of output in the early stage;
$\lambda_3 : \overset{\bullet}{e}_{0i}$——The first zero crossing rate of the error;
$\lambda_4 : t_{em}$——The interval time of error extreme value.
   The advantages of feature memory are as follows:
(1) It can directly affect the output of control and correction and improve the control effect;
(2) It can be used as the basis of self-tuning, self-adaptive and self-learning;
(3) It can be used as the basis of system stability monitoring;
(4) The memory effect is high and occupies less memory units [4]. Human control strategy is flexible, not only the control strategy is different, but also the control mode of the same object under the same dynamic response state or different control requirements will be different.

   The control (decision) mode set ψ is a set of quantitative or qualitative mapping relations F between the control output U and the output information E and the characteristic memory information Λ (collectively referred to as R), $\psi = \{\psi_1, \psi_1, \cdots\cdots, \psi_r\}$ where, $\psi_i : u_i = f_i\{e, \overset{\bullet}{e}, \lambda_i, \cdots\cdots\}$ or $\psi_i : f_i \rightarrow IF$ conditional THEN operations. According to the theory of intelligent control, this kind of control mode of changing strategy in intelligent control is called multi-mode control (decision-making). The process of identifying the characteristic motion state of the system through feature identification and taking corresponding control mode immediately can be regarded as an imitation of human heuristic and intuitive reasoning logic.

4   The Guarantee of Good Development of Artificial Intelligence in Colleges and Universities

4.1   Accurate Data

Data accuracy is very important for artificial intelligence. It is necessary to strictly avoid that the collected data can not accurately reflect the actual situation objectively or there are subjective structural deviations in the process of data collection. In Colleges and universities, the data precision of massive knowledge base of artificial intelligence terminal is very important for knowledge transmission. For the acquisition of artificial intelligence big data and cloud data, it is necessary to strictly control the knowledge and content entered into the knowledge base accurately, which is the key link for the next knowledge diffusion.

4.2 Legal Policy Protection

The law should protect the intellectual property rights, privacy and data security. In the process of providing services, the collection and use of user knowledge, personal privacy and data shall follow the principles of legality, legitimacy and necessity. In the Vocational Colleges of colleges and universities, it is not allowed to collect and provide the human–computer interaction knowledge, students' learning privacy and examination data other than those necessary for the university industry, or use the personal information of students for purposes other than that of the university industry, or collect and use the personal information of students by deception, misleading or coercion.

4.3 Strengthening Moral Standards

With the advent of the era of artificial intelligence, there are many new moral problems, which is also a common challenge that all human beings need to face. It will be an inevitable behavior for the government to participate effectively and timely in the process of artificial intelligence values and ethics. Philip BA11, a British science writer, said that the moral issue of robots is an issue that human beings must pay attention to and need to continue to discuss [5–8]. In Vocational Colleges of colleges and universities, in order to answer questions with racial discrimination, politically sensitive topics and intentional offense, AI terminals should interact with each other under the screening of ethical procedures to respect and protect others.

5 Five Union Mode of Production Education Integration

5.1 The Goal of Talent Training Mode in Industry College of Colleges and Universities Based on the Integration of Production and Education

Combined with the advantages of university industry application-oriented specialty construction, We should work together with industries, industries and enterprises to formulate talent training programs, carry out professional colleges and universities, build industry teams, evaluate the quality of personnel training, build experimental, practical training and practice bases, etc. to form a "five alliance" talent training mode of industry education integration, and through the deep cooperation between the school and industry, industry and enterprise, we can achieve seamless cooperation Then, we should further improve the quality of personnel training, further enhance the ability of scientific research and social service of colleges and universities, and further improve the operation ability of enterprises, highlighting the win–win situation of universities, industries, industries, enterprises and students.

5.2 Innovation of "Five Links" Mode of Production and Education Integration

In the past, the school enterprise cooperation was too loose and the development was unsustainable. We should build a new type of school property, school bank and school enterprise relationship of "mutual trust, mutual assistance and mutual benefit", give full play to the role of all parties in personnel training, and emphasize the "five links" in the process of realization, namely, "school industry alliance", "school enterprise joint operation", "school enterprise linkage", "learning and application connection", "learning industry joint development" [9–12]. In view of the purpose of teaching reform, we should focus on the development of the training scheme under the "five union" talent training mode of University, industry, bank and enterprise, as well as the research on the matching mode, method and means of the university industry. It mainly includes (see Fig. 2):

(1) The "five links" mode is a powerful guarantee for schools, industries, industries and enterprises to jointly formulate training programs, jointly carry out university industry activities, and jointly obtain interests, so as to enhance the continuity and closeness of cooperation between universities, industries, banks and enterprises.

(2) Through the organic integration of industry resources in Colleges and universities, the "five link" mode has established a curriculum module that meets the needs of the society, and fully respects the students' interests and specialties, so that students' learning is more targeted and practical.

(3) "Five couplets" mode can improve the learning interest of undergraduate application-oriented students. By controlling the credit of theory course, increasing the credit of practice course appropriately, and adopting a variety of practice assessment methods, the comprehensive ability of students can be effectively improved, and for the students who attach importance to practice and neglect theory, it is conducive to improve their interest in learning.

(4) The "five link" mode promotes the full exchange and interaction among students, schools and enterprises. Students not only have stronger employment competitiveness for enterprises in the industry, but also have stronger competitiveness for related industries in the industry, so as to improve the employment competitiveness of undergraduate application-oriented talents.

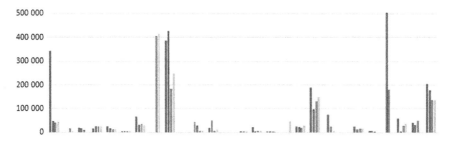

Fig. 2. Education integration effect

6   The Construction of "Integrated" Talent Training Mode Based on "Industry Education Integration, School Enterprise Cooperation"

6.1   "Integration of Industry and Education, School Enterprise Cooperation"

It aims to improve the quality of vocational talents training, solve the problem of the same direction between the supply of vocational education talents and the demand of industrial talents, realize the deep integration between the education and industry, and give play to the social responsibilities of enterprises. The mode of school enterprise cooperation is not only reflected in learning and employment, but also the cooperation between education chain and industry chain. Therefore, to build a more effective integrated talent training mode, we need the participation of "government, industry, enterprise, school and students", as shown in Fig. 3.

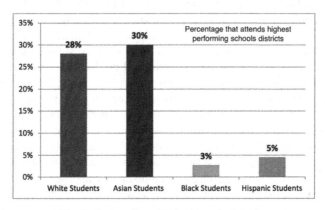

Fig. 3. Integration of industry and education

The government can participate in the personnel training of higher vocational education by publishing education planning topics and formulating relevant industry standards; the content of enterprises' participation in higher vocational education involves teaching resources, teaching staff, establishment of teaching units and training bases in the teaching process, learning to participate and practice, or using enterprise teaching and training platform and curriculum resources in the school; Industry associations can provide corresponding industry development trends for the development of higher vocational colleges, or industry experts can cooperate with higher vocational colleges in the form of part-time. Through the integration with enterprises in training team, teaching resource construction and operation, teachers and students can share enterprise projects, implement the industry specialization of school teachers, and truly realize the enterprise production of students' learning scene; Students can perceive e-commerce post cognition by visiting enterprises in person, accumulate social practical experience by practicing in e-commerce training bases inside and outside the school, and realize the integration of production and teaching.

6.2 Integration of Curriculum Construction

Through the "five party linkage of government, industry, enterprise, school and student", at the university level, through the analysis of national policies, education long-term planning policies, and the economic development status of the District, we can understand the development format of e-commerce industry; through sinking into e-commerce enterprises, we can obtain the setting of e-commerce posts and the requirements for e-commerce talents of leading enterprises, In order to make the curriculum construction plan of e-commerce specialty according to the actual demand, build various mutual aid platforms in accordance with the government, industry, enterprise, school and student resources, make the industry play the corresponding coordination function, and promote the in-depth and all-round integration of schools and enterprises.

The paper introduces the case of industry enterprise into classroom teaching, so that students can better grasp the application of curriculum knowledge in enterprise work [13]. Curriculum standards integrate professional skills standards. In the course of curriculum teaching, the learning objects are transferred from students to post employees. The curriculum objectives are transferred from knowledge mastery to job requirements of enterprises. The learning achievements of students will be transformed into the ability of enterprise posts. 13. The curriculum content integrates the vocational knowledge of post skills and makes the content post oriented and production process oriented, The knowledge goal and ability goal are transformed into the mark of the post by the enterprise production. The integration of the curriculum content provides the conditions and environment for setting up the enterprise personalized curriculum module and integrating the implementation of the curriculum into the post situation. Teachers design the teaching process in a similar environment to the work scene, which enables students to learn the relevant knowledge while solving problems in the close to the actual work situation, and construct a curriculum implementation mode composed of situation, project and task. The specific knowledge content is divided into tasks, tasks are integrated into the design projects, and projects are integrated into specific working situations. Classroom teaching does not only impart knowledge and skills to students, but also pay more attention to shaping their professional ability, and realize the organic combination of teaching process and production process.

6.3 Integration of Evaluation Standards

The evaluation after the implementation of teaching directly reflects the quality and effect of teaching and learning. How the evaluation standard directly reflects the curriculum objectives requires the integration of the evaluation standard, that is, the integration of student evaluation standard and industry evaluation standard, the integration of school teacher evaluation and enterprise expert evaluation, and the integration of academic examination and professional skill appraisal, as shown in Fig. 4. The student object is regarded as the evaluation standard of enterprise employee object. In this way, the students can better meet the requirements of the industry, meet the needs of the industry, realize the integration of curriculum evaluation, and record the whole process of students' curriculum learning in the form of students' curriculum portfolio, From the multi-dimensional perspective of knowledge mastery, technical skills shaping, professional quality and enterprise post competency, the assessment standard should be quantified and visualized, and the assessment results should be supported [14, 15]. School teachers and enterprise technical experts participate in the assessment as multiple identities to form students' learning portraits, so as to reflect on teaching, promote the improvement of teaching quality, and provide high-quality resources for enterprise talent transportation.

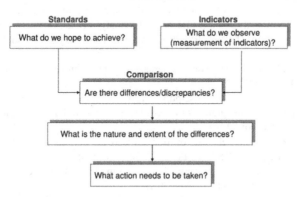

Fig. 4. Integration of evaluation standards

7 Conclusions

With the rapid development of artificial intelligence technology, financial robots are constantly updated. How to recognize the changes of the times, keep close to the pace of industrial development, assess the situation, speed up the transformation of higher vocational accounting information management professionals, and actively cultivate management accounting talents required by enterprise financial transformation, is an important proposition placed in front of each professional teacher. Only by further deepening the integration of production and education and strengthening school enterprise cooperation can the school successfully fulfill the historical mission entrusted by the times.

Acknowledgements. General topics of philosophy and Social Sciences Planning Office of Jiangsu Province in 2017: Research on the construction of Industry College of Application-oriented Universities under the background of industry education integration, Number: 17JYB007.

References

1. Li, L.: Understanding Artificial Intelligence in this Book. China Industrial and information publishing group, people's Posts and Telecommunications Press (2016)

2. Development plan of new generation artificial intelligence [EB/0l]. GF (2017) No. 35, 8 July 2017
3. Yang, H., Chi, J.: Exploration and reflection on the cultivation of digital media art talents under the background of integration of production and education
4. Sun, S.: Theoretical connotation and practical points of integration of production and teaching. China Vocat. Tech. Educ. **12** (2017)
5. Zhang, S., Gao, X.: Research on the cultivation of innovative and applied talents under the mode of industry education integration. J. Harbin Univ. **08**, 142–144 (2020)
6. Pan, K.: Practice and thinking of integration of production and education. J. Heilongjiang Inst. Technol. **12**, 69–71 (2019)
7. Luo, M.: Research on the Realization Mechanism of the Integration of Production and Education in Higher Vocational Colleges – Based on the Analysis of the Current Situation of Higher Vocational Colleges in Zhejiang Province. Zhejiang University of Technology, Hangzhou (2017)
8. Bao, J., Mao, Y., Yu, P.: Research on e-commerce talent training mode for enterprise demand. E-commerce **08**, 59 (2017)
9. Tang, L., Wang, M.: Engineering discipline construction in local universities under the background of deepening the integration of industry and education. J. Hebei Normal Univ. (Educ. Sci. Edition) **04**, 101–105 (2019)
10. Yang, K., Cao, Z.: "Internet plus" innovation of personnel training mode of school enterprise cooperation. China Occup. Technol. Educ. **32**, 50–55 (2018)
11. Zhang, H.: Research and practice on talent training mode of industry education integration. Sci. Technol. Chinese Univ. **08**, 42–44 (2018)
12. Fang, X., Ding, L.: Teaching reform and practice of computer application foundation course in higher vocational colleges based on ability standard. Hebei Vocat. Educ. **01**, 44–46 (2020)
13. Jiang, L., Zhang, X., Yan, M., Zhu, N.: Talent cultivation of e-commerce major in higher vocational colleges in the era of artificial intelligence — from the perspective of employment. Hebei Vocat. Educ. **03**, 40–43 (2020)
14. Hao, T., Shi, W.: From loose connection to entity embedding: the dilemma and breakthrough of the integration of production and education in vocational education. Educ. Res. **07**, 102–110 (2019)
15. Bai, Y.: Construction of first-class undergraduate course focuses on four integrations. J. Educ. Sci. Hunan Normal Univ. **02**, 23–26 (2019)

Computer Aided System for Swimming Teaching and Training

Han Guo[✉]

Northwestern Polytechnical University (NPU), Xi'an 710072, China
johnson0730@nwpu.edu.cn

Abstract. In the field of sports, the successful application of computer-aided system in various sports has been paid more and more attention by PE teachers and coaches. We know that the computer-aided system involved in the field of physical education and training, not only will improve the scientific training teaching to a new stage, but also bring the rapid improvement of the level of competitive sports. The application of high-tech achievements in sports training and teaching is the development direction of modern sports teaching and training. The emergence of computer-aided system technology provides a strong driving force for swimming teaching and training to a faster and better level. This paper expounds the composition and characteristics of the computer-aided swimming teaching system and the particularity of swimming teaching and training. This paper discusses the feasibility of the application of computer aided system in swimming teaching and training.

Keywords: Computer aided system · Swimming teaching · Swimming training · Application · Feasibility

1 Introduction

With the rapid development of computer technology, its application has penetrated into all fields of society, which has effectively promoted the development of social informatization. Mastering and using computer technology has become an essential skill for people. In recent 10 years, it has been widely used in aerospace machinery design, computer simulation and so on. With the increasingly fierce sports competition and the continuous improvement of sports training level, high-tech means are more and more widely used in sports competition and training teaching. However, the computer aided system (CAS) has not been developed in the field of sports due to technical personnel, funds, design difficulties and other reasons. We know that the intervention of high technology in the field of sports teaching and training not only improves the scientific training teaching to a new stage, but also brings about the rapid improvement of competitive sports level. It is the development direction of modern physical education teaching and training to seize the opportunity to apply high-tech achievements to sports training and physical education teaching [1]. With the development of sports teaching and the continuous

M. A. Jan and F. Khan (Eds.): BigIoT-EDU 2021, LNICST 391, pp. 43–52, 2021.
https://doi.org/10.1007/978-3-030-87900-6_6

improvement of sports training level, the deepening of specialization forces athletes and coaches to constantly improve and improve sports technology, training methods and with the help of high-tech equipment to adapt to the fierce competition of high-level competitions. It also makes PE teachers use high-tech means to improve the quality of physical education, and provides new methods and ideas. Therefore, the application of computer-aided system in swimming teaching and training has a very broad prospect and great significance.

2 Computer Aided Diagnosis Method Based on Random Forest

Image graying is to convert color images into images with pixel values between 0 and 25, that is, to convert them into images with different gray levels, so as to reduce the interference of color on the final imaging of national standard tumors. At present, there are kinds of image graying methods.

Component method:

$$Gray = B; Gray = G; Gray = R \tag{1}$$

Where gray is the gray value of the converted gray image. R. G and B are the three parts of color map.

Maximum method:

$$Gray = \max(B + G + R) \tag{2}$$

Image smoothing is to remove the noise in the image and improve the definition. In this study, wavelet de-noising method is selected for image flattening. Firstly, the image signal is decomposed by wavelet, and then the decomposition result is quantized by threshold [2–4]. Finally, the image signal is reconstructed by using two-dimensional wavelet to obtain the denoised image.

3 Application of Computer Aided System in Swimming Teaching and Training

3.1 Composition and Concept of Computer Aided System

3.1.1 Computer Aided System Includes

Computer aided design (CAD), computer aided manufacturing (CAM) and computer base education (CBE) are mainly used in swimming training. In As shown Fig. 1 and Fig. 2.

Fig. 1. Computer aided design

Fig. 2. Computer aided manufacturing

3.1.2 Computer Aided Design

Computer aided design (CAD) is to help all kinds of designers design with computers. Because the computer has the ability of fast numerical calculation, strong data processing and simulation, CAD technology has been widely used. For example: the innovative design of swimming techniques, the quantitative analysis of the world's elite swimmers' techniques. As shown in Fig. 3. The adoption of CAD not only improves the speed of technological innovation, but also improves the innovation quality and mastering speed.

3.1.3 Computer Aided Education

Computer Aided Education (be) includes CAI (Computer Assisted Instruction), computer aided test (CAT) and computer management (CML). Computer aided instruction (CA) is a kind of teaching method that uses computer as teaching medium to teach learners. It makes great changes in teaching mode, teaching content, means and methods of educators [5]. The situation of teachers in class (one person, one pen, one brush) has gradually become history. With the popularity of computers, CA has gradually become

Fig. 3. Computer base education

an important means of teaching. There are three kinds of Ca: network Ca, multimedia Ca and intelligent ca [3]. With the development of computer and network technology, cat and °C m are used for teaching management (exchange and transmission of teaching documents, test papers, etc.) and examinations.

3.2 Hardware Equipment for Computer Aided System

Host computer (PC, PC workstation), graphics and image processing system (input device and output device). hardware equipment required by cal (see Fig. 4). The hardware environment required by CBE is the same as above.

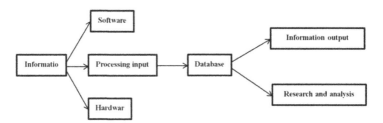

Fig. 4. Hardware equipment required by computer aided system

4 The Importance of Core Strength Training in Swimming Teaching and Training

4.1 The Meaning of Core Strength Training

The middle part of the human body is called the core, which is the muscles around the abdomen and buttocks. Collectively referred to as the "core muscle group", it is the main part of the whole body. It mainly includes abdominal muscles, hip muscles, and muscles connected with spine and bone box. The training of these muscle groups is called core strength training. Core strength plays a stabilizing and supporting role in motor skills and special technical movements, including posture. Therefore, the core strength is unstable, which has a great negative impact on people's mastery of the body, including posture. Before formally organizing the students to swim, the teacher must lead them to make preparations, so as to help them overcome the fear of water and lay a good foundation for the cultivation of water sense [6–8]. First of all, before swimming training, teachers should carefully combine the actual situation of students and the goal of water sense training, seriously formulate swimming training plan, and pay attention to organizing students to participate in preparatory activities before training. In this process, the teacher can directly teach the relevant theory to the students, use vivid language to describe the swimming process and visually demonstrate the specific action, so as to enhance the students' experience of water sense cultivation. For example, teachers can describe the state of a person swimming in the water as "floating objects in the water" and guide them to imagine the feeling of floating in the water.

4.2 The Necessity of Core Strength Training in Swimming Training

The muscle tissue of sex people can be divided into two types: superficial muscle and deep muscle. The superficial muscle is mainly responsible for strength and outburst, and the deep muscle is mainly responsible for stabilizing the body. The core muscle group can be divided into two parts: large core muscle group and small core muscle group. For these two parts, the core muscles are the superficial muscles, such as the extraabdominal muscles. The core small muscle group is the deep muscle, which plays a stabilizing role and plays a very important role in the body's trunk fixation. For example, the core strength training of internal abdominal muscles is the foundation of other sports training. A strong core muscle group can help us effectively improve our sports ability and efficiency. When upper and lower limbs are moving and exerting, the core muscles play a very important role in connecting the preceding and the following, helping us stabilize the body's center of gravity [9–11]. Therefore, when we swim and swing our arms and thighs, the core muscle group will help us better mobilize the muscles of the whole body, provide a support point for other parts of the force, reduce physical energy consumption, enhance sports ability, and improve sports efficiency. Scientific research results show that if swimmers want to improve their sports ability, they must strengthen the training of core strength. The core strength can mobilize the muscles of the whole body, maintain coordination, make the muscles combine with the nervous system in a relaxed state, instantly concentrate the strength, produce a huge resultant force, increase the swimming speed, reduce the resistance, and improve the performance.

5 Methods of Cycle Training

5.1 Using Statistical Software for Mathematical Statistics

Mathematical statistics method needs to be based on certain data. Two classes can be selected as experimental classes, and then the teaching experiment time of the two classes is controlled at 14 weeks. Before the cycle training experiment, the students' physical fitness, learning interest in swimming and swimming achievement are tested. After the experiment, these data are tested repeatedly to compare the two groups of data, All the data will be included in the statistical software for mathematical statistics, in order to test the practical role of cycle training method in swimming teaching.

5.2 Teaching Experiment Method

The traditional teaching method is used in the control class, that is, according to the swimming syllabus, the teaching plan is made, the breaststroke techniques are explained to the students in order and step by step, and then the corresponding training is carried out. The experimental class uses the circular training method to carry out the swimming teaching, that is, the teaching content of each class is divided into several parts, fixed multiple areas and swimming lanes to complete different parts of the training, and each swimming lane is set with different training time [12]. At the end of the training time, the students of each lane change their positions and continue to complete the corresponding part of the training after a short rest. The amount of training and training hours of the experimental class and the control class are completely consistent. The experimental class only set up four task sites (kicking, rowing, variable speed swimming, cooperative swimming) in each class, so as not to affect the efficiency and quality of students due to too many task sites.

6 Application of Cycle Training Method in Swimming Teaching in Colleges and Universities

6.1 Improve the Physical Quality of Students

Through the study of the data, it is found that after applying the circular training method to the swimming teaching in Colleges and universities, the physical quality of the students has changed significantly, mainly in the obvious changes of the trainer's ketchup index and skinfold thickness [13–15]. At the same time, the resting heart rate and vital capacity of the trainers have also been enhanced to a certain extent, The fat content of the trainers decreased in different degrees, so the swimming teaching under the circular training method can effectively improve the physical quality of the students.

6.2 It Improves the Interest of College Students in Swimming

Before and after the experimental teaching, the scores of students' learning interest test in the experimental class were (80.95 ± 485) and (90.57 ± 3.01) respectively, and those in the control class were (8152 ± 498) and (80.31 ± 3.95) respectively. From these data, we can see that the two classes are interested in swimming before the experiment, and the level of interest in swimming of the two classes is similar. After the experiment, the score of learning interest of the experimental class is significantly improved, which shows that the circular training method can effectively stimulate students' interest in swimming, which may be related to the different training content and training focus of each task site under the circular training method, which can give students more freshness and maintain a high degree of enthusiasm for swimming.

6.3   It Is Helpful to Relieve Students' Fatigue in the Process of Swimming

No matter in which sport, there will be different degrees of fatigue in the process of exercise, so in swimming, the trainer will also have a sense of fatigue. However, sports injury does great harm to the trainer's body, which will not only damage the trainer's body, but also affect the subsequent normal training of the trainer. Through the experiment, it is proved that when the reasonable cycle training method is used in swimming teaching, it can obviously reduce the fatigue of the trainers. This is mainly because the cycle training method can effectively divide the repeated training tasks into several simple and easy to complete small projects, and the students will not have too much exercise pressure during the training, reducing the probability of sports injury.

6.4   It Effectively Improves the Students' Swimming Performance

Because the circular training method divides the whole training into several small tasks, it enables students to train every swimming skill accurately [16]. Therefore, the circular training method is conducive to the comprehensive training of swimming skills, which is more conducive to students to master the basic skills of swimming, and can train leg muscles and increase arm training separately, So that students can fundamentally improve their swimming speed, and then improve their swimming performance.

7   Application of Computer Aided System in Swimming Teaching and Training

7.1   Application of CAD in Swimming Training

With the improvement of the level of competition, the athletes and coaches put forward higher requirements in the design of technical movements and learning advanced technology.

If athletes can absorb foreign advanced technology, learn from each other, and then form a set of their own near perfect technology according to their own characteristics, is the key factor to win the competition. In swimming training, the training and innovative design of action technology is still in the stage of artificial design mainly based on experience, only relying on the coach's language to explain and demonstrate, the athletes try carefully. This has many disadvantages, such as long design and training cycle, low efficiency, poor quality, narrow creative source, and can not simulate and demonstrate new movements unless the athletes train in person. So we can use CAD technology in the following two aspects.

7.2   Application of CAA in Swimming Training

The parameters of each part of the body are input into the computer to establish a set of human body model database. It can automatically simulate all kinds of swimming movements, and use computational virtual technology to establish site models and particle system models that are consistent with the real environment to replace flume experiments, so as to help people study hydrodynamic problems such as water resistance change and influence. Biomechanical analysis computer has many advantages, such as large data processing, accurate and rapid calculation, and no human error. Therefore, the prospect of introducing CAA technology into the field of swimming is very broad. For example, the United States power company has applied CAA technology to swimming. Its powerscan portable swimming technology analyzer can be used for biomechanical analysis of the whole race, average speed and instantaneous speed [17–19]. As shown in Fig. 5. A series of technical analysis, such as stroke frequency, stroke start, take-off, turn, sprint calculation and hand in angle, stroke angle and so on. Because powerscan instrument is compact and convenient, it is helpful to analyze and improve swimmer's technique.

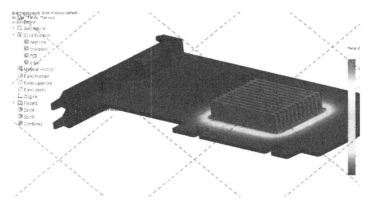

Fig. 5. Application of CAA in swimming training

7.3 Application of Computer Aided System in Swimming Teaching

In recent years, the development of network technology and multimedia technology has promoted the development of CBE. Online teaching and distance education have been carried out in many schools. The development of CBE makes great changes in teaching activities and teaching quality. In the field of swimming, the development of CBE provides an opportunity for sports colleges and other sports personnel training units to cultivate all-round development of high-quality swimming talents. The application of Ca in swimming teaching CA breaks away from the traditional teaching mode of human, pen and board, and introduces sound, light and image into teaching, which is intuitive and easy to understand. At the same time, CA teaching can solve the problems of improving teaching efficiency, lack of teaching staff and teaching standardization. In this regard, some researchers in China have achieved some research results [20]. For example, Zhang Zhaohui of Guangzhou Institute of physical education and Lu Peng of PLA Physical Education Institute have applied several kinds of swimming teaching CA courseware to swimming teaching activities, which has played a very good teaching effect and response.

7.4 Application of Cat in Swimming Teaching

Cat is a revolution of education examination in recent years. one side. It input examination Resources into λ database, and then randomly select test papers according to the difficulty for ability assessment. It realizes the test form of "test paper marking scoring automation". Can correctly and effectively determine the objective multiple choice questions [4]. On the other hand, with the development of CA technology in recent years, the research on the computerization of subjective examination papers has also appeared. For example, ETS has designed a set of CAT system combining GRE and GMAT composition examination, which implements double computer marking. That is to say, two computers simultaneously judge a composition paper. If the difference between the two computer scoring results is more than one point, manual marking is used [21–24]. After using the system, the marking time of GRE and GMAT compositions has increased from 30 min to 5 min. It has greatly improved the efficiency of examination scoring. Therefore, CAT technology for us in swimming teaching examination, referee examination or other content of the examination to create a new idea.

8 Conclusion

It is of great significance to apply CAS to swimming teaching and training. At present, there are many difficulties in the application of CAS in swimming training teaching, especially in the research of technical simulation. Using CAS to improve the level of swimming teaching and training is ultimately the improvement of people. With the continuous development of computer technology and related disciplines, computer aided design (CAS) will become an important force in swimming teaching and training. Intellectualization and precision will be the research direction of this kind of subject in the future. In many sports training methods, the circulation training method is a more common training method. The research shows that the correct cycle training method can not only have a very beneficial effect on the body's organ blindness, but also improve the athletes' training endurance and strengthen their muscle strength to a certain extent. Based on the swimming teaching in Colleges and universities, this paper compares the traditional training method with the circular training method, and discusses how to better apply the circular training method to the swimming teaching in Colleges and universities, so as to achieve the purpose of improving students' interest in swimming through the correct circular training method.

References

1. Yongsheng, W.: Feasibility study on the application of computer aided design in sports competitive action. J. Beijing Sport Univ. **2** (1998)
2. Qing, W.: Thoughts on sports science and technology. In: Proceedings of Scientific Research Institute of General Administration of sport of China (2000)
3. University Computer Committee. Basic Computer Knowledge. Beijing, Higher Education Press (2000)
4. Riewald, S.: Biomechanical simulation of hand and arm propulsion. Swim. Inf. **4** (2001)

5. Xinqi, L.: Research on the application of imagery training in swimming teaching in colleges and universities. Phys. Educ. Teach. Friends **44**(1), 41–44 (2021)
6. Lin, Z.: Swimming training "bravery" in the first place: exploration on the mode of psychological training in swimming course. Sports Sci. Technol. Lit. Bull. **29**(1), 82–124 (2021)
7. Xiufeng, H., Qiaoqin, W.: Research on the content and method of physical training in college swimming teaching. Youth Sports **12**, 87–89 (2020)
8. Fei, X.: Analysis of core strength training in swimming teaching and training. Sci. Technol. Inf. **18**(34), 240–242 (2020)
9. Gengyi, H.: Research on core strength training in swimming teaching in colleges and universities. Ice Snow Sports Innov. Res.
10. Xiaodan, Y.: Analysis of core strength training methods in swimming teaching and training. Farm Staff **18**, 261 (2020)
11. Lin, N.: Scientific research on swimming teaching and training methods in military academies. Contemp. Sports Sci. Technol. **10**(26), 72–73 + 76 (2020)
12. Jing, P.: Research on the application of core stable strength training in swimming teaching in colleges and universities. Res. Innov. Ice Snow Sports **13**, 27–28 (2020)
13. Cheng, Y.: The causes of "fear of water" in children's swimming teaching and the ways to overcome it. Contemp. Sports Sci. Technol. **10**(18), 204–206 (2020)
14. Zixuan, Z.: Analysis of core strength training in swimming teaching and training. Chin. New Commun. **22**(12), 194 (2020)
15. Bodong, Z.: Discussion on the practical application of circular training method in swimming training in colleges and universities. Res. Innov. Ice Snow Sports **10**, 59–60 (2020)
16. Ruilin, D.: Problems and countermeasures of training beginners in swimming teaching. Rural Staff **10**, 296 (2020)
17. Lei, W.: Research on the application of imagery training in freestyle teaching for students aged, pp. 10–14. Harbin Normal University (2020)
18. Xiaochen, J.: Optimization design and empirical research on the teaching of elementary breaststroke kick technique for boys aged, pp. 11–12. Capital Institute of Physical Education (2020)
19. Xinyu, H.: Experimental study on the effect of physical training on children's swimming teaching. Southwest University (2020)
20. Wei, W.: Research on the application of modern information technology in swimming training. Contemp. Sports Sci. Technol. **10**(11), 53–54 (2020)
21. Qian, Z.: Experimental study on the effect of gradual relaxation training method on swimming beginners' fear of water. Southwest University (2020)
22. Fangke, L.: Discussion on core strength training in swimming teaching and training. Contemp. Sports Sci. Technol. **10**(10), 63–65
23. Yuzhe, W.: Analysis of core strength training in swimming teaching and training. Sports Prod. **39**(3), 77–78 (2020)
24. Zhe, L.: Research on the influence of swimming teaching on the physical coordination ability of children aged, pp. 6–8. Shandong Institute of Physical Education (2020)

Computer Basic Course Teaching Based on Blended Learning

Lei Wang[✉]

Xi'an Haitang Vocational College, Xi'an 710043, China

Abstract. Blended learning is the latest trend in the development of international education. It integrates face-to-face learning in traditional classroom and Online Autonomous Learning Assisted by information technology. Its emergence is of great significance for the reform of the current basic computer teaching. This paper introduces the theory of blended learning. Based on the research of blended learning theory, this paper puts forward a blended learning teaching design mode of computer application foundation course, which is suitable for the current situation of university teaching. It can provide online learning and communication for students and teachers, and improve the shortcomings of traditional teaching mode, so as to help the reform of computer professional teaching development.

Keywords: Blended learning · Basic computer courses · Course teaching

1 Introduction

Nowadays, with the development of Internet and information technology, teaching methods have been improved, which has replaced the previous "chalk + blackboard" mode, making the expression of teaching content more intuitive, increasing the amount of classroom information and improving teaching efficiency. However, the relationship between teaching and learning is still "you teach me to learn". The difference is that the content of the teaching material is made into courseware, the content on the paper is projected to the large screen through the projection instrument, and the "electric irrigation" is adopted. It is still a teacher centered teaching mode, and students are always in the position of passive learning. In this teaching mode, the channel for students to obtain knowledge and information can only come from the teachers in the classroom. Unfortunately, teachers can not teach all the knowledge to students, and students can not learn all the knowledge. In fact, what students lack is how to learn how to learn and how to obtain information related to learning content through various channels. In addition, due to the differences in learning of students from the same learning starting point, it is difficult to adapt to students with different learning abilities by adopting a single teaching organization form, which is not conducive to teaching students in accordance with their aptitude, especially the teaching of "full regular irrigation" is not popular with students. As a result, students' learning initiative is ignored or even suppressed, which directly affects the teaching effect.

© ICST Institute for Computer Sciences, Social Informatics and Telecommunications Engineering 2021
Published by Springer Nature Switzerland AG 2021. All Rights Reserved
M. A. Jan and F. Khan (Eds.): BigIoT-EDU 2021, LNICST 391, pp. 53–58, 2021.
https://doi.org/10.1007/978-3-030-87900-6_7

2   A Summary of Hybrid Learning

The development of society and information technology has changed the way we communicate and learn, which inevitably changes the way we think. The form of communication and the management of information challenge our cognitive ability and the teaching paradigm of traditional classroom. The development of Internet promotes the popularity of distance education, and brings new learning form online learning. People define online learning as the process of learners using the Internet to obtain learning materials and complete the learning process through interaction with teachers and other learners. One of the most important problems faced by online learning is whether students can get better learning effect than traditional classroom teaching. The increase of students and the diversification of population structure, as well as the development of lifelong education and information technology, have brought opportunities for the emergence of new teaching models. The president of Pennsylvania State University in the United States thinks that hybrid learning is "the only recognized development trend in higher education today". Hybrid learning combines the advantages of traditional teaching and network teaching, which can effectively make up for their shortcomings, and thus has been favored by the society and the education community. Hybrid learning (BL) is a combination of traditional face-to-face teaching and modern information technology, and is being applied to teaching more and more. Some scholars predict that hybrid learning will become a "regular mode" in curriculum teaching [1].

The elements of hybrid learning can be represented by hexagon formed by two triangles. As shown in Fig. 1, the status of these six elements in hybrid learning is equally important. The six elements are divided into two systems, which support and integrate each other, reflecting the characteristics of hybrid learning.

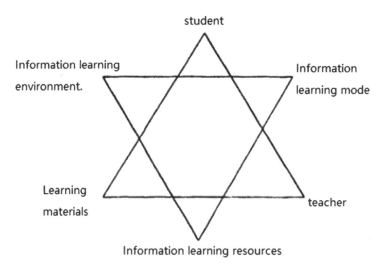

Fig. 1. Six elements of blended Learning

In the information-based learning environment, great changes have taken place in people's learning style. Information learning is different from traditional learning methods. Learners' learning not only depends on Teachers' teaching and textbook learning, but also uses information platform and information resources to carry out negotiation and cooperative learning between teachers and students. Through the collection and utilization of resources, they can explore knowledge, discover knowledge, create knowledge and display knowledge.

After the implementation of blended learning, the main elements of blended learning, including teachers, students and learning materials, have also changed, as shown in Fig. 2.

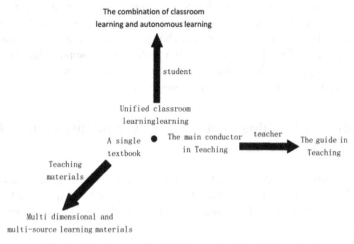

Fig. 2. The change of basic elements in blended learning

The construction of blended learning mode is an effective teaching mode in terms of teaching form, which breaks through the traditional single classroom teaching mode and improves teaching means; in terms of teaching content, it expands students' horizons, expands students' learning scope and enriches students' learning content; in terms of teaching content, it expands students' learning scope and enriches students' learning content; In terms of learning style, it breaks the boundaries of time and space, changes the cognitive style, and makes the "student-centered" white master learning a reality.

3   Shortcomings of Traditional Teaching Mode in Computer Teaching in Higher Vocational Colleges

3.1   The Use of Multimedia Courseware Is Too Much, with a Certain Degree of Dependence

In the traditional teaching mode of computer application foundation course, teachers use multimedia courseware excessively. Multimedia courseware should be used properly, in order to play a very good teaching effect. If it has a certain dependence on multimedia courseware, this kind of teaching method is not conducive to students' learning, which will lead to students not having their own thinking ability. Due to their own characteristics, students' basic computer knowledge is uneven, excessive use of multimedia courseware is not conducive to the improvement of students' practical operation ability, leading to teaching can not achieve the expected teaching objectives.

3.2 The Effect of Improving Students' Computer Professional Skills Is Not Obvious

For students, it is very important to improve their professional skills. But in the traditional teaching mode, we do not pay attention to the training of practical operation ability of the students in higher vocational colleges. Students should have certain computer professional skills and hands-on operation ability. But the students' own knowledge level is limited. Therefore, in the face of some professional computer knowledge, will not achieve the expected effect. This leads to students not enough interest in learning, so that they can not further improve their professional quality [2].

4 Research on Teaching Mode of Basic Computing Course Based on Blended Learning

In view of the new situation and new tasks of the current basic computer education, we believe that the reform of basic computer teaching is imperative, and the teaching mode based on blended learning will provide a new idea for deepening the reform of basic computer course.

4.1 The Mixture of Teachers' Leading Role and Students' Principal Position

In the teaching mode, mixing the leading role of teachers with the dominant position of students is from the perspective of teachers and students, which emphasizes the leading role of teachers in classroom teaching and the dominant position of students in the learning process. It is a teaching mode of "leading subject combination". In the initial stage of the teaching process, it is necessary to rely on teachers to stimulate students' interest in learning and help students form learning motivation; in the teaching process, it is also necessary to rely on teachers to connect the current new knowledge, new concepts and students' original cognitive structure about the current knowledge, so as to form meaningful learning. Therefore, the leading role of teachers should be emphasized in these stages. Students are the main body of information processing and the active constructors of knowledge meaning. Only by giving full play to their initiative and enthusiasm can they obtain effective cognition. This kind of active participation creates good conditions for students to give full play to their initiative and enthusiasm, so that students can truly embody the role of cognitive subject.

In the course of computer foundation, we should change the traditional teaching mode which takes the teacher as the center, and combine the teacher's leading role with the student's dominant position, so as to realize the optimization of teaching effect [3].

4.2   The Mixture of Classroom Teaching and Network Learning

The basic computer course is highly practical, the teaching content covers a wide range, and the difference of students' basic computer knowledge is very obvious. We should not only satisfy the classroom teaching, but use information technology to create a new teaching environment, For example, the application of network provides a good platform for practical courses. Therefore, we should build a website for basic computer courses and provide all the teaching resources of the course, including the material library, experimental instructions, teaching cases and expanded knowledge that students need for self-study.

The combination of classroom teaching and network learning in computer basic course can fully cultivate students' computer operation ability, problem analysis and problem solving ability, autonomous learning and cooperative learning ability, and meet the learning needs of students of different majors and levels.

4.3   The Mixture of Autonomous Learning and Cooperative Learning

Students' autonomous learning can be carried out through teaching materials, notes and other teaching resources before or after class, and they can also independently retrieve relevant resources through the network or carry out planned learning according to the guidance of network courses. The development of cooperative learning mainly refers to group discussion, communication in traditional teaching environment and online topic communication based on network environment.

The quality of students' autonomous learning and cooperative learning will directly affect their learning effect. How to guide students to integrate all kinds of learning methods, give full play to students' learning enthusiasm, enhance students' sense of participation, and cultivate the spirit of team cooperation is also an important issue for hybrid teaching.

4.4   The Combination of Process Assessment and Summative Evaluation

The key point of computer basic course examination lies in the cultivation of students' computer knowledge and ability. Therefore, the form of examination should be diversified. The examination system adopts the mode of "theory+. Computer", which can not only investigate the basic theory, but also test the operation skills. At the same time, a comprehensive design course design is arranged after each basic computer course, which is included in the final evaluation results of the semester. These measures cultivate and train students' practical operation ability and improve their comprehensive application ability.

The summative evaluation of the semester should include process assessment, curriculum design and final examination. At the same time, competition should be carried out to promote students' learning, to evaluate students' comprehensive ability and improve the assessment mechanism. For example, hold the annual computer skills competition, including computer basic knowledge, office automation application, database application system design, program design and other skills competition, in order to show students' quality and promote the improvement of students' comprehensive application ability.

5 Conclusion

In the process of deepening and improving the reform of basic computer teaching, First of all, we should set up the advanced educational thought of "teacher oriented, student-centered". Under the guidance of the advanced educational thought, we should explore new teaching means and methods mixed with various teaching modes, strengthen students' computer practical ability, pay attention to cultivating students' ability and quality, and promote the vigorous development of computer basic course teaching.

References

1. Lin, L.: Research on the application and practice of blended learning in the teaching of computer application foundation course in RTVU. Sci. Chin. **29**, 264–265 (2016)
2. Research Group of Computer Basic Education Reform in Chinese Colleges and Universities. Computer Basic Education Curriculum System in Chinese Colleges and Universities, 2008. Tsinghua University Press, Beijing, pp. 18–19 (2008)
3. ZhengJuan, L.: Application and practice of hybrid teaching mode in teaching reform of higher vocational education. Mod. Vocat. Educ. **11**, 31–39 (2018)

Construction of Fuzzy Comprehensive Evaluation Model of Physical Education · Teaching Based on Short Video

Jinyao Liu and Ronghan Wang$^{(\boxtimes)}$

Jiangxi College of Applied Technology, Ganzhou 341000, Jiangxi, China

Abstract. This paper draws on related teaching methods and designs a fuzzy evaluation index system for physical education quality based on short videos. On this basis, the maximum frequency interval method is used to determine the weights of the primary and secondary indicators. In view of the many factors affecting the quality of outdoor teaching of physical education teachers in colleges and universities, which are difficult to express and calculate with precise mathematics, the Fuzzy comprehensive evaluation model is used to deal with the qualitative factors among them, and with the help of case studies, designs are designed to affect the quality of physical education teaching. Several evaluation indicators, using fuzzy comprehensive scoring method, formulate a comprehensive evaluation table and calculation formula for physical education teaching, so as to realize the quantitative evaluation of physical education teaching. Case studies have shown that the use of fuzzy teaching methods to evaluate practical course teaching can effectively reduce the influence of subjective factors, the calculation method is simple and practical, and the evaluation results are accurate and reliable.

Keywords: Short video · Physical education · Fuzzy comprehensive evaluation · Model construction

1 Introduction

Physical education is an important part of school quality education. How to comprehensively evaluate the quality of physical education is related to discipline construction and reform and development [1]. Therefore, the use of scientific and reasonable multi-level evaluation is an effective way to standardize the evaluation of physical education teaching quality. Through student evaluation of teacher performance, we can clearly know the relationship between physical education teachers and students in teaching activities and their own shortcomings in the teaching process, so as to make up for the shortcomings in a targeted manner to improve physical education teachers' own comprehensive teaching ability [2].

At present, domestic and foreign scholars' research in the field of physical education mainly focuses on the following aspects. Some researchers mentioned that the current

M. A. Jan and F. Khan (Eds.): BigIoT-EDU 2021, LNICST 391, pp. 59–66, 2021.
https://doi.org/10.1007/978-3-030-87900-6_8

evaluation model of physical education teaching quality in ordinary colleges and universities has serious deviations from the content of the evaluation, the goal of the evaluation, and the concept of the evaluation [3]. Some researchers also believe that the purpose, content, standards, and methods of the new curriculum standard sports evaluation have changed, and the original evaluation indicators cannot be used [4]. In the current situation and reform trend of physical education evaluation, some researchers mentioned that teaching evaluation should be a combination of summative evaluation and formative evaluation, and a combination of qualitative evaluation and quantitative evaluation [5]. Although these studies have conducted various analyses on the evaluation of the teaching quality of physical education courses in colleges and universities, most of them have raised questions and analyzed the reasons, and have not established an evaluation index system and calculation method [6]. In the evaluation of physical education, due to the wide range of evaluation indicators, there are more reasons to be considered [7]. Some evaluation indicators can be evaluated using traditional methods, while some indicators have a certain degree of ambiguity and cannot be evaluated using traditional quantitative methods. It requires a combination of qualitative and quantitative evaluation [8].

In view of the fact that the quality of physical education is inherently vague, based on short videos, this article uses Fuzzy mathematics to evaluate the quality of physical education has a theoretical basis. The fuzzy comprehensive evaluation method is a combination of qualitative and quantitative methods based on fuzzy mathematics, and is especially suitable for evaluation methods with certain fuzzy indicators in the evaluation indicators. Therefore, this article discusses how to apply the fuzzy comprehensive evaluation method to comprehensively evaluate the quality of physical education. Through the use of logical analysis, based on the study of the development history and status quot of mobile short video, a teaching model of college physical education based on this is proposed. In practice, the Fuzzy comprehensive evaluation multi-level model has indeed broadened the evaluation thinking, expanded the evaluation scope, turned qualitative analysis into quantitative analysis, and promoted a more systematic physical education evaluation system.

2 Construction of Physical Education Teaching Model Based on Short Video

2.1 Principle of Fuzzy Comprehensive Evaluation

The basic idea of the fuzzy comprehensive evaluation method is: on the basis of determining the evaluation factors, the evaluation grade standards and weights of the factors, the fuzzy set transformation principle is used to describe the membership degree of each factor and the fuzzy boundary of the factor to construct a fuzzy evaluation matrix. The composite operation of the layers finally determines the level of the evaluation object. Based on fuzzy mathematics, aiming at the qualitative and quantitative ambiguities of the evaluation object, applying the principle of fuzzy relationship synthesis, according to multiple evaluation factors, comprehensive evaluation of the status of the research target is carried out. The framework is shown in Fig. 1. Considering the intricacies of the internal relations of objective things and the ambiguity of the entire system, this method

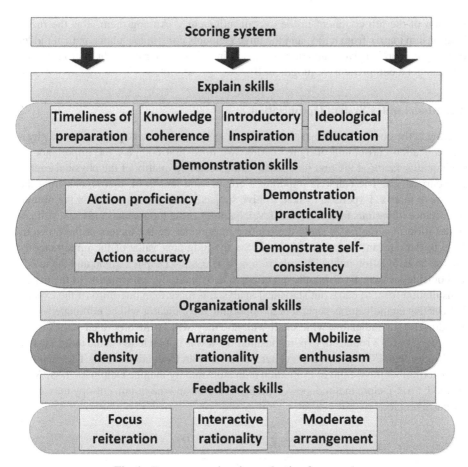

Fig. 1. Fuzzy comprehensive evaluation framework

can be used for the comprehensive evaluation of subjective indicators and objective indicators, especially the comprehensive evaluation of subjective indicators. The main steps are as follows:

There are two finite domains:

$$u = \{x1, x2, l, xn\} \tag{1}$$

$$v = \{y1, y2, l, yn\} \tag{2}$$

Among them: u represents the set of multiple factors of comprehensive evaluation, called the factor set; v is the set of multiple decisions, called the judgment set or comment set. Generally, the influence of each factor on the judged object is not consistent in the general factor concentration. Therefore, the weight distribution of the factor is a fuzzy vector on U. In addition, m comments are not absolutely positive or negative. Therefore, the comprehensive judgment can be regarded as a fuzzy set on y, which represents the position of the nth comment in the overall judgment y. Among them, T is the fuzzy relationship matrix from u to y, and the three elements constitute a mathematical model of fuzzy comprehensive evaluation. At this point, if you enter a weight distribution A, you can get a comprehensive judgment B.

2.2 Model Index System Optimization

Aiming at the comprehensive evaluation index system for the teaching quality of physical education curriculum designed earlier, we must first compare the importance of each quality factor at the first index level to the teaching quality of the physical education curriculum. The pairwise importance comparison matrix of, that is, construct the judgment matrix. Experts are asked to give subjective judgments based on the mutual importance of various factors at each level, quantify these judgments, and express them in the form of a matrix to show the relative importance of the factors at the previous level to the relevant factors at this level, Set the judgment value of the importance of the factor. Evaluation index The selection is based on the Delphi method and the inside and outside method. By using the quantitative and qualitative information of the expert consultation form to carry out statistical analysis, if more than one-third of the experts believe that an indicator is general or unimportant, the indicator will be eliminated soon. In addition, for indicators with small weights, they will be incorporated into Similar indicators. After 3 rounds of expert consultation, it was not included in the index system until more than 70% of the experts agreed to form an evaluation index. The methods for determining the weight of evaluation indicators mainly include Delphi method, AHP method, PAH-Delphi method, power gradient method and maximum entropy maximum variance method.

$$c = \frac{\sum\limits_{i=1}^{m} Ni(xi + 1 - xi)}{\sum\limits_{i=1}^{m} Ni} \tag{3}$$

$$[x, y] = \begin{cases} [x_m, y_m], m > n \\ [x_n, y_n], m < n \end{cases} \tag{4}$$

$$T = \begin{bmatrix} t_{11} & t_{1n} \\ t_{n1} & t_{nm} \end{bmatrix} \tag{5}$$

$$W = \sum T \bullet x = (w_{11}, w_{12}, \cdots, w_{1m}) \tag{6}$$

Set the weight distribution matrix of each index in the first-level index set as c, and the weight distribution matrix of each index in the first-level index set as E. The weights of the above indicators can be determined according to the Fuzzy statistical method: in the solicitation of the weight interval, n experts ($n \geq 10$) are asked to give a weight interval for each first-level indicator and second-level indicator. In the maximum membership frequency interval, find the maximum value of the left end of the weight interval [x, y] (i = I, 2,…, n). If the evaluation result is not applicable, the result will be normalized. The single-level fuzzy comprehensive evaluation method is used for problems with relatively few factors. If it is said that in a more complex system, there are more various factors that need to be considered, and there are often hierarchical divisions in each factor. You should consider dividing the set of factors U into several categories according to certain attributes. Make a comprehensive evaluation, and then conduct a high-level comprehensive evaluation between the "categories" of the evaluation results. At the same time, it is necessary to use a multi-user fuzzy comprehensive evaluation method in a complex system.

3 Application and Analysis of Physical Education Model Based on Short Video

3.1 Determination of Teaching Quality Evaluation Index and Weight Distribution

According to existing data and information, it is generally believed that the evaluation of physical education quality mainly includes four aspects: a teaching ability, b teaching effect, c teaching exercise volume, and d other ancillary factors. And each aspect contains several subsets, so that we can draw a relationship diagram based on these evaluation contents to clarify the relationship between the evaluation factors. The evaluation content of each subset has its evaluation language. The evaluation language is divided into four grades: excellent, good, medium, and poor, which constitutes the evaluation domain v: excellent, good, medium, and poor. For a certain physical education teacher to be evaluated, each factor can be estimated by the method of scoring by experts. If one item is prepared beforehand, if 40% of all experts think it is excellent. Then choose the weighted average operator, the main factor determining operator, the main factor prominent operator, etc. to calculate the teacher's evaluation results more objectively. The evaluation language has its own degree of membership, and the degree of membership can be obtained through investigation, that is, a certain number of questionnaires are issued, according to the four levels, the teaching of physical education teachers is evaluated according to the content of the evaluation, and the four levels of evaluation are carried out. There is a certain percentage, and its value is the membership degree mapping of the evaluation content, in which the weight distribution of indicators is shown in Fig. 2..

Since the evaluation factors in each subset have different effects on the quality of physical education, that is to say, the evaluation factors in each subset have different weights or weights, which means that in physical education, each evaluation factor cannot be completely equal. There is a difference in the number distribution. The weights assigned to the elements with greater influence are more important, and vice verse. But the total weight must meet the requirements of normalization. Then, using the "Delphi" method, the opinions of professors, senior teachers, and teaching management cadres were consulted in turn, and the factors with a concentration rate of more than 80% were analyzed and clustered regression. Finally, the correctness of the evaluation results was considered. The evaluation index system is determined by several factors, and the first and second index systems are obtained, and the weight coefficient is calculated according to the contribution rate of each factor in the evaluation.

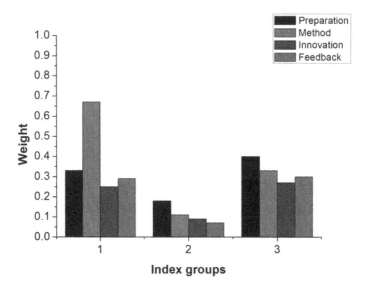

Fig. 2. The weight distribution of teaching quality evaluation index

3.2 Example Results and Analysis

The online short video media teaching quality evaluation was conducted for college physical education teachers participating in the "High School Sports Quality Class Competition" activity in a certain province, and the teacher numbered 9 was used as the evaluation object for a case study. Weight calculation: Use the maximum membership frequency interval method to determine the index weights at all levels. Data collection: Invite n(n ≥ 10) experts to score several indicators of the evaluation object ("very strong", "strong", "strong", "average", "bad"), and find out each teacher The proportion of the seed value is a 21 × 5 matrix. Matrix block: According to the division of the secondary index, the obtained matrix is divided into 5 corresponding sub-matrices. Second-level index score calculation: According to the second-level index weights obtained in advance, the corresponding sub-matrices are respectively multiplied to obtain the corresponding second-level index scores. The first-level index score calculation: multiply the first-level index weight obtained in advance and the obtained second-level index score to obtain the first-level index score. Fuzzy analysis of physical education teaching scoring in specific short videos is shown in Fig. 3, Most of the samples performed well, showing the practicality of this fuzzy comprehensive physical education system.

At the same time, in the 42 questionnaires recovered, 62% of the students' scores were in the excellent range, and 29% of the students' scores were in the good range. Within, 9% of the students' scores are within the general range. In Fig. 4, we can see the satisfaction of the physical education model under the short video, and the vast majority of people surveyed expressed satisfaction. Obtain the evaluation vector, teaching ability: (0.62, 0.29, 0.09); similarly, the teaching effect can be obtained: (0.71, 0.26, 0.03); the amount of teaching exercise: (0.65, 0.26, 0.09); professional ethics: (0.48, 0.38, 0.14); other ancillary factors: (0.57, 0.30, 0.13). Normalized to obtain the evaluation result

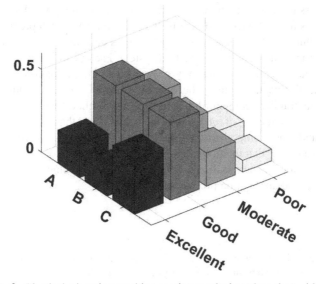

Fig. 3. Physical education teaching scoring results based on short videos

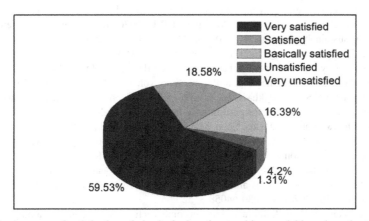

Fig. 4. A survey of satisfaction of physical education teaching model based on short video

description, and identify according to the principle of membership degree, the teacher's performance is: "excellent".

4   Conclusion

Based on the multi-user comprehensive evaluation method of Fuzzy mathematics under the short video, this paper designs a comprehensive evaluation model, which can integrate the opinions of various judges to the greatest extent, and more comprehensively reflect the quality of the teaching quality of the judged objects, thus increasing Judging the credibility and effectiveness of the results. In addition, this paper uses the analytic hierarchy process to determine the weights of various indicators, which has a scientific basis and reduces the influence of subjective factors; compared with previous methods, not only the influence of teachers' teaching factors is considered, but also the student learning system is included in the evaluation system. Factors are more comprehensive. The Fuzzy formula method can not only be applied to the evaluation of the teaching quality of physical education courses, but also can be applied to the scientific quantification of the group, training, competition, management of school physical education, and the comprehensive evaluation of related personnel. It is better than qualitative evaluation of experience and other comprehensive evaluations. The evaluation is easier to operate; the example also proves that the fuzzy comprehensive evaluation of the teaching quality of physical education teachers using the fuzzy set theory can obtain accurate evaluation results and has broad application prospects.

References

1. Wang, X., et al.: Simulation of physical education teaching video recognition based on FPGA and So-bel algorithm. Microprocess. Microsyst. 103519 (2020)
2. Wang, L., Wang, M., et al.: Application of MOOC in physical education teaching mode under the background of big data. J. Phys. Conf. Ser. IOP Publishing, **1744**(4), 042233 (2021)
3. Hei, X., Dong, F., Cui, Z., et al.: Intelligent fuzzy comprehensive evaluation of quality of public physical education based on HMM and AHP. In: 2020 3rd International Conference on Intelligent Sustainable Systems (ICISS), pp. 100–103. IEEE (2020)
4. Gou, X., Zhang, W., Zhang, J., et al.: Research on key technologies of elders' exoskeleton robot assisted by physical exercise based on fuzzy PID control. In: IOP Conference Series: Materials Science and Engineering, IOP Publishing, vol. 782(2), p. 022053 (2020)
5. Nazari-Shirkouhi, S., Mousakhani, S., Tavakoli, M., et al.: Importance-performance analysis based balanced scorecard for performance evaluation in higher education institutions: an integrated fuzzy approach. J. Bus. Econ. Manag. **21**(3), 647–678 (2020)
6. Olga, V., Sergey, S., Nikolay, B., et al.: Development of an expert information system for sports selection and orientation using fuzzy logic methods. In: Aliev, R.A., Kacprzyk, J., Pedrycz, W., Jamshidi, M., Babanli, M., Sadikoglu, F.M. (eds.) International Conference on Theory and Applications of Fuzzy Systems and Soft Computing. Springer, Cham, pp. 417–425 (2020). https://doi.org/10.1007/978-3-030-64058-3_52
7. Asadi, K., Bagheri, A., et al.: Initial training in combat activities in university training programs in physical education and health education. Int. J. Mod. Eng. Technol. **1**(1), 2639–2653 (2018)
8. Zhang, J.: Modernization process and traditional national sports inheritance research based on fuzzy clustering model. In: 2016 National Convention on Sports Science of China. EDP Sciences, p. 01015 (2017)

Design and Application of English Writing Training System Based on Web News Text Mining Technology

Yangxiameng Lu[✉]

Xi'an Medical University, Xi'an 710021, China

Abstract. Marking net, the largest online English composition marking platform in China, improves the speed of English writing feedback, and embodies the equal sharing of intelligence in learning. This paper focuses on the features of the new edition of the network, focusing on the technology of big data mining and learning analysis, discusses the application value of the visual graphics, charts and reports provided by the network, especially the classroom application value of error distribution and the role of guidance for accurate teaching and learning; points out that the ability of data analysis tests the multiple abilities of front-line teachers, which not only cultivates students' autonomous learning and learning abilityFinally, it briefly discusses the opportunities and challenges faced by intelligent technology itself.

Keywords: Correction network · Big data · Learning analysis · Error distribution · Accuracy

The Internet plus era is the era of rapid technological upgrading, and is the era of constantly updated ideas. Intelligent learning and intelligent teaching have gone deep into the behavior of teachers and students. However, the massive data provided by artificial intelligence is a challenge for teachers and students. "Data intelligence" provides technical support for accurate teaching in classroom, "teaching intelligence" will test teachers' decision-making and multiple action ability [1]."Data intelligence" also tests students' autonomous learning ability, constructs personalized adaptive learning habits, and conducts evidence-based intelligent learning. Customized teaching and learning based on big data analysis.

Teaching and learning will be the new mode and new power of learning in the future. This study specifically analyzes the application value of the new version of Junku correction network data in class and after class: through the bar chart, curve chart and word error report provided by the new version of correction network platform, the micro research on the two directions of data mining and learning analysis technology application of the new version of correction network is carried out, and it points out that only the integration of human and computer can implement effective correction [2].

An overview of the visualization and quantification of data in the latest edition of the online English composition and translation correction network, which is supported by corpus and cloud computing technology, is an online intelligent English composition

M. A. Jan and F. Khan (Eds.): BigIoT-EDU 2021, LNICST 391, pp. 67–75, 2021.
https://doi.org/10.1007/978-3-030-87900-6_9

and translation correction service platform. At present, it is the largest English online platform in China, which is used by teachers and students in more than 5000 schools. The automatic online correction service greatly shortens the time for College English teachers to correct their compositions. It is no longer a headache for students to correct their spelling and grammatical errors. It provides a strong technical support for teachers' intensive speaking in class and accurate tutoring after class. Students don't have to wait for delayed feedback from teachers. The score and comment of the composition will be given in time for reference.

And comment by sentence, so that every student using this platform can enjoy the dividend brought by technological innovation, bathe in the sunshine of educational technology intelligence, and enjoy the equal rights of everyone.

Junku correction network is developed by Beijing ciwang Technology Co., Ltd., which can present the data of students' writing behavior in many dimensions. The data of the new edition of the network not only includes the visualization of scientific calculation, but also includes the content of information visualization and knowledge visualization. The abstract data is displayed on the screen in the form of graph (pie chart, histogram, curve) and other intuitive ways, realizing the goal of data visualization of different levels of evaluation [3]. This kind of data mining can effectively help teachers to carry out technical analysis, dynamically understand and master the actual learning situation of students, formulate teaching plans integrating offline, online and classroom based on the characteristics of students and the content of teaching materials, carry out data-based learning analysis, and implement accurate teaching. The figures and tables below show the data of the first composition of the new semester in March 2018. The students of No. 1070070 composition does plastic surrymake women truly beautiful? Are non English Majors of grade 2016 (mechanic 1607–1609 and special education 1601–1602). The first layer of the data (teacher interface) includes eleven dimensions: data overview, student performance, error distribution, browsing composition, similarity statistics, word frequency, collocation, graded vocabulary, data comparison, dimension analysis and retrieval. Click each dimension and the drop-down item contains different subitems. In the composition preview screen of the marking website, click the "more" option and select "commonality analysis" to display the above 11 dimensions. Next, according to the classroom evaluation, after class guidance, academic research these three perspectives for the new version of the correction network data mining analysis.

1   Classroom Evaluation

The five dimensions of "data overview, student performance, error distribution, browsing composition, similarity statistics" belong to macro data: including the information of the old version, such as submission, score, number of words, similarity, modification times. Next, analyze the classroom application value of these five dimensions. "Data overview" provides three charts, the information has two parts, one is the chart, the other is the text: "submission statistics" histogram: including on-time submission (159), make-up (0), manual reading (0), similar (more than 40%) and text description "you received 159 compositions, a total of 28660 words, 1669 sentences, the longest sentence 75 words, the shortest sentence 3 words.

Score distribution curve: set score 60 as the starting point, 25 people as a group, divided into 5 segments. The information in Fig. 1 is as follows: 1 person scored less than 60, 8 persons scored 60–69, 50 persons scored 70–79, 98 persons scored 80–90, and 2 persons scored 90–100. The highest score of writing is 90.7 (Chen) and the lowest is 46.3 (MU). The average score was 80.6.

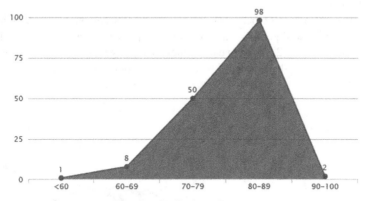

Fig. 1. Distribution of scores

Error statistics histogram: including the overall error text description, 399 errors were found in students' compositions. Among them, spelling and sentence composition are the most common mistakes made by students. Second, error statistics histogram. For example, 1070070 composition error distribution data histogram, according to the order from high to low, there are 17 sub items. The website visualized the general situation of this error release with a bar chart. The highest error was spelling error, with the data of 68. The lowest error was modal verb error, with the data of 1. (Fig. 2). There are many errors, which reflect the complexity of students' mistakes. It is related to students' personal English level and their attitude. If there are 68 spelling mistakes, students can correct them as long as they read carefully and follow the "warning" prompts. The data tells us that students need to correct their attitude to modify. They often type wrong words. Maybe they only pay attention to the meaning of Chinese when reciting words. If they memorize wrong words, they may make mistakes in typing. What's more, freshmen don't know much about English typing, resulting in wrong punctuation. Sentence structure, subject predicate consistency and misuse of part of speech are common mistakes made by Chinese students, which also reflects the challenges brought to Chinese students by different English and Chinese languages.

"Student performance" page includes expanding information, ranking (top 10), modifying ranking (top 10); using four colors to evaluate each student's individual situation (green stands for excellent, blue for good, yellow for general, red for poor), teachers can directly understand the overall performance of the students' composition by looking at the colors. Visual color data is convenient for teachers to analyze each student, and can also compare and analyze students. It is convenient for teachers to understand different classes of students as a whole by displaying visual information in intuitive colors. It is easier to identify students' learning attitude, good performance and general performance by color difference, and these comprehensive information can be understood in an instant. Visual color data reflects that the correction network is actively deepening the artificial intelligence technology, reflecting the development direction of educational technology to a certain extent, and constructing concise, time-saving and large amount of information educational big data. "Browse composition" page: including the composition score statistics, such as.

"More than 90 points (2 persons), 80–89 points (98 persons), 70–79 points (50 persons), 60–69 points (8 persons), and less than 60 points (1 person)". These data are the text expression in Fig. 2, showing each student's name, grade and modification times. You can click "comment by sentence" to view each student's composition.

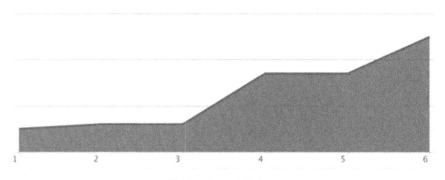

Fig. 2. Error statistics

"Similarity statistics" page: a general table shows the repetition rate of all 159 people, and the information is displayed in the order of repetition rate from high to low, such as "more than 40% (5 people), 20–40% (9 people), 10–20% (20 people), and less than 10% (125 people)". For example, in No. 1070070 composition, Li's similarity is 79%, ranking first; 14 students have more than 20%, so they must rewrite it. There are serious problems in students' learning attitude, so we must criticize education. Objective and fair data give the criticism strength, which plays a very good warning role for students' academic norms and integrity in the future. The comprehensive information provided by these five dimensions is in the form of both graph and word. Data overview and student performance are graph data, error distribution includes graph and word information, which can be easily used in classroom composition evaluation. The overall performance of the students in each class can be objectively and accurately displayed in the classroom, explained at the same time, reasonably educated students, guided students to make good use of "comment by sentence", and strive to be honest and trustworthy students.

2   After Class Guidance

The second level data of the new version of the network is the refinement of the first level data, including different numbers of sub data, which provides macro and micro data for teachers to comprehensively and accurately understand students. The error statistics chart (Fig. 2) and the word version of error distribution can be used for classroom analysis and individual student guidance. The data of this dimension makes clear the weak points of students' writing and provides good technical support for accurate after class guidance. At present, students' self adaptation, individual guidance strategies, error diagnosis and so on reflect the development direction of educational technology to a certain extent. Data mining and learning analysis is a hot topic in the field of international educational technology, and the domestic attention is also rising. With the combination of artificial intelligence technology, the network constructs its own intelligent data system. From a macro perspective, the "error distribution" in error diagnosis is the most characteristic. For teachers and students, the most practical type of data is "error release". The website provides a bar chart (as shown in Fig. 1 above). The data shows the distribution of students' writing errors from an overall perspective. The word version of the error evaluation report specifically shows each student's composition errors, points out the types of errors, and gives suggestions for revision. These wrong descriptions provide indispensable technical support for improving the accuracy of classroom teaching, one-to-one counseling after class, and the improvement of students' own ability. The combination of micro word and macro histogram provides reliable and evidential technical support for precision teaching. For example, the "growth track" (Fig. 2) records the historical version submitted by each student. Click on a specific student's growth track, the teacher can see the student's every revision, score change, submission time change, and can accurately guide the students to correct the composition, instead of 2 s, 3 s to submit, to see the score change. This reflects the students' speculative psychology. They want to get high marks, but they are not willing to spend more time revising. For students with too many modifications, viewing the historical version can accurately guide students and give pertinent guidance to their progress. For speculative students, criticize impetuous behavior and guide reasonable revision.

3   Academic Research

The last six dimensions "word frequency, collocation, graded vocabulary, data comparison, dimension analysis and retrieval" of the new edition of the website also include different numbers of sub items. For example, "data comparison" includes five sub items: "word statistical comparison, part of speech distribution comparison, collocation statistical comparison, sentence length distribution comparison and verb frequency comparison". For example, the word statistics comparison shows the comparison between a student and all the students. You can also compare the student with any one of the remaining 158 students in the same class or different classes. There are two kinds of data: histogram and statistical table. The reason why the data of six sub items are classified as micro level is that class explanation is limited by class hours and cannot be refined to this depth, but it is meaningful for deep academic research. From color histogram, curve chart, pie chart data to text description, it shows that the program design of the correction network is more refined and intelligent. As long as we users can understand the value of data, carry out data mining, and reasonably use these charts and tables for learning and analysis after class, we can overcome the disadvantages of poor adaptability and interactivity of data.

Second, the guiding role of data mining and learning analysis technology in teaching and learning.

With the advent of big data era and smart education mode, education reform has posed new challenges to front-line teachers. The teaching and learning mode of activities and tasks is no longer a single input, but the development and implementation of learning activities centered on students' autonomous learning. Modern education activities pay more attention to accuracy, autonomy, personalization and diversification. For teachers, only when they have higher ability of educational technology, actively participate in educational technology training, constantly explore in practice and constantly update ideas, can they not fall behind, better realize the role transformation, become the organizer of teaching and learning resources, the designer of process and the leader of behavior, and meet the requirements of important standards of teachers' professional quality. Since the report of enhancing teaching and learning through educational data mining and learning Analytics: an issue brief was released by the US Department of education in October 2012 [4], the academia has paid more and more attention to data mining and learning analysis technology. As the two directions of educational "big data" analysis and application, it is a late start and fast development discipline, technology empowerment learningLearning through technology [5] has become a new research path in the field of educational information technology and a new path to change learning. Sismesns and LAK (International Conference on learning analytics and knowledge) explain the concept of learning analysis from different aspects in the horizon report 2011 of NMC. Among them, the purpose of learning analysis has two prominent features: understanding the environment, optimizing the learning environment, measuring, collecting, analyzing and reporting the data generated in this situation [6]. He Kekang, a domestic scholar, has more concreted the exact connotation of learning analysis technology: "learning analysis technology tool, through collecting, measuring, analyzing and reporting massive data generated in the field of Education (the process of learning and the process of teaching management), extracts the hidden, potentially valuable, process and behavior information related to 'teaching and learning' or 'teaching management'It is a kind of information, knowledge and mode, so as to provide intelligent assistant decision-making technology for teachers' teaching, students' learning and teaching management [7]. The essence of learning analysis technology is to "support the implementation of evidence-based accurate teaching and effective teaching, emphasize the generation of efficiency or benefit, emphasize the guidance of teaching activities according to scientific principles, and strengthen the scientificity of teaching".

(1)   The role of teaching guidance for teachers

A large amount of data about students' writing behavior has been obtained and stored in the marking network. No matter its quantitative data or qualitative data have reached a higher degree of unity and sharing of data structure and data format of different systems, with a unified data format standard and information model. A reasonable data analysis model has a high reference value for classroom teaching and accurate management of students. The integration of intelligent decision-making and Intelligent Implementation of intelligent teaching is inseparable from the support of intelligent technology. For example, teachers dynamically manage students' writing behavior. During the writing period, teachers can read and correct students' compositions submitted online at any time. When they find that they are off topic or have similar red prompts, they can read and verify them. If the facts are consistent, they can cancel the composition, or click rewrite, and then use QQ in class.

The group small window informs them to rewrite, realizing real-time monitoring. You can check who didn't submit, how many students submitted last, and who didn't complete the minimum modification times by submitting date or student performance data. In the 1070070 writing, there are 6 students in class 07–09 who did not submit and did not make up for it. These 6 students scored zero in this composition; 25 students who submitted their compositions on March 28, the deadline, encountered the same problem in the process of submission: they did not submit successfully for many times, and they left a message on QQ to explain the situation. With the complete information obtained from data mining in Fig. 1, La technology can effectively help teachers to investigate whether students' performance and attitude are positive, and investigate students' integrity through similarity ratio, which provides a basis for timely education of students. Based on the technical support of correcting network data, learning analysis completely changes the biggest embarrassment of traditional manual correcting students' compositions plagiarism, and provides a scientific basis for teachers to make an objective, comprehensive, real and rapid evaluation of students. College English class, a teacher corresponding to a number of students, simply can not meet the requirements of everyone's correction, second correction. It is a good helper for teachers and greatly improves the feedback efficiency.

(2) The role of learning analysis technology in students' personalized and adaptive guidance

There are terminal consumers and students. As the largest user of the network, students' consumer experience should also be studied. When students submit their compositions, scores, comments and comments are generated instantly. For students, regardless of off topic, the first grade means the level of English writing, because in the student interface "my composition" window, the left side is students' composition (number of words, submission times), and the right side has the following four sub items: score, ranking, color viewable (yellow words, green sentences, blue chapter structure, light blue content related) and comments. Through the QQ survey, the students' feedback of "comment by sentence" has the most guiding role, and they think it is more practical. They modify according to the prompts, especially for those students whose grammar is not very good."Comment by sentence" is convenient for students to analyze their own learning and find out the relevant problems. Through many revisions, they can accumulate vocabulary and sentence patterns, and learn expressions in line with English Morphology and syntax habits, so as to improve their self-learning goal and improve their writing and translation ability.

The value of error distribution in three word versions Error distribution is an important data provided by the correction network. The data of visual histogram provides scientific and objective technical support for classroom precision teaching. In another word version of the same data, it clearly presents specific errors, comments and modification opinions, which is convenient for self modification. The teacher can get the student's name by clicking hide. Error distribution data is the most practical. Both the histogram and the display of specific wrong sentences provide convenient and reliable technical support for learning analysis. This kind of data provides a diagnostic basis for teachers' accurate classroom teaching and face-to-face accurate guidance, which is convenient for teachers to use the most appropriate teaching methods and teaching strategies for error analysis. The suggestions on spelling mistakes in Fig. 5 are correct. Start pay is also wrong. The correct one is start to pay or start paying; "our society are also had many change", which is a typical Chinese English sentence, "are" "Had" does not exist in English, "have" as a state verb, basically does not use in passive sentences; "change" lost the plural, the appropriate expression should be "many changes have taken place/happy in our society". It is a common mistake for many Chinese students to mistakenly regard Chinese topics as English subjects. It is a difficult point for students to learn English and a key point in classroom teaching. In the classroom composition evaluation, in addition to the above analysis, we should give more examples to explain the role of Chinese topics, the methods of English translation, and explain with Chinese sentences without subject, which is helpful to improve students' writing and translation ability. English SVC sentence pattern is also a kind of error prone type for Chinese students. In Chinese, the adjective directly follows the subject. If I am happy, he is happy, there is no need for the copula be; in English, there must be be be be to form the structure of the copula, SVCIt is one of the five core sentence patterns in English. Students are too familiar with it and make mistakes, which reflects that there are also problems in our teaching. We need to improve the explanation methods, emphasize the differences between English and Chinese, classify SVC and explain it systematically once, so as to avoid students making low-level mistakes again. When there are such errors, we can modify them by ourselves to improve the awareness of language self correction.

4   Opportunities and Challenges of Intelligent Technology

With more and more abundant data and higher intelligent performance, the feedback information from teachers and students in the new version is more detailed than that in the old version. For students, sentence comments and timely feedback improve their sense of participation, experience their own shortcomings in grammar and vocabulary, improve their awareness of prevention and optimize the learning process. Through the comments and the proportion of four colors, we can also understand the personal related problems and their performance in the class, which provides objective technical support for students' self-evaluation, and is conducive to personalized and adaptive learning, so as to improve the ability of English language expression. The development prospect of marking network is good, and its use value is very high for good, middle and upper middle school students. For teachers, the network faces more challenges. Many scholars have conducted in-depth discussion on this aspect, and I will not repeat it here. I just want to highlight two points: (1) the reliability and validity of the network.

It has been greatly improved. In the composition "how to tell Chinese stories in English" with the same title in May 2018, every student who misunderstands and doesn't write "how" has two red words of "digression". I have verified that the accuracy rate has reached more than 95%. In 1608 class, 8 students (8/30) only wrote stories related to Chinese idioms, such as the tortoise and rabbit race, Mencius mother moving, farmer and snake, etc., but did not write "how to tell", and manual reading is also off topic. (2) Batch.

It is necessary to improve the export of the error distribution of network change. At present, the export of a composition is not achieved by class, but the total export of all the students' errors of a teacher, 1070070 exported 38 pages of word text. College English teaching is generally large class, a teacher has more than 200 students, which is not conducive to teachers' feedback in class. Accurate feedback in class requires manual pasting one by one, which is too time-consuming. For intelligent technology, one instruction and one programming can save the trouble of front-line teachers and achieve efficient feedback: QQ class feedback and accurate classroom feedback. The construction of a new model of precision teaching in class is inseparable from the high development of intelligent technology.

5 Conclusion

Ten year development plan of education informatization (2011–2020). It is clearly pointed out that "the teaching mode of deep integration of information technology and teaching" is the direction of university reform. English composition correction network provides effective technical assistance for College English Teaching in large classes. It is a good helper for front-line teachers, making the dream of everyone's feedback and timely feedback come true. As a gradually improved intelligent technology, it has been widely used in practical teachingIt provides students with a flexible, personalized and adaptive information-based learning environment anytime and anywhere, and also provides certain technical support for front-line teachers' accurate classroom explanation and online and offline accurate guidance. Whether data mining and learning analysis technology can be deeply integrated with the classroom and how to integrate them will become an important mission of big data analysis in education, and also a key factor in building a lifelong learning system and a learning society.

References

1. Zhiting, Z., Hongchao, P.: The rise of smart learning ecosystem research. Chin. Audio Vis. Educ. **6**, 1–11 (2017)
2. Hongmei, L.: The value logic of "new" learning methods in the "Internet+" era. Chin Audio Vis. Educ. **6**, 102–107 (2017)
3. Bing, Y., Guoqing, L., Honggen, X., et al.: Research and implementation of data visualization in online learning system — taking sat platform as an example. Mod. Educ. Technol. **12**, 114–120 (2017)
4. Kekang, H.: New development of "learning analysis technology" in China. Audio Vis. Educ. Res. **7**, 5–13 (2016)
5. Kelin, L., Zhimin, X.: Technological change learning from the perspective of empowerment: a review of the "learning" part of the national educational technology program 2017 update. Mod. Educ. Technol. **3**, 26–32 (2018)
6. Yonghe, W., Dan, C., Xiaoling, M., et al.: Learning analysis: a new wave of educational informatization. J. Dist. Educ. **4**, 11–19 (2013)
7. Ronghui, G., Gaoda., H.: Research prospects of learning analysis and foreign language teaching in the era of big data. Audio Vis. Foreign Lang. Teach. **3**, 40–45 (2016)

Design and Implementation of Online English Writing Review System in Artificial Intelligence System

Qionghui Mei[✉]

School of Foreign Languages, Zhaotong University, Zhaotong 657000, China

Abstract. This paper uses nodejs based service to establish an online English writing review system, which has good application significance for online English teaching and other applications. This paper improves the original English text classification model through deep learning method, and gets better accuracy than the original classification results, which has certain reference significance for text classification based on deep learning.

Keywords: English text classification · Word correction · English online review · Artificial intelligence

1 Introduction

English writing ability is an important factor to measure students' English language development. The research background of this paper is based on the increasing demand of existing English learners for English communication and English learning review system. The existing English sharing and review system needs to be improved in content richness, user stickiness, article classification accuracy and so on. At present, there are few good English writing sharing and review systems in China. The existing writing review systems do not have a good user interaction experience [1]. Most of the articles are classified manually and labeled by users, which affects the accurate search of articles and the interaction between users to a great extent. Therefore, it is of great significance to improve user interaction, provide rich and detailed content, and enhance the accuracy of article classification.

2 System Requirement Analysis and Architecture Design

2.1 Requirement Analysis

The system layer needs to adapt to the changing needs, the software needs analysis and architecture design needs to meet the hierarchical structure, and the English online writing review system layer needs to provide continuous, stable and accurate data processing services for the application layer. There is no guarantee for the smooth operation of the

M. A. Jan and F. Khan (Eds.): BigIoT-EDU 2021, LNICST 391, pp. 76–85, 2021.
https://doi.org/10.1007/978-3-030-87900-6_10

system layer, the system layer needs to meet, the security and stability of the physical layer; the network layer needs to meet. The writing review system transmits data through the network in the form of HTTP request. In the process of transmission, there will be a large number of text data and image data; data consistency. Coordination among multiple systems and data unification among different processes of a single system are issues to be considered; timeliness of response; scalability. A good system needs to ensure the scalability of the system. In the process of iterative development of the system, new functions and new modules are often added. Application layer control and access security. The access control process and business functions of the English online writing review system include the permission audit of registration, login, writing, order placing, online payment, online review, blog publishing, etc.

2.2 Architecture Design

The overall architecture of the system is divided into front-end UI layer, display layer, user operation layer, nodejs service layer, database layer and neural network layer. Use these technologies to interact with the presentation layer, and display the data processed by the server on the interface. The neural network layer classifies the front-end access composition data and feeds it back to the nodejs server, so as to provide better content services for the front-end i layer and user operation layer. The functions of the neural network layer include model training, word error correction, text processing, etc. convolutional neural network is used to process and classify English text. The storage layer design is shown in Fig. 1. System storage structure the system adopts the form of separate storage to store the system data [2]. The system storage is divided into five parts, namely, Front end cache storage, system file storage, system database and other data information storage, word and text error correction results data storage and text classification model data storage, convolution neural network model of text classification is used to save the system for English Concerto text training results model, The system data saving module loads the new training result model into the running system after the model training.

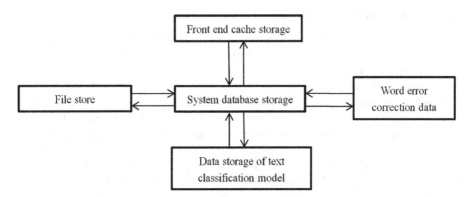

Fig. 1. System storage layer structure design

3 Design and Implementation of Text Classification Module

The English text classification process of the online writing review system can be divided into text preprocessing, neural network model training and training template updating, English text classification and other processes. The neural network training mode of the system adopts convolution neural network model of deep learning to train text classifier.

3.1 Text Preprocessing

Word vector is the symbol representation of words, which is convenient for machine language processing. Currently, the most commonly used word representation method is one hot representation method. The dimension of this representation method is the length of all words. Each word has its unique position marked as 1, and the rest positions are marked as 0. Every English word can be expressed as one of many data. The advantage of this way of English text representation is that it adopts sparse data storage, the way of data expression is also very simple, and the programming is also simple and convenient [3]. It only needs to assign a 10 to each word. However, this representation method has inherent defects for text classification, and cannot express the relationship between words and words, which cannot be fully expressed for English text with high text relevance. The co-occurrence matrix can be expressed as follows:

$$M_{to,human} + = 1 \tag{1}$$

$$M_{to,\text{instinct}} + = 1 \tag{2}$$

The co-occurrence matrix M of the text can be obtained by training the window with length of 5.

$$J = \sum_{i,j}^{N} (X_{i,j})(v_i^T v_j + b_i + b_j - \log(X_{i,j}))^2 \tag{3}$$

3.2 Convolutional Neural Network

Convolutional neural network, also known as convolutional neural network (CNN), is used to process data with similar network structure, such as two-dimensional image, one-dimensional time sequence.

The basic structure of convolutional neural network consists of feature extraction layer and feature network mapping layer. The feature extraction layer in the network layer is connected locally through the receiving domain between neurons. The local features determine the location relationship between the local region and other local domains or features. The mapping of each feature is composed of the mapping of many layers of features in the network layer. The mapping layer of each feature in the network layer is a plane represented by neurons with equal weights. In order to ensure the unique invariance of the feature mapping layer, the network layer will adopt the activation functions such as sigmoid activation function. In the network layer, the number of free parameters in the neural network can be reduced by sharing weights, so as to reduce the complexity of neurons. The frame of convolutional neural network is shown in Fig. 2.

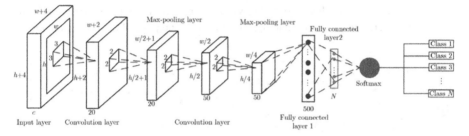

Fig. 2. Frame of convolutional neural network

4 System Implementation

This part introduces the specific implementation of the writing review system and the implementation of the word error correction module, introduces the implementation of the system from the perspective of front-end construction, and expounds the software flow of the word error correction module.

4.1 Implementation of Word Error Correction Module

The word error correction process of the system is mainly divided into word preprocessing, which is to de label and segment words; query the word dictionary to determine whether the words to be corrected are in the local word dictionary; word error correction; update the word error dictionary; query the word error dictionary.

The word text passed from the front end to the back end may contain HTML tags. The first step to deal with the word text is word segmentation. The word segmentation method adopted in this paper is regular expression processing method. The regular expression method uses JAV as (RPT) regular expression engine to generate specific string processing logic formula and replace HTML tags and their attributes with null. What is left is pure English text, and then according to the space between the words, the English text is divided into a single word and saved in the array, waiting for the subsequent error correction processing. After the word segmentation, the system will number each segmented word, so that the error result can be bound to the error correction word and returned to the client for processing.

4.2 The View Layer Implements the View Layer

Layer template parsing: template engine parsing is mainly divided into the following two aspects of data parsing. The data provided by the server, such as user's nickname, user's Avatar and article content, are loaded into the HTML tag. There are two ways to load the data into the HTML tag of the page in this English online writing review system. One way is to parse the data to be loaded into the data tag and coexist the data, another way is to parse all the data to be loaded into a string. The purpose of data processing is to process some data that cannot be processed by label parsing, such as buttons that can be parsed into different background colors according to the change of type [4]. The realization of view layer style is through the loading and rendering of CSS3 style file and the control of page by JavaScript. The view layer of the writing review system is to deal with the overall display style and page of the front-end page of the browser (Fig. 3).

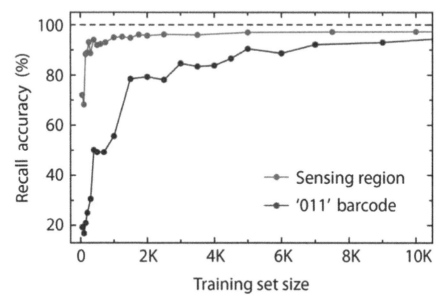

Fig. 3. Simulation for system implementation

5   Realization of System Front End Function

The front-end technology of the English writing and reading system adopts MVC and MVVM model driven, MVC is the model layer, control layer and visual layer. With the development of technology, the front-end technology is not only limited to page structure, page style, but also involves the development of background database, background control layer development, demand docking, product testing, product experience Optimization and other series of system development nodes [5].

5.1   Introduction of System Front End Technology

The front-end technology of the system mainly includes HTML (Hyper Text Markup Language), CSS (cascading style sheets), JavaScript, flash, XML and so on. Nodejs technology is a kind of server technology based on Google's Chrome browser engine. The language technology is built based on the V8 engine of Chrome browser. With the help of nodejs, we can quickly build our own server platform. The difficulties of the front-end technology of the system are as follows: 1. The page must be modular design to facilitate subsequent updates and system maintenance. 2. In order to ensure that the system can run smoothly in different versions and different types of browsers, special compatibility processing is needed. 3. The realization of the page effect, such as the realization of the article review function, the system in order to provide a comfortable operating experience [6].

5.2 View Layer Implementation

View layer template parsing: template engine parsing is mainly divided into the following two aspects: data parsing [7]. The data provided by the server, such as user's nickname, user's Avatar and article content, are loaded into the HTML tag. There are two ways to load the data into the HTML tag of the page in this English online writing review system. One way is to parse the data to be loaded into the data tag and coexist the data, another way is to parse all the data to be loaded into a string. Data processing. The purpose of data processing is to process some data that cannot be processed by label parsing, such as buttons that can be parsed into different background colors according to the change of type. The realization of view layer style is through the loading and rendering of CSS3 style file and the control of page by JavaScript. The view layer of the writing review system is to deal with the overall display style of the front-end page of the browser and the display effect after partial operation of the page [8].

5.3 Implementation of Control Layer

The control layer is the bridge between the view layer and the model layer. The information is saved to the database through the model layer through the control layer's data processing, detection and other operations. Session saving is the saving of user login information. The user only needs to log in once within the specified time to reduce the number of user login and increase the system user experience [9].

The security filtering of control layer includes XSS filtering, keyword filtering, MySQL database anti attack filtering, and anti web tag attack to ensure the security of database and the cleanness of system content.

2. Payment security, English composition marking needs to use the payment system, for payment security, the research adopts the following forms. The result of the payment will be consistent with the Alipay IP, and the result of Alipay's return will be encrypted to determine whether the encrypted data is the same as the encryption result of the Alipay public key after encrypting. The payment information is confirmed for the payment result, preventing the amount of error, the order error and so on [10].

6 The Construction and Functions of the Computer-Based Writing System

6.1 Technological Tools: JSP Technology and SQL Server 2000

After the consultation service of computer program from the computer majors, the JSP technology and SQL server 2000 are finally selected as the primary tools for developing the on-line writing learning system. Moreover, because of the limited knowledge of computer, the technical problems like the computer programs applied in the CALL software design are not studied in detail in this thesis. Only some of the key concepts will be introduced briefly in the following paragraphs one by one. For creating the database of the system, the computer program named SQL server 2000 is adopted. For creating the web pages of the system, the computer program named Myeclipse (belonging to the JSP technology) is adopted [11].

6.2 JSP Technology

JSP or Java Server Pages, was developed by Sun Micro-systems. JSP technology is object-oriented programming language and is based on Java language JSP is widely used for developing dynamic web sites and for creating database driven web applications because it provides superior server side scripting support. Here are some of the reasons for the popularity of JSP. Firstly, simplifies the process of development. It allows programmers to insert the Java code directly into the JSP file, making the development process easier. Although JSP files are HTML files, they use special tags containing the Java source code which provides a dynamic ability. Secondly, portability. The Java feature of "write once, run anywhere" is applicable to JSP. JSP is platform independent, making it portable across any platform and therefore multi-platform. It is possible for the programmer to take a JSP file and move it to another platform, JSP Servlet engine or web server [12].

6.3 SQL Server 2000

SQL server 2000 is taken as the main computer program for creating the database SQL server 2000 is a kind of database platform developed by Microsoft, which uses the SQL language to create all the relational tables and the view structures. Its main functions to deal with the B/S model where the design manager can maintain the web pages through the Internet and have the ability to directly access and manipulate configuration database files [13].

This module is to make students have a systematic and comprehensive study of one writing item. This module is basically constituted of two aspects: the brief introduction of one writing item and the general writing skills instructions of one writing item. The former part mainly includes these aspects: the definition (s) of this writing item, the general and specific classification of this writing item, the demands for writing this kind of writing item, a brief introduction of the situational use of this kind of writing item, the basic contents of this writing item and etc. The later part mainly includes the following aspects the general and specific conditions for applying this kind of writing item to the daily life the general statements and the specific introduction of the writing skill instructions.

7 Construction of Three Interfaces

Which will give you acomprehensive and better understanding of the general structure and ruming mechanism of the system. These three interfaces include the user Interface, here the user mainly referring to the students, the teacher Interface and the manager interface, which primarily refers to the computer professionals who designed the system and will be in charge of the background management [14].

7.1 User Interface

The user interface, as its literal meaning saying, means there is an interface in the system for students to work on. There are totally four modules provided by the system for students to study. They are the on-line learning module, the on-line testing module, the on-line evaluating module and the on-lime interacting module. There will not devote a lot of space to repeatedly introducing each module in detail, which has already been elaborated in the previous sections. To summarize into one sentence, students can have acomprehensive and systematic study of college practical English writing through this interface [15].

7.2 Teacher Interface

Just as the name showing, teachers launch the teaching activity mainly through this interface. Although to reach students' autonomous learning is one of the objectives for developing this on-line writing learning system, the important role of teachers cannot be totally neglected. In the traditional classroom-based teaching activity, teachers, class-rooms and textbooks are regarded as the center of teaching where students cannot have an overall development because they cannot full play their initiative and creativeness. This will be definitely improved by developing this on-line writing learning system where students can full play their initiative and creativeness. However, teachers are still the organizer and administrator in guiding students' study. They have just experienced a succession of changes from authoritative to neutral and finally to converting [16].

There are totally four modules provided by the system for teachers to launch their teaching activities of supplementary property as publishing the newly updating messages, on-line teaching of what students cannot understand by themselves, on-line evaluating and on-line answering FAQ. Publishing message means that if there appear new learning materials about the practical writing, teachers can update them in the system for students further study and teachers have to renew the testing questions for students to practice from time to time in order to guarantee that students can have a comparatively complete testing of what they have learned. On-line teaching relating to the on-line interacting means that during the process of on-line writing leaning, students may meet various difficulties, and then they can ask help for their teachers, so teachers must response to them immediately and give them proper answers or explanations through this module. On-line evaluating means that teachers are required to give them feedbacks after students hand in their literary compositions. As introduced in the previous sections, students' literary compositions of one writing item cannot be evaluated by the system itself, which need still revising by teachers. On-line answering FAQ is similar to the second module on-line teaching where teachers should give answers to any questions about the study raised by students.

7.3 Manager Interface

There will not take a lot of sentences to explain this interface any more. This interface belongs to the backstage management of this on-line writing leaning system. Teachers also play a significant role as a backstage supporter. However, they are different from each other: the former mainly focuses on the computer technology support and technical management of the system, whereas the latter is mainly responsible for dealing with the knowledge or the contents changing, updating and etc. of the system. It is always the computer majors who work on this interface. They provide the services such as technical support in managing people, managing curriculum, managing FAQ answering and managing the exam, system maintenance and operation support etc.

8   Conclusions

Through the process of requirement analysis, architecture design, function realization and iterative development, the system realizes the online English writing review system based on nodejs. The system can solve the problem that students can't practice after class and interact with teachers and students. On the other hand, it provides convenience for teachers to correct students' English homework after class. In addition, English text classification based on convolutional neural network achieves good text classification effect, and word error correction also achieves good error correction effect. For the system itself, it can provide users with more appropriate article service. However, there is still room for optimization in the stability of the system, and the design of the text classification system also needs to be optimized. Due to the limitation of code writing time, we will continue to optimize the simplicity of system code in the future.

References

1. Fen, H.:The application of online writing automatic assessment system in college English writing teaching -- a case study of Junku correcting net. Chin. Educ. Inf. **16**, 14–22 (2015)
2. Liguo, Z., Hongwei, Y.: Research on unified programming model of local application and web application based on nodejs. Electron. Technol. Softw. Eng. **12**, 25–31 (2015)
3. Ge, W.: Research on text classification method based on manifold learning. Hebei University of Technology (2012)
4. Ling, L.: A comparative study of college English writing teacher feedback and online correction feedback. Chin. Electr. Power Educ. **11**, 21–31 (2014)
5. Chongfeng, X., Xing, L.: Automatic text classification algorithm based on sequence. Acta Sin. Sin. **v12**, 134783 (2002)
6. Ke, W., Shengfeng, X., Ming, W.: Research on XSS attack and prevention. Sci. Tech. Inf. **217**, 610–611 (2010)
7. Longjie, W.: On the effective management of small and medium-sized software system development process in China. J. Decis. Mak. Inf. **16**, 5145–145
8. Tiantian, W., Yu, K.: Research on text dimension reduction based on variance and word vector. Comput. Syst. Appl. **5**, 29–34 (2016)
9. Lei, Z., Wei, Y., Yufeng, Z.: Problems and rethinking of co-occurrence matrix cluster analysis. J. Inf. **V22**, 32–36 (2014)
10. Wenbo, L., Le, S., Dakun, Z.: New text classification algorithm based on labeled LDA model. Acta Comput. Sin. **31**, 620–627 (2008)
11. Lei, H.: Research and design of text topic classification based on keywords. Beijing University of Posts and Telecommunications, pp. 78–83
12. Liu Tengfei, Y., Shuangyuan, Z.H., et al.: Text classification based on cyclic and convolutional neural networks. Software **1**, 43–51 (2018)

13. Huiping, C.: Research on short text classification based on convolutional neural network. Southwest University, vol. 5, p. 13 (2016)
14. Ge, W.: Research on text classification method based on manifold learning. Hebei University of Technology, vol. 19, pp. 61–89 (2012)
15. Ketkar, N.: Convolutional neural networks. Overv. Neural Netw. **55**, 113–118 (2017)
16. Xiaoqiang, J.: Research on error correction methods of English articles. Harbin University of Technology, p. 32564 (2015)

Design and Research of Curriculum Education Under Cluster Algorithm in English Hybrid Teaching Mode in Higher Vocational Education

Qin Guo[✉]

Shandong Communication Vocational College, Weifang 261206, Shandong, China

Abstract. Under the background of Internet, higher vocational English, as a general course, should be student-centered, make full use of the advantages of "Internet", integrate elements into the whole course teaching, and convey students' correct ideals and values. The concrete reform of Higher Vocational English can be considered from the perspective of blended teaching mode. Design and implement the development mode suitable for Higher Vocational English.

Keywords: Internet · Curriculum education · Higher Vocational English · Blended teaching mode

1 Introduction

With the development of educational philosophy and the advent of the "Internet plus" era, the application of multimedia and network technology in modern teaching is increasing [1]. However, at present, there are not many practical explorations on College English blended teaching, so there is a lack of deep experience and understanding of its positive role.

Under the background of the new era, the application of blended teaching mode in College English teaching can give full play to its positive role.

By means of questionnaire survey, the author finds that students' satisfaction with blended teaching is very high. The online learning content of blended teaching meets the needs of students, and the difficulty is moderate, which improves the learning interest. The mixed teaching mode makes most of the students' learning attitude more active than before, and the learning methods are more abundant and the effect is better. Through mixed teaching, students' abilities in all aspects are improved and learning methods are more diverse. 80% of the students think that the online learning effect is good or very good, and 90% of the students can basically or completely master the content. Mixed teaching mode is also conducive to improving teachers' teaching ability and information literacy [2–4]. The interviewed teachers believe that blended teaching has a certain role in promoting teaching reform and information-based teaching ability.

M. A. Jan and F. Khan (Eds.): BigIoT-EDU 2021, LNICST 391, pp. 86–95, 2021.
https://doi.org/10.1007/978-3-030-87900-6_11

2 Construction of Learning Community Between Teachers and Students Based on Blended Teaching Mode

The teacher-student learning community based on the blended teaching mode is centered on the exchange and transmission of curriculum knowledge, with the main purpose of online and offline mixed completion of teaching activities, and adhering to the learning goal as the guidance, to build a multi-level and multi-directional communication between teachers and students. The learning community between teachers and students can help teachers and students form a joint force, help each other and make progress together. A good learning community of teachers and students should have three elements, two levels and one core.

2.1 Elements of Teacher Student Learning Community Based on Blended Teaching Mode

There are three main elements in the learning community of teachers and students based on the blended teaching mode. First, students, who are the most important elements of the learning community and the originator of learning behavior, participate in the whole learning project and need to evaluate teaching through their mastery of knowledge. They are guides to guide students to understand and perceive the most fundamental law of the development of things, to discover and explore the mechanism contained in the discipline, and to use the knowledge to solve practical problems [5–7]. The third is the environment of students and teachers, which is the basis of learning and includes learning resources. The situation includes real situation and virtual situation. Real situation is the environment of interaction and actual communication between teachers and students, and it is a real learning environment. The virtual situation contains the emotional communication between teachers and students, which affects students' subjective initiative and potential way of thinking. Learning resources are used to support students' learning and provide necessary guarantee for the development of teaching activities.

2.2 The Level of Teacher Student Learning Community Based on Blended Teaching Mode

The teacher-student learning community based on the blended teaching mode mainly includes two levels, the first level is the low level, and the second level is the high level. The lower level is student student community and teacher teacher community, while the higher level is teacher-student learning network community.

2.2.1 Student Community and Teachers

Teachers' community and students' community is a low-level form of expression, which is a new mode of learning and discussion between students. Students communicate with each other, make progress together, share learning experience, new knowledge and new ideas in time. The novelty of it is that it is free from the constraints of time and space, and shares learning resources in real time with the help of information technology. Teacher teacher community is another form of low-level expression, which is based on the knowledge research model between teachers and teachers [8]. The main body of this level is the coordinator and organizer of the learning community between teachers and students. Teachers spontaneously form professional teaching discussion groups, establish teaching circle culture, hold regular meetings to report teaching experience, share knowledge resources, build discipline construction system, and uphold the idea of "one game of chess". The discussion group should organize the division of roles, divide responsibilities and tasks, and realize real-time communication and multi-point linkage for education and teaching.

2.2.2   Network Community of Teacher Student Learning

The higher level of student learning community is teacher-student learning network community, which is characterized by teacher-student interaction, teacher teacher interaction and student student interaction. Each participant of learning community can communicate with every member of the organization, and they are equal, promote and grow together. This kind of high-level sharing resources will increase several times, and the ideas in the network structure collide with each other, which will inevitably stimulate new ideas and new knowledge. The participation of information technology will make ineffective learning scenarios happen at any time, make knowledge resources flow freely in multi-dimensional space, and improve the probability and speed of knowledge dissemination.

2.3   The Core of Teacher Student Learning Community Based on Blended Teaching Mode

The core of teacher-student learning community based on hybrid teaching mode is that teachers and students can establish teacher-student learning community online and offline with the help of information technology, and cooperate to complete various learning tasks in order to obtain good learning results [9–11]. The transformation and development of application-oriented universities pay more attention to the cultivation of practical ability and comprehensive ability, which requires teachers and students to fully communicate and interact in order to efficiently complete teaching activities. The establishment of learning community between teachers and students based on the mixed teaching mode can further deepen the communication and contact between teachers and students, and help students master important knowledge and methods. It can be seen that in the whole process, the dominant position of teachers is not highlighted, but the main focus is on the bridge built by the teacher-student community to help students acquire knowledge, solve problems and improve their comprehensive ability.

3   Blended Teaching and Academic Warning

3.1   Disadvantages of Traditional Teaching Mode

In the 1990s, the development of multimedia technology and network technology promoted the emergence of network teaching mode, breaking the traditional teaching mode that students passively accept teachers' knowledge. However, the network teaching mode requires students to have strong self-learning ability and self-regulation ability, which has encountered great problems in practical application. Without effective monitoring means, students' learning effect cannot be guaranteed. In order to solve this problem, the concept of blended teaching came into being. Hybrid teaching was first proposed by foreign training institutions, aiming to make up for the lack of pure network teaching through the combination of online and offline, and has been gradually applied to the field of higher education [13]. At present, many domestic colleges and universities have accumulated a lot of teaching resources and teaching achievements in the hybrid teaching mode. Making full use of blended teaching can effectively enhance students' autonomous learning ability, increase students' opportunities for self practice, and reduce the situation of teachers' full house filling in traditional teaching mode.

3.2 Contrast Gap

In reality, the autonomy of online students still needs to be improved. In the process of offline teaching and guidance, teachers find that students' online learning effect is not good, so they repeat students' online learning content through offline teaching, which goes against the original intention of hybrid teaching design. Therefore, in order to better promote students to complete autonomous learning, under the background of blended teaching, colleges and universities need more comprehensive and effective monitoring means to monitor students' learning. Early warning means that colleges and universities use information technology means to establish a set of special programmed prediction, evaluation and processing mechanism in students' academic management, Ensure that the students whose evaluation results are in the early warning range can graduate smoothly in the future [14, 15]. Since the implementation of academic early warning system in China's universities in 2006, the academic early warning standards and early warning levels of various universities are similar, mainly through the completion of credits to grade early warning for students. However, in the information age, with the change of teaching mode and access to information, university teaching management should keep pace with the times, using more scientific and technological means to obtain more comprehensive data and information. By optimizing the academic early warning system, enriching the early warning content and improving the supporting measures, a set of academic monitoring management system is established to adapt to the mixed teaching mode and the needs of contemporary college students.

4 The Necessity of Optimizing the Academic Early Warning System in China's Colleges and Universities

4.1 Online Teaching Lacks Effective Monitoring Means, so It Is Difficult to Improve Learning Autonomy

The characteristic of blended teaching is the combination of online teaching and offline teaching. Online teaching mainly studies the course content through students' self-help, which requires higher autonomous learning ability of students. In practice, there will be the phenomenon that students hang up or do not participate in online learning. Therefore, in the absence of strong monitoring means, it is difficult to ensure the effect of students' online learning [16]. In view of this situation, colleges and universities need to rely on technical means to monitor students' online learning, timely remind students of their personal learning status, so as to enhance students' learning autonomy and give full play to the advantages of hybrid teaching.

4.2 The Content of Academic Warning Is Single, and the Problem Is Not Clear

China's colleges and universities mainly through the way of grading early warning to the students with poor academic performance. The early warning standard is mainly based on the completion of credits or academic performance, and the evaluation standard is relatively single. Students' credit completion or academic performance can only reflect the overall academic progress or level of students. Some students who get early warning are not clear about their graduation requirements and the school's talent training objectives. They cannot be aware of the purpose of setting early warning standards in time, let alone how to make up for the existing problems. Compared with the hierarchical early warning, the classified early warning can more clearly point out the problems that students need to pay attention to, and also help schools to provide help measures for students.

5   Analysis of Basic Learning Model

5.1   Interactive Internet Education Courseware

Internet education, as its name implies, is to teach and impart knowledge with the help of the Internet [17, 18]. Because of the convenience of the Internet, people can choose their own courses to study, and at the same time, it also avoids learning problems caused by time conflicts or explanation of important knowledge points due to distraction. It is this characteristic that makes it convenient for people to study anytime and anywhere. The Internet plays an important role in the education industry, which has a major feature - the sharing of resources. China has always attached great importance to the balanced development of various regions. At present, most of the work is to help the poor out of poverty. The popularization of Internet technology is the embodiment of poverty alleviation. The application of this technology solves the problem that students in backward areas cannot accept the same education as students in better developed areas due to lack of conditions, and saves teachers.

Internet education technology is characterized by convenience. Students only need to choose one course and reach a certain learning time to complete the final examination. They will be awarded a certificate of completion or certificate of completion. As shown in Fig. 1, the course of Internet distance education is generally composed of anti fake learning and anti substitution module, courseware learning timing system, final automatic evaluation system and courseware. The modules of anti fake learning and anti substitution learning mainly play the role of supervising learning, which are not included in the evaluation system of user standards. For the learning process, the determination of reaching the standard is given by the timing system. When the time of learning courseware reaches the target time and reaches the opening period of the final examination, the user can participate in the assessment, and the corresponding certificate or certificate will be granted after the assessment is completed.

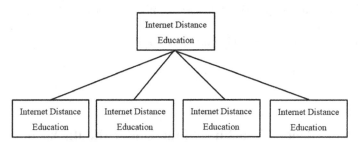

Fig. 1. Interactive network education course mode

5.2 Prior Probability Analysis

A priori probability refers to the probability of science and mathematics obtained from the previous experience of various experiments and the calculation and analysis of experimental data. The prior probability can represent most of the problems encountered in life. Taking the formula of total probability as an example, in all the problems of causality, the formula calculates the probability of "cause" in the problems encountered.

The pass rate of courseware refers to the pass probability of a certain courseware, which is the proportion of the total number of times (pass) of learning the courseware to the total number of learning the courseware. The total number of times that users who fail to pass the assessment of the courseware will increase each time they participate in the courseware learning [19, 20]. If and only if the user has not passed the assessment of the courseware and passed the assessment after learning, the total number of times of learning the courseware will be recorded. The courseware pass rate CP can be formalized as follows:

$$CPR = \frac{pass}{total} \tag{1}$$

Car (course accelerating rate) refers to the conditional probability of passing the Ci of another courseware after passing the examination of any courseware CJ. It is the ratio of the total number of times CP (condition pass) that passes the CJ and passes Ci to the total number of CI learning after passing CJ (condition total). When a user passes a certain courseware, all CP and CT based on the last passed courseware will increase; when the user fails to pass a certain courseware, only CT based on the last passed courseware will be increased. The car can be formalized as follows:

$$CAR(C_i \backslash C_j) = \frac{CP}{CT} \tag{2}$$

CMR (course master rate) refers to the probability of a certain courseware passing before learning. The comprehensive evaluation before the first learning course and the pre-school quiz before learning a courseware for the first time will record the user's assessment between the courseware before learning for the first time, The user whose score of pre-school assessment is greater than 85% is defined as the learned user who has mastered the knowledge of the courseware before participating in the courseware. Therefore, CMR is the proportion of the total number of times FP (first pass9 accounts for the total number of times of learning the courseware for the first time). The CMR of courseware early learning rate can be formalized as follows:

$$CMR = \frac{FP}{FT} \tag{3}$$

6 Design of Blended Teaching Mode Under the Background of Internet Plus

The focus of the mode design is the four core elements of information-based curriculum, namely platform, content, activities and evaluation methods. According to the teaching situation of Vocational English course in our college, this paper designs the information-based hybrid teaching mode suitable for the course [21]. The course design mainly includes three aspects: the design of learning environment, the design of learning activities and the design of learning content.

(1) Learning environment design

There are many understandings about the learning environment. Combined with the characteristics of Higher Vocational English curriculum, the author believes that the learning environment mainly includes classroom teaching environment, network learning environment and learning resources. According to the nature of the course, teachers of Higher Vocational English courses can use courseware such as computers, networks and projectors to teach in the multimedia classroom; according to the learning situation of the teaching objects, they can provide network and text learning resources, such as MOOC links of related topics, teachers' micro lectures, references, etc. [22]. The rich online resource library classifies the content, so that students can learn selectively according to their own level, and then assess according to the difficulty and quantity of the learning content selected by students.

(2) Design of learning activities

The learning activities of Higher Vocational English course include classroom learning, online learning, practical activities and collaborative learning. The combination of language learning and practical skills; the combination of group counseling and individual counseling; the combination of network resources and text teaching materials, so that students can set their own pace, choose their own time, work consciously and communicate freely. Online learning courseware, watching the video of micro class/Timothy class, completing the homework, participating in the test, strengthening the practical activities and collaborative learning of language skills in the classroom. On this basis, we can ensure the learning effect of students.

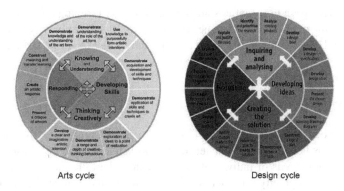

Arts cycle   Design cycle

Fig. 2. Learning content design

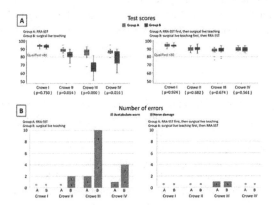

Fig. 3. Verification of test effect

(3) Learning content design

According to the needs and levels of students, the teaching contents with different levels are set up to give students more choices. The success of blended teaching largely depends on the construction of online content and resources. As shown in Fig. 2. Improve the proportion of online learning in assessment and evaluation. First of all, we should ensure that the assessment proportion of online learning is not different or consistent with that of online learning. Secondly, the proportion of online learning content in the examination content should be increased [23, 24]. Only by increasing the proportion of online learning content in the examination and strengthening the assessment, can the students pay attention to the online learning process and improve the learning effect.

7 Simulation Analysis

We verify the effectiveness of the proposed method from test scores and error rates. Because from all the teaching results, we can see that the test score is the most important, followed by the number of errors. As shown in Fig. 3

As can be seen from Fig. 3, after statistical analysis, the teaching effect of group A is not as good as that of group B. As can be seen in Figure B, the number of errors in group B is significantly less than that in group A. This shows that the proposed algorithm is effective.

8   Conclusion

In the process of teaching implementation, there are still some areas that need to be improved, such as the design of some teaching links is not detailed and reasonable, and the communication needs of individual students cannot be fully met. The information age of education has greatly impacted the concept, mode and evaluation system of traditional classroom teaching for English majors. Making full use of modern information technology and constructing the information-based hybrid teaching mode of English Curriculum in higher vocational colleges, its coverage effect and radiation effect will have positive guidance for other English major courses.

References

1. He, K.: Looking at the new development of educational technology theory from blending learning. Inf. Technol. Educ. Prim. Secondary Schools (3), 21 (2004)
2. Liu, D., Zhang, J.: Investigation and reform ideas of Public English Teaching in Higher Vocational Colleges. China Foreign Lang. **6**(6), 77–83 (2009)
3. Lin, X.: The practice of curriculum ideology and politics in English language teaching in Higher Vocational Colleges. Sci. Educ. Guide **12**, 144–145 (2018)
4. Zhao, Y.: Research on the multiple evaluation system of College English teaching quality – a case study of Chongqing University of science and technology. Foreign Lang. **28**(6), 169–173 (2012)
5. Fu, J., Sun, L., Zhao, X., Liu, W., Wang, X.: Exploration and practice of experimental teaching mode of data structure and algorithm based on ability training. Comput. Educ. (03), 99–103 (2021)
6. Liu, S., Xu, L., Zhang, Q., Cao, Z., Wang, Y., Hou, Y.: Hybrid teaching organization mode of computer composition principle based on engineering education professional certification. Comput. Educ. (03), 104–107 (2021)
7. Fang, L., Qin, D., Jing, B., Liang, Z.: Construction and implementation of hybrid experimental teaching mode of network interconnection technology. Comput. Educ. (03), 165–170 (2021)
8. Kang, M., Ling, W.: Implementation and summary of online teaching of BIM Technology Application Course. Shanxi Archit. **47**(06), 189–191 (2021)
9. Xiao, H., Zhu, Z., Xiao, H., Yu, F.: Research on online and offline hybrid teaching mode of radar principle and technology. Sci. Technol. Wind (07), 41–43 (2021)
10. He, W., Shi, X.: Research on mixed teaching innovation of self built resources of "road and Bridge Aesthetics" based on flipped classroom. Sci. Technol. Wind (07), 46–47 (2021)
11. Yu, J., Chen, X., Li, J., Liu, J., Liu, Z., Liu, M.: Research on online and offline hybrid teaching and practice of modern testing technology under the background of "new engineering". Southern Agric. Mach. **52**(05), 126–127 (2021)
12. Sheng, J., Ni, X.: The construction and application of SPOC Hybrid Teaching Mode under the background of "Internet plus" – taking the application project management course of the undergraduate course as an example. China Training (03), 78–79 (2021)

13. Li, S., Chen, S.: Exploration of online and offline mixed teaching mode of port logistics. Logistics Sci. Technol. **44**(03), 167–168 (2021)
14. Li, Z.: Research on online and offline integrated Internet plus teaching mode. Logistics Technol. **44**(03), 184–185 (2021)
15. Chen, W.: Research on online and offline hybrid teaching mode of electrical engineering. Hebei Agric. Mach. (03), 66–67 (2021)
16. Xian, X., Chang, H., Ding, P., Cao, Y., Zhang, Z., Li, J.: Discussion on the teaching of "hearing seeing testing thinking understanding" intelligent classroom in internal medicine of integrated traditional Chinese and Western medicine under the OBE + mixed teaching mode. Mod. Distance Educ. Chin. Tradit. Med. **19**(05), 9–13 (2021)
17. Shen, Q., Wang, S., Liu, H., Gu, Y.: Analysis of factors influencing the learning effect of online open courses in medical colleges and countermeasures. Mod. Distance Educ. Chin. Med. **19**(05), 19–21 (2021)
18. Cai, D., Jian, R., Zeng, D.: Application of flipped classroom mixed teaching mode in the course of X-ray of imaging equipment. Mod. Distance Educ. Chin. Med. **19**(05), 37–39 (2021)
19. Jun, L.: Research on Hybrid Teaching of mathematical modeling course in Higher Vocational Colleges Based on TPACK framework. J. Educ. (03), 68–73 (2021)
20. Fu, S., Zhu, S.: Research on the influencing factors of teachers' blended teaching based on TTF and UTAUT – taking X University as an example. China Educ. Inform. (06), 21–27 (2021)
21. Nan, D.: Operation demonstration skills training of computer normal students based on Hybrid Teaching. China Educ. Inform. (06), 68–71 (2021)
22. Jiang, S., Li, L., Ding, S., Yu, C.: Research on the cultivation of students' autonomous learning ability under the online teaching mode in Colleges and universities. Theor. Res. Pract. Innov. Entrepreneurship **4**(05), 63–65 (2021)
23. Ma, Z., Yong, W., Chang, P., Gao, C., Bian, H.: Design and practice of hybrid teaching mode based on the platform – taking College Physics Course as an example. J. Lanzhou Univ. Arts Sci. (Nat. Sci. Ed.) **35** (02), 113–120 (2021)
24. Zou, X.: Research and practice of Online + offline hybrid teaching mode. Educ. Inf. Forum (03), 7–8 (2021)

Design and Research of Teaching Support System for Urban Landscape Sculpture Course

Yujiu Liu[✉]

Ningxia Normal University, Guyuan 756000, China

Abstract. With the development of economy, the demand for landscape sculpture in urban development is higher and higher. At present, the level of landscape sculpture industry is uneven, and the lack of professionals hinders the healthy development of landscape sculpture industry. This paper expounds the connotation of the teaching mode of production, study and research, proposes to construct the teaching mode of production, learning and research of landscape sculpture course from the aspects of reasonable arrangement of teacher resources, development of studio teaching mode, establishment of assessment and coordination system, and analyzes the significance of implementing the teaching mode of production, learning and research in promoting the teaching reform of colleges and universities and the benign development of landscape sculpture course.

Keywords: Landscape sculpture · Production · Teaching and research · Teaching mode

1 Introduction

With the development of economy and the progress of society, people's pursuit of beauty is getting higher and higher. Because of its aesthetic nature, landscape sculpture has attracted more and more attention. The landscape sculpture industry has achieved rapid development under the rapid economic growth, but there are still many problems, such as the lack of professional personnel, lack of qualification, etc., which hinder the steady development of the landscape sculpture industry in the new period [1]. At present, under the promotion of the Ministry of education, colleges and universities implement curriculum reform to establish innovative education system and cultivate compound applied talents. The author believes that the application of industry university research mode in the curriculum reform of landscape sculpture in Colleges and universities can cultivate talents with professional quality and practical operation ability, and promote the development of landscape sculpture industry.

2 The Connotation of Teaching Mode of Production, Study and Research

The teaching reform of production, teaching and research in Colleges and universities can give full play to the autonomy and initiative of the University. With the cooperation of the school and enterprises, combined with the advantages of professional

M. A. Jan and F. Khan (Eds.): BigIoT-EDU 2021, LNICST 391, pp. 96–104, 2021.
https://doi.org/10.1007/978-3-030-87900-6_12

knowledge and enterprise market of colleges and universities, the complementary advantages of resources can be realized. Finally, a comprehensive talent training mode can be established to improve the teaching quality and enhance the market competitiveness of students [2].

The teaching mode of production, teaching and research is to achieve the effect of "1 + 1 > 2" through the cooperation between universities and enterprises. In the process of production, teaching and research, relying on the scientific research results and professional technology of university landscape sculpture, enterprises can obtain the latest research results of landscape sculpture industry, improve their comprehensive strength and develop rapidly. In the process of cooperation with enterprises, the landscape sculpture industry in Colleges and universities can obtain the latest market frontier information, timely adjust the undergraduate teaching structure and content, construct excellent landscape sculpture professional courses, and establish practical talent platform to solve the employment problems of college students.

The teaching mode of production, teaching and research cultivates applied talents matching the specialty and market demand. By integrating the resources of colleges and enterprises, the teaching mode of production, teaching and research provides college students with opportunities to contact enterprise projects by establishing a cooperation platform. Through school enterprise cooperation, students' comprehensive quality, especially innovation ability and practical ability, can be improved to meet the market demand. At the same time, the teaching mode of industry university research can also help students create landscape sculpture works that can be directly used in the market, and realize the combination of teaching and market.

Through the cooperation between universities and enterprises, the teaching mode of production, teaching and research aims to achieve the overall utility greater than the sum of all parts. It combines classroom teaching with social needs, reforms landscape sculpture courses in Colleges and universities, improves the quality of talent training, enhances the school running ability of colleges and Universities, and transforms relevant technologies and achievements into artistic products that can be directly produced, so as to realize the real connection between market and teaching, Promote professional development. The integration of production, teaching and research makes enterprises rely on the school's professional and technical advantages to transform the innovative achievements of colleges and universities into artistic works, shorten the development and design process, create more successful works to meet the market demand, improve the profit margin of enterprises, and make enterprises obtain long-term development.

3 Analysis of Basic Learning Model

3.1 Interactive Internet Education Courseware

Internet education, as its name implies, is to teach and impart knowledge with the help of the Internet [3]. Because of the convenience of the Internet, people can choose their own courses to study, and at the same time, it also avoids learning problems caused by time conflicts or explanation of important knowledge points due to distraction. It is this characteristic that makes it convenient for people to study anytime and anywhere. One of the characteristics of the Internet in the education industry is the sharing of resources. China has always attached great importance to the balanced development of various regions. At present, most of the work is to help the poor out of poverty. The popularization of Internet technology is the embodiment of poverty alleviation. The application of this technology solves the problem that students in backward areas cannot accept the same education as students in better developed areas due to lack of conditions, and saves teachers.

Internet education technology is characterized by convenience. Students only need to choose one course and reach a certain learning time to complete the final examination. They will be awarded a certificate of completion or certificate of completion. As shown in Fig. 1, the course of Internet distance education is generally composed of antifake learning and antisubstitution module, courseware learning timing system, final automatic evaluation system and courseware. The modules of antifake learning and antisubstitution learning mainly play the role of supervising learning, which are not included in the evaluation system of user standards. For the learning process, the determination of reaching the standard is given by the timing system. When the time of learning courseware reaches the target time and reaches the opening period of the final examination, the user can participate in the assessment, and the corresponding certificate or certificate will be granted after the assessment is completed. The organization of online distance education is shown in Fig. 1

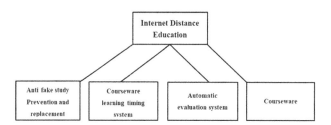

Fig. 1. Organization chart of internet distance education

The operation of personalized learning network means further innovation in the education industry. The construction of the network needs to meet two conditions. The user needs to accurately collect the user's own needs, including the user's own learning ability and parents' expectations. On the other hand, the lecturer also needs to introduce the course in detail, including the applicable objects of the personalized learning [4].

The pass rate of courseware refers to the pass probability of a certain courseware, which is the proportion of the total number of times (pass) of learning the courseware to the total number of learning the courseware [5]. The total number of times that users who fail to pass the assessment of the courseware will increase each time they participate in the courseware learning. If and only if the user has not passed the assessment of the courseware and passed the assessment after learning, the total number of times of learning the courseware will be recorded. The courseware pass rate CP can be formalized as follows:

$$CPR = \frac{pass}{total} \tag{1}$$

Car (course accelerating rate) refers to the conditional probability that one courseware passes the assessment and passes another courseware CI. It is the ratio of the total number of times CP (condition PAS) to the total number of CI learning after passing CJ (condition total) [6]. When all the users have passed a certain CT courseware, they will only be based on the previous CT courseware. The car can be formalized as follows:

$$CAR(C_i \backslash C_j) = \frac{CP}{CT} \tag{2}$$

4 Simulation for Measures of Landscape Sculpture Design Teaching

The teacher should lead the students out of the classroom and ask them to take a ruler to repeatedly observe the real scene, touch the material, experience the space, measure the volume of the sculpture, and take photos or sketches. Adhere to such teaching activities, after a period of time, students can get a lot of harvest (see Fig. 2) [7].

Regional culture is the best reference for the cultural form of landscape sculpture design, and it is also the embodiment of Fengge in landscape sculpture design. Regional culture reflects the historical events, natural characteristics, mineral resources and cultural features of a specific region. Most designers use concrete or abstract design forms to interpret regional culture in landscape sculpture design. However, this method is too simple to reflect the profound cultural connotation. On the basis of shaping the main cultural image, designers should integrate the characteristics of regional culture into landscape sculpture to express the connotation of regional culture. The simulation of land sculpture design is shown in Fig. 2.

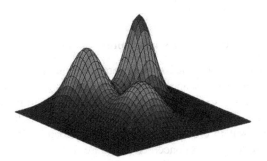

Fig. 2. The simulation of land sculpture design

5 Urban Sculpture Design and Environmental Art

With the development of the times, the application of urban sculpture in urban landscape design presents a diversified and diversified development trend in every corner of the urban public environment. They are in line with the aesthetic requirements of the times and meet the needs of the public for leisure and entertainment, and form a whole in the process of mutual dependence and integration with the environment. Urban sculpture stimulates people's creativity and imagination with its open position and pleasant scale. The different environment restricts the design of urban sculpture, which makes it present multi-level and multi angle expression of content. It is in this contradictory movement that urban sculpture and landscape art seek rationality and harmony [8].

5.1 Architectural Features and Urban Sculpture Design

The unique charm of the city reflects its charm. The architectural environment has become the creation of human beings in material form with a large volume. Its unique personality and characteristics not only reflect its own culture, but also faithfully reflect the different material civilization created in the process of human development. Architecture is solidified music. They are the rich achievements created by human beings in each era. While recording the material and cultural information, they also reflect certain era concepts, interests and hobbies through the morphological information. From a cultural point of view, each building is a collection of human ideals [9].

In modern society, the so-called space refers to the place of human communication. Therefore, with the development of communication, space is also moving towards a more advanced organic direction. People's spiritual world is a vast and boundless world, and human needs are more abundant and endless. The quality and improvement of people's spiritual needs is the performance of the improvement of social civilization. Therefore, in order to meet this demand, human beings should create an environment that is reasonable, scientific and humane, diversified rather than unit, rich and complex rather than simple. In addition, the architectural environment can also play the role of place and media in the process of dialogue with people, which makes the function of space get the greatest social effect [10].

5.2 Water Characteristics and Urban Sculpture Design

The design of water sculpture is the use and representation of rivers, lakes, waterfalls, streams, springs and other landscapes in nature. When designing, we should not only integrate with nature, but also use new techniques. According to the characteristics of water, there are three different forms of urban water landscape sculpture [11].

Using the water itself to create the main body of urban sculpture, water itself is public art. As far as waterscape is concerned, there are still water, moving water, falling water and gushing. Still water is a collection of water bodies in the garden, which can reflect the reflection of the surrounding space and produce a special visual effect of the landscape. Falling water is the falling curtain, water wall, water ladder, etc., which constantly glitters under the sunlight, and is accompanied by the sound of falling water. From the perspective of acoustics, we can enjoy the auditory landscape sculpture. The natural phenomenon of fountains is very wonderful, it is widely used in modern cities all over the world.

In the overall design of urban sculpture, water, as a part of the environment, plays a role of setting off, or it can be mainly one, supplemented by others, or it can be combined with several forms, especially with the perfect combination of modern sound control technology, to build a new type of sound control spray city landscape sculpture, which often attracts people to stop and watch for a long time [12].

The natural rocks in the abstract expression represent the water body with the polished water circle and water grain like white sand, and the mountains and islands with the upright or lying stones, which symbolize the eternity of nature and arouse people's infinite reverie like appreciating urban sculpture. Make full use of the communication and dialogue between water sculpture and the public to create a very rich hydrophilic experience. While redesigning the waterscape sculpture form, combining it with public art will make the water body more artistic in its natural form, and bring unexpected vividness and beauty to the space environment. The characteristics of water and urban sculpture design are shown in Fig. 3.

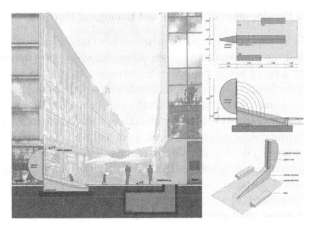

Fig. 3. Water characteristics and urban sculpture design

6   Urban Space and Urban Sculpture Design

Modern city is a public space full of people, logistics and information. The frequent exchange of information and culture inside and outside the city accelerates the pace of people's life and work in the city, so the trend of pursuing comfort and aesthetic feeling has become the basic feature of modern city. Therefore, it will become an important part of the cultural awareness and spiritual quality of the urban public environment to make urban sculpture from all aspects of the city with the artistic processing of urban landscape design [13].

Reasonable planning of urban public space, artistic recreation, because the material needs of urban residents, public aesthetic, etc. to provide effective services [14]. As urban landscape design, in the integration of environmental order and aesthetic concept, it should adapt to the overall planning of urban space, integrate into all levels of social life, so that the specific environment can become an organic part of urban public space culture and art. The central square of a city has always been an important public space environment in the long history of human settlement. It provides people with the convenience of gathering, communication, cultural entertainment and other public activities in an open space. The modern city square is praised by the city living room because of its multi-function, multi landscape. The main body of the square determines the orientation of urban sculpture design, and the rapid development of modern science and technology has also changed the aesthetic concept of citizens. In front of the simple and bright form of modern society, the landmark city sculpture of the square appears in front of the public in a new form. While beautifying the environment of urban public space, the public sculptures highlight the vitality, edify people's hearts and arouse the public awareness of citizens [15].

7 Humanistic and Ecological Harmony of Urban Sculpture

7.1 Sustainable Development of Human and Ecological Harmony

Urban sculpture is an important symbol of urban culture and civilization. The construction of urban public environment must adhere to the idea of sustainable development. In order to create a better urban public space environment, grasping this idea is the primary task. The ecological and humanistic conditions of a landscape environment are the basic contents of landscape matching and urban sculpture. Because they will have a variety of effects on the original environment, whether positive or negative, involving the optimization or destruction of the environment, involving the inheritance of history and culture, emotional identity in life and environment and other social problems. Therefore, public opinions should be widely adopted in the placement of urban sculptures, and their living habits should be respected, so as to develop harmoniously with the surrounding public space environment [16].

As an environmental art of public space, the design of urban sculpture works should play a positive role in the overall planning and design of the city, influencing the society and reflecting public opinion. Their design, implementation and maintenance should not be divorced from the geographical environment and natural resources of the city, but should focus on the protection of the natural resources on which the city depends and conform to the description of local characteristics, Research and integrate in a larger career. The intervention of urban sculpture in the space environment requires careful consideration of the attributes of the specific environment. At the same time, in the process of implementation, it should be actively integrated into the local ecosystem to form a certain place and properly handle the relationship between the part and the whole. The location of urban historical and cultural sites or important ecological and environmental protection areas should not only pay attention to the reasonable location of urban sculpture, but also pay attention to the volume, theme, tone, style tendency of urban sculpture itself. Because these factors will have a variety of effects on the atmosphere of the environment, involving the beautification or destruction of the environment, involving the inheritance of history and culture. Therefore, the location and methods of urban sculpture should be widely adopted by the public. It is an important social responsibility in contemporary landscape design to pursue the harmony between man and nature and the happiness and enrichment brought by spiritual culture. Part of the reason citizens live in cities is that the good structure of cities makes them wait for less energy, effort and cost to do more. City is the natural organization mode of cultural life. If a city is well planned and has relatively perfect functions, it is the best tool to adapt culture to nature. The design of urban sculpture should be combined with the urban macro planning, organically integrated into the original landscape of the city, become the constituent elements of different forms of urban culture and living scenes, become indispensable parts in the realization of urban functions, rather than become decorative objects contrary to the local human history and contemporary life.

7.2 Inheritance and Dialogue of Architectural Features

The appearance of architecture dominates the characteristics of urban public space design and the aesthetic value orientation of citizens. It is the most basic and prominent component of the city. The inheritance and dialogue of the architectural environment is also reflected in the urban sculpture, landscape sketches and public art around the architecture. Therefore, the urban landscape design should be adapted to local conditions, strengthen the communication between the architectural environment and urban sculpture, so as to make the connection between them closer and better bring the visual aesthetic enjoyment of urban landscape to the citizens. Enriching the content of architecture, simultaneous architecture has become a multi-dimensional art including other aspects, so that architecture itself is no longer a space tool only to meet the original function of wind and rain shelter. In today's boring environment of urbanization, the art function of architecture should be brought into play. As a pleasant living urban space, many buildings, to a certain extent, use the landscape to symbolize and beautify. It is the existence of urban sculpture that fully embodies the characteristics of architecture, which is indispensable in landscape sketches, installation art or large-scale urban sculpture.

7.3 Personality Construction of Business Environment

The intervention of urban sculpture and public art sketches in the business environment is not only to create a unique charm of urban business personality and attract people's shopping enthusiasm, but also to integrate the spiritual culture of products into the consumption environment, showing the new concept of modern business. In other words, the construction of urban public art needs the participation and sponsorship of enterprises and businessmen with diversified economy, as well as social activities accompanied by purposeful commercial activities. The functions of public sculpture are often various.

8 Conclusion

Through the cooperation between schools and enterprises, the learning research teaching mode combines classroom teaching with market demand, integrates the resources of colleges and enterprises, realizes complementary advantages, and innovates talent training mode, which is helpful to cultivate applied talents needed by the society. The teaching mode of production, teaching and research meets the needs of the current landscape sculpture education reform, has the characteristics of the times, and meets the needs of the development of market economy. At present, many colleges and universities have carried out the practice of teaching mode of production, teaching and research, but there are still some problems in the specific practice, which still need the joint efforts of colleges, enterprises and students, so as to make the teaching mode of production, teaching and research play an effective role and promote the reform of higher education and the sound development of enterprises.

References

1. Li, Y., Ye, B., Du, J., et al. Classification and selection of industry university research cooperation modes. Sci. Technol. Progress Countermeasures **10** (2004)
2. Zhang, J.: Some problems and reflections on the cooperation of industry, University and research in Colleges and universities. Technol. Innov. Manage. **1** (2006)
3. Wei, X., Shan, L.: On the construction of practical teaching system in Applied Universities. J. Liaoning Univ. Admin. **9** (2007)
4. Zeng, C.: On reconstruction of talent training mode of art design education in Colleges and universities. Art Educ. **3** (2008)
5. Shen, T.: Research on Landscape Sculpture Design in Urban Open Space. Shenyang University of technology (2011)
6. Liu, W.: Research on regionalization of landscape sculpture design. Shandong Forestry Sci. Technol. (2009)
7. Zheng, S.: Contemporary research on the expansion of Chinese figurative sculpture language. Dalian Univ. Technol. (2011)
8. Qian, B.: On the aesthetic characteristics of modern abstract sculpture. J. Suzhou Inst. Educ. (2006)
9. Guohui, J.: Research on the imagery of contemporary concrete sculpture. Northeast Normal Univ. (2009)
10. Chen, Z.: Discussion on modern urban landscape sculpture design. Anhui Agron. Bull. (2009)
11. Lin, B., Chen, X.: Shaping and production of urban sculpture art. China Construction Industry Press (2008)
12. Wu, W.: City is the container of culture. Shanwei daily (2011)
13. Zhang, J.: The influence of urban sculpture in society. Sci. Technol. (2011)
14. Qian, Y.: On sculpture materials and sculpture. Sculpture (1998)
15. Li, Z., Han, C.: How should public art enter Xi'an subway. Art and Design (1998)
16. Wang, Y.: The historical and cultural value of the big and small wild goose pagodas in Xi'an. Buddhist Culture (1998)

Design of Experimental Teaching System for Biochemistry and Molecular Biology in Cloud Course Platform

Yong Ma, Xiu-li Chen, Tu Ya, and Tong Wen(⊠)

Baotou Teachers' College, Baotou 014030, Inner Mongolia, China
{chenxiuli6666,wentong1029}@sina.com

Abstract. Biochemistry and molecular biology experiment is an important professional basic experimental course for biology majors, which plays a very important role in the cultivation of practical skills of related majors. Network teaching platform can expand the teaching time and space, and provide a public platform for the release of experimental course resources and the reform and innovation of teaching mode. This paper discusses the establishment of network assisted teaching of Biochemistry and molecular biology experiment course under the network environment combined with cloud course platform. Starting from the training objectives of the course teaching, the online course platform is used to promote the reform of practical teaching.

Keywords: Cloud course · Biochemistry · Molecular biology · Experimental teaching · Network platform

1 Introduction

With the continuous development of network technology, its application in teaching is more and more extensive. The great promoting effect of network teaching on teaching activities and the advantages of network teaching are becoming more and more obvious, which represents a development direction of modern education. In 2015, the Ministry of Education issued the opinions on strengthening the application and management of online open courses in Colleges and universities (Jiao Gao [2015] No. 3), pointing out that it is necessary to accelerate the construction of online open courses and platforms suitable for China's national conditions and promote the application of courses. Network teaching platform can expand teaching space and time, stimulate students' learning enthusiasm and autonomy, and provide a public platform for course construction and network teaching activities for the release of experimental course resources and the reform of teaching mode [1].

With the continuous development of biology, mastering its basic experimental operation technology has become the basic requirement for students majoring in biology, and also provides the necessary practical basis for their follow-up courses. Biochemistry and molecular biology experiment is an important professional basic course for

M. A. Jan and F. Khan (Eds.): BigIoT-EDU 2021, LNICST 391, pp. 105–114, 2021.
https://doi.org/10.1007/978-3-030-87900-6_13

biology majors. It is an extension of the theoretical teaching of Biochemistry and molecular biology. It is also an important link to master the two theoretical courses. It is a discipline to impart knowledge, train basic skills, and cultivate scientific research ideas and methods. Therefore, the teaching reform of the course should also meet the needs of the development of biology, it plays a very important role in the cultivation of practical skills of biology related professionals, and it is also one of the modes and ways to update educational concepts, actively promote innovative education, and strive to explore the cultivation of innovative talents.

In this paper, based on the online cloud course platform of Higher Education Press, how to establish the network assisted teaching of Biochemistry and molecular biology experiment course is discussed. Starting from the training objectives of course teaching, the online course platform is used to promote practical teaching.

2 Design of Cloud Course Platform System

The cloud course is mainly designed for teachers and students in Colleges and universities. In the design of course platform, the mainstream Web terminal is mainly considered to assist teachers and students to teach. The back-end of cloud course platform is mainly composed of B/S structure and SSH framework. The front end is composed of HT, JavaScript, CSS, J ρ uery, sass and bootstrap. The back-end page template is JSP page. The platform mainly adopts framework to develop, which can avoid repeated class library. Many function libraries have been implemented in popular frameworks, such as control inversion of spring framework and face slicing programming. Using framework can make developers focus on business implementation, and SSH framework also reduces the coupling of the system, When refactoring, extending or adding new functions occurs after the project, the project architecture can also adapt well [2].

Traditional recommendation algorithms mainly include: knowledge-based algorithm recommendation, content-based algorithm recommendation, collaborative filtering and hybrid recommendation. The classification of recommended algorithms is shown in Fig. 1.

This method uses vector to represent the user rating information of the project in the system, and the angle between vectors represents the difference between users. The smaller the angle, the smaller the difference and the higher the similarity. The specific formula for calculating the similarity between u and V is shown in (1).

$$Sim_{uv} = \cos(u, v) = \frac{\sum_{i \in Iluv} r_{ui} r_{vi}}{\sqrt{\sum_{i \in I_u} r_{ui}^2} \sqrt{\sum_{i \in I_v} r_{vi}^2}} \tag{1}$$

After calculating the similarity between users, some method is used to filter the target users to form a neighborhood set with similarity. According to the evaluation of adjacent users, the predicted value of target users is given. The prediction scoring formula is shown in (2).

$$P_{ui} = \overline{r_u} + \frac{\sum\limits_{v \in N} sim(u, v) \times (r_{vi} - \overline{r_v})}{\sum\limits_{v \in N} |sim(u, v)|} \tag{2}$$

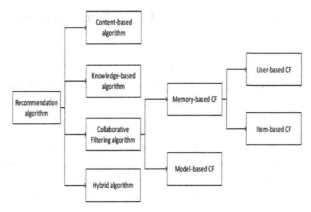

Fig. 1. Classification of recommendation algorithms

3 Increase Network Discussion and Deepen Experimental Understanding

After the experiment, students are required to complete the experiment report in time. One of the important components of the experiment report is the discussion and analysis of the experimental results. In the undergraduate learning stage, through this kind of learning and training, it can provide great help for the future graduate students to analyze and solve problems in the process of study and work, which is conducive to the cultivation of innovation ability [3]. With the network platform, students can discuss the experimental phenomenon on the network in time after completing the experiment.

Online discussion allows students to enter the cloud course platform at any time and place to express their opinions according to the problems set by the teacher, and also to view the views of other students. It provides a communication platform for students to enhance the universality of participation, which can be multi-directional communication between teachers and students, or even between students. At the same time, because the network platform can also upload text files, image files or multimedia files as the support of the argument, it can make the discussion more vivid and intuitive.

After the completion of all the experiments, the students were asked to consult the relevant literature, analyze their own problems, and compare the results of others' experiments, so that students can have an opportunity to show themselves on the platform, promote students' Thinking on the experimental results, and enable teachers to ask questions in person to check their understanding of these problems, At the same time, it enlightens and guides students how to analyze and solve the problems in the experiment by themselves, so as to let students explore extensively, so as to gradually exercise their innovation ability, problem-solving ability and scientific research ability of independently carrying out new experiments.

4   Changing Teaching Concept and Enriching Network Teaching Resources

Network teaching resources can consolidate, supplement and expand the contents of paper-based teaching materials, expand students' knowledge, enhance their awareness and ability to acquire knowledge independently, and promote students' autonomous learning [4].

Network teaching not only brings various advanced ideas, but also increases the workload of teachers. Teachers should become the guide of students' learning. Therefore, teachers need to change their original teaching concepts, organize network teaching effectively, and make extensive and in-depth communication and discussion between teachers and students, and students, so as to fully reflect the interactivity and flexibility of network teaching [5].

With the continuous reform of experimental course content, teaching video should be constantly updated. The teaching team should make corresponding teaching video according to the teaching content, and the video content less than 15 min should be used as the network platform resources, which is conducive to students' watching and learning.

In order to expand students' knowledge, teachers should also pay attention to collecting the development data of various disciplines, timely tracking the new development, so that students can have a better understanding of the subject development, which can also update the knowledge structure of teachers, improve the knowledge system of teachers, improve the teaching effect, and embody the connotation of "teaching and learning benefit each other". With the continuous development of science and technology, timely supplement and update teaching resources is also an important aspect of network assisted teaching mode reform (see Fig. 2).

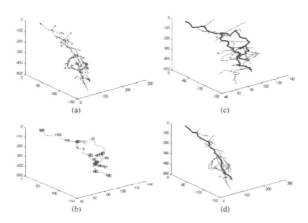

Fig. 2. Simulation for network teaching

5   Aggregation of Cloud Course Platform and Social Media

5.1   Design Concept

Formal learning and informal learning are two independent concepts. It is a formal learning environment with a clear learning goal. Before the concept of informal learning was put forward, the design of network teaching environment was centered on formal learning, also known as virtual learning environment (VLE), which was generally expressed as the hierarchical organization and activity design of learning units. With the continuous change and development of Web2.0 technology and learning philosophy, the network teaching environment with formal learning as the service object increasingly highlights the defects of learners' weak autonomy, lack of learning enthusiasm and low learning efficiency. The design of network teaching environment began to change from the informal learning environment, and the virtual learning environment was gradually replaced by the personal learning environment (PLE). Ple emphasizes that learning comes from the interaction, cooperation and sharing of learners. Learners become the center of all learning activities and master the main control of learning [6].

Based on the concept of integrating formal learning and informal learning, this paper proposes the aggregation mode of cloud course platform and social media. Cloud course platform, which serves for formal learning, is used as an organization platform for teaching activities such as course management, activity design and task arrangement, which provides direction guidance for learners' learning activities and cultivates learners' self-organization ability; social media is used as an auxiliary informal learning place, which allows learners to choose learning tools independently to meet their individual needs, It can control its own learning process at any time; through the aggregation mode, it can break through the boundary between cloud course platform and social media, integrate the advantages of formal learning and informal learning, and form a more perfect and adaptive learning ecosystem [7].

5.2   Design Principles

Based on the above design concept, the teaching environment design of cloud course platform aggregating social media should follow the following principles [8].

(1) In the teaching environment, the guidance and control of teachers to learners is an indispensable part. In the third chapter of the questionnaire survey, most learners pointed out that one of the major factors restricting their use of learning platform is the lack of teacher guidance. Therefore, the teaching environment design of cloud course platform aggregating social media should emphasize the guidance role of teachers in the learning process, which should be reflected in the guidance of the learning process, question answering and other auxiliary teaching levels, rather than surpassing the learners' thinking. The guidance for learning can be implemented in two ways. First, in the formal learning environment, teachers should organize and plan learning objectives, learning contents and learning plans according to different levels, and construct learning scaffolding and templates for learners to set their own learning pace. For example, learners can set learning time according to the curriculum offered by teachers. The second is that teachers can synchronize the updated content of teaching activities to social media to

guide learners in an informal learning environment. For example, the arrangement of activity time can be sent to learners through microblog, or questions can be answered on social networking sites [9].

(2) The principle of autonomy. Personalization, self-management and active participation are the key to effective learning. Therefore, in the construction of teaching environment, we should fully guarantee learners' autonomous management authority, embody the humanistic thought of taking learners as the center, and fully mobilize learners' subjective initiative. Although it is necessary for teachers to guide the learning process, learners can still carry out learning activities in a way of individual autonomy according to their own needs. Learner autonomy is mainly manifested in the following aspects: having the right to choose the use of learning tools and social media; being able to invite other partners to participate in learning discussion or collaborative learning, controlling the nature, process and participants of learning activities; having the right to decide whether individual learning records, discussion activities, comments and other contents are shared, and the choice of sharing objects. In the design of teaching environment, giving learners full autonomy helps to enhance learners' viscosity and interest, and improve learners' participation [10].

(3) Learning extension principle. According to relevance theory, today's knowledge is distributed in a network, and learning is the process of establishing connections among knowledge nodes in the network and transforming the original cognition. Therefore, learners' learning activities should not be limited to a certain platform, but should be transformed into the process of building knowledge network [11]. The design of teaching environment should help learners to find the relationship between knowledge, and constantly improve their personal knowledge system in the process of establishing the relationship. There are many ways to establish association, such as browsing related content, interactive discussion with others, and carrying out collaborative learning around the theme. The premise for learners to explore the relationship between knowledge is to extend learning, let more like-minded people join in learning activities, so that the original learning can spread to other nodes of the network. On this basis, learners can find more content related to learning activities, and establish links with them, so as to obtain a more comprehensive and in-depth understanding of knowledge.

6 Analysis on the Mode of Aggregating Social Media on Cloud Course Platform

6.1 Aggregation Mode of Cloud Course Platform and Social Media

The aggregation mode of cloud course platform and social media is not only a bridge between formal learning and informal learning, but also a key step to extend formal learning to informal learning. Learning is human learning. The extension of learning is inseparable from learners' subjective initiative. Learners' own social relations play a very important role in the transfer of learning. Professor Wilson (2008) emphasized the importance of social relations to the construction of teaching environment when redefining the teaching environment. He believed that the essence of social relations network is a collection of people, services and resources distributed in each node of the network. The establishment of teaching environment is to establish association between these elements through learning tools, extend learners' learning activities, and form a social learning network [12]. The aggregation mode of cloud course platform and social media is shown in Fig. 3.

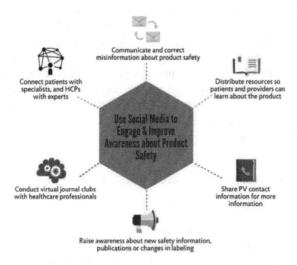

Fig. 3. Aggregation mode of cloud course platform and social media

6.2 Aggregation form of Cloud Course Platform and Social Media

The aggregation of cloud course platform and social media is based on mashup technology, which is mainly divided into two forms: content level aggregation and service level aggregation [13].

(1) The essence of content aggregation is the re organization of learning resources. Through the integration and presentation of relevant content, it can reduce learners' cognitive load and knowledge confusion in the face of massive resources, and reconstruct the application value of learning resources. In this paper, the aggregation form of content level is mainly the aggregation of blog and content sharing social media [14].

Content sharing social media provides rich learning resources, including videos, documents, pictures, slides and other types. It can make abstract concepts vivid and concrete, so as to arouse learners' interest. Content sharing social media is an effective medium to present structured courses. Effectively aggregating the learning content in this kind of social media into the cloud course platform can not only simplify the construction process of the course platform, but also realize the reuse and sharing of high-quality resources [15].

(2) The aggregation of service level is in cloud computing environment. Any business model that takes the Internet as the carrier and delivers and uses applications in the form of services can be regarded as SAS (software service) mode. From this perspective, all kinds of online social media are a service mode [16]. In the concept of SOA, the

functions of social media can be divided into multiple reusable and loose coupling service components, and can be packaged in the form of web service, and exposed to interface form through interface adapter. At present, most social media have disclosed their own API interfaces, such as user interface, relationship interface, friend grouping interface, user tag interface, search interface, etc. developers can easily call the required service interface and aggregate with other services to generate new service content. In addition to calling API interface, we can also use widget form to realize social media service aggregation some social media experience encapsulates common functions into widget components for developers to use. Because widget is implemented based on JavaScript and HTML, it can be embedded directly into web pages. Even if the programming ability is weak, developers can quickly master it, and can deploy multiple widget components in the same page as needed. When the widget provided by social media cannot meet the personal needs, the services required can also be packaged through widget API and uniformly scheduled on each page [17].

7 Architecture Design of Cloud Course Platform Aggregating Social Media

With the advent of the cloud era, computing power has become a service model that is ready to use. Cloud computing provides users with the most operational and collaborative technology platform, so that users can get rid of the shackles of technical ability and greatly reduce the complexity of application system development. In this paper, the aggregation of the course platform and social media is deployed on the cloud computing platform. The whole architecture is divided into four layers: infrastructure layer, application interface layer, application layer and user layer.

The infrastructure layer, also known as Las layer, mainly provides computing, data storage, network communication and other infrastructure resources (including physical hardware resources and virtualization resources) for high-level. Server, storage, network and so on are highly scalable services, which are provided to users in the way of on-demand distribution. The infrastructure layer provides dynamic and scalable underlying resources for the aggregation of cloud course platform and social media. In the development process, there is no need to care about the implementation details of the top-level hardware of the server, and there is no need to control the bottom hardware details, thus saving the allocation and maintenance costs of software and hardware resources. The application interface layer, or PAs layer, is the link between the application layer and the infrastructure layer. It directly faces the developers and provides an Internet-based application development and execution environment, including the running platform and the interface service application layer encapsulated by the bottom layer cloud computing capability, namely SaaS layer. It is also the presentation of cloud course platform and social media aggregation mode. Cloud course platform is the central platform for learners to carry out teaching activities. The aggregation of social media provides all kinds of learning support services for cloud course platform, and supports and expands functions for learners' knowledge acquisition, knowledge retention, knowledge representation, and conversion of explicit and implicit knowledge, connecting formal learning and informal learning environment. Learners can access the cloud course platform from the Internet and connect with social media through account binding. While learning in the cloud course platform, they can share and push resources to the selected social media, so that learning activities can continue to be maintained outside the cloud course platform, which is helpful for learners to explore learning community in a wider network, and then promote the formation of social learning network. At the same time, teachers can make use of the push mechanism of the cloud course platform to synchronize the updated information of the course to the social media, so that learners can effectively master the learning process in any environment. In addition, the content of social media will also be aggregated in the cloud course platform, which will avoid the dilemma of learners looking for useful resources in the vast ocean of information, and discover the new value of knowledge in the gathering of information. The user layer is the highest level of the whole architecture, directly facing the end users.

8 Conclusion

"Higher education law" points out that "the task of higher education is to cultivate high-level specialized personnel with innovative spirit and practical ability, develop science and technology culture, and promote socialist modernization construction". Therefore, modern higher education advocates strengthening the practice link and cultivating students' innovative spirit and ability. On the basis of strengthening scientific research training, the experimental teaching platform for cultivating high-quality innovative talents should be built, students' subjective initiative should be mobilized, students' strong desire for knowledge should be induced, and students' innovative ability should be cultivated. This paper explores the teaching reform of Biochemistry and molecular biology experiment from the aspects of enriching teaching content, expanding teaching methods and optimizing network resources, and constantly enriches and improves in teaching practice. Only in this way can we better mobilize students' learning ability.

References

1. Yichuan, L., Hu, L., Yongjie, S., et al.: Research on combined teaching mode and its teaching effect evaluation system under the network environment. Northwest Med. Educ. **18**(5), 876–878 (2010)
2. Limei, L., Ouyang, L., Zeng, F. : Biochemical practice teaching reform in Normal Colleges under the concept of innovative talent cultivation. Biol. Teach. Res. Colleges Univ. (Electr. Ed.) **2**(2), 30–32 (2012)
3. Molecular Biology and Experiment Press (2014)
4. Xiaoju, L.: Teaching reform of molecular biology experiment course with professional characteristics. Biol. Teach. Res. Colleges Univ. (Electr. Ed.) **4**(4), 43 (2014)
5. Yuqi, D., Zhengwei, B., Xiangyong, L.: CTCL: a new paradigm of Educational Technology Research (2) - from "media application", "curriculum integration" to "learning technology". J. Distance Educ. **2**, 3–12 (2013)
6. Xiao, J., Wang, L., Huang, H.J.: Research on the operation and management mode of education information cloud service. China Educ. Inf. (3), 18–21 (2013)
7. Lai, L., Zhou, X.: On the new model of open learning environment under cloud computing. Silicon Valley **6**, 17–178 (2010)

8. Discussion on cloud computing technology and application of Sun Lixin library. Huazhang (23), 317 (2012)
9. Chang, R.: Information architecture of social media. J. Nat. Sci. Hunan Normal Univ. (2), 37–41 (2011)
10. Yuhong, Z.: Research on the development of distance education in the United States before the 21st century, pp. 4–17. Hebei University, Hebei (2007)
11. Cai, J., Hu, X.: Discussion on the application of cloud computing in network course construction. E-Commerce **49**(3), 50 + 53 (2010)
12. Chen, W., Huang, H.X., Chen, H.: Comparative study on the development platform of online courses. Open Educ. Res. (5), 110–114 (2011)
13. Zhang, Y., Wu, Q.: Problems and Countermeasures of adult education network teaching platform. Continuing Educ. Res., 8485 (2011)
14. Mei, L., Yali, Y.: Introduction and educational application of cloud computing platform. China Inf. Technol. Educ. **7**, 73–76 (2010)
15. Jinhe, W.: Building a new model of College English teaching based on blog. China Press **8**, 269–270 (2012)
16. Huang, X., Ma, X.: Case study of open online education and research community based on social media. Educ. Inf. Technol. **201**, 11–14 (2003)
17. Yang, G., Huang, Y.: The influence of social media on Education. Sci. Technol. Horizon, 7980 (2012)

Big Data Analysis for Physical Education Teaching Evaluation

Huarong Deng[⊠]

Heyuan Polytechnic, Heyuan 517000, Guangdong Province, China

Abstract. In view of the absoluteness of Traditional P.E. teaching evaluation and the inconsistency of multiple evaluation conclusions, this paper constructs an independent advantage evaluation method that highlights its own advantages. In the evaluation, we use big data analysis to evaluate the advantages and disadvantages of the evaluation objects. By calculating the advantages and disadvantages of each evaluation object, we get the evaluation conclusion with probability information.

Keywords: Sports · Big data analysis · Education evaluation

1 Introduction

The theory of physical education teaching evaluation has been developed for many years in China. In view of this specific evaluation problem, even though the mechanism of the methods are different and the ways to solve them are not the same, most of the conclusions are determined in the same form, which is shown as "the absoluteness of distinguishing the advantages and disadvantages" and "the strictness of difference transmission". Generally, different evaluation methods will produce different evaluation conclusions for the same evaluation problem, at present, it is generally believed that "combination evaluation" is an effective way to solve the problem, but in fact, it is only a compromise, and does not solve the essence of the problem from the root. Therefore, this paper constructs an "independent advantage evaluation method highlighting its own advantages", in which a probability based random simulation algorithm is used, This method can produce the evaluation conclusion in the form of probability (reliability) and has stronger interpretability for practical problems [1]. From the perspective of innovation, this method puts forward the comprehensive evaluation method of "from the base to the top", which has high independence and joins the evaluation link in the form of "component", the effectiveness of the method is verified by an example.

2 The Main Evaluation Components of Physical Education Teaching Evaluation

Physical education teaching evaluation is an important part of physical education teaching, which plays an important role in the process of physical education teaching. Our

M. A. Jan and F. Khan (Eds.): BigIoT-EDU 2021, LNICST 391, pp. 115–124, 2021.
https://doi.org/10.1007/978-3-030-87900-6_14

country attaches great importance to teaching evaluation. In the "undergraduate teaching level evaluation program of ordinary colleges and universities (Trial)", it is clearly proposed that the state should further strengthen the macro management and guidance of the teaching work of colleges and universities through the level evaluation, urge the education authorities at all levels to attach importance to and support the teaching work of colleges and universities, and promote the colleges and universities to consciously implement the national policy, According to the law of education, we should further clarify the guiding ideology of running a school, improve the conditions of running a school, strengthen the basic construction of teaching, strengthen the teaching management, deepen the teaching reform, and comprehensively improve the teaching quality and learning efficiency. "Its purpose is to promote reform by evaluation, promote construction by evaluation, promote management by evaluation, combine evaluation with construction, and focus on construction" to achieve the purpose of improving teaching quality [2–5]. The idea of physical education teaching evaluation has been deeply rooted in the hearts of the people, and various evaluation methods have been widely used, but the scientific nature of evaluation methods needs to be studied. At present, the evaluation research mainly focuses on the theory of the macro evaluation method and the application steps of the micro evaluation method, and fails to discuss the limitations of the evaluation method in the application process. From the micro level, this paper studies the construction of indicators, the screening and testing of weights, the limitations of common evaluation methods and the problems that need to be paid attention to in the application. Its purpose is to improve the accuracy, objectivity and effectiveness of physical education evaluation, so as to provide theoretical and practical basis for improving the quality of physical education and the sustainable development of physical education.

3   The Design of P.E. Teaching Evaluation Scheme

The P.E. teaching evaluation scheme is the overall arrangement of the evaluation work. The advantages and disadvantages of the evaluation scheme are related to the success or failure of the evaluation work. In the process of implementation, improper selection of indicators, fuzzy evaluation criteria and unreasonable weight distribution will inevitably lead to one-sided evaluation conclusion, which cannot reflect the overall situation of the evaluated object, thus directly or indirectly causing adverse effects on the improvement and improvement of physical education teaching quality. In the procedure of design scheme, we must make clear the evaluation purpose, evaluation target and evaluation object, design and screen the evaluation index system, assign the weight of the index, formulate the evaluation standard, and demonstrate the evaluation scheme. Among them, the most important and key is the selection of evaluation index and the determination of index weight. From the perspective of the thinking mode in the process of putting forward the index and establishing the index system, it can be roughly summarized into two ways: the divergent construction method and the convergent construction method. The task of screening primary selection indicators is to merge those with the same connotation, remove the redundant indicators and find the missing important indicators. The main methods are Delphi method, brainstorming method, anti brainstorming method and counter acting method [6]. Since the traditional correlation coefficient screening method only represents the degree of linear correlation, but there may be nonlinear factors among indicators, a dynamic indicator selection method 6 can be used. The weight of an index is a value to measure the importance and role of an index in the whole evaluation index, which has an important impact on the evaluation results. There are many methods to determine the weight of the existing, but each method has a certain scope of application and limitations, according to the specific situation of the actual problem to choose different methods, the author recommends the use of analytic hierarchy process.

4   Diagnosis and Detection of Common Evaluation Methods of Physical Education

4.1   Fuzzy Comprehensive Evaluation Method

In the application process of physical education teaching evaluation, users often ignore the fact that there is "this and that" in the teaching phenomenon, but "either this or that" binary logic method to give evaluation. The fuzzy comprehensive evaluation method adopts the evaluation method of multi valued logic, which can have different degrees of membership for different grades. There are different degrees of fuzziness in the subject's understanding of the evaluation criteria and the nature of the evaluation object. In order to better deal with these fuzzy phenomena, to make a realistic evaluation of the various phenomena in the process of physical education teaching, and to improve the accuracy of the evaluation, the fuzzy comprehensive evaluation method has its unique application value. The selection of fuzzy operation model is the most important problem in the application of fuzzy comprehensive evaluation [7–10]. Different mathematical models of fuzzy comprehensive evaluation can be obtained by different definitions of "operation". Different mathematical models have different outstanding factors and different consideration of weight coefficient. Therefore, in the evaluation of physical education teaching, different models should be selected according to the evaluation purpose to be achieved in the teaching process. Due to the defects of understanding the essence of fuzzy comprehensive evaluation model, it leads to the abuse of the model in some literatures, resulting in the phenomenon of inconsistent evaluation.

4.2   Markov Chain Analysis

The advantage of Markov chain analysis in the evaluation of physical education teaching is that it considers the elimination of basic differences in the evaluation. For example, when evaluating the teaching effect of different teachers, the evaluation is always based on the final results of students taught by teachers. In fact, the differences in the original level of students in different teachers' classes affect the final examination results of students. If we simply evaluate the teaching effect according to the students' final scores without considering the students' basic differences, the conclusion does not necessarily reflect the actual situation, which is not convincing. Markov chain analysis considers the students' original state, and divides the students' original scores into the same level under the same standard, that is, to determine the state space [11]. Then the one-step transfer matrix is obtained. Finally, the limit vector is obtained according to the stationarity and ergodicity of Markov chain, and the comparison is made according to the limit vector. There are two problems here. One is that in the process of physical education teaching evaluation practice, we usually use the connection between two successive value states (such as two examination results) to describe the transition probability matrix, and then evaluate the practice that the evaluation object reaches the current state. However, whether the value scales used before and after the two times are consistent, and whether the evaluation scenarios used before and after the two times are consistent will affect the determined state matrix. Second, the process described by Markov chain is to use the transverse form of Markov chain to evaluate when k tends to infinity and the probability distribution of each state is stable. When using the obtained probability vector to solve the equations, the eigenvalue λ of the vector is artificially determined to be 1, and then the evaluation standard is established. As for whether each state is stable or not, the user should verify it by solving it. This condition has an important influence on the construction of stable probability distribution.

5   Basic description of physical education teaching evaluation

The evaluation process of physical education is described as a general transformation:

$$y_i = f(x_{i1}, x_{i2}, \cdots, x_{in}), i \in N \tag{1}$$

where f is a positive transformation function [12].

The purpose of evaluation is to promote the all-round development of students and fully reflect the educational policy. The traditional evaluation of physical education attaches importance to selection and results, pays attention to the evaluation of students' physical fitness and sports skills, and relatively ignores students' learning attitude, will quality, cooperation spirit and individual differences, and ignores the subjectivity of students' evaluation. In the process of teaching experiment, we use the evaluation method of combining quantitative and qualitative, self-evaluation and mutual evaluation, which makes the evaluation of students more reasonable and scientific.

Students' self-evaluation and mutual evaluation are not only a difficult point in teaching evaluation, but also a difficult link in PE teaching evaluation. There are many methods for students' self-evaluation and mutual evaluation. We try to use the "six step evaluation method". The "six step evaluation method" is a comprehensive evaluation combining students' self-evaluation, group evaluation, students' mutual evaluation and teachers' evaluation, which can better reflect the fairness and objectivity of the evaluation. Before the evaluation, according to the semester teaching plan, the evaluation content is classified and clearly listed, and each item is specific and clear. For example, the extent of learning progress, whether to participate in physical exercise frequently, the enthusiasm to participate in sports, the cooperation between students in the activities, etc. at the same time, it explains the requirements and standards, such as the implementation scale, defining the scope that should be concerned, and emphasizes the discipline and requirements in the evaluation. For individual students' technical confusion and subjective intentional violations, teachers should clearly and repeatedly emphasize the explanation [13, 14]. Then set up the evaluation team, give full play to the students' democracy, let the students elect the members of the evaluation team, the number of general control in about 20%.

6   Evaluation and description of independent advantage

Hypothesis 1: any evaluated object has the dual goals of "opening the gap between competitors" and "developing their own strengths", so as to comprehensively highlight their own advantages [15].

The quantitative description of the independent advantage evaluation thought in hypothesis 1.

The first step of the "six step evaluation method" is to send the form to the students, so that the students can give themselves a brief evaluation, and give them a grade, which is divided into four grades: A, B, C and D. Self evaluation is also a process for other students to understand (the one who knows the students most is the student himself, so he has the right to speak). Self evaluation of students is also helpful to mutual evaluation among students, because only by fully understanding the evaluated can the participants have the right to speak, so that they can really have the basis and substance.

As for whether to use big data or data mining algorithm, because these two algorithms involve many algorithms, when evaluating their data, which algorithm to choose will determine the timeliness of the algorithm.

Self evaluation or everyone's evaluation is something that many experts don't want to see, but for some experts, quantification is the best method, so we have a lot to consider when quantifying it [16]. as shown in Fig. 1. For example, in machine learning, we can quantify these parameters, in data mining, we can also quantify other parameters, which requires which evaluation method is used at the end of the evaluation.

Big Data & Data Mining ????

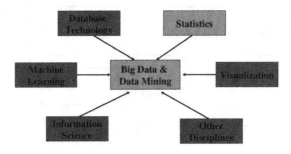

Fig. 1. Algorithm choice

7   Program implementation process

Before doing the technical support action, present the rubric to the students. Before presenting the rubric, the teacher first introduces the rubric evaluation concept and evaluation method, so that the students can have a correct and comprehensive understanding of the evaluation. Then bring the rubric to the classroom, let the students browse and communicate with each other, let the students express their own views and put forward some suggestions for revision in the discussion, the teacher combined with the suggestions put forward by the students to revise the rubric, and told the students where they have revised, and combined with the rubric to explain the specific requirements of learning and the final evaluation standard. From the effect of implementation, the process of students' participation can help students understand the requirements of the gauge, and greatly improve their learning enthusiasm and interest.

Provide action examples. The teacher will bring some videos of previous students' technical actions to the classroom, or put them on the teaching website. Let the students evaluate these technical actions according to the gauge. In the evaluation process, let the students experience and understand the requirements of the gauge, and think about how to achieve the excellent standard of the technical actions they will complete [14–18]. Action examples give students a visual learning goal, make the standard more specific, and improve the efficiency of learning. Practice shows that this link is very important. On the one hand, it can play the role of goal visualization, and let students use it as a reference and standard when they conceive their own learning actions. As shown in Fig. 2.On the other hand, it can help students understand the content of the gauge by evaluating other students' actions, reducing the time for teachers to explain the gauge and action requirements to students. Third, it can develop students' evaluation ability.

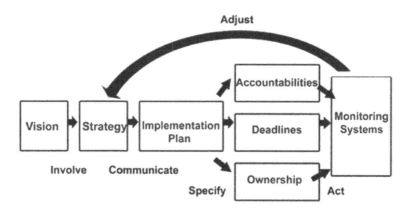

Fig. 2. Program implementation process

8   Stochastic simulation algorithm

Definition for any two evaluated objects, there are:

$$s(u_i' \succ u_i'') = p(f(u_i') > f(u_i'')) + 0.5p(f(u_i') = f(u_i'')) \qquad (2)$$

Where, the set function represents the event probability:

$$f(u_i') = \sum_{j=1}^{m} \lambda_i' \omega_j^*(i', i'') \qquad (3)$$

Students evaluate each other. Is to let all the students to evaluate the students, the mutual evaluation of the students a level. Students' mutual evaluation is the process of helping the evaluated to "know themselves" correctly, so that the evaluated can "wake up" in front of this "mirror", so that the students can clearly understand their strengths and weaknesses, and constantly improve themselves in the future learning activities.

The teacher makes an evaluation on the evaluated person according to all aspects of the situation. As a promoter, teachers should reasonably use the "authority" effect to put forward positive opinions to students. On the one hand, teachers should objectively give students a "exercise prescription" so that students can express their opinions along the correct track [19, 20]. On the other hand, teachers should avoid students' attachment and authority psychology when they finally express their opinions, so that students can fully express their opinions.

According to the actual situation, teachers, assessment teams and students should consider whether to modify the assessment for students with large gap in assessment, so as to fully promote democracy. In the process of evaluation, we have always grasped that giving priority to encouragement and promoting development by evaluation is not only the process of students' self-awareness and self-development, but also the process of promoting teaching.

Let the students to be evaluated talk about their satisfaction and feelings, as well as their own shining point, expertise, etc. for each level, several students can be selected for criticism and self-criticism. Changing bad habits through evaluation is conducive to the development of students.

9   Evaluation and Simulation

In the evaluation, teachers should pay attention to the phenomenon of "following the crowd", which is a psychological phenomenon caused by the pressure of different opinions of groups or most people in mutual evaluation or self-evaluation [21]. There is also "group phenomenon", which is an informal group with strong cohesion formed among teenagers. It has a great influence on students. It can not only change teenagers' external behavior, but also change their internal attitude and cognition, resulting in only starting from feelings, ignoring the objective situation, and one-sided exaggeration of their central position, blind self expansion and over emphasis on self, Attacking and retaliating against the students who put forward their opinions will lead to extreme evaluation, which is not conducive to students' objective and fair evaluation of themselves and others.

In addition, in the process of evaluation, we should adhere to the basic principles of seeking truth from facts and being objective and fair. Teachers should play the role of guidance and guidance, guide students where they don't know clearly, put aside personal emotional factors in the evaluation, and avoid making their own evaluation into a criticism meeting [22–24]. As shown in Fig. 3.We should be good at guiding students to pay attention to individual differences, attach importance to process, learning attitude and progress, so that every student has the feeling and joy of success. We should explain the reasons for the large gap in students' evaluation, avoid the phenomenon of students' groups, respect students' self-esteem and personality, fully affirm the progress and advantages of the evaluated, encourage and spur them, and truly embody everything for students' independent development in teaching.

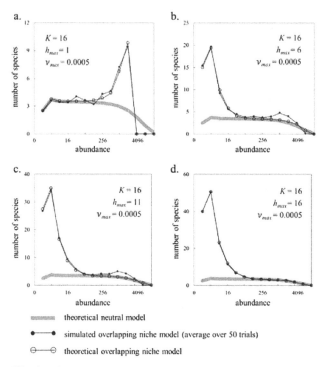

Fig. 3. The role of mathematical statistics in teaching evaluation

10   Conclusion

Teaching evaluation is a necessary link in school teaching activities. It is generally a comprehensive evaluation of teachers, students, teaching content, teaching methods, teaching environment, teaching management and other factors in the teaching process.

Teaching evaluation is an important way to understand the teaching situation and improve the teaching quality.

Teaching evaluation should not only provide feedback for teachers, but also provide feedback for students to understand their own learning situation, so that students can clearly understand the advantages and disadvantages of their own learning. Positive and positive evaluation can stimulate students' learning passion and build their self-confidence.

Acknowledgement. Heyuan Federation of Social Sciences,Research on the problems and Development Countermeasures of square dance in Heyuan City from the perspective of "healthy Heyuan"HYSK19QNO5.

References

1. Han, Y.: New development of teaching and learning in the era of Internet plus. Teaching in China University (12), 4–7 (2019)
2. Jin, Z., Wenjun, Z.: Zhang Rong strategies of university teachers to deal with teaching reform in the era of big data. J. Jiangsu Second Normal Univ. **35**(2), 102–105 (2019)
3. Bo, L., Lei, W., Chao, W.: Mathematical model and some problems of precision education in big data environment. Math. Model. Appl. **6**(4), 32–40 (2017)
4. Yahong, S.: Construction of classroom teaching evaluation system in Higher Vocational Colleges under the background of big data. Shaanxi Educ. (Higher Educ.) **12**, 51–52 (2019)
5. Xiaoqiong, L.: Exploration on the implementation of outward bound in College Physical Education. Hubei Agric. Mech. **20**, 115–117 (2019)
6. Zhang, Y.: On the infiltration strategy of moral education in junior middle school physical education. New Curriculum **2**(10), 276 (2019)
7. Hua, W.: Current situation and improvement methods of college physical education teaching evaluation. Educ. Teach. Forum **43**, 213–214 (2019)
8. Zhang, W., Sun, Z.: Connotation, value and realization path of "let learning" and "learn from others" in Physical Education. Educ. Theor. Pract. **39**(29), 57–59 (2019,)
9. Wei, Q.: Research on effective teaching evaluation in high school physical education. Contemp. Sports Sci. Technol. **9**(29), 125 + 127 (2019)
10. Xizeng, Y.: Research on teaching evaluation in lifelong physical education in Colleges and universities. Contemp. Sports Sci. Technol. **9**(29), 73–74 (2019)
11. Li, W.: Analysis of the learning evaluation strategy of primary school physical education. New Curriculum **1**(10), 219 (2019)
12. Changguang, H.: On the current situation and improvement methods of college physical education teaching evaluation. Sports Fashion **10**, 149 (2019)
13. Qinghua, G.: Research on the evaluation index system of college girls' physical education teaching quality based on analytic hierarchy process – taking China Institute of labor relations as an example. Sports Supplies Technol. **19**, 134–135 (2019)
14. Xinping, Z.: Research on the current situation and mode of College Physical Education Reform under the background of sunshine sports. Neijiang Sci. Technol. **40**(09), 128–129 (2019)
15. Jie, Z.: Research on the construction of the evaluation index system of rhythmic gymnastics teaching ability in Sports Colleges – Based on the application of WSR methodology. Contemp. Sports Sci. Technol. **9**(27), 198–199 (2019)
16. Qidong, L.: Practice and thinking of using social software to evaluate students' movement skills. Sports World (Acad. Ed.) **08**, 195–196 (2019)
17. Tang, X.: Research on Evaluation of physical education teaching under smart education [a]. Research Institute of digital education of people's education press. Digital teaching materials and digital teaching -- case collection of the 4th digital teaching seminar of primary and secondary schools [C]. Research Institute of digital education of people's Education Press: Digital teaching seminar of primary and secondary schools, 9, 4 (2019)
18. Lin, J.: Practice and exploration of hierarchical guidance of primary school physical education. Guidance New Curriculum **26**, 65 (2019)
19. Qin, M., Zhenghua, L.: Review and prospect of physical education teaching evaluation. Stationery Technol. (18), 85–8 (2019)
20. Chaohuo, Z., Junfeng, S.: The implementation of physical education in music schools under the background of cultivating people by virtue. Contemp. Sports Sci. Technol. **9**(25), 128–129 (2019)
21. Wenjing, X.: The opening of physical education and the development of students' subjectivity. Contemp. Sports Sci. Technol. **9**(25), 158–159 (2019)

22. Yaqi, Z.: Developing students' core literacy in Physical Education. Track Field **09**, 15–18 (2019)
23. Wu, J., Bingchun, J., Sheng, P.: Research on the quality evaluation system of middle school physical education from the perspective of people oriented. Sports Fashion, (09), 99 + 101 (2019)
24. Jun, X.: Research on teaching evaluation of junior high school physical education based on students' experience. Sports Fashion **09**, 264 (2019)

Development of a WEB-based Higher Education Management System

Yun Fu[✉], Ronal Judan, and Fei Han

University of the Cordilleras, 2600 Baguio, Philippines

Abstract. This system is mainly based on the current web to build an open format of higher education management system. The method is unified, open and secure. At the same time, it creates a good platform for the long-term use of the system.

Keywords: Web · Higher education · Management system

1 Introduction

In the use of the system, the reusable technology of component level is adopted, and the centralized storage of data is set up. In the constructed data center, it becomes an important technical form in the management information of high grade education. And also provides services for data. In this way, in the management of higher education, we can save, update, distribute and share data in time.

After the 1990s, information technology has made comprehensive progress, so it has been widely used in the development of various industries, and has realized the revolution of information communication technology. In such a rapid development of the technical background, but also the development of the field of education has been significantly affected. The information superhighway and satellite communication technology have been widely used in the world. Under the development of this technology, people's understanding of this technology has been greatly improved, so that people have a new understanding of the future development of the world.

The construction of educational information in our country has been developed in an all-round way after the 1990s [1]. At present, China has built educational research network, regional metropolitan area information network and campus network, and has formed a certain scale. For most campuses, they will be connected to the Internet, which can effectively provide students with a variety of high-quality teaching resources and realize the development of information education.

2 The Main Measures of Big Data Management in Colleges and Universities

2.1 The Importance and Urgency of Big Data to the Standardized Management of Colleges and Universities

In recent years, China's colleges and universities have developed rapidly and made great achievements, which has become an important part of higher education. It plays an

M. A. Jan and F. Khan (Eds.): BigIoT-EDU 2021, LNICST 391, pp. 125–132, 2021.
https://doi.org/10.1007/978-3-030-87900-6_15

important and positive role in meeting the diversified needs of the people to accept higher education, cultivating all kinds of suitable talents for the country, and deepening the reform of Higher Education system. At the same time, we must clearly see that there are many chaotic phenomena and serious problems in the enrollment, management, teaching and other aspects of some colleges and universities. In recent years, some local colleges and universities have occurred student mass incidents caused by the problems of student status, academic qualifications, fees and so on. Through the efforts of the local Party committee, the government and colleges and universities, these incidents have subsided, and the normal teaching order has been restored [2–4]. The occurrence of these events is not only the problems in the development process of colleges and universities, but also the result of the long-term accumulation of deep-seated contradictions in Colleges and universities. It mainly reflects that some colleges and universities are not well guided, the internal management system is not perfect, the property rights of legal persons are not implemented, and the school running behavior is not standardized. It also reflects that some colleges and universities are not well managed and supervised. If these problems are not paid great attention to and solved in time, it is bound to affect the healthy development of higher education and social stability. Colleges and universities should pay close attention to the management work as an important work at present.

2.2 Shortcomings and Problems in University Education Management Under Big Data

Although big data has been applied in university management for a period of time, there are still some problems to be improved in data management. First of all, there is no sufficient ideological understanding and preparation. Although the implementation of big data strategy and the public opinion atmosphere of technological innovation and application are increasingly strong, there are still some university managers who have not fully understood the beneficial side of big data to university education management. Secondly, although some universities have the conditions and resources for big data construction, they lack the platform to build big data system and apply big data technology. Third, some colleges and universities have the enthusiasm and intention to set up big data, but the investment in funds, equipment and professionals is insufficient [5]. Fourth, some colleges and universities do not conduct in-depth data mining in the process of data management, and the data mining is too simple to provide a deeper basis and decision-making for Colleges and universities. Fifth, the data communication between internal departments of colleges and universities is not smooth. The data ownership of different departments is independent, forming a physically isolated data fault. Data systems such as teaching, scientific research, administration and logistics are very difficult to connect and summarize, which is relatively common. Due to the lack of integration and connection mechanism, there are some difficulties in promoting data connection and integration. From a technical point of view, due to the inconsistency of application standards, the heterogeneity between departments and systems, and the compatibility problems of bottom layer digital entertainment library caused by technology iteration, the phenomenon of digital support fault is formed to a certain extent. All these problems restrict the deep development and application of big data in university education management.

3 Countermeasures of University Education Management Under Big Data

3.1 Improve the Big Data Literacy of Teachers

University management mainly depends on university teachers. After the introduction of big data, we still need to rely on teachers to work. Therefore, after the introduction of big data into university management, it is necessary for the teachers in charge of management to improve their scientific literacy in order to keep up with the pace of university big data management. In order to quickly improve the quality of teachers, first of all, the university managers need to reform the university management system, which is of great significance for universities to introduce big data [6–8]. Under the background of big data, the management team of university teachers should develop with scientific and technical talents. In the process of the development of such teachers, university managers should do a good job of guidance, so that teachers can deeply understand the awareness of big data and constantly improve their scientific and professional quality. College education management involves many aspects, including curriculum education management, student quality management, teacher evaluation management, etc. after the introduction of big data, colleges and universities should integrate the above information, analyze and centralize the integrated information, and transform the collected information into operational teaching practice, so as to do a good job in data aided teaching. Colleges and universities should do a good job in the guidance of teachers, let teachers consciously use big data, realize the reform of teaching methods, and let teachers fully realize the importance of using big data in teaching management, so as to constantly improve their own teaching work. Colleges and universities cannot ignore the professional talents of big data research. They should strengthen the cultivation of such talents, focus on the cultivation of comprehensive talents beneficial to the overall development of colleges and universities, and adopt various ways such as international exchange and training to provide a better learning environment for big data talents and strengthen the cultivation of talents.

3.2 Upgrade the Data Platform of Traditional Education

University data platform is an important carrier for university to carry out big data management, which plays a vital role in big data management. However, due to the limitation of funds and talents, the management and construction of data platform are limited, which leads to the situation that university big data platform cannot keep up with the pace of university big data management [9–12]. However, as long as colleges and universities make clear the relationship between big data development and big data platform construction, and the problems existing in the construction of their own big data platform, then colleges and universities will actively reform the original big data platform according to their own development needs under big data, so as to quickly establish a new big data platform to adapt to the background of the big data era. To integrate the data resources of the original platform more comprehensively and comprehensively, colleges and universities should understand their own development characteristics, take the data platform construction as an opportunity, actively integrate the original information and data resources, so as to develop a more practical and convenient data operation platform, implant the original data in the updated data platform, and open the new data platform, Ensure that data resources can be updated regularly. After that, we should comprehensively strengthen cooperation with enterprises, so that colleges and universities can build larger big data R & D bases and data centers, and effectively carry out core technology, education policy, system management and other work.

4   WEB-based Higher Education Management System

For the current higher education information management, as well as for the information decision-making system construction, mainly in order to make full use of the computer network this advanced technical means, further to the present higher education management entire process, Realize the improvement of management efficiency. For example, in higher education examination, professional evaluation, quality courses and teaching reform of the numerous work, can play a certain management ability. So that colleges and universities in the future information construction, the formation of information, modernization, intelligent management work, greatly promote the management level of colleges and universities [13, 14]. In such a system, we can also set up a good higher education examination management, professional evaluation, quality courses, teaching results and many other fields of resources. In this way, we can provide more quality resources for students and teachers in daily education and management. At the same time, it is also an important way to improve the ability of higher education management, especially in the management process of some higher education work, which can provide comprehensive and reliable services and data information for important decisions.

Education management system should include the following aspects: curriculum management, student organization structure, database, cost management, as shown in Fig. 1.

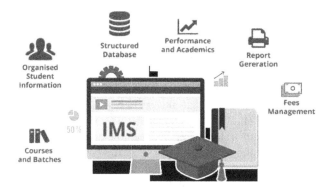

Fig. 1. Framework of education management system

4.1 Technical Standards, Architecture and Platforms

In the process of system development, it is necessary to design a system platform in accordance with the national standards based on the relevant regulations of the current state, the Ministry of Education and the information industry departments, and to optimize and adjust the process and index system at any time according to the needs of business process and education process.

Secondly, in the research of this paper, the research and development of system platform is mainly based on the architecture of J2EE multi-layer B/S/S, and the reusable technology of component level is used, which can effectively act on various types of mainstream operating systems [15–18]. And support many mainstream database systems.

4.2 System Functions

4.2.1 Online Examination Management

In this system platform, we can make full use of the Internet technology to realize the application, as shown in Table 1.registration, examination and printing of English proficiency examination, computer examination, advanced examination and so on. As shown in Fig. 2. And after the completion of the examination, you can query the test results on the system platform.

Table 1. System functions

Function	1	2	3	4	5
Name of name	Online examination management	Online evaluation system management	Higher education management	Decision Support System	Information exchange platform

4.2.2 Online Evaluation System Management

In the system function, can construct the specialty, the fine course construction, the teaching reform project very well, carries on the appraisal and the management work. In the actual operation, mainly in the online declaration, evaluation and administrative examination and approval of the operation.

5 System Architecture

In the current system architecture. It is mainly based on the current technology, products and related services that can be provided, as an important basic condition of the system architecture, so that the various construction objectives can be well integrated and utilized. Secondly, we should make full use of all kinds of advanced technology, mature products and various effective services to achieve the construction task.

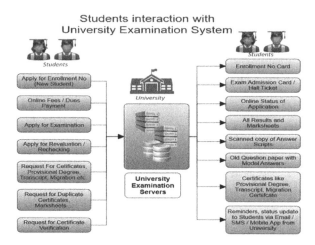

Fig. 2. Examination management

5.1 Construction of Information Integration Platform

As the core of the whole system, it has become an important design object for the construction of information integration platform. In different application systems, it is necessary to use different professional adapters to connect with the corresponding integration platform, and to realize the business interconnection between the systems by using the information mechanism.

In the current use of the integration platform, the application adapter is an important interface device with the application system. It can transfer the information between the systems in the daily use, and after the information transformation, form the execution action of the application system. The message queue is a kind of cache of new messages, which can store some messages processed by information workflow engine in the process of processing information [19, 20]. At the same time, the information policy library is built, which is the storage location of the formal description after the information flow. For message workflow engine, it mainly describes message forwarding between reference systems. This also assumes the system parameterized configuration storage function.

5.2 Application Integration Programme

In the actual interaction process, it is very easy to separate from the changing interface position, so that the data format change, interface mode and other content, are transferred to the independent middle layer, also come to the integration platform. For each external system integration platform, an adapter is needed to interact with other systems. The use of adapters in the system, mainly to achieve access protocols, data format conversion and other functions. In order to run the system, we can combine our own operation mode, make the corresponding request to the integration platform, and let the adapter be converted into the information form that the integration platform can accept.

5.3 System Reference Architecture

In the current system composition, from the point of view of application structure, it is a specific division based on business level, but also realizes the functional division. For different parts, there is often a clearer responsibility and independence. In different angles, we need to ensure the operation of the system, with independence, openness and security [21]. Therefore, the system can maintain a clear and smooth application structure type in the actual operation. In this paper, the object layer, support service layer, business logic layer and representation logic layer are designed.

In such an integrated platform, the interaction of its system will have high functionality. In the use of the design, it can help the relevant staff, realize the stable operation of the system, and realize the targeted management and operation according to the teaching contents of many aspects. In the current information construction, such a system can play a very important value, thus becoming an important part of the future information construction, the relevant staff should invest more energy, so as to realize the rational construction of the system. Improve the information management ability of higher education and expand the management category.

6 System Simulation

For the content described in the third part, we do a simulation through knowledge, experience and other content, and make a comparative experiment through five different dimensions. But through comparative experiments, we found that the neural network we used is more appropriate [22, 23]. A similar result can be seen in Fig. 3.

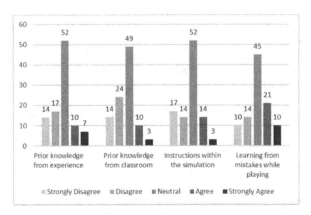

Fig. 3. The effect of simulation

7 Summary

To sum up, the information construction of education has become an important direction for the future development of education in China. Therefore, in the current information construction, we should design and optimize rationality based on the function and stability of the system, and provide more comprehensive and specific data information for the daily management of colleges and universities.

References

1. Luo, P.: A Study on the Development of Non-profit Private Colleges and Universities in China. Xiamen University (2018)
2. Yang, J.: [D]. of Information Management Platform for Self-taught Examination for Higher Education in Gansu Province Northwest. Normal University (2019)
3. Still Wins.: The Design and Implementation of Educational Administration System for Adult Higher Education Based on Web [D]. Univ. Electr. Sci. Technol. (2019)
4. Xia, G.: Research on General Item Bank Management System of Self Taught Examination and its Intelligent Test Paper Generation Strategy [D]. Tianjin Normal University (2008)
5. Fuyi, L.L.: Investigation and evaluation of computer "1 + X" teaching in Guiyang Medical College. J. Guiyang Med. Coll. (01), 88–89+91 (2008)
6. Linghui, T.: The development of higher education in Australia: a strategic perspective. Fudan Educ. Forum 01, 63–67 (2008)
7. Juan, C.: Optimizing the management system of adult higher education in China by using dynamic principle. Adult Educ. 01, 75–76 (2008)
8. Song, H., Li, X., Wang, C.: Thinking about teaching quality management system. J. Soc. Sci. Shanxi Univ. (12), 134–137 (2007)
9. In April 2007: The computer application test in the national self-study examination management system of higher education. Hebei Self-study Examination (11), 47-48 (2007)
10. Huang, R.L.: Research on educational administration system of Adult Higher Education. Continuing Educ. Res. (05), 94-96 (2007)
11. Hongliang, R., Bai, Y.: research on web based graduate management information system. Sci. Technol. Inf. (Acad. Res.) 27, 29–30 (2007)
12. Bingbing, B., Yan, Z.: Development and application of adult higher education information management system in Chongqing University. Higher Archit. Educ. 03, 160–162 (2007)
13. Zhang, Y.: Turn publishing industry into service industry – information construction exhibition of higher education press. Comput. Weekly 30, 22–23 (2007)
14. Zhang, Z.: Higher education society: from the free kingdom to the kingdom of necessity. Softw. World (13), 74–75 (2007)
15. Yiyun, X.: Research on teaching management system based on JSP. J. Guangxi Inst. Technol. S1, 31–33 (2007)
16. Zu, G.: Research on the implementation of credit system in adult higher education. Northeast Normal University (2007)
17. Hongwu, Z., ZeJian, L.: Construction of digital adult higher education management system. Agric. Netw. Inf. 05, 160–163 (2007)
18. Yang, D., Zhang, Y., Li, W., Ning, X., Wang, L., Jiang, H.: Development of graduate education information platform based on campus network. China Educ. Inf. (07), 38–40 (2007)
19. Zhenmei, T.: On teaching ability in the new era. Sci. Technol. Inf. 09, 99–100 (2007)
20. Luo, J.: Design and innovation of university quality management system. Chin. Market (z1), 130–131 (2007)
21. Xiaoyuan, Z.: MIS in postgraduate training management. J. Tianjin Manage. Coll. 01, 41–42 (2007)
22. Zhipeng, L.: Higher education press towards digitization. Chin. Editor 01, 7–9 (2007)
23. Xiaoyong, L., Yi, H.: Some thoughts and suggestions on building ERM in the construction of higher education information. China Educ. Inf. 01, 71–72 (2007)

Discussion on the Construction and Innovation of College Sports Training Platform Based on Computer Virtual Reality Technology

Jun Wu[✉]

Jiangxi Vocational Technical College of Industry and Trade, Nanchang 330038, China
qtmd1123@sina.com

Abstract. With the development of economy and the progress of science and technology, the leading role of virtual reality technology has been highly reflected. It has been widely promoted in the military and medical fields. It is a product of many related disciplines. It integrates many information technology branches, such as digital image processing, computer graphics, multimedia technology and sensor technology, and has great application prospects. In order to promote the level of efficient physical education to a new level and provide strong backup support for the development of sports in China, we should give full play to its technical advantages, combine it with college physical training, and establish a modern physical education service system.

Keywords: Virtual reality technology · Physical training

1 Introduction

With the rapid development of computer technology, the application of virtual technology is more and more widely. "Virtual reality" technology is based on a series of high-tech technologies, such as multi-functional sensing technology, three-dimensional computer graphics technology, interactive interface technology and high-definition display technology, etc., Including computer equipment, image acquisition equipment, position tracking, interaction and display equipment, mainly through the use of sensors to capture the real scene, and through the computer system simulation and reproduction, the characteristics of the technology include perception, imagination, interaction and immersion, using the computer environment to reproduce a lot of work, can also simulate the real world, Realize physical and functional environment and things.

Since the 21st century, computer technology has been developing rapidly, and it has gradually matured the technology of simulating the real scene, which has been applied in all walks of life. It can be predicted that it will be widely used in the field of college sports training. Participants use their ability of perceiving and recognizing external things to exchange relevant information in the computer virtual environment, It can greatly promote and inspire the thinking ability of the participants, which is conducive to the

M. A. Jan and F. Khan (Eds.): BigIoT-EDU 2021, LNICST 391, pp. 133–139, 2021.
https://doi.org/10.1007/978-3-030-87900-6_16

participants to obtain all-round information around things. Therefore, under such virtual conditions, the athletes can get good training and learning, which is not only conducive to the athletes' whole-heartedness, but also can maximize the function of the athletes' sensory system, Optimize the ideal training effect and learning effect of athletes [1].

2   Computer Virtual Reality Technology

2.1   The Concept of Virtual Reality

Virtual reality (VR) has become a new term of high-end technology of advanced human-computer interface in the computer industry. It is committed to the interactive, immersive and imaginative construction of the network. At present, it has achieved success, enabling users to have an amazing experience. It uses a variety of high-end technologies, such as artificial intelligence, computer network technology, computer graphics and multi-sensor technology. The application of computer virtual technology in physical education has been regarded as a revolutionary development of educational technology. It creates a "self-learning" environment, changes the traditional teaching and learning, promotes learning in new ways to learn knowledge and skills, and provides learners with the transformation of learning mode through the interaction of information environment. The use of computer virtual technology to create a virtual sports equipment, most of the scenes are virtual, can be at any time, according to the needs of new equipment to constantly update the training content, so that training to keep up with the development of technology. At the same time, the interaction of virtual reality is very strong, so that students can play a role in the virtual environment, and wholeheartedly into the human environment, which is very conducive to students' skill training. There is no danger in the virtual training system. Students can practice repeatedly until they learn [2].

2.2   Characteristics of Virtual Reality Technology

Virtual reality (VR), also known as psychic technology, is the use of three-dimensional graphics generation technology, multi-sensor interaction technology and high-resolution display technology to generate three-dimensional realistic virtual environment. Users can enter the virtual space by wearing special helmets, data gloves and other sensor devices, or by using keyboard, mouse and other input devices, and become a member of the virtual environment for real-time communication Interact with each other, perceive and operate all kinds of objects in the virtual world, so as to obtain immersive feelings and experience [3].

Virtual reality technology has the following five main characteristics.

(1)Immersion makes the virtual environment created by it make students feel "immersive", and make them believe that people really exist in the virtual environment, and it can play a role from beginning to end in the process of operation, just like the real objective world.

(2)Interactivity is that in the virtual environment, students interact with the tasks and things in the virtual environment just like in the real environment, in which students are the subject of interaction, virtual objects are the object of interaction, and the interaction between subjects and objects is all-round.

(3)Conceivability is a kind of virtual reality. It is a creative activity that can inspire people. It not only enables students immersed in this environment to obtain new instructions and improve their perceptual and rational knowledge, but also enables students to have new ideas.

(4)Action refers to that students can operate the virtual system with the actual actions of the objective world or in the way of human reality, so that students feel that they are facing a real environment.

2.3 Construction of Virtual Reality System

Virtual reality technology is a system composed of a series of hardware systems and software systems, as shown in Fig. 1.

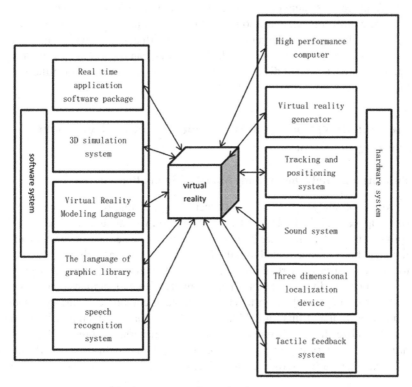

Fig. 1. Virtual reality technology system

The main components of the software system are: software package for building real-time 3D graphics application system; high fidelity 3D modeling and simulation system, which is a modeling software integrating 3D modeling, landscape and instrument graphics display; a language virtual reality modeling language (VRML) which can be used for online virtual world description; A language that can build a graphics library, and a speech recognition system supporting sound.

The hardware support needed for virtual reality mainly includes: high-performance computer, considering realistic generator, head, eye, hand, position tracking and positioning system, sound system, 3D space localization device, tactile and dynamic feedback device, etc. virtual reality generator is essentially a high-performance computer system which includes virtual world database to generate images. The database includes the description of the image of the object in virtual reality and the description of the object motion, behavior and collision. The sound system includes a sound synthesizer, a 3D voice localizer and a speech recognizer. The system can collect natural or platform sound signals, and use special processing technology to "stereoscopic" the sound signal in space; To combine other feelings, head, eyes, hands and body tracking positioning systems of the subject: in order to interact with virtual reality, we must perceive the human vision (i.e. tracking the position and direction of the head) and track and observe the position of each limb, so as to make people feel immersed. Tactile and dynamic system: virtual reality system must provide tactile stimulation of the object, such as the surface texture of the object, and also feel the movement resistance, but it is difficult to realize. Helmet display: provides a means to observe virtual reality, which must support two display sources and a set of optical devices, which can send images to the front of participants at predetermined distance, and enlarge the graphics to widen the viewing field [4].

3   The Role of Virtual Reality Technology in College Sports Training Platform

3.1   Building a Digital Human Body Model of Simulation Motion

In the process of studying virtual reality technology, virtual digital human plays an important supporting role. In the virtual reality system, virtual human model uses three kinds of node methods, which are human joints, gravity center and bone segment, The virtual human body is constructed into three structural layers, namely muscle, skin and skeleton. On this basis, the virtual digital human is studied and constructed. The human skeleton layer can be divided into three parts, namely joint part, human center of gravity and skeleton part. In general, the virtual human model is composed of surface model and skeleton model. In the virtual digital human model, no matter which part is around its joints, it can realize all kinds of movements according to certain degrees of freedom, By standardizing and determining the posture of the model, the fidelity and visualization of the model can be greatly improved, which is closer to the real human body.

3.2   Comparative Analysis of Virtual and Real Technical Movements

In the field of simulation, computer analysis and Simulation of human movement have always attracted much attention. In the process of analysis and research of sports technology, simulation technology plays a very important role. No matter what the project is, virtual simulation athletes can accurately imitate their standard movements, which is conducive to athletes' understanding of the details of ideal movements from different directions and angles, It is beneficial to improve the athletes' own skills, And the motion data is displayed in the form of three-dimensional human body animation, which is called "virtual" action. We record the video of athletes' real action as "real" action. 4. Through the special processing of virtual and real technology, we can maintain the consistency of viewing angle and viewpoint of simulation action and video motion display, and display them on the same screen at the same time, It can display the observation effect more accurately and intuitively.

3.3   Get 3D Information of Athletes

In the process of research and analysis of human 3D motion, the key and foundation is 3D information, including 3D coordinates and posture displayed by human body through bone joints from different angles in the whole process of human motion, as shown in Fig. 2, The human motion tracking method based on video is non-contact, which was first proposed by Wang Zhaoqi, a researcher of the National Academy of Sciences. Aiming at the disadvantages and technical problems of pasting special identification points, a better solution was put forward. This kind of motion tracking method is to arrange multiple sets of video capture equipment in the athletes' competition site or training place, The whole process of athletes' movement is captured from all directions and angles, and then all captured motion videos are processed by professional software, and all kinds of parameter data are provided to the follow-up three-dimensional human motion simulation research.

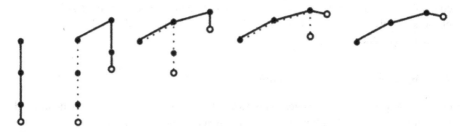

Fig. 2. Schematic diagram of angle and posture during human arm movement

4   Analysis of the Application of Virtual Reality Technology in the Field of Sports

The use of computer virtual technology in physical education will undoubtedly bring stormy changes to the classroom. It will make the physical education classroom from a single Professor into a comprehensive training of sports, and the physical education teaching work will also change from the oral transmission of training experience between teachers and students to high-tech training, so the monotonous trend of competitive sports will also change. Virtual reality technology in all walks of life have been varying degrees of development. The application in physical education training mainly includes the following aspects, as shown in Fig. 3:

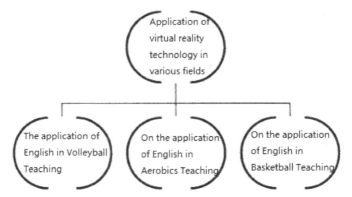

Fig. 3. Application of virtual reality technology in sports training

4.1 Application in Volleyball Training

The traditional volleyball teaching process is mainly through the teacher's explanation and demonstration, students' mastery of technology is affected by many factors. Teachers can observe students' mastery of technology by naked eyes, which greatly affects the teaching effect. The virtual reality technology can provide a new environment for the whole teaching process. For example, when explaining the front hand service technology, students can use the virtual reality technology to observe the virtual situation of the technical action, while communicating with the virtual human body body body language, feel the strength, order and range of the force of each part of the body, and produce movement synesthesia.

4.2 Application in Aerobics Teaching

Aerobics is a sport which combines gymnastics, dance and music to pursue the health and beauty of human body. It is highly artistic. In the teaching of aerobics, students not only get the training of coordination and flexibility, but also develop their thinking ability. In the traditional teaching, some contents are difficult for teachers to describe and students to understand and must master. The application of virtual reality multimedia technology can transform the basic actions into video information, with notes. According to the needs of teaching, the actions given can be played and explained repeatedly. With the correct demonstration of teachers, students will immediately form clear and complete technical actions in their brains. They can intuitively understand the essentials of actions and master actions faster, Practice will be more energetic and active. And can discover the mistake in time, discuss the cause of the wrong action, suit the medicine to the case, correct.

4.3 Application to Basketball Training

In basketball training, the traditional way of training is the coach to demonstrate and explain, but at present, virtual reality technology is gradually introduced in classroom training and courseware making. It can not only teach knowledge, but also teach skills and actions. First, the simulation library is constructed, and the virtual scene is displayed to the athletes through the instrument. The computer can monitor the whole training process, Therefore, players can adjust the training progress and difficulty according to the individual and human conditions. In basketball training, through the use of virtual computer technology, each action of players can be captured. According to the technical understanding of players, coaches can inform players of technical action errors by way of examples, At the same time, the virtual technology can also demonstrate the tactical cooperation. By showing the classic cooperation tactics, the outstanding technology in the cooperation action can be marked in the video, which is helpful for the athletes to observe the details of each movement. Teaching students in accordance with their aptitude can truly reflect the differentiated training and personalized training.

5 Conclusion

In the process of sports development, sports training is one of the important ways. From the perspective of athletes, it can effectively improve the technical movements and better grasp the technical and tactical cooperation. Through the application of virtual reality technology, the training platform can transform the action explanation into video information, and can also carry out playback and detail explanation, which can not only teach knowledge, but also teach action and skills at the same time. Therefore, the use of computer virtual reality technology can not only help athletes master the details of sports, but also effectively improve the efficiency of sports training.

References

1. Jianhui, W., Dengyue, L.: Discussion on using "virtual reality" technology to assist college physical education. Years (next ten days) **2**, 36–38 (2012)
2. Zhongxiao, W., Zhongxiang, W.: Research on the application of virtual reality technology in continuing education. Contin. Educ. Res. **11**, 69–70 (2010)
3. Tao, Z.: Discussion on the application of computer virtual technology in modern sports training. Electron. Test **11**, 264–265 (2013)
4. Wei, H.: Research on the application of virtual reality technology in difficult and beautiful skill event group. J. Jilin Inst. Phys. Educ. **3**, 95–97 (2010)

English Teaching Design in Language Learning from Pascal's Error Checking Function

Wei Li(✉)

Tianjin Light Industry Vocational Technical College, Tianjin 300350, China

Abstract. Because the computer has a strong logical judgment function, it is completely possible to use the computer to realize the selective self-test function. English self-test system is a kind of application software. Designing application software on computer is to write application program with computer language. There are many kinds of computer languages, such as basic FORTRAN, COBOL, C, P/1 and APLF. The computer languages configured on different machines are not the same. But most machines are equipped with basic, eortran and Pascal languages, among which Pascal is very suitable for writing application software.

Keywords: PASCAL · English · Classroom teaching · Teaching design

1 Introduction

At present, computers, especially microcomputers, have penetrated into all fields of human society. National defense, scientific research, culture and education, production, finance, health, management, transportation and even personal family life, such as financial management, stock market investment and Internet access, are inseparable from computer services. For non computer professional users, the current application platform such as Windows 98 and windows 2000 provides a very friendly interface [1]. The computer can provide the user with accurate information in the form of Chinese from the start to the operation. However, for students majoring in computer science and related majors, English is essential in the whole learning process, from DOS operation to reading of computer system configuration information, from learning algorithm language to reading application software tips and information, from reading prompt information in the process of hardware and software installation to visiting English websites, In particular, algorithm languages, such as basc, FORTRAN ALGOL, cobal, Pascal and C, are all native to English.

Take Pascal as an example, from programming to debugging menu operation, error message prompt reading to understanding of heip content, all are in English. Due to the characteristics of the computer itself, some of the information can't be translated into Chinese. At the same time, every command, every sentence and even every symbol of the computer need to occupy a certain space in the memory. Starting from the principle of saving, the computer usually uses the abbreviated form when storing and displaying the information. The statement is very simple and professional, Therefore, it is necessary

© ICST Institute for Computer Sciences, Social Informatics and Telecommunications Engineering 2021
Published by Springer Nature Switzerland AG 2021. All Rights Reserved
M. A. Jan and F. Khan (Eds.): BigIoT-EDU 2021, LNICST 391, pp. 140–148, 2021.
https://doi.org/10.1007/978-3-030-87900-6_17

and beneficial to learn English well while mastering professional knowledge, even in the process of learning professional knowledge. This paper will take pascai as an example to make a detailed discussion.

2   The Application and Understanding of English in Pascal

Pascal was proposed by N. Wirth of Switzerland, but it was written in English. Its most basic constituent units retain words, identifiers, standard functions and statements, all in English.

1. Reserved words

Pascal language has 35 reserved words. They are as accurate as possible, but they express their meanings in very concise or even abbreviated forms. The reserved words directly quoted from English original words are as follows:

If, in, Bel, nil, not, of, or, packed, procedure, program, ror, repeat, Se, Then, to, type, untl until When, with.

In these reserved words, except for wih sentence and procedure, the meanings of the rest are completely faithful to the original English.

The abbreviations of English words are used as reserved words:

Const (constant), div (divide, divide), MD (mu remainder, correction) and VaR (vanable variable).

2. Standard Identifier

Like reserved words, standard identifiers use English original words or abbreviations to express their meanings.

Such as flse (false), tre (true), integer (integer), real (real number), text (text), input (input), output (output), OD (odd), round (four in five), Mead (read), with (write) and so on:

For example, char (character character), aks (absolute value), EOF (end of file), eoln (end of line), RD (ER order), PRD (prdw leading), C (OD following), Sr (re Square), SGPT (square root square root), writeln (write line to write line skipping) are the abbreviations of English words to express the exact meaning.

It can be seen that reserved words and standard identifiers are basically based on the original English words, and these words are the primary common vocabulary of English. Therefore, if learners have a certain foundation of English, they can master these important elements in a short time, achieve twice the result with half the effort, and lay the foundation for learning complex procedures.

3. Statement

Pascal's program sentences express the idea of program design with very concise and accurate English syntax. The better the English grammar foundation of the learners is, the more accurate they can grasp the writing method of the program.

First of all, taking various loop statements as examples, let's look at three examples:

(1）for i:=s 1 to 10 do
Read from English, that is, "for the (for) loop variable I from 1 to 10 (1to10) do (do) loop". Simple and clear.
(2)while n< =100 do
When (will) n < = 100, do (d) loop
(3)repeat
......

until n > 100

Repeat the loop until (UIL) n > 100. Some beginners don't understand why the while statement makes a loop when the condition is true, while the CPE statement does a loop when the condition is false. This shows that they do not have a good command of the English original meaning of "when, especially uni". Untl means "always do it at the time point or condition point after unil" [2]. Therefore, when the condition after UMT is false, that is, when the condition is not met, the loop must continue. Only when the condition is true can the loop "stop here", that is, "end cycle".

The mathematical formulas used are as follows:

Mobius function μ:

$$\sum_{d\backslash n} \mu(d) = [n = 1] \tag{1}$$

Euler function ϕ:

$$\sum_{d\backslash n} \phi(d) = n \tag{2}$$

The relation between Mobius function and Euler function is as follows:

$$\sum_{d\backslash n} \mu(d)\frac{n}{d} = \phi(n) \tag{3}$$

The approximate number of functions is d:

$$d(ij) = \sum_{x\backslash i}\sum_{y\backslash j} \left[\gcd(x, y) = 1\right] \tag{4}$$

Using the properties of Euler function 1:

$$\gcd(i, j) = \sum_{d\backslash \gcd(i,j)} \phi(d) \tag{5}$$

However, this formula is rarely used. When gcd appears, it is usually enumerated directly, rather than converted into Euler function. 2:

$$\left[\gcd(i, j) = 1\right] = \sum_{d\backslash \gcd(i,j)} \mu(d) \tag{6}$$

3   The Special Importance of English in Computer Field

Through the above description of the functions of English in Pascal and other algorithmic languages, the importance of English in the whole computer field can be seen. A computer major student, in addition to the algorithm language, but also contact such as DOS operation, hardware and software installation and debugging, object-oriented programming language, network and some important application software such as AutoCAD, Photoshop and so on. In this process, the ratio of prompt information and sentence input in English is the same [3]. For example, the configuration information of the computer system is given in the form of a table in English culture.

If you don't understand English, you can't read or modify the configuration. For example, in AutoCAD, although there are Chinese culture drop-down menus, because there are hundreds of menu columns, it will be very cumbersome if the input of each command depends on the menu command, It is much more convenient to use the quick input method of English word abbreviation for common commands; in the process of in-depth mastering the function of application software and when encountering problems, it is necessary to read English prompts and consult help content, which requires students to have solid English skills. Without good English, it is unimaginable to master an application software and use it freely.

4   Simulation with Learning Methods of Computer English

1. For the commands and information composed of various abbreviations or original English words, we should not only memorize their Chinese meanings in the computer field, but also trace the source words and accurately grasp their original English meaning and derivative meanings in the professional field, so as to firmly grasp and grasp their usage [4]. When necessary, we should also use the method of root and affix to discuss. For example, a simple command like del in DOS comes from the English word delete, meaning "delete", so del means "delete". Deltree can be seen as delete the tree, that is, delete the tree (of course, not a tree, but a tree graph, branch graph) and delete, and more complex, such as the pred command in Pascal, comes from the English word "pre", meaning "before", With the root DCE, it means "guide, guide". Therefore, in Pascal, reduce is simply PRED, which means "leading". Therefore, in Pascal, it means "seeking the meaning of the previous variable of an ordered variable". However, there is no word "produce" in English dictionaries, which requires learners to infer based on their knowledge of English root affixes [5].
2. In the process of language learning, combined with its own grammar and morphology, analyze the meaning of sentences in programming language, and grasp its usage logically rather than memorize it [6].
3. Extensive reading of computer English textbooks, covering the professional vocabulary of various fields of computer, from the basis of computer software and hardware, to design methods, to operating systems, to computer applications, such as office automation, computer-aided design and manufacturing, multimedia, artificial intelligence, computer graphics, The network and other aspects of the article should read more, master professional vocabulary at the same time, but also familiar with the writing methods

and characteristics of professional English, such as in order to emphasize objectivity, strictness and conciseness, passive voice, analysis of sentences and a large number of abbreviations and so on.

The simulation of learning effect is shown in Fig. 1 and Fig. 2.

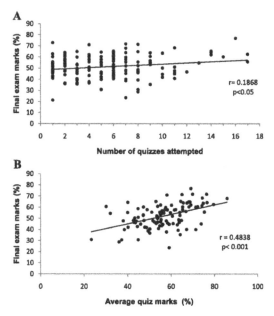

Fig. 1. Quiz simulation results

5 Quantitative Research on the Feasibility of Integrating Network Resources and Mobile Technology into Oral English Course

Integrating network resources and mobile technology, this paper discusses the experimental feasibility, demand feasibility, acceptance feasibility and technical feasibility of integrating it into oral English course [7]. The specific research methods are questionnaire method in descriptive research method and natural teaching experiment method in experimental research method: mainly discuss the feasibility of integrating the language learning function of network resources and mobile technology into oral English course, and for the interactive auxiliary effect of communication function of mobile technology on oral English course, predecessors have done a lot of research [8]. It has become a consensus that the communication function of mobile technology has a great auxiliary effect on the interactive teaching. The mobile technology discussed in this part focuses on the multi-modal information display function, multi-modal information editing function and interactive function of mobile technology in oral English teaching and learning [9].

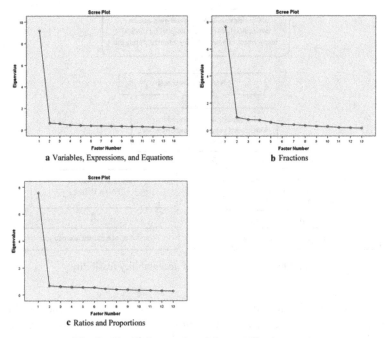

Fig. 2. Simulation results of factors affecting score

5.1 Quantitative Analysis of Acceptability Feasibility

Network resources and mobile technology assisted oral English course has its feasibility of acceptance. It is mainly reflected in the following aspects: first, the vast majority of contemporary college students affirm that the network resources or mobile technology can effectively assist oral English learning. Secondly, the course of spoken English assisted by network resources and mobile technology has a certain user base. Second, the network resources and mobile technology have been used to assist oral English learning, and the cognitive adaptability is high. Based on the above three points, the potential acceptance of fnmalls is already very high.

The feasibility of nma-usc is directly proportional to the acceptance of fnmalls, and nma-usc has its acceptance feasibility. The quantitative analysis of acceptability and feasibility is shown in Fig. 3.

5.2 Quantitative Analysis of Feasibility Based on Teaching Experiment Method

In order to avoid the influence of other factors in the pre-test, the students are not informed of the experimental situation in the classroom before the experiment, and in the early stage of the experiment in another parallel class that did not participate in the experiment to confirm whether similar experiments have been arranged in other courses. There are three research tools in this part of the feasibility study [10].

1) Objective oral test objective oral test is used to collect the learning effect after the end of oral English course, which is presented by the students'specific total score. There

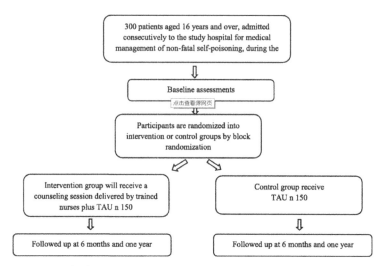

Fig. 3. Quantitative analysis of acceptability feasibility

are five questions in the oral test: the first is question and answer sentence reading, the second is declarative sentence reading, the third is long and difficult sentence reading, the fourth is situational question and answer, and the fifth is topic question and answer. In order to avoid the fuzziness of scoring, each scoring point adopts dichotomy.

2) According to Trifonov A and ronchetti, the time of single mobile learning should be controlled between 30 s and 10 min!. The previous NMA course content is aimed at the network resources, using mobile technology retrieval, after screening, 30 effective NMA course contents are obtained (the average duration of a single network resource is 58s, SD = 1.04).

3) The functions of cross tabulation, independent sample t-test and paired sample t-test of spss190 are used to analyze whether there are significant differences in the specific scores of the two groups.

6   Three Dimensional Framework of Oral English Course Design Assisted by Network Resources and Mobile Technology

6.1   Three Dimensional Framework of Oral English Curriculum Design

The three-dimensional framework of oral English curriculum design is based on the comprehensive summary of previous studies on oral English curriculum design from different perspectives [11].

It divides oral English curriculum design into "oral English curriculum principles, needs analysis, environment and teacher-student decision framework", "four elements circulation framework of oral English curriculum design" and "factors framework of oral English curriculum design", It also describes the relationship between the three categories and constructs the three-dimensional framework of oral English curriculum design.

These three categories have the characteristics of circulation, advance, decisive, integrity and dynamic. Circularity is reflected in the elements of oral English curriculum design, and the four elements are the dynamic process of circular design and continuous improvement; Decisiveness refers to the decisive role of the parallel framework in the whole process of the four elements of the round framework of oral English curriculum design elements; integrity and dynamism reflect that oral English curriculum design is a continuous cycle of development, revision, redevelopment and revision, in which all the contents of curriculum design are interrelated, Nonlinearity, mutual adjustment and adaptation are the norm [12].

6.2 A Cycle Framework of Elements in Oral English Curriculum Design

Oral English course objective design oral English. Curriculum goal design refers to the specific goals and intentions of oral English curriculum itself in the three aspects of "knowledge and skills", "process and method" and "emotional attitude and values", which is the most important criterion to guide the whole process of oral English curriculum design.

"Knowledge and skills" is not to be ignored in teaching, it is the premise for students to master the "process and method" of learning, but also the basis for students to form positive "emotions, attitudes and values". Method is ability, and method is a tool for people to benefit for life. Process is the media that produces value. Without process, there will be no development of cognition [13].

Without process, there will be no sublimation of emotion, attitude and values. "Emotional attitude and values" refers to the cultivation of students' correct learning attitude, high moral sentiment, positive attitude towards life and correct values based on the development of students [14, 15].

The goal design of oral English course should first clarify the general requirements of the country for oral English course, and the connection between oral English course and national English education, school English ability training objectives, so as to ensure that the oral English course design can reflect the general requirements of the country for English course teaching from the curriculum objectives, and combine the characteristics and advantages of the school with the training requirements [16].

7   Conclusion

Through the above examples, it is not difficult to find out the tasks that can be completed by using Pascal's powerful big data processing function combined with Pascal, especially in the later data processing of instructional design, Pascal plays a more important role, greatly saving production time and improving data quality, which is due to the importance of instructional design in language learning.

The research on College Oral English curriculum design assisted by network resources and mobile technology has important guiding significance for oral English and curriculum design, oral English ubiquitous learning in the information age, and has important enlightenment for oral English teaching design and other English subjects teaching.

In theory, the research on College Oral English curriculum design assisted by network resources and mobile technology expands the source of knowledge and technical conditions of oral English curriculum design from online video courses such as MOOCS and micro courses and computers to the practice of completely open massive network resources. It describes and designs the focus and curriculum tools of oral English curriculum design at present, It is of guiding significance to the teaching practice of contemporary oral English. At the same time, it uses quantitative and qualitative research methods to demonstrate the auxiliary feasibility of integrating network resources and mobile technology into oral English course, and explores the constituent elements and improvement path of fragmented mobile language learning ability, It can be used for reference to the specific design of each component of contemporary oral English course, the organization of oral English teachers' teaching methods, and the choice of oral English learning strategies of contemporary college students.

References

1. Ying, L.: The important role of English in algorithmic language learning and othersfrom Pascal. J. Jinzhu Univ. (Comprehensive Edition), (3), 83–84 + 64 (2000)
2. Yuliang, H.: The importance of instructional design in middle school English clasroom teaching. Henan Agric. (6), 34–35 (2017)
3. Rongding, G.: A method of designing a self-test system for English test questionswith Pascal language — analysis of the program of self-test for English test quetions implemented on an IMS microcomputer. Comput. Eng. Appl. (8), 32–37 (1990)
4. Weiguo, L., Xiaoyan, K., Hui, Y., Jian, T.: Teaching design of Ideological and political education of "fundamentals of computer programming" course. Ind. Inf. Educ. (11), 1–5 (2020)
5. Shuming, G.: Curriculum design and evaluation. Nanjing: Nanjing University Press, p. 9 (2015)
6. Guo, G.Y.: Analysis of multimedia and multimodal learning. Audio Vis. Foreign Lang. Teach. (2), 3–12 (2007)
7. Xiangyong, G.: The role orientation and function of teachers and students in the "double master" network teaching mode. Audio Vis. Educ. Res. (7), 447 + 54 (2002)
8. Xiaoqi, G.: Research on the application of mobile learning based on smart phone in English teaching. Shenyang Normal University (2014)
9. Kekang, H.: Looking at the new development of educational technology theory from blending learning (Part I). Audio Vis. Educ Res. (3), 1–6 (2004)
10. Kekang, H.: Looking at the new development of educational technology theory from blending learning (Part Two). Audio Vis. Educ. Res. (2002)
11. Kaibao, H., Lixin, X.: Research on the future development of college English teaching in China foreign language circles. (3), 12–19 + 36 (2014)
12. Huson.: Concise International Encyclopedia of Education: Curriculum, Beijing: Educational Science Press, p. 30 (1993)
13. Zhuanglin, H.: A review of foreign language teaching research. 1–30 (2009)
14. Dequn, H.: Research on web-based teaching evaluation. J. Dist. Educ. (4), 23–26 (2005)
15. Analysis on the application of Huang Yanyan's smart phone AP in english phonetics teaching in higher vocational colleges. J. Kunming Metall. Coll. 32(2), 26 (2016)
16. Yaoyi, J., Zhi, L.: Construction of mobile assisted language teaching mode in college English second classroom. China Forestry Educ. 33(3), 70–74 (2015)

English Translation Course Teaching Mode of SPOC Platform Under Artificial Intelligence System

YanYan Liu[✉]

Wuzhou University, Wuzhou 543002, Guangxi, China

Abstract. SPOC model is the model of online course opening in the post MOOC era, which has played a good role in promoting the teaching mode reform of Contemporary Colleges and universities. In this paper, through a detailed analysis of the current situation and problems of English translation course in Colleges and universities, and based on SPOC platform, a two-way research on the teaching mode of English translation course is carried out, so as to provide more effective teaching mode improvement strategies for contemporary students' English translation teaching. The study of English translation course based on SPOC mode can solve the problems and doubts encountered by contemporary students in English translation course, so as to lay a solid foundation for improving students' English level.

Keywords: SPOC platform · English translation · Course teaching · Mode exploration

1 Introduction

Through a comparative analysis of the current situation of College Students' English translation course learning, this paper fully discusses the improvement and research of English translation course teaching mode based on SPOC mode, and puts forward some specific curriculum reform suggestions and strategies, so as to better improve the contemporary students' English translation course learning problems. This paper makes a profound research and Analysis on the current situation of English translation teaching, and finds out the causes of the problem. Then, through the new teaching mode of SPOC, it successfully promotes the transformation of College English translation classroom, and provides some suggestions for the reform of English translation course teaching in Colleges and universities.

2 Brief Introduction of SPOC Mode

SPOC is the abbreviation of small private online course, which is translated into small-scale restricted online course, also called small-scale private open class, which is the

© ICST Institute for Computer Sciences, Social Informatics and Telecommunications Engineering 2021
Published by Springer Nature Switzerland AG 2021. All Rights Reserved
M. A. Jan and F. Khan (Eds.): BigIoT-EDU 2021, LNICST 391, pp. 149–157, 2021.
https://doi.org/10.1007/978-3-030-87900-6_18

product of the maturity of MOOC mode [1]. The model extends the advantages of small class teaching to the maximum by limiting the number of teaching and the threshold of access. The teacher can not only promote the interaction of the classroom to the greatest extent, but also stimulate the students' learning nature and instinct in time by making the course video through the content to be taught, and improve the teaching quality of the teachers while improving the learning efficiency of the students. Unlike MOOC, SPOC is a kind of auxiliary classroom learning, not an alternative classroom teaching. SPOC mode online communication learning has a significant teaching effect, not only can effectively promote students to deeply understand and interpret the curriculum, but also help students to analyze the text word by word, and through the teaching form of teacher self-made video to explain the knowledge to students. On the basis of retaining the advantages of traditional English translation classroom teaching, combining with the rich experience and excellent teaching ability of teachers, the essence and emphasis of the course content are shown to students by video. In this mode, students can relax and actively, better mobilize their learning enthusiasm and interest, and can get the answers from professional teachers whenever problems arise in the process of follow-up learning. At the same time, students can enjoy a continuous source of learning resources, which can be more quickly invested in English translation learning, and further promote the development of college teaching [2].

3   Current Situation of English Translation Teaching for Contemporary Students

3.1   Syllabus Out of Line with the Development of the Times

The common problem in many contemporary colleges and universities is that the students' overall English translation level is not improved qualitatively, the teaching process is delayed again and again, and the teaching results are also very low. In such a situation, it is inevitable that students' learning ability will be low, their enthusiasm for learning will decline, and their psychology of increasingly resisting English translation learning will appear. The primary reason for this problem is that teachers and students do not have a clear, standardized and professional syllabus, which will lead to the teachers' confusion in teaching. If the teachers are completely based on their own teaching experience, it will be possible to make the teaching direction deviate from the actual teaching goal and direction of English translation required by the country. Therefore, if we do not improve the English translation course in modern colleges and universities as soon as possible and set up a clear and clear syllabus, it will seriously hinder teachers to formulate the direction and content of teaching plans, and will indirectly affect the quality of students' learning.

3.2   The Modern Teaching Facilities are Backward

Due to the lack of adequate financial support and the situation of their own development is not optimistic, schools do not have sufficient economic strength to upgrade and improve the facilities needed for English translation classroom. In many colleges and universities, the situation of backward modern facilities is becoming more and more serious, which makes students unable to get the influence and drive of modern teaching technology, so they can only continue to suffer under the traditional English translation teaching mode until their learning enthusiasm and motivation are exhausted. In addition, due to the lack of professional English translation courses in many colleges and universities, the teaching of this course has not been given due attention, and teaching facilities are no exception. English translation learning itself is a process of cross-cultural and multi-cultural communication. Teaching methods and concepts must keep pace with the times and need a large number of multimedia network facilities. This problem should be paid attention to by the state and the government as soon as possible, and timely funding should be provided for the modern facilities of English translation in Colleges and universities, so as to enable the school to introduce a large number of modern teaching equipment, so as to improve students' English translation learning efficiency.

(x, y) represents the position of the center of the candidate frame relative to the lattice boundary; W and H are predicted relative to the whole picture; the confidence level of conf is shown in Eq. 1:

$$Conf(Object) = \Pr(Object) * IOU \tag{1}$$

In Formula 1, PR (object) indicates whether there is a target, if there is a target, the value is 1, otherwise it is 0; IOU is the intersection ratio of real value and actual value, which is calculated according to formula 2:

$$IOU = \frac{Area_{pred} \cap Area_{truth}}{Area_{pred} \cup Area_{truth}} \tag{2}$$

In order to ensure the accuracy of the model, it is particularly important to reduce the network volume and speed up the model [3]. In this paper, depth separable convolution is used to improve the convolution form and reduce the amount of computation in the convolution process. Depth separable convolution decomposes ordinary convolution into two parts: depth convolution and point by point convolution. Figure 1 is a comparison of the two forms.

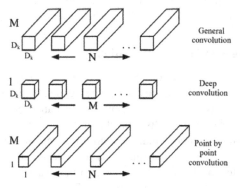

Fig. 1. Comparison of deep separable convolution and ordinary convolution

4 Specific Teaching Mode of SPOC + English Translation Course

4.1 Establishing Hardware Environment of English Translation Course

In the process of English translation teaching, we should make full use of digital multimedia teaching facilities, and the school should invest a certain amount of teaching funds to construct SPOC live teaching classroom [4]. By preparing sufficient SPOC classrooms for students, students can master their own time for autonomous learning, which not only cultivates students' ability to use time, but also provides students with an advanced atmosphere of modern multimedia learning, which makes students more interested in learning [5]. Only a good learning environment can promote the enthusiasm of students. In the modern multimedia classroom, students have been learning English translation knowledge in the traditional boring and boring education, which can arouse students' curiosity in the new mathematics field. In the process of SPOC + English translation teaching, students can choose the courses they want to learn and the teachers they like by themselves on the Internet, which can help the students to pay enough attention and enthusiasm in the early stage of learning, so as to make the follow-up learning more smoothly [6].

4.2 Training Teachers for Modern Teaching Skills

Since the application and operation of SPOC, a new teaching mode, has its own set of processes, so teachers need to learn and master it systematically [7]. We can invite the course lecturer to carry out corresponding experiential lectures, and let technical personnel of various departments explain and demonstrate the production process of SPOC, so that teachers can understand SPOC more clearly and use it skillfully. In the process of English translation teaching, SPOC belongs to an auxiliary teaching mode rather than a leading teaching mode. Therefore, teachers should reasonably plan the time arrangement for students, and when they feel that they are slightly tired in the process of daily classroom learning, they can let students choose their own time and way to learn the rest of the content on the Internet, This kind of education mode can make students better emancipate their body and mind, avoid fatigue learning, so as to reduce students' learning pressure and improve their autonomous learning ability more effectively. The simulation ranking of modern teaching skills is shown in Fig. 2.

4.3 Online Learning + Offline Consolidation

Online learning refers to the use of online course platform to build an online learning community for students. This community includes students, teachers and corresponding auxiliary teachers [8]. In this community, students can exchange their learning experience and experience to improve their English translation level. Offline consolidation refers to students' self-determination consolidation and improvement after learning relevant courses, and then through online test questions to understand their mastery of self-knowledge, and then feedback them to teachers, so that teachers can have a more in-depth understanding of students' learning situation, Therefore, it can provide guidance and suggestions for the direction and intensity of English translation in the follow-up study (Fig. 3).

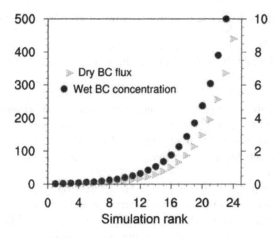

Fig. 2. Simulation rank for modern teaching skills

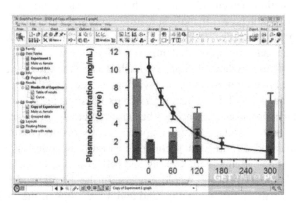

Fig. 3. Off-line education simulation

5   The Effect and Enlightenment of MOOC Translation Teaching Design Elements

The effect of MOOC translation teaching design needs to be investigated in the actual course [9]. Based on the results and discussion in Chapter 5, this chapter chooses the course of "English Chinese translation methods and techniques" on the platform of "MOOC of China University" as the research object, and takes the topic of "understanding and expressing word meaning" in this course as a case to analyze the teaching design elements, Considering the effect and deficiency of the specific design of MOOC translation teaching. On this basis, it puts forward eight suggestions to improve the teaching design of MOOC translation, which provides theoretical support for MOOC translation teaching design [10].

5.1   An Analysis of the Effect of Design Elements in MOOC Translation Teaching

Teachers are not only teaching designers, but also organizers of MOOC translation teaching. This section mainly analyzes the teaching style, external image, oral English and English teaching.

Lecturing style is a unique performance of teachers formed in the long-term teaching work. With the deepening of research, the unique role of lecture style in students' learning has also been paid attention to. The author believes that the teaching style of translation teachers in MOOC video can be mainly reflected in body language (including facial expression, head movement, arm movement, body posture), knowledge arrangement and explanation [11].

If the eye is the window of the soul, then the expression is the mirror of the soul. Psychological research shows that students' learning effect is related to learning mood, and one of the important factors affecting learning mood is teachers' facial expression. In the specific design of the topic "understanding and expression of word meaning", the main teacher's facial expression is not very rich, but it does not appear mechanical and rigid. In the introduction of each video into the theme, the teacher is smiling, full of spirit, and has a good eye, which is easy to make students expect and trust in the course learning. When explaining the examples, the teacher's expression will be a little more serious. This is because the main group of students facing the course is college students with mature cognition. These students do not pay much attention to the changes of teachers' facial expressions, but care more about the wisdom and connotation of teachers, while the lower grade students prefer teachers with rich expressions [12].

With the facial expression, the teacher's head movements, arm movements and body posture and other body language. Han Chunyan's survey results confirmed that teachers' body language had a significant priming effect on Academic Emotion, and had a significant impact on academic help seeking and self-evaluation results. In the course, the lecturer didn't show up in the whole process. In the 13 min video, it took about 3 min to show up, only in the beginning, end and a few clips in the middle [13]. The whole course of the teacher's standing posture is straight and straight, and there is no posture such as leaning forward and bowing back, which gives people a sense of full spirit. As far as the arm movement is concerned, it is relatively simple [14]. Put the arm on the waist in the whole process, and swing slightly with the lecture process. This kind of body language is in line with the teacher's temperament, natural and appropriate. In the head movement, the teacher will nod or shake his head with the emphasis on the knowledge points or considering the students' possible questions. The main teacher's body movements are in line with the teacher's personal temperament, conveying the unique elegance and wisdom of the linguistics teacher, and giving people a natural and sincere feeling [15].

5.2   The Design of Teaching Resources

Resources are the main learning objects of MOOC participants, which are convenient for students to obtain knowledge and information. The construction of teaching resources also provides conditions for MOOC translation learners' autonomous learning. In the questionnaire survey results, the average value of teaching resources is the highest, which also highlights the importance of this element. This section mainly analyzes the learning resources, translation strategies and subtitles in the teaching design of MOOC translation [16].

Generally speaking, the teaching materials of each unit basically include the carding of the knowledge points of this unit. Although it is a highly professional course, the language in the document is easy to understand and takes care of the understanding ability of students of different levels. In addition, the learning materials also include listening recordings and listening texts, and even upload the analysis materials of listening texts. It is worth noting that the original listening text and the analysis material are two documents, which are uploaded separately. In this way, for the learners who still have doubts through reading the original listening text, they can download the text analysis materials for secondary learning; for the learners who have a good foundation in listening and translation, they can choose whether to download or not according to their own time after listening practice, which fully takes into account the students' personalized learning needs. Moreover, teachers should organize the knowledge points timely according to the feedback questions of learners, which plays an important role in solving the common problems of students systematically [17].

6   Carry Out Multiple Interaction and Cooperation to Promote Real-time Interaction

The lack of effective interaction between teachers and students is considered to be one of the reasons for the low success rate of MOOC. In view of the problem that the discussion area is dominated by the interaction between teachers and students, and the interaction between students and students is not good, the author thinks that the teacher team should pay full attention to the learners' learning state, pay attention to the changes of learners' learning emotions in the discussion area, and pay attention to the students' learning experience. In order to achieve the above goals, we need to do a good job in teaching design: in addition to the knowledge, the discussion topics issued by teachers also need to consider the situation, and the discussion needs to be directional, so that the students participating in the discussion can have a clear discussion goal and stimulate the learners' expectation of learning. In addition, teachers can also set up learning groups to encourage students to carry out cooperative learning, and conduct in-depth discussions on the knowledge in videos, exercises, or translation learning questions, so as to form a "virtual learning community".

In view of the lack of real-time interaction, instructional designers can consider the following four points:

First, because the discussion and communication tool of MOOC is limited to the discussion area, and the energy of the lecturer is limited, it is unable to answer students' questions one by one in time. Therefore, the teaching team can arrange teaching assistants to assist in answering questions, so as to maintain learners' willingness to learn translation and realize the communication between teachers and students. In addition, we can also give a small number of learners certain rights, set up "student administrator", let students help manage the discussion area, which can also improve the enthusiasm of interactive communication.

In addition to effective communication, e-mail is also an effective way to communicate. The teaching team can not only complete the investigation of learners' situation through e-mail, but also comment on the translated works and comments of learners in e-mail, and encourage students to continue to communicate and maintain a good learning state. In this regard, Harvard University's "China" course regularly sends 2–3 e-mails to the learners every week. In addition to the course arrangement, the e-mail also affirms the learners' learning status and forum comments, so as to ensure the interaction with the learners.

Third, teachers can provide common social software as online collaborative learning and communication tools, such as QQ, wechat, microblog, etc. On these social software, learners can publish learning information, participate in discussion and interaction, exchange learning insights with other learners, and upload and share learning results. Compared with the discussion area, social software is more timely. Teachers and other learners can receive information reminders in time, so as to solve problems in time and improve the enthusiasm of learners. But on the other hand, it increases the pressure of teachers to manage students' speech, which requires the correct guidance and reasonable management of teachers, so as to avoid the interference of useless information released by students to other learners.

Fourth, with the rise of the current live platform, instructional designers may consider carrying out online live discussion to focus on solving learners' confusion. This kind of interactive mode has high real-time performance, can shorten the distance between teachers and students in online learning, and plays a very important role in eliminating learners' loneliness caused by online learning and solving learning confusion. In addition, the live video can also set up a bullet screen function, which is in line with the way of young people's communication and makes the interaction more interesting. It should be noted that due to the high development cost of MOOCS translation course, a certain fee can be charged for the live Q & a course, which is called the "business operation mode" of MOOCS. Relevant studies also show that the business mode can also improve the passing rate of MOOCS.

7   Improve Learning Support Services and Improve Learning Convenience

In video learning, the author found that "MOOC" can adjust the volume, full screen mode, pause and play, resolution, speech speed, subtitle selection and other functions, and is relatively complete in the construction of basic learning support services. On this basis, it is suggested to add the "cloud notes" function, so that students can open the cloud notes for recording at any time during the learning process, and realize the synchronous update of the terminal, so as to save the trouble of students carrying paper notebooks at any time, improve the convenience of learning, and encourage students to listen and watch at the same time, and form the habit of recording learning notes.

In teaching activities, MOOCS interactive platform is limited, only provides the discussion area interactive section, and according to the author's survey, the functional division of the three interactive sections is not obvious, students may have the confusion of not knowing which section to leave a message in. Here, the author suggests: first of all, teachers need to make students clear the functions of the three sections of the discussion area. At the same time, the MOOC platform can set up the related functions of topic paste classification in the discussion area, which can facilitate students to find related topics and avoid the trouble of Teachers to answer the same questions repeatedly. Secondly, more importantly, the MOOC platform needs to actively explore the function of real-time interaction, so that learners' questions can be solved in time and their learning willingness can be improved.

8 Conclusion

On the basis of studying the advantages and disadvantages of traditional resource database and combining with the characteristics of College Students' innovation and entrepreneurship projects, this paper designs and implements a personalized recommendation based College Students' innovation and entrepreneurship resource database system. In this system, the recommendation system successfully applied in e-commerce can improve the efficiency of resource dissemination to a certain extent. In the process of system implementation, theoretical knowledge should be applied to project practice.

References

1. Yan, Q., Hui, M., Jia, L.: Exploration and practice of college English flipped classroom under the background of SPOC. Heilongjiang Educ. (12), 9–12 (2017)
2. Wei, Z., Youlan. T.: Research on flipped classroom teaching based on SPOC translation course. Foreign Lang. Audio Vis. Teach. **39**(2), 27–32 (2017)
3. Li, H.: Research on the mixed flipped teaching mode based on SPOC. Comp. Study Cult. Innov. (28), 118–119 (2017)
4. Fengjia, G., Shusu, L., Xiaoqing, G.: Investigation and analysis of micro learning status. Open Educ. Res. **14**(3), 94–99 (2008)
5. Murray: A study of translation teaching in China, 1st edn. Shanghai Foreign Language Education Press, Shanghai, Dec 1999
6. Meifang, Z.: A study of translation textbooks in China (1949, 1998), 1st edn. Shanghai Foreign Language Education Press, Shanghai, July 2001
7. Miqing, L.: Translation teaching: practice and theory. China International Translation and Publishing Company, Beijing, Mar 2003
8. Guifen, F.: Correction of Punctuation and Collation. Zhongzhou Ancient Books Publishing House, Zheng Zhou (1998)
9. Zhengqing, F.: Cambridge Chinese Late Qing History 18001911, vol. II. China Social Sciences Press, Beijing (1985)
10. Zhen, S.J.: The Whole Process of Repairing and Preparing for the Affairs of Yi Was Xianfeng Dynasty. Zhonghua Book Company, Beijing (1979)
11. Tieya, W.: Collection of Chinese and Foreign Old Testament, vol. 1. Sanlian Bookstore, Beijing (1957)
12. Weixing, G.: A study on the history of English teaching in Beijing Tongwen library. Foreign Lang. Foreign Lang. Teach. (3), 59–69 (2004)
13. Ran, S., Hua, Z.: Translation teaching. Foreign Lang. World, 32–38 (1994)
14. Jinde, L.: On translation teaching. Foreign Lang. Stud. (1), 19–25 (1997)
15. Jun, L.: Translatology -- a special field of communication studies. Foreign Lang. (2), 178–189 (1997)
16. Miqing, L.: Contemporary Translation Theory. China Foreign Translation Press, Beijing (1999)
17. Funk: History of Foreign Language Education in China. Shanghai Foreign Language Education Press, Shanghai (1988)

Information Collection and Data Mining Technology of Open University Distance Education Website

Junrong Guo[✉]

Hebei Open University, Shijiazhuang 050051, China

Abstract. With the development of information technology, how to reasonably develop the information collection and data mining of distance education courses in Open University to make network courses play its great role and potential is a subject worthy of study. At the same time, it also provides more reference for the design of education website. It is of great significance to use data mining technology to process the data information and access information of distance education website.

Keywords: Open University · Distance education · Information collection · Data mining

1 Introduction

It is one of the important goals of popularizing basic education and constructing lifelong education and learning socialization after the rapid development of information technology and the arrival of information society to establish modern distance education website to transfer knowledge and information to learners and provide relevant services [1].

The so-called distance education is not just a new thing. Taylor, a western scholar, thinks that distance education has gone through five stages and points out the characteristics of its technological application: the first stage is the correspondence teaching mode, which is mainly based on printed teaching materials; the second stage is the multimedia mode, which uses printed materials, sound recording, video recording, computer and interactive video recording technology for learning; The third stage is the electronic remote mode, using audio conference, video conference, acoustic communication, radio/TV/radio and teleconference technology for learning; the fourth stage is a more flexible learning mode, using interactive multimedia, Internet based access to world wide web materials, computer transmission communication technology as the media of education. In the fifth stage, the key point is to establish an online automatic response system. At this time, distance educators focus on cost-effectiveness and teaching quality. In a word, distance education in the 21st century aims at the development of open, flexible and lifelong education [2, 3]. It is not only the continuous development of traditional

M. A. Jan and F. Khan (Eds.): BigIoT-EDU 2021, LNICST 391, pp. 158–167, 2021.
https://doi.org/10.1007/978-3-030-87900-6_19

education, but also a great change to traditional education. It breaks the limitations of traditional education and has incomparable advantages over traditional education, And take it as an important form to realize the popularization of higher education, continuing education and lifelong learning. The organizational form of Open University is shown in Fig. 1.

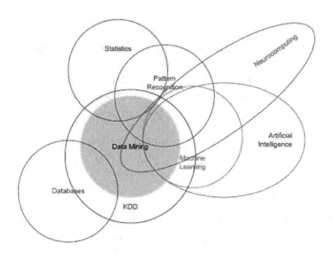

Fig. 1. The organizational form of Open University

2   Log Preprocessing and Algorithm Description of Distance Education Website

The information on distance education website is presented in the form of unstructured or semi-structured, and data mining needs structured data. The original log file is a simple flat text file, which contains some incomplete, redundant and wrong data. It needs to be processed, otherwise it will directly affect the effect of mining [4]. In addition, the implementation of mining algorithm also needs the support of standardized data sources, so the format of data storage collected in the first stage needs to be adjusted to suit the mining method. Therefore, the data preprocessing stage is the basis of the whole process of Web log mining and the premise of implementing effective mining algorithm, which plays a very important role in Web log mining. This chapter focuses on the preprocessing process and algorithm of distance education website log.

2.1   Definition and Properties of Association Rules

A typical example of association rule discovery is shopping basket analysis. This process finds the relationship between different products in the shopping basket and analyzes customers' buying habits. By understanding which products are frequently purchased by customers at the same time, the discovery of this association can help retailers make marketing strategies [5, 6]. This is the original form of association rule mining.

The support degree of implication x → y refers to the ratio of the number of records and the total number of records that simultaneously support item set X and Y in the database. It describes the probability that X and Y occur at the same time and indicates the importance of the rule. The support degree of association rule x → y is defined as:

$$Support(X \to Y) = \text{supp}(X \cup Y) = |T \in \text{Dand}(X \cup Y) \subseteq T|/|D| \qquad (1)$$

The confidence degree of implication formula x → y refers to the ratio of the number of records supporting both X and y to the number of records supporting X in the database. It can be understood as the probability of occurrence of y when x occurs. It indicates the correctness of the rule. The confidence degree of association rule x → y can be expressed by the following formula:

$$Confidence(X \to Y) = \text{supp}(X \cup Y)/\text{supp}(X) \qquad (2)$$

2.2 Introduction of Apriori algorithm

Apriori algorithm graph is a famous association rule mining algorithm, which uses the downward closure of frequent itemsets, that is, any subset of a frequent itemset must be a frequent itemset, and any superset of a non frequent itemset must be a non frequent itemset, so as to achieve the purpose of pruning frequent itemset candidates.

Apriori is a width first algorithm, which can find all frequent itemsets through multiple scans of database D. in each scan, only all itemsets with the same length (that is, the number of items in the itemset) are considered. In the first scan, Apriori algorithm calculates the support of all single items in D and generates all frequent item sets with length of In each subsequent scan, firstly, new candidate itemsets are generated based on all frequent itemsets generated from k-1 scans. Then, database d is scanned to calculate the support of these candidate itemsets, and the itemsets whose support is lower than the minimum support given by users are deleted. Finally, all frequent itemsets with length of K are generated [7]. Repeat the above process until no new frequent itemsets are found. So Apriori algorithm is mainly composed of two processes, that is, out connection and pruning.

2.3 Partition Technology

Partition technology only needs two database scans to mine frequent itemsets. Savasere and others designed an algorithm based on partition. This algorithm first logically divides the database into several disjoint blocks, considers one block each time, and generates all frequency sets for it. Then the frequency sets generated are combined to form all possible frequency sets. Finally, the support of these itemsets is calculated. The size of the blocks should be selected so that each block can be put into main memory, and each stage only needs to be scanned once. The correctness of the algorithm is guaranteed by every possible frequency set at least in a block [8]. The algorithm discussed above can be highly parallel, and each block can be assigned to a processor to generate frequency set. After each cycle of generating frequency set, processors communicate with each other to generate global candidate k-item set. Usually, the communication process here is the main bottleneck of algorithm execution time; on the other hand, the time for each independent processor to generate frequency set is also a bottleneck.

Confidence level:

$$C\% = Confidence(X \rightarrow Y) = \mathrm{supp}(X \cup Y)/\mathrm{supp}(X) * 100\% \tag{3}$$

The purpose of data mining is to find out the representative and credible rules. Support indicates the importance of the rule in all data, and credibility means the trustworthiness of the rule. If the degree of support is too low, the rule is not general, if the degree of confidence is too low, the rule's trustworthiness is poor.

3   Current Situation Analysis

3.1   Application Basis

This paper introduces the teaching reform of DACUM method based on CBE Mode to cultivate senior applied talents of geographic information data acquisition and processing specialty.

Higher engineering college is a part of higher education in China. It is the direction of higher education reform in China to cultivate cross century senior applied talents for the 21st century. In 1998, the Ministry of Education approved the first batch of experimental teaching reform of the specialty of geographic information data collection and processing. In order to meet the requirements of knowledge economy in the 21st century, we adopt the CBE (competency based education) ability target education mode to develop and practice the new education mode for the experimental specialty of geographic information data acquisition and processing [9–11]. Through the practice of teaching reform, this paper explores the mode and way of cultivating cross century high-tech post type talents, forms the school running characteristics of cultivating new technology post type talents in higher engineering colleges, and transports high-tech and high-quality applied talents for the construction of information superhighway and digital earth in China.

3.2   Development of Teaching Mode

In the practice of teaching reform, according to the geographical education theory put forward by experts outside school. According to the DACUM (developing a curriculum), this paper designs the teaching plan, arranges the teaching contents and methods, and establishes the ability based education mode for the specialty of geographic information data acquisition and processing in engineering colleges. The teaching reform of this major focuses on the basis of public courses, foreign language and computer teaching, with the knowledge and technology of Surveying and mapping, geography as the guide, and the cultivation of the three abilities of geographic data collection, data editing and geographic information management as the goal. The theory and practice of geographic information system run through the whole teaching process, Improve the structure of students' knowledge, ability and quality of professional system development and maintenance spatial analysis [12]. According to the responsibility/task table, the decomposition and comprehensive choice of the curriculum system of various disciplines is the starting point of building a new curriculum. Arming the new curriculum with new high-tech knowledge, retaining the essence of the original subject curriculum system, appropriately adding new content; developing new teaching plans, syllabus and compiling some new teaching materials; in theory, striving to build a new teaching system, update and enrich the teaching content, innovate teaching methods and teaching means, and compile suitable teaching materials.

3.3 Responsibility Requirements

According to the requirements of duties/tasks, the geographic information data acquisition is divided into four modules: ground spatial data acquisition, global positioning, map digitization, digital photogrammetry and remote sensing. Among them, the ground spatial data acquisition module is composed of three major technologies: topographic survey technology, geodesy foundation, and geodetic instrument operation. Various technologies are based on the framework of modern new technology system, boldly giving up a lot of old and unused knowledge and adopting a brand-new framework. The instruments required for ground spatial data acquisition are organized independently according to the type, function and precision series, Systematically and comprehensively teach the basic principles, functions, usage and operation skills of various instruments. It avoids the repeated, scattered and unsystematic teaching of geodetic instruments in the traditional course of topographic survey and control survey. Make the new curriculum module structure system more compact, systematic and perfect. In this course, the teaching of Surveying and mapping instruments is based on the mastery of conventional instruments, with electronic total station, electronic level and electronic handbook as the theme framework, to meet the needs of the development of new surveying and mapping technology.

4   Preliminary Evaluation of cbe-dacum Education Model

In 1999, the major of GIS data acquisition and processing first enrolled 36 students. After two years of teaching practice, from the students' learning and knowledge, the effect is satisfactory. It basically meets the requirements of the syllabus, and has obvious teaching effect compared with the similar courses of Surveying Engineering Grade 99.

4.1   The Study Time Is Greatly Shortened and the Effect Is Good

According to the teaching plan, "Xincai" 99 pilot class will concentrate the series of professional courses of ground spatial data acquisition in one academic year, and carry out relevant practical teaching at the same time. According to the plan, three courses of topographic survey technology, geodesy foundation and surveying instrument operation technology were set up in the second semester. Digital mapping technology was set up in the second semester. The above courses were set up in the teaching plan of surveying engineering class 99, which entered the school together with the "Xincai v 99" pilot class, respectively in the first, second, third, fourth and fifth semester [13–15]. The course names and main contents of the two majors are shown in the table below.

The time of learning and mastering the content of "Surveying and mapping discipline" is greatly shortened, and the learning is more concentrated. The curriculum structure system has been adjusted, especially emphasizing the current and practical technology, paying attention to the combination of knowledge system and technological process, and improving the teaching efficiency and effect through the renovation, reduction and reconstruction.

4.2 The Practice Links Have Been Greatly Increased, and the Operation Ability Has Been Enhanced

In the teaching plan of Xincai 991, the practice link is increased, and the total number of practice weeks is 43 weeks (99 classes of Surveying Engineering), accounting for 39.2% of the total number of teaching weeks. The classroom teaching follows the practice teaching closely. For example, in combination with the practical courses, the experiment was taught independently, and five experimental weeks were set up for centralized training. According to the skill test, most of the students have a good command of it, which basically meets the requirements of the experimental syllabus. Taking the computer grade examination results as an example, 75% of the 99 classes of "Xincai" have passed the second and third level examinations for non computer majors, and the passing rate exceeds the average passing rate of undergraduate education in Jiangsu Province. In the map digitization and GPS survey professional skill appraisal organized by the professional skill appraisal department of the Ministry of labor and social security of the people's Republic of China, 45 people in 99 classes of Xincai obtained the intermediate skill appraisal certificate issued by the Ministry of labor and social security of the people's Republic of China with a high passing rate of 98% [16]. It can be seen from the analysis table 6 of the weekly examination results of professional measuring instrument operation experiment that the rate of reaching the standard at one time is more than 70% by adopting the same skill test standard of measuring engineering specialty, and all of them can meet the requirements of measuring engineering specialty through three skill tests.

5 Application of Information Collection Technology in Distance Education Website

With the accumulation of time, the webh log file in the web server will be larger and larger, which contains more and more customer information. The web log records the information of users visiting the site, including the number of users, the URL of the requested file, the protocol version number, the number of bytes transferred, the URL of the reference page, etc. Combined with the user database, the effective collection and analysis of Web log files can not only effectively evaluate the performance of the website, but also provide decision support for educational website service positioning and improving user relationship.

5.1 Application of Information Collection Technology in Distance Education Website

The application of information collection technology in distance education website mainly includes the following aspects:

(1) Through the data collection of the user's past visit history, we can know the user's frequent visit path, obtain the needs of the visitors, more fully understand the needs of the users, classify the users, and provide targeted services, which is conducive to improving the user's satisfaction and recognition, and truly realize the design of personalized website for users with the user's needs as the guide.

(2) Analyze the potential needs of users and optimize the service mode of distance education website. According to the historical data of users, we can not only predict the demand trend, but also evaluate the change of demand trend, which is helpful to improve the utilization rate of distance education website.

(3) Optimize the web site, improve the organizational structure of the web space. Website designers can no longer completely rely on the qualitative guidance of experts to design the website, but modify and design the structure and appearance of the website according to the information of visitors, find out how to optimize the organizational structure of a website, and determine which pages to pre transmit to the user, so as to improve the efficiency of the website [17].

A visual data acquisition and analysis system based on web is designed. According to the previous discussion, we use the object-oriented design method to design a visual acquisition and analysis experimental system for text content. The system can flexibly process all kinds of information, such as filtering useless information according to the needs of users, or cataloging, sorting and saving the collected information according to the needs.

5.2 Simulation Analysis

In this section, we first give the basic structure of data mining, as shown in Fig. 2, and then use this basic structure to do simulation. In this basic structure, we can see that a basic data structure contains two parts: database and mining. So next, we will simulate these data, as shown in Fig. 3. The simulation data can be obtained from Sect. 2.

6   Main Application Effects

6.1 Most of the Requirements Are Solved

Cbe-dacum teaching development mode can effectively solve the problem that higher engineering education does not meet the needs of employers for high-tech post talents under the socialist market economy environment. Through the market-oriented reform and exploration of the professional teaching and training program, the most important thing is to shift the focus of the training objectives to how to adapt to the employing units and help students to obtain employment [18–20]. The primary key of cbe-dacum mode reform is how to solve the demand of talent market and the problems of students.The interface between employment intention and school education plan.

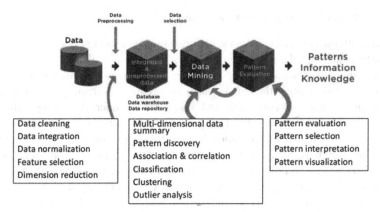

Fig. 2. Structure of data mining

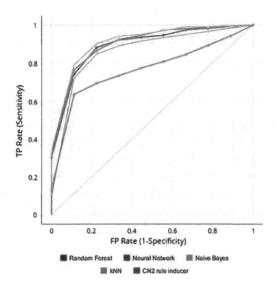

Fig. 3. The simulation with data mining

6.2 Skill Development

CBE → DACUM teaching mode has a set of standardized and standardized ability training methods, which is helpful to the cultivation of students' skills. Through the combination of production and learning, the skills training will be socialized, so that the students' skills will eventually get the identification of the application position and the market certification. It shortens the distance between employers and schools, enhances the transparency of teaching, and is conducive to the two-way choice between employers and students.

6.3 Domestic and International Integration

Combined with the national conditions and learning from foreign cbe-dacum teaching mode, the teaching goal of foreign cbe-dacum teaching mode is relatively single, which is due to the developed education and less job types. In China, geographic information data acquisition and processing is the foundation of Surveying and mapping, computer, geography, management and environment, and a platform for interdisciplinary infiltration. Students should adapt to more jobs. Therefore, we have formulated 20 responsibilities and 203 tasks, which are much broader than the training objectives of foreign majors [20–23]. Cbe-dacum mode has no clear provisions on theory teaching, and it is essential to ensure sufficient theoretical basis. How to deal with the relationship among the theoretical basis, professional knowledge and practical skills in the teaching plan according to the national conditions is a problem that needs to be deeply discussed and solved. It is also a common situation in China that the combination of industry and education is hot. How to make the industry hot, we must explore a new way according to the characteristics of China's socialist market economy.

Specialty construction is a huge system engineering, which needs to constantly update the concept and make unremitting efforts to achieve the expected goal.

7 Conclusion

Through the mining of distance education website, we can extract the useful knowledge we need from a large number of log information. Through the analysis of the total user access behavior, frequency, content and so on, we can get the general knowledge about the group user access behavior and way, provide personalized services for users, improve the service efficiency of the system, improve the website design structure, determine the user needs of the distance education website, and effectively evaluate the website, Through the understanding and analysis of these user characteristics can help to carry out personalized education service activities.

References

1. Deng, P., Xiaoshe, D., Maishun, Y.: Mining frequent access patterns from web data. J. Xi'an Jiaotong Univ. **36n0.6**, 631–644 (2002)
2. Shi Jianchen, W., Lina, W.L., Yiling, Y.: Research on mining user browsing patterns from web logs. J. Xi'an Jiaotong Univ. **35**(6), p621-624 (2001)
3. Baoshu, C., Qimin, J.: Data preprocessing in web data mining. Comput. Eng. **28**(7), 14–19 (2002)
4. Guixia, J.: Research on association rules and application in data mining, Master's Thesis. Lanzhou University of Technology, Lanzhou, Two Thousand and Six Point Four (2012)
5. Dynasty, S., Xiuying, S.: Asp.net. Comput. Knowl. Technol. **14**, 325–326 + 344 (2011)
6. Party Construction Online (within the province). Jianghuai **16**(1), 36–37 (2011)
7. Xiaohong, Y., Fangyu, L.: Research on digital resources integration of modern distance education for rural party members and cadres. China Dist. Educ. **21**(1), 88–91 (2011)
8. Qijie, G.: The enlightenment of Japanese and Korean models on online Chinese distance teaching. Capital Foreign Lang. Forum **5**, 658–665 (2001)
9. Songhe, Y.: Research on the content framework of modern distance education network course construction. J. Guangdong Radio Telev. Univ. **19**(6), 13–18 (2010)

10. Special training for application administrators of "Qilu pioneer" distance education website in Dongping County. Guide Getting Rich Sci. Technol. (34), 10 (2010)
11. Jie, C.: Comparison of modern distance education websites. Lib. Sci. Res. 4(22), 46–48 + 80 (2010)
12. Modern educational technology. 20(10), 153–158 (2010)
13. Aiyun, J., Baofeng, Z., Pingzhu, W., Jingchao, Z.: Design and implementation of computer aided design distance education website. China Sci. Technol. Inf. 32(19), 232–233 (2010)
14. Yajun, L.: Analysis on the current situation of network question answering system. J. Xichang Univ. (Natural Science Edition) 24(3), 68–70 (2010)
15. Minggang, Y.: Analysis and countermeasures of campus culture construction in modern distance education pilot colleges — taking the website construction of four pilot colleges in Shanghai as an example. China Dist. Educ. 8(9), 53–57 (2010)
16. The characteristics of teaching Chinese as a foreign language in Gansu Province. 3, 26–35 (2010)
17. Hong, S.: Research on the current situation and strategies of online education resources construction in primary and secondary schools. Lib. Work Res. 21(7), 107–109 (2010)
18. Juncai, G.: Solutions for browsing distance education resources in LAN. China Educ. Technol. Equip. 22(20), 41–42 (2010)
19. Guoqing, L.: Analysis of the characteristics of American primary and secondary education websites and its enlightenment to China. Audio Vis. Educ. Prim. Sec. Schools 15(z2), 43–45 (2010)
20. Hafezi, S., Mehri, S.N., Mahmoodi, H.: Developing and validation a usability evaluation tools for distance education websites: Persian version. Turk. Online J. Dist, Educ. 11(3), 22–29 (2010)
21. Moore, M., Dongjie, X.: New power of network: teaching method and organization. Open Educ. Res. 16(3), 100–109 (2010)
22. Yan'er, T.: An analysis of the development of Chinese international education based on 3G. Res. Mod. Dist. Educ. (3), 26–31 (2010)
23. Lanlan, J.: Research on new type of farmers' Entrepreneurship Education Based on Network. Zhejiang Normal University (2010)

Research on System Platform Design of Applied Statistics Teaching in Colleges and Universities

Chengping Liu(✉)

Zhaotong University, Zhaotong 657000, Yunnan Province, China

Abstract. The characteristics of Applied Statistics in Colleges and universities determine that practical teaching is an important part of applied statistics teaching system. Starting from the training objectives of statistics major, this paper analyzes the construction ideas of practical teaching system of applied statistics major, puts forward the practical teaching system of statistics major, which is composed of four subsystems and practical teaching platform, and puts forward the implementation scheme of the system.

Keywords: Applied · Statistics · Practical teaching system

1 Introduction

With the popularization and development of information technology and statistical application, statistics, as a method and technology of data processing and analysis, has become a necessary knowledge for everyone in modern society. However, the education of statistics major in Colleges and universities is always faced with three challenges: first, the continuous innovation and development of statistical methods in the application lead to the change of statistical content system; second, the continuous innovation and development of statistical methods lead to the change of statistical content system; Secondly, the development of information technology has led to the continuous innovation of statistical software tools; thirdly, the change of educational philosophy centering on students' development and social needs [1]. These challenges require the development of statistics in Colleges and universities, In particular, the application-oriented statistics teaching should change the educational concept, absorb new methods through case teaching, use new tools, and face the application and practice. The construction, innovation and implementation of the practical teaching system of statistics specialty are the key to the teaching reform of application-oriented Statistics Specialty in Colleges and universities.

2 The Orientation of the Training Goal of Applied Talents of Planning and Learning

The major of applied statistics is to meet the actual needs of China's socialist economic construction, have good mathematical and economic literacy, master the basic theories

M. A. Jan and F. Khan (Eds.): BigIoT-EDU 2021, LNICST 391, pp. 168–174, 2021.
https://doi.org/10.1007/978-3-030-87900-6_20

and methods of statistics, skillfully use computers for data processing and analysis, and be able to engage in statistical investigation, information management, quantitative analysis and other work in enterprises, institutions and economic management departments, Or statistical talents engaged in teaching and research in the scientific research department of the University.

2.1   Have Solid Statistical Theory and Knowledge Level

Have the ability of applying statistical thinking to analyze things and solve problems. In the process of constructing students' theoretical knowledge system, we should pay attention to the cultivation of practical application ability of knowledge. However, in the process of practical teaching, it is often found that teachers pay more attention to the introduction of formula derivation methods, but ignore the application of practice, resulting in students blindly master some basic formulas, but do not know how to solve practical problems.

2.2   Have a Certain Level of Macroeconomic Theory and Knowledge

It can analyze and understand the internal logical relationship between data at a higher and more macro level, deeply excavate the meaning behind data, and comprehensively improve the ability of analyzing and solving problems. Many students of statistics major, including some teachers, only emphasize the study of statistical knowledge, lack the guidance of economic theory, and the conclusions drawn from statistical methods to analyze economic problems are not convincing.

2.3   Proficient in Operating a Variety of Commonly Used Statistical Analysis Software

It can skillfully apply modern information technology to the practice of statistical work, making the complicated statistical calculation and analysis process simple, efficient and fast. Because many colleges and universities have not established a perfect practice teaching system and lack of practice teaching platform, practice teaching and theoretical teaching can not be well connected, which makes the effect of practice teaching difficult to play.

3   Thoughts on the Construction of Practical Teaching System of Applied Statistics Major

The construction of the practical teaching system of statistics major should meet the needs of social development, with the purpose of cultivating high-level applied statistical talents with strong statistical theoretical knowledge and practical innovation ability, highlighting the characteristics of practical teaching of statistics major [2]. The practice teaching system of statistics specialty is different from curriculum experiment and extracurricular practice. It is a multi-level, hierarchical and progressive practice system, as shown in Fig. 1.

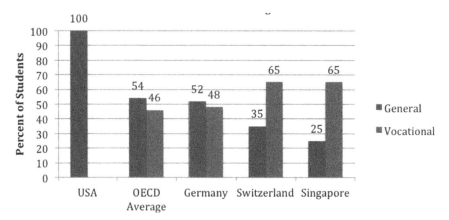

Fig. 1. Practice teaching system of statistics major

3.1 Statistics Practice Teaching System Is Divided into Three Dimensions, Progressive Layer by Layer

Many colleges and universities regard practical teaching as experimental teaching, and only set up simple experiments in some statistical courses, which does not reflect the characteristics of practical teaching of statistics. In the process of constructing the practical teaching system of statistics, we should first emphasize the practical teaching of professional courses, and then promote the training of professional skills and the second classroom learning, so that students can master the application of statistical theory in an all-round way.

3.2 Diversification of Practical Teaching Forms

In the process of designing the practice teaching system of statistics major, we mainly adopt the way of combining the on campus experiment with the off campus practice. The professional course of statistics is mainly to teach the whole working process of statistics, from the design of the scheme to the collection, collation, display, analysis and interpretation of data [3]. The combination of on campus experiment and off campus practice can not only cultivate students' ability to comprehensively use statistical methods and statistical analysis tools, but also cultivate and train students' ability to observe and understand society, improve students' ability to analyze, solve and adapt to society, and better combine theoretical knowledge with practical application.

4   Design of Practical Teaching System for Applied Statistics Major

According to the training objectives and specifications of statistics professionals, combined with the construction idea of practical teaching system, this paper thinks that the practical teaching system of statistics major should be composed of two main lines, four subsystems and practical teaching platform. The two main lines are: the practical teaching system running through the professional theory courses and the practical teaching system running through the four academic years to guide and cultivate students' innovative ability and practical ability. The four subsystems are preparation practice teaching subsystem, curriculum practice teaching subsystem, practice teaching subsystem and innovative practice teaching subsystem. The details are shown in Fig. 2.

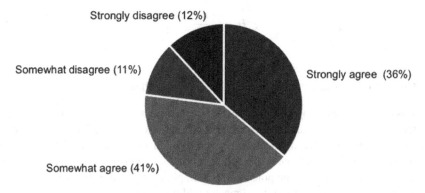

Fig. 2. Practice teaching system of statistics major

4.1 Preparation Practice Teaching Subsystem

Generally, the basic theory courses of statistics major mainly include two parts: public courses and subject basic courses. The setting of public courses is considered from the perspective of the basic moral quality and political quality of a college student. The subject basic courses are mainly set from the perspective of professional learning, so as to lay a good foundation for the future study of professional courses. The practice teaching subsystem of this link is mainly manifested in the cultivation of political quality and basic knowledge system, which lays the foundation for the study of basic knowledge.

4.2 Course Practice Teaching Subsystem

The main purpose of the system design is to enable students to use these methods for practical operation on the basis of mastering the theoretical knowledge of professional courses. For example, using SPSS to establish and manage data files, descriptive statistical analysis, parametric test, ANOVA, nonparametric test, correlation analysis and regression analysis, cluster analysis, discriminant analysis, factor analysis; using Eviews and SAS software to establish random time series model; using Excel, Eviews and SPSS software to make economic forecast and decision.

4.3 Comprehensive Practice Teaching Subsystem

In order to cultivate high-level application-oriented statistical talents, in addition to the introduction of professional basic theory, we should also set up some comprehensive simulation training, so that students' professional skills can be effectively refined. Through comprehensive simulation, comprehensive design, comprehensive analysis and other links, students can participate in the process of statistical work, understand the nature, characteristics and requirements of statistical work, truly understand the connotation of accounting major, and improve their comprehensive ability to deal with and analyze statistical problems.

$$H = \frac{n}{\sum \frac{1}{x}} \tag{1}$$

4.4   Construction and Practice of Practice Teaching Platform

The construction of teaching platform can ensure the effective development of the practical teaching system of statistics major, and can monitor and feedback in real time to realize the two-way communication between students and teachers. Many materials, including case sets, exercise sets, practice manuals and practice reports, can be transferred and filed through the practice teaching platform to improve work efficiency. The purpose of learning is not only to master and use theoretical knowledge, but also to innovate. The practice teaching subsystem can improve the innovation ability and comprehensive analysis ability of statistics students through extracurricular research, undertaking projects, entrepreneurship planning system development and other ways, and can effectively use the knowledge to solve practical problems in a complex and changeable environment.

$$M_e = L + \frac{\sum f}{f_m} - s_{m-1} * d \tag{2}$$

$$AD = \frac{\sum |x - \bar{x}| * f}{\sum f} \tag{3}$$

5   Implementation Path of Practical Teaching System of Applied Statistics Major

The practical teaching system of statistics is a complex system composed of many aspects and elements, which must be carefully designed and organized to achieve the goal of optimization. The specific implementation path is as follows. Professional practice leading group should be set up to be responsible for the planning, organization, coordination, monitoring and evaluation of professional practice teaching, and actively give play to the enthusiasm and creativity of professional teachers and experimenters. The implementation of any practical teaching scheme must be specifically organized and implemented by professional teachers and experimenters. Therefore, it is necessary to fully mobilize professional teachers and experimenters to study practical teaching problems, develop and design practical teaching projects, and improve the enthusiasm and creativity of practical teaching effect. To formulate the implementation plan of practical teaching in statistics major, we should formulate not only the overall implementation plan, but also various special implementation plans, And strive to be systematic, scientific and operable. 4. Compile books related to experiments, organize professional teachers and experimenters to write and design experiment instructions, teaching cases, teaching projects, simulation training topics, exercise sets, topic design sets, practical teaching CA courses and multimedia courseware, and strengthen the basic construction of professional practical teaching [4]. Establish and perfect the practical teaching management system, such as practice syllabus, practice code, practice record, practice appraisal form, practice performance evaluation method, extracurricular scientific research reward method, student research group and community management method, laboratory management system, in class experiment report system and so on. Strengthen the system construction of professional practice teaching.

6 Case Teaching Thought

6.1 Main Ideas

The case teaching mode originated in 1920 and was advocated by Harvard Business School. It is on the basis of students' mastering the basic knowledge, according to the teaching purpose and teaching content requirements, through negotiation and careful design of typical cases, to bring students into specific practical problems for exploration and research. Case teaching advocates a multi-directional and divergent way of thinking, cultivates students' creativity and imagination, focuses on practice and case explanation and analysis, and enlightens students' positive thinking. 2) actively participate in and guide students to solve practical problems with what they have learned. Designing classic and practical teaching cases has become a key issue in teaching.

6.2 Case Design Factors

To design a good case, we need to consider the following factors: professional relevance, moderate difficulty, collaborative learning, before and after contact and other factors. The first factor considered in the selection of visual basic (hereinafter referred to as VB) cases is professional relevance. The teaching object of VB programming course is non computer major students. Students do not have systematic training in programming, so computer programming is undoubtedly a very difficult thing. In addition, in the current teaching materials, the relevant examples are basically universal, lack of professional pertinence, resulting in students' interest and initiative in program design is not strong, and the effect of classroom teaching is not ideal. In order to ease students' fear of programming, arouse students' interest in programming with VB, better master programming skills, and enhance classroom teaching effect, I consider that students of different majors have different concerns. From the professional perspective of teaching objects, I introduce professional related cases for teaching, so that students can learn programming at the same time, Be able to solve professional problems.

7 Concluding Remarks

The cultivation of manufacturing engineering undergraduate talents is the human support and intellectual guarantee for the implementation of "made in China 2025" manufacturing power strategy under the new normal of China's aerospace development. The reform of training program is the key for Aeronautics and Astronautics colleges to actively adapt to the leap forward development of Aeronautics and Astronautics and promote the construction of a strong manufacturing country. Through the above-mentioned reform, we can build a modern and demanding talent training curriculum system; keep pace with the times, deepen the reform of curriculum teaching content; enrich teaching means, creatively use a variety of new generation information technology to organize students' learning activities; and finally achieve the purpose of improving the training program of aircraft manufacturing engineering.

References

1. Mingfeng, H.: Some thoughts on the practical teaching system of statistics major. Gen. Educ. **11**, 32–33 (2005)
2. Yangan, Y.: Statistical research on statistics discipline construction, personnel training and teaching reform. **2**, 10–14 (2005)
3. Min, F.: Construction and implementation of open experimental teaching system of statistics. Stat. Educ. **1**, 24–25 (2008)
4. Jian, H.: Exploration and practice of the "tetrad" practice teaching system for statistics major, research and exploration of u laboratory. **2**, 121–123 (2011)

Research on the Application of Clustering Analysis Algorithm in the Construction of Film and Television

Jie Hang[✉]

Xi'an FanYi University, Xi'an 710061, Shaanxi Province, China

Abstract. With the rapid development of Internet and the popularization of personal computer, distance network teaching as a new and advanced teaching mode is becoming increasingly popular, and has become a focus in the field of education in recent years, so the research and development of online teaching platform has become a hot topic. However, there are many problems in the existing online teaching platform: the website structure is complex, the level is not clear, the goal is not strong; the teaching form is simple and boring, which can not mobilize the students' interest in learning; the teaching pertinence is poor, and different students adopt the same teaching methods. The existence of these problems has affected the teaching results of online teaching platform to varying degrees, and also restricted the development of distance network teaching.

Keywords: Intelligent teaching platform · Clustering analysis · K-means algorithm · Grid clustering

1 The Importance of Film and Television Culture Education

1.1 The Theory of Film and Television Culture Education

At present, there are many theories about film and television culture communication, among which the book "film and Television Culture Communication" analyzes the content of film and television culture communication in Colleges and universities from the background of humanistic thoughts, and discusses the content and system of film and television culture education in Colleges and universities combined with Digitization and the reform of visual culture system. As we all know, film and television culture is a part of cultural undertakings. The quality of film and television culture communication also affects the reform of social and cultural system. Strictly speaking, the spread of culture depends on the public. Especially in the context of humanistic trend of thought, the concept and thinking of the public have undergone major changes. More and more people take the initiative to accept the art form of film and television culture, Therefore, the effect of film and television cultural communication is closely related to the humanistic spirit, and the two are in direct proportion. In other words, under the humanistic trend of thought, the humanistic quality of the public has opened up a new way for the

M. A. Jan and F. Khan (Eds.): BigIoT-EDU 2021, LNICST 391, pp. 175–180, 2021.
https://doi.org/10.1007/978-3-030-87900-6_21

film and television cultural communication, and is the core of the film and television cultural communication. For example, in the aspect of film distribution, compared with the 20th century, the number of film production, film output, distribution and influence have been improved. In terms of teleplays, China is a big country in the production and broadcasting of teleplays.

1.2 The Main Analysis Angle of Film and Television

Starting from the background of humanistic trend of thought, this paper explores the content of film and television culture education in Colleges and universities. As one of the viewpoints, theory and case are also recognized by the author as an important basis for the reform of film and television culture communication system. Among them, the concept and viewpoint of the public have changed with the improvement of humanistic quality. In the research and understanding of film and television culture, the "exclusion phenomenon" in the traditional mode can be abandoned. Especially in the context of cultural diversity and social informatization, more and more people have realized the practical significance of humanistic quality, which also brings opportunities and challenges to the film and television culture communication, At the same time, it also provides an opportunity for the development of visual culture education in Colleges and universities. In addition, from a theoretical point of view, the author summarizes symbolism and film art, surrealism and visual art, expressionism and film art, postmodernism and film art, etc., all of which can be demonstrated by communication, so it is certain that communication theory has become the basis in the process of film culture education in Colleges and universities [1]. At the same time, due to the influence of many factors, the film and television culture education in Colleges and universities is facing challenges at this stage, and even presents a bad phenomenon that flowers are becoming more and more attractive and colorful.

2 Research on Clustering Analysis Algorithm

2.1 Cluster Analysis Algorithm is Mainly Introduced

With the explosive growth of information, the emergence of massive data and the rapid increase of data dimensions, people can not effectively distinguish the data and get reliable judgment basis. To find the information that users are interested in from these massive data, we must make appropriate processing of the data, so how to effectively organize the massive data, that is, data mining, has become a hot topic It is an important subject and plays an important role in a wide range of fields.

Cluster analysis has been applied in many practical problems. Biologists use cluster analysis to analyze a large amount of genetic information. For example, cluster analysis has been used to discover genomes with similar functions; Clustering analysis can also be applied to web search engines, which divides the search results into several clusters, each cluster captures a specific aspect of the query, and each cluster can be divided into several subcategories, thus generating a hierarchical structure to support users' further query; Cluster analysis can also be used to find polar and oceanic atmospheric pressure patterns that have significant impacts on land climate, etc. in short, cluster analysis is more and more widely used in various fields.

2.2 Clustering Algorithm Analysis Algorithm

2.2.1 The Principle of Cluster Analysis

Clustering analysis is an important task in data mining. Clustering is one of the most common technologies in the field of data mining, which is used to discover unknown object classes in database. This kind of object class division is based on "clustering of birds of a feather", that is, investigating the similarity between individuals or data objects, dividing the individuals or data objects that meet the similarity conditions into a group, and the individuals or data objects that do not meet the similarity conditions into different groups. Each group formed through the clustering process is called a cluster [2]. According to the above description, we get the mathematical description of clustering problem.

According to the above description, we get the mathematical description of clustering problem:

$$\cup_{i=1}^{k} c_i = V \tag{1}$$

$$G_i \cap G_j \cup \cdots \cup G_k = X \tag{2}$$

Members G1, G2 Each class is described by some features, such as representing a class of points in n-dimensional space by their center of gravity or the (boundary) points of relationships in the class, representing a class graphically by nodes in the cluster tree, or representing a class by logical expressions of sample attributes.

2.2.2 Models in Cluster Analysis

There are two types of data structure in data analysis. (1) Data matrix (or object and variable structure) uses P variables (also known as measures or attributes) to represent n objects, such as age, height, weight, gender, race and other attributes to represent the object "person". This data structure is in the form of relational table, or as a matrix of n × P (n objects, n × P attributes).

$$\begin{bmatrix} x_{11} & \cdots & x_{1f} & \cdots & x_{1p} \\ \vdots & \vdots & \vdots & \vdots & \vdots \\ x_{i1} & \cdots & x_{if} & \cdots & x_{ip} \\ \vdots & \vdots & \vdots & \vdots & \vdots \\ x_{n1} & \cdots & x_{nf} & \cdots & x_{np} \end{bmatrix} \tag{3}$$

Cluster analysis originated from statistics, and most of the traditional analysis methods are based on numerical data. However, the object of data mining is complex and diverse, which requires that the clustering analysis method can not only deal with the data whose attribute is numerical type, but also adapt to the change of data type. Generally speaking, in data mining, the common data types of object attributes are interval scale variable, binary variable, nominal, ordinal, proportional scale variable and mixed type variable. Interval scale variable is a continuous measure of rough linear scale.

2.3   K-means Clustering and Grid Clustering

The time complexity of K-means clustering algorithm is O (TkN), where t is the number of iterations, K is the number of clusters, and N is the size of sample space. K-means clustering algorithm has less computation than hierarchical clustering algorithm, and is suitable for processing large sample data. However, the initial clustering centers of K-means clustering are randomly selected, which makes it possible to obtain different clustering results by selecting different initial clustering centers, K-means clustering can only find convex clusters, and can not deal with outliers well. At the same time, it is not efficient in time, and it does not have good scalability.

3   Construction of Film and Television Culture Education Platform

3.1   The Original Intention of Platform Construction

With the development of science and technology art and the improvement of the demand level of human life, film and television art gradually rises and develops rapidly. After music, writing, fine arts, sculpture, architecture and drama, it has the most extensive impact on social civilization. At present, it has been involved in various regions of the world, infiltrated into all aspects of people's daily life, and has increasingly broad and profound repercussions on social life and cultural progress [3]. It is an important and creative subject for physics teaching to apply campus film and television to high school physics teaching. At the same time, campus film and television can combine space-time, audio-visual, dynamic, visual and aesthetic into one, and also become a new and flexible education mode of combining sound and painting. Through the analysis of the requirements of the new curriculum, it is considered that the application of campus film and television can adapt to the requirements of the new curriculum system. Because of its own flexibility and innovation, it can be easily applied to physics teaching and promote the reform of physics teaching.

3.2   The Positive Role of the Construction of the Platform of Film and Television Culture Education

The use of film and television is well adapted to the education mode with the development of students as the main goal. First of all, the use of campus film and television based on the open exploration learning network platform can improve the enthusiasm of teachers to constantly update and restructure the teaching content according to the latest technological development process, and make the curriculum content in school in line with the most cutting-edge technology. At the same time, it can also vividly show the physics knowledge which is difficult for teachers to explain and understand to students. The teachers should use the campus film and television selectively and pertinently, not blindly. As shown in Fig. 1. Clustering results based on Grid.They should adopt different teaching methods according to different teaching contents and requirements, so as to improve the teaching quality better. For example, for the content with strong knowledge and difficult to understand, students can fully display the learning content and experiment details in combination with the latest campus video broadcasting operation process.

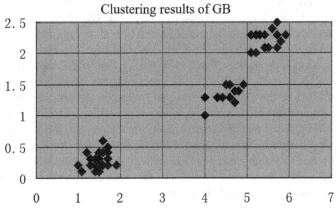

Fig. 1. Result of grid-based clustering method

We also use INS data to conduct several K-means clustering experiments and compare the initial clustering centers of each time. It is found that the initial clustering centers are randomly selected for k-means clustering each time, which makes the initial clustering centers of each time very different. As shown in Fig. 1, the initial clustering centers of the first, second, third and fourth times are very different, In the graph, the broken line fluctuates greatly. Obviously, the more the clustering center can not be well captured, the more computation and time the algorithm will pay, and the higher the cost of the algorithm.

4 Development Tools and Models

4.1 Development Tool

After a detailed investigation of the development tools, the system decided to use JSP (Java Server Pages) technology framework to generate dynamic and interactive web server applications. JSP technology is to insert Java program segment (scriptlet) and JSP tag tag into the traditional HTML file (* HTM, * HTM) to form JP file (* JSP). JSP uses tags and scriptlets to encapsulate the processing logic of generating dynamic web pages, access the application logic of resources existing in the server, separate the web page logic from web page design and display, support reusable component-based design, and make the development of web-based applications fast and easy [4]. The web server of this system uses Tomcat 5.0, Tomcat as a servlet container, When the user requests to visit a servlet, it encapsulates the user's request information in the ServletRequest object, and then transmits the request object and response object to the servlet requested by the user. The servlet writes the response result to the servletresponse object, and Tomcat transmits the response result to the user.

4.2 Development Model

It is composed of a system of collecting, storing and transferring information by computer. With the development of science and technology, the expansion of information and the explosion of knowledge, how to effectively collect information and transfer knowledge has become the development purpose of the system. Therefore, it is very important to develop a system which can give consideration to both development efficiency and operation efficiency and satisfy the asynchronous real-time processing function. The MVC mode is adopted in the development of this system. MVC mode is the abbreviation of "model view controller", which is translated into "mode view controller" in Chinese. That is to say, the input, processing and output processes of an application are separated according to the mode of model, view and controller, and are divided into three layers: model layer, view layer and control layer. View represents the user interface. For web applications, it can be summarized as HTML interface. Applications can have many different views, MVC design pattern only deals with the data collection and processing on the view, as well as the user's request, not the business process processing on the view. The business process is handled by the model.

5 Main Conclusions

Distance network teaching is a kind of teaching method which is paid close attention by many experts and scholars at present. We are constantly improving its teaching mode and implementation mode from different angles and aspects in order to better carry out distance network teaching activities. In this paper, the clustering analysis algorithm and its application in the field of teaching are deeply studied, the traditional clustering analysis algorithm is improved, and the gbkm clustering analysis algorithm is proposed. In this paper, the convergence and effectiveness of gbkm clustering analysis algorithm have been verified by standard test cases, and it has been successfully applied to the actual system – the personalized intelligent learning system of embedded online intelligent teaching platform, which greatly improves the intelligence of the teaching platform.

Acknowledgements. Scientific research team of Xi'an FanYi University XFU18KYTDC01.

References

1. Shen, G., Chen, M., Cheng, F., Wei, S.: Research on the construction of lifelong education big data application model and service platform. China Distance Educ. **12**, 59–68 (2020)
2. Deng, B., et al.: Construction and application of agricultural product quality and safety monitoring platform based on spring boot microservice architecture. Shanghai Agric. Sci. Technol. **6** 49–51 + 58 (2020)
3. Sheng, W.: Analysis of application platform construction based on agricultural Internet of things. South. Agric. Machinery **51**(22), 87–88 (2020)
4. Bai, M., Wang, R., Ren, L.: Construction and application of project collaborative management platform based on BIM Technology. Housing Real Estate **33**, 143–154 (2020)

Research on the Application of Information Technology in Physical Education Teaching in Colleges and Universities

Jun Yuan(✉)

JiangXi Police Institute, JiangXi, China

Abstract. With the development of the times, most of the students do not pay attention to physical exercise, which leads to their failure in the physical test, and the school does not make good use of the physical test data. Therefore, this paper uses the tensor flow platform, uses the deep neural network classification method, and uses SPSS pairing analysis to get the problems existing in College Physical Education Teaching in China, so that the school can accurately grasp the physical condition of students, so as to make the physical education teaching plan. The experiment shows that DNN can not only improve the accuracy and reduce the error, but also put forward the scientific class division strategy.

Keywords: College students · Physical fitness · BP neural network · MATLAB program

1 Introduction

College students are the important talent resources of the country, and their physical quality is the basis of all qualities, which not only directly affects their own healthy growth, but also affects their ability to serve the society in the future. According to the monitoring results of the Ministry of education in recent years, college students' physical fitness continues to decline, and the situation is worrying. Therefore, it is of great significance to establish a scientific and objective evaluation model to evaluate the physical quality of college students.

College Students' physical quality evaluation refers to the overall evaluation of College Students' physical quality according to their body shape, physiological function and sports ability. From the previous research results, most of the mathematical models reflecting the relationship between College Students' special performance and physical fitness use the methods of probability statistics and multiple regression analysis. However, probability statistics and multiple regression analysis are greatly affected by the sample space of sampling test, and the prediction accuracy is not high. Therefore, this paper uses BP neural network algorithm to solve the problem accurately, in order to further optimize the evaluation of College Students' physical fitness [1].

© ICST Institute for Computer Sciences, Social Informatics and Telecommunications Engineering 2021
Published by Springer Nature Switzerland AG 2021. All Rights Reserved
M. A. Jan and F. Khan (Eds.): BigIoT-EDU 2021, LNICST 391, pp. 181–185, 2021.
https://doi.org/10.1007/978-3-030-87900-6_22

2 Basic Theory of BP Neural Network

Artificial neural network is a kind of simulation of the working mode of human neural network. It is an information processing system that imitates the structure and function of brain neural network. It is a large-scale nonlinear adaptive system which can carry out complex logic operation. It has strong adaptive, self-learning, associative memory, high error tolerance and other characteristics. It is suitable for dealing with problems with complex information, incomplete data and difficult to accurately describe by mathematical model [2].

The artificial neuron (processing unit) model can be simulated by Fig. 1, and the symbols in the figure are given by formula (1).

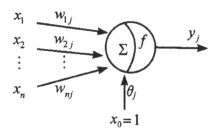

Fig. 1. Schematic diagram of artificial neuron (processing unit)

The relationship between input and output can be expressed as:

$$\begin{cases} s_j = \sum_{i=1}^{n} w_{ij}x_i - \theta_j \\ y_j = f(s_j) \end{cases} \tag{1}$$

BP neural network is a kind of artificial neural network which is more mature and widely used. It is composed of input layer, hidden layer and output layer. The processing units between layers are fully interconnected, and the processing units in the same layer are not connected. The basic idea is that the information processing process consists of two processes: forward propagation and error back propagation. In forward propagation, the input information is input from the input layer and output from the output layer after being processed by each hidden layer. If the output information of the output layer is inconsistent with the expected information, the output error is transferred from the output layer to the input layer in some form, and the error is allocated to the processing units of each layer to gradually correct the calculation error. Because BP neural network model can approach any continuous function with high precision, and can achieve good fitting effect for complex problems with multi factors and nonlinearity, this paper uses BP neural network to establish the evaluation model of College Students' physical fitness.

3 Design of Flipped Classroom and Volleyball Teaching Experiment Based on MOOC

The main purpose of experimental teaching of volleyball skills is to test the influence of flipped classroom of sports skills teaching based on MOOC on College Students' sports skills learning, and to test whether this teaching mode can improve students' learning efficiency and teachers' teaching efficiency, Whether it can enhance students' learning interest, learning initiative, learning self-confidence and learning will in the learning process, so as to provide certain data support and practical basis for the application research of MOOC based flipped classroom in motor skill teaching [3].

The flipped classroom based on MOOC consists of traditional teaching classroom and MOOC classroom. Relying on the normal use of the network MOOCS platform in teaching experiment, the students who participate in the experiment also need to have intelligent mobile terminals for MOOCS learning. According to the understanding of the experimental objects before the teaching experiment, they all use mobile phones as the media of MOOCS learning. Now there are many MOOCS platforms to choose from. The MOOCS platform of Xuetang online is the online platform in this experiment. Xuetang online, a Chinese MOOC platform developed and launched by Tsinghua University in 2013, is an online course platform for the whole world. As long as there is a network around the students can be in this platform for video learning courses. In 2016, Xuetang online was rated as one of the top three platforms with "the most excellent courses" in the "global MOOCS ranking". The diversity and quality of the number of courses attract more users to register and select courses.

4 BP Neural Network Evaluation Model of College Students' Physical Fitness

The input layer of the evaluation model consists of six indexes: height, weight, vital capacity, endurance performance, flexibility and strength performance; speed and dexterity performance; the output layer has only one neuron y, representing the physical quality of college students.

$$n_1 = \sqrt{n + m} + \alpha \tag{2}$$

n. M represents the number of neurons in the input layer and the output layer respectively, and a is a constant between 1 and 10.

In the flipped classroom based on MOOC, the in class link is the offline classroom teaching link. Teachers should design the classroom teaching according to the teaching objectives, teaching content and students' learning results before class. In the classroom teaching, the teacher first checks the students' learning results according to the pre class learning tasks to determine whether the students have seriously completed the pre class MOOCS learning; and then answers the students' problems in the process of MOOCS learning. This part of the check and answer is convenient for the teacher to more intuitively understand the effectiveness of students' pre class MOOCS learning. Organize teaching activities according to the students' mastery of the teaching content: combine the classroom teaching content and students' acquired knowledge, carry out the internalization and immediate evaluation of knowledge. In the classroom, teachers organize students to group or students to carry out any group for cooperative learning and inquiry learning, so as to increase the communication and discussion between teachers and students and students in motor skill learning.

5 After Class

After the end of classroom teaching, teachers need to evaluate the class in time: To evaluate the students' learning, to evaluate their own teaching, and to make the teaching reflection of this class. In view of the unsolved problems in the classroom, this paper provides corresponding guidance after class, and points out the knowledge points they need to pay attention to in MOOC learning. According to the learning progress of most students, determine the teaching content of the next lesson. In the arrangement of collective learning tasks at the same time, supervise the slow learning progress of students to follow the pace of the collective, strengthen the learning and practice after class. In the whole teaching process, teachers often need to reflect on teaching, and students are also required to summarize and reflect on their own learning process, so as to find problems in the reflection. Through wechat group to seek the help of teachers or save their problems in learning to the next class, and then focus on feedback to teachers, and seek solutions to provide guidance and help for students, at the same time, urge students to complete homework arrangement after class, timely review and preview learning content, improve classroom teaching in continuous communication and reflection [4].

The flipped classroom based on MOOC is different from the traditional physical education classroom in its teaching mode, and their learning places are different, but it can not change the cognitive law of sports skills and its teaching essence. After class, students summarize and reflect on their learning process before and during class, which is another stage of improving motor skills. Teachers can constantly improve teaching design and classroom teaching by reflecting on students' learning situation and classroom teaching effect.

In the teaching experiment, because the students in the experimental class learned MOOCS before class, they can quickly establish the initial movement representation in the initial stage of each technology. Teachers only need to explain the movements a little, students can quickly understand the essentials of the movements and practice, no longer need teachers to repeat in the classroom, for students to save learning time in the classroom, leaving more time to carefully polish their own movement technology, at the same time, it also increases the opportunity and time for teachers to guide students one-to-one. In the classroom practice of students, correct each student's movement, and provide guidance for students to further improve their movement skills, and flexibly master various sports skills in volleyball. Compared with the students in the experimental class, the students in the control class need teachers to repeatedly emphasize the basic essentials of the action in the classroom. Teachers also need to spend more time explaining the details of the action and demonstrating. At the same time, students need to spend more time in the classroom to practice in order to grasp the action essentials of various techniques. Class time is limited. Facing all students, teachers spend enough time on explanation and demonstration, and the time left for students to practice independently is correspondingly reduced. Teachers can not take into account the learning situation of each student. Students' mat practice in class lacks personalized guidance, and it is difficult for students to accurately grasp each sports technology.

6 Conclusion

Using the powerful function mapping ability of BP neural network, this paper establishes the neural network model of the correlation between the total test score and the physical fitness of college students, and realizes it by MATLAB software. The research example shows that the model has higher prediction accuracy and operation efficiency than the multiple regression analysis model, and does not need to determine the expression form of the mathematical model in advance. The operation is simple, and the evaluation results are scientific and reasonable. It can be used as an effective method for the evaluation of College students' physical fitness in the future.

References

1. Liu, J.: Discussion on how to improve the physical quality of college students. Contemp. Sports Sci. Technol. **15** (2014)
2. Wang, J., Zhao, J.: Analysis and countermeasures of influencing factors of College Students' physical quality. J. Phys. Educ. Coll. Shanxi Normal Univ. **2** (2000)
3. Liu, G.: Application of improved BP neural network in college students' physical fitness evaluation. Shaanxi Educ. (Higher Educ. Ed.) **11** (2013)
4. Duan, Y.: Research on the evaluation model of College Students' physical fitness test based on neural network. J. Wuhan Inst. Phys. Educ. **8** (2005)

Research on the Application of User Interest Model and Apriori Algorithm in College Students' Education Recommendation

Peng Zhang$^{(\boxtimes)}$

Harbin Finance University, Harbin 150030, Heilongjiang, China

Abstract. In order to realize the intelligent recommendation and interest matching of College Students' employment, a college students' employment recommendation model based on user interest model and Apriori algorithm is proposed. This paper constructs the user interest information collection and big data distribution model of College Students' employment, uses the big data association information mining method to match the interest features of College Students' employment, and constructs the interest correlation feature quantity of College Students' Employment under the control of association rules, so as to optimize and fuse the interest feature big data of College Students' employment recommendation. Apriori algorithm is used to adaptively match the interest feature points of College Students' employment recommendation, and fuzzy adaptive optimization method is used to optimize the recommendation of College Students' employment behavior. The simulation results show that the reliability of this method is good, and the employment satisfaction level of college students is improved.

Keywords: User interest model · Apriori algorithm · College students employment recommendation · Big data optimization fusion processing · Feature point matching · Adaptive matching

1 Introduction

With the continuous expansion of the scale of education and the transformation of social economy, the employment pressure of college students is also increasing. It is necessary to build an optimized recommendation model of College Students' employment, combine with the interests of college students to actively recommend, and provide employment guidance for college students [1]. According to the needs of Minwei, the automatic matching of College Students' employment Minwei is carried out, so as to improve the satisfaction level of College Students' employment. Research on the employment recommendation model of college students, combined with the big data statistical analysis method to optimize the employment recommendation of college students, promotes the increase of employment of graduates, and the related research on the employment recommendation model of college students has received great attention.

2   User Interest Sampling and Interest Feature Matching for College Students' Employment

2.1   User Interest Characteristics Sampling of College Students' Employment

In order to realize the employment recommendation of college students, we first build the user interest information collection and big data distribution model of College Students' employment [2]. This paper establishes a big data model for the distribution of user's personalized interests and hobbies in college students' employment recommendation, and uses the association rule scheduling method to match the interest feature points in the process of College Students' employment recommendation. The user interest information of College Students' employment is sampled, and the user interest information fusion characteristic quantity p(x) of personalized recommendation of College Students' employment is obtained:

$$p(x) = x_m / \sum_{i=1}^{n} I_i \cdot u_m \tag{1}$$

Where u_m is the interest characteristic index of college students.

Based on this, the feature sampling model of user interest distribution of college students is constructed:

$$P\left(k = \frac{p(x)}{\sum_{i=1}^{n} I_i(l(k) \cdot q(k))}\right) \tag{2}$$

Where: k is the interest parameter; i is the amount of interest employment information; l is the employment project index; q is the employment intention index.

According to the above analysis, using the method of fuzzy association rules mining, this paper constructs the big data evolutionary game model of personalized recommendation for college students' employment, realizes the user interest feature sampling of College Students' employment, and carries out employment recommendation and pattern recognition according to the feature sampling results.

3   User Modeling Based on Ontology and Concept Frequent Interest Cluster

Behavior record module. It is mainly responsible for collecting the behavior log files formed by users' browsing of page links, clicking and downloading of resources, feedback information and other behaviors, forming the user interest range of comparative entities, which is used for query and reasoning operation of resource ontology. For user interest model, user interest represented by behavior record is the basis of all work.

Resource ontology module. It is mainly used for the description function of resources. The content of each resource is represented by the combination of some concepts of resource ontology. The resource ontology module is the core of the whole system. When behavior records are transformed into concept interest strings, and potential user interests are mined through behavior records, resource ontology should be used for query and reasoning [3].

Interest mining module. It uses the improved Apriori algorithm to form a non redundant and non repetitive concept frequent interest cluster which can represent the user's long-term interest direction. It also uses SPARQL ontology query language and mining algorithm to dig out the user's potential interest from the concept interest cluster, Improve the accuracy of user interest model and get rid of the bottleneck of user resource recommendation.

User interest model module. The concept frequent interest cluster and potential instant interest are combined to form the final user interest model.

The four modules are in the process of linear link. The behavior record module is the input part of the whole system. The resource ontology module receives the behavior record set to query the resource RDF documents involved in the behavior record set, and forms the user's concept interest string set as the input part of the interest mining module. When the update cycle arrives, the interest mining module will process the input information with Apriori algorithm, mine the potential interest, form the concept of user interest, frequent interest clusters and potential instant interest clusters, and input them to the user interest model module. In the user interest model module, according to the update algorithm, the frequent interest clusters and the potential instant interest clusters are combined to form the final user interest model as the output of the whole system.

4   Simulation Experiment and Result Analysis

The statistical analysis software Excel2007 and spss19.0 are used to analyze the statistical data of College Students' employment recommendation model. Combined with MATLAB simulation tool, college students' employment recommendation is carried out. According to the above simulation environment and parameter setting, the simulation of College Students' employment recommendation is carried out to test the accuracy of the recommendation, and compared with the traditional SVM algorithm and BP algorithm. The comparison results are shown in Fig. 1 [4].

The analysis of Fig. 1 shows that the accuracy of this method for college students' employment recommendation is high, which improves the ability of interest feature matching of College Students' employment, and thus improves the level of satisfaction of College Students' employment.

5   User Interest Model Module

The updating of user model is a periodic process, and the updated data information is the real-time interest model formed by the user's behavior records. To a certain period of time, the incremental user concept frequent interest cluster is formed by Apriori algorithm, which is fused with the weight of the original user long-term interest model concept frequent interest cluster.

User's interest has a certain time, with the passage of time cycle, some interest may decrease, but some interest will increase. The increased interest will be reflected in the

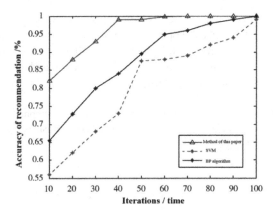

Fig. 1. Accuracy test of College Students' employment recommendation

incremental model of user interest. For the decrease of user interest, we introduce an attenuation factor T, which makes the user's long-term interest model attenuate according to the attenuation factor t to describe the process of user interest decrease.

With the continuous updating of long-term user interest model, some interests will be attenuated to a great extent when they cannot be updated for a long time, which indicates that users lose interest in frequent interest clusters of this concept. Therefore, we give a minimum attention threshold confisin. When the attention of frequent interest clusters of a concept is lower than this threshold, confisin can be used to calculate the interest of frequent interest clusters of this concept, It will be eliminated directly from the user's long-term interest model.

The abscissa interestnum of the experiment represents the number of interesting topics involved in user behavior. When the number of topics involved in user behavior records is more, the probability of users having potential interest is greater, and the precision of resources recommended by user model is improved. However, in general, the precision is slightly lower than that of frequent set clustering user model, because the more interests are involved, The larger the base of potential interest, the lower the precision.

6 Conclusion

Research on the employment recommendation model of college students, combined with big data statistical analysis method to optimize the employment recommendation of college students, promote the increase of employment of graduates. This paper proposes an employment recommendation model for college students based on user interest model and Apriori algorithm. Association rules scheduling method is used to match interest feature points in the process of College Students' employment recommendation, and adaptive matching is carried out for jobs in different fields and college students' interests. The spatial fuzzy clustering model is established, the preference distribution model of College Students' employment recommendation is constructed by using the method of preference information mining and interest alignment, and the Apriori algorithm is used for the adaptive matching of interest feature points of College Students' employment recommendation to realize the optimization of employment recommendation. The test results show that the accuracy of this method for college students' employment recommendation is higher, the interest matching ability is better, and the reliability level of employment recommendation is improved.

Acknowledgements. A New Characteristics of the Ideological Development of Poverty University Students in Universities and Colleges by the Provincial Basic Business Fee Project of Harbin Institute of Finance (2018-KYWF-E017).

References

1. Chen, W., Zhang, S., Wang, D., et al.: College course selection recommendation algorithm based on nearest neighbor model and probability matrix decomposition. J. Liaoning Univ. Eng. Technol. (Nat. Sci. Ed.) **36**(9), 976–982 (2017)
2. Yang, F., Zheng, Y., Zhang, C.: Hybrid recommendation algorithm based on probability matrix factorization. Comput. Appl. **38**(3), 644–649 (2018)
3. Gong, Y., Lu, J.: Cooperative training algorithm combining active learning and density peak clustering. Comput. Appl. **39**(8), 2297–2301 (2019)
4. Meng, X., Liu, S., Zhang, Y., et al.: Research on social recommendation system. Acta softw. Sin. **26**(6), 1356–1372 (2015)
5. Chen, J.X., Zhao, Q.L., Qin, Z.Y., et al.: Research of regional user interest model based on agricultural ontology. J. Libr. Inf. Sci. Agric.
6. Xu, Z., Lu, R., Xiang, L., et al.: Discovering user interest on twitter with a modified author-topic model. 422–429 (2011)
7. Jing, S., Gong, Z., Qiu, H., et al.: Intelligent information retrieval system based on user interest model – PCSICE. J. China Soc. Sci. Tech. Inf. (2003)
8. Liu, B., Xiong, H., Papadimitriou, S., et al.: A general geographical probabilistic factor model for point of interest recommendation. IEEE Trans. Knowl. Data Eng. **27**(5), 1167–1179 (2015)
9. Cheng, W.H., Chu, W.T., Kuo, J.H., et al.: Automatic video region-of-interest determination based on user attention model. In: IEEE International Symposium on Circuits & Systems. IEEE (2005)
10. Gündüz, S., Özsu, T.M.: A user interest model for web page navigation. In: Proceedings of the International Workshop on Data Mining for Actionable Knowledge (2003)
11. Gündüz, S., Özsu, M.T.: A user interest model for web page navigation. In: Proceedings of International Workshop on Data Mining for Actionable Knowledge, pp. 46–57. Seoul Korea (2003)
12. Gong, S.: Learning user interest model for content-based filtering in personalized recommendation system. Int. J. Digit. Cont. Technol. Appl. **6**(11), 155–162 (2012)

Research on the System Design of Cooperative Foreign Language Teaching Mode Under Data Analysis

Xiaohua Guo[✉]

Ganzhou Teachers College, Ganzhou City, Jiangxi Province, China

Abstract. With the development of English education, the requirement of College Students' English ability is higher and higher. However, the lagging teaching mode restricts the learning of College English writing. As a new learning mode, the cooperative foreign language teaching mode combined with ant colony algorithm is of great significance in the study of College English writing teaching.

Keywords: Ant colony algorithm · Collaborative · Foreign language teaching mode

1 Introduction

College English writing is a key link in College English education, especially in the current social environment of questioning the writing ability of college students, College English writing has become the most difficult link faced by English educators and all college students. As we all know, English writing is a collection of English knowledge. Through the reasonable collocation and application of vocabulary, sentence patterns and grammar, the final English article is formed, which reflects students' English knowledge, English thinking ability and comprehensive ability of English application, and becomes an important development orientation of English learning. In the traditional English teaching classroom, teachers instill knowledge points into Yu students through one to many teaching mode, which can not cultivate students' comprehensive ability according to their knowledge level and interest.

2 Ant Colony Algorithm

Ant colony algorithm is an algorithm to solve combinatorial optimization problems based on natural foraging behavior [8 scientific observation shows that ants in nature can always find the shortest path from ant nest to food source, and release substances in the process of searching for food, which is called pheromone. The higher the concentration, the more likely the ants will move in this direction. Therefore, more ants will leave more pheromones on the path, and most of them will eventually go through the optimal

© ICST Institute for Computer Sciences, Social Informatics and Telecommunications Engineering 2021
Published by Springer Nature Switzerland AG 2021. All Rights Reserved
M. A. Jan and F. Khan (Eds.): BigIoT-EDU 2021, LNICST 391, pp. 191–201, 2021.
https://doi.org/10.1007/978-3-030-87900-6_24

path [1]. The core of ant colony algorithm is mainly based on ant state transition rules and pheromone update rules, but ant colony algorithm has the defects of slow convergence speed and easy to fall into local optimal solution. In order to improve the convergence speed and the accuracy of the mosquito swarm algorithm, the ant state transition rule, heuristic function and pheromone update rule are improved based on the basic ant colony algorithm. The initialization process is shown in Fig. 1.

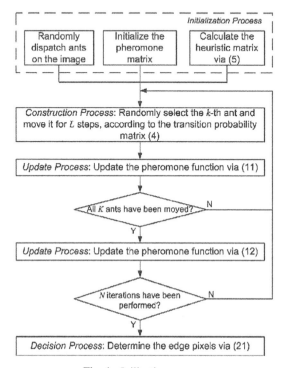

Fig. 1. Inilization process

2.1   Improvement of Ant State Transition Rule and Heuristic Function

The basic ant colony algorithm state transition formula is:

$$S_{uu}^{k}(t) = \begin{cases} \arg\max\{[\tau_{uu}(t)^{a}]\} \\ 0, other \end{cases} \tag{1}$$

Where, S_{uu}^{k} is the opportunity value of the ant with number k to select the next node V at the moment, u (knowledge (1) represents the pheromone concentration, expectation degree and transition probability of the ant from node u to V at the moment, where k is the heuristic function. a is a fixed threshold, $t \in (0,1)$ is a uniformly distributed random variable, alow is the set of all nodes satisfying the constraint conditions, α and β represent the importance factor of pheromone and heuristic function respectively [2–4]. When the random variable Q is less than the fixed threshold a, a non random search method is adopted by using the known information, that is, the node with the largest product of pheromone and heuristic function is used for state transition; otherwise, the transition probability of all nodes meeting the constraint conditions is calculated, and the state transition is carried out according to the node with high probability.

2.2 Optimized Ant Colony Algorithm

In order to optimize the logical routing problem in PTN network, an optimal path model with multiple constraints is constructed, and an improved ant colony algorithm is used to search the optimal path satisfying the QoS constraints. The optimal path is taken as the optimal solution to solve the logical routing problem. By improving the state transition rule, heuristic function and pheromone update rule in the basic ant colony algorithm, the algorithm gives full play to its strong optimization ability, at the same time, it avoids the "premature stagnation" phenomenon of the algorithm, and speeds up the convergence speed of the algorithm. The experimental results show that the improved algorithm has obvious improvement in operation efficiency and optimization effect [5–7]. In the future, with the increase of the number of networks, the running time complexity will also increase. It is an effective solution to study the idea of partitioning and parallelizing large PTN networks. The simple and easy-to-use ant colony algorithm will play an important role in PTN network planning and optimization. The algorithm provides a certain practical value for the study of network optimal path problem.

3   The Concept of Collaborative Task Orientation

Collaborative is widely used in network teaching, such as collaborative network education. It refers to the teachers in the same field or different fields, the teachers in the same college or different colleges, the teachers in the same country or different countries, using and using the Internet for the same course or the same group of educatees, in the time and content of the education process, highlighting the interaction and connection of network education. In this paper, the collaborative mode takes its literal meaning, which means "cooperation together", that is, the teaching objects (students) are divided into groups to complete a task together. "Task oriented" originates from "task driven", which strongly emphasizes the guiding and regulating role of task. When applied in teaching activities, task orientation is to induce, strengthen and maintain learners' achievement motivation through tasks in teaching activities, and achievement motivation is the dynamic system of learning and completing tasks [8]. Task, as a bridge of learning, is driven by task to achieve the purpose of learning. Specific to this article, "task oriented" refers to the specific teaching content in the teaching plan as a task. Generally speaking, "collaborative task orientation" is to take the specific teaching content of the course as the task, and divide it into several groups according to the number of teaching objects (students). The groups are required to correspond to the task. After careful discussion and study before the group class, it explains some details of the task completion for other students and teachers in the classroom. In this teaching activity, the requirements for teachers will be more strict. In addition to mastering the basic knowledge of this course, teachers also need to accurately master the knowledge related to this teaching task, because the explanation content of group students can often be expanded beyond the teaching materials.

4 Composition of Collaborative Task Oriented Teaching Mode

The core idea of collaborative task oriented teaching mode is that in the whole teaching activities, teachers and students are in the same position, and teaching tasks are completed by students, including preparation before class and teaching in class. But in the process of students' teaching, the teacher should make a detailed record of the whole teaching activities, so as to comment, supplement and improve after each student's explanation.

4.1 "Collaborative task oriented" team building

Whether the school can cultivate compound talents with professional skills and practical ability, independent working ability and good communication ability, innovative ability and teamwork spirit is the standard team to measure the success of the quality education of the school. It refers to the collective that can complement, unite and share the responsibility and mission [9, 10]. Collaborative task orientation is implemented in the way of team, and the formation of team is the premise of collaborative task orientation. As shown in Fig. 2. The size of the team depends on the total class hours and the total class size. If the number of members in each group is too many, it will be difficult to understand the task. The formation of the team is completed by teachers before class, and students' interests, learning level, learning ability, personality differences and other factors should be considered comprehensively.

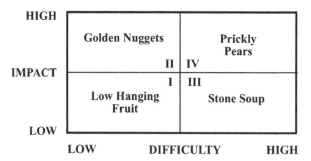

Fig. 2. Collaborative task oriented team building.

4.2 "Collaborative Task Oriented" Task Decomposition

In the higher vocational colleges which pay attention to the cultivation of technical ability, the guidance task often focuses on the skills involved in the professional post and ignores the learning of theoretical knowledge. In application-oriented universities, in addition to technical learning, we also need to master solid theoretical knowledge. Therefore, a specific guidance task can not cover all of a skill or a textbook. Sometimes a task may be a complex theoretical derivation or an example of combining theory with practice [11]. Specifically, the guiding task should be arranged according to the syllabus and teaching plan, and each team should arrange the teaching task that can not be returned. Then, each team member should learn independently, and encourage students to expand the content beyond the teaching materials, that is, to consult the materials and essays related to the guiding task, and the guiding task should be completed by the students of this group. If the class size is small and the total class hours are large, each team can assign different guidance tasks and explain them several times.

4.3 "Collaborative Task Oriented" Evaluation System

The collaborative task oriented teaching evaluation system includes four evaluation criteria. One is scientific, which requires each team member to understand the content accurately and not deviate from the scientific truth. The other is fluency, It emphasizes that all members of each team should use modern teaching methods (multimedia, network, etc.) and traditional teaching methods (blackboard writing) to explain. It requires members to be continuous in the content of explanation and pay attention to the speed and intonation of language expression. Thirdly, interactivity is not only a simple transposition of teachers and students in collaborative task-based teaching activities, We should also pay attention to the interaction between the subject (narrator) and the object, and strive to mobilize every student's learning enthusiasm. The fourth is standardization [12–14]. After the collaborative Task-oriented Teaching activities, each member is required to make a systematic arrangement of their own tasks, and on this basis, write a scientific paper, and the paper format meets the requirements of the journal.

4.4 "Collaborative Task Oriented" Teachers' Role

In the collaborative task-based teaching mode, teachers play an important role. In this process, teachers play two important roles. First, the role of "guide" is to skillfully guide the acquisition of knowledge after task decomposition, the collection of data, the requirements of cooperation, the details of explanation and other specific matters, The role of "summarizer" is that teachers need to make a complete summary of the specific issues such as knowledge combing, content improvement, students' comments, individual questions and so on.

5   The Role of Teachers in Collaborative Task Oriented Teaching Model

5.1   The Role of Teachers in Collaborative Task Oriented Teaching Model

In the traditional teaching mode, teachers are the main body of teaching. Teachers make teaching plans according to the syllabus, and then complete the teaching content step by step according to the teaching plans to achieve the teaching objectives. In the collaborative task oriented teaching mode, teachers are no longer the main body of teaching, but play the role of chief designer [15]. According to the syllabus, the teaching content is divided into guided tasks according to the chapters, the completion time of guided tasks is planned, and then the teaching team is established according to the difficulty of guided tasks. The teaching team can be divided into three groups according to their interest, learning level, learning ability and personality differences.

5.2   The Teacher is the Director of the Team in the Collaborative Task Oriented Teaching Mode

In the collaborative task oriented teaching mode, the teacher is more like a tutor. From students' access to information, collective lesson preparation, explanation of content to classroom explanation of details, the teacher should play the role of a mentor. In addition, after the team members get the task, teachers need to point out the difficulty of the task. One of the characteristics of collaborative Task-oriented Teaching mode is that each team and members have to explain. When a member begins to explain, on the premise of no mistakes. Teachers should not interrupt the explanation at the beginning, so as to maintain the integrity of members' thinking [16–18]. After the member's explanation, make comments. The main points of comment are the accuracy of the content, the grasp of the scope of knowledge, and the voice, posture, writing on the blackboard, sense of rhythm, content proficiency, coherence, language expression, interaction of the members. Teachers' comments can help students understand their own strengths and weaknesses. For example, atiho's comments can also help other team members learn, learn advantages and overcome disadvantages.

6   Practice of Collaborative Task Oriented Teaching Mode

In the practice of collaborative task oriented teaching mode, the author takes "mining system engineering" course as an example to illustrate the application of collaborative task oriented teaching mode.

6.1   Making Guidance Tasks According to the Syllabus

"Mining system engineering" is a professional basic course of mining engineering. Through the study of this course, students can master the basic principles and methods of system engineering and its application in mining industry. The course requires students to master the theory and application of mathematical programming, shortest path problem, network analysis, analytic hierarchy process fuzzy comprehensive evaluation, system reliability, etc. the total class hours of the course is 30. The main details of each chapter are explained by students in class.

6.2   Determine the Number of Team Members According to the Number of Students in the Class

As this course is 30 class hours, the teacher should summarize and perfect it once after each chapter, and the remaining 10 class hours. If the class size is 30, a team of 3 people can be divided into 10 teams to complete the guidance task. If the class size is 60, each team needs to arrange 6 people. Team members are determined according to students' interests, learning level, learning ability, personality differences, etc. 3) based on classroom explanation + lecture + scientific papers as the assessment basis, the same task orientation has reformed the traditional test paper evaluation method, and replaced by classroom explanation + lecture + scientific papers comprehensive evaluation method. The accuracy of the content of classroom explanation, the grasp of the scope of knowledge, and the voice, posture, writing on the blackboard, rhythm, proficiency, coherence, language expression, interactivity and other evaluation indicators of the members account for 50% of the total score, 20% of the lecture notes written by each member, and 30% of the scientific papers. Scientific papers are in the form of oral defense, and each student will participate in the oral defense when submitting their own papers.

6.3   Strengthen the Understanding of Teaching Content by Teachers' Comments, Summary and Thesis Defense

A class of a team is generally arranged to be completed in about 70 min, and the rest of the time is for teachers to comment on each member. It also includes the summary, carding, improvement and expansion of the team's teaching content, so as to make students of other teams have a systematic understanding and mastery of the team's teaching content [19]. At the same time, while affirming the advantages of the explanation group, correct its shortcomings, and provide help and guidance for other team members in the follow-up explanation. In addition, after the conclusion of each chapter, the teacher will give a systematic, difficult and forward-looking lecture on the content of this chapter in combination with the students' explanation, so as to further consolidate the learning achievements. In order to supervise and identify the authenticity, accuracy and innovation of the scientific and technological papers of each member, the scientific and technological papers submitted by each member shall be defended. Since the first experiment of "mining system engineering" course in class 1, mining engineering grade 07, Heilongjiang University of science and technology, the collaborative task oriented teaching mode has been implemented in all classes of mining system engineering grade 08 and 09 through continuous summary, revision and improvement, It has been listed as a key support project of heilonghui University of science and technology, and has held teaching observation classes and promoted in the whole university.

7   Connotation of Multimodal Cooperation

7.1   Definition of Multimodal Collaboration

Multimodality, that is, a variety of information transfer patterns, including language, posture, materials, music and other multimodal co symbols are integrated to form a benign interaction. This interaction is not necessary for multimodal people to use the most effective expression mode in the system to infiltrate into College English, because there are different forms in the system, which can meet the advantages of different levels of modes.

7.2 Multimodal Cooperation Principle

The first is multimodality, that is, a variety of information transmission modes, including language, posture, materials, music, etc. multimodal collaboration is to integrate these information transmission symbols to form a benign interaction. This interaction is not simply to input information to the information receiver, but through multimodal high interaction, the information receiver uses the most effective expression mode in the system to promote understanding, It is necessary to the infiltration of the first mock exam into College English writing teaching, because there are different ways of expression in this system to meet the needs of students at different levels of learning [20]. Therefore, we should make use of this model to improve students' interest in writing and writing.

Secondly, multimodal cooperation has the principle of efficiency. Multimodal collaboration can effectively process dynamic visual images, rich audio materials or vivid teaching animations, so that they can cooperate harmoniously and achieve high-quality teaching, which makes students more efficient in the process of learning. By organizing the content expressed by various information transmission modes, these knowledge can be more deeply rooted in the hearts of the people, Multimodal synergy can also improve the amount of memory information of students in a short time, so that students can understand the key knowledge more deeply.

8   Simulation for Improving College English Writing Mode by Multimodal Cooperation

In the face of the diversification of social information technology, the traditional teaching mode has been far from meeting the needs of students for the improvement of their comprehensive English ability. In the process of English writing learning, on the one hand, teachers can promote the transmission of multiple information through the use of multimodal collaboration, and effectively express non-verbal information such as pictures, audio and video, so that students can interpret it in multiple languages; On the other hand, students can also make use of multi-modal collaboration for learning feedback in such an environment to realize the two-way communication between teachers and students.

8.1   On the Main Research Direction of College English Writing Teaching

For multimodal collaborative mode, we should update our understanding with the development of the times. In addition to the application of multimedia in PPT, in the future, we should grasp it from the following aspects: first, students' imitation ability should be promoted in the process of multimodal collaboration. At present, College English writing teaching pays more attention to the inculcation of theoretical knowledge and writing skills, and ignores the students' understanding and application of these contents [21, 22]. Therefore, we should adopt imitation activities based on computer network system in the multimodal collaborative development teaching environment, so that students can watch network video, animation and other non text information, This kind of interesting classroom activity can also enhance students' interest in writing. It not only helps students to use logical sentences and paragraphs correctly, but also improves students' ability of deep level structure, The cultivation of this ability makes students have a deeper understanding of English writing and abandon the original stereotyped writing routine. The mathematical model of constructing multi constraint shortest path objective function is as follows:

$$C(Pod) = \frac{1}{\sum_{L_{uu} \subset Pod} \delta |L_{uu} + W_{uu}|} = \frac{1}{\delta |Pod| + \sum_{L_{uu} \subset Pod} W_{uu}} \tag{2}$$

8.2 The Enlightenment of Multimodal Collaboration on College English Writing Education

The improvement of teachers' ability and quality [3, 4]. Through the research, we can know that multimodal collaboration has an important impact on College English writing. First of all, as the participants of teaching activities, teachers should make sufficient preparations before class. In terms of content, they should pay attention to that language and words are always the main modal forms in the process of writing teaching, and other modes can play an auxiliary role in the collaborative process. As shown in Fig. 3. They can not only focus on the diversity of forms, but also ignore the meaning of writing itself. Secondly, teachers should pay attention to the coordination of the interaction between various modes, choose the main mode and the secondary mode, and combine the primary mode and the secondary mode in the process of practice, so as to avoid the confusion of words, sounds and pictures, interfere with students' writing learning logic, and strive to create a natural writing learning environment. Finally, teachers themselves should improve their reading and writing ability, and actively deepen the learning of multimodal knowledge [23, 24]. Multimodal interaction in China's education is still in its infancy, many research results are not perfect, so teachers should explore in classroom teaching practice, to find more conducive to students' English writing learning multimodal collaborative environment.

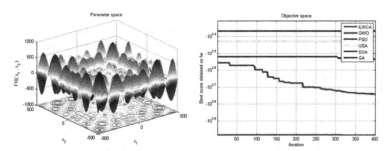

Fig. 3. Results of simulation with improved colony algorithm

9 Conclusions

To sum up, the multimodal collaborative teaching mode can combine multiple social symbols, including words, images, sounds, etc., which can not only fully mobilize the sensory stimulation of college students, but also stimulate their interest in learning, so that they can actively participate in classroom learning. In the process of English writing, it can also help students to effectively understand the basic knowledge of English and improve their comprehensive ability of English writing, Therefore, we should make full use of multimodal collaborative teaching in the future college English writing course. Taking the specific teaching content of the course as the task, it is divided into several groups according to the number of teaching objects (students), and the groups are required to correspond to the tasks. After careful discussion and study before the group class, it is a new teaching mode to explain some details of the task completion for other students and teachers in the classroom. The practice shows that the teaching mode has the following characteristics: The whole teaching task of collaborative task oriented is completed by students, including from pre class preparation to classroom teaching, which is a completely "student-centered" teaching mode; Collaborative task oriented teaching mode is composed of student team, oriented task, evaluation system and teacher's role, Its performance evaluation system consists of classroom explanation, lecture notes and scientific papers. Teachers only play the role of guiding task allocation, team building, classroom comments, content summary and knowledge carding.

References

1. Qingmin, Z.: Research on the effectiveness of multimodal audio visual oral teaching mode in the development of listening and speaking ability. J. Foreign Lang. Coll. PLA **06**, 72–76 + 128 (2011)
2. Caihong, W., Xuyang, G.: Research on collaborative service mode of College English writing supported by IC. Library Sci. Res. **11**, 84–87 (2011)
3. Jian, W.: Multimodal interaction mode in Multimedia English Writing Teaching. Audio Visual Foreign Lang. Teach. **06**, 14–19 (2010)
4. Xiaohui, L.: Cognitive multimodal training mode of English writing thinking. Audio Visual Foreign Lang. Teach. **01**, 43–49 (2015)
5. Chaoyi, H.: Enlightenment of foreign language education mode of Fujian shipbuilding school on ESP teaching in Higher Vocational Colleges in China. J. Jiujiang Polytechnic **03**, 47–48 (2013)
6. Chaohong, L., Min, L., Tong, L.: Research on embedded Emotional Moral Education Mode in college foreign language classroom. J. Beihua Univ. (Soc. Sci. Ed.) **14**(04), 144–147 (2013)
7. Yanfei, Z., Shunde, Z., Weiqing, Q.: Research on software engineering curriculum system based on CDIO model. Comput. Knowl. Technol. **9**(10), 2415–2417 + 2422 (2013)
8. Kunxue, X., Fengjuan, L., Yuanlian, S.: A new exploration of foreign language teacher education in the context of curriculum standards for Teacher Education – a summary of the 2012 National Joint Conference of Presidents (directors) of foreign language colleges (departments) of normal universities. Contemporary Foreign Lang. Stud. **02**, 66–68 (2013)
9. Yuxia, L.: Practice of "discussion teaching method" for Foreign Language Majors Based on text dialogue humanistic education model. J. Heilongjiang Inst. Educ. **32**(01), 166–167 (2013)

10. Liumei, S., Yanhong, L.: On the necessity of general education mode of basic English for English majors. Xueweekly (33), 5 (2012)
11. Xuefang, W., Huajie, L.: Using CBE to promote the reform of adult foreign language education model. Vicissitudes (05), 148–149 + 152 (2012)
12. Yan, L., Pai, C.: Analysis of "second classroom" education mode in foreign language colleges. Chongqing World (Acad. Ed.) **29**(09), 75–78 (2012)
13. Bin, L.: On the reconstruction of foreign language curriculum system in art colleges. J. Jilin Inst. Educ. (Last Ten Days) **28**(09), 22–24 (2012)
14. Xiaojing, H.: Reflective practical teacher education model and Its Enlightenment on pre service foreign language teacher education. Educ. Career **26**, 80–82 (2012)
15. Cuiping, M.: Chinese and western general education model and Its Enlightenment on English Teaching. Teach. Manage. **24**, 101–102 (2012)
16. Jianfeng, L., Jia, L., Xiaolin, Z.: Hierarchical analysis of post-90s college students' group characteristics and innovative ideological and political education model. Foreign Lang. **28**(S1), 219–224 (2012)
17. Enzhi, Z.:. Exploration and practice of foreign language compound talents training mode in application oriented universities. J. Jiamusi Inst. Educ. (04), 303 + 305 (2012)
18. Haiyun, J.: On the foreign language education model of Japanese Secondary Education. Health Vocat. Educ. **30**(07), 30–31 (2012)
19. Kai, Y., Jianhua, L.: On Graduate English Teaching under CDIO education mode from Bachman's perspective. J. Hebei Univ. Technol. (Soc. Sci. Ed.) **29**(01), 110–112 (2012)
20. Jing, W., Fuli, L.: Between affective view and methodology: an exploration of the education mode of Crazy English. Crazy English (Teacher Ed.) (04), 53–56 + 199–200 (2011)
21. Hongmei, L., Qinyan, Y.: Research on immersion foreign language teaching mode in primary schools in western minority areas. Sci. Technol. Western China **10**(32), 78–79 + 86 (2011)
22. Libin, F., Chunxia, W.: Establishment of Tsinghua School and its foreign language education model. Lantai World **20**, 47–48 (2011)
23. Zhiwei, L.: Discussion on the "talent" education mode of Foreign Languages University. J. Chifeng Univ. (Sci. Educ. Ed.) **3**(04), 25–26 (2011)
24. Kang, L.: Talking about both sides of learning and teaching in English classroom teaching under "student based education." Sci. Educ. Wenhui (Zhongxunjiao) **07**, 106–107 (2011)

Response System Design of College Students' Education Management with Data Analysis

Qing Li[✉]

Baoshan College, Yunnan Province, Baoshan City 678000, China

Abstract. The research on the design of the response system of College Students' Education Management Based on data analysis has brought impact and pressure. How to actively deal with the negative impact of education management is an urgent task of College Students' education and management. From their own point of view, colleges and universities should establish and improve the service mechanism, democratic participation mechanism, information disclosure mechanism and rapid response mechanism, and actively deal with the adverse effects of student management.

Keywords: Data analysis · University · Student education management · Coping mechanism

1 Introduction

Management system is a complete organization management system composed of various management institutions, management systems, management processes and management methods with specific management functions and internal relations for the management objects to achieve the organizational objectives. In an enterprise, the total system can be divided into planned operation, production technology, labor and personnel, financial costs and life services. There are differences and connections between them. The objective of subsystem should be subject to the general goal of enterprise management system. The functions of each subsystem are not listed in parallel, among which one subsystem plays a leading role in achieving the overall goal. If we consider enterprise management as a system, we can adopt the method of systematic analysis, comprehensively study the professional management of the enterprise, combine the internal conditions of production and operation activities with external environment, quantitative analysis and qualitative analysis organically, and choose the best scheme to improve economic benefits and promote production development. A good management system is shown in Fig. 1.

2 Research on Theory and Technology of Genetic Algorithm

The research of genetic algorithm mainly includes three fields: the theory and technology of genetic algorithm; optimization with genetic algorithm; machine learning of classification system with genetic algorithm. The theoretical and technical research of genetic algorithm mainly includes coding, crossover, mutation, selection and fitness evaluation.

© ICST Institute for Computer Sciences, Social Informatics and Telecommunications Engineering 2021
Published by Springer Nature Switzerland AG 2021. All Rights Reserved
M. A. Jan and F. Khan (Eds.): BigIoT-EDU 2021, LNICST 391, pp. 202–210, 2021.
https://doi.org/10.1007/978-3-030-87900-6_25

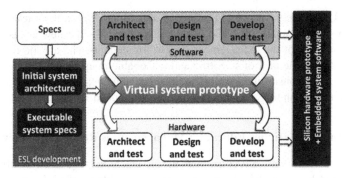

Fig. 1. Basic framework of management system

In many problems solving, coding is the most important problem in genetic algorithm, which has a very important impact on the performance of the algorithm.

1) Binary coding Holland first put forward the most commonly used coding method in genetic algorithm [1]. It adopts the principle of minimum character encoding, which is characterized by simple and easy operation of encoding/decoding, which is conducive to the realization of crossover and mutation operations. It can also use pattern theorem to analyze the algorithm theoretically. However, when binary coding is used in the optimization of multi-dimensional and high-precision numerical problems, it cannot overcome the mapping error of discretization of continuous functions, and cannot directly reflect the inherent structure of the problem, with low precision, large individual length and large memory consumption.

2) Gray code coding in order to overcome the shortcomings of binary code in discretization of continuous function, people put forward the method of coding with gray code, which is a variant of binary code. Suppose there is a binary code $X = x_m x_{m1} \ldots x_2 x_1$, If the gray code of $Y = y_m y_{m1} \ldots y_2 y_1$, then

$$\begin{cases} y_m = x_m \\ y_i = x_i + 1 \oplus x_i \end{cases} i = m-1, m-2, \ldots, 2, 1 \tag{1}$$

The methods of mutation were as follows:

$$v_{zt} = \begin{cases} v_{zt} + (v_{zt} - v_{max})h(g) \\ v_{zt} + (v_{min} - v_{zt})h(g) \end{cases} \tag{2}$$

$$h(g) = r_0(1 - g/G_{max}) \tag{3}$$

3 The Present Situation of Educational Management in Colleges and Universities

3.1 The Management System of Higher Education is not Perfect

The important guarantee to improve the level of educational management in Colleges and universities is the good management system that most colleges and universities have established. Under the influence of traditional education concept, the relevant management system which cannot meet the development needs of the new era is still in its infancy. The reform of the management system for students who are too rigid and too strict is very slow. The lack of scientific and reasonable management system to stimulate the sense of responsibility and work enthusiasm of university teachers leads to slack work, which is not conducive to the development of education.

3.2   The Content of Higher Education Management is Relatively Backward

As far as the present situation is concerned, the old teaching mode and inflexible method of education in China, which is affected by the backward ideas before, has not considered the students' ideas and teachers' interests in the traditional education management mode and education mode, which has brought certain obstacles to the education management of colleges and Universities, Even under the influence of backward ideas, it wastes a lot of teaching resources under the management system of higher education, which leads to a great reduction in the efficiency of China's higher education management in practice. Because of the traditional teaching concept still deeply existing in people's heart, the education management of colleges and universities hinders the overall development of colleges and universities.

3.3   The Management Mode of Higher Education is Too Monotonous

At present, with the decrease of elective courses and the increase of cultural courses in Colleges and universities, many education methods are still outdated. Many colleges and universities adopt the credit system which cannot unify new knowledge and new information. The implementation of the credit system which lacks the concept of people-oriented leads to the serious phenomenon of fewer subjects in most colleges and universities in China, And at present, the educational management means which cannot reflect the students' situation in our country is too simple. The overall quality of high students affects the development of students to a certain extent [2]. At the same time, it cannot improve the education management of colleges and universities in the next step, and cannot guarantee its scientificity and rationality in the development of education management.

4   The Importance of Reforming and Innovating the Educational Management System in Colleges and Universities

4.1   Conducive to Social Development

With the rapid development of social economy and the reform of education management system, the future promotes the sustainable development of society [3, 4]. In order to improve the overall quality of the society and prevent any bad atmosphere from damaging the rapid development of China, colleges and universities have trained more talents representing China's hope and future, and have the courage to innovate, To provide the society with a continuous stream of talents who undertake this arduous task. The young strong are the strong in China. In the era of fierce war, countless patriots and talents were trained by colleges and Universities under extremely difficult circumstances. With the power of these people, now there is China. Nowadays, with the development of international competition, there is an urgent need for innovative talents [5, 6].

4.2 It is Conducive to the Development of Education

Under the influence of the old management system with many drawbacks, the reform and innovation of the education management system is stagnant, which cannot give full play to the role that colleges and universities should play in personnel training. The most important task of colleges and universities is to train people. The education management system has no way to deal with the current unbalanced development of college students, which restricts the development of society. In order to promote the development of education in the new situation, we can start from a more fundamental point of view, develop student development plans with students as the main body, so as to cultivate more high-level talents to meet the social needs (see Fig. 2).

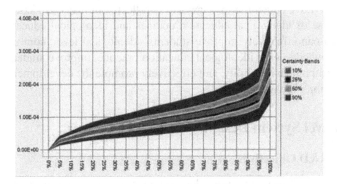

Fig. 2. Effect simulation of manager system

5 The Innovation Strategy of University Education Management Mechanism

5.1 Changing the Concept of Education

In the new situation of classroom teaching, teachers should give full play to students' subjective initiative, actively interact with students, strengthen communication with students according to different students' learning conditions, and formulate teaching programs and reasonable teaching plans suitable for most students' learning conditions [7].

5.2 Innovation Evaluation System

Teachers should have a complete student evaluation system based not only on their academic achievements but also on their social behaviors, not only in their daily work but also in students' feedback to teachers. The evaluation of students should not only pay attention to their daily behaviors, but also their communication and cooperation with teachers, and explore their interest and potential. Through the evaluation of students, we can better understand the students. Teachers should also have a complete evaluation system based on the students trained by teachers. In order to strengthen the supervision of students, improve the competitiveness of teachers and promote the development of colleges and universities, the evaluation of teachers should be carried out from the aspects of students' examination, daily life, participation in competitions and sports activities [8].

5.3 Innovating the Content of Education Management

In order to promote the effective implementation of university education management, under the condition of educational management mode innovation, the content of university education management should fully consider the development needs of students, meet the needs of talent training and the development needs of the information age, so as to effectively promote the rationality and scientificity of higher education [9]. The content of innovative education management is reflected in many aspects, such as reasonable increase of ideological education courses and ideological education practice courses which can effectively improve students' ideological level, combine students' theoretical knowledge with ideological education practice, improve students' personal quality and comprehensive ability, and effectively promote the development of China's Higher Education Management [10].

6 High-Level System Design

6.1 System R&D Objectives

The expected goal of the system is to take the adult education teaching activities of Civil Engineering College of Jiaying University as the center, take the students as the link, realize the whole process management of educational administration, teaching, assessment and graduation, strengthen the comprehensive inquiry and analysis function through information means, free the educational administration staff from the heavy offline labor, devote themselves to teaching activities, and improve the quality of education [11].

6.2 System Architecture Design Principles

According to the business needs of student information management system, the system architecture design realizes unified architecture technology system, unified business control processing system, unified system maintenance, backup and development management system. The system architecture design follows the principles of data stratification, low coupling, scalability, practicability, reliability, practicability and security [12].

1. Principle of data layered design: the data of the system includes system rules and business application data, which should be classified and stored in different data layers during design. 2. Low coupling layered design principle: in the system architecture

design, under the condition of meeting the system requirements, the low coupling of system design can be achieved by adopting the component design of each functional module, which creates convenient conditions for team members to develop independently and work together, and can greatly provide development efficiency, The whole system will not stagnate due to local obstacles, which greatly reduces the project risk [13]. 3. Expansibility principle: the system must have good expansibility to meet the more requirements of system functions brought by the expansion of business. We can follow the business component modular design principle, factory design pattern to design functional components and add new business processing components to achieve the scalability of the system. 4. Practicality principle: no matter how complex the system logic is, it must be simple and easy to use for users, and try to follow the user's operating habits and business processes. 5. Reliability principle: the system should be reliable, and the application system should be able to describe the abnormal error report in detail, so that the administrator can deal with the problem in time. At the same time, the system should have high fault tolerance ability to meet the robustness requirements of the system [14].

6.3 Application System Structure

Student information management system is a three-tier application software system based on J2EE industrial standard enterprise level distributed technology architecture. The system is developed with Java language. By making full use of the cross platform, extensibility, security and stability, reliable technical functions and features of Java language, the system also realizes a large number of integrated application interfaces, It not only makes the system have strong technical advantages, but also greatly improves the flexibility and expansibility of the system [15].

The system adopts browser/service (B/S) architecture. This architecture greatly reduces the workload of system development and maintenance, and also reduces the difficulty of users. The whole system is divided into three layers of web structure, that is, the system access structure is logically divided into three layers: presentation layer, application service layer (business logic) and data layer. The presentation layer enables users to understand and efficiently locate application services through the implementation of the graphical interface of application services. The application layer between the display layer and the data layer not only encapsulates the application model associated with the system, but also provides the connection between the client application and the data service, thus providing a clear level for the realization of the business logic of the college, and separating the user presentation layer from the database code. At the same time, the application layer also implements the application strategy and encapsulates the application pattern, And present the encapsulated pattern to the client application. The application system structure is shown in Fig. 3.

7 System Detailed Design

Detailed design is the key to realize the functions of the system. It gives the diagram of the software structure of the student information management system, describes each

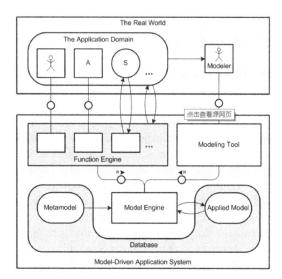

Fig. 3. Application system structure

function module in detail, including algorithm and logic, and is the basis of the implementation and test of the student information management system. The detailed design of the system directly affects the smooth level of the development progress of the system. An excellent detailed design can reduce the occurrence of development iteration and reduce the development time and reduce the development cost; at the same time, the detailed design also gives the development testers a common standard, which is convenient for the development and test of the detailed design of the student information management system from the teaching management needs of the college, The main functions of student management, course selection management and examination management are described [16].

The student management module mainly includes student basic information management, payment rules setting, student status management, inquiry statistics management and other sub functions. Students' basic information management realizes the management of students' basic situation, which is basically static and serves as the basis of College Students' management. At the same time, it can also be updated with the occurrence of some events, such as the adjustment of students' majors, so the professional attributes can be updated. The setting of payment rules realizes the setting and management function of students' payment rules, which serves as the basis for students to collect fees from enrollment to graduation. Student status management mainly realizes the functions of student status change management, specialty transfer management and student status information audit. When a student's status changes, such as graduation or withdrawal, such information will be recorded and saved. Inquiry statistics is mainly to realize the student-centered, comprehensive query of students' various information, and statistical analysis by category. Server security refers to the server security reinforcement and configuration with the operating system as the core. It is the most basic requirement of server security. Doing well in server security, ensuring the stable operation of the server, enhancing the anti attack ability, and configuring the audit function are the necessary measures for security forensics [17].

8 Database Design

Database design is the basis of the realization of student information management system. The quality of database design determines the success or failure of the realization of student information management. Therefore, in the process of database design, designers should make full use of the principles, standards and norms of database design in order to achieve good design results. Database design is the core work in the development and construction of information system. Through database design, the physical design model of database can be obtained. In the process of database design, not only to support the excellent performance of related programs, but also due to the complexity of the database application system itself, these factors lead to the database design has become a very complex work. Since the database design has the characteristics of great difficulty and long time, it is impossible to get the best design results overnight. Designers can only get better and better design results in the process of planning and structuring the data objects in the database and the relationship between these data objects. Database design includes conceptual structure design stage, logical structure design stage and physical structure design stage.

9 Conclusion

The innovation and development of education mode and teaching quality, since the reform and opening up of new China, has been under the background of the integration of education mode. In order to better develop and cultivate high-quality talents and cultivate better talents for the society, higher education management has to adhere to the road of innovation. As an important part of China's colleges and universities, it has an urgent demand for the standardization, standardization and informatization of teaching management, which is not only the need of its own management, but also the need of many students. Based on the in-depth discussion of the urgent need of adult education of civil engineering in Jiaying University Based on teaching management information, according to the theory of software engineering, this paper analyzes and designs the student information management system, including the system requirements analysis, the main technology of application, the system outline design, the detailed design of the main functions of the system, and the database design. The design goal of this system is to realize the informatization and intellectualization of student management, teaching management and educational administration management, and improve the level of adult education management.

References

1. Xue, X.: Research on coping mechanism of College Students' Education Management under the new media environment. Ind. Innov. Res. **20**, 185–186 (2020)

2. Wei, W.: On the coping mechanism of College Students' Education Management under the new media environment. Int. Public Relat. **06**, 35–37 (2020)
3. Jiang, L.: Analysis on the transformation of College Students' education management mode in the era of big data and Discussion on coping strategies. Ind. Sci. Technol. Innov. **2**(03), 95–96 (2020)
4. Qingbiao, X., Jun, L.: Research on the education and management mechanism of college student party members in the new era — from the perspective of "thinking, speaking and doing". Youth (09), 200 + 199 (2019)
5. Yichun, Z., Yuxi, W.: The current situation of information teaching ability of higher vocational teachers and Its Improvement Countermeasures – Based on the survey of 74 Higher Vocational Colleges in Jiangsu Province. Vocat. Techn. Educ. **36**(36), 70–75 (2015)
6. Yun, P.: The development of adult education under the concept of Lifelong Education. Sci. Educ. Wenhui. **3**, 102–103 (2017)
7. Yun, T.: Research on the deep integration of entrepreneurship education and lifelong education. Chizi. **3**, 108–109 (2017)
8. Nanguonong: New stage and new mission of China's education informatization development. Audio Visual Educ. Res. (12), 10–12 (2011)
9. Youju, Q., Xuesong, Y., Yi, L.: Construction of lifelong education system under the environment of modern information technology. J. Dist. Educ. **28**(05), 79–83 (2010)
10. Ding Shaoliang, X., et al.: Construction and practice of multimedia network teaching mode in Higher Vocational Education. J. Jiangxi Police Coll. **01**, 125–212 (2008)
11. Xiaohua, L.: UML Foundation and VI isio Modeling. Electronic Industry Press, Beijing (2004)
12. Ning, W.X., Ping, W.X.: JSP General Module and Typical System Development Example Navigation. People's Posts and Telecommunications Press, Beijing (2006)
13. Peixin, Q., et al.: Essence of Java Project Development Case. Electronic Industry Press, Beijing (2010)
14. [American] Brown, S., et al.: JSP Programming Guide, 3rd edn. Electronic Industry Press, Beijing (2004)
15. Yuhui, F.: SL Basic Course. People's Posts and Telecommunications Publishing House, Beijing (2009)
16. Chun, S.K.: Selected Examples of JSP Information System Development. China Machine Press, Beijing (2006)
17. Jin, L.: Research and Development of Integrated Educational Administration System for Adult Education. Shandong University of science and technology, Qingdao (2005)

Strategy Exploration of Educational Administration in Colleges and Universities from the Perspective of Information Construction

Yiping Zhang[✉]

YunNan Economics Trade and Foreign Affairs College, Beijing 6501114, China
linlv543@sina.com

Abstract. Since the 21st century, the application of information technology in various industries has gradually deepened, and the importance of information technology in the administration of colleges and universities has gradually become prominent. As an important symbol of modern education reform, informatization has become a booster to improve teaching quality. Schools rely on information technology to realize the information construction of administrative work. From the perspective of information construction, this paper speeds up the process of administrative education reform in colleges and universities by renewing ideas, increasing financial support and building information platform.

Keywords: University education · Administration · Information construction

1 Introduction

In fact, information management is the application of scientific theory and management concept, combined with advanced information technology to deal with information resources, so that the management work towards the direction of institutionalization. Give full play to the technical advantages of information technology, establish information exchange and transmission platform for university administration, construct university administration platform, integrate financial management, scientific research management, personnel management and other data, establish database, and realize the information construction of administrative education management.

2 Analysis on the Necessity of Information Construction of University Administration

2.1 Modern Education Can not Be Separated from Information Technology Support

In fact, educational informatization is to use information technology in the field of education, to realize the effective integration of technology and educational work, and to

M. A. Jan and F. Khan (Eds.): BigIoT-EDU 2021, LNICST 391, pp. 211–215, 2021.
https://doi.org/10.1007/978-3-030-87900-6_26

promote the innovation of educational concept and the transformation of teaching mode. Online education and wisdom education are the common achievements of information teaching reform and play a vital role in teaching practice. In this field, the state put forward the integration of information construction into school administration, which is the only way to realize the modernization of education.

2.2 Informatization is the Driving Force to Realize Educational Mission

The goal of school education is to train advanced talents who meet the needs of social development and make them better serve the society. Under the background of information age, in order to complete the mission of human education, it is necessary to speed up the pace of information construction, apply information technology to carry out modern management work, and innovate the administrative management mode. At present, the competitiveness of colleges and universities is mainly reflected in the work of information management, and information has gradually become an important embodiment of the modernization of school administration.

2.3 Information Management is a Necessary Means to Realize Modern Management in Colleges and Universities

When the school administration work enters the modernization, the school only then formally has the modernization management pattern. In the past, schools did not improve the intelligent level of administration in the process of information construction, and school administrators and staff generally lack understanding of information management. The establishment of school website is regarded as the standard of information construction, but the evaluation of its application effect is ignored. Therefore, many people say that the cost of information construction is too high but not much, even administrators regard these contents as a kind of work burden and do not want to participate in it.

In the face of this situation, schools must realize that information management is a necessary means to realize modern administration, which is the key to improve the competitive strength of schools. First of all, to realize the modernization of management, the application of information management system for information collection, collation, analysis and transmission, to achieve the automation of administrative office, so that administrators can obtain information in time. Secondly, it realizes the intelligence of information processing, uses the information technology means to collect the school management information by using the campus network, and realizes the school financial management, teaching management and so on by establishing the database. Thirdly, to realize the standardization of documents and materials, the informatization of university administration has changed the working mode of manual records in the past and reduced the probability of mistakes. Finally, the real-time sharing of teaching management resources is realized. Under the influence of the network environment, the information resources are used efficiently, and people can communicate more conveniently. For example, in the aspect of subject setting or administrative function division, the resources are transmitted by the network. To realize resource sharing and improve administrative efficiency [1].

3 Strategy Analysis of Educational Administration in Colleges and Universities from the Perspective of Information Construction

3.1 Renewal of the Concept of Administration and Progressive Realization of Information Management

According to the above information, some school leaders and teachers have prejudice to the information construction at present, and think that there is little connection between the administrative management work and the information construction, so it is good to follow the previous work mode and need not be improved. In the school organization, the administrative department undertakes the important management and the service function, this is the school carries out the teaching and the scientific research work safeguard, relates to the talented person training effect in order to satisfy the school administration mechanism reform request, the university administration department innovates the management service pattern, introduces the information management idea, creates the green, the wisdom management service idea, creates the administration management new situation. In order to promote the development of information management in colleges and universities, we should first set up the concept of modern management and guide teachers to establish the concept of information administration. The school administration system is not a single technical system, but needs to make comprehensive consideration to the personnel, the management system and the teaching resources. The information construction should be managed by the school leaders as a whole, pay attention to the development process of the school informatization, plan and design the system as a whole. The school should set up the information management group, establish the coordination mechanism of the information construction, unify the planning content, clarify the responsibility of each department, and carry out the post responsibility.

3.2 Increased Financial Support to Create Software and Hardware Conditions for Modern Management

The construction of administrative information system needs to invest funds, do budget work in advance, and use special funds. In general, the purchase of school hardware equipment is a one-time investment, in the budget should be added to the cost of software and other auxiliary equipment, schools can combine their own economic conditions to promote the development of hardware and software equipment information, Overall planning for information projects, gradually improve school infrastructure construction. Moreover, with the development of information technology, government functional departments and educational units should give school support in policy, especially in terms of financial funds, and distribute funds to schools for campus network infrastructure and network maintenance. Table 1 shows the cost of the construction of an administrative information center in a school in recent years. Through the value of the data, the school has increased its investment in the information media in the administrative reform according to the needs of social development. Popularize new media equipment and play the role of information technology in school administration [2].

Table 1. Details of the construction cost of a university information center

	2018	2019	2020
Information centre fund building	$650,000	$0.7 million	$0.8 million
Information centre technical staff training funds	$70,000	$87,000	$92,000
Network maintenance funds	$150,000	$170,000	$210,000

3.3 Establish a Complete Database System and Optimize the Administrative Information Platform

In the construction of information administration platform in colleges and universities, we should make reasonable management plan according to the actual situation, and follow the principles of "overall planning" and "hierarchical implementation" to promote all kinds of work. Schools should effectively develop existing resources, improve the efficiency of resource utilization, maintain the existing management system in time, establish a complete database system, and realize the sharing of resources among departments and disciplines in the system. In order to ensure the true, accurate and rapid transmission of information, the construction of public database breaks the time and space limit of information transmission, establishes the information database in the whole school, and emphasizes the effectiveness of information transmission.

At the same time, we should consider the influencing factors of administrative work, introduce advanced information technology in combination with the direction and goal of school administration, and scientifically construct an integrated administrative management platform. Improve the level of school administration information. Information construction is a systematic and complex work, involving more content, schools should stand on the basis of overall planning to formulate information platform construction process, with the help of big data and cloud computing to establish information administration system, Develop a teaching administration system that integrates teaching and research, personnel and financial management. The system is divided into three parts: supervision and management module, risk evaluation module and data analysis module. By setting up module index system, resource sharing database and administrative database are established, each database is coordinated and unified in the platform. And under the interaction of hardware and software facilities to improve the integration of school administration. In order to avoid the phenomenon of isolated information island, it is necessary to link administration with other daily work and apply information data reasonably based on multi-level business cooperation so that school managers can understand the current situation of administration. In order to better play the role of university administration, we should optimize the means of information management. In order to protect the safe operation of the administrative information platform, we should use firewall technology and identity authentication technology in time, increase the security control of the platform, upgrade the platform regularly, and improve the comprehensive ability of school administration with the help of all people in data mining and analysis [3].

Summary: to sum up, the school wants to deepen the administrative work from the theory and practice, and on the basis of innovating the administrative thinking, it should start from three aspects: management idea, equipment and facilities, system platform, and integrate information into it. By using big data and Internet technology, we can update the concept of administration in time, realize information management step by step, create software and hardware conditions for modern management by increasing financial support, and establish complete database system by relying on information technology. Optimize the administrative information platform, improve the efficiency of school administration, education and talent training.

References

1. Wang, J.: Discussion on the construction of university administration information under the background of "Internet+." Res. Practice Innov. Entrepreneurship Theory 3(15), 154–155 (2020)
2. Lucoshio: Exploration and design of personnel management system in colleges and universities. Inform. Comput. (Theor. Ed.) 32(14), 89–91 (2020)
3. Zhu, M.: Discussion on the strategy of administration management in colleges and universities from the perspective of. Construct. Econ. Manag. Abstracts 21, 70–71 (2019)

The Algorithm and Implementation of College English Teaching Comprehensive Ability Evaluation System

Yanxia Li and Xinchun Wang[✉]

School of Aviation and Tourism Management, Chongqing Aerospace Polytechnic College, Chongqing 400020, China

Abstract. The evaluation system of English teaching comprehensive ability can complete the evaluation and ranking of College English teaching comprehensive ability. By using the attribute method, seven attribute indexes are obtained. The example shows that the structure of the system is clear and the process is simple. It can flexibly adjust the evaluation parameters such as the school scheme set model and relevant psychological weight according to the user's requirements. It can compare the overall teaching quality of different grades or the same grade universities after considering various influencing factors (internal factors and external factors) according to the characteristics of the school, and objectively reflect the overall teaching level of the school.

Keywords: English teaching · Evaluation · Attribute theory

1 Introduction

It is a misunderstanding that the passing rate of the examination is used as the basis for evaluating the overall teaching quality of a school. The results of this one-sided approach are as follows: (1) from the perspective of the administrative department of teaching, ranking each school according to the simple passing rate is very easy to cause schools to compete with each other and form an inappropriate invisible pressure. In fact, each school has different conditions and different sources of students, there is no basis for simple comparison (2) from the perspective of school. In order to improve the passing rate, we should link the passing rate of CET-4 and CET-6 with the degree and Diploma of the students. In some places, we only want to pass but not improve. This is against the law of English teaching, It is easy to frustrate the enthusiasm of teachers and students. Besides, the passing rate of the examination can only reflect how many students have reached the passing line of CET-4 or CET-6, but not at what level these students have reached the corresponding requirements of the syllabus. (3) From the perspective of students, the purpose is to obtain a certificate, not to improve their practical ability to use English [1]. In order to scientifically reflect the overall teaching level of a school, the author has developed such an English teaching comprehensive ability evaluation system to more accurately describe the actual situation of students.

© ICST Institute for Computer Sciences, Social Informatics and Telecommunications Engineering 2021
Published by Springer Nature Switzerland AG 2021. All Rights Reserved
M. A. Jan and F. Khan (Eds.): BigIoT-EDU 2021, LNICST 391, pp. 216–224, 2021.
https://doi.org/10.1007/978-3-030-87900-6_27

2 Attribute Analysis of Evaluation System

2.1 Basic Introduction

The English comprehensives IV e evaluating system (ECE) is a complex large-scale system involving various factors or attributes, and there are various complicated causal relationships among the factors. Therefore, the ECE is a complex system, a series of theories and methods of systematic analysis and decision-making have emerged. Accordingly, all kinds of decision-making and evaluation have gradually moved from the past empirical decision-making to the stage of scientific decision-making and intelligent decision-making with the help of computer tools. Therefore, scientific decision-making theory and the most advanced decision-making aids must be used as much as possible in the evaluation of English teaching comprehensive ability. It makes the assessment of English teaching comprehensive ability go on the road of scientization and modernization.

2.2 The Function of Comprehensive Ability Assessment in English Teaching

The function of the English teaching comprehensive ability evaluation system is to compare the situation of English Teaching in several schools after considering the internal and external factors of various English learning, regardless of the grade of the school, and compare the overall quality of learning in different grades and the same grade universities, which can more accurately reflect the overall level of the school and help the school to reduce costs, So that the teaching level has been improved.

Through the analysis, it is necessary to extract the attribute features of teaching quality evaluation among schools. Therefore, the evaluation system of comprehensive ability of English teaching has the following attributes: internal cause, external cause and capital investment, specifically speaking, the learner's personal factors, environmental factors and the cost paid.

3 Personal Factors

Learners' personal factors include intelligence, personality, motivation and attitude. The ability to grasp and use various learning skills in general, the learners with good intelligence learn faster, and the learners with low intelligence can not produce miracles in learning even under the best learning conditions, In personality psychology, personality can be divided into "extrovert" and "introvert". People once tended to think that extrovert learners, because of their lively personality, dare to speak in the process of learning, have more opportunities to practice English, and their performance will be better than introvert learners. But this is not the case. Learners with different personalities use different learning strategies to deal with different learning tasks. For learners with extroversive personalities, their good talk is conducive to obtaining more opportunities for input and practice. However, they often do not pay much attention to language forms. Introverted learners may be better at making use of their redundant and quiet personality to make a more in-depth and detailed formal analysis of limited input, especially in the teaching environment that pays attention to language forms and language rules [2]. Personality factor refers to whether the school adopts different English education for different personalities.

4 The Application of Attribute Theory

4.1 The Indicators of Each School Will Be Converted into Sex Scores

In order to express clearly, three factors (attributes) are taken for analysis. For example, considering only three important factors of investment, intelligence training and learning environment, three schools are set up to compare the quality of English teaching. The investment of school a is 800000, that of School B is 400000, that of school C is 600000, that of school a is 0, and that of School B is 100, The score of school C is calculated as: $(100 - 0)/(40 - 80) = (y - 0)/(60 - 80)$, $y = 50$, which can transform the attribute of capital input of the above three schools into a hundred point system. Similarly, school a attaches great importance to the intelligence training of the three schools, ranking first among them, school a gives 100 points, school C pays the least attention to the cultivation of cohesion, school C gives 0 points, and school B can score by experts, Compared with school a and school C, the score of intelligence factor is the same. The school with good learning environment has higher score, while the school with poor learning environment has higher score.

4.2 Applied to Horizontal Type of Gravity Center

First of all, each school should be graded, and then they should be divided into several grades. In this way, we can compare the same grade. There are two methods for grading. One step archiving method is to directly grade the school into the grading grade of the comprehensive ability system of English teaching. Experts are invited to grade the seven English Teaching Indicators of the schools participating in the evaluation, or conduct online survey, The students of the evaluation school are asked to score their own school on seven indicators, and then, according to the level of scoring, 5 points or 10 points are divided into one grade, Secondly, the two-step filing method first classifies the evaluation schools according to the scoring and ranking of some authoritative institutions (for example, the famous website of China Netcom University ranks all the schools, and the top 200 can be classified as category 1, the $200 - 400$ as category 2, and the $400 - 60$ as Category 3). Using the close degree formula of spatial distance and human brain cognition in attribute theory, the satisfaction degree of a certain school grade is set as:

$$C_s(X) = \exp(-(\sum_{i=1}^{n} w_i|x_i - y_i|)) \tag{1}$$

In order to compare the schools in different grades, a regulation coefficient λ is used in front of the grade satisfaction function:

$$C_t(X) = \lambda C_s(X) \tag{2}$$

Where: $C_s(X)$ is the grade satisfaction degree of school $\lambda C_s(X)$ is related to the total score of school attribute of school x, and selects an entry:

$$\lambda = (\sum x_i)^{\alpha}, a > 0 \tag{3}$$

5   System Flow and Result Simulation Analysis

The experimental data are evaluated by 200 universities. Considering the seven attributes of universities, the lowest score is 520, and the highest score is 700, There are 30 grades, 6 grades, and one grade is 610 (the 15th grade, $520 + 15 \times 6 = 610$), including 12 schools with total scores from 605 to 610. Their attribute scores. The psychological standard point of this grade is (854259389681013868668761 9, 83.750.91.898) [3]. It can be seen from table 1 that the closer to the standard score point, the greater the grade satisfaction of the school, and the greater its space satisfaction, Such as school 46, school 147, the system flow is shown in Fig. 1.

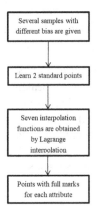

Fig. 1. Flow chart of English teaching comprehensive ability evaluation system

For this system, we mainly look at the evaluation effect from the error rate. Two different controllers are used, one is synovial controller, the other is mechanism controller. The simulation results are shown in Fig. 2. From Fig. 2, we can see that with the blessing of the two controllers, the error rate is reduced, which also verifies the effectiveness of the algorithm [4].

6   Research Design

The aim of the present research is to check whether the task-based approach is effective in improving students speaking ability in Integrated Skills of English Course to English major A semi-experiment is designed, with an experimental group and a control group, pre-test and post-test on speaking performance, a questionnaire and informal interviews to collect data. In this chapter, the research aim, subjects, materials and procedures will be reported [5].

6.1   Research Aim

The present research is intended to check the effects of the task-based teaching in improving students speaking ability in Integrated Skills of English Course to English majors

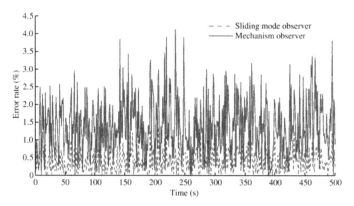

Fig. 2. Simulation results for estimate effect

[6]. To be concrete, the researcher hopes to find the effectiveness of the task-based app-roach on the improvement of the students' speaking ability as well as their motivation. It is hypothesized that task-based teaching through communicative tasks can function positively in speaking training to English majors and their motivation [7]. The general research questions are 1. Will the teaching through tasks in Integrated Skills of English Course lead to the improvement of the students speaking ability? 2. Will the teaching though tasks have positive effect on the students motivation?

6.2 Subjects

Students participating in this research are72 freshmen of English majors enrolled in two classes in Foreign Language College in Beihua University. They were probably at different level of English proficiency as a whole, however they may have attained similar level of speaking competence, since the condition of speaking teaching at secondary schools is generally discouraging. In addition, they have been trained in the college by the researcher for one temn. Therefore the students in the two classes were believed to be at similar level of speaking proficiency, and this was proved by the pretest at the beginning of the research [8].

6.3 Instruments

In Beihua university, English Department of foreign Language College has Oral Test at the end of every term. The score of the Oral Test will be added to the final score of the Integrated Skills of English Course [9]. Every temm, the Oral Test will be conducted strictly. The scores of each student will be given by two teachers, then the average scores given by the two teacher swill be the final one. So we set the Oral Test at the end of the 1 temn of 2005–2006 as the pre-test, then the post-test will be the Oral test at the end of the 2 term of 2005–2006. The two tests were administered in this research in order to check the effect of task-based approach in teaching of speaking in the Integrated Skills of English Course to English majorsReliability of the tests was guaranteed since they were both administrated under the same circum stances and at the same time.

6.4 Procedure

The goals of the speaking training in the Integrated Skills of English Course are to improve the students' speaking ability and provide opportunities exercising initiative, leadership, and practicing organizational and participation skills in group situations [10].

TBLT carried out teaching through accomplishing tasks in class. If the tasks couldn't be accomplished, the teaching process would be hindered and the students' confidence and initiative would be decreased. Therefore, the difficulty of the task was a key factor. Besides, the students' available resource was limited. If the task is too difficult the students would focus on the accomplishment of the task and overly depend on communicative strategies and vocabulary, neglecting language forms, even not using target language. Then the accuracy and complexity couldn't be achieved. So the tasks should be designed at an appropriate level of difficulty to achieve balanced goal development. In general, the language skill that the students employed to accomplish the task was a little beyond their current stage of development. It would drive the students to develop and achieve success [11].

7   Refine Formative Assessment Indicators

The process evaluation includes many forms: Students' self-evaluation, students' mutual evaluation, teachers' evaluation of students, educational administration department's evaluation of students, etc. Process assessment has the characteristics of "subjectivity, process, diversity, development and openness". Therefore, the graded teaching evaluation of College English course should adopt a combination of various ways and means, increase the intensity of evaluation, refine and quantify the usual performance, increase the score items of classroom performance and group activity performance, duty report, effort degree and so on. At the beginning of each semester, teachers can publish the evaluation criteria and proportion, so that students can make clear their learning objectives. There must be a clear percentage of formative assessment and summative assessment. For example, formative assessment accounts for 50%, including daily written work (5%, 5 points), daily oral work (5%, 5 points), attendance (10%, 10 points), classroom performance (20%, 20 points), daily test (10%, 10 points), and summative assessment accounts for 50%. When evaluating various awards or scholarships, each department can refer to the students' overall evaluation results. At the end of each semester, a, B and C classes still take the form of standardized level closed book examination. The following formula can be used to calculate the total score of English: the total score (100 points system) = 5% of the usual written homework + 5% of the usual oral homework + 10% of the attendance + 20% of the classroom performance + 10% of the usual test + 50% of the final term [12].

7.1 Diversity of Classroom Evaluation Indicators

The indicators of classroom evaluation should be diversified, including academic achievement test and potential investigation [13]. The form should be diversified, including: written test, examination of knowledge and skills, comprehensive evaluation of

emotion, attitude, values, innovative consciousness, group coordination ability, organization ability, information extraction and processing ability, practical ability, etc. (1)
Discourse flow evaluation. The data of students' oral expression in class can be collected
and recorded periodically, including the time of discourse flow, the fluency of discourse,
the number of language defects, the clarity of thinking, etc. (2) Classroom participation. Classroom evaluation should also include students' interaction, initiative and the
actual effectiveness of their actions in the classroom. (3) Cognitive acceptance. In the
classroom, we can use various means to understand students' thinking process, master
students' understanding of teaching information, and students' ability to accept new language learning projects. (4) Responsiveness. Students' flexibility, creativity and adaptability to learning situations can also be examined in class. The diversity of classroom
evaluation indicators is shown in Fig. 3.

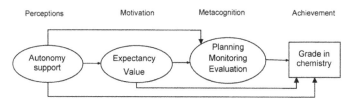

Fig. 3. Diversity of classroom evaluation indicators

7.2 Diversification of Evaluation Subjects

Classroom evaluation involves teachers and students. Teachers as the subject of evaluation, evaluation object can be divided into: (1) a teaching class. Teachers make immediate
evaluation on the overall performance, group advantages and disadvantages of a teaching
class. (2) Different groups at different levels [14]. Evaluate the actual performance of
different levels of class groups, and compare the classroom performance changes of each
group. (3) Study group. Sub activity or group activity is an important evaluation index of
classroom evaluation. Grouping should follow the principle of heterogeneity in the same
group and homogeneity between groups to conduct scientific and reasonable grouping,
and observe the activities of the group, the strength of organizational ability, information
communication, the process of completing tasks, the effect of solving problems, etc. (4)
Individuals. For each individual evaluation, it is necessary to collect and compare data
in the form of individual cases [15].

Give full play to students' subjectivity and regard students as the main body of
evaluation.

Students as the main body of classroom evaluation, is a more open evaluation model.
The evaluation object is the participant who completes the learning task with the evalu-
ator, which mainly includes: (1) students record their learning process, reflect on themselves regularly, and describe their learning behavior. (2) A member of a sub activity.
That is to say, the two people participating in the antithetical activities evaluate each
other. (3) Study group. That is, the evaluation of cooperation within the group.

To cultivate students' good cooperative evaluation behavior, we should guide students to manage group activities and implement group evaluation tasks independently in class. (4) There are three teaching classes as a whole. Students evaluate the group learning of the whole teaching class [16].

7.3 Rationalization of Evaluation Methods

In the hierarchical teaching mode, we should adopt the method of combining dynamic and static evaluation mechanism [17]. At present, the practice of most schools is the traditional, static horizontal evaluation, that is, the synchronic comparison between individual students, and the quantitative performance management within the teaching class. The commonly used evaluation methods are as follows: (1) test; (2) measurement of attitude and emotion in classroom teaching; (3) observation; (4) questionnaire and interview as the main form of investigation; (5) establishment of portfolio; (6) anecdotal record, that is, continuous and objective description of behavior in a certain time, place and environment.

This kind of horizontal comparison evaluation method pays too much attention to the results of individual learning activities and ignores the progress, change and effort of the evaluated. Therefore, in the hierarchical teaching, we should also comprehensively use dynamic and vertical evaluation, that is, on the premise of respecting individual differences, we should pay attention to the individual development process, and not only evaluate the results at the end of the student development process. Its evaluation object can be a single individual, a learning group, a teaching class or even the whole grade or school class. It emphasizes the collection and preservation of all the key information in the process of students' development, so as to help teachers form a correct and comprehensive understanding of students' learning process, development and change. It is an evaluation mechanism with incentive or guidance function for the evaluation object. It is a kind of evaluation method of individual difference, that is, based on the status of the evaluated object itself, according to the development of the evaluated individual, to make a vertical comparison, so as to judge its value.

8 Conclusions

The evaluation system of English teaching comprehensive ability is a comprehensive evaluation model with multiple indexes (factors and attributes). Its design is unique and novel. It takes into account the weight change of evaluation indicators (factors and attributes) and the mutual restriction and connection between evaluation indicators (factors and attributes). The comprehensive ability evaluation system of English teaching involves social environment factors, learning environment factors, natural environment factors, investment funds, intelligence training and personality education. There are a lot of uncertain and fuzzy factors in a multi-attribute decision-making question in many aspects, such as learning, motivation and attitude. The system discussed in this paper can complete the evaluation and ranking of English teaching comprehensive ability. The structure of the system is clear, the process is simple, and the evaluation parameters such as the scale of the school scheme set and the relevant psychological weight can be flexibly adjusted according to the requirements of users.

References

1. Guangdong Education Examination Center: Lecture notes on social psychology of Peking University. http://www.gd.edu.com/selfstudy/study/9study6.htm (11 March 2002)
2. Xie, X., Feng, J.: Attribute barycenter partition model in college entrance examination. J. Guilin Instit. Technol. **20**(3), 287–290 (2000)
3. Xie, X., Liu, J., Lu, Q.: Decision algorithm in college entrance examination. J. Guilin Instit. Technol. **21**(4), 402–406 (2001)
4. Wu, Q., et al.: Evaluation decision model based on attribute coordinate analysis and learning. J. Nanjing Univ. (Nat. Sci. Ed.) **6**, 183–188 (2003)
5. Yang, H.: Language Testing Research: Development, Evaluation and Research Guide. Foreign Language Teaching and Research Press, Beijing (2001)
6. Luo, S.: Research on Formative Assessment of English Classroom Teaching. Foreign Language Teaching and Research Press, Beijing (2003)
7. Hedge, T.: Teaching and Learning in the Language Classroom. Shanghai Foreign Language Education Press, Shanghai (2002)
8. Liu, R., Wu, Y.: Research on English Education in China. Foreign Language Teaching and Research Press, Beijing (2000)
9. Meng, C., Zhang, J.: The function of classroom assessment in English teaching. Sci. Tech. Inform. **35**, 444–445 (2007)
10. Wang, Z.: Exploration of graded teaching management mode and evaluation system in college English class of newly established universities. J. Hebei Energy Vocational Tech. College **4**, 76–78 (2012)
11. Li, B., Nie, J.: Summary of domestic formative assessment application research. J. Shanxi Agric. Univ.: Soc. Sci. Ed. (2010)
12. Li, L., Guo, Y.: A study on the promotion of formative assessment in college English listening teaching. J. Shanxi Radio TV Univ. (2011)
13. Chen, Y.: Evaluation of the effect of formative assessment in college English teaching. Chin. J. Out School Educ.: Subject Educ. (12) (2010)
14. Zhang, M., Zhang, R., Yuan, C.S.: Research on Formative Assessment Based on Network. Jiangxi Radio and TV University (2007)
15. Ma, L., et al.: The practice and application of formative assessment "open English I multimedia learning system". English News Mech. Electr. Univ. (3) (2005)
16. Wang, Y.: Investigation and reflection on the use of multimedia learning system in open English I. J. Nanjing Radio TV Univ. (2009)
17. Aijing, M., Xiaonan, Z.: The teaching mode and practice of contemporary college English [J]. Journal of Cangzhou Teachers College (3) (2005)

The Influence of Diversified Teaching Modes on College Students' Comprehensive English Ability Under the Background of Mobile Internet

Xiaotian Zhang[1], Wang Zhao[2], and Yan Tang[1(✉)]

[1] School of Western Languages, Harbin Normal University, Hain 150025, China
[2] Universiti Putra Malaysia, Kembangan, Malaysia
gs60525@student.upm.edu.my

Abstract. Technology has changed the mode of education and teaching. The mobile Internet model not only breaks the constraints of space and time, but also enables interaction and communication with famous teachers. This article analyzes the impact of diversified modes of teaching on college students' comprehensive English abilities in the context of mobile Internet from the three dimensions of student experience, comprehensive language skills and comprehensive language application capabilities, and explores the application value of mobile Internet in college English teaching.

Keywords: Mobile Internet · Diversified teaching mode · College students' comprehensive English ability

1 Introduction

The rapid development of modern information technology has caused tremendous changes in the world. It has changed the way people live, work and communicate, and affects the quality of education with its flexibility, convenience and effectiveness. The Internet provides learners with unprecedented learning opportunities. People can not only share learning resources, but also overcome the obstacles of time and space. All this brings new prospects for education and teaching. With the rapid development of network information technology, the concept of education has undergone tremendous changes. The goal of achieving rapid development of education in our country today is to promote the modernization of education with network information technology. For the foreign language teaching circle, the reform of information teaching has attracted more attention. The integration of information technology and courses is the dominant course learning method in the information age, and the integration of information technology and college English courses is an important way to promote the transformation of college English from traditional to modern teaching. As the country attaches great importance to education, it is particularly important to explore the impact of diversified teaching modes

M. A. Jan and F. Khan (Eds.): BigIoT-EDU 2021, LNICST 391, pp. 225–234, 2021.
https://doi.org/10.1007/978-3-030-87900-6_28

in colleges and universities on the comprehensive English ability of college students in the mobile Internet environment to promote the development and reform of education in our country.

2   Research Purpose and Significance

Research Purpose: As a brand-new teaching form, the diversified college English teaching under the background of mobile Internet surpasses the traditional college English classroom teaching form with its openness, individuality and richness. At the same time, it has brought about the impact of teaching concepts, learning methods, teaching modes, etc., and has put forward new challenges to the teaching ability of teachers, students' autonomous learning ability and the scientific nature of the teaching environment. The main goal of this research is to explore the impact of the use of mobile social networks, flipped classrooms, cloud classrooms and other diversified teaching methods on the comprehensive English ability of college students by mining and transplanting the teaching functions of the mobile Internet.

Research Significance: From the perspective of the development law and trend of global education informatization, the realization of the in-depth integration of information technology and education and teaching is the key stage and the only way for the in-depth development of education informatization worldwide. It is also an important way and core move to realize the revolutionary impact of information technology on the development of education. How to achieve the in-depth development and high-level advancement of education informatization, how to transition from the initial application stage to the integration and innovation stage, and how to explore the effective path to promote the modernization of education through education informatization, are unavoidable arduous tasks and major issues that cannot be looked down upon in the field of education informatization. Because of the mobile internet technology gene and social activity value concept that mobile social network is rich in, its influence and effect on social and cultural dissemination have gradually become prominent. Undoubtedly, it has also become a brand-new social discourse system. For the comprehensive reform of the education field, as well as the overall concept and overall action of education informatization, there must be appropriate and close theoretical care and practical guidance. Therefore, to carry out research on the impact of diversified modes of teaching on the comprehensive English ability of college students based on the background of mobile Internet is not only a theoretical perspective that has a profound grasp of academic research levels such as social development, educational innovation, information construction, and higher education connotative development, but also has the value coupling to improve the quality and efficiency of practical applications such as the scientific layout, continuous promotion, and innovation of educational informatization.

3   Related Concepts and Literature Review

(1) Concepts and Research Related to Mobile Internet and English Learning.

In terms of foreign research, learning based on mobile social networks is mainly concentrated in the field of higher education, which is related to the fact that college students generally have smart phones and prefer to socialize on the Internet. Therefore, relevant scholars have carried out research on the application of mobile social networks in education and teaching. Regarding the popularity of the Internet among young people, the well-known American survey organization Pew Research Center released a research report on the Internet and American Life Project in 2010. This report found that social media technology has become an important part of personal life. The ubiquitous social media technology is changing the way students communicate, collaborate and learn.

In terms of the application of the Internet to teaching research, Greenhow and Lewin (2016) constructed a social network learning space model that includes formal and informal learning attributes and forms, laying a corresponding theoretical foundation for the in-depth application of social networks in education in the future. Ahrens and Zasćerinska (2015) conducted a research and analysis on the impact of students' attitudes towards distance learning using mobile social networks. Studies have shown that students' conception of distance learning and blended learning will dominate their attitudes towards learning using mobile social media. Tess (2013) pointed out that with the increasing appearance of social media in the field of higher education, many scholars generally believe that purposeful social media can be used as an integrated educational tool, and teachers can adjust and use social media technology. Enhancing their teaching process, at the same time, it can also promote students' active learning at the level of students' use. Tess (2013) pointed out that with the increasing appearance of social media in the field of higher education, many scholars generally believe that purposeful social media can be used as an integrated educational tool. Teachers can use social media technology to adjust and enhance their teaching process, and at the same time, it can also promote students' active learning at the level of student use.

In domestic research, the teaching application of mobile social network has only gradually emerged in recent years, and most of the previous researches are aimed at the discussion of traditional social networks. For example, Yang et al. (2010) analyzed the status quo of the online learning community and the characteristics of SNS, and based on this, proposed the basic model and constituent elements of the SNS-based learning community. And from the perspective of changes in the roles of members, the construction process of learning and sharing is explained. Feng (2010) discussed the important characteristics of the SNS-based postgraduate inter-school network learning community, the basic components of the community network platform and the basic principles of building the community, and then designed its organizational structure.

(2) Concepts Related to Comprehensive English Ability.

With the continuous deepening of reform and opening up, college English teaching in China has gradually formed its own teaching system. College English teaching has made great progress in various aspects such as teaching level, textbook construction, curriculum setting, teaching methods, teaching methods, teaching environment, and teaching staff. In the new century, college English teaching is also facing development opportunities and new challenges to a new level. Therefore, it is very important and urgent to explore the training mode of College Students' English and improve their comprehensive English application ability in order to promote the reform of College English teaching and establish a curriculum system and teaching mode suitable for personalized development.

Comprehensive English ability is the ability to "listen, speak, read, write, and translate" in English through the cultivation of multiple abilities. It includes language cognitive ability, reading comprehension ability, thinking ability, innovation ability, emotional understanding and expression ability, cross-cultural communication ability, etc., that is to say, the skills of "listening, speaking, reading, writing, and translation" in English Exercising is based on these abilities. Only by cultivating students' comprehensive abilities in language application, can students truly improve their Comprehensive language skills of "listening, speaking, reading, writing, and translation" in English.

1. Cognitive ability: refers to the ability of students to use pronunciation, word meanings, phrases, rhetoric, grammar, idioms, sentence structure, etc. to achieve the correct use of pronunciation, that is, a sublimation process of perceptual recognition of rational cognition. Students can consolidate the knowledge they have learned through preview, review, individual exercises and group exercises, connect the cultural differences between their mother tongue and foreign languages, create moods, stimulate associations, and have a thorough understanding and accurate use of the language they have learned.

2. Reading ability: Reading is a kind of language activity, and the ability shown in the reading process is called reading ability. The reading process is a dynamic and positive thinking process, as well as a process of interaction and reaction between old and new information in the human brain. It includes two aspects of form and content, forming an abstract image, and finally reaching the communicative intention of understanding the discourse. To have this ability requires students to have a rich knowledge structure, have an understanding of social culture, astronomy, geography, customs, literature and history, etc., so that students can not only understand the content mentioned in the text, but also be able to understand the content of the text. The proposed content is connected with the related content not mentioned in the text, to understand the connection between the language content and paragraphs, improve the thinking understanding and generalization ability, and promote the students' understanding of the deeper meaning of the article.

3. Thinking ability: refers to the ability of students to evaluate the entire learning process, including textbook content, classroom teaching, and after-school exercises, so that students can correctly evaluate their own learning process and the degree of knowledge mastery. Thinking is based on the driving force, setting new goals and requirements for yourself. Through thinking, students can make self-assessment and adjustment of learning strategies in a timely manner and improve their ability to understand and solve problems.

4. Innovative ability: It is students' creative thinking through existing knowledge in the process of language learning and application. It is required to train students to be bold in exploration, practice, bold ideas, independent thinking, actively participate in teaching content in classroom learning, enhance language accumulation and improve language application ability, instead of rigidly and passively accepting teaching content. This kind of innovation ability is based on the mastery of knowledge and skills, to explore newer and more effective learning methods, seek diversified learning strategies, and improve the ability of original problem-solving.

5. Emotional understanding and expression ability: Teachers need to adopt appropriate teaching methods to mobilize students' enthusiasm for learning, cultivate interest, and enhance self-confidence according to the differences in personality of students. At the same time, teachers need to inspire and guide students' thinking so that they can ask questions, analyze, summarize and summarize them during the learning process. In addition, the school should cultivate students' love of the motherland and life, broaden their international horizons, understand different cultures, and encourage students to experience unfamiliar emotions and corresponding language expressions, and be able to carry out effective language through language learning and application activity.

6. Cross-cultural communicative competence: Language is a communicative tool. The purpose of any language teaching is to cultivate students' ability to communicate in written or oral ways. And effective communicative competence includes language input and output. This requires students to have the ability to express their own cultural concepts and behaviors, to deepen their understanding of other cultures in the world, to learn from and absorb the essence of foreign cultures, to achieve the purpose of mutual communication and mutual learning, to have the ability to communicate with foreigners in correct language and behavior, and to generate effective communication and resonance in language and thought.

To sum up, it is a prerequisite for college students to have comprehensive English ability, and it also requires students to have the ability to learn by themselves and master learning strategies. It is a process from quantitative change to qualitative change for students to transform the knowledge they have learned into practical language application ability. This process can only be completed through a lot of language practice by the students themselves, which includes different learning modes (individual, group, multimedia) and learning strategies.

(3) Current Research Status of Foreign Language Proficiency Standards at Home and Abroad.

The definition and exploration of foreign language proficiency standards on a global scale has a history of more than sixty years. Through comprehensive elaboration of various documents, the mainstream standards of foreign language proficiency are mainly divided into: examples of proficiency levels mainly used in the United States, The cross-grade continuous scale used in the United Kingdom and other European developed countries, and the grade-by-grade achievement map represented by Australia. In the first half of the 20th century, the ISLPT standard was proposed under the guidance of behaviorism and structuralism. From the formulation of listening, speaking, reading, and writing standards in the early stage to the evaluation of translation ability in the later stage, this standard uses language knowledge as an indicator for evaluation. Taking the 1980s as the dividing line, the foreign language proficiency standard mainly relied on the input-driven form before that, and then gradually evolved into the output-driven. Among them, the United States has promoted the cultivation of foreign language ability to a strategic height, and through the cultivation of national foreign language ability, it has promoted the cultural combat effectiveness and core competitiveness of the nation. At the end of the last century, the United States put forward the "5C" competency standards: culture, communication, comparison, colony and correlation in five aspects, and established the strategic position of foreign language teaching in national education. The ALTE competency standard system is the first to propose the use of communicative competence as a part of language competence. On the basis of the traditional four major competence measurement, the test of communicative pragmatic competence is added, which is of innovative significance. After that, foreign language communicative competence has become an important part of language competence standards. Among them, Heimsky's communicative competence theory is the most famous, which played an important role in related language research later. Whether it is basic education or higher education, the quality of education has always been the focus of social concern, and no matter at which stage, the core standard of foreign language ability is the cultivation of communicative application ability.

The definition of foreign language competence standards in our country started relatively late. For a long time, there is no clear foreign language competence standard system. It only evaluates and analyzes the students' learning conditions based on the foreign language courses and syllabus and training objectives of each stage. The definition and explanation of foreign language ability standards are mainly concentrated in related documents and outlines such as "Graduate English Course Teaching Requirements" and "English Course Standards". The 2007 "Teaching Requirements" described the foreign language ability of graduate students: able to understand and accept lectures in English, fluent in English for communication and discussion during the learning process, and complete writing tasks, and have a higher English ability for graduate students than before. The "Planning Outline" also proposes to train international talents who can meet the needs of international development and can cope with international competition. The core criteria of talents are to have an international vision, adapt to international rules, and be able to handle international affairs smoothly.

4   Research Process

The questionnaire method is that the survey implementer reasonably designs the questionnaire structure, items and answers on the basis of clarifying the purpose of the survey and the main survey content, and distributes the questionnaire to the appropriate survey subjects, and obtains the status quo, questions, suggestions, etc. of the relevant issues according to the feedback of the survey subjects. This research takes four classes of freshman students in Harbin Normal University as a sample, and takes the impact of diversified teaching modes on the comprehensive English ability of college students under the background of mobile Internet as the starting point. This research combines quantitative and qualitative investigations from three dimensions: student experience, comprehensive ability of language skills, and comprehensive ability of language application.

There are two types of tool sentence software involved in the survey process. One is a questionnaire implementation tool, and the other is a statistical analysis tool for statistical questionnaire results. In terms of questionnaire implementation tools, the questionnaire use "Questionnaire Star https://www.wjx.cn/newwjx/manage/myquestio nnaires.aspx" to implement online surveys, mainly considering the fact that it is difficult for college students and teachers to fill in collectively. The website provides functions such as questionnaire production and release, statistics, etc. The questionnaire can be answered through mobile WeChat, computer online and other platforms, and detailed basic data statistics can be provided according to the situation of each question. In terms of questionnaire results statistics and analysis tools, SPSS statistical software is used.

5 Data Analysis

(1) Reliability and Validity Test.

The quality of the questionnaire is generally considered through two perspectives: the reliability value and the validity value of the measurement data. Reliability refers to the degree of internal data consistency, and validity refers to the degree of data validity. Generally, the reliability refers to the judgment by observing the a value of the data. It is generally considered that a value between 0.8 and 0.9 is an acceptable range value, and the reliability above 0.9 is very good. The general validity value is judged by the KMO value of the observation data, that is, the KMO value is obtained by the KMO and Bartlett sphericity test. It is generally believed that the KMO value is above 0.7 and the questionnaire has passed the validity test, and the scale data is suitable for factor analysis.

The questionnaire of this research is based on the standardized item Cronbach's coefficient a = 0.909. The Cronbach's coefficient a of "Student Experience" is 0.912, the Cronbach's coefficient a of "Comprehensive Ability of Language Skills" is 0.903, and the Cronbach's coefficient a of "Comprehensive Ability of Language Application" is 0.914, both of which are greater than 0.9, indicating that the project is internal There is a high degree of consistency. As shown in Table 1, the KMO value obtained is 0.703 greater than 0.7, which passes the validity test.

Table 1. Cronbach's coefficient test

KMO	0.703
Questionnaire category	Cronbach's alpha
Student experience	.912
Comprehensive ability of language skills	.903
Comprehensive language application ability	.914

(2) Questionnaire survey data analysis.

Aiming at the improvement of college students' comprehensive English ability by the diversified teaching mode under the background of mobile Internet, the author conducted a questionnaire survey on three items in the dimension of student experience, namely to increase interest, concentration and efficiency. The results of the questionnaire are shown in Table 2. It can be seen from the table that the proportions of students who choose "conformity" and "very conformity" from the three perspectives of increasing interest, concentration and efficiency are 67.3%, 50.32%, and 56.6%, respectively. Among them, more than 65% of the positive options are selected from the perspective of increasing learning interest, and less than 60% are selected from the perspective of improving concentration and learning efficiency. This phenomenon shows that the diversified mode of teaching under the background of the mobile Internet is effective in enhancing students' interest, but the effectiveness in the two perspectives of concentration and efficiency is average.

Table 2. Results of the questionnaire survey on the dimensions of student experience

Question type	Very non-conforming	Non-conforming	Difficult to determine	Conforming	Very conforming
1. Increase interest	6.29	6.29	20.13	52.83	14.47
2. Improve focus	7.55	16.98	25.16	36.48	13.84
3. Improve efficiency	8.18	8.81	26.42	41.51	15.09

Aiming at the improvement of college students' comprehensive English ability by diversified teaching models under the background of mobile Internet, the author conducted a questionnaire survey of 5 items in the comprehensive language skills dimension, namely improving listening, speaking, reading, writing, and translation. The results of the questionnaire are shown in Table 3. It can be seen from the table that the proportions of students who choose "conformity" and "very conformity" in improving the five language skills of listening, speaking, reading, writing and translation are 74.84%, 62.89%, 61%, 54.09%, 57.23% respectively. Among them, the improvement of listening ability is the most obvious, and the improvement of writing and translation ability is generally effective.

Table 3. Questionnaire results of comprehensive language skills

Question type	Very non-conforming	Non-conforming	Difficult to determine	Conforming	Very conforming
4. Listening	5.66	4.4	15.09	55.97	18.87
5. Speaking	5.66	10.06	21.38	45.91	16.98
6. Reading	6.92	8.81	23.27	45.28	15.72
7. Writing	6.29	14.47	25.16	40.88	13.21
8. Translation	7.55	8.18	27.04	42.14	15.09

Aiming at the improvement of college students' comprehensive English ability by diversified teaching modes under the background of mobile Internet, the author conducted a questionnaire survey of 7 items in the dimension of comprehensive language application ability. They are to improve language cognitive ability, text comprehension ability, thinking ability, innovation ability, cultural understanding ability, expression ability and cross-cultural communication ability. The results of the questionnaire are shown in Table 4. It can be seen from the table that the proportions of students who choose "conformity" and "very conformity" in the 7 language application comprehensive ability are 66.67%, 79.24%, 69.18%, 73.59%, 71.7%, 69.81, 70.44, respectively. All of them are higher than 65%, indicating that the diversified teaching mode under the background of mobile Internet has a significant effect on improving the comprehensive ability of college students in English language application.

Table 4. The results of the questionnaire survey on the comprehensive ability of language application

Question type	Very non-conforming	Non-conforming	Difficult to determine	Conforming	Very conforming
9. Language cognitive ability	5.66	3.77	23.9	49.69	16.98
10. Text comprehension ability	3.77	3.77	13.21	57.23	22.01
11. Thinking ability, innovation ability	3.77	6.29	20.75	50.94	18.24
12. Cultural understanding ability	3.77	6.29	16.35	55.35	18.24
13. Expression ability	3.77	7.55	16.98	53.46	18.24
14. Cross-cultural communication ability	4.4	5.66	20.13	52.83	16.98
15. Language cognitive ability	5.03	7.55	16.98	51.57	18.87

6 Conclusion

To sum up, in college English teaching, diversified teaching mode under the background of mobile Internet plays an important role. It can not only effectively mobilize students' enthusiasm and interest in learning, but also can effectively exercise the students' comprehensive English ability. In terms of language skills and abilities, diversified teaching methods under the background of the mobile Internet have significant effects on the improvement of students' listening, speaking, and reading abilities, with the most significant improvement in listening ability. In terms of the comprehensive ability of language application, the diversified mode of teaching under the background of mobile Internet has obvious effects on the improvement of students' speech cognition, text understanding, thinking ability, innovation ability, cultural understanding, expression ability, and cross-cultural communication ability. Therefore, it is necessary to conduct a comprehensive research on the teaching mode of diversified teaching mode under the background of mobile Internet, so that it can play its role in college English teaching, and then provide more new ideas for the new development of the education industry in the 5G era.

Acknowledgements. 1. Heilongjiang Province Educational Science Planning Project: Research on the Application of Output-Oriented Method in Oral English Teaching in Senior High Schools (Project Number: JJB1319002).

2. Harbin Normal University Postgraduate Training Quality Improvement Project.

References

Ahrens, A., Zasćerinska, J.: A comparative analysis of educator's and peers' influence on students' attitude to mobile social media in distance learning. Literacy Inform. Comput. Educ. J. **6**(1), 1289–1298 (2015)

Feng, X.: Research on the Establishment of an SNS-based Inter-school Network Learning Community for Postgraduate Students. Nanchang University, Nanchang (2010)

Greenhow, C., Lewin, C.: Social media and education: reconceptualizing the boundaries of formal and informal learning. Learn. Media Technol. **41**(1), 6–30 (2016)

Tess, P.A.: The role of social media in higher education classes (real and virtual)—a literature review. Comput. Hum. Behav. **29**(5), 60–68 (2013)

Yang, H., et al.: Research on the construction of SNS-based network learning community. Mod. Educ. Technol. **5**, 95–98 (2010)

A Follow-Up Investigation on the Measurement Data of College Students' Mental Health Effectiveness Based on Big Data Analysis

Deming Qiu[✉]

Harbin Finance University, Harbin 150030, China

Abstract. The mental health level of college students not only directly affects their own growth, but also affects the stability of the campus, and then affects the social harmony and the improvement of the quality of the whole people. Therefore, the psychological problems of college students have aroused widespread concern. College Students' psychological intervention has become a hot topic in college students' mental health research. With the development and maturity of big data analysis technology and its successful application in all walks of life, this technology has incomparable advantages in discovering hidden rules or patterns in data. In this paper, the effectiveness of mental health measurement data tracking research.

Keywords: Big data analysis · Mental health · Effectiveness · Tracking analysis

1 Introduction

Data mining, also known as knowledge discovery, is to discover hidden mineral resources knowledge from massive data. It is a comprehensive application of statistics, artificial intelligence, database and other technologies. Using the tools and methods of data mining, valuable knowledge can be extracted from the rich data, otherwise the vast "data ocean" will become the "data grave" of lack of information.

Some research shows that most of the students' weariness, dropout, suicide and hurting others are caused by mental health problems, and the number of students with poor mental health has been on the rise [1]. According to a survey of 126000 college students in China, 20.3% of them have psychological problems, mainly manifested as terror, anxiety, obsessive-compulsive disorder, depression and neurasthenia.

According to the survey, the current college students' psychological problems mainly include three aspects: psychological confusion, psychological obstacles and psychological diseases. Among them, the students with psychological confusion are more common. Although they are mild psychological problems, they do not affect their health. However, if the minor problems can not be adjusted and dredged in time, they will develop into mental disorders [2–4]. If psychological barriers are not timely adjusted and treated, they will develop into mental diseases. Mental illness will seriously affect their physical and mental health and all-round development, and even lead to malignant events.

© ICST Institute for Computer Sciences, Social Informatics and Telecommunications Engineering 2021
Published by Springer Nature Switzerland AG 2021. All Rights Reserved
M. A. Jan and F. Khan (Eds.): BigIoT-EDU 2021, LNICST 391, pp. 235–243, 2021.
https://doi.org/10.1007/978-3-030-87900-6_29

2 Data Mining Technology

2.1 Cluster Analysis

Clustering is to classify data objects into several classes or clusters according to the principle of "maximizing the similarity within a class and minimizing the similarity between classes". The similarity of objects in the same class is very high, but the differences of objects in different classes are very high. Clustering analysis is the process of classifying according to some similarity of data and analyzing the formed multiple classes [5]. Clustering methods mainly include hierarchical method, partition method, grid based method, density based method, model-based method, etc.

2.2 Classification of Data Mining System

Data mining technology comes from many disciplines, which will have an impact on data mining, as shown in Fig. 1.

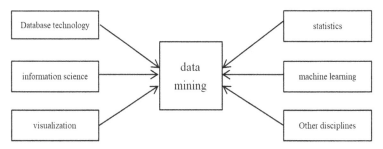

Fig. 1. Multiple disciplines influence data mining

Because data mining is an interdisciplinary subject, data mining will produce many different types of data mining systems [6]. Accurate classification of data mining system can provide scientific basis for users to choose the most suitable data mining system.

2.3 Decision Tree

In data mining, decision tree is mainly used for classification. Each node represents the distribution method of the top-level tree, and each node represents the distribution method of a class, and each node represents the distribution of a class. According to different characteristics, the decision tree uses tree structure to represent the classification, which is used as the basis for generating rules [7–9]. The main advantages of decision tree are simple description, fast classification speed, easy to understand the generated model, and high precision. It is widely used in all kinds of data mining systems. Its main drawback is that it is difficult to construct a decision tree based on multiple variables.

3 Application of Data Mining in the Analysis of College Students' Psychological Problems

Attribute selection measures, also known as splitting rules, determine how to split samples on a given node. Here are two popular attribute selection metrics: information gain and gain rate.

1. Information gain.

Let node n store all samples of data partition D [10]. The expected information required for the classification of samples in D is given by the following formula:

$$Info(D) = -\sum_{i=1}^{m} p_i \log_2(p_i) \tag{1}$$

Where p_i is the probability that any sample in D belongs to C_i.

The expected information required for sample classification of D Based on attribute A can be obtained as follows:

$$Info_A(D) = \sum_{j=1}^{v} \frac{|D_j|}{|D|} \times Info(D_j) \tag{2}$$

Where $\frac{|D_j|}{|D|}$ is the weight of a subset of value a_j on attribute A.

Classification is actually to extract information from the system to reduce the confusion of the system, so as to make the system more regular, more orderly and more organized [6, 7]. The more chaotic the system, the greater the entropy. Obviously, the optimal splitting scheme is the splitting scheme with the largest entropy reduction.

In this chapter, according to the requirements of decision-making analysis of College Students' mental health education, the whole process of classification and mining of College Students' psychological problems is fully realized. The first is the determination of mining objects and data mining objectives: decision tree model of whether students have interpersonal sensitivity symptoms or not. Then preprocess the data to get the training sample set. According to the characteristics of the training sample set, C4.5 algorithm of decision tree is selected to construct the decision tree model of whether students have interpersonal sensitivity symptoms and prune it [8]. Then the classification rules are extracted from the decision tree model and analyzed. Finally, the accuracy of the model is evaluated. This paper also compares the original tree with the pruned tree in terms of scale, extracted classification rules and classification accuracy. The conclusion is that the pruned decision tree model is simpler, easier to understand and has higher classification efficiency than the directly generated decision tree.

4 Simulation for College Students' Psychological Data Management System

The collection and analysis of students' psychological evaluation data is a necessary basic work for colleges and universities to carry out mental health education. With the rapid increase of enrollment and the improvement of the connotation of psychological data analysis, more and more psychological data need to be analyzed and processed more deeply. Although some well-known and powerful psychological assessment software has appeared in China, these software are expensive and have not applied data mining technology [9, 10]. Therefore, it is necessary to develop a college students' psychological data management system based on data mining technology and BS mode, so as to improve the work efficiency of psychological evaluation data collection and increase the depth of psychological data analysis.

The student function module is oriented to students, which mainly realizes the collection of students' basic information and psychological evaluation information, and establishes psychological files for students. After students enter the system (see Fig. 2), the system generates a dynamic psychological file for them. Students can modify their personal password by modifying the password sub module; modify the personal basic information by modifying the basic information sub module; at the same time, the system can collect the students' basic information; through the psychological evaluation sub module, online psychological self-assessment can be realized, and the evaluation results can be viewed, and the system can collect the psychological evaluation data.

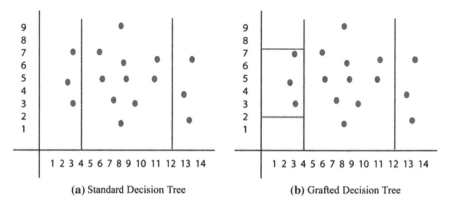

(a) Standard Decision Tree   (b) Grafted Decision Tree

Fig. 2. Decision tree with grafted and standard

The administrator function module is used to retrieve the administrator, mainly to modify personal password, customize psychological questionnaire, information management, data mining, psychological prediction and other functions [11]. The administrator realizes the management and import of the questionnaire through the self-defined psychological questionnaire sub module, realizes the self-determination of the students' basic attributes, the management of the students' basic information and the management of the psychological evaluation information through the information management sub module; realizes the data preparation, the generation of the decision tree and the generation of the classification rules through the data mining sub module; Through the psychological prediction sub module, students' psychological problems can be predicted (see Fig. 3).

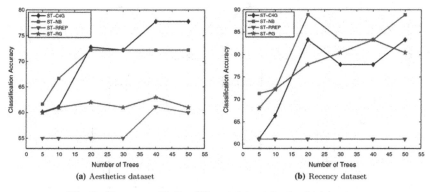

Fig. 3. Compare with the different dataset for the decision tree

5   Phase Difference Detection Technology of CMF System

5.1   Introduce

According to the basic principle of Coriolis force measurement, the output signals of the left and right vibration detectors on the U-tube of CMF are two sinusoidal signals [12, 13]. When there is flow in the measuring tube, because of the Coriolis force, the phase difference between the two signals is very small and increases with the increase of the flow in the measuring tube. The mass flow rate of fluid has a linear relationship with the phase difference. In order to get the accurate flow rate, the accurate phase difference must be measured. Phase difference detection technology is one of the key technologies of CMF system. Which phase difference detection technology is used directly determines the composition of the system and the accuracy of the instrument.

5.2   Common Phase Difference Detection Technology

(1) After adding, subtracting or multiplying two sinusoidal signals of the same frequency by vector method and phase multiplication, the sine or cosine value of the phase difference can be obtained through a low-pass filter, and the value of the phase difference can be obtained after anti sine or anti cosine operation [14]. According to the different operation methods, they are called vector method and phase multiplication. These two similar methods are suitable for the measurement of high frequency sinusoidal signal with single spectrum and large phase difference. If the frequency of the signal is low, then the low-pass filtering is difficult to achieve very accurate, and if the phase difference is small, the cosine value is close to 1, As shown in Fig. 4 and the sensitivity is very low. In addition, the signal must have a single spectrum, noise and interference have a great impact on the measurement results.

(2) In practice, the most commonly used detection methods are zero crossing phase detection method and improved two-way zero crossing phase detection method. The basic method is to shape the two signals after zero crossing comparison, then get the phase pulse signal by phase discrimination, and finally get the phase difference by high frequency counting. There is also a process of offset pulse square wave correction in

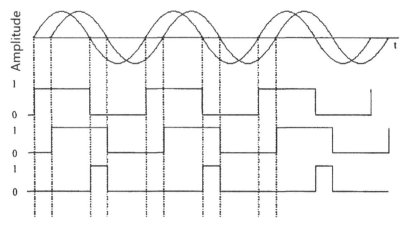

Fig. 4. Waveform diagram of zero crossing phase discrimination

the two-way zero crossing phase detection. The two-way zero crossing phase detection method can well solve the influence of temperature drift and comparator offset on the measurement error [15]. However, the noise and interference also have a great influence on the measurement error, and when the phase difference is small, the phase difference accuracy will be reduced due to the influence of counting clock accuracy.

(3) There is another phase detection method based on least square method (LMS). Through some matrix transformation and calculation, the amplitude and phase angle of two signals can be obtained simultaneously. The calculation of this method is more complex, and it can get high accuracy ($<1‰$) when the noise and interference are small and the signal spectrum is single. However, the measurement accuracy will deteriorate sharply with the distortion of signal waveform and the increase of noise and interference, and the actual implementation is also more complex, which requires a higher processor [16–19]. These methods have their own advantages and disadvantages, but they can not overcome the influence of signal zero drift and waveform distortion on the measurement error.

6   Research on CMF Signal Processing Method based on DPLL

6.1   Introduction of Application Technology

In practical application, the signal is not an ideal sine signal because of various harmonic interference and noise in industrial field. The frequency of the output signal of Coriolis mass flowmeter sensor falls into the frequency range of many industrial noises, and the amplitude of the output signal of the sensor is relatively small, which is not significantly greater than the amplitude of the noise signal in many cases, which limits the sensitivity of the flowmeter, makes it difficult to obtain the useful signal, and leads to the reduction of the measurement accuracy [20]. In addition, the vibration frequency of the U-tube varies with the fluid density, so that it is not equal to the driving frequency, resulting in the frequency change of the output signal of the sensor. In this way, the spectrum of the output signal of the sensor can not be a single spectral line corresponding to the sinusoidal signal, and its composition will become very complex. At present, the commonly used zero crossing equal phase measurement methods are based on amplification, filtering, shaping and counting. The use of analog filter will inevitably change the amplitude and phase of the sensor output signal, which is undesirable, because the phase delay between the two signals is used to calculate the basic information of fluid characteristics [21]. This leads to the final measurement of the phase difference of the sine useful signal output by the synthetic wave rather than the sensor, and the measurement results are easily affected by the waves and random noise, resulting in measurement error.

6.2 Signal Processing based on DPLL

6.2.1 General Overview

Phase locked loop (PLL) is a closed-loop phase control system. Its theoretical basis is automatic control theory. The theory of synchronous detection proposed by dbellesize in 1932 first published the description of PLL. Since the 1960s, PLL began to be digitized, and some digital loops and integrated loops appeared [22]. The common characteristics of these digital PLLs are high reliability, stable performance and easy integration. Now, PLL has become an indispensable part of communication, radar, navigation, deep space exploration, electronic instruments and other equipment The reason why it can be widely used is that it has a unique narrow-band tracking performance, and can complete the tasks of frequency synthesis, modulation and demodulation, synchronous extraction, velocity and moment measurement, micro frequency conversion and so on. Narrowband tracking performance includes two meanings: one is the tracking function of input signal; the other is the narrowband filtering performance of input noise.

The DPLL consists of digital phase detector, digital loop filter and digital controlled oscillator. According to the type of digital phase detector used in the loop, digital phase locked loops can be divided into four types: lead lag digital phase locked loop (ll-dpll), trigger digital phase locked loop (ff-dpll), zero crossing detection digital phase locked loop (zc-dpll) and Nyquist digital phase locked loop (nr-dpll).

6.2.2 Down Sampling Filter

In this system, although the required useful signal frequency is very low, only about 100 Hz, but the signal is complex, high-frequency noise and interference have great influence. In order to eliminate the influence of noise and interference after AD sampling, the sampling rate of ad is much higher than twice of the highest frequency of the useful signal, so we need to pay attention to the spectrum aliasing of the sampled signal. In the traditional down sampling system, in order to avoid spectrum aliasing, the input sampling data must be de aliased first, so that the highest spectrum component contained in the signal is lower than the Nyquist frequency after sampling, $/(2 m)$. In this system, the fundamental frequency component of the signal after digital mixing has moved to the zero position, and the harmonic interference has been eliminated by integral comb filtering, so the sampling frequency can be reduced very low [23]. The anti aliasing filtering is not needed before sampling.

6.3 Simulation Analysis Data

Before the simulation analysis, it is necessary to obtain the parameters of all filters in the whole DPLL loop, in addition to the frequency offset Δ – y data table. It is very easy to get the filter parameters by using the computer-aided design method under the MATLAB platform. We will not repeat here, but only discuss the acquisition of 4-y data table in detail. After that, we will simulate and analyze the data of several different cases to verify and analyze the performance of the whole DPLL system. In the simulation process, the most important thing is the evaluation of frequency tracking and the calculation accuracy of the final phase difference results, which will be verified and analyzed later. All the work of this part is completed in the MATLAB simulation software platform [13, 14]. The hardware system based on CPLD and MCU overcomes the contradiction between the low processing speed of MCU and the high speed of data acquisition, and greatly eliminates the redundant data collected by AD converter, which reduces the volume of the system and the difficulty of MCU software system development. The MCU system completes the final data processing, calculates the phase difference and mass flow [24–26]. Because the data processing is relatively simple, the software system of single chip microcomputer is designed with assembly language, which realizes many functions including data processing, display and communication modules, and enhances the data processing and auxiliary functions of CMF system, especially the communication between CMF and PC.

7 Conclusion

This paper analyzes the key technologies of data mining, deeply studies the classification in data mining, and analyzes and compares several commonly used classification algorithms, which provides the basis for the application of decision tree algorithm in the analysis of College Students' psychological problems. The classification rules are extracted from the optimal decision tree model, which provides an important reference for the school psychological consultation work, and realizes the classification and prediction of new data by using the model, which provides a scientific basis for the early warning and intervention research of College Students' psychological problems.

Acknowledgements. A New Characteristics of the Ideological Development of Poverty University Students in Universities and Colleges by the Provincial Basic Business Fee Project of Harbin Institute of Finance (2018-KYWF-E017).

References

1. Mao, G., Duan, L., Wang, S.: Principle and Algorithm of Data Mining. Publishing House of Tsinghua University, Beijing (2005)
2. Wang, P.: Research on the Application Of Data Mining in the Identification Of College Students with Difficulties. Northeast Normal University, Changchun (2011)
3. Li, W.: Application of Data Mining Technology in Secondary Vocational Enrollment Information System. Northwest Normal University, Lanzhou (2008)

4. Le, G.D.: Application of data mining in college students' psychological problems. Wireless Internet Technol. **2**, 196–197 (2013)
5. Zhou, H., Jiang, Z., Wang, D.: Maneuvering Target Tracking. National Defense Industry Press, Beijing (1991)
6. He, M., Wang, Z., Zhu, J.: Real time field elimination method for multi-sensor target tracking. Acta Astronaut. Sin. **23**(6), 34–37 (2002)
7. Zhu, J.B.: Data fusion technology of incomplete trajectory measurement. Sci. Bull. **45**(20) (2000)
8. Sun, H., Ding, X., Chen, X.: Real time field culling method based on data fusion for range optical measurement data. J. Command Technol. Coll. **10**(4) (1999)
9. Zhu, X., Han, R., Yang, R.: Outlier elimination method based on fuzzy prediction system. Syst. Eng. Electron. Technol. **28**(3) (2006)
10. Xu, Z.: Principle and Application of Total Station. PLA Press, Beijing (2003)
11. Luo, Y.: Application of Measuring Robot in Fast Feed Dynamic Tracking Measurement. University of Information Engineering, Zhengzhou (2003)
12. Yang, Y.: Adaptive Dynamic Navigation and Positioning. Surveying and Mapping Press, Beijing (2006)
13. Ni, W.: Phase Difference Measurement Method and Device for Coriolis Mass Flowmeter. Institute of Automation, Hefei University of Technology, Hefei (1999)
14. Xu, K., Lv, X., Chen, R.: Research on key technology of DFT method in signal processing of Coriolis flowmeter. Ind. Instrument. Autom. Device (5), 7–10 (1998)
15. Xu, K., et al.: Development of excitation circuit for Coriolis mass flowmeter. J. Hefei Univ. Technol. (Nat. Sci. Ed.) **23**(1), 37–40 (2000)
16. He, H., Liu, Q., Xu, Y.: Hardware circuit analysis of remote transmitter rft9712 for Coriolis mass flowmeter. Autom. Instrum. **18**(10), 32–34 (1997)
17. Sara, D., Fateme, D., Marzieh, A.: The relationship of maternal anxiety, positive and negative affect schedule, and fatigue with neonatal psychological health upon childbirth. Contraception Reprod. Med. **6**(1) (2021)
18. Hu, Z.: Research on local government emergency management of public health emergencies. Anhui University of Finance and Economics (2021)
19. Cheng, K., Xu, J.: Improving the mental health service system for Tibetan adolescents. China Soc. Sci. J. 2021-04-01 (005)
20. Sun, Q.: Tolerance is a magic weapon for mental health. Modern Health Preserv. **21**(7), 52 (2021)
21. Yang, H.: Problems and measures of moral education of primary school head teachers in the Internet age. Knowledge Base **7**, 58–59 (2021)
22. Chen, L.: On the influence of family factors on College Students' mental health and countermeasures. Knowledge Base **7**, 177–178 (2021)
23. Zeng, J.: Analyzing the realistic demands and paths of adult mental health education. Knowledge Base **7**, 181–182 (2021)
24. Lu, B.: Old things and new play are beneficial to the mental health of the elderly. Shanxi Elderly **4**, 64 (2021)
25. Educating people with heart, cultivating wisdom, cultivating heart, moistening life. Mental Health Educ. Primary Second. Schools 10, 2 (2021)
26. He, Y., Yu, G.: The influence of cultural trend and social transformation on the mental health of Chinese teenagers. Primary Second. School Psychol.

Design Conception of Web Based Chinese Wushu Distance Education Platform (WEB-WTS)

Mingyuan Zhao and Chen Li[✉]

School of Physical Education and Health, Zhaoqing University, Zhaoqing 526061, Guangdong, China

Abstract. This paper analyzes the development status of Wushu distance education based on Web. On this basis, the design of Wushu distance education system platform is macro and overall conceived. The requirements, objectives, functions and functions of the system platform are described and analyzed in detail. Through the decomposition and design principle of Wushu distance education system function, through the development of system platform, the distance education platform (wts-web) is developed, which promotes the popularization of Chinese Wushu.

Keywords: Wushu distance education platform (web-ws) · Wushu teaching · Design concept

1 Introduction

Wushu is the quintessence of China. As a traditional folk sport, it has existed for thousands of years in China, and Wushu education also has a long history. There are written records that from the spring and Autumn period, there have been martial arts masters specializing in martial arts. However, due to the influence of feudalism such as "different schools", "pass on inside but not outside, pass on male but not female" and the limitation of Wushu education methods and techniques, many Wushu schools and techniques disappeared. Nowadays, the rapid development of computer technology and network technology has triggered a revolution in the dissemination of knowledge and information [1]. Modern educational technology has also developed from audio-visual education to the real combination of teaching and network, which has forced the long-standing educational ideas, methods, means and modes to be updated, Distance education has become a very effective way of universal education, continuing education and job training. In order to meet the challenge of information society and break the limitation of traditional Wushu education, it is urgent to conduct in-depth research on Wushu distance education. This paper analyzes the current development status of Wushu distance education, on this basis, the design of Wushu distance education system platform for a macro, overall concept, focusing on Wushu distance education system needs, objectives, functional decomposition and design principles for a more detailed elaboration and analysis, in order to promote the sustainable popularization of Wushu through the construction of the platform, And then promote the development of national traditional culture.

M. A. Jan and F. Khan (Eds.): BigIoT-EDU 2021, LNICST 391, pp. 244–252, 2021.
https://doi.org/10.1007/978-3-030-87900-6_30

2 The Current Situation of Wushu Distance Education in China

Long distance education is a new generation of education mode combining computer technology and multimedia technology. With the popularity of computers, the convenience of broadband Internet access and the change of people's concept, distance education, as an industry, is in a period of rapid development in recent years. Compared with traditional education, distance education can break through the limitations of traditional education in terms of educational resources (teachers, teaching materials, experimental and demonstration equipment) and educational methods (Unified progress, centralized and one-way teaching, etc.), and realize the sharing of educational resources and educational methods without constraints of time and space, While the educated can arrange their own learning plan and progress according to their own professional level and time, so as to realize the "personalized education" that traditional education can not achieve. In addition to the advantages of distance education itself, in the case of uneven distribution of educational resources, distance education is to informationize some traditional education, especially some of the best educational resources. For traditional education, distance education is a necessary supplement [2].

In order to facilitate the analysis and research, constraints are given to the multi-objective task scheduling problem, which is expressed by the formula:

$$\sum_{k=1}^{M} x_{ijk} = 1 \tag{1}$$

It means that any sample can only select one machine for calculation.

$$S_{k(j+1)} - n_{kj} \geq 0 \tag{2}$$

It means that the machine has no parallel computing ability, that is, it can only compute one sample at a time.

In addition, we also need to assume that: the samples of each task can not be stopped in the process of calculation; the same task samples are constrained by calculation order, and different task samples have the same priority; all tasks can be calculated at zero time.

3 System Requirement Analysis and Outline Design

3.1 The Goal of Web WTS System

Martial arts is a professional course for college students majoring in martial arts or physical education. There are teachers or coaches for systematic learning. For martial arts lovers, it is a non systematic educate. The web-wts system provides a network teaching and learning platform for these two types of teachers and students. Through the use of the system, we can consolidate and strengthen the effect of classroom teaching and make up for the lack of classroom teaching. Through the teaching system, teachers can release and manage the teaching content and related teaching information, arrange homework, organize discussion, communicate with students in real-time or non real-time, understand the problems in students' learning, and guide students [3–5]. According to their own situation, students independently choose to learn related content, ask questions, participate in discussion, online practice and simulation test.

3.2 Function Decomposition of Web WTS System

(1) Students learn. Students enter the web-wts system, take the title structure of each project as the navigation on the Internet, browse the teacher's multimedia teaching plans, lecture notes, lecture videos and other materials, and download or browse them directly for autonomous learning. Students must pass the system's identity authentication as legitimate users, in order to learn the core part of the content. According to the learning progress, unit test can be carried out, with each chapter as the unit). The unit test is maintained by the teacher in charge of the chapter (questions, test management, etc.). Teachers can maintain and modify their own chapters and unit test questions.

(2) Online examination. Student examination part: students log in and enter the examination subsystem. According to the number of questions set by the management module, question type, score and so on, the system randomly selects questions to form a test paper. Students test online. After the test, they submit the answers. The system automatically marks the test paper, records the scores, and intuitively feeds back the test results to students [6–9]. For the wrong questions, the system gives the correct answers, So that students can summarize and improve.

(3) Answer questions online. When students encounter questions in the process of learning after class, they can ask questions or get answers in time through the web WTS teaching system. The system provides students with the function of leaving messages and asking questions for a certain course chapter. After the teacher in charge of the chapter logs in, the unanswered questions will be automatically prompted for teachers to answer online.

(4) Teachers' personal classroom. According to the concept of web20, we set up a personal classroom for teachers. Teachers can use the professional courseware making tools provided by the website to make exquisite courseware, upload their own courses and price them. Teachers can manage their own students, manage homework, exams, answer questions, and provide teaching aids. Teachers can manage their own curriculum system. According to the charging items, teachers can participate in the sharing and query all kinds of data, including the charging situation of students. Teachers can participate in forums, chat and other exchange activities. At the same time, teachers themselves are students, and they can complete all the operations as a student.

4 Test and Analysis of Web WTS System

4.1 Software Testing Tools

Generally speaking, testing tools can be divided into white box testing tools, black box testing tools, performance testing tools, as well as testing management tools (test process management, defect tracking management, test case management) [10]. These products are mainly products of mercuryinteractive (m), segue, IBM Rational, Compuware and Empire "x", while Mi company's products are the mainstream.

White box testing tools are generally used to test code. The defects found in testing can be located at the code level. According to the different principles of testing tools, they can be divided into static testing tools and dynamic testing tools.

Static test tool: analyze the code directly, do not need to run the code, do not need to compile the code link, generate executable files. Static testing tools generally scan the code syntax to find out the places that do not conform to the coding specifications, evaluate the quality of the code according to a certain quality model, and generate the call diagram of the system. The representatives of static testing tools are: Logiscope software of telelog company; prqa software of PR company.

Black box testing tools are suitable for black box testing. Black box testing tools include function testing tools and performance testing tools. The general principle of black box testing tool is to use the script recording and playback to simulate the user's operation, and then record the output of the tested system and compare it with the pre-determined standard results [11, 12]. Black box testing tools can greatly reduce the workload of black box testing, in the process of iterative development, it can do regression testing well. Representatives of black box testing tools are: team test and robot of rational company; qacenter of Compuware company (see Fig. 1).

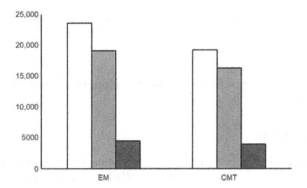

Fig. 1. Simulation for software testing tools

4.2 Analysis of Factors Affecting Service Performance

Bandwidth: bandwidth includes server outlet bandwidth, network line bandwidth and user access bandwidth. In case of insufficient bandwidth of any segment, for example, from the server to the student client PC, only 20K bandwidth can be obtained. The bandwidth occupied by video playback is usually higher than this value, and streaming playback appears intermittent or mosaic.

Server performance: for small and medium-sized websites, server performance has little impact on Web access, but has great impact on streaming media services [13]. Loading many services on a server at the same time, such as database, mail and other resource consuming services, affects the response speed of the server.

IIS: Microsoft's is, including Microsoft's windows 2003 operating system, is easy to be infected with viruses or hackers, and is sometimes congested and has to restart the server.

Programming: programming structure affects efficiency. For example, bad programming style, not paying attention to program structure and cumbersome processing.

Deployment mode: server and software configuration mode may affect performance. If traffic distribution, load balancing and server cluster strategy are carried out, the service effect will be greatly improved (see Fig. 2).

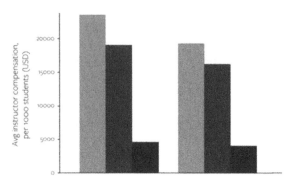

Fig. 2. Analysis of factors affecting service performance

5   School Martial Arts Between Social Expectation and Realistic Dilemma

5.1   Development Status

Throughout the hundred year history of the development of school Wushu, it is not difficult to find that since modern times, School Wushu has been formed and integrated into the new education between the "Shiyang sports debate" and the "Chinese and Western culture debate". It plays a unique value and function in inspiring the national spirit and strengthening the nation. It shoulders the historical mission of Wushu education and Wushu culture inheritance. Since the founding of new China, martial arts, as an important part of school education, has always been promoted and promoted by the education authorities. Whether it is the formulation of the syllabus or the compilation of teaching materials, the content and hours of teaching are strictly stipulated in different sections of our education system, From the objective data of Wushu education, such as curriculum, teaching content, popularity and talent training level, the development of Wushu in school is undoubtedly remarkable [14–16]. However, there are many problems in the quality and effect of Wushu education, "Although the party and the government have always attached great importance to the importance of Wushu in school education, the current situation of the development of Wushu education in schools is worrying. Although Wushu has been listed as a sports item in school education, Wushu teaching has not taken root in schools. 2." from 1987 to 2001, the content of Wushu education in schools has been revised many times However, there are still many problems to be solved.

5.2 The Trembling of Ideas: The School Wushu Education of "using Western Learning in Chinese"

Mr. Liu Sanyuan once said that the core and fundamental mistake of carrying forward national culture is that we are not lack of excellent traditional culture, but the education of excellent traditional culture. China's modern school education is a new type of education based on western education. 4. After the founding of the people's Republic of China, under the background of surpassing the United Kingdom and catching up with the United States, the Soviet Union's sports model entered China and accelerated the process of "Wushu Sports" in the process of copying and imitating. After that, Chinese martial arts voluntarily or involuntarily entered the circle of sports friends. "After our" processing and transformation ", Chinese martial arts has become a kind of sports. It can be said that the modern transformation of Chinese Wushu education is a process of transforming itself into Chinese style sports in the competition with western sports in the tortuous road of business difference and return 151. But we forget that "the western sports represented by the modern Olympic movement is the product of western industrial culture, It takes the scientific spirit as its leading culture, guides the competition, and pursues different ideas and goals from Chinese martial arts under the influence of traditional culture, With the feelings of cosmopolitanism and the vision of world holism, he regards the world as a family, emphasizes to view the world from the world, thinks about problems and governs the world from the perspective of the world as a whole, and thinks that conflicts and confrontations are only temporary disorder, which is characterized by the implicit nature of Chinese traditional culture. So there is a culture, there is a concept of movement, from the concept of movement, the eastern and western regional culture will have different colors. Obviously, Wushu education is different from physical education [17]. Chinese Wushu should be an independent discipline with its own discipline system. In a deeper sense, Wushu education is the education of Chinese culture, and physical education is the education of western culture. From the perspective of Tuyang sports.

5.3 Lack of Own Culture: "specious" School Wushu Inheritance

The cultural tradition of a nation is embodied in its national spirit. Cultural tradition is the immortal soul of a nation. It comes from the life of a nation through the ages, grows up in the repeated practice of a nation, and forms the collective consciousness and collective unconsciousness of a nation. In short, cultural tradition is national spirit. Therefore, the differences of national cultural spirit will inevitably lead to different cultural forms and expressions. In the education system, Wushu has always been different from any kind of foreign sports. It has the cultural tradition and emotional belonging of the Chinese nation. Because of this, the national culture embodied in Chinese Wushu is the fundamental reason for its inheritance, and it is the key to maintain the position of Wushu in the school education system. In a more fundamental sense, the reason why martial arts enter the campus is to spread K culture, carry forward national spirit and stick to cultural recognition. In the specific implementation process, we only take martial arts technology and martial arts movement as the foothold [18]. This method seems to inherit the national principle of "cultural inheritance", but it is actually a kind of blind behavior of "changing beams and columns", This phenomenon of "reading the classics askew" directly leads to the reduction of martial arts education into a kind of martial arts education. As shown in Fig. 3. From the perspective of cultural inheritance and cultural education, martial arts with cultural functions has only become a sport with sports attributes. It can be said that this kind of "specious martial arts teaching sound" has nothing to do with its own cultural inheritance room.

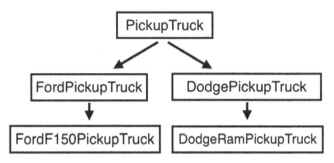

Fig. 3. The method of inheritance

6   The Way Culture of Chinese Wushu

6.1   Boxing Theory and Technique Theory in "Dao"

It seems that the idea of "the theory of all things in Taoism" is helpful to the liberation of sensibility and the equality of personality, so it is conducive to the development of Keji sports. However, its spiritual pursuit of simplicity and selflessness weakens the consciousness of Kezheng and the enthusiasm of adventure of Chinese people to a great extent. However, Taoism takes "Tao" as the core, thinks that Tao does nothing and advocates that Tao follows nature, which is in line with the idea of the unity of man and nature advocated by Wushu. In the view of Taoism, Tao is the origin of all things and the root of all things. "Qi" is a subtle, omnipresent, moving and changing material entity between nature and all living bodies, which constitutes the noumenon and law of Yumu. "Tao is the core of Taoist thought, and Tao is the innate condition for things to produce, move and change [19–21]. The so-called "Tao begets one, life begets three things." therefore, Taoism believes that without Tao, there would be no other things in the world. The Tao is also the principle, the method and the law. That is to say, if you master the Tao, you will get the Tao. Just as Mr. Jin Yuelu said: the most lofty concept and basic motive force in Chinese thought is the way that is not the way, the way that every family wants to say but can't do, the way that Chinese people naturally admire, the way that everything has to come from, have to follow, and have to return.

6.2   The Expression of the Idea of "integrity" and "Inaction" in Wushu

Tao Te Ching says: nothing is the beginning of heaven and earth; being is the mother of all things. Therefore, often without, want to see its wonderful; often have, want to see its emblem. Generally speaking, it is: before the birth of heaven and earth, everything is nihilistic and nothing is called "nothingness". When heaven and earth produce all things, it is the beginning of all things, which is called internal angle. Observe its beauty, and conversely observe its boundary from some angles. Being and nothingness are two sides of the same thing, so the two are different from each other in name, such as wind. Wind can't be seen, but it really exists, and its function is self-evident. The great form has no shape. But we are often hearing about the folklore, school spirit, family tradition, style of work and style. In the same way, spirit, theory and belief are all invisible, but what people must have is that people have no spiritual world but only physical body, which is just like walking dead. For example, the cup is empty as if it were nothing, and the shape of the cup is something: the interior of the house is empty as if it were nothing, and the wall is in its shape as if it were something. But people tend to see only some parts, and suddenly No. If you fill in the interior of the house, is the house still a house? Chinese wood seems to contain such a truth. Wumu ancient proverbs practice muscles and bones and skin outside, practice one breath inside and sink into the elixir field to express one's mind [22, 23]. Whether Qi exists has always been one of the hot spots of researchers. Although we hold the view that invisible may not exist, we also need to test its authenticity from many aspects. There are many different opinions about "Qi", which can be summarized as follows: breathing and breathing Qi; the other refers to the original Qi of the ancients.

7   Conclusion

Web WTS system design and development, access to a large number of information, research the latest development of distance education technology, and computer, network technology experts, distance education experts and martial arts educators were discussed, listened to their views and suggestions. During the test run, some martial arts enthusiasts were invited to try. The actual operation shows that due to the full use of system engineering theory guidance and practical development tools, the system design is rigorous, the layout is reasonable, the function is complete, and the user interface is friendly, which achieves the expected scientific research and design purposes.

Acknowledgement. Guangdong Province Educational Science "Thirteenth Five-Year Plan" Project, Project Number: 2019GXJK207.

References

1. Fang, G., Jie, W.: Research on web based distance education system reference model. Comput. Eng. **12**, 37–39 (2000)
2. Zhang, J.Z., Lu, J.: Design of a graphical object-oriented requirement definition language. Acta Sinica Sinica **9**, 76 (2003)
3. Hu, X.: classification and comparison of information system modeling technology. Comput. Modern. **12**, 65 (2004)
4. Lu, F.: Good man Zhang Youfeng. Chin. Martial Arts **11**, 34–37 (2020)

5. Jie, S.: 2020 Shaanxi Youth traditional Wushu Invitational competition will be held in Xi'an. Chin. Wushu **11**, 54 (2020)
6. Zhenjing, L, Zhixue, X.: Analysis on the inheritance and development of luohanquan in Huojia County, Henan Province. Chin. Wushu **11** 122–124 + 78 (2020)
7. Dan, Z., Wenbo, W.: Hot topics and core issues of cross-cultural communication of Taijiquan in Chinese academic circles in recent 20 years. Chin. Wushu **11**, 98–105 (2020)
8. Rong, C.C., Jun J.Y.: Research on Wushu culture from the perspective of Confucianism, Buddhism and Taoism. Chin. Wushu **11** 95–97 + 105 (2020)
9. Traveling across the sea to Shaolin, seeking truth for nothing, from a Shaolin foreign disciple to a foreign minister. Shaolin Taiji **11** 43–44 (2020)
10. Shaolin and Taiji show off China. Sidelights on the award presentation of Henan Wushu "double evaluation" activity in 2017. Shaolin Taiji **11** 51 (2020)
11. The editorial department of this journal. Communicating with the world with the wisdom of Shaolin Zen and martial arts. Wanakuni: diplomatic envoy under the understanding of Chinese culture. Shaolin Taiji **11** 52–53 (2020)
12. Hongbin, L., Jiandong, H., Zheng, H.: Cold thinking on the development of school Wushu in the new era. Zhejiang Sports Sci. **42**(6), 44–47 (2020)
13. Linlin, L.: Research on the issue of Chinese Wushu entering the olympic games – taking Wushu entering the fourth youth olympic games as an example. Sport. Goods Technol. **21**, 128–129 (2020)
14. Mingjie, Z., Hexia, W., Ding, H.: Analysis of the two-way path based on the internationalization of Wushu. Sport. Goods Technol. **21**, 3–4 (2020)
15. Zhenyan, F., Jun, L.: Training both inside and outside the body and mind, practicing Bajiquan. Tourism **11**, 86–93 (2020)
16. Shengchuan, H.: Paradigm crisis and reconstruction of Chinese Wushu research. J. Xi'an Inst. Phys. Educ. **37**(06), 731–736 (2020)
17. Ruolin, W.: One belt, one road, the development of martial arts culture. Martial Arts Res. **5**(10), 37–40 (2020)
18. Jiankang, N., Xupeng, W., Jie, L., Xuemei, Y.: New exploration on the strategy of Chinese Wushu entering the olympic games – enlightenment of judo development. Wushu Res. **5**(10), 5–7 (2020)
19. Wanliang, T.: Tradition and modernity: on the origin of Chinese martial arts. Martial Arts Res. **5**(10) 14–16 + 26 (2020)
20. Yuchao, L., Zezheng, Z.: Unified understanding in the process of internationalization of Chinese Wushu. Wushu Res. **5**(10), 11–13 (2020)
21. Xue, Y., Xiaoshuang, W.: Research on professional competition operation of Wushu Sanda. Wushu Res. **5**(10), 45–48 (2020)
22. Zhengning, Y.: Exploration of Wushu culture communication and development mechanism under the environment of media integration. Wushu Res. **5**(10), 24–26 (2020)
23. Xuepeng, L., Qiuyan, L.: Research on traditional Wushu values. Wushu Res. **5**(10), 29–32 (2020)

Development and Utilization of Folk Game Intelligent Program in Children's Activities of Big Data Information Education

Lijuan Zhong[✉]

XianYang Normal University, XianYang 712000, China

Abstract. With the continuous development of the times, people have higher and higher requirements for education. Therefore, the intelligent folk games need to pay more. How to improve the development and utilization of folk games in children's activities has become the focus of teachers' research. At the same time, the concept of education is also changing. Therefore, when carrying out educational activities, we should fully integrate folk intelligent game resources and give full play to the advantages of folk game resources.

Keywords: Intelligent folk games · Kindergarten activities · Development and utilization

1 Introduction

The current education stage has started from kindergarten, but kindergarten education belongs to a special stage of education, there are some difficulties in the process of education, if there is no scientific and effective education methods, it will lose the role and significance of education. The students in the early childhood stage are the golden age of the common development of morality, intelligence, sports and beauty, so it is very important for the correct education of children [1]. Children's age is low, and their cognition of things is not comprehensive. If we adopt the indoctrination education mode in the process of education, it will seriously affect the normal development of children. Therefore, teachers should make full use of folk game resources, start with children's interests and hobbies, and drive them to learn by means of games. The schematic diagram of children's games is shown in Fig. 1.

2 Related Work

2.1 Combined with children's Teaching Objectives, the Introduction of Local Folk Games

In the early childhood stage, students are very interested in the game, so in the process of teaching activities, making full use of game resources can effectively stimulate children's

© ICST Institute for Computer Sciences, Social Informatics and Telecommunications Engineering 2021
Published by Springer Nature Switzerland AG 2021. All Rights Reserved
M. A. Jan and F. Khan (Eds.): BigIoT-EDU 2021, LNICST 391, pp. 253–262, 2021.
https://doi.org/10.1007/978-3-030-87900-6_31

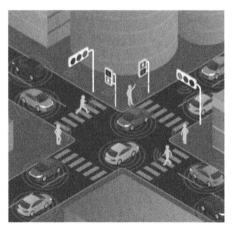

Fig. 1. The schematic diagram of children's games

interest in learning, so that children have a more forward understanding of learning. In the process of playing games, self innovation awareness can also be effectively improved, and it can also help children establish a correct ideological and moral sentiment [2–4]. The introduction of game resources in kindergarten activities can make children become more confident. In the activities, children can make their moral, intellectual, physical and aesthetic development better by playing games. In this way, it is of great significance for children's healthy and comprehensive development.

At present, there are many folk game resources that can be used in kindergarten activities, but many folk game resources cannot be used directly. We need to innovate on the original basis, so as to better play the role of game resources. Therefore, kindergarten teachers should constantly innovate the traditional folk game resources, and use the methods of expansion, combination and divergent thinking in specific activities to make the innovative folk game resources more in line with children's cognition, so as to continuously improve children's enthusiasm to participate in education, At the same time, we also need to innovate the use of folk game resources [5]. Will use the form of design interesting, can effectively attract young people.

2.2 Based on children's Reality, We Should Choose Folk Games that Are Conducive to children's Physical and Mental Development

As the most important content of early childhood education activities, the design of teaching activities is very important. According to children's age and psychological characteristics, teachers should not only pay attention to the theoretical basis of the game, but also pay attention to the cultivation of their comprehensive ability. Therefore, teachers must consider the following aspects, such as children's age, gender, hobbies and their cooperation ability [6–8]. Because of this, the introduction of games should be combined with the actual situation of children to make it more targeted and effective. In addition, the local characteristics of folk games should be integrated into it, and teachers should choose suitable folk games for children. For example, younger children, because of their poor cooperation ability, are more independent in the game and often do not like to be disturbed, so they are more suitable for individual games, while older children like to play with other children, so they are more suitable for group games. For another example, boys like challenging and sports games, while girls like relatively quiet games. From these points of view, teachers in the introduction of folk games must be based on children's reality, so as to better play the positive role of folk games in promoting children's physical and mental health development.

2.3   Creating Folk Game Situation and Developing children's Learning Potential

In the introduction of folk games, teachers should also pay attention to the creation of relevant game situations, which is not only conducive to the innovation of the form of game teaching, but also conducive to enrich the content of game teaching. To provide children with a vivid game field with more diversified game situations and give full play to its value, develop children's intelligence and develop their learning potential. In addition, teachers can also make use of the advantages of information technology to create vivid game situations for children, such as video, animation, pictures and so on. At the same time, they can provide props for them to give them sufficient space for performance, so that they can feel the fun of the game, so as to achieve the goal of education [9]. Teachers gradually guide children to learn by playing and play in learning to promote their development in many aspects. Teachers must also realize that folk games, as the essence of national culture, can guide children to learn the excellent traditional culture of the Chinese nation in game teaching.

3   Optimization Strategy of Big Data Technology in College Education

3.1   Building a Complementary System to Break the Information Island

In order to ensure the effective formation of education data and break the information island, it is necessary not only to strengthen the information construction, but also to strengthen the technical support, system maintenance and so on. At the same time, we should strengthen the use of relevant education data. Through the establishment of relevant leading groups, we can clarify the business responsibilities of different departments, so as to promote the further use of big data and help it to play its value. All business departments should also conduct comprehensive data exchange and complementation, and verify the inconsistent data information again, so as to ensure the standardization and authenticity of data collection. In addition, all business departments should collect relevant information in a unified format, which is conducive to the later data analysis, inspection and evaluation [10–12]. For example, information collection standards and databases can be unified, and the popularization and promotion of information collection standards can be promoted, so as to ensure the effectiveness and uniformity of data collection.

3.2 Strengthen Data Integration, Application and Research

It is necessary to strengthen data integration, application and research, and enhance the auxiliary frequency of education data in higher education teaching and education management, so as to promote the modernization of education teaching and education management. First of all, it is necessary to further integrate the scattered information among the business departments of colleges and universities, not only to fully realize the automation of data collection, modernization of education and teaching, automation of scientific research management and informatization of financial management, but also to integrate all the education data, divide and stack the simple data structure, so as to increase the analysis of the relevant dominant data, So as to provide relevant data support for colleges and universities [13–15]. For example, we can strengthen the effective management of the collection way in the data collection stage. Different collection ways will form different collection forms. We can unify, sort and transform different data collection, hoping to lay the foundation for later data analysis and integration by forming a new data set.

3.3 Strengthen Systematic Management and Overall Planning

Colleges and universities should strengthen the overall management and planning of educational information, so as to strengthen the analysis and use of the original data. First of all, it is necessary to formulate long-term data collection standards and development plans, so as to promote the improvement of data collection, analysis and application, and strengthen the maintenance and summary of initial data. At the same time, the relevant data statistics work should also be evaluated regularly, so as to strengthen the macro management of relevant data and information; secondly, colleges and universities should constantly coordinate and organize various business departments to carry out information work, so as to promote the construction of school affairs network platform [16–18]. At the same time, it is also necessary to strengthen the maintenance and management of university websites, and timely warn the relevant network public opinion, so as to ensure that bad information can be handled in time; finally, it is necessary to strengthen the development of big data information system, establish a unified big data computing system, and promote the diversification of computing, so as to meet the different computing needs of educational data, It can also manage and plan education data in a unified way,

4 Relevant Strategies to Strengthen the Organic Combination of Kindergarten Activities and Folk Game Resources

4.1 Effective Integration of Folk Game Resources and Outdoor Game Activities

Most of the folk games are carried out outdoors, so when teachers carry out activities, they can fully combine folk game resources with outdoor sports, so that children can exercise in the process of playing games. In this way, children's participation enthusiasm can be improved, and students' perception ability can be cultivated. The moral quality of students can also be good edification. In addition to combining folk game resources with sports activities, teachers can also combine folk game resources with intellectual activities, such as radish squatting, counting frogs and other games. In this way, children can not only enjoy themselves, but also exercise their thinking, which can be said to kill two birds with one stone [19]. In order to improve the data transmission rate and energy efficiency, the following energy efficiency maximization resource allocation problem is established:

$$\max = \frac{P_U Ew\%GF}{P_t EwF} \tag{1}$$

$$G_2 G\|w\|^2 \le P_{\max} \tag{2}$$

4.2 Effective Integration of Folk Game Resources and Indoor Activities

Although most of the folk game resources are carried out outdoors, it is impossible to organize children to go outdoors every time in the process of carrying out activities. Appropriate indoor activities can also effectively improve students' personal ability. Therefore, teachers should fully combine folk game resources with indoor activities in the process of carrying out activities. Fully explore the characteristics of folk game resources, so as to select some activities suitable for indoor development. For example, tangram, checkers or jigsaw puzzle. Indoor activities often focus on training students' thinking ability, so scientific and effective indoor activities can continuously improve students' thinking ability. To lay a good foundation for future learning and development. In addition to carrying out some intellectual activities indoors, we can also carry out some manual activities, such as paper-cut, clay sculpture and so on. Through this activity mode, students' hands-on ability and action coordination ability can be well improved, which is of great help to children's future life [20]. Although folk game resources are dead, but the content and form can be innovated. Therefore, teachers can encourage students to innovate the original activities in the process of carrying out activities, and add their own interested elements in the activities, so as to improve students' innovation and creativity.

4.3 Effective Integration of Folk Game Resources and Spare Time

Children's daily time in school is very limited, and the time in class is even more limited. Therefore, it is basically impossible to give full play to the role of folk game resources only by the activity time in class. Therefore, teachers should seize the spare time and combine the spare time with folk game resources scientifically and reasonably, So as to maximize the role of folk game resources. When children enter the kindergarten in the morning, they are easily bored. If they don't adjust the students' mood in time, it is easy to directly affect the students' learning state all day. Therefore, teachers can carry out some game activities in the morning. For example: hawk catching chicken, radish squatting and other activities. When students participate in activities, they will soon forget some unhappy emotions. Dependence on parents.

4.4 Infiltrate Folk Games into the Whole Process of Teaching and Develop children's Thinking

In children's daily teaching, teachers can carry out folk games in their spare time. Such as tug of war, stone, scissors, cloth and so on to enhance the sense of participation in children's activities, not only to integrate folk games into the whole teaching process, but also to meet the needs of children through various forms of folk games. Under the guidance of teachers, they complete the game together, which adds a sense of achievement to children's game experience [21]. At the same time, teachers can also select appropriate game items according to the classification of games and children's wishes, so as to fully mobilize their participation in activities and successfully complete the teaching objectives. In the game, teachers can guide children to role play, so that they can better understand the characters and stimulate their desire for performance. Such as doctors, police and teachers, if you are a doctor, how would you treat patients, if you are a police, how would you do it, if you are a teacher, how would you teach children to learn knowledge, etc. In the creation of this kind of problem situation, it can stimulate children's curiosity and creativity, not only meet their desire for performance, but also spread children's thinking and innovation ability.

5 Simulation Analysis

For children's activities, we mainly need to develop children's intelligence level, so we use different games to match children's hands-on ability, etc. we can get the simulation distribution as shown in Fig. 2. From Fig. 2, we can see that different strategies and games have different effects on children. Among them, the proportion of events in the competition has reached 30%. That shows that children should not only do things but also think about problems in games with comparison [22]. On the other hand, it also shows that people will develop a higher level of intelligence in the process of moving.

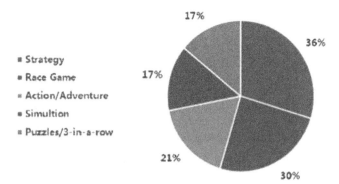

Fig. 2. The influence of different projects on children

To get rid of the chronic disease of "five only" education evaluation and implement the inevitable choice of establishing morality and cultivating people and running people's satisfactory education.

The plan points out that we should take the effectiveness of moral education as the fundamental standard, improve the system of moral education, speed up the modernization of education, build a powerful country in education, and run a satisfactory education for the people. In terms of promoting the development of students, education evaluation must adhere to the principle of "moral education as the fundamental task" and point to the life growth of students. However, traditional education evaluation pursues utilitarian value too much, especially the chronic disease of "five only evaluation" is making teachers and students instrumental, profit oriented and one-sided in school education. The development of individual teachers and students is dominated by the evaluation index dimension, system and inherent evaluation standard. Personality and spiritual pursuit are gradually lost and declined, and life vitality is covered. The original reason is that the "five only evaluation system" is the product of China's specific historical stage. In the past, in order to cultivate and select catch-up standardized talents, we chose quantitative and objective external benchmarking indicators that are easy to see, catch up and surpass [23]. However, the current evaluation system seriously suppresses people's life vitality, conceals personality and creativity, and is seriously contrary to the goal of cultivating new people with harmonious and healthy body and mind and all-round development in the new era. It is an urgent task to get rid of the "five only" stubborn disease and realize the modern transformation of education evaluation.

6 Application of Big Data Technology in Higher Education

6.1 There is Information Island Phenomenon

At present, there is a lack of communication in the business departments of many colleges and universities, which also leads to the independent existence of many data resources in the business departments, which is not conducive to information sharing, but also makes the data stored between various departments deviate. This will also affect the business collaboration of different departments, which will easily lead to waste of storage space and low utilization rate of storage space. At the same time, the phenomenon of information island is also difficult to recessively analyze the dominant data, even if the formation of relevant recessive data, its authenticity and value also need to be considered. For example, at present, many business departments of colleges and universities will use Oracle, visual FOX PRO, Sybase and other databases, and some departments will use traditional Excel to save relevant data. This kind of storage form is not unified, which also makes data fusion difficult. As shown in Fig. 3. Moreover, some universities lack of long-term planning, data independence between business departments, and many businesses can not share data, which not only wastes storage space, but also makes the phenomenon of information island exist all the time.

6.2 The Data Caliber of Each Department is not Unified

It is necessary to strengthen the cooperation between the two business departments in Colleges and universities to make joint efforts for data integration, application and research. But at present, each business department in Colleges and universities has their

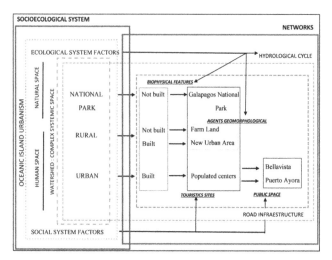

Fig. 3. Island phenomenon

own struggle, which also leads to the data caliber is not unified, a lot of education data can not be effectively applied in education teaching and education management, which also hinders the deep mining of the value of education data to a certain extent. For example, the alumni system does not share the data of enrollment, employment, student management and so on with the University, which also causes a lot of inconsistent information input and makes it lack of certain integrity.

7 Conclusions

To sum up, early childhood education plays a very important role in children's growth and development. Folk game resources are a very important part of Chinese traditional culture. In the process of early childhood education, making full use of folk game resources can continuously improve children's learning interest and comprehensive learning ability, which plays a very important role in children's growth and development. The ultimate purpose of evaluation is to promote the fullness and perfection of learners' life meaning based on educational goals. At present, in order to ease the big data education evaluation becoming the means, methods and processes of producers, avoid becoming a discipline technology and fall into the pattern of simply focusing on instrumental rationality, we must regain the value of big data evaluation, stick to it and drive the reconstruction of education evaluation system [24]. The persistence of value rationality of big data reflects students' value pursuit and life significance. Instrumental rationality is the source of students' rationality and innovation. The combination of the two becomes the Ariadne line to guide students to realize the ultimate value of life. On the one hand, we should promote the diversification of evaluation subjects and give full play to the role of professional institutions and social organizations.

Acknowledgements. Education and Teaching Reform Research Project of Xianyang normal University 2019" Research on the Reform and Innovation of Art Curriculum system of Preschool

Education Specialty under the background of excellent Preschool Teachers training "Project No.: Y07;2019 "Young Backbone Teachers" No. XSYGG201907, Xianyang Normal University, 2019 Xiamen University from 2018 to 2019.

References

1. Dang, G.: The application and strategy of folk game resources in kindergarten activities. Basic Educ. Forum **22**, 63–64 (2020)
2. Liu, Z.: Analysis of the use of folk game resources in kindergarten activities and its strategies. Acad. Wkly. **21**, 165–166 (2020)
3. Li, Y.J.: Exploring the use of folk game resources in kindergarten activities and its strategies. New Curriculum (Comprehensive Ed.) **9**, 155 (2019)
4. He, W.: The application and strategy of folk game resources in kindergarten activities. Intelligent Learning and Innovation Research Committee of China Intelligent Engineering Research Association. Research on Educational Theory (Part 7), p. 1. Chongqing Dingyun Culture Communication Co., Ltd. (2019)
5. Chen, Q.: Strengthening teacher child interaction to support deep learning: a case study of children's construction game activities. Read. Writ. Arithm. **4**, 53–54 (2021)
6. Chen, W.: Innovative strategies of game education in early childhood teaching activities. Contemp. Fam. Educ. **4**, 55–56 (2021)
7. Hong, M.: On the application of natural resources in children's art teaching activities. Contemp. Fam. Educ. **4**, 67–68 (2021)
8. Sun, H.: Let the melody of life play the music of happy growth – pursuing the educational value of children's daily life activities. Education **6**, 75–76 (2021)
9. Zhang, X.: On the development and application of school-based teaching materials guided by children's mathematics activities. Mod. Voc. Educ. **8**, 48–49 (2021)
10. Sun, J.: Analysis on the prevention countermeasures of hidden dangers in children's outdoor activities. Everyday Love Sci. (Educ. Front.) **3**, 5–6 (2021)
11. Zhu, J.: On the strategy of introducing nursery rhymes into children's independent play activities. Love Sci. Every Day (Front. Educ.) **3**, 33–34 (2021)
12. Yi'er, N.: How to use picture books to create interesting preschool education activities. Love Sci. Every Day (Teach. Res.) **3**, 127–128 (2021)
13. Li, Q.: Strategies of safety education for children in art activities. Basic Educ. Forum **4**, 78 (2021)
14. Wang, X.: The cultivation of children's effective reading in parent-child activities. Parents **4**, 185–186 (2021)
15. Yu, X.: Play talk record exhibition: deep learning for children: a case study of "how high are bamboo shoots" in large class measurement activity. Child. Health **2**, 26–27 (2021)
16. Ma, Y.: "Woodworking workshop" activity: improving children's multiple abilities. Child. Health **2**, 36–38 (2021)
17. Liu, T.: Reflections on the improvement of preschool teachers' observation skills. Child. Health **2**, 44–45 (2021)
18. Mao, L.: Open materials expand the possibility of children's learning – taking the construction activity "tree house" as an example. Early Educ. **5**, 48–49 (2021)
19. Lu, L.: Effective strategies for supporting children to participate in planting activities. Tianjin Educ. **4**, 154–155 (2021)
20. Liu, X.: Training strategies of cooperative ability in children's game activities. Tianjin Educ. **4** 156–157 + 160 (2021)

21. Hua, Y.: Research on children's independent choice in regional activities. Happy Fam. **3**, 15 (2021)
22. Liu, S.: Practice Tao Xingzhi's educational thought and build a living environment for kindergarten. Happy Fam. **3**, 18–19 (2021)
23. Shao, L.: The application of teachers' observation ability in children's planting activities. Happy Fam. **3**, 46 (2021)
24. Zhang, X.: The significance of Tao Xingzhi's educational thought on curriculum gamification. Happy Fam. **3**, 57 (2021)

Educational Informatization in the Reform of Physical Education Teaching

Kang Lei[⊠]

Shaanxi Xi'an Eurasia University, Xi'an 710065, China
leikang@eurasia.edu

Abstract. In the Internet age, education has also entered the information age. The informatization of subject teaching has become the inevitable result of the development of education. Physical education is no exception. How to better apply information technology to all aspects of daily teaching is one of the major problems faced by PE teachers. Based on the general trend of education informatization, this paper discusses how to embody informatization in all aspects of physical education reform.

Keywords: SAS · Physical education

1 Introduction

With the vigorous development of sports and more scientific sports research, the role of sports statistics shows its importance more and more. We know that the factors, including physiological, psychological, technical and environmental factors, which come from the extremely complex factors that affect the human body's sports, undoubtedly affect the sports performance. Because of the fierce competition, it is obviously not enough for people to analyze human motion only by experience and simple data. At present, sports research generally needs to go through scientific analysis, that is, through quantitative analysis to qualitative analysis, so as to draw correct conclusions and carry out quantitative analysis, usually using the commonly used statistical methods and multi factor analysis methods in sports statistics. With the in-depth study of sports statistics, people are more and more aware of its role in the field of sports, especially with the continuous development of new technology, the introduction of information theory, cybernetics, system theory and electronic technology, sports statistics method has become one of the indispensable means in sports scientific management and training. At present, with the rapid development of China's sports and level, the number of sports in the leading position in the world is gradually increasing, and some backward sports in the past are gradually catching up with the world's advanced level. The improvement of sports performance, on the one hand, is the improvement of athletes' own quality, on the other hand, because we now have scientific management methods and training means, in which the use of sports statistical methods has been gradually promoted. In sports statistical methods, common statistical methods have been widely used in management and training, with

© ICST Institute for Computer Sciences, Social Informatics and Telecommunications Engineering 2021
Published by Springer Nature Switzerland AG 2021. All Rights Reserved
M. A. Jan and F. Khan (Eds.): BigIoT-EDU 2021, LNICST 391, pp. 263–271, 2021.
https://doi.org/10.1007/978-3-030-87900-6_32

the deepening of research and the popularization of computers, the use of multivariate analysis methods is also increasing. We have made statistics on Sports Science from 1984 to 1994. The following information can give us some enlightenment.

2 The Application of SAS System in the Teaching Reform of Sports Statistics

In sports science magazine, the proportion of sports statistical methods used in papers is about 50%, and it has reached about 60% since the 1990s. It can be seen that sports statistical methods are widely used in scientific research.

Common statistical methods still account for a large proportion in sports research. With the popularization of computers in the 1990s, multi factor analysis methods are gradually used in sports research, accounting for about 20% in the 1990s.

Due to the more and more important role of sports statistics in the field of sports, sports statistics courses have been set up in sports universities, sports colleges and sports departments of various colleges that train sports research, training and management talents [1–4]. At present, both undergraduate and college students in Beijing Normal College of physical education have set up the course of sports statistics, and graduate students have set up the course of multi factor analysis. Therefore, from the perspective of teaching in physical education colleges, more and more attention has been paid to sports statistics.

3 Q-Learning Algorithm

Q-learning algorithm is a milestone reinforcement learning algorithm, which was proposed by Watkins in 1987. It is a Markov decision process (MDP) in essence. It is a simple and widely used reinforcement learning algorithm, which has been widely concerned by experts and scholars in the field of artificial intelligence [5]. Q-learning algorithm does not need to establish an accurate environment model. It only learns the evaluation value of a certain action after it is completed, instead of learning the evaluation function of each state. In this paper, the Q-learning algorithm is introduced into the coordination control of SAS and EPS, which is just in consideration of the complexity of vehicle driving environment. By introducing the algorithm, it does not need to consider the impact of complex environment on the vehicle, only needs to evaluate the action after the action, and select the action through the evaluation value obtained.

The updated formula of Q value is as follows:

$$Q_{t+1}(S_{t+1}, A_{t+1}) \leftarrow Q_t(S_1, A_t) + a_t\big[R(S_t, A_t) + \gamma maxQ_t(S_{t+1}, A_{t+1})\big]$$

Where γ is the discount factor and a is the learning rate.

The main advantage of q-learning is that it integrates the time difference method TD of Monte Carlo and dynamic programming, while calculating the value function under the cover of walking, of course, it is solved by Bellman equation (dynamic programming) [6]. The value of each state is determined not only by the current state but also by the later state, so the current state value V (s) can be obtained by the cumulative reward expectation of the state:

$$V_\pi(s) = E(U_t|S_t = s)$$

$$V_\pi(s) = E_\pi\left[R_{t+1} + \gamma\left[R_{r+2} + \gamma[\cdots\cdots]\right]S_t = S\right]$$

$$V_\pi(s) = E_\pi\left[R_{t+1} + \gamma V\left(S^{'}\right)S_t = S\right]$$

The optimal cumulative expectation can be expressed by V * (s), and it can be seen that the optimal is the highest expectation of the current strategy

$$V^*(s) = max_\pi E\left[\sum_{t=0}^{H} \gamma^t R(S_t, A_t, S_{t-1})\pi, S = s\right]$$

Q-learning is an incremental online learning algorithm, which is mature and effective, and its convergence has been proved.

4   The Application of SAS System in the Teaching Reform of Physical Education Measurement and Evaluation

With the popularization of computer in our country, the data processing in statistics can be completed by computer, which brings us great benefits. The calculation speed is doubled and accelerated, and when we use large samples to analyze problems, we will not worry about the calculation problems. But in the past computer data processing, we have to write a program first to carry out the operation, which brings inconvenience to many people, because not everyone can easily master the method of programming [7–9]. In this case, computer experts solved this problem for us, they developed a software package for statistical processing, including SAS statistical software.

For SAS statistical software, people can generally master how to use it by learning for a short time. SAS software includes data processing methods of common statistics (such as calculation of mean and standard deviation, hypothesis test method, variance analysis, etc.) and data processing methods of multi factor analysis (such as regression analysis, discriminant analysis, cluster analysis, principal component analysis, etc.), It is easy to master, so the introduction of SAS software has brought great benefits to our statistics teaching.

5   The Logical Origin of Practical Teaching Reform of Physical Education Major

5.1   Develop Various Abilities

The goal of P.E. teaching speech major is to cultivate excellent P.E. teachers. The training process focuses on students' ability to master sports knowledge and skills, P.E. teaching speech teaching ability and P.E. competition organization ability, so as to meet the needs of the country and Society for P.E. teaching speech talents. Results from the perspective of attributes, P.E. teaching talents should belong to applied talents, which is, to be exact, dynamic brain Good application, willing to do, hands-on type sports professionals. It can be seen that the various abilities of the students are determined based on the professional attributes, which is the natural responsibility of the physical education professional training unit [10]. In January 2018, the Ministry of Education promulgated the notice on the implementation of the measures for the certification of normal education majors in Yintong University (temporary), which highlights the importance of improving the ability of P.E. teachers to cultivate professional talents. The ability based orientation should become the concept of sports education professional talents training, It should be said that as an important part of the cultivation of physical education professionals, practical courses and teaching play an extremely critical role in improving the ability of physical education professionals.

5.2 Practical Courses

It is no exaggeration to say that the various abilities of physical education professionals are mostly obtained from the practice course teaching. However, for a long time, the training mode of physical education major in China has been subject oriented, and following this logical thinking has restricted the individuality and flexibility of talent training. The acquisition of students' ability is mostly just an accessory in the process of sports knowledge and skills teaching [11–14]. This kind of training logic orientation is easy to ignore students' sports practice ability, which is why many graduates of physical education major are difficult to understand the reason of being competent for the post of PE teachers in local primary and secondary schools. Therefore, the traditional discipline logic can not meet the needs of the training of sports business talents in the new era. We should shift from the discipline academic logic to the application ability oriented logic, reconstruct the ability oriented talent training program, and build a sports practice teaching and training system to meet the needs of the country and society.

6 SAS Can Improve the Teaching Effect of Physical Education Theory Course

The computer teaching and research section of our college has set up SAS software course for postgraduates since 1989. Students' study has laid a good foundation for the completion of graduation thesis. In recent years, according to the graduate thesis, when doing statistical analysis, we usually complete the data processing work through SAS software. But there are teaching problems [15]. On the one hand, the computer teachers are not very clear about the statistical content that students need to master when explaining SAS. As a result, some of the content should be introduced to students in detail but not specifically. Some of the content can be roughly understood but takes up a lot of time to explain. On the other hand, the statistics teachers still use the previous book method when explaining the multi factor analysis for students. The calculation process talks a lot, but the effect is not good, As a result, the teaching problems of repetition and disconnection of the two courses are caused. In order to solve this problem, our computer and statistics teachers try to combine the multi factor analysis teaching of postgraduates with SAS statistical software teaching, That is to say, the statistics teacher explains the theoretical problems in the multi factor analysis, emphatically introduces the significance, concept, experimental design and data analysis of various statistical methods, while the computer teacher introduces the data content in the SAS software in the calculation part, so that the teaching difficulty in the statistics, that is, the calculation part, can be completed by the computer. In the second semester of the 1993–1994 academic year, we conducted the first round of combined teaching experiments. Before each chapter is taught, teachers of our two majors are discussing the content of statistics. Computers are going to talk about the content. After each class, they are going to discuss the problems they encounter. The general teaching process is: first, statistics teachers explain the meaning and concept of a certain method (this is the key explanation). The calculation method is just a rough introduction to the types and approximate steps of calculation methods [16]. After that, in the computer class, the computer teacher introduces how to use SAS software to process this statistical method and get the calculation results. In the statistical class, first analyze the SAS software calculation results made by examples in the computer class, and then talk about the new content. The introduction of each statistical method is basically completed according to this process. After a round of teaching, we have tasted the real significance of the teaching reform and found out many experiences.

7 Application of SAS Software in Statistics Teaching

The introduction of SAS software into statistical teaching has brought unexpected results to our statistical teaching, especially the teaching of multi factor analysis. First, it solves the calculation problem that has been perplexing the teaching of statistics. The data processing of various methods can be completed by SAS. The calculation speed is doubled, and the calculation result is accurate and reliable. Second, the focus of statistical teaching is shifted from the calculation method of the main lecture to the use and significance analysis of various methods of the main lecture. The problem of blind use of statistical methods by less students can be solved, which undoubtedly improves the quality of teaching. Third, because of solving the calculation problem, students' enthusiasm for learning has been improved, and teachers' enthusiasm for teaching has also been improved, which has played a positive role in promoting teaching. Fourth, the popularization of this kind of teaching will promote the scientific research of the college [17–19]. After many people master the method of statistical processing with SAS software, they can make more teachers join the ranks of scientific research, increase the number of scientific research articles using statistical methods, and indirectly improve the quality of scientific research. Of course, this combination teaching method is just in its infancy, and there are still many problems:

1) the teaching content of SAS software and multi factor and element analysis needs to be further determined, that is to say, their teaching characteristics and clear teaching content need to be established in the combination;

2) There is no doubt that the two courses will bring inconvenience to their teaching. Once a link is not well connected, it will disrupt the overall teaching effect. Although there are still some problems in the introduction of SAS software into statistics teaching, its advantages cannot be estimated. As shown in Fig. 1 and Fig. 2. It is necessary for us to constantly summarize our experience in the future teaching and solve the problems that may arise in time. We can also imagine that we can integrate the two courses in the next two years, that is, SAS software teaching as an experimental course of statistics teaching, which requires statistics teachers to master the SAS software teaching or computer teachers.

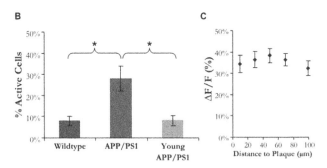

Fig. 1. Effect of SAS software teaching

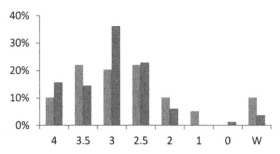

Fig. 2. Simulation for statistics teaching

8   Problems Existing in Practice Teaching of Physical Education Major Under the Guidance of Traditional Disciplines

8.1   The Characteristics of the Training Objectives of Teachers' Education Fail to Highlight

The nature of teacher training is the fundamental characteristic of education major, including physical education major, the focus of physical education talents training is to cultivate practical and applied physical education talents rather than scientific research talents. As shown in Fig. 3.The objects of physical education talents training are mainly the prospective physical education teachers at all levels and all kinds of schools in the future, especially the middle and small-sized physical education teachers with comprehensive teaching theory literacy and solid Sports skills literacy. One of the important dimensions to measure the quality of physical education professional training is the training quality of physical education normal students' professional practice teaching ability, which directly determines whether the physical education normal students can effectively and qualitatively complete the physical education teaching task after entering the post [20]. The traditional subject oriented physical education personnel training pays more attention to the cultivation of normal students' subject knowledge and subject content knowledge, but lacks the cultivation of normal students' subject teaching knowledge, especially the cultivation of practical teaching ability.

Fig. 3. Traditional sports discipline

8.2 The Construction of Practical Curriculum System Lags Behind the National Education Policy

Curriculum is the core carrier of education. The key to the cultivation of high-quality rest education talents lies in the curriculum system of physical education. As the practical teaching curriculum of the curriculum system of physical education, it is an important part of the curriculum that the rest education normal students must master. In any era, the development and practice of any curriculum need to consider three elements: one is the important basis to be followed. Among them, education embodies the national will, what kind of people to cultivate, how to cultivate, how to evaluate and other educational tasks, must follow the national education reform policy, and must be closely related to the spirit, instructions and requirements into the curriculum system [21]. At present, the practice teaching curriculum construction of physical education curriculum system in most colleges lags behind the national education policy, mainly as follows. In the face of the new era education, such as sports power construction, moral education, curriculum ideological and political education, sports education platform and so on, especially the new policy of physical education and sports education reform, the professional practice of physical education is facing The sensitivity of the curriculum to the spirit of relevant policies is insufficient, and the integration of the spirit and requirements of the new policy to guide the construction of practice curriculum system is not enough.

8.3 The Richness of Practice Teaching Mode and Teaching Mode Needs to be Strengthened

It can effectively complete the strong support of practice teaching, and the specific performance is as follows. The staff of the practical teaching team is mainly composed of full-time physical education teachers in physical education institutes and departments. It is true that the solid theoretical course teaching and practical course teaching of full-time physical education teachers in physical education institutes and departments can provide guarantee for the physical education normal students to accept the practical course learning. However, in the face of the rapid changes and new forms of physical education in primary and secondary schools, Over reliance on or even only relying on the full-time teachers of physical education institutions to carry out practical curriculum teaching can not fully provide strong support for practical curriculum teaching [22]. Although some colleges have adopted the measures of joint training of physical education talents, They invite excellent PE teachers from primary and secondary schools to participate in the learning guidance of normal students' practical courses, but they are still limited to helping normal students get familiar with the development of PE Teaching in primary and secondary schools or teach them textbooks, teaching methods and other knowledge through excellent PE teachers from the grass-roots level entering the campus to carry out PE teaching lectures in primary and secondary schools [23]. The characteristics of scattered and individual combat are far from forming an institutionalized and large-scale talent joint teaching mode.

9   Conclusions

To sum up, we believe that the significance of teaching reform is very significant. We can not only summarize teaching experience, but also find solutions to problems, and improve the professional level of teachers. We believe that through our efforts, our teaching achievements will be recognized. Introducing SAS into PE teaching is a new way to reform PE teaching. It is of great practical significance to reform education mode and improve teaching efficiency. In the teaching of SAS, computer hardware is the foundation, it is the basic guarantee to realize the supporting function of SAS goal, and the design and development of software is the key to the effective application of SAS in practice, which needs to organize experts to select the subject, design the courseware, and realize the teaching goal According to the teaching objectives and the actual situation of different types of students, the basic program to achieve the objectives is planned to ensure the realization of the task objectives of the courseware.

References

1. Mingli, Z., Xiulin, Y. (eds.): Methods and Procedures of Multivariate Statistical Analysis, p. 5. Beijing Institute of Physical Education Press, Beijing (1991)

2. Compilation group of sports statistics data. Sports Statistics. People's Sports Publishing, Du, Beijing (1987)
3. Compiled by Lu Wendai. Practical Technology of SAS/PC Statistical Analysis Software. State Industrial Publishing Du, Beijing (1996)
4. Jinning: Innovative practice of College Physical Education Teaching from the perspective of agriculture, rural areas and farmers culture. J. Nucl. Agric. **35**(5), 1256 (2021)
5. Zhendong, M.: The feasibility study of adding rural leisure sports courses in Colleges and universities in the new period. J. Nucl. Agric. **35**(5), 1260 (2021)
6. Rongping, Z., Nina, J.: Significance and function of cheerleading teaching on aesthetic education of rural college students. J. Nucl. Agric. **35**(5), 1267 (2021)
7. Melina, S., Alina, K., Sarah, S., Simon, B., Filip, M.: What makes a physical education teacher? Personal characteristics for physical education development. Br. J. Educ. Psychol. (2021)
8. Morrison, H.J., Gleddie, D.: Interpretive case studies of inclusive physical education: shared experiences from diverse school settings. Int. J. Inclusive Educ. **25**(4) (2021)
9. Xiaoli, Y.: Research on the penetration path of emotional education in primary school physical education. Parents **9**, 20–21 (2021)
10. Haiying, Q., Zimeng, G.: Research on the cultivation of "demand oriented" excellent PE teachers in primary and secondary schools. J. Liaoning Normal Univ. (Nat. Sci. Ed.) **44**(1), 130–137 (2021)
11. Chao, F., Bin, H.: Can physical exercise promote the development of teenagers' cognitive ability? An empirical study based on China's education tracking survey data. J. East China Normal Univ. (Educ. Sci. Ed.) **39**(3), 84–98 (2021)
12. Yuan, G., Chunbin, D.: Characteristics of college physical education in Yan'an period and its contemporary enlightenment. J. Yan'an Univ. (Nat. Sci. Ed.) **40**(1), 99–102 (2021)
13. Yangmin, Z., Shirong, L., Zhenshan, L.: Analysis on the promotion path of continuing education to the professional ability of primary and secondary school physical education teachers. J. Yan'an Univ. (Nat. Sci. Ed.) **40**(1), 117–120 (2021)
14. Lei, Z., Wei, Y., Minqing, Y., Jinlong, L.: Analysis and cultivation of PE Teachers' professionalism in the new era. Educ. Theory Pract. **41**(8), 35–37 (2021)
15. Alhumaid, M.M., Khoo, S., Bastos, T.: The effect of an adapted physical activity intervention program on pre-service physical education teachers' self-efficacy towards inclusion in Saudi Arabia. Sustainability **13**(6) (2021)
16. Yijun, L., Aihua, L.: On the necessity of setting up children's interesting track and field events in physical education. Sci. Technol. Wind **8**, 164–166 (2021)
17. Mingfen, L., Jie, L.: Analysis on the integration path of sports and medicine in Colleges and universities in Yunnan under the background of healthy China strategy. Sci. Technol. Wind **8**, 175–177 (2021)
18. Guo, Y.: Don't let "physical education" become another kind of "exam oriented education". China Population Daily, 2021-03-18 (003)
19. Bo, L., Honghao, F.: Practice and prospect of online physical education teaching in Colleges and Universities under the background of education informatization. Innov. Talent Educ. **1**, 16–22 (2021)
20. Qi, C.: Analysis on the application of positive psychological suggestion in junior middle school physical education and health teaching. New Curriculum **11**, 223 (2021)
21. Guo, Y.: Don't let physical education become another exam oriented education. Changchun Daily, 2021-03-16 (006)
22. Jizhen, F., Pingzhou, X., Peng, T.: Practical research on the integration of physical education and moral education. College Entrance Exam. **10**, 145–146 (2021)
23. Jianjun, Y.: Practice and thinking of integrating diet education into College Physical Education – review of food nutrition and health. Food Mach. **37**(3), 243–244 (2021)

English Autonomous Learning Platform with Constructive Teaching Mode

Juan Xie[(✉)]

Yunnan Land and Resources Vocational College, Kunming 650041, China

Abstract. This teaching reform mainly uses the advanced modern education technology to promote the English teaching based on the network technology. This is the inevitable result of the development of modern information technology. This paper mainly studies the design and implementation of English Autonomous Learning Platform Based on constructive teaching mode. Through the existing neuron model, it studies the individual needs of "teaching" and "learning", and puts forward a constructive autonomous learning mode based on RBF algorithm to realize "both learning and teaching". We should try our best to give full play to the leading role of teachers and fully reflect the cognitive main role of students. We should pay attention to both teachers' teaching and students' learning, and mobilize the initiative and enthusiasm of both teachers and students.

Keywords: Constructivist teaching · Neuron · RBF · English autonomous learning

1 Introduction

With the continuous development of English autonomous learning theory, student-centered teaching research has become a hot spot in the field of educational technology. If it goes on, autonomous learning platform is inevitable.

We can carry out the research and development of the courses online, and we can also publish the contents of the existing courses on the Internet. This platform regards the Internet browser as the development environment client of our course. For course creators, WebCT is the best tool that can provide them. These creators can easily use this platform to create, reuse or improve some courses and their contents [1]. All of the above operations can be implemented in a relatively simple and user-friendly mode of development. It is very simple and efficient to implement all operations such as course design and release by WebCT platform. Teachers can have sufficient time to improve the course content, display their talents, and guide students with pertinence and purpose [2].

At present, the relatively popular general network teaching platforms in China include Tsinghua Education online, 4a, network ladder teaching management platform,

M. A. Jan and F. Khan (Eds.): BigIoT-EDU 2021, LNICST 391, pp. 272–281, 2021.
https://doi.org/10.1007/978-3-030-87900-6_33

Anbo online, TVU online, etc., while in foreign countries, ukeu, WebCT, frontier, blackboard learning space and so on are 131 [3–5]. These international online teaching platforms can not fully meet the actual teaching needs of domestic English teaching platforms, Many of the domestic network teaching platforms are some teaching institutions or software manufacturers simply transplant the teaching content and their own resources or courseware to the network, without considering the unified application of all the technical platforms or teaching functions. In contrast, due to the absence of large-scale learning of non-native language skills as in China, foreign online teaching platforms are basically unable to adapt to domestic teaching. This puts forward new requirements for the application of network technology and English teaching methods in China (see Fig. 1).

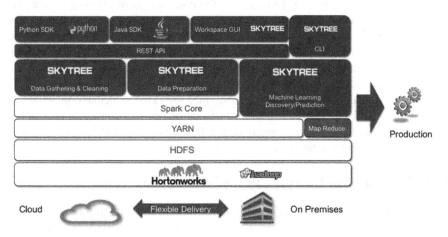

Fig. 1. Autonomous learning platform

2   Constructive Teaching Mode

2.1   Classification of Teaching Mode

In English teaching mode, there are still various problems in the past and present advantages. There is no perfect teaching mode, the optimization of teaching mode is always relative, after all, it is impossible to give an absolute ideal scheme. For a long time, there is no independent English teaching program in China. The design and implementation of English mortar main learning platform based on constructivist teaching mode are modeled on foreign teaching mode, which is worthy of filling. According to China's national conditions, combined with its own actual situation, the teaching mode with Chinese characteristics should be innovated [6]. The optimization of teaching mode must also start from the domestic national conditions and Chinese characteristics, and fully combine the characteristics of pedagogy, psychology and English discipline. Teachers should form full interaction with students, and integrate learning psychology harmoniously to achieve the ideal teaching effect.

2.2 Constructive Teaching Mode

The teaching mode of the teaching structure of "paying equal attention to learning and teaching" mainly includes individual tutoring mode, lecturing mode, exploring learning mode, discussing learning mode and cooperative learning mode. The teaching plan mainly focuses on "learning environment" and "autonomous learning strategy" [7]. The former is to provide the necessary environment and conditions for students' active construction (external factors of learning); the latter is the core content of the whole teaching design, which is to stimulate students to construct the meaning of knowledge independently (the internal cause of inducing learning) through various learning methods. There are three design objects of instructional design: learning environment, learning activities and media transmission, and these three design objects have hierarchical relationship. Design learning activities must be treated as the core content of teaching design. The design of learning activities is ultimately embodied in the design of learning tasks. The design of learning environment is mainly reflected in the combination of learning tools and learning resources by specifying the task objectives, activity contents, achievement forms, activity strategies and methods to promote learners' internal cognitive quality and thinking, so as to achieve the purpose of developing learners' psychological ability. The task of media communication design is to customize what kind of media form, what kind of organizational form, and what kind of presentation order to convey information to learners. The design of classroom teaching and the development and design of teaching media materials belong to this level of activities [8–10].

3 College English Learning in the Network Environment

The media of network science is the presentation form of computer information, which is completely different from the traditional classroom. It shows the characteristics of electronic multimedia, such as massification, diversification, visualization and three-dimensional. This is especially required for the study of College English. The support of Internet for College English learning shows a series of advantages [11].

3.1 Provide More Practical Opportunities for College English Learners

College English learning needs a certain intensity of skill training, and the training density of students is directly proportional to the improvement of a certain ability [12]. In the traditional classroom, due to the limitation of the number of students, teaching time and teachers' energy, this kind of skill training is relatively insufficient, and the network teaching software can replace the work of teachers, overcome the defect that the traditional classroom model can not increase the time and intensity of listening and speaking training, and students can carry out unlimited training on their ability according to their own needs [13].

3.2 Equal Communication on the Internet Is Conducive to Improving Students' Listening, Speaking and Expressing Abilities

As a kind of language ability learning, College English learning needs to be acquired in a certain natural environment or situation. One of its purposes is to narrate things and express ideas in language, so as to achieve the goal of developing students' intelligence and cultivating students' ability. Under the traditional teaching mode, creating a good college English language environment is a key and difficult point in Teachers' teaching. The traditional methods include setting up extracurricular activity groups, English story club, reading or report Club (which can cultivate students' listening and speaking ability, but focus on imitation and performance), "English corner" (the most successful way to create language environment among the existing methods). Its advantages are that the content and object are relatively open, the sense of reality is strong, the ability to put learning in fun, and the ability is appropriate; The biggest disadvantage is: in a completely real language environment, students with shy and introverted personality can not participate, resulting in some students with strong desire for performance have stronger and stronger language control ability, while the other students have less and less words due to inferiority, so it is difficult to improve their language application ability. The use of network technology to establish a virtual language environment as a supplement to the real language environment will be conducive to the cultivation of all students' listening and speaking ability [14].

3.3 Rich and Authentic Network Resources Are Conducive to Creating a Real Language Learning Environment

(1) The network environment can provide a large number of authentic language materials, to a certain extent, to overcome the disadvantages of the lack of authentic language environment for College English learners. The language carrier of picture, text, sound and image and multi form information input provided by multimedia, such as background knowledge and vocabulary examples with film and television effect, not only make the teaching content rich and colorful, but also make the teaching more vivid, three-dimensional and vivid, which can greatly stimulate learners' interest and memory, and improve learning efficiency [15].

(2) College English teaching as a language course, the most ideal is to use native English speakers as teachers. But the vast majority of schools still can't do this. Even in the key universities with relatively strong economic strength, the number of foreign teachers is limited. Multimedia can make up for this by adopting the standard pronunciation of native English speakers, which overcomes the personal differences of Chinese teachers in pronunciation, It also enables all students to hear the pure pronunciation and intonation of native speakers throughout the learning process, which is very helpful for strengthening students' listening, adapting to the speed and intonation of foreigners, and training students to be familiar with and issue standard pronunciation.

(3) Foreign language learning needs an effective environment for language learning and use. Most of the language exercises in the classroom are carried out in hypothetical situations. Students often learn language for the sake of learning language. On the Internet, students can directly order English movies. Satellite TV English programs and English teaching reference films can communicate with teachers and even native English speakers in English. This kind of language environment is conducive to consolidating students' language knowledge and improving their communicative competence [16].

In short, the network constructs a self-regulation mechanism for learners, which is in line with the teaching framework based on the input and output of language information. In this real, open and interactive teaching environment, students can actively participate in the whole teaching process for autonomous learning [17].

4 Research on the Characteristics of Autonomous Learning Based on Neural Network

Neuron is the basic unit of neural network. It is imitated from biological neuron. The characteristics of neurons determine the overall characteristics of neural networks in a certain program. Many simple neurons are interconnected to form a neural network. A very classical neuron model with input of n-dimensional function is shown in the Fig. 2.

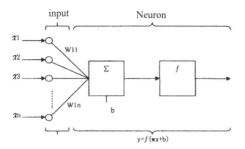

Fig. 2. Neuron model.

$x_1, x_2 \ldots, x_n$ represents n inputs of neurons. It is expressed by $n \times 1$ column vector X.

$$X = [x_1, x_2, \ldots x_n] \tag{1}$$

The weight of network and the corresponding threshold of network can be changed. It is a kind of adjustment based on the dynamic aspect of the weight of the neural network and a threshold value corresponding to the weight value that makes our neurons and even our neural network show a certain behavior characteristics. Therefore, the adjustable characteristics of weights and thresholds of neural network are the basic connotation of the characteristics of neural network learning.

5 Design and Implementation of Learning Platform

5.1 System Overview

The wooden platform is a software platform for English learning based on campus network, which is based on various colleges of higher education, vocational education and general education. The platform comprehensively designs the main scenes in the process of English teaching, including classroom teaching, autonomous learning, communication between teachers and students, unified examination, resource management, educational administration management, etc. According to the teaching scenarios mentioned above, the platform can be divided into six English learning function modules, including information center, tutoring training, autonomous learning, online examination, listening and speaking training, and system management. The six learning modules can fully provide teaching, homework, practice, examination and evaluation functions for the teaching methods in the teaching link, meet the needs of different teaching objects, and provide convenience for school leaders, teachers, students and administrators. The design process of the learning platform is shown in Fig. 3 below:

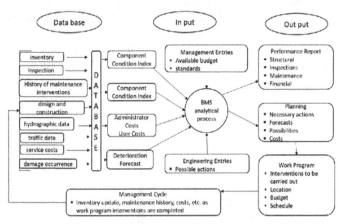

Fig. 3. Design flow chart of learning platform

In addition to learning texts, learners can also browse learning resources, use the tools provided by the platform, write their own blogs, learning experiences and learning plans, etc., make speeches, reply and modify their speeches in BBS, and select test questions from the question bank according to their own needs, You can view your own learning records, understand your own activity records in the learning support platform, and evaluate your own learning. In addition to the function of publishing texts, teachers can also add content and modify their own content in the learning resource database and test question database. In addition to an independent book or extracurricular, the added content can also enrich a certain knowledge point of others, or supplement multimedia materials. Managers manage BBS categories, moderator authorization, teacher identity confirmation, user permissions, teacher upload content audit. No matter what kind of users, they will first enter the landing interface of the platform. After landing, they can browse the course content. After students log in, the platform will automatically record their relevant information, such as landing time, landing times, browsing page times, etc., but learners can't publish courses and test questions. Only teachers can publish and manage courses and test questions. New users can register in the login interface by clicking the "new user registration" link button [18].

5.2 System Architecture Simulation

The overall architecture of the system is implemented by the platform based on modern computer network communication technology and multimedia technology [19, 20]. The platform closely integrates teachers, students and teaching resources, applies intelligent methods such as teaching methods and learning skills assessment to the teaching management process, achieves the organic integration management of various subjects (teachers, students, courseware, auxiliary), teaching mode (organization, management, evaluation, evaluation, strategy), teaching behavior, and shows the function of students' personalized learning and voluntary system In addition to the conventional examination, homework, audio and video on demand, autonomous learning test functions, the day ahead system also provides functions such as answering questions, situational teaching, interactive communication and oral pronunciation training. The system is designed and implemented in the English speaking center of constructive teaching mode, and the functions are logically divided according to teachers, students and managers, Users with different roles will directly enter their own virtual workspace after logging in (see Fig. 4).

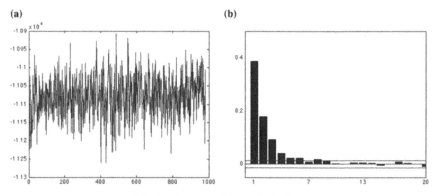

Fig. 4. Teaching platform test effect

6 System Usage Evaluation

Item 3–11 mainly refers to the relevant evaluation of the platform by learners after using the platform. Among the evaluation of item 3, 83% of the learners choose to feel that the interface of the platform is concise, which indicates that the platform is recognized by most learners for its simple interface. At the same time, it also shows that learners care about whether the interface of mobile learning resources is concise, and 4% choose "uncertain", According to the survey, the main reason is that they don't understand the simplicity of the interface. Item 4 examines whether the structural design of the platform is reasonable and whether it brings convenience to learners. 46% of the learners choose "very good", which indicates that learners basically agree with this interface and interaction mode. Because the development of the platform is not perfect,

37% of them choose "general" and 17% choose "unreasonable", which indicates that the friendly interface and interaction mode of the platform still need to be corrected. Item 5 examined whether the individual test module in the platform could help learners improve their individual skills, 53% thought it was helpful, indicating that the module did help learners improve their individual skills; 19% thought it was not helpful, 28% thought it was uncertain. Item 6 examined whether the learners were interested in the recording function of oral English training on this platform. 67% of them said that they had used this function, which indicated that most of the learners were very interested in this function; 18% did not use this function very much, and 15% said that they had not used this function, which indicated that this function still did not attract them and needed to be improved. Item 7 examines whether the oral training of this platform is helpful to learners' oral practice. 51% of them think it is helpful, 27% think it is not helpful, and 22% think it is not helpful. This shows that this function has certain effect on learners' oral training, but there are also some shortcomings that need to be improved. Item 8 and Item 9 investigated the learners' utilization and satisfaction of the network resources of the platform. Among them, 73% often used these network resources, 17% seldom used them, 10% never used them, 49% were very satisfied with the network resources provided here, 23% were average, and 28% were uncertain. This shows that learners hope to have the support of learning tools when they carry out autonomous learning, However, the learning resources of the platform need to be further enriched. Item 10 and item 11 investigated the rationality and effectiveness of the design of the learning evaluation module of the platform. Among them, 53% thought it was reasonable, 24% thought it was general, and 23% thought it was unreasonable; 48% thought it could promote their learning, 28% thought it was general, only a little promoting effect, and 24% thought it was not helpful, which indicated that it was very important to do a good job in the learning evaluation of the autonomous learning platform. As shown in Fig. 5 below.

Item	Statement	Strongly disagree	Disagree	Agree	Strongly agree
1	"If I sufficiently practice English pronunciation, I will be able to master a native-like accent."	6 (5.17%)	19 (16.38%)	59 (50.86%)	32 (27.59%)
2	"It is important to understand varieties of English, e.g., Indian English, Singaporean English, Chinese English, etc."	12 (10.34%)	20 (17.24%)	57 (49.14%)	27 (23.28%)
3	"The feature that causes miscommunication in English the most is a non-native accent."	31 (26.72%)	41 (35.34%)	36 (31.03%)	8 (6.90%)
4	"I am proud of my own English accent."	21 (18.10%)	45 (38.79%)	31 (26.72%)	19 (16.38%)
5	"It is important to acquire native-like competence in pronunciation."	11 (9.48%)	31 (26.72%)	45 (38.79%)	29 (25.00%)
6	"We should not tolerate varieties of English that differ from native speakers'."	31 (26.74%)	61 (52.59%)	14 (12.07%)	10 (8.62%)

Fig. 5. Feedback chart of system usage

7   Conclusion

This paper analyzes the research and application status of Web-based English autonomous learning platform at home and abroad, and analyzes the application of constructive teaching mode in English teaching process (learner testing, evaluating learners, arranging teaching plans, self-study, completing self-study assignments, retesting and evaluation process), This paper analyzes the application of traditional teaching methods in the process of computer multimedia network teaching (resource management, courseware management, personnel management, self-study status tracking management). According to the characteristics of the above analysis, the architecture of the platform is designed, and the software design specifications of relevant modules are formulated.

References

1. Yu, W., Xuezhen, Z.: on the construction of network teaching resources in Colleges and universities. Audio Visual Educ. Res. **06**, 54–56 (2004)
2. Sun, B.: Research on the management and application of network teaching in Colleges and universities. Audio Visual Educ. Res. **10**, 53–55 (2010)
3. Pang, W.: Some progress of foreign autonomous learning research since 1990s. Psychol. Trends **04**, 12–16 (2000)
4. Dong, N.: The enlightenment of autonomous learning mode in foreign universities. Foreign Lang. Teach. Res. Jiangsu **02**, 12–15 (2008)
5. Cao, H.: Application and research of blended teaching mode in College English teaching practice. Neijiang Sci. Technol. **42**(02), 149–150 + 152 (2021)
6. Yafeng, L.: Research on the construction of College English autonomous learning curriculum based on classroom style. J. Hubei Open Vocat. Coll. **34**(03), 186–187 (2021)
7. Dan, L.: New ideas of College English education reform based on network . Mod. Vocat. Educ. **06**, 208–209 (2021)
8. Runlu, Z., Yingxue, H.: Research on English autonomous learning of higher vocational students in the era of big data: a case study of Guangzhou Panyu Polytechnic . Sci. Technology Horizon **01**, 73–75 (2021)
9. Jia, L., Yuhong, Z.: Exploration and research on College English autonomous learning classroom from the perspective of mobile Internet – taking American education curriculum under Sino foreign cooperative education as an example. Sci. Technology Horizon **35**, 37–38 (2020)
10. Juan, F., Minfang, L.: Practice and effect evaluation of ubiquitous learning mode in College English listening class under the guidance of Poa theory . Campus English **49**, 16–17 (2020)
11. Tian, T., Yujian, L., Shasha, X.: An analysis of College Students' autonomous learning of English from the perspective of social cognitive theory . English Square **34**, 126–129 (2020)
12. Wu, J.: Construction of autonomous learning mode for English majors based on wechat platform. Overseas English, (21), 67–68 + 76 (2020)
13. Jiao, F.: Research on the hierarchical teaching of public English in higher vocational colleges based on MOOC . Chin. J. Multimedia Netw. Teach. (Zhongxun) **11**, 41–43 (2020)
14. Zhang, M., Li, X., Chen, Y., Xu, Y., Wang, H.: The study of mobile English autonomous learning of College English vocabulary under the background of "Internet plus." Comput. Knowl. Technol. **16**(31), 160–161 (2020)
15. Shao Xinjie, Y., Qingqing. : Applied research on College English autonomous learning mode based on wechat public platform. J. Jiangxi Electr. Power Vocat. Tech. Coll. **33**(10), 30–31 (2020)

16. Wenqin, H.: Research and Practice on the application and effect evaluation of autonomous learning platform – taking higher vocational public English as an example . Public Stand. **20**, 176–177 (2020)
17. Xu, M.: Typical problems and countermeasures of English autonomous learning in higher vocational colleges based on network platform. J. Yanbian Inst. Educ. **34**(05), 62–64 (2020)
18. Zhang, G., Hu, W.: Design of autonomous learning resource platform for English majors in independent colleges based on metacognitive strategy. Lang. Culture Stud. (02), 75–80 (2020)
19. Yu, Q.: Research on the construction of mobile learning platform for College English based on WeChat official account. J. Jiangxi Vocat. Tech. Coll. Electr. **33**(09), 37–38+40 (2020)
20. Ling, C.: Research on extracurricular learning training mode based on wechat platform . Sci. Technol. Econ. Guide **28**(26), 171–172 (2020)

English Teaching Ability Evaluation Algorithm Based on Big Data Fuzzy k-means Clustering

Jiayun Tang[✉]

Yunnan Land and Resorces Vocational College, Kunming 650000, China

Abstract. Based on the rise of cloud applications and the use of various forms of digital devices, data is growing explosively. In the face of such a huge amount of data, the traditional data analysis tools only deal with the simple statistics, query and management of data, and can't deeply mine the potential useful information. Therefore, how to use big data to mine valuable information is particularly important. Clustering analysis is one of the big data analysis technologies. The traditional single machine clustering algorithm can not meet the requirements of big data information processing in terms of operational efficiency and computational complexity. The development of cloud computing technology provides a new research direction for big data clustering analysis. The English teaching comprehensive ability evaluation system can complete the evaluation and ranking of College English teaching comprehensive ability. By using the attribute method, seven attribute indexes are obtained. The example shows that the system has clear structure, reasonable process, and can flexibly adjust the evaluation parameters such as the scale of school scheme set and relevant psychological weight according to the user's requirements.

Keywords: Big data · Cloud environment · Data integration · FCM · MapReduce

1 Introduction

With the rapid development of Internet technology, data storage and data compression technology, the emergence of microblog, wechat, social networking and other interactive applications, the rise of cloud based applications, and the use of various forms of digital devices, data is growing explosively. All sectors of the society, such as academia, enterprises and government departments, have paid close attention to the problem of big data, and began to really pay attention to how to effectively use these data to generate greater wisdom and value [1]. For example, banks can identify potential credit card users who can not repay by analyzing user data, The traffic department can manage the traffic more effectively by integrating the data of weather, traffic situation and driver's geographic location information. Data has become a new asset, which can bring endless social and economic benefits. Big data is gradually becoming a new powerful tool for people to understand and transform the world, making it easier for people to grasp the laws of things and accurately predict the future. There are still many questions and controversies about the basic concepts and key technologies of big data.

© ICST Institute for Computer Sciences, Social Informatics and Telecommunications Engineering 2021
Published by Springer Nature Switzerland AG 2021. All Rights Reserved
M. A. Jan and F. Khan (Eds.): BigIoT-EDU 2021, LNICST 391, pp. 282–291, 2021.
https://doi.org/10.1007/978-3-030-87900-6_34

2   Fuzzy C-means (FCM) Algorithm in Cloud Environment

2.1   Fuzzy C-means Algorithm (FCM Algorithm)

Fuzzy C-means (FCM) algorithm is a clustering analysis method based on objective function. The algorithm transforms clustering into optimization problem with constraints, and then determines the final classification and fuzzy clustering results by solving the optimization problem [2].

The main difference between FCM clustering algorithm and HCM clustering algorithm is that FCM clustering algorithm introduces the idea of fuzzy partition, so that each given data object uses the value in (0,1) interval to express its degree of belonging to each group, and the values of all data objects belonging to each group constitute the membership matrix U. for any data object, the sum of its membership is always equal to 1, that is to say:

$$\sum_{i=1}^{c} u_{ij} = 1 (j = 1, \cdots, n, \text{Represents the j - th sample}) \tag{1}$$

Then, the general form of the objective function of FCM clustering algorithm can be expressed as:

$$J(U, c_1, \cdots, c_c) = \sum_{i=1}^{c} J_i = \sum_{i=1}^{c} \sum_{j}^{n} u_{ij}^m d_{ij}^2 \tag{2}$$

2.2   MapReduce Analysis of FCM Algorithm

The membership degree of each data object to a cluster center is calculated with the data object, and then it is obtained through the accumulation sum. This part can be calculated in the map stage of the map node, and then it can be calculated corresponding to the data point, and then the accumulation of the upper part of the formula calculated by the map node in the combine stage is as follows:

$$sumo0_k = \sum_{j=1}^{N_k} u_j \tag{3}$$

$$suml_k = \sum_{j=1}^{N_k} u_j \tag{4}$$

The judgment of convergence condition. In this step, the difference between the two objective functions is not used for judgment, because there will be a lot of data transmission in the whole MapReduce process, and the difference between each cluster center before and after clustering is less than a certain threshold for judgment. This step can be done after this clustering.

3 Simulation Analysis of Evaluation System

With the development of system science, management science and scientific decision-making theory, the comprehensive evaluation system of English teaching ability (ECE) is a complex system, which involves various factors or attributes, A series of theories and methods of systematic analysis and decision-making have emerged. Accordingly, all kinds of decision-making and evaluation have gradually entered the stage of scientific decision-making and intelligent decision-making with the help of computer tools from the past empirical decision-making. Therefore, the evaluation of English teaching comprehensive ability must make full use of scientific decision-making theory and the most advanced decision-making aids, It makes the assessment of English teaching comprehensive ability scientific and modern [3].

The function of English teaching comprehensive ability evaluation system is: no matter what the grade of the school is, after comprehensively considering the internal and external factors in various English learning, compare the English teaching situation of several schools, and compare the overall teaching quality of different grades and the same grade universities, which can more accurately reflect the overall level of the school and help the school to reduce costs, Through the analysis, the attribute characteristics of English teaching quality evaluation among schools are extracted: attributes are internal and external. One can not think that one attribute is important and ignore other attributes. The understanding of things should be multi angle and multi-directional. Therefore, the evaluation system of English teaching comprehensive ability has the following attributes: internal cause, external cause and capital investment, Specifically speaking, they are learners' personal factors, environmental factors and costs (see Fig. 1).

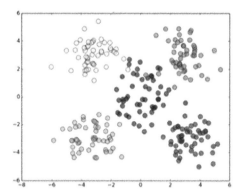

Fig. 1. K-means clustering simulation for teaching effect

3.1 Internal Cause -- Learner's Personal Factor

Intelligence. Under the same condition of mastering and using all kinds of learning skills, the learners with good intelligence learn knowledge faster, and the learners with low intelligence can not produce miracles that surpass the normal learners even under the best learning conditions, The importance of intelligence training.

Character. In psychology, personality is divided into "extrovert" and "introvert". People once tended to think that extrovert learners, because of their lively personality, dare to speak in the process of learning, have more opportunities to practice English, and their performance will be better than introvert learners, However, this is not the case. Learners with different personalities use different learning strategies to deal with different learning tasks: for extroverts, they are good at talking, which is conducive to obtaining more opportunities for input and practice, but they often do not pay much attention to language forms; Introverted learners may be better at making use of their quiet personality to make more in-depth and detailed formal analysis of limited input, especially in the teaching environment that pays attention to language forms and language rules. In the comprehensive ability assessment system of English teaching, personality factor refers to whether the school adopts different English teaching methods for different personalities.

Motivation and attitudinal motivation are the internal motivation and strength to motivate people to take action (including personal intention, desire, psychological conflict or the purpose they are trying to achieve). It is a kind of psychological state to initiate and maintain action, Among them, a considerable number of female students answer "very like" or "just interested". Attitude refers to: first, learners' attitude towards English and its culture; second, attitude towards language teachers and learning environment. In the comprehensive ability assessment system of English teaching, the factors considered are: the proportion of male and female students, students' learning attitude and teachers' teaching attitude.

3.2 External Factors -- Environmental Factors

Social and environmental factors. With the deepening of reform and opening up, international cultural exchanges become more and more frequent [4]. English, as a communicative tool, is becoming more and more important, which stimulates learners' interest in learning English, Other factors are: Students' family economic status, family atmosphere and parents' role models, family structure, social practice and so on.

Natural environmental factors. The natural environment and cultural environment around the school. For example, because Guilin is a world-famous tourist attraction, there are many foreign tourists, which makes the atmosphere of learning English for college students in Guilin stronger than some colleges and universities in other places [5].

3.3 Cost

In order to get a higher passing rate of CET-4 and CET-6, some schools reward students, teachers, open a large number of training classes, invite foreign teachers, and hold various foreign affairs activities to improve students' interest in learning. However, the effect is not directly proportional to the money invested. Therefore, the cost (capital investment) is also an important factor affecting the quality of English teaching, but it is not a decisive factor (see Fig. 2).

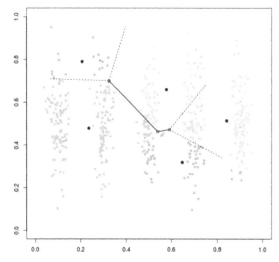

Fig. 2. Simultation for some factors.

4 The Current Situation and Problems of English Teaching Quality Evaluation in Higher Vocational Colleges

4.1 The Current Situation of English Teaching Quality Evaluation in Higher Vocational Colleges

In recent years, higher vocational colleges continue to deepen education and teaching reform, and actively promote theoretical innovation and practical exploration [6]. Teaching quality evaluation is undoubtedly an important link in the teaching management system of higher vocational education, which plays an important role in promoting the overall level of higher vocational colleges, teaching management, quality improvement and the formulation of teaching strategies. In terms of the establishment of teaching quality evaluation system and personnel allocation, colleges and universities have also actively promoted and implemented it. First of all, at present, the process of teaching quality evaluation in higher vocational colleges is generally in the charge of teaching management department. The educational affairs office, departments and supervision group are the macro-control, evaluation support and direct implementers of teaching supervision and evaluation, respectively. The supervision group is composed of retired teachers and some teachers in office. Good ethics, excellent teaching level and good communication are the selection criteria of supervision teachers. They play a stable and positive role in promoting the teaching process and improving the teaching quality. Secondly, the educational administration department of higher vocational colleges, usually the office of educational administration, has introduced corresponding teaching management system for English theory courses and practical training courses in higher vocational colleges [7]. The teaching materials are distributed uniformly, and the teaching management documents are studied regularly. Especially in the training of new teachers, they will lead them to study in-depth the documents of educational evaluation.

The establishment of these measures is to lay a good foundation for the teaching quality evaluation, to ensure that the evaluation is institutionalized, standardized and scientific, to consider all kinds of possible problems in advance, and to actively deal with and solve the work. The establishment of teaching quality evaluation system in higher vocational colleges is uneven, and it is impossible to achieve complete uniformity and consistent standards. However, most colleges are gradually improving according to the indicators of the Ministry of education "about the teaching excellence and qualification evaluation system of Higher Vocational Colleges". Third, the teaching quality evaluation of higher vocational colleges mainly focuses on classroom explanation, paying attention to the teacher's classroom activity setting, teaching content arrangement, complete teaching materials and attendance assessment, so as to form the basic evaluation of the overall teaching work of teachers. The evaluation of students' learning effect is mostly reflected in the way of final evaluation, with the summative evaluation standard as the main. As a basic course of pragmatic competence, it follows the unified standard of teaching evaluation. At present, the teaching quality evaluation results of most schools are linked with the assessment of the evaluated teachers, which reflects the college's emphasis on teaching evaluation and the awareness of promoting teaching self-improvement [8].

4.2 Problems and Analysis of English Teaching Quality Evaluation in Higher Vocational Colleges

Higher vocational English teaching quality evaluation has made some achievements, but there are also many problems. The direct participants of English teaching quality evaluation in higher vocational colleges are teachers and students. Their understanding and attitude towards teaching quality evaluation are directly related to the results of teaching quality evaluation, and also have an important impact on the establishment of teaching quality evaluation system and the formulation of teaching strategies. The author designed the interview question and interviewed 15 English teachers in higher vocational colleges, aiming to understand their cognition and attitude towards the quality evaluation of Higher Vocational English teaching, the existing difficulties and problems in the teaching process, so as to better improve the quality evaluation of English teaching. At the same time, through the small program of questionnaire star, the paper makes a questionnaire survey on the evaluation of English teaching quality in higher vocational colleges. Specifically understand the students' cognition and views on the teaching process, teaching quality and teaching evaluation [9]. The problems and analysis of Higher Vocational English teaching quality evaluation are shown in Fig. 3.

The vast majority of teachers think that the object scope of teaching quality evaluation is relatively old, and the teaching quality evaluation of English Curriculum under the background of the new curriculum reform does not really reflect the real evaluation of students' language use. Nowadays, with the increasingly rich teaching media, all kinds of small programs, application software and big data information resources integration and analysis technology are not advocated in classroom teaching and teaching quality evaluation, resulting in the backwardness of Higher Vocational English teaching quality evaluation reform [10].

163 students believe that the object of the current English teaching evaluation in higher vocational colleges is mainly limited to the teaching effect of English language

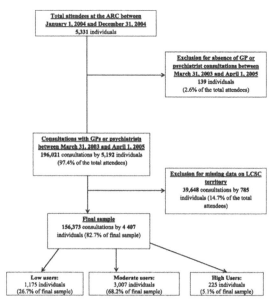

Fig. 3. Problems and analysis of English teaching quality evaluation in Higher Vocational Colleges

knowledge and skills test or competition results and the final evaluation of the final examination, and is limited to the teaching quality evaluation of basic language knowledge such as pronunciation, grammar, vocabulary and reading. 112 students think that the current evaluation of Higher Vocational English teaching quality ignores the evaluation of non-verbal knowledge and skills such as learning attitude, teaching strategies, teaching methods and innovative consciousness, while 65 students think that the current evaluation of Higher Vocational English teaching ignores the extended evaluation of teaching quality such as employers and social needs, 72 students think that the current evaluation of Higher Vocational English teaching quality ignores the evaluation of information teaching resources [11].

The reference documents of English teaching quality evaluation in higher vocational colleges are "basic requirements of English Teaching in Higher Vocational Colleges" and "basic requirements of English Teaching in Higher Vocational Colleges". The former only explains the most basic requirements of English teaching, but does not explain the teaching evaluation alone [12]. Although the latter explains the evaluation of Higher Vocational English teaching, it does not explain the subject, object, evaluation method, feedback effect of Higher Vocational English teaching evaluation more accurately, and the implementation rules are lack. According to the questionnaire survey and interview conducted by the author, more than 80% of the teachers surveyed think that there is no standard to determine the qualification of the evaluation subject in the evaluation of Higher Vocational English teaching quality. Because there is no unified standard for the selection of supervision teachers, the evaluation subject often has no professional background knowledge and practical teaching experience in English linguistics, pedagogy, psychology, etc., This will easily lead to the teaching evaluation is more one-sided and subjective [13]. More than 60% of the teachers think that the current English teaching evaluation in Higher Vocational Colleges lacks the evaluation system of different admission levels and different teaching levels, while the students in higher vocational colleges come from senior high school, secondary vocational school, secondary technical school or junior high school, and the students' English level is quite different from that in the early stage of English teaching, It is easy to lead to the overall evaluation of Higher Vocational English teaching can not achieve the different evaluation of students from different sources. 70% of the teachers think that the current higher vocational English teaching evaluation lacks the reward and punishment guarantee system for Higher Vocational English teaching evaluation [14].

5 Suggestions on Strengthening the Evaluation of English Teaching Quality in Higher Vocational Colleges

English Teaching in higher vocational colleges should follow the requirements of "service-oriented, employment oriented, practical oriented, sufficient and application-oriented". This requirement makes a clear distinction between English education in Higher Vocational Colleges and ordinary colleges [15]. "National vocational education reform implementation plan" puts forward: in the further deepening of education reform and innovation, economic development, the position of vocational education should be further highlighted, the "double high" construction plan is put forward, and it is clear that higher vocational colleges should cultivate high-quality workers and technical talents. Therefore, in the English Teaching of higher vocational colleges, we need to pay more attention to the cultivation of pragmatic competence and professional competence, which should be reflected in the evaluation index of teaching quality. In the design of the evaluation index, we should not only combine the actual situation of students' English learning in higher vocational colleges, but also consider the actual operation ability of teachers, and reflect the development direction of the college. First of all, in the teaching quality evaluation, the teaching quality evaluation tables of professional courses and basic courses in higher vocational colleges should have their own teaching quality evaluation indexes to reflect the specific evaluation elements of different disciplines, so as to have a better reference and guidance for teaching. Secondly, in English teaching, we should pay attention to the evaluation of the practical teaching of Higher Vocational English, distinguish the evaluation of theoretical courses and practical courses, and the evaluation index should reflect the curriculum objectives, teaching characteristics and inspection focus of the two courses. As a public basic course of Liberal Arts in higher vocational colleges, the teaching quality evaluation form should show the characteristics of the course and the specific evaluation indicators. If there is no scientific and reasonable quantitative indicators, the concept of evaluation is not clear, which will affect the objective and fair evaluation of English teaching quality to a certain extent. Third, in the evaluation of teachers' teaching process, we should focus on the evaluation of teachers' professional quality and professional English teaching ability while examining teaching design, teaching methods and teaching attitude, which is the special feature of English Teaching in higher vocational colleges. Finally, in the evaluation of teaching effect, we can increase the evaluation index of teachers guiding students to participate in the English pragmatic competence competition, so as to "replace evaluation with competition", and enhance the cultivation and practice of students' pragmatic competence [16].

Teachers are not only the key to improve the teaching quality, but also an important part of education quality evaluation. Building a high-level teaching team is the key to improve the teaching quality of higher vocational colleges, and also helps to improve the teaching quality evaluation ability of the supervision team. Teachers engaged in Higher Vocational Education and teaching supervision should have a more comprehensive knowledge reserve, higher professional technology application ability, and constantly update knowledge, enrich practical experience, improve teaching level, and apply the teaching of innovative ideas to students' innovative ability training courses and teaching practice activities, so as to ensure the smooth realization of the goal of high-quality skilled personnel training.

6   Conclusions

In recent years, the hot research direction of big data as the background, this paper analyzes the characteristics of big data, the technology that can be used for big data, and the basic process of big data processing. The first work of big data analysis is the integration of heterogeneous data sources, and the data clustering in data mining technology is one of the technologies that can be used for big data. Therefore, this paper first studies the integration method of heterogeneous data sources, On this basis, the FCM algorithm, which is widely used at present, is studied. At the same time, combining with the advantages of cloud environment, the FCM algorithm is implemented by MapReduce.

References

1. Hongying, F.: Research on Data Preprocessing Method in Data Mining . Southwest University, Chongqing (2009)
2. Zhiye, S.: Model Design and Research of A-FCM Algorithm. Central China Normal University, Wuhan (2011)
3. Yu, Q., Dai, Y.: Parallel fuzzy c-means algorithm based on MapReduce. Comput. Eng. Appl. **49**(14), 133–137 (2013)
4. Qiusheng, P., Wenhong, W.: Parallel fuzzy clustering algorithm based on kernel method. Comput. Eng. Des. **29**(8), 1881–1883 (2008)
5. Rong, M.: University Management , p. 96. Nanjing University Press, Nanjing (1997)
6. Yanguo, T.: New theory on the historical development of Education. Educ. Res. Exp. **9**, 4 (2007)
7. Xiaodong, C.: Research on the reform of public English teaching evaluation system in Higher Vocational Colleges. J. Tianjin Bus. Vocat. Coll. **9**, 39 (2013)
8. Xianhui, R.: On the principles of teaching quality evaluation in Vocational Colleges. J. Xiangfan Vocat. Tech. Coll. **1**, 113 (2010)
9. Jigang, C.: Adjustment of foreign language teaching evaluation system in the context of internationalization of Higher Education. Audio Vis. Foreign Lang. Teach. **1**, 3 (2013)
10. Cui, H., Feng, X.: Building a teacher self-evaluation mechanism to promote the professional development of English teachers in Higher Vocational Colleges. J. Changsha Vocat. Tech. Coll. Civil Affairs, **3**, 126–127 (2012)

11. Weiliang, D.: Research on the diversification of Higher Vocational English teaching evaluation. Comp. Study Cultural Innov. **5**, 115–116 (2017)
12. Zhao, L., Jifa, G.: Comparative study on evaluation methodology between East and West. School Manage. Sci. **1**, 90 (2000)
13. Jizhen, L.: Research on the Sinicization of the fourth generation education evaluation theory. Tianjin Normal Univ. **5**, 3 (2019)
14. Weiqiang, P.: The experience and reference of foreign language curriculum reform in contemporary foreign countries . Comp. Educ. Res. **4**, 39–43 (2002)
15. Li, Z.: Research on quality monitoring and evaluation system of Higher Vocational English Teaching . Res. Priv. Educ. **5**, 8–11 (2010)
16. Jie, G.: Problems and countermeasures of professional English teaching in Higher Vocational Colleges: a case study of mechanical major in college a [D]. Jiangxi Agric. Univ. **6**, 5 (2016)

Exploration of Individualized Foreign Language Teaching Mode Based on the Integration of Multimedia and Traditional Methods

Qian Xu(✉)

Jiguang Vocational and Technical College, Shanghai 201901, China

Abstract. When we turn our attention to subject teaching, we can't help asking: how practical and widely applied are the things studied by experts to practical teaching? Especially when subject teaching is facing the impact of curriculum reform and digitization, How can researchers help teachers and learners break through the bottleneck of teaching? The author thinks: blindly pursuing the new and seeking the difference can not solve the practical problems in the classroom, which is in line with the actual teaching situation in China. For example, in foreign language teaching in China, there are many ideas to explore reform and innovation, and a lot of energy has been invested in the network, but the effect is very little. In basic education, the classroom is the strongest position. It is unrealistic to try to solve the problems in the classroom completely through network teaching. Therefore, based on the middle school classroom, this paper attempts to explore some ideas and methods of personalized foreign language teaching mode based on the integration of multimedia and traditional teaching to build a personalized learning environment for learners in the classroom, and verify its effectiveness through experiments, so as to seek some enlightenment for improving the teaching efficiency in foreign language classroom, This paper will learn from the idea of building personalized learning scene in the network environment, and build a personalized foreign language learning environment in the foreign language classroom according to the individual characteristics and needs of learners. By building a personalized foreign language learning environment and verifying its effectiveness, we hope to explore a new integration way of teaching design, information technology and foreign language teaching through the application of personalized learning environment.

Keywords: Multimedia teaching · Individualized foreign language teaching · Traditional teaching

1 Introduction

English multimedia teaching is an effective way to cultivate high level foreign language application ability. The theory of Constructivism emphasizes that students are the center, students are the active constructors of knowledge, and teachers are the helpers and promoters [1]. This theory has greatly changed the traditional teaching mode. With the

M. A. Jan and F. Khan (Eds.): BigIoT-EDU 2021, LNICST 391, pp. 292–301, 2021.
https://doi.org/10.1007/978-3-030-87900-6_35

application of computer technology, it can process and display a variety of language information forms, which provides a great possibility for improving teaching efficiency and realizing scientific foreign language teaching.

Multimedia teaching refers to in the teaching process, according to the characteristics of teaching objectives and teaching objects, through teaching design, reasonable selection and use of modern teaching media, and organic combination with traditional teaching means, to participate in the whole process of teaching, with a variety of media information on students, to form a reasonable teaching process structure, to achieve the optimal teaching effect. In fact, multimedia teaching has existed since ancient times. Teachers have been teaching with the help of text, sound and pictures. But in the 1980s began to use a variety of electronic media, such as slide, projection, recording, video and other comprehensive use and classroom teaching, this teaching technology is also known as multimedia combination teaching or audio-visual teaching, since the 1990s, with the rapid development and popularization of computer technology, multimedia computer has gradually replaced the previous comprehensive use of a variety of teaching media. Therefore, what we usually call multimedia teaching now refers to the process of teaching activities carried out with the help of multimedia computers and pre made multimedia teaching software. It can also be called computer assisted instruction (CAI). Multimedia computer aided instruction refers to the use of multimedia computer, comprehensive processing and control of symbols, language, text, sound, graphics, images and other media information, the various elements of multimedia according to the teaching requirements, organic combination and display through the screen or projector projection, at the same time, according to the need to add sound cooperation, as well as the interaction between users and computers The teaching or training process can be completed by human-computer interaction between teachers and students.

Therefore, multimedia teaching usually refers to computer multimedia teaching, which is a combination of multiple media realized by computer. It has the characteristics of interactivity, integration, controllability and so on. It is only one of a variety of media.

It uses computer technology, network technology, communication technology and scientific and standardized management to integrate, integrate and comprehensively digitize all information resources related to learning, teaching, scientific research, management and life services, so as to form a unified user management, unified resource management and unified authority control. It focuses on that students can access campus network and Internet at any time through WiFi to obtain learning resources conveniently. Teachers can use wireless network to check students' learning situation, complete lesson preparation and carry out scientific research at any time. Its core lies in the implementation of paperless teaching and the extension of campus wireless network.

2 Advantages and Disadvantages of Multimedia Teaching

2.1 Advantages of Multimedia Teaching

1. Media teaching can make the original abstract and boring learning content become vivid and intuitive, and enhance students' interest in learning. Teachers can easily, quickly and fully use modern teaching methods to teach, so that the teaching content is more intuitive, and even can not be limited by time and space. The introduction of new

content can not only save valuable time, increase the amount of information in the classroom, but also activate the classroom atmosphere, and fully mobilize the enthusiasm of students.

2. Multimedia teaching can improve teaching efficiency. 11% of people learn knowledge through hearing and 83% through vision. In addition, psychologists also pointed out that people can remember 10% of what they read, 20% of what they hear, 30% of what they see, 50% of what they see and hear, and 70% of what they say when they talk. This conclusion shows that the memory effect will be better if the visual and auditory are used at the same time. The multimedia teaching method just provides the language environment of "text, sound" and "image".

3. Multimedia teaching makes individualization possible. To learn what you need at your own convenient time and place. They can learn by themselves according to the teaching requirements, and can use computers to test and evaluate themselves.

2.2   The Shortage of Multimedia Teaching

1. Multimedia teaching puts forward higher requirements for teaching staff, and teachers' technical level needs to be further improved. As a matter of fact, some teachers lack the proper technical level in the use of multimedia equipment, which affects the effect of multimedia teaching.

2. What multimedia teaching provides is man-machine communication, which is not as good as natural language communication between people. For example, students ask questions in class, but the knowledge and courseware involved are rarely related, which will cause difficulties in explanation.

3. Due to the discontinuity and delay in projection operation, the teacher's language expression will also be intermittent [2]. At the same time, students focus on the screen and ignore the teacher's teaching. Sometimes, it is difficult for teachers to organize or adjust the teaching content.

4. Due to the large amount of multimedia information, fast presentation speed and short residence time, students not only can't keep up, but also have visual effects. Experiments show that if the projection plays for more than 20 min in a class, students are prone to fatigue, leading to the decline of knowledge acceptance ability. The original s I ope one algorithm uses a linear function $(x) = x + B$ to predict, where parameter X represents the target user's score of the project, and parameter B represents the average score deviation between the projects. Therefore, in the process of rating prediction and recommendation, we first use formula (1) to calculate the average score deviation matrix ev1d between the target project and other projects (representing the target project, I represents some other project), and finally use formula (2) to predict the corresponding project score. Prediction (U) represents a project, and u represents a student:

$$Deu_{i,j} = \sum_{u \in S_{ij}} \frac{R_{u,j} - r_{u,j}}{count(S j, \ i(x))} \tag{1}$$

$$Perdiction(u)_j = \frac{1}{count(r_j)} \tag{2}$$

3 Give Full Play to the Advantages of Science and Technology, Optimize the Classroom Atmosphere

3.1 Research Process

Psychological research shows that the environment has a profound impact on the efficiency of people's work. High school students are in a critical period of physical and mental development. Teachers should optimize the teaching atmosphere according to their personality characteristics and lay the foundation for students' development. But at present, the efforts of English classroom teachers in China are not proportional to the final results. The effect of improving students' learning enthusiasm is not high, which has a negative impact on the development of the classroom [3]. A good classroom atmosphere requires teachers to consider many things. First of all, the creation of the atmosphere should be in line with the development characteristics of students, based on which to promote a good teaching atmosphere to further enhance the enthusiasm of students to participate in classroom knowledge exploration. In the traditional way of guidance, teachers are mainly oral guidance, but English is a language discipline, many knowledge points need students to recite, teachers monotonous way of guidance is difficult to drive students' learning enthusiasm, affect the normal learning efficiency of students. Secondly, many teachers are influenced by exam oriented education, and the construction of classroom atmosphere is too formalized, focusing on the process of indoctrination of students' knowledge, resulting in poor effect of final guidance, wasting limited time in the classroom and reducing the original teaching efficiency. A good beginning is the key to success. If teachers want to improve the guiding efficiency of classroom atmosphere, they can appropriately use multimedia technology to bring students into a new teaching environment, so as to stimulate their enthusiasm for learning knowledge.

3.2 Relevant Conclusions Drawn

For example, during the teaching of "the Olympic Games", teachers can use rich network resources to find stories about the development of the Olympic movement and tell them to students. Through history, teachers can guide students to have the desire to explore the contents of textbooks, expand their horizons, and help students participate in the learning of knowledge in a better mental state, And in this process, teachers can also let students say their understanding of the Olympic Games, strengthen the interaction between teachers and students, and push the classroom teaching atmosphere to a higher level. In addition, teachers can also play the elegant demeanor of Chinese athletes in the Olympic Games, as a starting point to enhance students' enthusiasm for learning knowledge, encourage students to improve their learning status, and lay a solid foundation for efficient English classroom. Multimedia technology contains rich image materials. Teachers can make rational use of it and change their own guidance methods, which can make students have a fresh feeling of English learning, help them to participate in the process of knowledge learning, and promote the efficiency of students' English learning.

3.3 Improvement Measures

In the process of students answering questions, teachers should adopt a kind tone, and give some encouragement when students answer wrong, so that they can always keep a high enthusiasm for exploring questions, and help students find their thinking defects, improve their English learning methods, and accelerate their development process. In addition, in view of the knowledge points that high school English needs students to memorize, teachers should effectively grasp the classroom teaching methods, turn the black and white text in textbooks into colorful pictures, so that students can have the enthusiasm to explore English knowledge learning, and promote them to participate in the actual knowledge learning in a better state, And then drive students to experience more learning fun in the process of knowledge learning. In addition, teachers should also use multimedia teaching technology to help students review their English knowledge points. First, they should have a detailed understanding of students' mastery of knowledge points by asking questions, and then use the large screen to intuitively show students the internal relationship between knowledge points, so as to help students build a more complete knowledge model in their mind. Then teachers should strengthen the interaction between teachers and students, and pay attention to students' personal learning situation in time.

4 Simulation Analysis for Advantages and Disadvantages of Traditional Teaching

Traditional teaching means that teachers impart knowledge to students by means of language, blackboard writing, wall charts and models. The traditional teaching method has three centers: Teacher centered, classroom centered and Book centered. In the traditional teaching mode, the teaching process consists of three basic elements: teachers, students and teaching content.

(1) The advantages of traditional teaching methods an excellent teacher can often express the teaching content with vivid language and graceful body language in class, so as to achieve good teaching effect [4]. Different teachers will explain the same teaching content in different ways and means. Traditional teaching is convenient for communication between teachers and students. Teachers pay great attention to coordinating the relationship between lecture speed, students' emotion and blackboard admonition. Lecture content and admonition degree will be adjusted according to students' reaction [5].

(2)The disadvantages of traditional teaching methods, teachers often take up a lot of time to give lectures and write on the blackboard. In recent years, with the expansion of college enrollment, large classes are more common. As a result, students can't see what is written on the blackboard when they listen to what teachers teach. In the face of hundreds of students, teachers also feel powerless, even out of control in the classroom. Media alone, it is difficult to stimulate students' interest in learning, it is difficult to produce a variety of sensory stimulation of students, it is difficult to stimulate students' learning, it can be seen that single multimedia teaching or traditional teaching can not meet the needs of modern teaching. Therefore, in the process of teaching, only by organically combining traditional teaching and multimedia teaching, learning from each other's strong points and choosing diversified teaching methods according to different teaching contents, can better teaching effect be achieved [6, 7].

In the process of teaching, teachers should develop a good teaching attitude, fully display their good temperament and constantly improve their own quality, which is also very necessary.

From Fig. 1, we can see that the advantages and disadvantages are relatively uniform, but from the fitting effect, the advantages are obviously better than the disadvantages. Therefore, for English multimedia teaching, using the algorithm proposed in this paper is very advantageous [8].

From Fig. 2, we can also see that in all the teaching effects, the teaching effect of using multimedia is far better than that of not using multimedia.

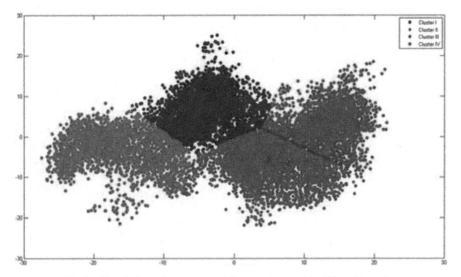

Fig. 1. Simulation advantages and disadvantages of traditional teaching

5   The Definition of Individualized Foreign Language Learning Environment in Classroom

5.1   On the Definition of Individualized Learning Environment of Foreign Language in Classroom

From the traditional point of view, The understanding of the learning environment is mostly from the external factors relative to learners or even very macro perspective [9]. such as: Learning environment refers to the classroom structure that enables teachers to teach and learners to learn smoothly, It includes a series of requirements such as how to set up and maintain the learning area in the classroom, draw up the calendar and daily work and rest, plan free activities, group activities, the time of the whole class activities, and

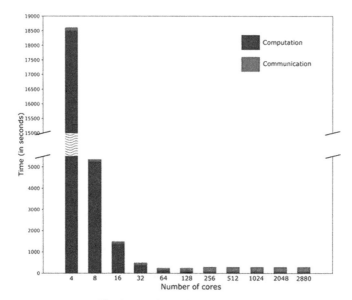

Fig. 2. Teaching effect simulation.

create a classroom community. From this angle, The researchers believe that: Learning environment refers to social environment, learning education, family influence, campus culture and other external factors. The definition of personalized learning environment in foreign language classroom is shown in Fig. 3.

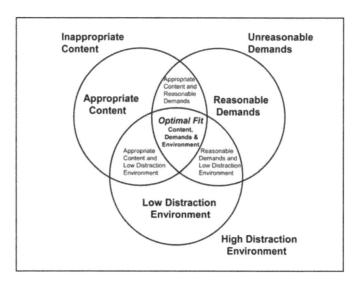

Fig. 3. The definition of individualized learning environment in foreign language classroom

To sum up the above understanding of learning environment, it can be summarized into three aspects:

1. Learning environment is the place where learning activities take place. As an external factor, it mainly includes classroom, campus, family and other social places. It is a learning environment based on teaching and behaviorism. It aims to promote learners' learning through external hardware facilities or equipment [10, 11].

2. Learning environment is the support of all kinds of learning resources for learning activities, which is still from the external factors. It includes knowledge resources, tool resources, human resources, and of course also includes the place where learning activities take place. But it emphasizes the use of these resources to assist the occurrence or continuation of learning activities. Obviously, resource view is a step further than place view, because it puts learners and learning activities in the center.

3. Learning environment is a kind of task which is different from place and resource. It includes not only place and resource, but also learning requirement for achieving learning task. Integrating place, resource and task, we call it learning situation, which can be supported by situational cognitive theory. The theory of Situational Cognition holds that learning and thinking are based on situations. They can not be embedded in the individual brain in isolation, but occur in the human brain through cultural activities or tools in situations. Those learning and knowledge separated from activities, tools and culture are inert [12]. Knowledge must be presented in real situations in order to stimulate learners' real cognitive needs. This is because knowledge exists in specific activities, situations and cultures. Only when people enter them can they learn the so-called knowledge [13].

5.2 Construction and Experiment of Individualized Foreign Language Learning Environment in Classroom

The purpose of this observation is to acquire and accumulate perceptual materials about learners and their learning environment through scientific and rational observation. Through the analysis of the interaction between teachers and students, learners and learners in the classroom, the use of multimedia and other teaching aids by learners, and the adoption of teaching methods and strategies, we can understand the appearance and internal mental activities in the classroom environment. The first-hand materials from the classroom are used to provide the basis for subsequent hypotheses and experiments. The subjects of observation and experiment should come from the same learning group and environment [14, 15]. Moreover, the observation and experiment should maintain the stability and continuity of time, content and scope, that is to say, the observation and experiment of the object should be carried out on the same sample in a relatively short period of time. Such observation can provide reliable and reliable basis for the experimental stage; on the contrary, if the time interval is long or the sample changes, the cognitive and mental level of the observation object is likely to have changed, then the observation based experiment will lose its reliability and validity. The author determines the object of observation from three aspects: the subject of the object, the time and the scope of knowledge.

The multimedia model in personalized learning environment is the multimedia integration that can't meet the needs of learners' learning activities. This model is more stable than learners and learning activities. In foreign language learning, the media supporting learners include listening, speaking, reading and writing. The stability of multimedia needs to be able to fully meet the learning needs of each learning group and each learning stage. Multimedia model is a collection of cognitive tools to support learning activities.

6 Conclusions

Teachers using multimedia technology in high school English classroom teaching can reduce the negative impact of traditional education mode in students' mind, which will have a far-reaching impact on their future study and life. It will help to deepen the impression of knowledge points in the minds of students and play a positive role in promoting them to meet the challenges in the future. Visual memory is one of the main ways of human memory. Teachers use multimedia technology to create a colorful classroom, which can let students focus on the teaching of knowledge points, and will play a positive role in promoting students' learning efficiency.

References

1. Huang, R.: Constructivism and multimedia foreign language teaching mode. Audio Vis. Foreign Lang. Teach. (2) (2000)
2. Wang, S.: On the advantages and possibilities of Multimedia Teaching. J. Taiyuan Teachers Coll. (4) (2000)
3. Huang, A.: A preliminary study on the effect of foreign language multimedia teaching. J. Gannan Med. Coll. (12) (2003)
4. Yang, L.: Tentative practice from traditional teaching to network. J. Yanbei Normal Univ. (6) (2006)
5. Jonathan, D.H.: Theoretical Basis of Learning Environment. Shanghai: East China Normal University Press, pp. 6-22 (2002)
6. Huanqi, Z.: Prospects for Foreign Language Education . East China Normal University Press, Shanghai (2001)
7. Zhixian, Z.: Informatization Teaching Mode – Theory Construction and Practice Example, p. 253. Science Education Press, Beijing (2003)
8. China Institute of curriculum and textbook, Thomson Learning press, USA. go for it!. Beijing: People's education press, Deng Zhiwei. Personalized teaching theory. Shanghai Education Press, vol. 202, pp. 55-57
9. Weisheng, L., Experimental research guidance. Beijing: Educational Science Press, : Introduction to educational research methods , p. 1997. Educational Science Press, Translated by Yuan Zhenguo. Beijing (2002)
10. Normal Education Department of Shanghai Education Bureau: Statistical Methods of Education. Higher Education Press, Beijing (1993)
11. Research Group on training in the process of new curriculum implementation. New curriculum and student development. Beijing Normal University Press, Beijing (2001)
12. Zhang, B.: Case Study on Description, Acquisition and Inference of Personalized Demand. Graduate School of Chinese Academy of Sciences, Beijing (2005)

13. Zhu, B., Wen, Z.: Research and application of learner model standard. Comput. Eng. (8), 300–304 (2002)
14. Sun, Z.: Research on the organization strategy of personalized learning content. Wuhan: Central China Normal University, 2006, Li Xinguo. Exploration of network foreign language teaching and education mode innovation. Jiangsu Foreign Lang. Teach. Res. (1), 33 (2006)
15. Wenjing, W.: Situational cognition and learning theory: the development of constructivism. Global Educ. Outlook **4**, 3 (2005)

Research on College Students' Health Education Based on Feature Extraction Algorithm

Wanjun Chen(✉)

South China Institute of Software Engineering,
Guangzhou University, Guangzhou 510990, China
cwj@sise.com.cn

Abstract. The research of students' mental health education is the need of the development of the times, the need of the development of higher education practice in our country, and also an important measure to comprehensively implement the party's education policy, implement quality education, and strengthen moral education in Colleges and universities. It is of great significance to promote the healthy growth and success of college students, deepen the teaching reform of College Students' mental health education, promote and steadily implement quality education, and realize the talent training goal of higher education.

Keywords: College students · Mental health · Educational countermeasures

1 Introduction

In recent years, the mental health problems of college students have caused widespread concern from all walks of life, and the investigation and Research on the mental health of college students are also increasing. On the basis of inheriting the traditional mental health education thoughts, China has formed a mental health education mode with local characteristics. It has made positive progress in classroom teaching, team building, publicity and education, and carrying out consultation and counseling activities. It has also accumulated rich experience, which has laid a good foundation for us to further promote college students' mental health education. But we should also be aware that the work of mental health education for college students is facing more complex environment and arduous tasks [1]. On the whole, the current work is far from meeting the needs of the development of the situation. This work has been carried out unevenly in various places and schools, and its importance is not fully understood, and it has not been put in its proper position; some colleges and universities lack sufficient exploration and Research on the tasks, characteristics and laws of College Students' mental health education under the new situation; some colleges and Universities need to strengthen the construction of College Students' mental health education team.

SIFT (scale invariant feature transform) is an algorithm for detecting local features. It searches for extremum points of a pair of images in spatial scale, extracts its position, scale, rotation invariants and other descriptors, obtains features and matches image feature points to detect and describe local features in images.

M. A. Jan and F. Khan (Eds.): BigIoT-EDU 2021, LNICST 391, pp. 302–307, 2021.
https://doi.org/10.1007/978-3-030-87900-6_36

It is based on some local features of the object. SIFT features are the local features of the image, which keep invariance to rotation, scaling and brightness changes, and also keep a certain degree of stability to the changes of viewing angle, affine transformation and noise; The detection rate of partial object occlusion using SIFT feature description is also quite high, even more than three sift object features are enough to calculate the position and orientation.

The essence of SIFT algorithm is to find the key points (feature points) in different scale space, and calculate the direction of the key points. The key points found by SIFT are some very prominent points that will not change due to illumination, affine transformation, noise and other factors, such as corner points, edge points, bright spots in dark areas and dark spots in bright areas.

Lowe decomposes the SIFT algorithm into the following steps:

(1) Input image, suggest double (width $*$ $=$ 2, height $*$ $=$ 2, size $*$ $=$ 4), and Gaussian filter for smoothing.

(2) Decide how many towers to build according to the image size, and how many layers of each tower (generally 3–5 layers). Layer 0 of tower 0 is the original image (or the image after you double). Each layer up is Laplacian transform (Gaussian convolution, where the Sigma value gradually increases. For example, it can be sigma, K $*$ sigma, K $*$ k $*$ sigma…). Intuitively, the higher the image is, the more blurred the image is. For example, the 0 th layer of tower 1 can be obtained from the 3 rd layer of tower 0 by down sample, and then Gaussian convolution operation similar to tower 0 can be performed.

(3) Build the dog pyramid. The dog pyramid is calculated from the Gauss pyramid generated in the previous step. The number of towers is the same, and the number of layers of each tower is less than 1, because each layer of the dog is obtained by subtracting two adjacent layers of Gauss.

(4) The extremum points are detected in the dog tower, and the illegal feature points are removed according to the preset contrast threshold and principal curvature threshold. Non maximum suppression is used to detect extreme points, that is, the gray value is compared among 3 $*$ 3 $*$ 3 points, and the minimum or maximum is passed.

(5) The scale of each feature point is calculated. Pay attention to the scale relationship between towers, sigma $*$ 2.0 $\hat{}$ (octvs $+$ intvl / intvls).

(6) The gradient modulus and direction of each feature point are calculated. The feature point is described by a point in a patch around the feature point, and the histogram of the feature point is used to count the modulus and find the main direction, which can be more than one.

(7) Finally, we need to generate 64D or 128d feature descriptors. Align the main direction and calculate the 2D array of direction histogram. If each histogram has 8 bin, then 64D (2 $*$ 2 $*$ 8 bin) or 128d (4 $*$ 4 $*$ 8 bin).

2 Feature Extraction Algorithm

2.1 Main Design Ideas of Feature Extraction Algorithm Database

The speed of data index and query directly affects the efficiency of subsequent data feature extraction and data mining. Therefore, this paper uses the full-text search engine to process the full-text index, spatial index based on spatial location, and abstract index of image, audio and video open-source intelligence; uses mys α 1 to establish the open-source intelligence data cataloging index and association search based on relational model of each United States; Mongo DB is used to build summary information index based on key value pairs and spatial location index based on R-tree.) parallel computing framework is used to solve the efficiency problem of massive open-source intelligence data processing. In this framework, map reduce component is mainly used to provide heavy parallel processing functions such as feature extraction and mining of large-scale open-source data [2]. The component adopts the map reduce parallel computing model, as shown in Fig. 1.

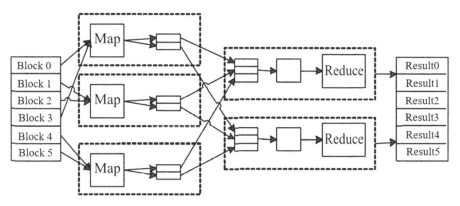

Fig. 1. Map reduce parallel computing model.

2.2 Overall Flow of the Algorithm

Among them, the method based on word frequency statistics has the advantages of easy to understand, simple process and good feature differentiation, so it is most widely used in practical applications. Tf-df (TEM frequency inverse document frequency) method is one of the most representative feature extraction algorithms. TF-IDF algorithm uses term frequency TF (term frequency) and inverse document frequency IDF (inverse document frequency) The word frequency represents the frequency of a specific keyword in a single text file, and the inverse text frequency represents the ability of the same keyword to distinguish categories in the whole document set. Finally, the weight of keywords is obtained by combining TF and IDF frequencies.

$$TF = \frac{N_{i,j}}{\sum_{k} N_{k,j}} \tag{1}$$

$$IDF_i = \log \frac{|D|}{1 + |\{ j | i \in d_j \}|} \tag{2}$$

$$TF - IDF_{(i,j)} = TF \times DF \tag{3}$$

3   The Standard of College Students' Mental Health

According to the definition of mental health, combined with the psychological characteristics of college students and their special environment and social roles, college students with mental health should meet the following standards.

3.1   Normal Intelligence, with a Strong Interest in Learning

Intelligence refers to the comprehensive ability of observation, attention, memory, imagination, thinking, creativity and practical activities. Normal intelligence is the most basic psychological condition for people to engage in life, study, work and other activities, and it is also the necessary psychological guarantee to adapt to the changes of the surrounding environment. The intelligence of college students is generally excellent, they have a strong ability of learning or understanding, the ability to acquire and update knowledge, the ability to quickly and accurately respond to new things, the ability to use reasoning to effectively solve problems and so on [3]. Learning is the main content of university life. Students with mental health have clear learning objectives, can maintain a strong interest in learning and desire for knowledge, are willing to accept new things and dare to challenge, are good at overcoming difficulties in learning, have stable academic performance, can maintain a certain learning efficiency, and can experience satisfaction and happiness from learning.

3.2   Good Environmental Adaptability

Living in a complex and changeable world, people will encounter a variety of environments and changes. Therefore, having a good ability to adapt to the environment is an important symbol of College Students' mental health. The ability to adapt to the environment includes the ability to correctly understand the environment and the ability to correctly deal with personal and environmental relations. College students with mental health can keep good contact with the environment, have a clear understanding of the current social situation, face the reality when the environment changes, make an objective understanding and evaluation of the environment, and timely correct their needs and wishes according to the changing environment, so that their personal behavior can meet the requirements of the new environment; when there is a contradiction between personal needs and the society, the students with mental health can face the reality, They can choose a positive way to adjust the conflict between themselves and the society, so that they can keep in harmony with the society in thought and behavior. College students with mental health also have a strong sense of competition and innovation, dare to face the changes and challenges of life and society, and constantly realize self-improvement and self transcendence.

4   The Contents, Methods and Countermeasures of Strengthening College Students' Mental Health Education

4.1   Strengthening the Mental Health Education of College Students

Cognitive development education cognitive ability includes the ability to know oneself, others and everything. The university stage is an important period for college students from youth to adulthood, and it is also an important stage for the development and improvement of College Students' cognitive ability. Correct cognition of self and others is an important premise for college students to correctly evaluate themselves, learn to get along with others, and then better develop themselves. In real life, many college students have contradictions between ideal and reality, ups and downs in emotion, inferiority and depression in the face of setbacks, and paranoia and paranoia in character, all of which are due to the deviation of cognitive development. Therefore, the cultivation of correct cognitive ability, correct treatment and evaluation of themselves and others will help college students deal with the relationship between ideal me and reality me, between me and others, between me and society, and establish a healthy and good self-image [4]. By learning the basic knowledge of emotion management and regulation, college students can strengthen the understanding and control of their own emotions, master the skills of self emotion management, actively regulate their own emotions, and be the masters of emotions.

4.2 Methods and Countermeasures of Strengthening College Students' Mental Health Education

Strengthening college students' mental health education is an urgent requirement of social development and college students' own development. At present, society, school, family and other aspects have realized the importance of College Students' mental health education. In the face of the psychological problems and obstacles among college students, we should attach great importance to them, strengthen the mental health education, timely prevent and solve the psychological problems faced by college students, and improve their physical and mental health. Based on the above analysis, we think we should start from the following aspects to carry out the mental health education of college students.

5   Conclusion

The mental health of college students is affected by many factors, including the internal reasons of individual physiology and psychology, as well as the external reasons of society, family and school. We should take positive and effective measures to deal with the current situation of College Students' mental health and its influencing factors, mainly through the opening of mental health education courses, the establishment and improvement of psychological counseling institutions, the development of campus culture, the strengthening of the construction of teaching staff and other channels, Mental health education on cognition, emotion, personality, learning communication, love, job hunting and so on should be carried out to cultivate college students' good psychological quality and improve their mental health level.

Acknowledgements. I would like to express my gratitude to all those who helped me during the writing of this thesis. A special acknowledgement should be show to Professor Huang, from whose lectures I benefited greatly. I am particularly indebted to Mr. Ke, who gave me kind encouragement and useful instructions all through my writing. Finally I wish to extend my thanks to my parents for their support. It is a great help for me to finish this thesis successfully.

References

1. Hu, W., Chen, P.: Research on the innovation of mental health education in Colleges and universities in the era of big data. Sci. Technol. Innov. (01), 24–25 + 29 (2021)
2. Chen, Y.: Big data and Internet plus: innovative Exploration of mental health education for frontier university students in Yunnan Province. Dig. World, (01), 188–189 (2021)
3. Xin, H.: Key research on Ideological and political education and mental health education of College Students under the background of epidemic situation. Sci. Educ. Wenhui (Next Issue) **12**, 44–45 (2020)
4. Jingjing, H.: Application of "narrative therapy" in college students' mental health education. Mod. Commun. **24**, 186–187 (2020)

Research on Teaching Reform Algorithm of Modern and Contemporary Literature Education in Colleges and Universities with Data Mining Technology

Jing Li[✉]

Liaoning Jianzhu Vocational College, Liaoning 111000, China

Abstract. This paper first expounds the current situation of the teaching of modern and contemporary literature course in Colleges and Universities under the background of data mining algorithm, and then discusses the teaching reform strategies of modern and contemporary literature course in Colleges and Universities under the background of network resources, including carrying out diversified teaching based on network resources, using teaching software to carry out information-based teaching, and changing the traditional single evaluation mode, Finally, the significance of the teaching reform of modern and contemporary literature in Colleges and Universities under the background of network resources is put forward.

Keywords: Data mining · Modern and contemporary literature teaching · Teaching software

1 Introduction

Teaching reform is the reform of teaching content, method and system, which aims to promote the progress of education and improve the quality of teaching. There are many reasons to promote the teaching reform, mainly including: (1) the progress of science and technology and the development of social productivity; (2) social change, including the change of political and economic system and ideology; (3) the development of educational science and other marginal disciplines affects the change of educational concept. Teaching reform can be divided into: (1) single reform. Only the content of a certain subject, a certain system (such as examination system), a certain principle and method should be reformed. (2) Overall reform. It refers to the overall coordinated reform of relevant teaching plans, tasks, contents, methods and systems.

The ways of reform are as follows:

(1) Reform under the guidance of new theories and policies. After a long period of planning and expert argumentation, a reform plan is formed and carried out in a planned and step-by-step manner. Such reform is often carried out in a country or a large scope.

M. A. Jan and F. Khan (Eds.): BigIoT-EDU 2021, LNICST 391, pp. 308–316, 2021.
https://doi.org/10.1007/978-3-030-87900-6_37

(2) Experimental reform. Under the guidance of certain theories, we should carry out the whole or single reform experiment in a certain area or school to obtain data and accumulate experience and lessons.

(3) We should promote the reform. After the selection and optimization of the excellent teaching experience or reform experimental results which have been tested by long-term practice, it is planned and step-by-step to promote them in a larger area and scope (see Fig. 1).

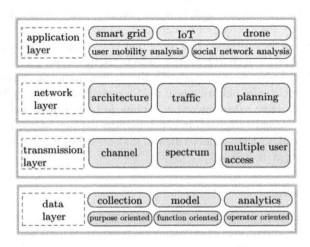

Fig. 1. The frame of big data with data minging

2 Data Mining Algorithm

2.1 BP Neural Network

BP neural network includes input layer, output layer and hidden layer. If the input of input layer is x_i, then its output is:

$$O_i^{(1)} = x(i), i = 1, 2, \ldots, n \tag{1}$$

If the weight coefficient of BP neural network hidden layer is $W_{ij}^{(2)}$, and $f[\cdot]$ is the mapping function, then the input and output calculation formulas are respectively expressed as:

$$net_i^{(2)}(k) = \sum_{j=1}^{m} w_{ij}^{(2)} O_j^{(1)}(k) \tag{2}$$

$$O_i^{(2)}(k) = f[net_i^{(2)}(k)] \tag{3}$$

The initial values of some parameters of BP neural network, such as: $w_{ij}^{(2)}$ and $w_{ij}^{(3)}$ are determined by experience, so it is difficult to train the optimal BP neural network. In this paper, adaptive genetic algorithm is introduced to determine their initial values.

3 The Present Situation of Modern and Contemporary Literature Teaching in Colleges and Universities

3.1 Main Courses

Chinese modern and contemporary literature is the main course of Chinese language and literature major in Colleges and universities. The course mainly includes the context of Chinese literature history, famous writers' works and literary phenomena since the beginning of new literature, so as to cultivate students' ability to read literary works, appreciate writers' creation and analyze literary phenomena. With the development of Internet technology, the teaching of modern and contemporary literature has rich network resources, but the utilization rate is not high [1]. At present, most teachers only use multimedia to teach, such as playing related films, music, pictures and using electronic courseware, and even some teachers only use oral narration. In such a teaching mode, showing a relatively old-fashioned, rigid teaching status quo, students will feel monotonous, boring, easy to lose interest in learning, just mechanical learning and exam. What's more, it is "dumb" teaching, in which teachers explain the whole process, students listen passively, teachers write on the top, students write down below, and students actively participate in the course.

3.2 Course Nature

On the one hand, the above problems are due to the nature of the course. Before the teaching of the relevant works, a lot of reading and background introduction are involved. Inevitably, teachers and textbooks are the main ones, while teachers rely on explanation and use less modern information technology. On the other hand, it is also related to teachers' teaching philosophy and the popularity of school teaching informatization [2]. Due to the special nature of the curriculum, teachers are more willing to use the traditional teaching mode, but they have less understanding of new technology and concept, and the operation of new technology is more complex. Therefore, the actual teaching effect is not ideal. For example, the production and application of micro class can greatly improve the teaching efficiency of teachers, Rich teaching mode, but the technical requirements of teachers are too high, and there is no relevant technical training and supporting teaching facilities, teachers in the production of micro class hours spend a lot of energy, little achievement. Some teachers are older and less receptive to the new teaching mode and concept.

4 Teaching Reform Strategy of Modern and Contemporary Literature Course in Colleges and Universities Based on Data Algorithm

4.1 Carrying Out Diversified Teaching Based on Network Resources Based on Data Mining Algorithm

Although it is difficult for teachers to complete the production of online courses, teachers can rely on rich network resources to carry out diversified teaching and enrich teaching mode. At present, many institutions and universities have set up teaching teams to produce excellent courses, such as MOOCS, love courses and other websites. There are many courses on modern and contemporary literature, such as Suzhou University, Capital Normal University, Nanjing University, Jilin University and so on, as well as some special studies, Such as Mo Yan's novel research, contemporary popular novels and network novels, the essence of Chinese culture and literature, and the introduction of Nobel Literature Prize Works. Teachers can search for relevant teaching resources according to the needs of the course through the Internet. For example, when teaching Mo Yan's works, teachers can combine the research course of Mo Yan's novels set up by Beijing Second International Studies Institute on moocnet as an extension of classroom teaching. Because the teaching time is limited and the interpretation of writers' works is unlimited, students' horizons are expanded. Students can self-study online, complete the course tests and exercises, and then initiate discussions in class [3]. At the same time, students can also find their concerns and share network resources according to their own interests. For example, students are more interested in online literature and popular literature, but the proportion of this part in teaching materials and teaching is not high. Students can find course resources according to their interests and conduct interactive communication, To form a good learning atmosphere. Therefore, it can change students' passive learning into active learning, take a certain topic as the starting point, expand research horizontally or vertically, gain more for students, and make classroom teaching more flexible, stimulate students' interest and enrich teaching staff (see Fig. 2).

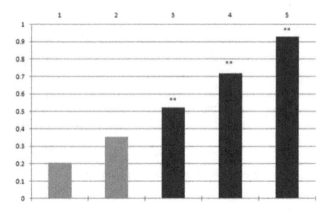

Fig. 2. The effect of teaching reform simulation

4.2 Using Teaching Software to Carry Out Information Teaching

At present, there are many kinds of teaching software, such as rain class, classroom school, bisection, etc., but the utilization rate of modern and contemporary literature teachers is generally not high. On the one hand, due to the complexity of the software application program, people are deterred; on the other hand, the nature of modern and contemporary literature curriculum causes teachers to rely on the traditional mode and are unwilling to make changes. Practice has proved that information-based teaching is of great help to classroom management, and the key lies in the change of concept. At present, many teaching software can complete many aspects of classroom management, such as attendance, assignment and correction, communication between teachers and students, and can realize continuous communication after class. The traditional home-work arrangement and marking will cost more manpower and material resources. The homework finished by the teacher is piled up like a mountain, and the teacher can't give feedback to the students in time. The teaching software provides a network virtual platform for teachers and students. In the teaching process of modern and contemporary literature, teachers can arrange homework in the network class. For example, students can complete the reading of Lu Xun's cry within two weeks and submit a 300 word reading impression. Students can immediately get information and have time nodes to remind them. After students submit their homework, they will also show it clearly, Omit the teacher - after correcting the homework, you can also feedback to the students in time, and you can have one-to-one communication with students. In addition, teachers can also put the homework in the place similar to forum or post bar to share resources, so that all students can see the feedback submitted by others and make comments and discussions. In addition, the teaching software can also be connected with classroom teaching equipment and applied to classroom teaching management (see Fig. 3).

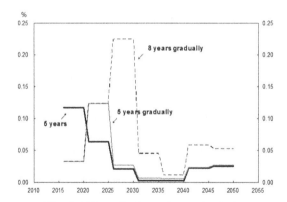

Fig. 3. Effect of using software simulation

5   The Significance of Teaching Reform of Modern and Contemporary Literature in Universities Under the Background of Data Mining Algorithm Combined with Network Resources

The development of Internet has not only changed people's life, but also changed people's thinking mode. The current college students are growing up in the environment of the Internet, their thinking mode and learning state are very different from the past, the network can search for a variety of information, these information give people more choices, but also formed a fast-food cultural atmosphere, leading to the current college students almost lost the patience of literature reading, weakened the feeling of literary ability. As Professor Wang Weiping said when talking about the curriculum reform in Colleges and Universities: "the social influence of literature is gradually shrinking, the charm of literature as a major is slowly declining, and the attraction of literature, as the main course of Chinese department in universities, is also quietly weakening. Today's college students tend to pay more attention to practicality than quality, utilitarianism and humanism. They do not feel the great potential of deep literature and culture for shaping people [4]. Their pursuit of foreign language and computer grade certificate seems to be far greater than their love of literature. It is an undeniable fact that scholars are worried about students' curriculum learning and social education. In contrast, the rich and diverse network information is more attractive to students. However, there are advantages and disadvantages in the way of obtaining these information. On the one hand, it makes people's access to knowledge more efficient and intuitive, on the other hand, it also dispels the depth and charm of literature and art itself. As some scholars have said: "when we are immersed in the perceptual intuition and vulgarization of modern visual cultural images, there will be a thousand Hamlets in a thousand readers in literary reading, and there will be only one Hamlet in a thousand audiences [5].

6 Analysis of the Current Situation of College Students' Core Literacy and College Classroom Teaching Based on Investigation and Research

6.1 Analysis on the Current Situation of College Students' Core Literacy

According to the questionnaire, this paper analyzes the core literacy of college students. There are three questions in the literacy of humanity. 76.04% of the students who can actively listen to other people's opinions and suggestions choose to conform to it. If I do something wrong, even if I am embarrassed, I will admit it [6]. 78.7% of the students think it conforms to it, I will take the initiative to find that 79.53% of the people who choose to meet the requirements of all things that make people feel good in life. Through the above data, we can draw a conclusion that college students have good cultural heritage literacy. Through the data investigation and analysis of scientific spirit literacy, when I can correctly evaluate whether the information meets my own requirements and will not blindly pursue, 79.7% of the students choose to meet the requirements, I can resolve other people's conflicts with a rational and peaceful attitude. 74.7% of the students choose to meet the requirements. 62.4% of the students think that they can meet their own requirements when I use the professional knowledge I have learned. From the above analysis, it can be seen that college students lack the ability to deal with and solve problems [7].

6.2 Analysis of the Current Situation of Classroom Teaching in Colleges and Universities

Through the analysis of the questionnaire and exploratory factor analysis, four factors affecting college classroom teaching are found. The following four factors are analyzed on the current situation of college classroom teaching. The analysis of the items of classroom teaching methods shows that 77.7% of the students choose the items that teachers often use the teaching method for classroom teaching, 42.1% of the students choose the items that teachers will explain the corresponding examples, and 75.88% of the students choose the items that are in line with the requirements of perfect hardware facilities, 72.04% of the students met the requirement of the teacher's association that students should be in the front row [8]. Among the items that the teacher's Association encouraged students to help each other in their study, 79.53% of the students chose to meet the requirement. Among the items that the teacher would assign practical activities and ask students to share in the classroom teaching, 77.7% of the students chose to meet the requirement, According to the results of data analysis, it can be seen that most of the classroom teaching methods in Colleges and universities choose teaching method, the method is single, and the interaction between teachers and students is less [9].

7 Problems in College Classroom Teaching Based on College Students' Core Literacy

7.1 Single Teaching Method, Lack of Interactive Thinking

According to the survey results, teachers will explain the teaching content directly by teaching method. Teaching method is to directly use language to make statement and explanation of problems, and improve students' understanding of teaching content through language expression. The non repudiation teaching method is the most direct and effective way to explain knowledge, but the teaching method mainly focuses on the teacher's "mono" explanation, which is not conducive to students' independent discovery and understanding of knowledge. At the beginning of the new century, China has put forward the concept of classroom teaching which encourages students to take initiative, interactive cooperation and mutual research and exploration, which guides them to fully demonstrate their interaction in the activities. However, according to the survey, teachers choose teaching method mainly based on Teaching in the classroom teaching of colleges and universities. Teachers explain in a single way according to the knowledge structure, and students listen to and take notes, The interaction frequency is less, and the classroom atmosphere is dull [10].

First of all, most teachers at this stage are deeply influenced by Herbart's "four stages" theory of teaching. In the whole class teaching, they often adopt the following steps: introducing new content, explaining new lessons, consolidating new knowledge and reviewing and arranging homework content after class. The specific performance is that teachers teach through language or with the help of multimedia and other technical means, Most of the knowledge that students need to master in a class is mainly in the form of teachers' language explanation, and students' listening is a passive form of instilling knowledge. Secondly, the teaching content and plan of each class need to be carried out according to the outline stipulated by the state and the school. In order to complete certain teaching tasks within the specified time limit, most teachers rarely use the methods and models of group cooperation or free exploratory learning, while some teachers adopt more conservative teaching methods in order to complete the tasks within the appropriate scope, To achieve a certain effect. Thirdly, most of the current college teachers use lecture method as the main method of classroom teaching for many years, and change the teaching method in a short time, so it is difficult for teachers to find their own teaching method, so they continue to choose the relatively suitable lecture method [11].

7.2 The Goal of Classroom Teaching Is Knowledge-Based, Ignoring the Change of Emotion, Attitude and Values

The goal of classroom teaching is a sign of value orientation. It is mainly to achieve a desired effect through teaching. What kind of method is used in classroom teaching is mostly based on the given teaching goal. The goal of classroom teaching is also an index to evaluate the quality of classroom teaching. The goal of classroom teaching in the new era should not only be the acquisition of theoretical knowledge taught by teachers, It should be the cultivation of students' thinking ability, judgment ability and practical ability. However, at this stage, the classroom teaching goal of colleges and universities is mainly to impart and accumulate knowledge, ignoring the continuous changes of personality and ability in this process [12].

On our way forward, we need a clear goal to guide the direction. No matter what action we take, we need to have a specific goal in line with the reality to guide [13]. The goal of classroom teaching is to guide the direction of teachers' teaching. The mastery of subject knowledge is not only the center of contemporary classroom teaching, but also a series of evaluation criteria for students and teachers. In order to complete the planned teaching content within the specified time, the best and most direct teaching method is adopted, which can not only avoid the possible interference in the classroom, but also greatly avoid some students challenging teachers' knowledge and ability. This kind of classroom teaching simply optimizes the whole teaching process. Students only need to listen to the ready-made knowledge and experience or problem-solving steps or memorize them by rote to master the content of a lesson in a short time, which excludes students' active participation in thinking and cultivates students who only master knowledge but do not know how to think and ask questions [14].

Teachers play an important role in classroom teaching, and their ideas on classroom teaching will have an impact on the whole classroom to a great extent [15]. Every teacher should have the ability to have a clear awareness of the curriculum and a clear and vivid understanding of the curriculum, and reasonably treat the goal of classroom teaching and the mechanism of classroom teaching. In the process of classroom teaching, every teacher should be able to adjust his own performance according to various sudden changes, choose the corresponding response methods, complete the significance of classroom teaching, and realize the value. With the development and progress of the times, classroom teaching no longer only pays attention to the transfer of knowledge, but more attention to the generation of ability, from teaching to learning. But at present, many teachers are still not strong in curriculum consciousness, or focus on "teaching", and it is difficult to change to the direction of "learning" [16].

8 Conclusion

To sum up, the data mining algorithm combined with the network resources environment is very urgent and significant, which is not only applicable to the teaching reform of modern and contemporary literature, but also applicable to the curriculum reform of many majors in Colleges and universities. This paper is only a brief discussion and analysis, and it is urgent to conduct more in-depth research and exploration in the actual teaching.

References

1. Xie, H.: Discussion on the teaching method reform of modern and contemporary Chinese literature in Colleges and universities. J. Jilin Univ. Educ. **72**(11) (2010)
2. Lili, Z., Qiao, C.: Analysis of the necessity of curriculum system reform under the background of big data. Ind. Technol. Forum **17**, 154 (2018)
3. Yan, F., Liping, M.: Statistics and decision making of university teaching quality evaluation model based on Optimized BP neural network, vol. 34, no. 2, p. 8082 (2018)
4. Zhilan, Y.: Some thoughts on the teaching reform of modern and contemporary Chinese literature in Colleges and universities. J. Heilongjiang Univ. Educ. **5**, 53 (2015)
5. Chongde, L.: Research on the Core Literacy of Students' Development in the 21st Century. Beijing Normal University Press, Beijing (2016)
6. Guangxiong, H., Qingtian, C.: Core Literacy: New Theory of Curriculum Development and Design. East China Normal University Press, Shanghai (2017)
7. Zhong, Q., Cui, Y.: Core literacy and Teaching Reform. East China Normal University Press, Shanghai (2018). Zhong, Q., Cui, Y.: Core literacy research. East China Normal University Press, Shanghai (2018)
8. Vincent, Y.: Core Literacy Oriented Classroom Teaching . Shanghai Education Press, Shanghai (2017)
9. Learning basic literacy project group: How Literacy Grows in the Classroom. East China Normal University Press, Shanghai (2018)
10. Qiquan, Z.: Ten Lectures on Core Literacy. Fujian Education Press, Fujian (2018)
11. Jinzhou, Z.: 50 Details of Classroom Teaching. Fujian Education Press, Fuzhou (2007)
12. Hu, Y.: Transformation of instructional design for core literacy. Teach. Manage. (34) (2017)
13. Xiong, Q., Zhu, D.: Theory on the transcendence of teaching content in the era of core literacy. Educ. Theory Pract. (2019)
14. Zhang, S.: Deep learning committed to quality cultivation: concept and mode. Curricul. Teach. Mater. Teach. Methods (2018)
15. Ma, Z., Yu, T., Lei, H.: Point to the curriculum theory and practice of core literacy - Summary of the 15th Shanghai International Curriculum forum. Global Educ. Outlook (3) (2018)
16. Xie, H., Liu, C., Liu, L.: Smart classroom construction in colleges and universities guided by classroom teaching reform. Modern Educ. Technol. (2018)

Research on the Construction and Development of General Education Curriculum in German Universities Under the Background of Information Education

Xiaofen Li[✉]

Wuhan Business University, Wuhan 430056, China

Abstract. With the development of society, it is an era of globalization, information and resource sharing. Under the mode of Sino foreign cooperation in running schools in the field of teaching, with the emergence of German, it has realized the integration of new educational methods and elements into the West under the Chinese educational system, and refined a set of development mode that is suitable for the development of Chinese education, suitable for Chinese students to absorb, and can be combined with foreign educational concepts. So as to improve the quality of German teaching in major schools in our country, and improve the development mode of students' open thinking..

Keywords: German teaching · Cross cultural awareness · General education · Practical exploration

1 Introduction

The term "general education" is translated from "general education". It was first proposed by nine Ivy League schools in the United States. At the beginning, it was called "liberal arts education". Its main subjects were seven arts (culture, logic, rhetoric, geometry, astronomy, mathematics, music) and liberal arts. It was mainly used to train lawyers and teachers [1]. After that, Harvard University added Chinese, humanities, society, natural science and other disciplines on this basis, and gradually developed into what we call general education today [2].

General education in higher education should be regarded as a kind of educational thought and idea, which should run through the whole process of higher education. If higher education is a person, then general education is the blood of a person, and professional education is the skeleton of a person. General education should flow in all the muscles of higher education, so as to provide reasonable nourishment and correct guidance for higher education. In order to adapt to the development trend of the times, the education system is constantly updated, and new education models are springing into teaching. The development of German classroom teaching in China is bound to be the integration of new elements in China's original education system. The school

M. A. Jan and F. Khan (Eds.): BigIoT-EDU 2021, LNICST 391, pp. 317–326, 2021.
https://doi.org/10.1007/978-3-030-87900-6_38

running mode of Sino foreign cooperation will realize the integration and innovation of teaching models, and extract a set of teaching methods that are suitable for Chinese and foreign education Chinese students, including German advanced teaching philosophy and German teaching mode with rich experience, are of great significance to improve the teaching quality of German professional knowledge and cultivate excellent students with leapfrog thinking [3].

2 The Development Trend of German Classroom Teaching

With the increasingly close cooperation and exchanges between China and Germany in various fields, those with good German expression ability and a deep understanding of German culture and economy have become the resources that enterprises in Huade and other enterprises closely cooperate with Germany, and the international talent demand is increasing. Many universities in China actively integrate with the advanced education mode in Germany, and run schools in combination with German universities, and implement the international talent training mode. The graduates who run a school in cooperation have good German language ability and are interdisciplinary and complex talents. For them, language is both a goal and a medium for acquiring professional knowledge. Therefore, the establishment of German classroom teaching is in line with the needs of the times and economic development, and is a teaching project with great potential for development [4].

3 The Mode of Chinese Foreign Cooperation in Running a School

The establishment of any foreign language major in China is closely related to the inherent educational model of the school. The teaching management mode of Chinese foreign cooperative German course mainly includes demonstration class, mutual listening and collective listening system [5].

The demonstration class mainly invites some senior German majors or senior lecturers to attend lectures, or completes the teaching tasks in the form of demonstration class within the prescribed teaching time. Through this mode, the latest teaching tasks and advanced teaching methods are introduced into German class to achieve the teaching objectives [6–8].

The main purpose of listening to each other is to let one German teacher attend another German teacher's curriculum, and then discuss the teaching method and teaching method. Then the teacher will attend the course of another German teacher. The main purpose of this is that teachers can learn from each other in this way, learn from each other and make up for each other, so as to improve the teaching quality.

Listening to a group of teachers is to listen to a German teacher's teaching, and then discuss the teacher's classroom, summarize the advantages and disadvantages, and finally let each teacher express his own feelings, and extract the essence of his own harvest, so as to create a good teaching atmosphere and improve the quality of teaching. Figure 1 shows the pattern of Sino foreign cooperation.

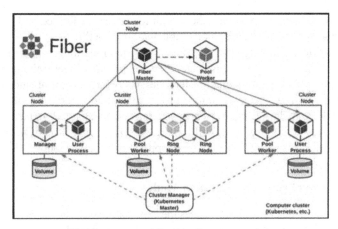

Fig. 1. Pattern of Sino foreign cooperation

3.1 The Curriculum Setting of German Class

Generally speaking, our German teaching course is divided into three stages: learning stage, reinforcement stage, professional training stage.

When we first came into contact with German courses, it must have started from the simplest listening, speaking, reading and writing stage, and it is the cultivation of interest and hobbies. We will often have a basic introduction to study through some German films, TV, songs or plays. Then, it is the strengthening stage. Through the training of listening, speaking, reading and writing in the early stage, what we should achieve at this stage is to strengthen and improve the language on the basis of the previous people, so as to prepare for the use of the later language [9]. Finally, it is the professional training stage. German application is not only a simple understanding in our life development, but also needs us to apply it as a professional skill to the future life and work. The school will improve and train the language specialization degree of students by exchanging students and interviews between schools. And will use the way of assessment to get the students' final results in the German course, complete the credit of the course [10].

3.2 Problems in the Sino German Cooperative School Running Project

German learning is to adapt to the development of the whole social globalization, and is a course to improve the overall quality of students. In the current degree of completion of the course, students generally respond to the heavy task of learning. The three courses of German learning are a gradual process from primary to advanced, from basic to professional. Students mostly stay in the primary stage of listening, speaking, reading and writing, and then to a deeper level, they need to make up for their own shortcomings [11].

In the classroom, teachers and students communicate poorly and knowledge is broken. According to the teaching in books, the knowledge that is taught is generally written, and can not be expressed as the skills needed for daily work and life. Besides, the better way to learn German is to really understand the life habits and daily life of Germany as exchange students abroad. However, the school resources are limited and can not give all the students who study German a favorable learning condition.

Not professional. Although the last stage of German learning is specialized training, only a few can really go to this stage, then enter professional training and finally use German vocabulary professionally. Here, the misunderstanding of students is to be familiar with the first two stages, and the third stage is often ignored, and the formation of professional vocabulary is inadvertently generated or understood. In fact, in different contexts, different writers' writing will have a word polysemy. It is difficult to read a work with strong professionalism only by the previous basic vocabulary [12–14].

3.3   The Reform of German Education Mode

In the basic German teaching class, besides the explanation of basic German vocabulary, the daily German listening, speaking, reading and writing should be completed, and the explanation of professional vocabulary should be appropriately increased on the basis of the basic vocabulary. It is not enough to study through the third stage of students, and it is difficult for students to complete the transformation of their major. This requires teachers to help students in the early teaching tasks, guide students to understand professional vocabulary, and finally improve their professional literacy [15].

We can also understand the learning effect of students through the communication between the two sides, and enhance the interaction between teachers and students [16].

In the third stage, the teacher can make the classroom teaching easier, strengthen the communication and discussion between students, summarize and put forward suggestions on the problems in the application and specialization of German, and deepen the students' understanding of the professional terms in a relaxed and pleasant learning atmosphere.

In a word, the German teaching in the mode of Chinese foreign cooperation is a foreign language teaching in such a large environment in China. It needs a strong integration and plasticity between the two. The audience group is the group of students in the Chinese education system. We can neither abandon the original teaching mode nor admire the foreign language. We should combine the two better and achieve "Chinese and western use", and do not worry too fast, so as to create a strong and professional German talent.

4   Research Status of Ant Colony Optimization Algorithm

Thirdly, the negative feedback mechanism is introduced. Every time an ant moves from one node to another, the pheromones on the path are eliminated according to the following formula, so as to realize the local adjustment of pheromones, so as to reduce the probability of the selected path being selected again.

$$\tau_{ij} = (1 - \varsigma) \cdot \tau_{ij} + \varsigma \cdot \tau_0 \tag{1}$$

Another improved algorithm for as is rank based version as. Similar to "elite strategy", the pheromone on the better process is always updated in this algorithm, and the selection criterion is its travel length, $(L^1(t) \leq L^2(t) \leq L^m(t))$, and the intensity of pheromone placement for each ant is determined by the ranking weighting in the following formula, where W is the total number of ants placing pheromones after each iteration.

$$\tau_{ij}(t+1) = (1 - \rho) \cdot \tau_{ij}(t) + \sum_{r=1}^{w} (w - r) \qquad (2)$$

5 The Importance of General Courses in German Teaching in Universities

5.1 To Meet the Needs of Globalization

In recent years, the development of global economy and trade, science and technology is more and more rapid, and close ties have been formed between countries [17]. The awareness of global coordinated development is widely recognized, especially the cultural exchanges are more and more frequent. The spread and development of culture has already exceeded the boundaries of regions and countries [18]. The formation of cross-cultural awareness is a necessity for the development of globalization. Cross cultural communication can not only promote the wide spread of excellent culture, but also provide spiritual support for national development and strengthen the close ties between countries. College German teaching must conform to the development trend of the times, change teaching concepts, and integrate German teaching with the spirit of the times. This integration is not limited to teaching German, but also allows students to indirectly learn the history and national conditions of Germany through German learning, so that students can truly understand German culture and the differences between Chinese and German cultures, so as to cultivate students' cross-cultural awareness. To train a large number of cross-cultural language workers for the development of the country [19–21].

5.2 Basic Principle of Ant Colony Algorithm

The essence of College German teaching is to let students learn to use the language, form a dialectical thinking of cultural differences, and improve students' ability of cross-cultural communication, rather than simply teaching words and grammar. In the process of German teaching, teachers should cultivate students' language ability from four aspects: listening, speaking, reading and writing, Cross cultural awareness in this process reflects its role. The traditional teaching mode and exam oriented education mode seriously restrict the German teaching. Most students study German with a utilitarian exam oriented attitude. Their goal is to test rather than to achieve a deep understanding of culture through language learning, which runs counter to the essence of German teaching [22].

6 General Education

According to the purpose of general education and the goal to be achieved, the curriculum and its process are designed. In undergraduate colleges and universities, it generally refers to all courses except professional courses. (see Table 1).

Table 1. Undergraduate general education curriculum

Formal courses	Basic skills	Political morality course
		Language, writing
		Computer
Hidden curriculum	Core curriculum	It is to promote the construction of students' personality and balance their knowledge structure. To social sciences, etc
		Social investigation, practice, campus culture, environment, campus landscape, campus tradition, school spirit, school motto, community environment, etc

(1) General education model and core curriculum plan of Harvard University

The general education model and core curriculum plan of Harvard University the core curriculum of Buddha university is divided into 70 fields, including foreign culture, historical research a, historical research B, literature and art a, literature and art B, literature and art C, ethical speculation, quantitative analysis, science a, Science B, social analysis, etc. [23]. The above core courses are mainly arranged in the first and second year of the University. From the listed courses, Harvard's core courses are widely distributed in content, which can be used to describe and describe astronomy, geography, science and humanities from ancient times to the present. In addition to quantitative analysis and science, the others belong to humanities and social sciences. From this, we can understand Harvard's educational philosophy and innovative talent training philosophy. First, regardless of whether students major in science or arts, all students must have a knowledge base across the two fields of Arts and science [24]. For example, the more they major in classical literature, history, anthropology and other majors that seem to have nothing to do with science, the more they are required to take science courses as a compulsory course, The organic unity of humanity and science, ethical speculation and pragmatic verification embodies the basic purpose of Harvard's human cultivation and education, that is, to cultivate people's comprehensive quality and comprehensive innovation ability in the multi-disciplinary knowledge synthesis. Second, the content of the course covers a wide range, each field contains a large number of specific courses, even its content only involves a certain country, a certain historical fragment, for students to choose freely. Obviously, here, we can understand the obvious flexible or flexible characteristics of Harvard's rigid core curriculum plan. Therefore, it takes care of the interests of different students and reflects the personalized and diversified characteristics of general education. Third, the curriculum covers a wide range of regions. Although it is difficult to determine whether a specific curriculum has the tendency of western centralism, the overall distribution structure and framework of the curriculum undoubtedly contain the civilizations of all countries, regions and nationalities in the world. Therefore, the core curriculum plan has a strong international color (see Fig. 2).

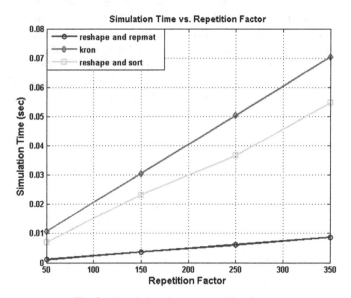

Fig. 2. Simulation time vs repetition factor.

7 Current Situation of General Education

7.1 Misunderstandings in Curriculum Understanding

(1) Today, with the emphasis on marketization and commercialization, universities are facing the great challenge of utilitarianism. Undergraduate education falls into the trap of "professionalism" and "professionalism" [25]. General education courses are only additional courses besides the main courses for undergraduates, which are additional, secondary, dispensable and at most icing on the cake. Most of these courses do not have strict requirements and training, It is often a mixed credit course for students, or a course to increase extracurricular interest at most [26].

(2) In terms of concept, the independent significance of undergraduate general education is not emphasized. Instead, the idea of graduate education is used to support the reform of undergraduate education. General education has become the preparatory stage of graduate education. I'm afraid that such a guiding ideology is still the continuation of the previous "professionalism" education thought and tradition, and

does not really regard the undergraduate education stage as having an independent purpose and goal.

7.2   On the Credit Allocation of General Education Courses

Take the undergraduate teaching plan of East China Normal University published in 2005 as an example. In this plan, the average total number of credits for four-year undergraduate students is 160, of which the average number of general education courses is about 57, accounting for 36% of the total credits [27]. In general education courses, the average number of general compulsory courses is 41 credits, accounting for 72% of the total number of general education courses, and the number of general education elective courses is 16 credits, accounting for 28% of the total number of general education courses, Other credits can be offset by professional elective courses. In addition, due to the school's curriculum resources, students have little autonomy in their choice of study (see Fig. 3).

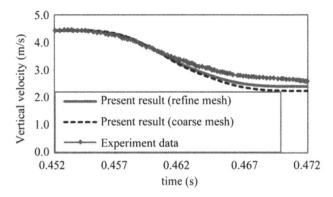

Fig. 3. Estimated results of general education courses

8   Epilogue

Learning German teaching must pay attention to the cultivation of students' cross-cultural awareness, which is a long-term and systematic process. We should strengthen the infiltration of cross-cultural awareness in German teaching by cultivating excellent German teachers, changing teaching methods and ideas, and strive to achieve the cultivation goal of cross-cultural awareness.

Acknowledgements. Research on the construction and development of general education course "German culture and German" in applied undergraduate universities.

References

1. Fujun, Y., Lijuan, W.: Practice of general education curriculum system construction in local universities. J. Anshan Normal Univ. **14**(01), 90–93 (2012)
2. Haizhou, Q.: Difficulties and practical exploration of general education curriculum construction. Teach. Educ. People **03**, 117–118 (2012)
3. Back to the origin: Practice and exploration on the construction of excellent courses of general education in higher vocational colleges. J. Liaoning College Public Secur. Judicial Manage. **03**, 96–98 (2010)
4. Yonghong, M.: Practical exploration of undergraduate general education curriculum construction. Teach. Educ. Res. **05**, 53–55 (2006)
5. Wu, k., Xia, X.: Error analysis and teaching strategies of foreigners' Chinese acquisition -- based on the analysis of German native speakers' Chinese learning corpus. Educ. Rev. (03), 124–128 (2021)
6. Yuanyuan, C.: Effective classroom teaching of German for students with core literacy. College Entrance Exam. **11**, 45–46 (2021)
7. Yang, C.Y.: The practice of SPOC based online and offline hybrid teaching reform of basic german: mode, method, content and effect. Chin. J. Multimedia Netw. Teach (First Issue) **03**, 20–22 (2021)
8. Yanli, W.: Application of game teaching method in German teaching for non German majors. Modern Commun. **03**, 182–184 (2021)
9. Hong, R.: Teaching design of German as a second foreign language in Colleges and Universities Based on output oriented method. Modern Vocat. Educ. **06**, 180–182 (2021)
10. Li, J.: Cultivating students' autonomous learning ability through "task driven blended teaching" – taking basic German as an example. Intelligence **03**, 135–137 (2021)
11. Xiaofang, C.: An exploration of the ideological and political elements in the classroom teaching of intermediate German. Sci. Educ. J. **01**, 186–188 (2021)
12. Jia, Z., Yugui, W.: Analysis of German reading test in colleges and universities and its washback effect on teaching. J. Yangzhou Inst. Educ. **38**(04), 85–88 (2020)
13. Yuan, L.: Research on the mixed teaching reform of "College German" based on Bloom's classification of educational objectives. Sci. Educ. Guide (Next Ten Issues) **36**, 163–164 (2020)
14. Wenxi, Z.: The application of behavior oriented teaching method in German teaching: a case study of vorkus 6, contemporary college German 1. J. Yanbian Inst. Educ. **34**(06), 87–89 (2020)
15. Juan, G., Fen, J.: How to integrate German as a second foreign language into ideological and political education. J. Taizhou Polytech. **20**(06), 19–21 (2020)
16. Zhao, Y.: An empirical study of second language transfer from the perspective of third language acquisition. Changjiang Series (34), 1–2 + 7 (2020)
17. Chaoqun, L.: Cultural research and teaching in German curriculum. Forum Lang. Culture **04**, 61–69 (2020)
18. Fu, R., Weng, Z.: Comparison of modal particles between Chinese and German and Its Enlightenment on Chinese teaching in Germany. Literat. Educ. **2**(11), 47–49 (2020)
19. Liangyu, L.: Teaching design of College German under boppps teaching mode – taking "weather expression" teaching as an example. Modern Vocat. Educ. **45**, 90–91 (2020)
20. Qianli, Z.: A survey of German learning motivation of students in Sino german cooperative education project – taking sino German college of engineers of Zhejiang University of science and technology as an example. J. Zhejiang Univ. Sci. Technol **32**(05), 446–451 (2020)

21. Hanzi, X.: German classroom error correction and the establishment of language autonomous learning mechanism: a case study of German teaching reform in China German Institute of engineers, Zhejiang University of science and technology. J. Zhejiang Univ. Sci. Technol. **32**(05), 460–465 (2020)
22. Xiaoyu, Z.: The important role of German art songs in vocal music teaching. Northern Music **20**, 206–208 (2020)
23. Jin, Z., Xiong, Z.: Interpretation of College German teaching guide in the context of public foreign language teaching reform. Foreign lang. Circles **05**, 24–30 (2020)
24. Qisheng, L.: A guide to undergraduate teaching of German major and the disciplinary turn of German major. J. Foreign Lang. **05**, 1–6 (2020)
25. Rui, Z.: Research on the cultivation of intercultural competence in college German Teaching . Sci. Tech. Inf. **18**(25), 123–125 (2020)
26. Lin, G.U.I.: on the way to improve the online teaching ability of University Teachers - learning from the online teacher training project of Goethe college. Chin. J. Multimedia Netw. Teach. (Last Ten Days) **09**, 16–17 (2020)
27. Xiaodong, X.: Strategies for optimizing the effectiveness of German classroom teaching in Colleges and universities. Comparat. Study Cultural innov. **4**(25), 76–78 (2020)

Research on the Construction of Scientific Research Evaluation System for Teachers in Higher Vocational Colleges Based on Computer PCA and ANP

Jing Lv[✉]

Xi'an Aeronautical Polytechnic Institute, Shanxi 710089, China

Abstract. With the rapid development of Higher Vocational Education in China, a series of problems need to be solved, especially the performance appraisal of teachers. At present, the scientific research assessment system of teachers in higher vocational colleges is not perfect, which restricts the development of higher vocational colleges to a certain extent. Establishing a scientific performance appraisal system is the key to improve the teaching quality and highlight the characteristics of higher vocational colleges. This is also the premise of the healthy development of higher vocational education, which has strong theoretical and practical significance for the sustainable development of higher vocational education. According to the working characteristics of teachers in higher vocational colleges, this paper establishes the performance evaluation index system of teachers in Higher Vocational Colleges from five aspects of teaching, scientific research, social service and discipline construction, and studies and grows through investigation and principal component analysis (PCA). On this basis, the use of network analytic hierarchy process (ANP) to determine the construction of Higher Vocational College Teachers' performance evaluation model.

Keywords: Higher vocational colleges · Performance appraisal · Appraisal system

1 Introduction

Talent competition is the main content of today's international competition, people are more and more deeply aware of the strategic importance of talent. In the current situation, only by vigorously developing all kinds of education can we be invincible in the future international competition. Higher vocational education is the inevitable product of economic development and the development of modern social science and technology. The rise of new technological revolution after World War II has promoted the rapid development of economy in the world, and the economic structure and labor employment structure have also changed significantly, thus promoting the great development of higher vocational education. All countries in the world recognize that the development of higher vocational education plays an important role in promoting economic

M. A. Jan and F. Khan (Eds.): BigIoT-EDU 2021, LNICST 391, pp. 327–335, 2021.
https://doi.org/10.1007/978-3-030-87900-6_39

and social development and employment growth. Therefore, they regard the reform and development of higher vocational education as an important part of planning the education system in the 21st century. In 1999, the decision of the CPC Central Committee and the State Council on deepening education reform and comprehensively promoting quality education put forward: "higher vocational education is an important part of higher education, and we should vigorously develop higher vocational education. Since then, higher vocational education began to expand on a large scale, and its development has been widely concerned by all sectors of the society. It has provided great support for the rapid leap of China's higher education from the elite stage to the popular stage.

2 Summary of Performance Appraisal

2.1 The Meaning of Performance Appraisal

From the perspective of human resource management, performance is efficiency, which refers to the input-output ratio of an organization or individual in a certain period of time. There are various forms of performance, generally speaking, mainly reflected in the work efficiency, the quality and quantity of work tasks and work efficiency. From the perspective of management, it is the expected work behavior, performance and results of an organization, including organizational performance and individual performance [2]. The realization of organizational performance is based on the realization of individual performance, but the realization of individual performance does not necessarily guarantee the realization of organizational performance, it is not a simple superposition. However, if the organizational performance can be decomposed to everyone according to a certain logical relationship, as long as everyone realizes the requirements of the organization, the organizational performance can be achieved. If higher vocational colleges want to achieve the goal of running a school, they should first decompose the development goal of the college to each teacher. As long as the performance of each teacher is achieved, then the performance of the college can be achieved.

2.2 Main Methods of Performance Appraisal

Key performance indicators (KPI) is a mode of performance appraisal based on the analysis of the characteristics of work performance and the selection of a series of indicators that are the most critical for a job. It is a tool to decompose the strategic objectives of an organization into operational long-term objectives and the basis of the organizational performance management system. The specific steps of establishing key performance indicators are as follows: first, clarify the strategic objectives of the organization, and the top management of the organization will reach a consensus on the key points of the future development objectives of the organization, that is, the key points of the organization value evaluation, and then analyze each key business focus and relevant performance standards and their proportion through the "fishbone chart", Finally, according to the qualification requirements of the post, the corresponding performance standards are re decomposed to determine the KPI indicators corresponding to the post, which are the elements of employee evaluation. All KPI indicators point to the key points of organizational success, and can play the guiding role of indicators themselves.

3   Design of Higher Vocational College Teachers' Performance Appraisal Model Based on ANP

3.1   ANP Overview

ANP and AHP are both faced with unstructured and semi-structured decision-making problems. AHP is a multi project decision-making method combining qualitative and quantitative analysis [3]. In the 30 years since its birth, Saaty and many other scholars have done a lot of work in the development and application of the theory. At present, AHP has been widely used in the world, especially in the field of economy. AHP is a multi criteria evaluation and decision-making method, which quantifies people's subjective judgment objectively through relative scale, and reasonably combines qualitative and quantitative decision-making. As shown in Fig. 1. To analyze a relatively complex problem, first of all, the problem to be analyzed is hierarchically divided into several groups with the same or similar attributes. It divides the system into different elements by analyzing the relationship between various factors and their subordination, and divides these elements into different levels, thus forming a multi-level analysis structure model.

Let W be the hypermatrix of the system, and let the k-th power of W be:

$$W_k = (W_{ij}^{(k)}) \tag{1}$$

$$W_{ij}^{(k)} = \sum_{m=1}^{N} W_{im}^{(1)} W_{mj}^{(k-1)} \tag{2}$$

Therefore, the matrix reflects the relative ranking of index I for the cumulative K steps of index J.

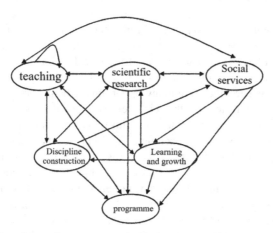

Fig. 1. ANP based teacher performance appraisal index system of higher vocational and technical college

3.2 Analysis of Performance Appraisal Index System

The purpose of teachers' performance appraisal in this higher vocational and technical college is clear, and appraisal is only a means, and the ultimate goal is to promote the teaching and scientific research level of teachers. Through the way of performance appraisal, it can form certain pressure and motivation for all teachers, and promote each teacher to constantly dig out his own strengths in the work. But in the actual implementation of the performance appraisal work, it has not played too much effect, mainly because the current performance appraisal ignores the development of teachers, which has greatly hit the enthusiasm of teachers. In order to manage, there is a lack of communication and feedback, and the performance appraisal index system is not perfect.

The orientation of teachers' assessment is vague, which fails to combine with the orientation, development strategy and purpose of the college, and lacks a clear purpose. In order to assess, the assessment becomes a mere formality, which costs a lot of time, manpower and material resources. In the process of formulating and designing the indicators, the college does not widely solicit teachers' opinions and carry out in-depth research, which will inevitably lead to the low or high level of indicators, and the assessment standards can not reflect the actual working conditions. The orientation of performance appraisal is the core of performance appraisal. Unreasonable positioning will lead to the inconsistency between the assessment process, the application of key points and the assessment objectives. The fundamental purpose of teachers' teaching performance appraisal is to reward advanced teachers and enhance their sense of responsibility for teaching quality. On the other hand, it is to make some teachers realize their shortcomings, improve teaching methods and improve teaching quality. But at present, teachers' teaching performance evaluation has become the focus of teachers' professional title evaluation. Performance evaluation is only for rating, selecting excellent teachers and granting subsidies, rather than focusing on improving teachers' quality and enhancing the future competitiveness of the college through performance evaluation [4].

If the teaching workload is set at 380 class hours, teachers are busy completing the workload, and it is difficult to pay attention to the improvement of teaching quality, let alone improve themselves. As mentioned above, the requirement of scientific research workload leads to the lack of academic spirit. Most of teachers' scientific research focuses on publishing papers and compiling teaching materials, while topics are just embellishments. Even in the papers, there are many opportunistic behaviors. Many papers have changed their faces or registered with each other. Although the number is large, there is no new idea. In the project selection, tend to "short, fast" project. Moreover, for college teachers, most of them have heavy teaching tasks. Many teachers have 16 class hours a week, among which most full-time teachers are also class teachers, so they have no time to write papers, and there are conflicts between teaching and scientific research [5–7]. The time of engaging in scientific research is not guaranteed, which is not conducive to mobilizing teachers' enthusiasm for scientific research, let alone the quality of scientific research. Therefore, the effectiveness of this assessment policy is very poor, which is not conducive to the long-term development of scientific research.

3.3 System Simulation Analysis

PCA (principal components analysis) is principal component analysis technology, also known as principal component analysis. Principal component analysis, also known as principal component analysis, aims to transform multiple indicators into a few comprehensive indicators by using the idea of dimension reduction.

In statistics, PCA is a technique to simplify data sets. It's a linear transformation. This transformation transforms the data into a new coordinate system, so that the first major variance of any data projection is on the first coordinate (called the first principal component), the second major variance is on the second coordinate (the second principal component), and so on. Principal component analysis (PCA) is often used to reduce the dimension of data sets, while maintaining the features of data sets that make the largest contribution to the square error [8–11]. This is achieved by retaining the lower order principal components and ignoring the higher order principal components. In this way, low-order components can often retain the most important aspects of the data. However, this is not necessarily, it depends on the specific application.

We use PCA and ANP technology to evaluate teachers, and the evaluation results are shown in Fig. 2 and Fig. 3. Figure 2 shows the results of using PCA technology to evaluate teachers, and Fig. 3 shows the results of ANP technology to evaluate teachers.

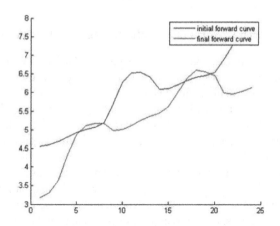

Fig. 2. PCA technology to evaluate teachers

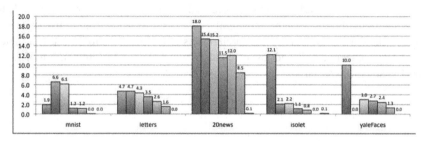

Fig. 3. ANP technology to evaluate teachers

4 The Main Problems in the Evaluation System of the Achievements of Scientific Research of University Teachers

4.1 Research Performance Evaluation of Digital Quantity

The quantitative evaluation index of teachers' scientific research performance can avoid the interference of human factors to a great extent, which is relatively fair. However, there are some problems in the performance evaluation system of scientific research of teachers in some colleges and universities, such as over quantification and standardization. For example, the scientific research situation of teachers in the past year, whether the research projects they presided over or participated in were national, provincial, municipal or school level; whether they were vertical or horizontal projects, and how much funds they had. How many papers are published in authoritative journals, core journals or general journals? How many papers are included in SC and E? How many monographs are published? Implement digital management, simply pursue quantity, and ignore the weight of quality in evaluation. Since the amount of remuneration for teachers' scientific research work is calculated and paid according to the amount of scientific research work completed by the teachers themselves in that year [12–14]. Therefore, teachers will only focus on the number of academic papers, and ignore the quality of papers, which is not conducive to the improvement of the level of scientific research.

4.2 Scientific Research Performance Evaluation Ignores Discipline Differences

Because different disciplines and their academic research have their own special regularity, the ways and methods of research exploration, the length of research cycle, and the form of achievements are all different. It is impossible to use a unified scientific research quantitative evaluation system and standard to evaluate the research of all disciplines. For example, the evaluation of liberal arts research involves value judgment, historical judgment and nature judgment, which needs time precipitation and historical evaluation. The scientific research of science and engineering is mostly applied technology research, with high conversion rate of scientific research achievements, obvious direct economic benefits, more invention patents, and easy to quantify the evaluation index. According to the classification of university scientific research, university scientific research can be divided into three categories: basic research, applied research and technology industrialization. Due to the emphasis of disciplines and the conditions of scientific research, the workload of scientific research varies greatly between basic disciplines and professional disciplines, between liberal arts and science and engineering. As shown in Fig. 4. In order to facilitate the assessment, most colleges and universities usually use the same evaluation standard to evaluate the research results of different disciplines. It is difficult to achieve the objective, fair and just evaluation, which affects the enthusiasm of some teachers in scientific research.

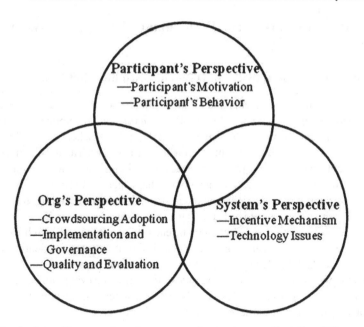

Fig. 4. Scientific research performance evaluation ignores discipline difference

4.3 Excessive Quantification Is Easy to Make Teachers Eager for Quick Success and Instant Benefit and Academic Misconduct

At present, there are some problems in the performance evaluation system of scientific research in Colleges and universities, such as ignoring the process and paying attention to the results. Scientific research performance evaluation is mainly based on the level of published articles, the level of scientific research projects and the amount of funds. The assessment results are directly linked with each person's year-end remuneration and professional title promotion [6, 9, 12]. Under the guidance of this policy, in order to meet the requirements of assessment scores, some teachers lack of academic innovation and are willing to engage in the research and development of short and quick small projects, resulting in few influential high-level scientific research achievements and low level of scientific research achievements. Some teachers even divided a high-quality article into several articles to publish, or pieced together to cope with the assessment. From the academic research achievements of colleges and universities in recent years, there are more tracking projects and less original articles. Although the number of papers is rising sharply, the number of papers cited by the international academic community is very few. Even academic misconduct such as "plagiarizing and plagiarizing other people's scientific research achievements" occurred.

5   Measures to Improve the Performance Evaluation System of University Teachers

5.1   Scientific Research Activities of Different Disciplines and Types

Different evaluation index systems and methods should be adopted, and the evaluation objectives and contents should be different. Because different disciplines have different ways of research and forms of achievements. For example, teachers engaged in science and engineering research should evaluate their scientific research achievements from the aspects of scientific research projects, scientific research funds and the economic benefits generated by the transfer of achievements. For teachers engaged in Humanities and social sciences research, the representative papers published in domestic influential academic journals and their citation should be taken as the important reference index for evaluation. In addition, there are obvious differences in each teacher's age, research experience, professional expertise and career goals. In the design of teachers' scientific research performance evaluation index system, we must analyze the bainite situation, determine the reasonable weight of each evaluation index, and refine the evaluation standard. Only in this way can we objectively and positively reflect teachers' achievements in scientific research and improve their enthusiasm in scientific research.

5.2   Implement the Organic Combination of Quantitative Assessment and Qualitative Assessment

The advantages of quantitative method of scientific research performance evaluation system lie in its high degree of standardization and accuracy, strong operability and little influence by subjective factors. However, scientific research performance evaluation system, not only quantitative analysis, but also qualitative analysis, to achieve the organic combination of qualitative and quantitative. We should accord with the law of academic development, put innovation in the first place, and gradually change from "quantity centered evaluation" to "quality centered evaluation". For example, to measure the level of academic papers, we should not only see whether they are published in authoritative and core journals, but also make a more scientific evaluation by comprehensively examining the cited times, online download rate and other indicators of papers. We should not only see how many scientific research projects teachers have, how many patents they have applied for and how many awards they have won, but also see the potential social benefits, so as to achieve the organic combination of quantitative assessment and qualitative assessment [10, 13]. We should pay attention to the quality of scientific research while evaluating the quantity of scientific research, so as to make the evaluation of teachers' scientific research performance more fair and equitable.

6   Conclusion

To vigorously develop higher vocational education, we must fully mobilize the enthusiasm of teachers. Only by establishing a performance appraisal system suitable for higher vocational colleges, can we give full play to the guiding role of appraisal, promote the independent development of teachers, and finally promote the development of higher vocational colleges. On the basis of expounding the relevant theories of performance appraisal, this paper compares and analyzes the performance appraisal of teachers in Higher Vocational Colleges with that of colleges and secondary vocational and technical schools. Combined with the working characteristics of teachers in higher vocational colleges, this paper analyzes the problems existing in the performance appraisal of teachers in Higher Vocational colleges, and conducts research in some higher vocational colleges in Suzhou, Wuxi and Changzhou to obtain relevant index data, And try to use principal component analysis (PCA), combined with sps8 statistical software, finally, from the teaching, scientific research, social services, discipline construction, learning and growth five dimensions to build a higher vocational college teacher performance appraisal index system.

Acknowledgements. 2018 Shaanxi Provincial Social Science Fund Project, Research and Practice of Research Evaluation System of Higher Vocational Colleges Based on Need Level Theory, 2018Q09 .

References

1. Yuqin, X., Yonghong, J.: Enterprise Salary and Performance Management System Design, 1st edn. China Machine Press, Beijing (2004)
2. Zhaofeng, L.: The construction of teachers' performance management system in higher vocational colleges. J. Hunan First Normal Univ. **3**, 143–145 (2008)
3. Wu, J., Yue, N.: Does interest relevance affect the objectivity of evaluation results: a study on the selection of performance evaluation subjects based on simulation experiments. Manage. Rev. 58–62 (2007)
4. Li, C.: American university teacher performance evaluation. J. Nat. School Educ. Admin. (5), 91–95 (2007)
5. Xu, Y.G., Yu, G.R.: Guidance and rationality of scientific research evaluation system for university teachers in China. J. Sichuan Normal Univ. (Soc. Sci. Edition) (3), 119–123 (2011)
6. Junjie, L.: Problems and improvement of scientific research performance evaluation of university teachers. Educ. Dev. Res. **7**, 74–76 (2011)
7. Chunyan, Z.: Evaluation and suggestions on scientific research performance of university teachers . Sci. technol. Progress Countermeasure. **11**, 210–212 (2008)
8. Weijin, D.: Analysis on the current situation and improvement of scientific research evaluation in Colleges and universities. High. Educ. Res. **4**, 61–64 (2004)
9. Yu, J., Zhou, L.: Problems and thinking in the evaluation system of scientific research performance in Colleges and universities. Res. Sci. Technol. Manage. (18), 73–75 (2010)
10. Xing, L.: Research on the scientific research performance evaluation of university teachers. Sci. Technol. Industrializat. Chin. Univ. **5**, 40–41 (2010)
11. Xi, Z., Xiaofeng, S.: On the thinking of the non material incentive of university scientific research teachers. Res. Sci. Technol. Manage. **4**, 185–186 (2010)
12. Tian Zai, L.A.N.: Research on optimizing the scientific research performance evaluation system of university teachers in China. J. Econ. Res. **18**, 238–239 (2009)
13. Wenyan, Z.: Problems and countermeasures of scientific research evaluation in Chinese universities. J. Jishou Univ. (Nat. Sci. Edition) **7**, 119–121 (2006)
14. Ping, J., Tingting, Y., Song, L.: Research on discipline construction of open university. Modern Dist. Educ. **2**, 28–33 (2012)

Research on the Construction of Teaching Quality Guarantee System in Application-Oriented Universities Under the Background of Informationization

Jingjun Shu[(✉)]

Wuhan Business University the School of Business and Management, Wuhan 430056, China
20160165@wbu.edu.cn

Abstract. With the deepening of education reform, it is an important measure to formulate and improve the teaching quality assurance system which is more suitable for application-oriented colleges and Universities under the background of informatization to alleviate the contradiction between the current social demand for application-oriented talents and the cultivation of talents in Colleges and universities. This paper mainly discusses the goal, basic structure and implementation focus of the construction of teaching quality assurance system in application-oriented universities, in order to make contributions to the reform and development of China's application-oriented universities.

Keywords: Application oriented universities · Teaching quality · Guarantee system

1 Introduction

In recent years, due to the increase in the number of Application-oriented Universities and the improvement of the quality requirements of enterprises for application-oriented talents, the teaching quality of application-oriented universities has attracted much attention. The teaching quality assurance system of undergraduate colleges is a kind of management system of internal supervision, and also a feedback promotion system that can improve the teaching quality. Therefore, how to build a qualified, appropriate and reasonable teaching quality barrier system of application-oriented universities is an urgent problem to be solved.

2 Research on Clustering Algorithm of Data Mining

Considering that the traditional data mining clustering algorithm can not meet the requirements of efficient and accurate mining clustering for massive data [1]. Therefore, the use of cloud computing database to store data and intelligent mining of these data has become a key research topic. In the research of data mining clustering algorithm based on cloud computing, firstly, the whiten weight of data mining clustering is determined, and then the data mining clustering based on cloud computing is realized.

M. A. Jan and F. Khan (Eds.): BigIoT-EDU 2021, LNICST 391, pp. 336–344, 2021.
https://doi.org/10.1007/978-3-030-87900-6_40

2.1 Introduction to Data Clustering

Data clustering is to divide data into multiple aggregation categories according to the inherent properties of data. The elements of each aggregation class have the same characteristics as much as possible, and the characteristics of different aggregation classes are different as much as possible. The purpose of cluster analysis is to analyze whether the data belong to their own independent groups. The members of the group are similar to each other and different from the members of other groups. It can analyze the collection of data objects, but different from classification analysis, the classification of clustering analysis is unknown. It groups data objects into multiple classes or clusters, and the objects in the same cluster have high similarity, and the objects in different clusters are quite different. In the practical application of clustering analysis, each data object in a cluster can be treated as a whole [2]. Cloud computing is a kind of distributed computing, which mainly refers to decomposing huge data processing programs into numerous small programs through the network "cloud", and then processing and analyzing the results through a system composed of multiple servers and returning them to users. Large scale data clustering algorithm based on cloud computing technology takes cloud computing technology as a container to carry large-scale data clustering computing.

2.2 Determine the Whitening Weight Function of Data Mining Clustering

As the most important index of data mining clustering algorithm based on cloud computing, whiten weight function of data mining clustering must be determined to ensure the accuracy of data mining clustering algorithm based on cloud computing. This paper uses this method to determine the whitening weight function of data mining clustering. Let the set of data mining clustering be i = 1,2,3,…n. The calculation formula of whitening weight function of data mining clustering is:

$$f(x) = (w.x) + c, w \in Rn, b \in R \tag{1}$$

$$dist(Z_p, C_j) = \sqrt{\sum_{k=1}^{N_d} (Z_p - C_j)^2 N_c N_k} \tag{2}$$

2.3 Realize Data Mining Clustering

According to the whiten weight function of data mining clustering, choose an index which can accurately evaluate the data mining clustering algorithm based on cloud computing. In the iterative process of data mining clustering, with the number of clustering centers decreasing, the position of each clustering center will change. We must use cloud computing technology to establish data mining clustering database, and store the location of clustering center in the form of integrated data in the database. The database built by cloud computing technology is the integration and management of massive data mining clustering, which transforms massive data mining clustering files of the same type into isomorphic database. Then, through the iterative process of data mining clustering, the coordinates of the remaining clustering can be very close to the real clustering

[3]. The data mining clustering algorithm based on cloud computing can maximize the data mining clustering coverage and realize the data mining clustering based on cloud computing.

3 Basic Structure of Teaching Quality Assurance System

3.1 Dynamic Teaching Goal Setting System

Application oriented universities need to cultivate high-quality talents more close to the needs of enterprises. Therefore, the dynamic teaching goal setting system should be based on the social survey, enterprise survey, school survey, student survey, previous graduates' return visit, relevant regulations of the Ministry of education and other information for comprehensive analysis, so that the formulation of teaching objectives and teaching programs can be closer to the "application" and "market-oriented" training of talents, and effectively improve the comprehensive quality of students.

3.2 Functional Teaching Quality Control System

There are many disciplines involved in application-oriented universities. If the "top leaders" such as the president and the director of education simply control and supervise the teaching quality, it is easy to lead to poor supervision effect. Therefore, it should be built on the basis of the special leadership of the school management and the subordinate functional teaching quality monitoring department. Functional departments can supervise all disciplines of the school, realize time effective teaching quality control activities, and improve the quality of personnel training.

3.3 Practical Educational Administration System

Almost all the application-oriented universities have the conventional educational administration system, but the educational administration system often only has the task of managing teaching activities and allocating teaching resources, and the supervision of teaching quality is mere formality, and the arrangement of related activities is more limited by personnel problems and superficial. Therefore, the practical educational administration management system should start from the management of teachers, through the standardized and scientific arrangement of teaching tasks, implement the normal supervision of teachers, and arrange the teaching quality from the guide of teaching tasks.

4 Implementation of Teaching Quality Assurance System

4.1 Establish a Normal Inspection System

Many colleges and universities often check the quality of teaching only at the end of the term, so there will be nearly five months of regulatory vacuum. Therefore, the teaching cycle should be divided, and each teaching cycle should be checked 3–4 times, and the inspection objectives should be detailed and specific. Different inspection objectives should be set according to different majors, and the completion of teaching quality objectives of each major should be checked, and the positive notification should be made.

4.2 Establish a Comprehensive Listening System

The system of attending classes should not only arrange the periodic and fixed system of attending classes. For a given class time, teachers usually make targeted preparation, which will lead to unreliable results. Therefore, the management, teachers of the same subject and even interdisciplinary teachers should be arranged to attend classes from time to time within the specified time range. The purpose of teaching quality supervision can only be effectively guaranteed by the form of spot check, and the enthusiasm of teachers' work and students' learning can be improved from the side.

4.3 Strengthen the Internet Educational Administration System

The construction of Internet educational administration system has been popularized in Colleges and universities [4]. The Internet educational administration system can achieve the task of teaching objective evaluation, such as online student questionnaire survey, teachers' teaching completion score, students' knowledge mastery test, etc. through the addition of some auxiliary small programs, the construction progress of modern education quality assurance system can be promoted. Fourth, pay attention to teaching information feedback, obtain opinions and suggestions on teaching quality from teachers, students, enterprises, school leaders and other parties through special channels, form relevant records, and then make a comprehensive report to the management of teaching quality assurance system. Through information integration, the management can make

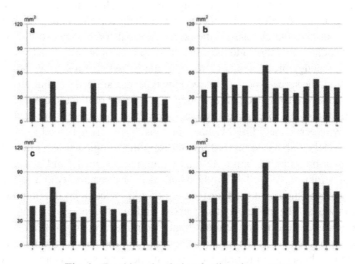

Fig. 1. Teaching simulation for listening system

a comprehensive analysis of related issues, and then revise the whole teaching quality assurance system (see Fig. 1 and Fig. 2).

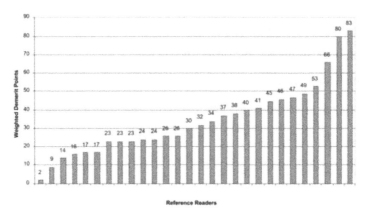

Fig. 2. Simulation for internet educational administration system

5 The Relationship Between the Transformation of Knowledge Production Mode and the Reform of Teaching Evaluation in Application Oriented Universities

5.1 Specific Performance

The traditional view of knowledge holds that knowledge is objective and separated from the subject. People can only discover, summarize and use knowledge. However, with the development of society and the popularization of higher education, the "advanced knowledge" that higher education adheres to has changed. This change is not only its own change, but also the change promoted by external forces. Due to the continuous expansion of social foundation and the rapid development of information technology, the number of knowledge producers is increasing, the knowledge resources are becoming more diversified, the spread speed of knowledge is accelerating, the radiation coverage is expanding, and so on. Knowledge is no longer a privileged product that only a few elites can have, and the social dispersive knowledge production system is formed [5–7]. Six science policy experts, including Michael gibbons, have distinguished two knowledge production models, one based on traditional disciplinary logic and the other characterized by application situation, multiple interaction, heterogeneity and interdisciplinary of knowledge structure, as well as emphasis on social accountability and self reflection, and put forward the theory of the transformation of knowledge production model from model 1 to model 2. The mode is not subversive and revolutionary, but a supplement to mode 1, which is derived from the traditional discipline structure of science and technology. The characteristic of the mode is "between the foundation and the application, and between the theory and the practice.". The mode creates a new organizational picture of knowledge production, and makes knowledge production develop to a new stage with more open research mechanism, knowledge flowing at the boundary of disciplines and abundant human resources. University organization is closely related to knowledge production. The change of knowledge production mode is imperceptibly influencing the knowledge production and organizational activities of universities. The application-oriented undergraduate school is born under the background of knowledge transformation, and it is the specific performance of the transformation of knowledge production mode under the background of higher education structure adjustment. The emergence of application-oriented universities is to distinguish traditional research-oriented universities from higher vocational and technical universities, which is the inevitable mission of higher education entrusted by social development.

5.2 Main Differences

The biggest difference between application-oriented universities and research-oriented universities lies in the context, mode, carrier and function of imparting knowledge. Due to the change of the context of knowledge production, the orientation of teaching function, the content and method of specific teaching will also be adjusted according to the objectives. Education evaluation is an inherent part of systematic education reform, It is an indispensable part of any education reform, which is both meaningful and logical. However, in the practice of education reform, as evaluation is always the last link, its reform motivation often shows the problem of insufficient stamina, lagging behind the reform of other education links. The improvement of monitoring and evaluation can support the daily operation and strategic planning of education system. Therefore, it is of great significance to pay attention to the reform of education evaluation. The teaching evaluation system of application-oriented universities is directly related to the real knowledge production situation and social production and life. The transformation of Application-oriented Universities in China is entering a deep water area, and the reform of teaching evaluation can be used as a breakthrough for the transformation of application-oriented universities. Teaching evaluation is a process in which a school evaluates the effect of teaching work by using relevant evaluation means and methods according to teaching objectives and requirements. As one of the important internal guarantee measures to promote teaching quality, teaching evaluation is the focus of the development of application-oriented universities. Teaching evaluation is not only the technology and method of education internal quality assurance, but also a management tool at the school level. The key mechanism of teaching evaluation and feedback plays an important role in improving the school's improvement ability and tool effectiveness.

6 The Dilemma of Teaching Evaluation in Application Oriented Universities

6.1 Improving the Working Conditions of Teaching Secretaries

With the help of modern technical means to improve the level of teaching management. Such as timely updating the educational administration management system, providing more diverse means of upload and release, establishing direct contact between students and teachers and the educational administration system, so that teachers and students can query the examination, class, score and other teaching arrangements by themselves through mobile app, computer and other modern means. The number of teaching secretaries in local undergraduate colleges should be adjusted according to the number of students and teachers. Instead of one teaching secretary in each college, the workload and difficulty of teaching secretaries should be considered [8–12]. As shown in Fig. 3. At the same time, the dissatisfaction caused by the comparison of teaching secretaries between secondary colleges should be avoided, so as to stabilize the healthy development and stability of teaching secretaries in the whole college.

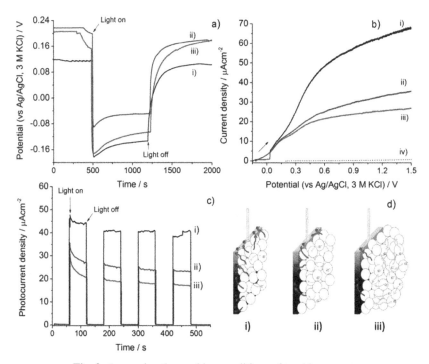

Fig. 3. Improving the working conditions of teaching secrets

6.2 Broaden the Career Development Path of Teaching Secretary

Local colleges and universities should realize the importance of teaching secretary position, reasonably plan the position of teaching secretary, and set up promotion ways. If you can compete with full-time teachers and evaluate professional titles, you can be promoted from professional title to intermediate and senior professional title after completing certain work. In addition, we should improve the salary system structure of teaching secretaries, improve the assessment mechanism, narrow the salary gap between teaching secretaries and full-time teachers, so that teaching secretaries can work in their own jobs, pay attention to the training and training of teaching secretaries, and local universities should pay attention to the work of Teaching Secretaries, and give full play to their role in the process of carrying out teaching activities. We should provide more learning opportunities for teaching secretaries, create conditions for their further study and exercise platform, and let them feel the space for improvement and the value of existence. In addition, we should speed up the construction of relevant training mechanism and form a practical training plan as soon as possible [13]. Through temporary training, academic promotion, special training and other ways, we can constantly improve the teaching secretary's understanding of new knowledge, new ideas and the use of new technology, so as to expand their ideas and broaden their field, so as to better serve the teaching. In addition, the school should allocate enough funds to set up corresponding research and research projects for teaching secretary, strengthen innovation of new methods and ideas of teaching management, and help improve teaching management.

6.3   Lack of Social Accountability for Teaching Evaluation Results and Teachers' Self Reflection

Paying too much attention to the evaluation system, policies, theories and indicators will encounter many problems in the real situation, among which the neglect of social accountability of teaching evaluation and teachers' self reflection is a challenge [14, 15]. The transformation of application-oriented universities needs corresponding changes in the whole internal structure and operation form. However, at this stage, academic research ability is still the key standard to evaluate the teachers of application-oriented universities. Rigorous academic research requires peer review, academic exchanges and discussions are only in a concentrated and highly closed academic circle, lacking social accountability and self reflection. "Ivory tower" is the image of this situation, closed system brings professional extension and strong controllability, but also brings limitations, because the internal resources and influence are very unlimited, unable to break through the academic barriers. Social accountability requires first of all to make sure that the construction of applied knowledge files is a continuous and dynamic process, which needs constant adjustment and revision [16]. In this process, teachers are required to redefine the content they teach. The social feedback of applied knowledge is very strong, and the problems involved usually have certain social impact. From knowledge production, dissemination to teaching evaluation, every environmental responsibility permeates the self-discipline of social accountability teachers My reflection is another challenge, because teaching evaluation is mainly based on other evaluation, which leads to a lack of teachers' self-evaluation. Teachers think that self-evaluation and reflection are too subjective to reflect the real internal evaluation of learning evaluation [17, 18]. Another important reason for teachers' lack of self-evaluation is that they regard teaching as accountability rather than improvement. In the context of accountability, external teachers need to bear pressure, but in the context of improvement, teachers can better reflect and adjust for optimizing their knowledge structure and teaching ability.

7   Epilogue

The construction of teaching quality assurance system in application-oriented universities is not achieved overnight. The training goal of talents needs to be changed according to the market demand, so the system also needs to be adjusted dynamically. To some extent, the teaching quality assurance system is more dependent on the particularity of the University, so it should be formulated according to the specialty, teaching and employment situation of the University.

Acknowledgements. The construction and research of teaching quality assurance system under the background of undergraduate teaching work qualification evaluation.

References

1. Jianquan, H., Huabin, Y., Qi, Y.: Research on quality assurance system of practical teaching in local universities. J. Higher Educ. **9**, 44–45 (2016)
2. Haiyan, Z., Qi, W.: Research on the construction of university teaching quality assurance system based on the concept of "student-centered" . Educ. Rev. **3**, 51–54 (2016)
3. Feng, X., Shiwei, L.: Reflections on the construction of undergraduate teaching quality assurance system in Colleges and universities. J. Higher Educ. **11**, 56–57 (2016)
4. Jiang, H., Cheng, X., Xiao, X., et al.: Based on the "three learning", construct and improve the "four in one" teaching quality assurance system. China Univ. Teach. (8) (2016)
5. Xue, J.: Difficulties and countermeasures of graduate teaching secretaries in local universities. Continu. Educ. Res. **10**, 107–108 (2016)
6. Huang, R.: Research on problems and countermeasures of teaching secretary team in colleges and universities. East China Normal University (2009)
7. Jing, L.: Analysis on the standardization of teaching secretary work in Colleges and universities. Heilongjiang High. Educ. Res. **02**, 75–76 (2016)
8. Liping, M.: Research on coping strategies of job burnout of teaching archives management personnel – taking academic secretaries of colleges and departments as an example. Contemp. Educ. Forum (Comprehensive Res.) **03**, 35–43 (2011)
9. Qiao, Y., Zhang, G., Zhang, C.: Practice and optimization strategy of student teaching information officer system in local universities. High. Educ. Forum (04), 76–79 (2011)
10. Zhang, N., Zhang, K.: Practice and thinking of student teaching information officer system in local universities. J. Xinzhou Normal Univ. 30(05), 125–127 (2014)
11. Clark, B.: Higher Education System, Translated by Wang Chengxu, pp. 13–16. Hangzhou University Press, Hangzhou (1994)
12. Gibbons, M.: A new model of knowledge production. Trans. Chen Hongjie, Shen Wenqin, et al., pp. 12–17. Peking University Press, Beijing (2011)
13. [UK] Michael Gibbons: a new model of knowledge production, p. 7.
14. Zeng, G., et al.: Ziman: True Science: What it is and What It Means, pp. 84–97. Shanghai Science and Technology Education Press, Shanghai (2008)
15. Jiangzimala: [France] Pierre Bourdieu: Sense of Practice, p. 124. Yilin Press, Nanjing (2003)
16. Qi, W., Hui, F.: Research on Performance Evaluation of Higher Education, pp. 42–63. Higher Education Press, Beijing (2012)
17. Weimin, L.: Financial Dictionary, p. 11. Heilongjiang People's Publishing House, Harbin (2002)
18. Qin, L., Jiang, Y.: [US] Egon g. Gubei: The Fourth Generation Evaluation, pp. 1–14. China Renmin University Press, Beijing (2008)

Research on the Protection and Inheritance Path of Higher Education Informatization in Folk Music

Jing Wen[✉]

Music Education College of Xi'an Conservatory of Music, Xi'an 710061,
Shaanxi, China

Abstract. Shaanxi is rich in regional music and cultural resources, from Xi'an ancient music to northern Shaanxi folk songs, from southern Shaanxi folk songs to Qin Zheng, Qin Hu and other Qin ethnic instrumental music, with various forms and far-reaching influence. How to better protect and inherit Shaanxi folk music with higher education informatization depends not only on the folk music organizations preserved in society, but also on the power of higher education.

Keywords: Higher education · Informatization · Folk music

1 Introduction

Regional culture refers to "all material and spiritual achievements and achievements created, accumulated, developed and sublimated by people in a region through physical and mental labor in the long-term historical development process". It includes material culture and spiritual culture, reflecting all aspects of social life such as local economic level, scientific and technological achievements, values, religious beliefs, cultural accomplishment, artistic level, social customs and habits, life style, social behavior norms, etc. "① Shaanxi is one of the birthplaces of Chinese civilization, a province with large cultural resources and rich traditional cultural resources. As a kind of regional culture, "Shaanxi culture occupies a prominent position in the history of Chinese cultural development. To a certain extent, it is the source and backbone of Chinese traditional culture, representing the main source of Chinese culture. Shaanxi regional music and culture resources are rich and have a long history [1]. Shaanxi has a unique geographical location. The different natural features of Guanzhong, northern and southern Shaanxi in the three Qin Dynasties have also achieved different regional music characteristics and styles, and jointly constructed a rich and colorful regional music and cultural resources in Shaanxi. Because of its unique history, folk custom and artistry, Shaanxi local music enjoys high popularity and influence in the country, and is also an important source of material and inspiration for modern music creation. Therefore, the inheritance and development of Shaanxi regional music is of great significance to the promotion of national music culture and the inheritance of Chinese culture.

© ICST Institute for Computer Sciences, Social Informatics and Telecommunications Engineering 2021
Published by Springer Nature Switzerland AG 2021. All Rights Reserved
M. A. Jan and F. Khan (Eds.): BigIoT-EDU 2021, LNICST 391, pp. 345–353, 2021.
https://doi.org/10.1007/978-3-030-87900-6_41

2 Geographical Distribution of Regional Music Cultural Resources in Shaanxi Province

"Shaanxi folk music is rich in content, various in types, distinctive in features, artistic beauty, great in value, long in origin and widely spread, which is unparalleled in many provinces and regions." The most influential ones are Xi'an drum music, Northern Shaanxi folk song, Yulin Xiaoqu, Northern Shaanxi suona, southern Shaanxi folk song, Guanzhong Qinqiang, Huayin bowl tune and other musical cultures reflect the unique regional culture and folk customs of Shaanxi through various forms of expression, and reflect the belief and value system of people in Shaanxi for thousands of years [2]. Shaanxi local music is famous for the Northern Shaanxi folk song "new journey to heaven", which is the most recognized music in Shaanxi folk songs in China, and also the most influential music in Chinese folk songs. "The folk songs in Northern Shaanxi are full of vitality and appeal. The ups and downs of the Northern Shaanxi plateau and the rugged terrain reflect each other, showing a bold and simple musical feelings. Famous folk songs in Northern Shaanxi include cattle drive, orchid, red flower, etc.

The music in Guanzhong area is represented by Xi'an drum music. Xi'an drum music, also known as Chang'an ancient music, Chang'an drum music, Xi'an drum music and so on, has a history of more than 1300 years and is known as the "living fossil of music" by the music industry. It is mainly distributed in the ancient capital of Chang'an. It is an ancient percussion ensemble of Sheng and flute. It inherited the music tradition of Tang and Song Dynasties, absorbed the essence of folk music in yuan, Ming and Qing Dynasties, and gradually developed and perfected. In ancient music scores, the music scores often played include "boshouzi", "nutu drum", "Huatu drum", etc.

Besides the influence of Xi'an drum music in Guanzhong area, it belongs to Qin opera. Qin opera is one of the oldest operas in the history of China, and it is the originator of Bangzi opera. Qin opera was introduced into Beijing in Qing Dynasty, which had a certain influence on the formation of Peking Opera. The music characteristic of Qin opera is high, excited, fast and warm. There are two kinds of music in Qin Opera: bitter and music, sad, sad and deep; music is Ming, Ming and Zhuang. Its singing fully embodies the bold, straightforward and generous personality of Shaanxi people, and reflects the simple, simple, industrious and brave folk customs of Shaanxi people. The representative repertoires of Qin opera include "three drops of blood", "three niangs and godsons", "suwu herdsman", etc.

3 The Effect of College Art Education in the Inheritance and Development of Shaanxi Regional Music Culture

Shaanxi has the leading educational resources in China, ranking first in the western region, third in the country, second only to Beijing and Shanghai. Shaanxi has gathered many well-known universities such as Xi'an Jiaotong University, northwest Polytechnic University, Northwest University, Shaanxi Normal University, and many students from all over the country. They study culture here, receive professional education and quality education. Every year, a large number of graduates enter different positions in all walks of life. Therefore, we can give full play to the advantages of higher education in Shaanxi, rely on the advantages of scientific research and talents in Colleges and universities, take art education in Colleges and universities as the platform, realize the effective inheritance and dissemination of regional music, combine regional music and cultural resources with the advantages of higher education, and promote the characteristics and charm of regional music in Shaanxi.

3.1 The Role and Significance of Art Education in Colleges and Universities in Inheriting Regional Music Culture

Regional music culture is mainly spread among the people. For a long time, its inheritance belongs to unconscious communication, which mainly depends on the spiritual instructions of folk singers and folk art groups. This kind of communication is not systematic, purposeful and continuous. This kind of characteristic often makes these fresh music with deep life background and regional culture background spread freely and primitively. Its beauty and truth are often wrapped and blocked by geographical boundaries and barriers, unable to break through and create a broader value space. When the field workers engaged in national music found and recognized them, they were deeply moved by their unique charm and color [3]. However, only relying on the field work group of ethnomusicology to excavate, organize and develop these music, the strength is still too weak and the effect is limited.

4 The Function and Significance of College Art Education in Inheriting Regional Music Culture

"For a long time, there have been two main modes of communication of traditional music, one is unconscious communication, the other is conscious communication. The so-called unconscious communication refers to the folk songs, folk dances, operas, quyi and other folk musicians' singing (performance), which are handed down from folk songs, folk dances, folk music, operas, quyi and so on. Its communication is either for self entertainment, or for survival, often in a state of confusion and self destruction. This is the main channel of traditional music. However, conscious communication is in a secondary position, which is reflected in the skills taught by masters and apprentices, as well as the publication and distribution of a few folk characters and Kungfu manuscripts."

Regional music culture is mainly spread among the people. For a long time, its inheritance belongs to unconscious communication, which mainly depends on the spiritual instructions of folk singers and folk art groups. This kind of communication is not systematic, purposeful and continuous. This kind of characteristic often makes these fresh music with deep life background and regional culture background spread freely and primitively. Its beauty and truth are often wrapped and blocked by geographical boundaries and barriers, unable to break through and create a broader value space. When the field workers engaged in national music found and recognized them, they were deeply moved by their unique charm and color. However, only relying on the field work group of ethnomusicology to excavate, organize and develop these music, the strength is still too weak and the effect is limited.

As we all know, the process of learning, understanding and understanding mainly depends on school education. College students are mature in age and psychology [4–6]. They can accept and learn knowledge quickly and persistently. College students come from all over the country. After graduation, they will bring the music culture with the school as the regional background to a broader region, which is more conducive to the national communication and development of Shaanxi regional music culture.

5   Construction of Art Education System and Mode in Colleges and Universities with Regional Music Culture Characteristics in Shaanxi Province

In the traditional college public art education, regional music is not a very important field. Generally speaking, the content of music art is mainly based on the Chinese and Western classical art music. Although these music have high aesthetic value and artistic value, students can not experience and perceive the cultural background of music in the process of appreciation and learning, and their understanding of music can not rise to the cultural level. And regional music is formed in the area where they study and live. Students can go into this cultural context in person, pay attention to various details, and further understand the social significance behind music.

Therefore, in the public art education of colleges and universities, it is necessary to recognize the importance and necessity of regional folk music learning, and reasonably allocate the proportion of regional music in the curriculum. Through art education, let students first understand and understand these music. Only by fully contacting and learning these music can students enter the circle from the outside and really like these music. In addition, the influence of art is also very important. In addition to increasing theoretical teaching, regional music and cultural activities should also be widely carried out. Regional music has its advantages in this respect. This kind of close learning will

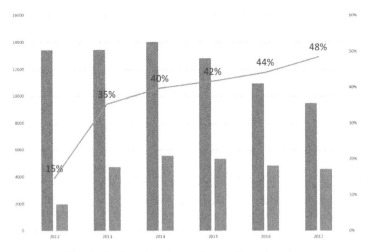

Fig. 1. Online education and non-online education

enable students to deepen their experience and understanding of regional music culture. Online education and non-online education are shown in Fig. 1.

In the public art education of colleges and universities in China, music education plays an important role in popularizing music knowledge and improving music literacy. Fully understand the current situation and characteristics of art education in Colleges and universities, and introduce the representative works with artistic value and cultural charm in Shaanxi regional music culture into the art education system of colleges and universities on the premise of conforming to its operation and development laws [7–9]. Through the platform and resources of higher education, realize the effective communication of regional music culture.

Colleges and universities can choose music works with certain familiarity and familiarity as the main content, combining with their own geographical location, school philosophy and school philosophy, and take a variety of teaching forms for innovative practice and research. For example, Yan'an University, located in the north of Shaanxi Province, can increase the proportion of students in the exploration and study of music in the north of Shaanxi Province because they are in the generating environment of music. In this state, it is easy to connect the cultural background and artistic expression of music, find the relationship between them, and appreciate the original cultural feelings. Shaanxi University of science and technology and other colleges and universities in southern Shaanxi can fully organize students to deeply understand and learn the local music in southern Shaanxi, guide students to deeply experience the original ecological music on the ground, or invite folk musicians to give lectures in the school, which is more vivid, more infectious and convenient than teachers. Guanzhong area is the main position of universities in Shaanxi Province. These schools can learn more about Qin opera, Xi'an drum music and other music. Students immersed in the zero distance contact between the soil and music will certainly stimulate their inner feelings and strength of music.

Therefore select music content for learning in a timely and selective manner, realize paste teaching, and form their own music characteristics [9–11]. At ordinary times, colleges and universities should arrange more art exchanges and cooperation, exchange

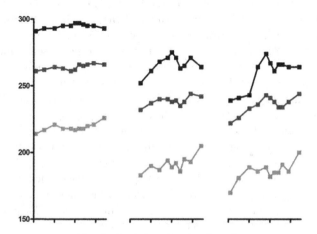

Fig. 2. Statistics of regional music

and study in places they are familiar with and do well, so as to make the research of regional music live, and realize the purpose of characteristic, which will be a very useful attempt (see Fig. 2).

6 The Ingenious Transformation of the Singing Language of Folk Music in Modern Creation

6.1 Many Excellent Shaanxi Minority Songs Have Been Excavated

In the process of exploring the folk music in the new era, modern artists constantly dig out many excellent Yunnan Minority Songs, such as Bai's love song under the moon, Hani's place where the sun turns around, Lisu's meet music, Lahu's happy Lahu, Jingpo's chongmi song, Manchu's running Nanhai, etc., These works are very true to reflect the music characteristics of different ethnic minorities and different cultural customs. In addition, in the process of music creation, Chinese modern music artists have also found the cultural characteristics of Yunnan ethnic minorities outside the music art and melody, and their unique music feature is music. There are differences between different minority languages and cultures in Yunnan. These differences are caused by different regions and environments in Yunnan. These different environments also make Yunnan folk songs form a different musical force in these different regions [12]. The rhyme of Yunnan folk music is related to the local dialect, and the content is also quite different. There are also some minority songs in Yunnan, which are similar to the chanting style of "singing and reading". This way of singing makes the melody and melody not very clear, and the trend of music also changes with the change of dialect. This change of singing style is the unique feature of folk music, and it is also the national feature that can not be ignored, and it highlights the characteristics of Yunnan minority music.

6.2 Accurately Grasp the Characteristics of Shanxi Minority Music

In the creation process of modern music, artists also deeply understand the characteristics of Yunnan minority music, and combine it with modern music. In the process of creation, musicians use a very simple borrowing way to combine folk music with modern music, so as to better inherit Yunnan's folk music. Ethnic folk music processed by modern music has more characteristics. Although some ethnic words have no meaning in themselves, they are just some language habits or songs in the process of daily work or life. People's daily life habits and songs can be used as a supplement to life. They usually appear at the end of music sentences, sometimes as the decorative language of songs, sometimes to reflect a special cultural characteristics. As shown in Fig. 3. For example, the Zhuang folk song "toasting song" sings "bennon ah: the Zhuang family toasts to sing, singing with wine, the more guests, the warmer the heart; the Hani folk song" the place where the sun turns around "in salalalala, salayisai, Sasa, salayisa, the magical city of Tropic of cancer, how many people you make you fascinated by the Manchu folk song" running South China Sea "in" southeast wind, come, hey, northwest wave, Come, go out of the South China Sea, go over the hills, go over the hills, and so on.

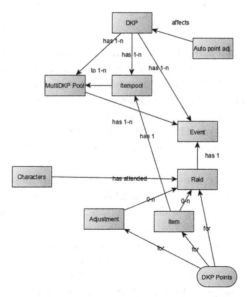

Fig. 3. Accurately grasp the characteristics of Shanxi Minority Music

6.3 Integrating Personal Emotion into Yunnan Music Singing

The tone of Shaanxi dialect is also closely related to the emotion of songs. In the contemporary creation, we should not only imitate the sound and form, but also integrate the emotion. In the work plateau woman, it interprets the characteristics of dialect logic and forms a unique work. The work combines the dialects of ethnic minorities in western Yunnan and integrates the pronunciation into the collocation of lyrics and melody to restore the simple and honest feelings of the local atmosphere. The rhythm and pitch in the lyrics are created by imitating the characteristics of Yunnan dialect, and fully grasp the relationship between language and singing. For example, when the cold wind blows on the old man's head, the woman takes her back to the crack of the door to block the middle. She combines the pentatonic, hexatonic, rhythmic, and declarative sounds, and divides them into three and eight intervals to describe the intonation vividly. There are many works of this kind, such as "the school song of forest primary school" adopts the song words of "solo" in Yunnan dialect, which imitates the scene of primary school students reading textbooks with closed eyes and straight neck in Putonghua mixed with dialect; in "the water hen", it holds the characteristic of "the water hen is pronounced as chirp, relying on the language characteristic of wearing the whole song all the time, It grasps the distinctive characteristics of Yunnan folk songs, so that the audience can join in and enjoy the simple, flowerless and resounding music of Yunnan folk music [13, 14]. In the process of understanding the folk music culture of Yunnan, musicians also observed the amazing decorative sounds in Yunnan folk music, such as whistles, tongue flicks, trills, shouts and other unique skills.

7 Conclusions

Only by fully learning and understanding the rich and colorful Shaanxi local music can we inherit and develop. In order to realize the inheritance and development of regional music culture through the platform of art education in Colleges and universities, the research of regional music culture should not only stay at the level of appreciation, but also let everyone actively participate in the performance and practice of music. Regional music can not only be performed by a small number of people, but also need to mobilize the enthusiasm of the majority of groups, so that the regional music culture spread more in-depth and in-depth.

Therefore, in addition to classroom learning and various music activities, students should also be encouraged to participate in art scenes. Students can sing and play after study [15]. They are familiar with and consolidate their understanding of music and improve their enthusiasm for learning music. If conditions permit, more people should enter the folk, listen to and experience these music, watch music performance, and participate in music performance activities. Invite experts to perform and introduce on site to enhance the vitality and participation of learning.

Colleges and universities are the main places of cultural exchange. The music education in Colleges and universities can inherit the regional music culture more systematically and comprehensively, grasp the most fundamental content of the national traditional music culture, and then spread the core cultural concept, with a wide audience. It is an important means and method to develop regional music culture. Strengthening regional music education in Colleges and universities is conducive to the inheritance of national traditional music and the development of art education in Colleges and universities [16–19]. At the same time, the inheritance of regional music culture is also an unshirkable responsibility and task of colleges and universities. We should give full play to the good platform role of art education in Colleges and universities, and truly inherit and develop Shaanxi's long and colorful music culture.

Acknowledgements. Research on the protection and inheritance method of Shaanxi folk music based on online music platform(19JK0777).

References

1. Yansheng, W.: Research on the regional characteristics in the construction of university culture. Xue **4**, 4 (2007)
2. Qinkaifeng: Research on Shaanxi regional culture and Chinese cultural renaissance. J. Xi'an Univ. Finan. Econ. (9), 111 (2013)
3. Radar: Give full play to Shaanxi's regional advantages to protect folk music heritage. Music World (1), 7. (2005)
4. Xiaolu, L.: An analysis of the relationship between the creation of folk music in Qin opera and Shaanxi regional culture Yes. Symphony **1**, 56 (2013)
5. Guangyu, F.: Inheritance of national music culture and school music education. Chin. Music. **1**, 20 (2003)
6. Haoran, P.: Exploring the national flavor of Hulusi . National Music **06**, 22–24 (2020)

7. Jingjing, Z.: Development protection and exploration of badatao in Shanxi Province Based on AR technology. Voice Yellow River **24**, 7–9 (2020)
8. Xianying, Y.: Research on the curriculum of Tongren local folk music in music teaching of primary and secondary schools . Voice Yellow River **24**, 133–135 (2020)
9. Libby, W.M.: Lessons from the country music industry on closing the gender gap: conversation is not enough. JAMA Surgery (2020)
10. Shuang, H.: The penetration of folk music in preschool music education . Northern Music **24**, 140–142 (2020)
11. Jiaying, O.: On a Bing's Erhu performance art . Northern Music **24**, 48–50 (2020)
12. Tan Zhi, O., Xiao, Y.Z.: The significance of "folk evaluation" in oral texts to the theoretical and practical research of ethnomusicology . Res. Ethnic Art **33**(06), 138–144 (2020)
13. Cristina, W.M.: Music education and folk music. Int. J. Soc. Sci. Stud. **9**(1) (2020)
14. Hong, W.: Protection and inheritance of folk music intangible cultural heritage . J. Hebei Univ. Technol. (Soc. Sci. Edition) **37**(04), 116–120 (2020)
15. Jing, M.: Practice of Xinjiang folk music in ballet basic skills accompaniment music . Popular Literature Art **24**, 89–90 (2020)
16. Shi, Y.: A brief history of Jiangsu Modern erhu. Symphony (J. Xi'an Conservatory Music) **39**(04), 30–40 (2020)
17. Tang, Y., Liu, X.: Performance analysis of lute Concerto Loulan girl. Symphony (J. Xi'an Conservatory Music) **39**(04), 107–112 (2020)
18. Nan, Z.: Practical research on intangible cultural heritage work of urban canal cultural belt – taking Hengshui folk music intangible cultural heritage project as an example. Meiyu times (City Edition) **12**, 107–108 (2020)
19. Yue, L.: Inheritance and practice of folk culture in the process of urban cultural development – taking folk music as an example . Beauty Times (City Edition) **12**, 109–110 (2020)

Research on the Reform of English Smart Classes Teaching Model Based on Network Informatization

Yan Tang[1], Zhao Wang[2], and Xiaotian Zhang[3]([✉])

[1] School of Western Languages, Harbin Normal University, Hain 150025, China
[2] Universiti Putra, Putra, Malaysia
gs60525@student.upm.edu.my
[3] School of Western Languages, Harbin Normal University, Hain 150025, China

Abstract. Smart classes is the inevitable result of education modernization condensed in classroom teaching, education informatization converges on teacher-student interaction, and education intelligence is converged on students' smart thinking in the context of the post-epidemic era. It is a hot topic of current education intelligence research. This article conducted a questionnaire survey of teachers and students who used the Smart classes cloud to teach during the epidemic. The author analyzes the application of the Smart classes teaching model before, during and after class from three perspectives: student attitude, student input, and teacher input, hoping to provide a new perspective for improving the efficiency of network information Smart classes teaching in the post epidemic era and exploring the integration of information intelligence and contemporary education reform.

Keywords: Network information · Smart English classroom · Teaching mode

1 Introduction

With the rapid development of information technology, repetitive and mechanical work will gradually be replaced by machines. The traditional classroom teaching model that emphasizes indoctrination by teachers and memorization by students is increasingly unsuitable for social development. "National Medium and Long-term Education Reform and Development Plan Outline (2010–2020)" and "Ten-Year Development Plan for Education Informatization (2011–2020)" pointed out that education informatization work should be closer to the major practical issues in education reform and development, and education reform and development should be included in the core area to promote education development. In the age of network information, various new teaching models that subvert traditional classrooms have emerged one after another, such as Smart classes, bisection classrooms, flipped classrooms, etc. Their core is to reconstruct the form of teaching organization, of which Smart classes are the most typical. Smart classes is the inevitable integration of new technology and education reform under the background of network information age. It is the focus of current education reform research that cannot be ignored.

© ICST Institute for Computer Sciences, Social Informatics and Telecommunications Engineering 2021
Published by Springer Nature Switzerland AG 2021. All Rights Reserved
M. A. Jan and F. Khan (Eds.): BigIoT-EDU 2021, LNICST 391, pp. 354–366, 2021.
https://doi.org/10.1007/978-3-030-87900-6_42

2 Research Purpose and Significance

The purpose of this research is to use literature research, questionnaire surveys, interviews and other methods to study the current situation of the research and application of English Smart classes under the background of network information, and to judge the advantages and disadvantages of the Smart classes teaching model, so as to maximize the strengths and avoid the weaknesses. It provides suggestions for the reform of English Smart classes teaching mode under the background of network informatization in the post-epidemic era.

In terms of theoretical significance, according to the constructivist learning theory, the learner's knowledge is obtained by the learner with the help of others, using certain learning resources, and by means of meaning construction. The ideal learning environment includes four elements: context, collaboration, conversation and meaning construction. Smart classes can very well meet the higher requirements of constructivist learning theory for the learning environment. It utilizes a variety of new media, new technologies and smart devices today, aiming at closed-loop English teaching before, during and after class. Smart classes can create and display various learning situations that tend to be realistic, and enhance the three-dimensional communication between teachers and students, and between students and students. This model is conducive to the development of collaboration, inquiry learning, and helps learners construct the meaning of knowledge.

In terms of practical significance, Smart classes can promote the sharing of high-quality educational resources and teacher power through the Internet, so as to promote the development of educational equity. The intelligentization of the Smart classes from lesson preparation to class and then to after class saves teachers a lot of time and reduces the burden on teachers. Smart classes have the advantages of rich English teaching content, individualized learning, real-time performance analysis, and diversified English teaching forms, which significantly increase the classroom capacity and improve the efficiency of English teaching.

3 Literature Review

The master and doctoral dissertations reflect the research hotspots in a certain field to a certain extent, and the master and doctoral dissertations are relatively long, with relatively complete theoretical expositions and comprehensive coverage of experimental data. Therefore, the author of this study used "English Smart classes" as the keyword and searched the master and post database in the CNKI database. After manually removing irrelevant data, a total of 11 valid data were selected. The author uses the quantitative visual analysis function of the CNKI database to visually analyze these 11 data with a higher frequency. The visual analysis of the "main theme" reflects the hot issues in the research field of "English Smart Class" to a certain extent. The results of the visual analysis are shown in Fig. 1.

"Smart classes" is the subject of this research, so it is not included in the statistical results. It can be found that in the school stage, Smart classes have more research in the "junior high school" stage; in teaching research, the "teaching model" and "application

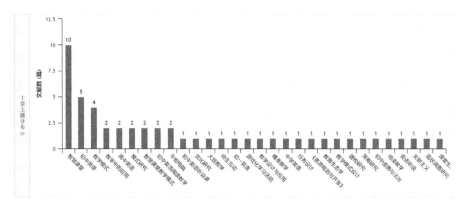

Fig. 1. Distribution of main themes of CNKI quantitative visualization analysis of "English Smart classes"

in teaching" of the Smart classes have a higher degree of attention; in terms of the types of courses selected in the experiment, the "reading" and "listening and speaking" courses are selected more frequently. The specific research summary of related master and doctoral theses is as follows:

Wang Hongbo (2018) summarized the characteristics of English listening and speaking teaching in junior high schools in Smart classes and the choice of task types. He proposed methods and processes for different types of task design and conducted empirical research. Xie Xiangcao (2018) analyzed the teaching cases using Smart classes tools based on the theory of relevance and explored the construction model of the junior high school English Smart classes. Zhong Chongyan (2018) uses the "dual classroom" education cloud platform to conduct empirical research on the teaching model of Smart classes. Zhang Yan (2018) comprehensively described the composition of the information environment of the Smart classes, effectively constructing an intelligent and flexible teaching environment for the Smart classes. Chen Mengqi (2018) explored the presentation, progress, development, and changes of the interaction between teachers and students under the Smart classes teaching model by using a combination of qualitative and quantitative research methods. And he analyzed the effects of teacher-student interaction, in order to explore better models and strategies that are conducive to the development of education.

Guo Ying (2019) introduced micro-classes into teaching design and optimized the teaching process of the Smart classes and the teaching mode of different course types. Li Yuting (2019) started with the design of Smart classes teaching from the perspective of information technology, conducted research on teaching practice, and analyzed the current status of the implementation of classroom reforms and the results achieved with the support of information technology in Xinjiang. Combined with the teaching process of the Smart classes, Liu Yujing (2019) proposed a strategy for the interaction of the junior high school English listening and speaking classes supported by the Smart classes.

Zhao Lei (2020) uses the "Le Class" platform to investigate students' English learning self-efficacy and performance under the English Smart classes teaching model. Zhang Liqiong (2020) explores and implements the English reading teaching model of boarding ethnic middle schools based on Smart classes through the Internet, mobile smart phones, online reading exchange groups and other modern information technology means. Juan Li (2020) analyzes the status quo of high school students' learning input in Smart classes English learning through a questionnaire on English learning input of high school students in a Smart classes environment.

4   Related Concepts

4.1   The concept of Smart classes

The proposal and development of Smart classes is actually the inevitable result of school education informatization focusing on teaching, classrooms, and teacher-student activities. Regarding the meaning of Smart classes, there are different understandings from different perspectives. "Zhihui" in Chinese usually includes the meaning of "smart, insightful, and strategic" in the psychological sense and "intelligence" in technology (Liu Xiaolin et al. 2016). Therefore, there are two perspectives to understand the concept of Smart classes: One is based on the educational perspective, that classroom teaching is not a simple process of "knowledge imparting", but a process of comprehensive quality training and generation with "smart" as the core. The concept of "Smart classes" here is relative to "knowledge classroom". The other is based on the perspective of informatization, which refers to the use of advanced information technology to realize the informatization and intelligence of classroom teaching and build Smart classes teaching environment. The "Smart classes" here is in contrast to the "traditional classroom" that uses traditional teaching methods. In fact, the above two perspectives are closely related. The fundamental purpose of using information technology to create Smart classes teaching environment is to promote the transition from "knowledge classrooms" to "Smart classes" and to achieve the development of students' smart. The definition of "Smart classes" in this research is put forward by focusing on the latter perspective. Establishing the concept of "Smart classes" from the perspective of informatization is a prerequisite for the development of informatization teaching research. It is also the logical starting point for constructing a theoretical and practical system of Smart classes teaching in the age of network information.

4.2   Theoretical basis

(1) Constructivism theory

According to the constructivist learning theory, the learner's knowledge is obtained by the learner with the help of others, using certain learning resources, and by means of meaning construction. The ideal learning environment includes four elements: context, collaboration, conversation and meaning construction. Smart classes can very well meet the higher requirements of constructivist learning and theory on the learning environment. Using mobile smart devices to create and display a variety of realistic learning situations for the closed-loop English teaching before, during and after class, which is helpful to help learners construct the meaning of knowledge.

(2) Programmed Instruction

Programmed Teaching Method follows the principles of small steps, positive response, timely reinforcement, self-paced and low error rate. It divides the overall goal of a course into several units, and then divides each unit into many small steps. The autonomous learning system of the Smart classes allows students to set their own learning pace to achieve the overall learning goals in accordance with their own learning ability and learning habits. Therefore, programmed teaching provides a solid theoretical foundation for the construction of smart English classrooms.

5 Research Process

5.1 Purpose of Investigation

The purpose of this survey is to understand the use of Smart classes by students and teachers. On the one hand, it can understand students' performance, existing problems and their own needs when using Smart classes learning. On the other hand, it can understand the teacher's feelings when using the Smart classes teaching, including the advantages and disadvantages of the Smart classes. This survey took the teachers and students of Harbin Normal University as the object. The author hopes that the investigation can discover the problems of teachers and students in Smart classes teaching and learning, so as to find a suitable entry point to solve or improve existing problems and provide effective support for the use of English Smart classes teaching and learning.

5.2 Survey Content

This survey is mainly carried out in two parts: student questionnaire and teacher questionnaire. In the research part of the student questionnaire, the main content of the questionnaire includes the attitudes and input of students before, during and after class in the smart English class. In the survey part of the teacher questionnaire, the main content of the questionnaire includes the teaching methods of teachers, the organization of learning activities, and the time for teachers to prepare lessons in the English smart class.

5.3 Research Objects and Tools

The main subjects of this survey are teachers, freshmen and sophomores from the English Education Department of Harbin Normal University. A total of 36 teacher questionnaires and 333 student questionnaires were collected. Two types of tool software are involved in the survey process, one is the questionnaire implementation tool, and the other is the statistical analysis tool used to count the results of the questionnaire. In terms of questionnaire implementation tools, the author used the "Questionnaire Star" (https://www.wjx.cn/) to implement online surveys, mainly considering the actual situation that the epidemic situation is difficult to fill in collectively. The website provides functions such as questionnaire production and release, statistics, etc. After the questionnaire is released, the questionnaire can be answered through mobile phone WeChat, computer online and other platforms, and detailed basic data statistics can be provided according to the situation of each question.

In terms of questionnaire results statistics and analysis tools, SPSS1.19 statistical software is used.

6 Data Analysis

6.1 Reliability Analysis

Whether the questionnaire is consistent and reliable must be proved by analyzing the reliability of the questionnaire. Alpha coefficient is a measure of reliability (Table 1). The author has tested the reliability of the questionnaire of the Internet-based English Smart Class teaching model. The analysis results are shown in Table 2 and Table 3. This questionnaire is divided into teacher questionnaire and student questionnaire. The Cronbach's alpha of the two questionnaires in each dimension are all above 0.7. The Cronbach's alpha of the student questionnaire is 0.975, and the teacher questionnaire is 0.858. This shows that the online information-based English Smart classes teaching model has good internal consistency.

Table 1. Cronbach's Alpha is a measure of reliability

Reliability Coefficient	Significance
>0.80	Reliability is very good
0.70–0.80	Reliability is quite good
0.65–0.70	Minimum acceptable reliability value
<0.60	give up

Table 2. Reliability table of student questionnaires on the teaching situation of the Internet-based intelligent English class teaching model

Dimensionality	Items	Cronbach's Alpha
Student input before class	5	0.847
Student attitudes before class	5	0.930
Student input in class	5	0.759
Attitudes of students in class	5	0.948
Student input after class	5	0.759
Student attitudes after class	5	0.947

6.2 Validity Analysis

Validity reflects the degree of validity of the measurement content. The KMO value is the standard of whether the data obtained from the test is suitable for factor analysis,

Table 3. Reliability table of teacher questionnaires on the teaching situation of the Internet-based intelligent English class teaching model

Dimensionality	Items	Cronbach's Alpha
Teacher input before class	5	0.767
Teacher input after class	5	0.747
Teacher input in class	5	0.767

and the value range of KMO is 0–1 (Table 3). When the factors between variables increase, the more suitable factor analysis is, the larger the KMO value. After analyzing the collected student questionnaire data, Table 4 can be obtained. The result of the student questionnaire test is that the KMO value is 0.970, and the Bartlett's sphere test is approximately 12838.523, and the significance is less than 0.001, indicating that the institute's measurement table is suitable for factor analysis. After analyzing the collected teacher questionnaire data, Table 5 can be obtained. The teacher questionnaire test result is that the KMO value is 0.856, and the Bartlett's sphere test is approximately 928.615, and the significance is less than 0.001, indicating that the institute's measurement table is suitable for factor analysis.

Table 4. KMO value range and meaning

KMO Value Range	Significance
0–0.5	Unacceptable
0.54–0.6	Bad
0.6–0.7	Medium
0.74–0.8	Okay
0.84–0.9	Rewardable
0.9–1.0	Excellent

Table 5. KMO and Bartlett test of the student questionnaire

Kaiser-Meyer-Olkin		0.970
Bartlett	Approximately Chi-square	12838.523
	Df	435
	Significance	0.000

Table 6. KMO and Bartlett test of teacher questionnaire

Kaiser-Meyer-Olkin		0.856
Bartlett	Approximately Chi-square	928.615
	Df	505
	Significance	0.000

6.3 Result Analysis

In the questionnaire, the author considers the three perspectives of student attitude, student input, and teacher input, and designs the questionnaire from three dimensions: before class, during class, and after class. The purpose is to count the actual situation of the smart class teaching mode in the teaching practice process.

1) Student Attitude

According to students' attitudes about applying Smart classes before class, during class and after class, the author designed 15 items and conducted a questionnaire survey. The results of the questionnaire are as follows:

Table 7. Results of the interest questionnaire of students applying smart classes before class

Question	A. Very disagree	B. Not agree	C. Difficult to determine	D. Agreed	E. Very agree	D + E
Q1	4.2%	8.41%	18.32%	50.75%	18.32%	69.07%
Q2	5.11%	8.11%	20.12%	49.55%	17.12%	66.67%
Q3	3.3%	11.11%	15.02%	51.65%	18.92%	70.57%
Q4	4.8%	15.62%	21.92%	39.94%	17.72%	57.66%
Q5	4.5%	12.61%	20.42%	44.44%	18.02%	62.46%

Table 8. Results of the interest questionnaire of students applying Smart classes during class

Question	A. Very disagree	B. Not agree	C. Difficult to determine	D. Agreed	E. Very agree	D + E
Q6	4.2	10.21	21.02	46.55	18.02	64.57
Q7	4.5	11.11	15.62	50.45	18.32	68.77
Q8	3.3	7.21	18.02	53.45	18.02	71.47
Q9	5.11	10.21	19.22	48.95	16.52	65.47
Q10	4.2	6.91	18.32	52.85	17.72	70.57

Table 9. Results of the interest questionnaire of students applying Smart classes after class

Question	A. Very disagree	B. Not agree	C. Difficult to determine	D. Agreed	E. Very agree	D + E
Q11	4.5	11.41	20.72	46.55	16.82	63.37
Q12	4.8	13.81	19.82	45.65	15.92	61.57
Q13	3.6	9.91	21.02	47.75	17.72	65.47
Q14	3.6	10.81	24.02	43.84	17.72	61.56
Q15	3.3	7.21	19.82	53.15	16.52	69.67

From Table 6, Table 7, and Table 8, the Q1–Q15 questionnaire results selected "agree" and "Very agree" options are more than half of the number. This result shows that students have a strong interest in using Smart classes related tools to study before class, during and after class. which is conducive to stimulating students' interest in learning, motivating students' learning internal drive, and cultivating students to learn independently.

2) Student input

According to the students' learning input in the application of Smart classes before class, during class and after class, the author designed 15 items and conducted a questionnaire survey. The results of the questionnaire are as follows:

Table 10. Statistics of student input questionnaire results of students applying Smart classes before class

Question	A. Very disagree	B. Not agree	C. Difficult to determine	D. Agreed	E. Very agree	D + E
Q16	4.2	11.11	23.12	43.24	18.32	61.56
Q17	4.2	11.41	21.02	45.05	18.32	63.37
Q18	8.71	24.62	26.73	30.03	9.91	39.94
Q19	3.3	8.11	18.92	53.45	16.22	69.67
Q20	4.5	9.31	23.12	46.5	16.52	63.02

In Table 9, Table 10, and Table 11, Q18, Q24, and Q29 are reverse questions, and others are all positive questions. From the above statistical results, it can be seen that before and after class the number of people who chose the "agree" and "very agree" options for the positive questionnaire results exceeds 60%, while the questionnaire result for the reverse question is less than 40%. This result shows that most students believe that the use of Smart classes related tools to preview before class and review after-school can increase students' understanding of knowledge, as well as are conducive to improving the efficiency of students' autonomous learning. The results during the class show that

Table 11. Statistics of student input questionnaire results of students applying Smart classes during class

Question	A. Very disagree	B. Not agree	C. Difficult to determine	D. Agreed	E. Very agree	D + E
Q21	3.3	6.61	16.22	53.15	20.72	73.87
Q22	3.3	7.21	21.02	49.25	19.22	68.47
Q23	4.5	11.41	23.42	42.64	18.02	60.66
Q24	7.51	24.92	23.42	32.13	12.01	44.14
Q25	4.5	11.41	25.53	42.64	15.92	58.56

Table 12. Statistics of student input questionnaire results of students applying Smart classes after class

Question	A. Very disagree	B. Not agree	C. Difficult to determine	D. Agreed	E. Very agree	D + E
Q26	3.9	9.61	23.12	46.85	16.52	63.37
Q27	3.9	9.61	23.42	47.45	15.62	63.07
Q28	3.9	9.31	23.12	46.25	17.42	63.67
Q29	7.51	23.72	26.13	20.33	12.31	32.64
Q30	3.3	9.91	26.43	44.14	16.22	60.36

Smart classes teaching methods can improve students' learning input during the class, but there are still disadvantages that it is easy to distract learning and it is difficult to concentrate (Table 12).

3) Teacher Input

According to the teacher's use of Smart classes before class, during class and after class, the author designed 15 items and conducted a questionnaire survey. The results of the questionnaire are as follows (Table 13, 14 and 15):

In Table 9, Table10, and Table11 Q31, Q34, Q35, Q39, Q44, and are reverse questions, and others are all positive questions. By analyzing the data above, It is also concluded that before class smart classroom teaching methods have been affirmed by teachers, but it increased the teacher's lesson preparation burden; during the class the smart classes cloud teaching model completely separated from the physical classroom does not guarantee the teaching effect; after class student data analysis function in the smart classroom tool has been affirmed by most teachers, which has improved the teacher's work efficiency after class, but the frequency of teachers using smart classroom tools after class is not very high.

The author believes that the reasons for this phenomenon are as follows: The author believes that the reasons for this phenomenon are as follows: (1) Teachers and students are

Table 13. The results of the questionnaire on teachers' application of smart classes before class

Question	A. Very disagree	B. Not agree	C. Difficult to determine	D. Agreed	E. Very agree	D + E
Q31	0	22.22	22.22	41.67	13.89	55.56
Q32	2.78	36.11	25	33.33	2.78	36.11
Q33	0	27.78	19.44	44.44	8.33	52.77
Q34	0	33.33	30.56	36.11	0	36.11
Q35	2.78	36.11	30.56	27.78	2.78	30.56

Table 14. The results of the questionnaire on teachers' application of smart classes during class

Question	A. Very disagree	B. Not agree	C. Difficult to determine	D. Agreed	E. Very agree	D + E
Q36	2.78	33.33	33.33	27.78	2.78	30.56
Q37	0	16.67	44.44	36.11	2.78	38.89
Q38	8.33	16.67	33.33	36.11	5.56	41.67
Q39	0	27.78	25	42.67	5.56	48.23
Q40	0	13.89	36.11	44.44	5.56	50

Table 15. The results of the questionnaire on teachers' application of smart classes after class

Question	A. Very disagree	B. Not agree	C. Difficult to determine	D. Agreed	E. Very agree	D + E
Q41	0	5.56	27.78	55.56	11.11	66.67
Q42	0	0	22.22	63.89	13.89	77.78
Q43	0	0	11.11	69.44	19.44	88.88
Q44	11.11	36.11	27.78	25	0	25
Q45	2.78	30.56	22.22	36.11	8.33	44.44

not used to arranging and completing homework in smart classroom tools. (2) Teachers and students are not proficient in the operation steps of smart classroom tools, so that it wastes time to use them. (3) Smart classroom tools are cumbersome to operate, which is not conducive to popularization.

7 Conclusion and Recommendation

This study conducted a questionnaire survey of teachers and students who used the cloud to teach in the smart classroom during the epidemic, and used SPSS1.19 for data analysis. The author introduces from three perspectives of student attitude, student input and teacher input, and summarizes from three dimensions before class, during class, and after class. In terms of student attitudes, smart classroom teaching methods are conducive to stimulating interest before class, improving driving force during class, and stimulating independent learning after class; In terms of student input, smart classroom teaching methods can increase students' understanding of knowledge before class and improve the efficiency of students' independent learning after class. However, it is easy to distract learning and difficult to concentrate during the teaching process; In terms of teacher input, smart classroom teaching methods have been affirmed by teachers to a certain extent before and during class, especially the data analysis function. However, the teacher's lesson preparation burden is virtually increased, and the teaching effect is affected.

The above research shows that the teaching methods of smart classrooms have been affirmed by teachers to a certain extent, but the teaching tools of smart classrooms still have a lot of room for improvement, and the integration of traditional classrooms and smart classroom models should be further promoted. In the post-epidemic era, the reform of the Internet-based English smart class teaching model should focus on "integration and development" "inheritance and development" and "innovation and development". The construction of the Internet-based English smart class teaching model should rationally design the teaching content, innovate teaching methods, and gradually meet the teaching needs. It should be noted that the application of network information technology is a practical, convenient and novel way to improve the quality of English teaching, and making good use of the advantages of network information technology is also an indispensable boost for English teaching innovation.

Acknowledgements. 1. 2018 Heilongjiang Provincial Department of Education's Higher Education Teaching Reform Research Project: Building a Mobile Cloud Classroom of "English Literature" Based on Mobile Learning Theory (Project Number: SJGY20180266).

2. 2018 Harbin Normal University's Mixed Teaching Model Reform Pilot Project: English Literature (Project Number: HJG20080014).

References

Li, J.: An Empirical Study on high school students' English learning engagement in smart classroom environment. Minnan Normal University (2020)

Zhao, L.: Research on the influence of English smart classroom based on LECO platform on senior high school students' English learning self-efficacy. Southwest University, 2020

Zhang, L.: Research on English reading teaching in boarding ethnic middle school based on smart classroom. Southwest University (2020)

Liu, Y.: Research on interactive strategies of junior middle school English listening and speaking class supported by smart classroom. Guangxi Normal University (2019)

Li, Y.: Design and application of intelligent classroom teaching in senior high school English. Kashgar University (2019)

Guo, Y.: Optimization design and application of smart classroom teaching mode in junior high school English large class teaching. Central China Normal University (2019)

Zhong, C.: Research on the design and application of teaching mode based on smart classroom. Beihua University (2018)

Xie, X.: Exploration on the construction mode of junior high school English smart classroom based on relevance theory. Chongqing Normal University (2018)

Wang, H.: Research on task design method of intelligent classroom in junior middle school English listening and speaking class. Northeast Normal University (2018)

Chen, M.: Investigation and research on the status quo of teacher-student interaction in junior one English class under the smart classroom mode. Shaanxi University of technology (2018)

Zhang, Y.: Research on the construction of middle school English smart classroom. Chongqing Normal University (2018)

Xiaolin, L., Ronghuai, H.: From knowledge to smart: smart education in the perspective of real learning. China Audio Vis. Educ. **3**, 14–20 (2016)

Shuhui, S., Bangqi, L., Xinyi, L.: Construction and application of smart classroom in big data era . China Inf. Technol. Educ. **7**, 112–114 (2015)

The Application of Information Education in the Teaching of Passenger Cabin Sales of Civil Aviation

Feng Guo[✉]

Sanya Aviation and Tourism College, Sanya City 572000, Hainan, China

Abstract. This paper introduces the concept and process of information education and its application in the teaching of engine room sales. This paper constructs the application process of information education in civil aviation cabin teaching, points out the problems existing in the application of information education, and prospects the application prospect of information education.

Keywords: Information education · Civil aviation cabin sales · Sales teaching

1 Introduction

With the in-depth development of domestic and foreign markets, the marketing direction of civil aviation express has gradually transformed from "product driven" to "market driven" and "customer driven", which requires the civil aviation express to adopt the marketing strategy centered on market demand. And in the process of enterprise informatization promotion, a large number of sales data have been accumulated in the enterprise business database, including purchasing, inventory, sales and other business information. How to obtain useful data from these data to help enterprises analyze the actual needs of customers and provide diversified and hierarchical personalized service solutions has become an important issue for civil aviation express to increase sales revenue and profit, improve customer satisfaction and loyalty.

InMajor developments.

With the increasing number of software and hardware resources in schools, the amount of data generated each year is also increasing. The main sources of data include the following square character software systems [1–4]. When such systems can play a very important role in teaching management, we should make reasonable optimization according to the actual content of educational institutions, This can better enhance the application effect of digital software, data management system; this kind of system is mainly used to manage the input and output data information and important documents, so that the security of data storage can be effectively improved. The composition of data management system comes from the document format, which can effectively record management information.

M. A. Jan and F. Khan (Eds.): BigIoT-EDU 2021, LNICST 391, pp. 367–376, 2021.
https://doi.org/10.1007/978-3-030-87900-6_43

1.1 Definition of Data Aggregation

Aggregate data is composed of program supply system, process sensor and other parts. Information management system covers complex and diverse information management tables, information duplication, errors and other issues. Therefore, program control in aggregate data can effectively screen, process and correct the wrong information, and sort out and classify the correct information, So as to better ensure the accuracy of information and data. Hardware resource data: this kind of data mainly includes: computer, router, wireless controller and other parts, and the way of use mainly includes: data exchange, router exchange link interworking and so on. If you want to ensure the smooth network, you can make use of these devices, so as to further mine the data resources, And then better school network and relevant departments to make analysis, decision-making, to provide favorable conditions for support. Other data: this kind of data mainly includes: video resources, defense equipment, mobile Internet data and other frequency management resources. It is an important incidental management resource of data management system, and the network system in some areas is not perfect, so there is no extensive application of video resources, which makes it difficult to play its role.

2 Related Work

2.1 Data Mining Technology

Data mining is a process of extracting useful information and knowledge from massive data. It can help enterprises to carry out micro, meso and even macro statistics, analysis, synthesis and reasoning of data, so as to use the existing data to predict the future and help enterprises win competitive advantages. For example, data mining can be used to analyze the massive data of enterprises, including customer types, demand tendency of various customers, loan repayment forecast, customer credit policy analysis, customer churn analysis, etc.; conduct market research, including commodity market share prediction, market expansion plan simulation, and business strategy research, Including operating cost and income analysis, risk control, fraud screening and so on.

2.2 Data Mining Algorithm

Regression analysis is a method of trying to find some rules from actual data. Regression analysis establishes and analyzes the functional relationship between a response y (dependent variable) and an important factor X. Regression value represents any conditional expectation value. In data modeling, it is often the conditional expectation value of dependent variable under given variable. The prediction attribute is regarded as independent variable and the prediction target is regarded as dependent variable.

Linear regression models are commonly used:

$$Y_i = \alpha + \beta X_i + E_i, i = 1, 2, 3 \cdots n \qquad (1)$$

Where E_i is a random variable, which should satisfy the following requirements:

$$E(E_i) = 0 \qquad (2)$$

$$\text{cov}(E_i, E_j) = 0, i \neq j \tag{3}$$

Obviously, a good value of and β should make the error between X, y and the actual data as small as possible, so the value of a and β is directly related to the measurement standard of error.

The expression of multiple linear regression is as follows:

$$Y = \alpha + \beta_1 X_1 + \beta_2 X_2 + \cdots + \beta_m X_m + E \tag{4}$$

The data mining method in civil aviation cabin sales mainly uses association rule algorithm.

3 Analysis of the Current Teaching Situation of the Course "Civil Aviation Cabin Sales Skills"

3.1 Curriculum Background

In recent years, with the rapid development of China's aviation industry, carrying out on-board sales has become a common practice for a long time. Most of the domestic and foreign airlines carry out their own on-board direct selling to provide high-quality and low-cost business for passengers. The course "cabin sales skills" is set up based on this background. It is a professional course that must be mastered by the graduates of aviation service related majors who are engaged in civil aviation sales related positions after graduation. The purpose of this course is to broaden the students' knowledge, Let the students master more professional cabin sales skills, master the purchase psychology of passengers and the solution of environmental problems, so as to provide more intimate purchase experience for passengers and improve the purchase rate of passengers. "Civil aviation cabin sales skills" course is an important course for students majoring in aviation service, which can not only effectively improve the professionalism of communication, Moreover, it can achieve the maximum efficiency of economic development for enterprises. In this regard, relevant educators must pay attention to teaching reform, so that aviation professionalism can be effectively improved [5, 6]. From the current situation of our civil aviation sales course, the course content needs to be reformed according to the changes of the times and consumers, teaching students in accordance with their aptitude and combining with the characteristics of the subject.

3.2 Civil Aviation Cabin Sales Skills

Curriculum assessment is one of the important means to reflect the teaching effect. The important reference of curriculum reform is the students' curriculum examination results. Therefore, whether the curriculum assessment method is scientific and correct and whether the students' scores can accurately reflect the real situation is related to the adjustment of curriculum teaching content, the selection of teaching methods and the change of teaching progress. Before the teaching reform of the course "civil aviation cabin sales skills", the examination method was still based on the closed book written examination [7, 8]. However, for the course like this, which focuses on improving students' ability, the examination method should not stay in the theoretical knowledge examination on the paper surface, but should choose the more suitable and more comprehensive assessment method to reflect students' level. In addition, there should be a variety of assessment methods. Theoretical knowledge assessment is more suitable for memory based courses. In order to better test the teaching effect of the course, understand the deficiencies in teaching and improve it in time, the assessment method of the course can be changed to the general assessment of classroom performance, sales performance and usual homework performance. Compared with the previous written examination, this method is more scientific and can reflect the real learning level of students.

4 Application of Various Teaching Methods

The original intention of the course of civil aviation cabin sales skills is to provide high-quality skilled talents for the flight attendant industry, so that they can flexibly use what they have shown in their respective jobs and contribute their strength. Therefore, in the course teaching, we should not only teach students the basic knowledge of sales, but also find ways to improve students' sales ability. Colleges and universities should change the traditional teaching method of emphasizing theory and neglecting application ability. The teaching direction should focus on improving students' sales ability. We can try to use the following new teaching methods.

4.1 Case Teaching Method

Case teaching method is that when the students have mastered the basic theoretical knowledge of sales, the teacher can quote specific sales cases to the students. Through the explanation of the cases, the students can be inspired to have a more specific and in-depth understanding of the theoretical knowledge of sales. The plain and direct theoretical explanation is usually boring, not vivid and not vivid, just with the help of cases. The analysis of typical cases can not only explain the truth of sales theory, but also provide students with the direction of thinking and solving problems, so that students can understand how to deal with similar situations accurately and properly in their future work. Case teaching method is an innovative teaching method for the course of "civil aviation cabin sales skills". It can help teachers to concretize abstract theoretical knowledge, which is more convenient for students to accept and understand.

4.2 Situational Teaching Method

The situational teaching method is to create the working situation of simulated bainite, let the students understand and role in advance, get familiar with the cabin sales process, and experience the sales work content. Create different situations, when students really face in the work, there are also coping strategies. The teacher is teaching to simulate the creation of work situation, and the students answer how to do when they encounter this situation. For example, when the flight attendants are selling goods to some passengers, when they are disturbed by the reaction of passengers, will the flight attendants stop selling or insist on continuing to sell? Or do they have a panacea for solving the problem? Throw this question to the students for thinking and discussion, so that the enthusiasm of students to participate in the classroom will be significantly improved [9, 10]. When the students think for a moment and have their own ideas, the teacher should provide the students with the opportunity to speak and listen carefully to the students' opinions. This kind of flexible question has no case. It is not the teacher's answer, but the standard answer. As shown in Fig. 1.Therefore, the teacher should encourage the students to speak boldly, and divide their answers for reference, so as to provide them with ideas. For example, tell the students that one of the tricks in the cabin sales process is to apologize in advance. The so-called hand does not smile, in advance to express apology, passengers reflect the probability of being disturbed will be much lower.

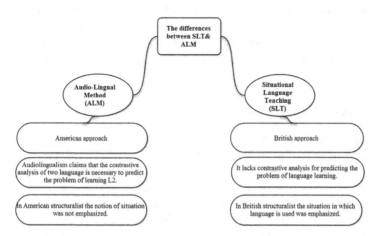

Fig. 1. Situational teaching method.

5 Practice Teaching Method

This teaching method is adopted at the end of the course in order to test what students have learned and strengthen the teaching effect. Students participate in the real cabin sales activities, which is more real and effective than the simulation scene teaching method. It can consolidate the knowledge of time and test the students' adaptability and basic knowledge of sales. The practice link is basically equivalent to work, but students can also find out what is missing in this link. In the work, they can observe more and consult with an open mind. If they don't understand, they can find their own advantages and find their own shortcomings in time, so as to make full use of their strengths and avoid weaknesses in future work, and strive to cope with the real cabin sales [10, 11]. There are many things that can be learned in the process of practice, many of which are not in the classroom. Teachers should tell students the importance of practice, let students pay attention to the practice link, seize the opportunity, exercise and improve their ability level.

6 Summary and Practice Analysis of Big Data Technology

The data on the experimental platform mainly includes application system data, server access log, Snort information, security device syslog log, network access log, port image data and so on. Because the amount of data in syslog log and network access log is relatively large, the journal update speed is relatively fast and the amount of data is large, In the lnux server in the experimental environment, tomcat8, zookeeper 3.4.6 and other programs can be installed and started. Using the scheme of collecting and storing data and logs such as fume + HBase, fume can customize different data senders, collect data, and make simple processing of data in the log system. At the same time, it can also collect data on RPC, text, exec and other data sources. HBase system is more significant in reliability, performance, scalability and so on. On the experimental platform, Tomcat can be selected as the web server, flume can be used to monitor the network logs in real time, and effectively collect and process the newly added logs. Finally, it can be saved in HBase, which can be used in the analysis of spark and other related distributed computing frameworks.

7 Application in Sales Management System

Data mining technology has been widely used in marketing. It is based on the market segmentation principle of marketing, and its basic assumption is that "the past behavior of consumers is the best explanation of their future consumption tendency."

Through collecting, processing and processing a large amount of information related to consumer behavior, the interest, consumption habit, consumption tendency and consumption demand of a specific consumer group or individual are determined, and then the next consumption behavior of the corresponding consumer group or individual is inferred [12, 13]. Based on this, targeted marketing of specific content is carried out for the identified consumer groups, Compared with the traditional large-scale marketing method which does not distinguish the characteristics of consumers, it greatly saves the marketing cost and improves the marketing effect, thus bringing more profits for enterprises.

The main applications of data mining technology in marketing are as follows:

Consumption pattern analysis: it is to carry on the correlation analysis to the long-term customer's consumption situation and the customer's file material and so on related data, unifies the customer's classification, may carry on the analysis and the forecast from the consumptive ability, the expense custom, the consumption cycle and so on, thus provides the basis for the related management decision-making.

Market promotion analysis: using data mining technology to realize the simulation of commodity selection and preferential strategy, according to the model of commodity sales, the simulation results can reveal the problems existing in commodity selection and preferential strategy, and make corresponding adjustment and optimization, so as to maximize the revenue of preferential promotion activities.

Customer churn analysis: according to the existing customer churn data, establish the mathematical model of customer attribute, consumption data and customer churn probability, find out the relationship between these data, and give a clear mathematical formula.

Then according to this model to monitor the possibility of customer churn, if the possibility of customer churn is too high, we can improve customer loyalty by means of promotion to prevent the occurrence of customer churn. This has completely changed the past in the successful acquisition of customers can not monitor the loss of customers, can not effectively achieve customer care.

Customer demand analysis includes: consumption habits, consumption frequency, product type and service mode, transaction history, demand change trend and other factors.

Customer loyalty analysis includes: customer service duration, total number of transactions, customer satisfaction, customer geographical distribution, customer consumption psychology and other factors.

Customer rating analysis includes: customer consumption scale, consumption behavior, customer performance, customer credit and other factors.

Product sales analysis includes: regional market, channel market, seasonal sales and other factors.

8 Teaching Reform of Civil Aviation Cabin Sales Skills Course

8.1 Teaching Content Setting of Civil Aviation Cabin Sales Skills Course

The basic knowledge of cabin sales, the professional ability of cabin sales, the skills in the process of cabin sales, the psychological analysis of customers' purchase and the actual combat of cabin sales. Obviously, it is impractical to teach so much knowledge in the course. Considering that theoretical knowledge is for practical operation, the working environment of students after graduation tests their sales ability more than conceptual sales theoretical knowledge. Therefore, in the curriculum, we should take improving students' sales ability as the goal, and convey sales skills to students as the main purpose. We can focus on explaining cabin sales combat and cabin sales skills. In the teaching of cabin sales practice part, the whole sales process should be explained clearly to students, including pre-sale preparation, sales steps, etc., and specific sales cases should be cited to imitate the sales situation, so that students can have the feeling of being personally involved in the sales and be trained repeatedly, so as to effectively improve the sales ability and level of students. In the content teaching of cabin sales skills, teachers should teach students as much as possible the skills in sales work, including the methods of communication with people, conscious social style training, how to have a comprehensive sales service level and so on. These are the key contents after the teaching reform of "civil aviation cabin sales skills". Only by grasping these key points can we distinguish the theoretical teaching before the reform and improve the teaching quality and students' ability level.

8.2 Using a Variety of Teaching Methods

The original intention of civil aviation cabin sales skills course is to provide high-quality skilled talents for the flight attendant industry, so that they can flexibly use what they have learned in their respective employment positions, and contribute their own strength to the development of the industry. Therefore, in the course of teaching, we should not only teach students the basic knowledge of sales, but also try to improve their sales ability. In order to achieve this goal, colleges and universities should change the traditional teaching method of emphasizing theory and ignoring application ability. The teaching direction should focus on improving students' sales ability. The following new teaching methods can be tried.

Case teaching method. Case teaching method is that after students have mastered the basic theoretical knowledge of sales, the teacher can quote specific sales cases to students, and inspire students to have a more specific and in-depth understanding of sales theoretical knowledge through the explanation of cases. The plain and straightforward theoretical explanation is usually boring, not vivid and vivid, with the help of case teaching is not the same. The analysis of typical cases can not only explain and understand the truth of sales theory, but also provide students with the direction of thinking and solving problems, so that students can understand how to accurately and properly deal with similar situations in their future work. Case teaching method is an innovative teaching method for the course of "civil aviation cabin sales skills". It can help teachers to make abstract theoretical knowledge concrete, which is more convenient for students to accept and understand.

Situational teaching method. In particular, situational teaching method is to create a simulation of specific working situation, so that students can understand and role in advance, be familiar with the cabin sales workflow, and experience the sales work content. Create different situations, when students really face in the work, there are also countermeasures. Teachers can simulate the creation of working situations in teaching, so that students can answer what to do when they encounter such situations. For example, when the flight attendants are selling goods to some passengers, when they are disturbed by the passengers' reaction, do they stop selling, or do they insist on selling? Or do they have a perfect solution? Throw this question to students for thinking and discussion, so that students' enthusiasm for participating in the class will be significantly improved [14]. When students think for a moment and have their own ideas, teachers should provide students with opportunities to speak and listen to students' opinions carefully. There is no fixed answer to this kind of flexible question. It is not the teacher's answer or the standard answer. Therefore, teachers should encourage students to speak boldly and share their answers with students for reference and ideas. For example, tell students that there is a trick in the cabin sales process, which is to apologize in advance. The so-called people who don't smile will be much less likely to be disturbed after they express their apologies in advance.

9   Simulation Analysis

In order to evaluate the application effect of data mining technology We can deduce Table 1 from the data obtained in in teaching. As shown in Fig. 2 we give an example to verify the effectiveness of the algorithm proposed in this paper.

We can see from the figure that as time goes on, the variances obtained are almost the same, and the teaching effect is distributed evenly.

Table 1. F-test two sample analysis of variance

	A Class	B Class
Average	74	84
Df	14	14
f	1.2	1.4

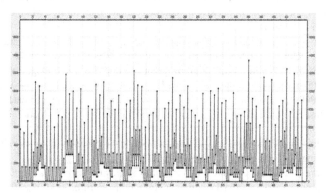

Fig. 2. Data mining simulation analysis

10   Conclusion

To sum up, the course of civil aviation cabin sales skills plays an important role in flight attendants related majors. However, at present, the teaching process of the course needs continuous innovation of the course content. Combined with the actual situation of students' knowledge, targeted education courses are carried out to effectively guarantee the quality of teaching courses. In addition, we can learn from foreign advanced teaching methods, so that the curriculum can be closer to the development of internationalization, so that students can deal with all emergencies after real employment, ensure the professionalism of aviation personnel, and make students really apply their knowledge to work.

References

1. Xu, Y.: On the role of civil aviation cabin culture in improving service quality . Cul. Educ. Mater. **21**, 74–75 (2017)
2. Liu, X.: Analysis on the teaching reform of civil aviation marketing course . Sci. Educ. Wenhui (last xunjian) **2**, 61–62 (2013)
3. Mo, X., Jin, R.: Analysis of vocational post ability oriented online marketing curriculum reform in higher vocational colleges – taking civil aviation business major as an example. Mod. Econ. Inf. **6**, 423–425 (2015)
4. Chi, R.: Countermeasure analysis on improving the teaching quality of cabin service and emergency response training course. J. Civil Aviat. Flight Univ. China **29**(03), 70–73 (2018)

5. Maggie, J., Li, Z., Cui, K.: Teaching evaluation research of practical courses based on data mining. Sci. Educ. Guide (zhongxunyuan) (8) (2020)
6. Wadewar, Wei, X.: Design of network experiment teaching evaluation system based on data mining. Mod. Electron. Technol. v.43(554)(03), 150–153+157 (2020)
7. Qi, L., Guo X., Junying, M., et al.: The application of data mining technology in teaching evaluation of colleges and universities. J. Shijiazhuang Univ. **22**(121)(03) 67–70 (2020)
8. Cui, K., Ma, J.: Application of data mining and analysis in teaching evaluation of practical training courses. Equipment Manufact. Technol. **309**(09), 117–120 (2020)
9. Gao, G., Guo, Y., Cai, F., et al.: The establishment of teaching evaluation database and the application of data mining in classroom teaching quality monitoring . Med. Educ. Manage. **006**(002), 15–19 (2020)
10. Wang, J.: Evaluation of computer application basic teaching based on data mining and visualization technology. Chin. Foreign Entrepreneurs, **679**(17), 206–206 (2020)
11. Liang, Q.: Evaluation and optimization of talent training mode in colleges and universities based on data mining technology . J. Dalian Univ. Nationalities **22**(01), 94–98 (2020)
12. Zhang, X.: Path research of constructing adaptive learning model under data mining technology – Based on the analysis of higher vocational education . Inf. Record. Mater. **21**(03), 189–190 (2020)
13. Li, X.: A study on the model of Ideological and political evaluation of college students based on data mining. J. High. Educ. **5**, 189–190 (2020)
14. Yan, Z., Wang, X., Gu, L.: Research on the quality verification of graduate student evaluation based on emotional analysis and data mining. High. Educ. Forum, 000(005), 80–86, 91 (2020)

The Development of Creative Writing Thinking Under the Educational Information

Xiaoci Yang[✉]

Xi'an Fanyi University, Xi'an 710105, Shanxi, China

Abstract. The purpose of creative writing thinking training course is to cultivate students' practical ability and creative writing ability. From the teaching content, classroom concept, evaluation and evaluation, teaching methods and other aspects of the attempt and exploration. Under the background of education informatization, we should strengthen the practice strategy in the classroom training and timely evaluate and feedback in the course assessment.

Keywords: Education information · Writing thinking · Thinking development

1 Introduction

Writing thinking training is a professional support course for students majoring in cultural market management. In the teaching process of this course, the author has carried out a series of attempts and explorations for college students who have uneven writing foundation but need to improve their writing skills, in order to achieve more obvious teaching effect in a short time. In the past two years, researchers at home and abroad have devoted themselves to the research of in-house virtual network mapping algorithm. However, in essence, the problem of dynamic resource allocation is the essence of online virtual network mapping. When the virtual network mapping requests constantly arrive and leave, a large number of fragmented resources may appear in the physical network [1]. On the other hand, the excellent level of the existing mapping scheme may be reduced, which will reduce the utilization rate of the underlying physical network resources and the request acceptance rate of the subsequent virtual network mapping.

2 Mapping Mathematical Model for Reconfiguration of Secure Virtual Network

This paper analyzes the following mathematical model of multi-objective secure virtual network reconfiguration mapping.

$$\min \sum_{n^i \in N^p} f(n^i) \tag{1}$$

© ICST Institute for Computer Sciences, Social Informatics and Telecommunications Engineering 2021
Published by Springer Nature Switzerland AG 2021. All Rights Reserved
M. A. Jan and F. Khan (Eds.): BigIoT-EDU 2021, LNICST 391, pp. 377–386, 2021.
https://doi.org/10.1007/978-3-030-87900-6_44

$$\max \sum_{G^i \in G} G(G_m^v, rb) - C(G_m^v, ra) \qquad (2)$$

In formula (1), there is a binary variable TF (n). If the fragmentation of physical node Ni is larger than the threshold value FD, then it has a value of 1, otherwise it has a value of zero. In Eq. (2), the mapping cost of virtual network G is expressed by CG (RB) before reconstruction, and C (g, RA) after reconstruction. The constraint conditions of nodes can be seen in detail. See formula 6 and formula 7 for link constraints and formula 8 for security constraints. Among them, the set of virtual nodes carried by physical node n represents the value range of variables, which is represented by formulas 1 and 2.

3   From Applied Writing to "Applied Creative Writing"

Since 2016, writing thinking training course has been set up for the major of literary management. In the previous professional curriculum, practical writing was the only course to cultivate writing skills. In 2015, with the rise of WeChat official account, more and more graduates entered WeChat's official account and WeChat copywriting. Therefore, new media operation is regarded as an important goal of talent training for the major of cultural management. In this way, the demand for writing ability will rise. The traditional practical writing course obviously can not meet the requirements of the new training objectives.

For this reason, the author considers setting up a writing thinking training course. The training of writing ability can not be equal to literary writing, but it can not only be limited to mastering the work plan, work summary, report, meeting minutes and other practical styles [2]. The writing of practical writing pays more attention to the format and the organization and logic of the text. Although the new media copywriting has a certain "routine and mode", it pays more attention to creativity and wonderful words. In my opinion, the writing of new media copywriting that students will be engaged in is actually a kind of "Applied Creative Writing", which has become the teaching theme of writing thinking training course. The reason why the name of the course is "writing thinking training" is that writing courses seem to teach a kind of ability, but the essence is to construct a set of thinking mode in students' minds through teaching activities. This is the reason why writing courses are easy to teach, but not easy to teach well.

4   The Content Composition of Writing Thinking Training Course

The teaching content of writing thinking training course is mainly composed of sensory writing practice, rhetorical writing practice and practical writing practice.

4.1   Feeling Writing Practice

The internal point of this part is that although everyone has not received special training in his childhood, he is often curious about the world and has a keen sense, but with the growth of age, his sense is becoming increasingly dull. There is a certain side to the dullness of feeling. It is the nature of effect in the process of socialization. However, this change is not conducive to one's creative writing and expression. Therefore, "to be a dreamer of life" is my first proposition. how to be a sleeper of life? We need to wake up the feeling of dullness and deep sleep. The design of this part comes from the borrower. In the creative writing system of the United States, the practice of feeling writing is the most basic training. Its starting point is that feeling is not only the premise of writing, but also the basis and source of people's understanding of the world.

There are five groups of exercises in this part, which are tactile writing exercise, taste writing exercise, olfactory writing exercise, auditory writing exercise and visual writing exercise. Although the method has long been there, but in the specific teaching process, the author has carried out a small innovation, and strive to bring fresh and stimulating to students, in order to stimulate the writing trend. For example, in the tactile writing practice class, the writing materials are the leaves picked up from under the tree before class, and each leaf is not completely matched. In the taste writing practice class, different food is brought each time. In the olfactory writing practice, the writing materials try to bring special liquid that students have not touched. The reaction of the students is that they have never had a writing class like this since primary school. The primary purpose of writing teaching has been realized.

4.2   Rhetorical Writing Practice

When it comes to rhetoric, most people don't think so. From primary school to middle school, there are all kinds of rhetorical learning units. The emphasis of rhetoric teaching in primary and secondary schools is to explain the definition and characteristics, pay attention to the learning of knowledge, and ignore the use and practice. It can be said that people have misunderstood and neglected rhetoric for a long time. "Rhetoric, as the name suggests, can be interpreted as the words that need to be cultivated." rhetoric is not a dispensable skill, but a higher level of language use and an advanced state of expression. The density of rhetoric is one of the typical characteristics of good writing [3]. Therefore, the focus and goal of rhetoric writing practice is to practice the density of rhetoric. The density of rhetorical practice needs targeted training and carefully designed practice. Rhetorical writing practice is the key link of writing thinking training course.

There are dozens of rhetorical devices in modern Chinese, but they have different effects on writing. In the part of rhetorical writing practice, there are five units, which focus on the training of metaphor, contrast, parallelism, exaggeration, pun, allusion, and other rhetorical devices. The reason for doing so is that the above rhetoric can produce good expressive effect and enhance the expressiveness of words. Metaphor is the "trump card" rhetoric in many rhetorics. Whether it is a literary text or a theoretical article, metaphor can add color to it. It can almost be said that "no metaphor, no speech". Contrast can form tension between words, highlight the essence of things, and promote the evolution of words. Parallelism is often the "glue" of a paragraph or text, which can express rich ideas, enhance the momentum of language and enhance the communication effect. Exaggeration is not a rhetorical device that any writer likes to use, but it is more common in oral expression or new media writing. As for pun, allusion and Dingzhen, they are all euphemistic figures of speech, which are seldom used. However, if they can be used properly in the article, they can add color to the article, so they are also paid attention to.

5 Innovation of Writing Thinking Training Course

5.1 Intensive Practice

The first innovation of writing thinking training course is intensive practice. How intensive is it? Unit 1 "feeling writing exercises, one exercise in each class. Of course, the exercises are very short. If you write 200 words, you will reach the standard. However, to give a few drops of inexplicable liquid, it is easy to write a complex smell in 200 words. Unit 2 rhetorical writing exercises are more complex. Each class has 80 min of practice. At the beginning, it is required to write more than 600 words. The starting point of setting up intensive exercises is very simple, and the writing level can only be improved in a large number of writing exercises (see Fig. 1). If you don't have enough practice speech and Jia Pingwa to teach, you can't teach writing if you ask a famous reporter from Xinhua news agency to teach.

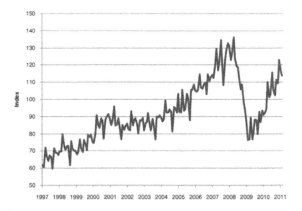

Fig. 1. The effect simulation of writing thinking training course.

5.2 Immediate Evaluation and Feedback

The second innovation of writing thinking training is immediate evaluation and timely feedback. More than half of the exercises are graded in class, so the three-point evaluation method is adopted, that is, 1 point for writing, 2 points for passing, and 3 points for excellent, so that each student's grade can be given quickly in class. In addition to scoring, it's better to give written comments to each student [4]. Of course, it's impossible to write written comments to each student (see Fig. 2). What can be done is to score while giving comments to the outlet head, such as "there is potential and room for improvement". The real-time scoring of writing exercises in class is rough and fuzzy, but at the end of a semester, the sum of the scores of all previous exercises can still reflect the students' real level more accurately [5–7]. As compensation and correction, two exercises with higher score, certain difficulty or time-consuming can be set up, such as "figurative writing exercise" and "family history writing", so as to widen the score gap between students of different levels, The evaluation is more accurate.

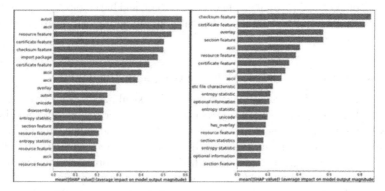

Fig. 2. Simulation for Immediate evaluation and feedback.

6 Stimulate the Desire for Knowledge and Develop Innovative Thinking

6.1 Important Conditions

Confucius said, "those who know are not as good as those who are good, and those who are good are not as happy as those who are happy." Einstein, a great scientist, thought, "interest is the best teacher." In geography teaching, the key to curriculum reform is to give full play to students' subjective initiative and change passive receptive learning into active inquiry learning. One of the most important conditions for students to study actively is to stimulate their interest in learning. Stimulating interest is an effective way to arouse students' learning enthusiasm and develop creative thinking [8–10]. How to take students as the main body, stimulate students' learning interest and develop students' creative thinking? This requires effective and appropriate methods and skills. All the wisdom of geography teachers should be reflected in the design of teaching methods and means to attract and shock students, so that they have a strong desire for knowledge, in the enjoyment of art to accept knowledge, enlighten wisdom, develop creative thinking, cultivate sentiment.

6.1.1 A Space for Students to Highlight Their Subject Status

Classroom teaching is a process that can not be ignored and the main battlefield of quality education. In class, let all students participate in learning activities, highlight the main role of students, give students a space to move forward; give students a condition to exercise; give students a time to arrange; give students a problem to grasp; give students a conflict to discuss; give students a right to discuss, Let the students create by themselves. In the process of observation, thinking, practice, self exploration and independent activities, the students have interest and found the law of cognition [11–13]. From "I want to learn" to "I want to learn", teachers focus on guiding students with learning difficulties, students' differences get teachers' attention, overcome the "one size fits all" of students' reading practice, brain, mouth and hands-on, teachers seize the opportunity to guide, so that students' logical thinking ability and divergent thinking ability can be developed.

6.1.2   Using Various Methods to Make the Geography Class Lively

Lu Shuxiang once said: "successful teachers are successful because they have made the class lively. If teaching method is a key, then there is a master key on top of all kinds of teaching methods. Its name is" live. "In order to effectively stimulate students' interest in active learning in geography teaching, it is necessary to avoid thousands of rules and boring, to be vivid, flexible and diversified as far as possible, to show their charm, and to become a real art course. Czech educator Comenius once said: "the desire for knowledge and learning should be stimulated in all possible ways in children." Therefore, changing the "tricks" in teaching and mobilizing the enthusiasm of students through new stimulation are in line with the characteristics of students' curiosity, changeable emotions and diverse interests.

6.2   Enhance Interest in Learning

Using multimedia teaching skillfully. Multimedia can create a lively and interesting teaching situation, turn silence into sound, turn static into dynamic, make students into a kind of pleasant and lively atmosphere, overcome the static and rigid text and blackboard writing defects. For example, in the lesson "a video clip of the Yangtze River is played. The music is pleasant, the picture is beautiful, the explanation is beautiful, and the students are lively, relaxed and novel. It enhances the artistic appeal and stimulates the thirst for knowledge. Use new data to impart new information. As shown in Fig. 3. Geography involves politics, economy, military, history and many other subjects. Teachers can pass on the new information to students by reading newspapers and listening to radio, film and television [14]. For example, when talking about China's industrial and trade, they can timely quote the latest data released by the National Bureau of statistics and understand the great achievements of reform and opening up, which can strengthen the students' sense of pride and enhance their interest in learning.

7   Create an Equal, Harmonious and Pleasant Learning Atmosphere

7.1   Respect Every Student

"The revolution of learning" believes that "real learning should create a relaxed atmosphere." facts have proved that students like a certain subject, to a large extent, because

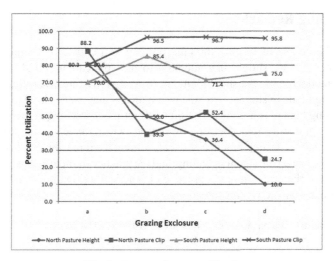

Fig. 3. Increase interest utilization

they like the teacher. To stimulate students' interest in learning and develop creative thinking, we must create an equal and harmonious relationship between teachers and students, eliminate the emotional distance between teachers' condescension and students' submissiveness, strengthen the spiritual communication between teachers and students, and enhance the emotion of mutual trust and love. And it's up to the teachers [15–17]. Teachers should be full of enthusiasm to infect students, the language is funny and vivid, the intonation is just right, the blackboard writing is simple and clear, so that students can get a kind of artistic enjoyment in learning, at the same time, they should respect every student and show their love to students timely.

7.2 Actively Guide Students to Think Actively

Looking forward to the eyes, knowing smile, nodding approval, kind touch, etc., will inject energy into the students' mind, will make students feel a kind of love inspiration, a kind of emotional blend, become the driving force to motivate him, and sometimes even affect his life. Only by actively creating a harmonious, democratic and mutual help relationship between teachers and students, can we realize the transfer of students' interest from teachers to the study of the subject, make students "believe in their teachers and their way", and cultivate their love for learning [18–20]. Only harmonious and equal relationship between teachers and students, students can be active in thinking, questions can be put forward at any time, ideas can be published, teachers and students have equal dialogue and common discussion, students can communicate freely, people can devote themselves to others, all of them are masters of learning, and the whole learning process is full of interest.

8 Concluding Remarks

In essence, the course of writing thinking training is a course of "Applied Creative Writing". Although we should pay attention to the application and skill training of students in practical work, we should not ignore creative writing. Therefore, we should build a thinking mode in students' minds, which means that the teaching task of writing thinking training course is arduous. Therefore, in terms of teaching content, the author first establishes a new system, focusing on sensory writing practice, rhetorical writing practice and practical writing practice [21, 22]. Among the three, the practice of sensory writing tries to wake up the sleeping feeling, and the practice of rhetorical writing focuses on the density of rhetoric, while the practice of practical writing hopes to improve the writing ability in realistic writing situations.

Acknowledgements. Drama Adaptation Research (XFU18KYTDC01).

References

1. Huang, J.: From trigger to secondary: exploring the thinking training path of high school narrative writing. Res. Class. Teach. Prim. Secondary Schools **12**, 31–33 (2020)
2. Lu, R.: Analysis on the effective development of thinking training in senior high school English writing teaching. Middle Sch. Engl. **44**, 25 (2020)
3. Ying, J., Ding, N.: Research on English writing teaching based on sub item thinking training in virtual community . J. Jilin Inst. Educ. **36**(11), 84–87 (2020)
4. Li, F.: Thinking training in senior high school English writing teaching. Gansu Educ. **21**, 96–97 (2020)
5. Yang, Y.: Developing students' intelligence and cultivating their thinking ability. A collection of research achievements in basic education theory, **1** (3): editorial board of China Education and teaching series: 205 (2005)
6. Yu, C.: Train children's thinking, Actively develop intelligence China Education Association, China dialectics of Nature Research Association, Jiangsu Education Association, Suzhou Education Association, Zhangjiagang Social Science Association, Zhangjiagang Education Association, Zhangjiagang wisdom Research Association. Selected papers of the second national wisdom academic seminar. China Education Association, China dialectics of Nature Research Association, Jiangsu Education Association, Suzhou Education Association, Zhangjiagang wisdom Research Association Federation of Social Sciences, Zhangjiagang education society, Zhangjiagang Intelligence Research Association: China Intelligence Engineering Research Association, 239–241 (2004)
7. Zhangjiagang Intelligence Research Association: China Intelligence Engineering Research Association, pp. 278–280 (2004)
8. Xiao, H.: Innovative thinking – the key to develop wisdom potential China education association, pp. 165–168. China Education Zhangjiagang Education Society, Zhangjiagang Intelligence Research Association, China Intelligence Engineering Research Association (2004)
9. Xiao, H.: Innovative thinking -- the key to develop wisdom potential. China dialectics of nature research association. In: Proceedings of the second National Symposium on wisdom (3). China dialectics of Nature Research Association: China dialectics of Nature Research Association, pp. 126–131 (2004)

10. Qiao, D.: Macroscopically grasping systematic thinking: interpreting the urbanization strategy of central and Western China from the real connotation of large-scale development. In: Urban Planning Society of China. Proceedings of 2004 annual meeting of urban planning (Part I). Urban Planning Society of China: China Urban Planning Society, pp. 48–51 (2004)
11. Jiang, G.: Transforming the subjective world, developing innovative thinking and practicing Three Represents. Heilongjiang Federation of social sciences circles. The most precious spiritual wealth -- the collection of the Symposium on the theory of commemorating the 100th anniversary of Deng Xiaoping's birth in Heilongjiang Province. Heilongjiang Federation of social sciences circles: Heilongjiang Federation of social sciences circles, pp. 590–594 (2004)
12. Xu, Y.: Planning thinking and procedures for the preservation and development of historic sites in Taiwan: a case study of Jianguo brewery in Taipei. China National Architecture Research Association; China National Architecture Research Association; China National Architecture Research Association. Proceedings of China national architecture. China National Architecture Research Association; China National Architecture Research Association; China National Architecture Research Association: China National Architecture Research Association, pp. 198–205 (2001)
13. Huang, Y., Ma, L.: Sports · architecture · riverside · symbiosis -- new thinking of waterfront development in Wuhan China Association for construction education, Tianjin University, Tianjin Institute of urban construction. Theses of the University Student Forum of the 46th IFHP World Congress. China Association for construction education, Tianjin University, Tianjin Institute of urban construction: Research Center for urban development and environment, Chinese Academy of Social Sciences, pp. 288–290 (2002)
14. Xu, Y.: Planning thinking and procedures for preservation and development of historic sites: a case study of Jianguo brewery in Taipei. In: Proceedings of 2002 Cross Strait Symposium on traditional dwellings. China National Architecture Research Association: China National Architecture Research Association, pp. 70–90 (2002)
15. Zhang, J.: Developing creative thinking and cultivating innovative learning ability. China Association for science and technology, Jilin Provincial People's government. New opportunities and challenges in the new century: knowledge innovation and development of high-tech industry (Volume I). China Association for science and technology, Jilin Provincial People's Government: Academic Department of China Association for science and technology, p. 99 (2001)
16. Troiano, G.M., et al.: Exploring How Game Genre in Student-Designed Games Influences Computational Thinking Development. Human Factors in Computing Systems (2020)
17. Trojano, G., et al.: To explore the influence of game types on the development of computer thinking in the design of games by students. Human factors in the calculation system (2020)
18. Ratnasari, D., Supriatana, A., Hendayana, S.: The development of critical thinking in collaborative learning. Education and information technology (2020)
19. Li, C., Li, J.: The cultivation of critical thinking in College English teaching. Atlantis press (2020)
20. Jing, J.: Development and practice of digital mind map of middle school chemistry. Research center of basic education curriculum reform, Ministry of education. In: Proceedings of 2020 Quality Education Innovation Research Conference in primary and secondary schools. Research center of basic education curriculum reform, Ministry of Education: Research Center of basic education curriculum reform, Ministry of education, p. 206 (2020)

21. Wang, Y.: Optimizing classroom questioning and promoting thinking development. Fujian business association and Xiamen new curriculum reform research group. Collection of papers of South China education informatization research experience exchange meeting (5). Fujian business association and Xiamen new curriculum reform research group: Fujian business association, pp. 221–222 (2020)
22. Wang, J.: On how to cultivate students' thinking ability in primary school mathematics classroom teaching. Guangdong ChenYue Education Development Co., Ltd

The Online Teaching Practice of Flip Classroom

Bin Huang and Xinyu Yang[✉]

School of Education, China West Normal University, Nanchong 637009, Sichuan, China

Abstract. After the Western flipped classroom concept was introduced into higher education, how to effectively carry out the reform of information education has been plagued by many educators. Taking the college network course as an example, this paper analyzes the problems existing in the process of information teaching, and probes into the new ideas of the future information teaching reform from the perspective of the combination of network teaching and flipped classroom teaching.

Keywords: Flipped classroom · Classroom design

1 Introduction

The outbreak of the novel coronavirus pneumonia has led to the separation between teachers and schools, students and schools, students and teachers, students and students in education. In response to the call of "stopping courses but not stopping studying, learning not delay", the Ministry of Education emphasizes the need to guide teachers to select suitable MOOC, SPOC and campus online curriculum resources, to carry out online teaching, make full use of learning behavior analysis data, and understand the students' online learning [1]. During the epidemic, teachers are the key for education to take a turn to be out of danger, so they should optimize the teaching mode, make good use of the teaching platform to cultivate students' ability of self-learning, critical thinking, communication and cooperation, and at the same time, achieve the effect of integrating "quality, depth and temperature" in the online classroom. Therefore, this study proposes the online teaching mode of flipping classroom based on "SPOC + MOOC Class + Tencent Meeting", which provides a reference for the research of online teaching mode in the post-epidemic era through the practice in "Information Technology course Teaching Theory".

2 Preparation of Teaching Practices

"China University on the MOOC" platform selected Nanjing Normal University Zhu Cailan's "Information Technology Teaching Method" curriculum resources as the master version for secondary editing, the chapter order was adjusted, the teaching content was screened, the teaching resources was increased (such as 8 multimedia coursewares,

© ICST Institute for Computer Sciences, Social Informatics and Telecommunications Engineering 2021
Published by Springer Nature Switzerland AG 2021. All Rights Reserved
M. A. Jan and F. Khan (Eds.): BigIoT-EDU 2021, LNICST 391, pp. 387–394, 2021.
https://doi.org/10.1007/978-3-030-87900-6_45

2 microlectures, 12 topic discussions, 6 chapter tests, 10 chapter assignments, 12 questions from MOOC Class practice library, etc.), and the asynchronous SPOC courses was created according to the syllabus. Students need to log in the iCourse, and "student certification" through the "School Cloud". After successful certification, students can "sign up" for the course [2–4]. Thus, teachers can control the students' learning progress and learning quality through the following links: ①In the "Announcement" and "Scoring standards" section issues the curriculum dynamics, curriculum examination and the schedule arrangement and other content. In the "Courseware" and "Quizzes and assignments" sections upload units PPT, microlecture, chapter tests and assignments. ③In the "discussion area" section, teachers actively participate in the discussion, timely response to the questions raised by students, give responses to students' feedback and Suggestions, and think about improvement measures.

The teaching object of this teaching practice is the 2018 undergraduate students majoring in Educational Technology of X normal University (48 students). The class hours are arranged for 2 class hours per week, a total of 32 class hours.

3   The Process of Teaching Practice

3.1   SPOC + MOOC Class "pre-Learning"

"SPOC + MOOC Classroom" is the first step to implement flipped classroom. First, a QQ group will be established to share the teaching arrangement, online learning notice and requirements, Tencent conference number, two-dimensional code in the classroom. Secondly, related and created MOOC Class on the SPOC platform (input class name, class year, semester time, class time, etc.), and the classes were prepared online according to teachers' own teaching time, and relevant teaching activities was added based on teaching design, such as setting in-class exercises, questionnaires, class announcements, topic discussion, etc. [5, 6]. Finally, PPT, video and other teaching resources will be released on SPOC platform for students to learn independently online. Students are required to watch the teaching resources on time on the SPOC platform. If they have any doubts when learning, they can ask questions in the discussion area of the SPOC platform. Teachers will give timely replies.

We use the function of "random grouping" of MOOC Class to divide the students into 8 groups and use group cooperation and task-driven form to guide the students to complete their autonomous learning before class. As shown in Fig. 1. According to the teaching plan of each class, make detailed guidance arrangement, and publish it to MOOC Class. The before-class guidance mainly consists of four sections: Learning goal: help students to clarify the learning goal of each class. Guide tasks: Make a list of tasks for students to learn independently, so that students can quickly locate teaching resources to improve learning efficiency. Live teaching plan: let students understand the next live teaching process in advance and prepare for class. ④Thinking before class: ask enlightening questions to stimulate students' interest in learning.

3.2   Mutual Assistance in the "MOOC Class + Tencent Meeting" Class

In order to ensure that "teaching standards are not reduced", to create a "face-to-face" classroom atmosphere for students and to meet the needs of real-time interaction between

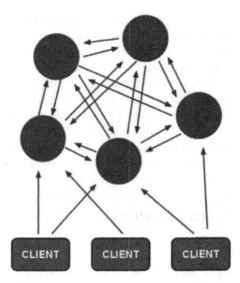

Fig. 1. MOOC class + tent meeting "class"

teachers and students, we choose MOOC Class and Tencent Meeting to complete the control and guidance of students' online learning [7]. During the live broadcast classroom of Tencent Meeting, The basic content that has been explained on SPOC platform will not be repeated by teachers, but focus on the key and difficult points of knowledge, the students' doubts and the evaluation of the students' group homework. This teaching process can not only check and consolidate students' online learning situation before class, but also improve students' ability to analyze and evaluate problems and cultivate their higher-order thinking.

"MOOC Class + Tencent Meeting" helping students during class is the second step in the implementation of the flipping classroom, which achieve online live broadcast from "indoctrination classroom" to "dialogue classroom ". As follows: ①The first 10 min of the first class, Teachers and students enter the Tencent Meeting, Teachers open "check-in" and issue pre-class tests in the MOOC Class, and through Tencent Meeting video and audio or chat area text function to remind students to complete check-in and testing in the MOOC Class, Teachers check students' attendance rate and autonomous learning in the MOOC Class. ②In the last 30 min after the first class, teacher first explained the pre-class test, then use the "roll call" function of MOOC class to randomly select 4 groups to let them share the gains of pre-class learning and answer "thinking before class" questions. Group representatives can display learning results through Tencent Meeting "shared screen" function.

3.3 SPOC + MOOC Class "after-School Inspector"

After class supervision of "SPOC + MOOC Class" is the third step to implement flipping classroom. After class, the teacher publishes the chapter test and the discussion question through the SPOC platform, the student needs to complete the test within the specified time and participate in the discussion by consulting the data. Besides, students can watch the teaching resources on the SPOC platform repeatedly after class to consolidate knowledge. Teachers promote students' thinking and help students to internalize and absorb knowledge by supervising student learning [8, 9]. The relevancy between SPOC and MOOC class can count the number, frequency, duration, document browsing, class answering, in-class discussion, chapter test and so on of each student's video viewing. Teachers can master the learning situation of each student at any time on the computer terminal of the MOOC class and analyze the students individually according to the statistical data of the learning situation. They can not only urge the backward students, but also provide the advanced learning materials for the students who have spare time during their learning to truly achieve precision teaching.

4   Practical Results and Reflections

4.1   Results of Practice

Learning effect is an important basis for testing the effectiveness of teaching mode. We use the Classroom Real-time Observation Scale to record the learning situation of each lesson before, during and after class in detail. After the course, summarize and analyze the records. First of all, about 88% of the students can complete the task of autonomous learning before class, 63% of the students can participate in the topic discussion, indicating that most of the students have high initiative and enthusiasm for learning, and can reconstruct the new knowledge from the existing knowledge and experience [10–12]. Secondly, the interaction between teachers and students, and among students is generally active, and through classroom observation, it is found that the number of students participating in discussion and communication or class summary increases with the advancement of class hours. Finally, although 96% of the students can complete the chapter test on time, only 21% of the students can put forward more depth or breadth of views, which shows that most students only master the basic knowledge of the classroom, but do not pay much attention to the understanding and transfer of knowledge.

Learning effect also needs to stand in the perspective of students to experience and feel, so that teachers can easily ask questions to guide students to think, to improve the quality of teaching to a greater extent. To this end, we distributed the Learning Feedback Questionnaire to understand the impact of the flipped classroom teaching model based on "SPOC + MOOC Class + Tencent Meeting" on students' learning effect. According to the survey data, 90% of the students indicates that they were adapted to the application of this model in "Information Technology Curriculum Teaching Theory"; 75% said that the use of the SPOC platform is very convenient and the teaching resources are rich and diverse, which can stimulate learning enthusiasm and improve learning efficiency to a certain extent; 79% of students believe that the SPOC platform helps to review and consolidate what they have learned; As shown in Fig. 2 believe that the model can improve their autonomous learning ability and group cooperation ability, and better solve the problem of not grasping the key points of learning [13–18]. 85% say that flipping the classroom enhances the sense of learning participation, and the interactive communication between teachers and students, and among students can promote the internalization and absorption of knowledge, achieving the effect of drawing inferences from one to the other; 62% of the students said that they could communicate with teachers and classmates in time and have a sense of belonging in the.

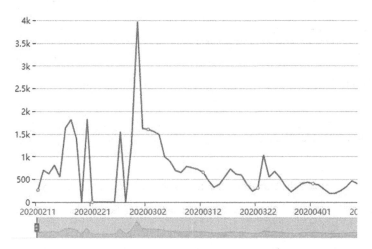

Fig. 2. Data chart of online course selection

In addition, 44% of students think that the model requires a high degree of autonomous learning ability. As shown in Fig. 3. Although it is more likely for students with poor self-control to affect their learning progress, it can also play an encouraging role to some extent; 25% of students want group reporting section to be more interesting, most groups are mainly lecturing, lack of interaction and attraction; and 10% of students show that they are difficult to adapt to the model because of their lack of ability to accept new technologies. Overall, the flipping classroom, which based on "SPOC + MOOC Class + Tencent Meeting" transformed "online closed classroom" into "face-to-face open classroom" during the epidemic period, promotes teachers' supervision of students and students' thinking and learning of knowledge, realizing that teaching and learning benefit each other.

4.2   Reflection

4.2.1   Can Improve Learning Efficiency, and Enhance Autonomous Learning Ability

The flipping classroom teaching mode based on "SPOC + MOOC Class + Tencent Meeting" can give full play to the main position of students' learning, improve their ability of autonomous learning and increase the opportunity of self-thinking. Since teacher will provide the task list to guide the students' self-study direction before class, students with weak learning ability can also finish the learning task on time, which improve the learning efficiency. In addition, teachers do not need to repeat the content of knowledge in the live classroom, but only need to answer the students' questions, which not only lightens the burden of teachers, but also cultivates the students' critical thinking.

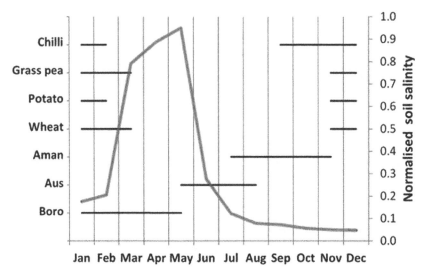

Fig. 3. Detrended graph of main calculation results.

4.2.2 Can Activate Classroom Atmosphere, Strengthen Communication and Expression Ability

Although college students are independent in mind, they need an active and free atmosphere in their study. By SPOC platform the independent learning of the platform before class, students already have a certain knowledge base, and have more time to express their opinions, ask questions, participate in the discussion in the live class, which can maximize the sense of classroom participation and learning identity. Moreover, the flipping classroom teaching mode based on "SPOC + MOOC Class + Tencent Meeting" provides an opportunity for discussion and communication, and students can exercise their language expression ability, which is helpful for enriching the teaching content, helping students enlighten their wisdom and consolidating their knowledge in the collision of thinking between teachers and student, and among students.

4.2.3 Should Advance with the Epidemic and Change the Teaching Concept

In the face of the changes in learning situation caused by the epidemic, teachers should actively change their teaching concepts. They should not only give full play to their leading role, be good guides and participants in students' learning, but also help students play the main role of learning [19–22]. Through appropriate teaching methods and teaching design in line with distance education, the students' learning enthusiasm, initiative and creativity can be fully aroused and the role of students from passive knowledge receiver to active learning participant can be transformed. Enable students to "learn at home with mind" and realize the substantive equivalent of teaching quality between online learning and offline classroom.

5 Conclusion

The flipping classroom based on "SPOC + MOOC Class + Tencent Meeting" is an innovative practice of curriculum teaching reform in the era of "Internet +" and during the epidemic situation, which enables teachers and students to form an organic whole of co-learning, co-research and co-progress before, during and after class. SPOC can bring students a fine, interactive, seminar-oriented and professional learning experience; MOOC Class can objectively and truly integrate all the data of classroom teaching, make the learning effect digital and visual, and help teachers to manage and evaluate students efficiently [23, 24]. Tencent Meeting live teaching can strengthen teachers and students' online classroom participation and teaching identity; flipping classroom can increase teachers and students' communication and interaction, making students broaden the depth and breadth of knowledge in the class. The four teaching methods complement each other to ensure the quality of online teaching.

References

1. Li, M., Zhang, H.: China Audio-Visual Education, (04), 8–15 2020
2. The Ministry of Education shall address the novel Coronavirus pneumonia outbreak Task Force office.On ordinary institutions of higher learning online during the epidemic prevention and control guidance of teaching organization and management [EB/OL]. [2020–9–28]. http://www.gov.cn/zhengce/zhengceku/2020-02/05/content_5474733.htm
3. Zhiyi, L.: My opinion on water course and golden course. Chin. Univ. Teach. **12**, 24–29 (2018)
4. Zhang, J., Liu, L., Yao, S., Zhang, Y.: Online teaching practice based on SPOC+mooc classroom + Tencent conference + WeChat group -- taking instrumental analysis course as an example [J/OL].University chemistry: 1–7 [2020–10–20]. http://kns.cnki.net/kcms/detail/11.1815.O6.20200707.1350.014.html
5. Wang, H., Wang, Z., Wang, Q., Cui, Y., Gao, X.: Online teaching Model of SPOC+ Tencent Conference in the context of coVID-19. J. Nanchang Norm. Univ. (03), 61–63 (2020)
6. The Ministry of Education higher education department director Wu Yan curriculum construction in colleges and universities put forward clear requirements for the future [EB/OL]. [2020–10–11]. http://www.pjtime.com/2020/5/352712691839.shtml
7. Li, W., et al.: Bibliometric analysis of the application of LAN Moyun class in nursing field in China. Gen. Nurs. **19**(08), 1009–1012 (2021)
8. Yin, J., Li, S., Zhang, X.: Multi center and multi-dimensional teaching method framework construction and its application research. Sci. Educ. Wenhui (Zhongxunjiao), (03), 59–63 (2021)
9. Liu, Y., Huang, W.: Application of flipped classroom model in fruit and vegetable processing technology. Sci. Educ. Wenhui (Zhongxunjue), (03), 90–91+96 (2021)
10. Bai, L.: Application of flipped classroom in medical microbiology teaching under the background of Internet plus. Sci. Educ. Wenhui (middle and low) (03), 117–118 (2021)
11. Chunxing, L., Yong, Z.: Research on the application of flipped classroom in middle school physics teaching . Sci. Educ. Wenhui (Zhongxun J.), (03), 163–164 (2021)
12. Chaorong, Y., Cai, Y., Xie, M., Huang, W.: Investigation and analysis on the status quo and demand of standardized training for operating room nurses in 45 secondary and above hospitals in Guangdong Province. Gen. Nurs. **19**(08), 1129–1132 (2021)
13. Li, Y.: Discussion on the core course teaching of Engineering cost specialty in application-oriented Universities under the background of informatization. J. Heilongjiang Ecol. Eng. Vocat. Coll. **34**(02), 133–135+160 (2021)

14. Yao, Z.: Research on flipped classroom blended teaching mode based on higher vocational learning situation – taking Hotel communication skills course as an example . J. Manage. Cadre Coll. State Forest. Grassland Adm. **20**(01), 50–56 (2021)
15. Haiyan, L., Gan, L.: Application of flipped classroom teaching in fixed vision training before femtosecond laser small incision corneal stromal lens removal . Med. Vocat. Educ. Mod. Nurs. **4**(02), 175–178 (2021)
16. Xuefeng, L., Junxian, M.: Two wing flipped hybrid online teaching practice based on improving digital autonomous learning ability – taking physical chemistry course as an example . High. Educ. Forum (03), 23–28 (2021)
17. Wang, X., Kangyuan, W., Liang, X., Lu, H.: The experimental teaching design ofInternet plus flip classroom. China Mod. Educ. Equipment, (05), 25-28 (2021)
18. Yongqiang, W., Ruili, J., Ming, L., Han, L., Wenchao, T.: Exploration on teaching mode of MATLAB image processing course combining science and education . China Mod. Educ. Equip. (05), 111–113 (2021)
19. Yang, X.: Research on mixed teaching mode based on MOOC, SPOC, micro class and flipped classroom –Taking engineering survey course teaching as an example . Fujian Build. Mater. (03), 116–118 (2021)
20. Changbin, Y., Li, M., Zhang, J., Li, R., Wang, H.: Online and offline same frequency resonance: reflections on classroom teaching reform in the post epidemic era. J. North China Univ. Technol. (Soc. Sci. Ed.), **21**(02), 86–91+103 (2021)
21. Huiying, Z.: Exploration on the application of flipped classroom mode of micro Curriculum – taking college English teaching as an example. J. North China Univ. Technol. (Soc. Sci. Ed.) **21**(02), 92–98 (2021)
22. Cai, H., Nafen, B., Lu, D.: Application of target management teaching method combined with flipped classroom in nursing teaching in operating roo. China Clin. Res. **34**(03), 380–382 (2021)
23. Yin, B., Xu, W.: Teaching practice of graduate quantum chemistry based on flipped classroom concept . J. Southwest Norm. Univ. (Natl. Sci. Ed.), **46**(03), 201–205 (2021)
24. Chen, W.: Application of flipped classroom in junior high school chemistry teaching under micro class platform. Math. Phys. Chem. Middle Sch. Stud. (Teach. Learn.) (03), 10 (2021)

Application of Computer Visualization Technology in Intelligent Education Management

Dongxiao Mo[1], Jiaqi Yan[2], Tingting Li[3], and Chun Jiang[4(✉)]

[1] Faculty of Educational Studies, Universiti Putra Malaysia, Selangor, Malaysia
[2] Management and Science University, Alam, Malaysia
[3] Multimedia University, Cyberjaya, Malaysia
[4] Nanning University, Nannning, China

Abstract. The rise of education informatization, big data and cloud computing has brought new opportunities for education management. Combined with the development of artificial intelligence and the needs of education in the new era, this paper introduces the concept of visual management to build a smart education management system of smart teaching, smart environment, smart management, smart evaluation, smart research and smart service. Taking Hunan Industrial and Commercial University as an example, this paper explores the practical contents and application scenarios of the construction of education management system through the application of visualization technology in intelligent education management, and promotes the school management behaviors such as educational resources, teaching environment, teaching evaluation, teacher-student activities, security and other school management behaviors to a new height, Finally, the adjustment and optimization direction of visual application of education management system is prospected.

Keywords: Smart education · Education management system · Big data · Visualization

1 Introduction

With the rapid development of Internet of things, cloud computing, big data, ubiquitous network, artificial intelligence and other new technologies, China's education management has entered the intelligent era rapidly. Artificial intelligence has rapidly promoted the change of educational ecology and has a wide application prospect in the field of education, which can effectively overcome the shortcomings of traditional education [1]. In the era of intelligence, it is an inevitable trend of history to carry out wisdom education in an all-round way. The integration of cloud computing and big data and other information technologies into the society provides a support platform for smart education. The horizon report (Higher Education Edition) released by the new media alliance has repeatedly mentioned that intelligent information technologies, such as artificial intelligence,

© ICST Institute for Computer Sciences, Social Informatics and Telecommunications Engineering 2021
Published by Springer Nature Switzerland AG 2021. All Rights Reserved
M. A. Jan and F. Khan (Eds.): BigIoT-EDU 2021, LNICST 391, pp. 395–403, 2021.
https://doi.org/10.1007/978-3-030-87900-6_46

virtual technology, robot, Internet of things, blockchain and visualization technology, are helpful to education reform. Under this background, the ten-year development plan of education informatization (2011–2020) puts forward the requirements of "promoting the deep integration of information technology and education teaching"; while the action plan of education informatization 2.0 proposes to promote the construction of intelligent teaching system of colleges and universities facing the new generation network, and comprehensively build the public service system of education informatization, We should strive to achieve the three major goals of the "two high" strategy.

2   Construction of Intelligent Education Management System

The construction of intelligent education management system is the direction of the development of higher education informatization in China, which can promote the development of school education and teaching and meet the needs of selecting innovative talents in the new era. In the future, the development of education informatization in Colleges and universities in China will develop towards the trend of full integration of teaching resources, informatization of data, unification of management standards, and intellectualization of evaluation system. Based on the smart campus data center, this research has built a smart education management system by making full use of the digital campus environment, Internet of things, cloud computing, big data, ubiquitous network and other technologies. This system realizes six kinds of smart education businesses, including smart teaching, smart environment, smart evaluation, smart management, smart research and smart service, and provides new interactive application scenarios for teachers, students, parents, managers and other users, integrating teaching, evaluation, scientific research and management with the new big data application platform, It is used to realize the visibility of information perception, the clarity of application interaction, the flexibility of educational means and the timeliness of service response. At the same time, the availability of intelligent education management system is guaranteed by visual security platform, which reflects the fusion characteristics. It makes intelligent and advanced classroom teaching environment, ubiquitous network learning platform, transparent and efficient education management system, innovative network research environment, accurate and reliable teaching evaluation system and online and offline intimate teaching service platform become reality [2].

3   Interactive Technology of Surface Rendering and Visualization Based on MC Algorithm

3.1   Fundamentals of Surface Rendering Algorithm

Definition of voxel: eight adjacent points in the upper and lower layers of volume data field, as shown in Fig. 1. These eight points are called voxel corners, and their gray values are called voxel values. If medical imaging equipment samples uniformly in X, y and Z directions, the voxel values of any point in voxel can be represented by the combination of voxel values of eight vertices of voxel. In order to determine the way of

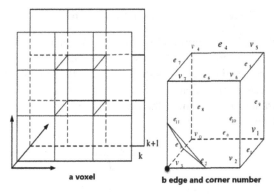

Fig. 1. Definition of voxels.

contour cutting voxels and find the configuration of voxels quickly and conveniently, 8 corners and 12 edges of voxels are labeled.

If the layer spacing is much larger than the pixel spacing, the volume data field should be normalized, that is, the spacing of voxel x, y, Z is changed to 1:1:1. The normalization of volume data field is mainly divided into three steps: first, determine the standard value D of data field normalization, find out the minimum distance from X, y, Z, and regard it as the standard value, which is generally selected from the XY direction; second, two-dimensional image normalization, changing the spacing of X and y to D; third, normalizing the image sequence along the z-axis direction, so that the spacing of X, y, Z becomes D, so that x, y, Z are changed to d, The distance between Z becomes 1:1:1.

3.2 Isosurface

The purpose of surface rendering algorithm is to construct isosurface which can represent three-dimensional object from volume data. In the introduction of voxels, we learned that the voxel values of non sampling points can be represented by the combination of voxel values of eight corners of voxels, so any point in voxels has physical significance, because according to the principle of MRI image and CT image imaging, the same tissue should have the same pixel value [3]. The combination of points with the same voxel value will inevitably form one or more surfaces, such a surface is called isosurface. Different tissues of human body can be represented by selecting appropriate isosurface. According to the above expression, the isosurface can be expressed as:

$$\{x, y, z | f(x, y, z) = c\}, c \text{ is a constant} \tag{1}$$

In the process of 3D reconstruction, the general 3D reconstruction algorithm uses geometric patches to simulate the isosurface in voxels to simplify the calculation. The moving cube algorithm introduced in this chapter is to generate triangular patches in voxels, which are used to simulate the isosurface, and finally draw the three-dimensional model.

3.3 Calculation of Vertex Position of Triangular Patch

The basic assumption of MC algorithm is that when the density of 3D discrete data is large, voxel values can be considered to vary linearly along the edges of voxels. Based on the above assumptions, the spatial positions of the vertices of the triangular patch can be calculated by linear interpolation.

When L is parallel to x direction, the threshold value of isosurface is c, and the calculation formula of x is as follows:

$$x = i + \frac{c - f(v_1)}{f(v_2) - f(v_1)} \tag{2}$$

4 Simulation for Teacher Portrait and Student Portrait System

Through the data fusion and mining of teaching administration system, personnel system, scientific research system, library system, network behavior management system and other data samples, we can record, track and master the students' learning characteristics, life rules and network usage in the whole process and all-round way, so as to design flexible learning and life paths for students, and dynamically adapt and adjust education policies, The implementation of intervention education management will eventually return to the "student-centered" nature of education. The student portrait system shows the trend of students' personal achievement, the optimal value of GPA, and the comparison of the optimal value of excellent courses. It can provide learning suggestions for teachers and students through the predictive analysis engine [4]. Simulation for Teacher portrait and student Portrait System are shown in Fig. 2 and Fig. 3.

In order to ensure the safe and stable operation of the education business system, the campus network has deployed the next generation firewall, network behavior management, database audit, intrusion detection, vulnerability scanning system and other security systems. Due to the massive security logs generated by various security systems

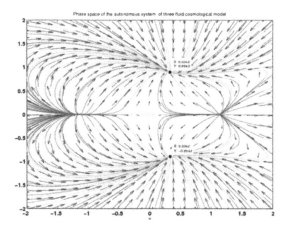

Fig. 2. Teacher portrait system

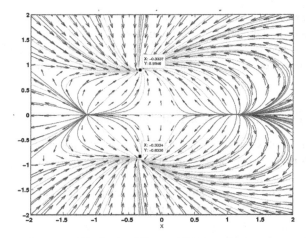

Fig. 3. Students portrait system

every day, and it is difficult for system administrators to analyze the security status, weak links and attacked objects of campus network from these text information, in order to make the systems more easily perceived and respond in time, the university has developed various visual security platforms, So as to ensure the stable and safe operation of various businesses.

5 Demand Analysis and Development Strategy of Smart Education Platform

5.1 Demand Analysis of Smart Education Platform

Based on the analysis of the current situation and problems of the existing smart education platform, we can find that a perfect smart education platform needs to realize the following aspects: smart learning and teaching, provide students with diversified online learning methods and real-time interactive functions, and carry out knowledge construction with information technology, so as to realize personalized learning. We need to gather excellent teachers in the field of education, establish a huge network teaching team, realize teachers' timely online guidance and resource sharing, and let teachers become the designers, organizers and instructors of students' platform learning and platform activities. In terms of intelligent management, the teaching management of the platform needs more effective, faster and more convenient technical environment support. Visualization and automation of the platform operation, real-time monitoring of the education and teaching status of the platform, and the realization of comprehensive remote guidance. The real-time communication and cooperation of each system of the platform can realize seamless information exchange and business cooperation. The corresponding teaching information, teaching resources and platform services are pushed to users through the situational perception of learning and teaching [5].

In terms of intelligent scientific research and evaluation, the platform's scientific research and evaluation need to rely on big data technology, change from experience based to data-based, and conduct more diversified and intelligent analysis and evaluation of various sources in the platform's teaching process. At the same time, cloud storage technology is applied to permanently store the classified data in the cloud, so as to regularly evaluate the development of users and put forward more targeted development suggestions [6].

5.2 Development Strategy of Smart Education Platform

From the demand analysis of smart education platform, we can find that the current smart education platform has many shortcomings in platform construction and development, smart teaching, smart learning, smart management, smart research, smart evaluation, smart service and so on. Therefore, for the future development needs of smart education platform, the following aspects should be realized:

(1) The construction and development of smart education platform should show the educational concept of smart education and realize the educational demand of smart education. The most important thing is that the national government must formulate specific theoretical guidance, overall planning, unified industry construction standards and operation specifications for the construction and development of the smart education platform, so that the smart education platform has a clear development direction and goals in the process of construction, development and operation, Unified construction planning industry standards and reasonable platform organization classification and system guarantee. So as to ensure the infrastructure construction and system application development of the intelligent education platform, promote the large-scale promotion and comprehensive application of the intelligent education platform, and improve the dynamic monitoring and supervision mechanism, fundamentally promote and ensure the construction and development of the intelligent education platform, and avoid all kinds of problems caused by the system confusion.

(2) In the initial stage of platform construction, it is necessary to formulate the corresponding internal comprehensive and standardized construction and operation scheme of the platform. From the classification and arrangement of teaching courses to the certification and examination of curriculum resources; from the certification of teachers' technical ability and qualification level to the empirical investigation of schools (educational institutions); from the integration of education and teaching forms (video broadcast, online live broadcast, real classroom assistance, etc.) to the intelligent teaching process (interactive classroom, virtual practice, etc.); From diversified teaching exchange and discussion methods to reasonable and humanized platform service settings, from standardized and concise platform management mechanism to scientific and empirical scientific research data analysis and evaluation, we must formulate platform construction and operation standards with comprehensive scope, continuous development and scientific theoretical basis [7].

(3) To establish a smart education platform serving users, smart education platform should be truly integrated into the current people's learning and life, and become a necessary tool and primary way for all kinds of users in the process of education and learning. First of all, it is necessary to improve the information technology

literacy of all kinds of users (including students, teachers, schools, etc.) in the intelligent education platform learning, so that all kinds of users in the platform can achieve barrier free learning and communication; at the same time, according to the education and teaching needs of all kinds of users, the platform should be able to develop a perfect online course learning system [8].

(4) Strengthen the management system of smart education platform. The construction and operation of smart education platform need a comprehensive, standardized and mandatory platform management system. The comprehensive management of smart education platform, first of all, is that the platform should aim at the different needs and behaviors of all kinds of users, and formulate a management system that can cover all aspects of platform operation. Then, the management system of smart education platform should be in line with the actual experience needs of users and relevant platform development specifications. Finally, the management system of the platform should be enforced to every aspect of the platform operation and development. Only by strengthening the management system of smart education platform, can we effectively regulate, control and improve the platform curriculum production and teaching practice of teachers (lecturers) and schools (educational institutions), and create a safer, more reasonable and more scientific learning environment for students.

6 Research on the Design of Smart Education Platform

6.1 Overall Design Architecture of Smart Education Platform

From the research on smart education platform, we can see that information technologies such as Internet, cloud computing, big data, mobile communication, Internet of things and artificial intelligence are the foundation of smart education construction, so the construction of smart education platform framework is destined to be a project set up at the top of information technology and education resources, It is a systematic education project with large scale, high technical difficulty, complex frame structure and extensive aspects. Therefore, we must make a unified overall planning for the construction of the platform, so that the construction and development of the platform can truly meet the needs of the concept of wisdom education, adapt to the needs of the development of education, integrate the educational resources of all parties, solve the current situation of the wisdom education platform, and design a scientific and reasonable wisdom education platform [9].

In the construction of smart education platform, infrastructure/equipment providers, software/application developers and banks/financial institutions should make full use of cloud computing, Internet of things, big data and other resources, and rely on cloud storage, parallel computing, data mining and virtualization technology (mware) to design cloud server and various virtualization software for smart education platform, In order to develop the necessary mobile learning system, intelligent teaching system, intelligent management system, data resource center system and other systems, as well as the application software to meet the development requirements. At the same time, all the daily maintenance and security protection of the platform (storage data security, network system security, terminal platform security, data backup) also need the technical and financial support of various providers and financial institutions. Local governments and education departments play a leading and regulatory role in the construction and development of smart education platform. National education guidelines and policies are conveyed to all departments of platform construction and maintenance through local governments and education departments; similarly, for all kinds of situations in the operation of smart education platform, local governments and education departments also play a regulatory role, so as to make the construction of platform follow the development direction of national education.

6.2 Overall Hierarchical Structure of Smart Education Platform

In the intelligent education platform, the design and construction of the platform can be divided into user layer, terminal layer and application layer according to different organizational stages [10].

(1) User layer. The user layer of smart education platform includes two aspects: users and administrators. Specifically, it mainly includes students, teachers, parents, the public, administrators, schools and educational institutions. In the smart education platform, different users can log in to the corresponding platform service section according to different permissions, and use or manage all kinds of smart education services within their permissions [11].

(2) Terminal layer. The terminal layer of smart education platform refers to the necessary intelligent terminal devices for all kinds of users to use the platform system [12]. Specifically, it includes smart phones, iPads, computers, cameras, infrared sensors, heart rate sensing bracelets and other smart education wearable devices. The use of all kinds of intelligent terminal devices can not only optimize the user's experience in the learning service of the intelligent education platform, but also enable the platform to collect all kinds of relevant data through the use of users, providing data support for the mining and analysis of educational big data [13].

(3) Application layer refers to all kinds of application systems specifically set up for different levels and directions of learning needs and service needs in the smart education platform [14]. It mainly includes smart campus, smart classroom, digital library and distance teaching. Smart campus and smart classroom are oriented to all kinds of students and teachers. Through the construction of smart education platform, the data center, multimedia classroom, voice classroom, computer room, staff office, student dormitory and Library in real middle school can be connected with each other; at the same time, the schools can be connected with each other [15]. So as to realize the effective integration and sharing of various educational resources and optimize the distribution of educational resources. Shuyu library is an educational and learning sharing resource that is open to all users in the intelligent education platform through the Internet by using digital technology to process and store the existing library resources.

7 Conclusion

With the prevalence of big data and artificial intelligence, colleges and universities need to integrate all kinds of resources inside and outside the school, build a data sharing platform, improve the digital literacy of teachers and students, accelerate the deep integration of modern information technology and teaching practice, and explore a new education management system and a new mechanism of education and teaching operation in line with the era background. At present, the visualization application of smart education management system is still in the primary stage, which needs to be continuously adjusted and optimized, and implemented and promoted step by step. Knowledge map, word cloud and 3D technology are the means and tools of knowledge visualization for harmonious integration of education and technology. Whether it is static or dynamic graphics and images, whether it is two-dimensional or three-dimensional space, technology can give it new functions to change the teaching mode and method of teachers, optimize the cognitive ability of learners and promote their learning ability. The goal of wisdom education is no longer to cultivate knowledge-based talents, but innovative talents. To achieve this goal, the innovation of teaching means is indispensable.

References

1. Yang, X., Zhang, H., Guo, L., et al.: The development problems and breakthrough paths of educational artificial intelligence. Mod. Dist. Educ. Res. (3), 30–38 (2018)
2. Song, L., Xu, L.: The logical starting point and boundary of the application of artificial intelligence in education – taking knowledge learning as an example . Audio Vis. Educ. China (6), 14–20 (2019)
3. Li, B.: Research on 3D visualization technology in 3D conformal radiotherapy planning. South China University of Technology (2007)
4. Dayang, J., Yao, Q.: Design and research of intelligent visual teaching environment . China Mod. Educ. Equipment (21), 96–99 (2016)
5. Wei, W.: IBM's smart earth strategy and China's countermeasures . Henan Sci. Technol. (10), 236 (2013)
6. Haiquan, A.: Intelligent education and informatization teaching. Off. Autom. Acad. Ed. (1), 31–32 (2015)
7. Yang, X., Tang, S., Li, J.: Big data of development education: connotation, value and challenge . Res. Mod. Dist. Educ. (1), 50–61 (2016)
8. Zhang, H.: The influence of learning analysis technology on distance education teaching mode under the background of big data. New Campus J. (3), 89–90 (2016)
9. Xin, N., Wang, L., Wang, F.: The role of modern educational technology in teaching reform and innovation . Sci. Educ. Guide Electron. Ed. (13), 37 (2013)
10. Shao, S.: Survey and analysis on learning needs of distance education learners of aopeng . J. Chongqing Radio TV Univ. 21(3), 15–17 (2009)
11. Yang, X.: Discussion on the construction and key issues of regional intelligent education comprehensive service platform . Mod. Dist. Educ. Res. (1), 72–81 (2015)
12. Hu, L., Zhang, X., Tang, L.: Research on the construction of smart education cloud platform under the background of big data . Comput. Knowl. Technol. 11(7x), 109–111 (2015)
13. Ge, H.: Exploration on the construction of regional smart education based on the concept of cloud computing . China Educ. Informatization (20), 72–74 (2012)
14. Zhang, J., Huang, R., Zhang, L.: Smart education cloud service: a new mode of education Information Service . Open Educ. Res. 18(3), 20–26 (2012)
15. Chen, Y., Yang, X., Che, I, Yao, H., et al.: Development strategy of international smart education and Its enlightenment to China. Mod. Educ. Technol. 24(10), 5–11 (2014)

Research on the Design of University Sports Teaching System Based on Cloud Computing

Ronghan Wang[✉] and Jinyao Liu

Jiangxi College of Applied Technology, Ganzhou 341000, Jiangxi, China

Abstract. In this paper, we conduct an in-depth analysis and research on physical education teaching systems in colleges and universities through cloud computing-related technology, and design a physical education teaching system. The historical process of developing and utilizing educational resources, promoting knowledge innovation, and sharing, and promoting profound changes in educational ideas, concepts, models, contents, and methods. Education informatization is conducive to optimizing the structure of the educational community, rationalizing the allocation of educational resources, and improving the quality and management of education. Its technical characteristics are digitalization, networking, and intelligence, and its basic features are openness, sharing, interaction, and collaboration, and information technology penetrates all kinds of educational management, teaching, and scientific research, influencing and determining the overall situation and direction of educational reform and development. A more comprehensive and integrated quantitative process evaluation of students' physical education performance at school will also yield more objective evaluation results.

Keywords: Cloud computing · Physical education teaching system · Design research

1 Introduction

The physical education model in colleges and universities refers to the implementation of a system of educational strategies that use physical activity to promote the overall physical and mental development of students. It contains physical education cognitive education, physical education curriculum implementation, physical education teaching content, physical education extracurricular activities, and physical education performance evaluation in five aspects [1]. Physical education cloud refers to a comprehensive college sports model built according to the general rules and principles of college physical education by using cloud computing as technical support to achieve more optimal college sports implementation, monitoring, and management.

However, according to the results of the questionnaire, 423 out of 500 school students, or 84.6%, were willing to receive scientific physical fitness instruction in extracurricular physical education activities, which means that most students are still willing to receive scientific knowledge in sports-related aspects [2]. At present, colleges and universities

M. A. Jan and F. Khan (Eds.): BigIoT-EDU 2021, LNICST 391, pp. 404–412, 2021.
https://doi.org/10.1007/978-3-030-87900-6_47

do not pay enough attention to the teaching of physical education cognitive aspects, and the development and cultivation of students' motivation are not enough.

College students have studied physical health and education for nearly 12 years, but few of them know a series of basic knowledge of exercise physiology and exercise rehabilitation. They only know to follow the teacher's requirements to complete the tasks in a physical education class, but they do not know why they should do these exercises, what are the benefits of doing these exercises, or whether these exercises are suitable for them. Most of the students are only concerned about their grades in physical education classes, and the exercises they do outside of class are usually for exams, not for spontaneous scientific physical exercise. However, according to the results of the questionnaire, 423 students out of 500 university students were willing to receive scientific physical fitness instruction in extra-curricular activities of physical education, accounting for 84.6%, which means that most students are still willing to receive scientific knowledge in sports-related aspects.

2 Related Studies

Shaw supplemented his students' lessons by recording instructional videos and then dubbing the videos [3]. Today, the flipped classroom continues to play a role in changing the traditional teaching model from one in which the teacher explains the knowledge in class and the students do the homework after class to one in which the teacher sends the learning tasks to the students in advance and the student's study and complete the tasks outside of class time through the system; in class, the teacher answers the questions that the students encounter during their study [4]. The teacher has changed from being a teacher to a tutor.

Yang et al. collected video resources through channels such as TV recording, videotape conversion, CD conversion, network download, and network integration, and after format conversion, designed a platform for sports video integration through the integration of these resources, integrating various sports videos of various disciplines and specialties to play a reference role for teaching and research; secondly, playing the specialties of school sports, the various sports videos are specialized cutting, description, and analysis for special research; the authors describe in detail the whole process of this characteristic video library from conception to concrete implementation, especially focusing on the characteristics and installation and use of the open-source system, which is powerful and scalable [5].

Because each student is influenced by genetic factors, physical performance varies. Some students do not need to work very hard in a physical education class and do not need to spend effort after class, and they can achieve excellent grades in physical education class because of their good innate qualities, while some students can only achieve just passing grades because of genetic factors, even if they take physical education class seriously and work hard after class. In this respect, the fairness of our evaluation criteria is not ideal [6]. Therefore, we need to add process evaluation to outcome evaluation. To objectively evaluate students' learning, both outcome and process evaluations need to be quantified. While outcome assessment can be quantified, process assessment has not been a good quantified solution in the current physical education management system.

3 Cloud Computing Physical Education System Analysis and Design

3.1 Cloud Computing Design

Currently, there is no uniform and clear definition of cloud computing in the industry, but there are several expressions of cloud computing that are widely accepted. According to Wikipedia, cloud computing is an Internet-based computing method that provides on-demand supply for computers or other devices through the sharing of hardware and software resources and information in a grid-like manner [7]. In this paper, cloud computing is based on virtualization technology and Internet-based technology to manage numerous distributed hardware and software resources and to realize the unified management of resources, and collaborative work. Since this paper mainly applies cloud computing technology to realize enterprise project management from the perspective of enterprise project management, we understand cloud computing technology from two aspects: on the one hand, we use Hadoop technology to manage many hardware and software resources, and provide a resource storage platform with huge storage capacity for enterprise project management system; on the other hand, we unify project management-related information management to provide services for all parties of the project management system. On the other hand, the information related to project management is managed in a unified manner, and a standardized and unified information service interface is provided for all users of the project management system.

Hadoop Distributed File System (HDFS) is a distributed file storage system with high throughput, suitable for storing large amounts of data at the PB level. HDFS adopts a master/slave master/slave structure, including a Name Node master node with master task and several Data Node slave nodes with worker task. The HDFS uses a master/slave architecture, which consists of a Name Node master with the task of master and several Data Node slaves with the task of worker. The overall architecture of HDFS is shown in Fig. 1.

The Data Node is the worker node responsible for storing the file blocks and responding to the operations of the Name Node on the data blocks and client read and write requests. Name Node processes the data stored on the Data Node after receiving heartbeat information from the Data Node. The Data Node is organized using racks, and each file in the HDFS file system has two backup data blocks. Different backup data is stored on different racks to ensure the security of Data Node data nodes on different racks.

A data warehouse integrates historical data information over some time, rather than simply recording current state information [8]. Therefore, most of the data in the data warehouse carries time information, which provides data support for changes in transactions and analysis of future trends. Data in the data warehouse is mainly used to be queried and statistics, and is rarely modified. Therefore, the stability characteristic of the data warehouse means that the data in the data warehouse will not be changed by another. However, new data will be added to the data warehouse periodically, so the stability of the data warehouse is only relatively stable. The relative stability characteristic of a data warehouse ensures the continuity of data in a data warehouse, and ensures that the operation of data in a data warehouse does not need to consider concurrency control.

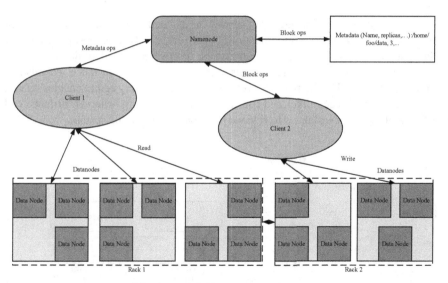

Fig. 1. HDFS file system architecture

3.2 Design of Physical Education System in Colleges and Universities

We can adopt a one-library-one-table model for the system, i.e., a microservice corresponds to a separate data house. This one-library-one-table model can realize the features of a separate process, separate deployment, separate development, and separate maintenance for each service [9]. When a microservice needs to be upgraded or maintained, it can well avoid the shadow of other services. The system has 5 functional modules and is designed into 5 microservices, each of which contains business source code and database, namely: statistics centre service, information management service, data centre service, micro-video on-demand service, and teaching interactive service. Each microservice in the system corresponds to a different functional module, and the services are developed, installed, and maintained separately from each other. The teaching support platform also includes many Spring Cloud service base components for implementing the microservice architecture to assist in realizing the whole system architecture. The system architecture design is shown in Fig. 2.

Microservices exist in the system as separate program modules, and developers can manually modify the parameters to configure various parameters of the services such as ports and addresses in the configuration files of microservices so that they can realize mutual remote invocation between services and achieve mutual invocation implementation. As the parameters of the microservice are modified, other services will not be able to find the modified service directly, and as the project grows, the configuration file will also become bigger after the project becomes bigger, then the manual maintenance of the configuration parameters will become unsuitable, which is not conducive to the weak coupling feature of microservice. The registration of configuration parameters can be solved by the Service Registration and Discovery Centre, which can register the service list for discovery and reduce the maintenance of programmers. When the parameters of a microservice module are changed, other services associated with it can continue to communicate with it without other modifications, which effectively improves the scalability of the system [10]. A single service can also be discovered and identified by service governance if it runs several instance units at the same time, and instances can also be combined as needed. The microservice registration and discovery centre enables service processes to identify each other and can resolve the failure rate when an instance call fails by invoking other instances to achieve high availability of the system.

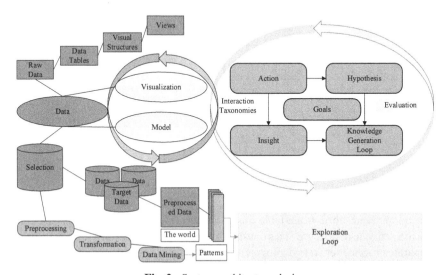

Fig. 2. System architecture design

This project adopts the microservice architecture system. Docker is a set of opensource programs that enables virtualization-based packaging of container technology, which is currently used in many industries. Docker's container technology has many advantages, such as Docker containers have the runtime environment required for a single microservice, which makes it very convenient to shift the value of the program and reduce the deployment time of the deployer through a unified deployment implementation; program design engineers can simulate the user scenario in the design coding scenario to achieve the design coding scenario and the user scenario Consistent, preventing errors caused by different environments; when changing the physical location of deployment, it can achieve rapid migration and deploy specific microservices to different environments.

4   Results Analysis

The results of the survey of 30 physical education teachers showed that all of them gave feedback on the evaluation results after the evaluation. In terms of the content of feedback, 53.33% of physical education teachers were not clear about the specific content of feedback, so that more than half of the physical education teachers were not clear about the results of evaluation feedback, and the content of feedback was relatively single; in terms of the timing of feedback, as shown in Fig. 3, the timing of feedback was mainly at the beginning of the new semester before giving feedback to teachers and after some time (this semester), so the feedback In terms of the timing of feedback, as shown in Fig. 3, the timing of feedback is mainly at the beginning of the new semester and after a while (this semester), so the feedback is not timely, which leads to most physical education teachers not paying attention to the feedback results; from the way of feedback, the way of feedback is mainly private conversation feedback, posting on the public board and written feedback, which is old and lack of openness, so the way of feedback should keep up with the times, such as online feedback, and the feedback should be more open, so that physical education teachers pay attention to the feedback results.

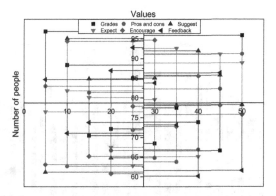

Fig. 3. Feedback content

From Fig. 4, the content of the evaluation of students' physical education is based on physical education theoretical knowledge, motor skills, classroom performance, and

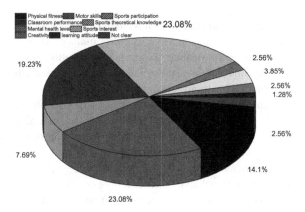

Fig. 4. Evaluation content

physical quality, and neglects the evaluation of students' innovation ability, sports interest, and mental health level, so the content of the evaluation is too much emphasis on some common contents and neglects the differences of individual students.

As shown in Fig. 5, the average number of 13 secondary indicators in the first round was greater than 3.5, indicating that the primary design of secondary indicators was approved by experts; 11 items had coefficients of variation less than 0.25, but the coefficients of variation of physical fitness and physical quality were still greater than 0.25, indicating that these two items needed to be adjusted, and some experts pointed out that the indicator of physical quality included the indicator of physical fitness. These two items should not exist side by side, and the indicator of basic knowledge of sports theory also needs to be considered again. The Kendall's harmony coefficient in the graph is 0.087, which indicates that the experts' evaluation results are consistent but not highly coordinated.

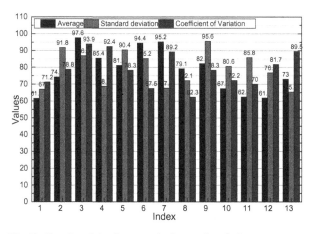

Fig. 5. Results of the first round of secondary index parameters

Education modernization and education informatization are the main strategies for us to promote teaching reform and improve teaching quality. As a computer science graduate student who has been working in secondary vocational schools for a long time, to promote the deep integration of information technology and education teaching and improve the quality of classroom teaching, this paper combines my work reality, analyses in detail the teaching problems existing in secondary vocational education, and proposes an education informatization strategy to optimize the traditional classroom teaching process and improve the quality of teaching through information technology. In other words, a distributed teaching aid system is developed to assist teachers in the classroom teaching process, and a series of traditional teaching behaviours are integrated with information technology to achieve better teaching results.

When users use the system, if the system response time is too long, it will cause a very poor experience. In general, the system users have a tolerance for the system response time within 5 s. Therefore, this system uses response time to test the performance of the system. The performance of the system is evaluated by simulating concurrent accesses

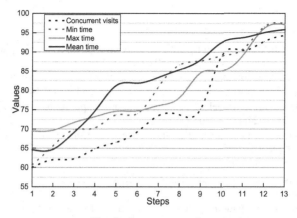

Fig. 6. Stress test results

to the system by different orders of magnitude of users at the same time, as shown in Fig. 6.

According to the test results, we can see that the system can maintain a good response time despite the increasing number of concurrent accesses to the system. The API gateway is the exit portal of the system, and it is the transit station of the system, which is directly facing the users, so the API gateway is chosen here to test the performance of the system. JMeter is used to test the performance of the API gateway to get a general understanding of the performance of the whole system.

5 Conclusion

This paper analyses the architecture system used in this system, and concludes the development and characteristics of microservices, and studies the core technologies Spring Cloud and Spring Boot to implement microservices, through which the system is developed and designed to improve the performance and concurrency of the system. The feasibility, business requirements, performance requirements, and functional requirements of the system were analysed in the context of the actual situation of the secondary school, and the specific problems and functions to be solved by the system were clarified. Based on the requirement analysis, the system architecture is designed, and the teaching support system is divided into 5 functional modules, which are encapsulated into 5 independent microservice modules for design and development. This paper also designs and implements the core components of Spring Cloud such as service registration discovery and governance and API gateway. Finally, the system was tested to verify that the system functions properly, and the performance of the system was also tested to verify that the system has a good performance and can strongly support the real-time use of thousands of people in the university.

References

1. Zhang, X.Q., Tian, H.Y.: Research on digital education resource sharing platform based on cloud computing. Electr. Des. Eng. **3**(4), 502–513 (2017)
2. Wu, H., Li, G.: Visual communication design elements of Internet of Things based on cloud computing applied in graffiti art schema. Soft. Comput. **24**(11), 8077–8086 (2020)
3. Shaw, J.N., De Sarkar, T.: Model architecture for cloud computing-based library management. New Rev. Inf. Netw. **24**(1), 17–30 (2019)
4. Wang, J., Yang, Y., Wang, T., et al.: Big data service architecture: a survey. J. Internet Technol. **21**(2), 393–405 (2020)
5. Yang, J., Lee, T.Y., Chen, B., et al.: A comprehensive teaching reform model for a computer networks course based on integrated information systems. Int. J. Emerg. Technol. Learn. **14**(18), 76–91 (2019)
6. Yao, F.: Design and simulation of integrated education information teaching system based on fuzzy logic. J. Intell. Fuzzy Syst. **37**(4), 4687–4695 (2019)
7. Zhu, L., Wang, W., Shen, G.: Resource optimization combination method based on improved differential evolution algorithm for cloud manufacturing. Comput. Integr. Manuf. Syst. **23**(1), 203–214 (2017)
8. Jian, L., Youling, C., Long, W., et al.: An approach for service composition optimisation considering service correlation via a parallel max–min ant system based on the case library. Int. J. Comput. Integr. Manuf. **31**(12), 1174–1188 (2018)
9. Çakiroğlu, Ü., Erdemir, T.: Online project based learning via cloud computing: exploring roles of instructor and students. Interact. Learn. Environ. **27**(4), 547–566 (2019)
10. Cai, J.Y., Zhang, P.P.: The support environment construction for teaching and research of physical education based on emerging information technology. J. Comput. Theor. Nanosci. **14**(4), 2015–2020 (2017)

An Intelligent Piano Teaching System and Method Based on Cloud Platform

Qian Guo[✉]

College of Music Lan Zhou City University, 730070 Lanzhou, China

Abstract. This paper studies the intelligent piano teaching system and methods based on cloud platform, and the research results are as follows: combined with the current situation of piano teaching management and the needs of information construction, this paper analyzes and expounds the background, purpose, significance and feasibility of the design and implementation of the system, and summarizes the overview of the research progress of the system at home and abroad. The system uses B/S architecture as the system architecture, MVC pattern as the design pattern, SSH framework as the hierarchical structure of the main body of the system, and uses Java language to design and implement the system on the basis of structured design idea. The design and application of the system can provide a new idea for piano teaching management, and provide a normative and scientific technology management platform for the work.

Keywords: B/S structure · Piano teaching system · Cloud platform · Intelligence

1 Introduction

With the rapid development of computer science and technology, teaching methods are not becoming conventional, but a variety of teaching methods. Since the formulation and implementation of China's reform and opening-up policy, especially from the late 1980s to the early 1990s, with the rapid development of China's economy and the overall improvement of national quality, piano art has also shown a blowout development in China, and the number of people who can play and like piano has also increased significantly, and in many areas There has also been an upsurge of piano learning, and the number of people taking piano grade examination is increasing year by year, which shows that piano has been more and more loved by Chinese people. According to statistics, since China began to implement the piano amateur grade examination in 1990, the number of people participating in the piano grade examination has exceeded 300000, and is still increasing year by year, especially since the enrollment expansion of colleges and universities in our country, the number of people in higher education has been increased, followed by a further upsurge of piano learning, although many students have a better piano foundation Weak, but have a unique understanding of the piano and hobbies, have also joined the piano learning, also makes the school originally relatively weak piano teaching resources is difficult to meet the requirements of the new era of

© ICST Institute for Computer Sciences, Social Informatics and Telecommunications Engineering 2021
Published by Springer Nature Switzerland AG 2021. All Rights Reserved
M. A. Jan and F. Khan (Eds.): BigIoT-EDU 2021, LNICST 391, pp. 413–419, 2021.
https://doi.org/10.1007/978-3-030-87900-6_48

students on piano learning, and because of the traditional face-to-face teaching based piano teaching mode is also constantly, because of the increase in the number of students and make teaching more and more difficult Therefore, there is an urgent need for new piano teaching mode to improve this situation and provide better teaching services for piano learners.

The design and implementation of intelligent piano teaching management system based on cloud platform allows teachers to arrange piano teaching tasks with pertinence, including the overview of piano history, the study of basic piano theory, the training of piano cultivation, the creative style of piano score and piano playing skills and other theoretical knowledge related to piano, thus allowing students to use piano teaching software On the one hand, it reduces the teaching burden of teachers, but also provides students with a more optimized piano learning mode. Piano learning no longer needs to be limited by the learning site, the number of students and other conditions. It also provides a guarantee for better cultivating students' understanding of the piano score content and the sublimation of artistic experience.

When the intelligent piano teaching management system of cloud platform is implemented, MVC design idea is taken as the guidance, struts is used as the view display control component of program control, spring is used as the business logic processing control component, and Hibernate is used as the data access model, It not only realizes the sharing of data coupling between piano teaching data display and business processing, but also realizes the openness of piano teaching management system through the application of B/s, which allows piano teaching software to be better compatible with new application requirements according to the actual application requirements of teaching without affecting the previous operation functions, thus providing a more convenient platform for online promotion of piano teaching Stable support.

2   System Structure Analysis

2.1   B/S Structure

In the traditional two-tier C/S architecture, the system is divided into two layers, namely the presentation layer and the data layer, corresponding to the client and server respectively. In the three-tier C/S architecture, a function layer is added between the presentation layer and the data layer of the two-tier C/S architecture. The corresponding functions are added to process messages, applications, transactions, etc. the addition of the function layer avoids the shortcomings of the two-tier structure and greatly improves the scalability and stability of the designed system. The three-tier mode of C/S architecture is shown in Fig. 1.

B/S architecture is developed to improve the shortcomings of C/S architecture. B/S architecture has distinct characteristics, and most functions of the system are completed by browser [1]. The server side undertakes most of the functions and passes them to the user, while the script program has few functions. This kind of system running mode reduces the pressure of the server and the task of the client. Therefore, the scalability of the system is improved, and the maintenance cost in the later period is also alleviated to a certain extent. The B/S architecture is shown in Fig. 2. The reality of computer aided translation is very interesting: on the one hand, it is confused and ignored by translation

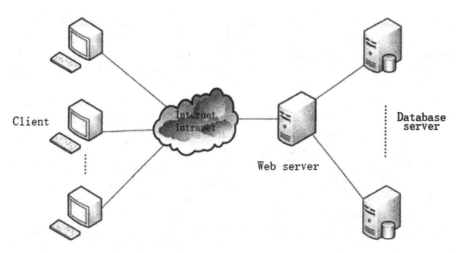

Fig. 1. Three tier C/S architecture

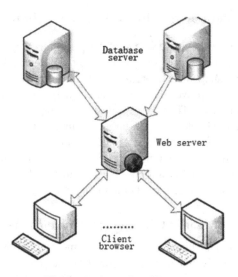

Fig. 2. Typical BS architecture

theories and teaching circles.Why computer-aided translation is ignored by teaching circles. The query process is shown in Fig. 2.

2.2 C/S Architecture

C/S architecture appeared in the 1980s. According to different layers, C/S architecture can be divided into three types, namely multi-layer structure, three-layer structure and two-layer structure. In CI/S architecture, two-layer structure is the most common. This section will discuss the basic principles of C/S architecture implementation and application from two-tier structure.

The two-tier C/S architecture divides the system into two parts, and the two parts are different. The roles and uses of each part in the system are different. The two parts complement each other to achieve the functions. The client sends the request to the server to complete the transaction. After receiving the request, the server processes the information and returns the result.

The work of C/S architecture is undertaken by the server and the client. The nature of the work undertaken by the two parts is different. The work undertaken by the server is the most important and the heaviest task. It is mainly to process the requests of the system users and return the processing results to the user interface. Different from the server side, the client side is simple in function implementation, and its main work is to interact with the customer, and transmit the customer's situation and data to the server side for processing. CIS architecture has obvious advantages, such as high computing efficiency and complete functions, but it also has many disadvantages, such as poor scalability, difficult maintenance and poor operability. These shortcomings of C/S architecture make its application subject to certain limitations, usually dealing with some simple transactions such as small data and non real time.

3 The Establishment of Intelligent Piano Teaching System

The design and implementation of the intelligent piano teaching management system based on cloud platform mainly provides a convenient, efficient and reasonable platform for the piano teaching management departments of colleges and universities or independent teaching units, and improves the scientific, electronic and scientific management level of the management work. Therefore, the design and implementation of piano teaching management system should have the target requirements of reliability, efficiency, integrity and integration. Reliability and efficiency are the basis, while integrity and integration are the basis for better improvement and expansion of the system. At the same time, when designing and developing the system, we should pay attention to the principles of practicality, advanced, aesthetic, maintainability and integrity [2].

3.1 Analysis on the Function of Curriculum Information Management

Another basic function in the piano teaching management system is the course information management function, which mainly realizes the management of all the course information involved in piano teaching, including adding courses, editing courses, querying courses and deleting courses. The use case diagram of course information management is shown in Fig. 3.

3.2 Analysis of Student Information Management Function

In the piano teaching management system, the most basic function is to manage the information of all the students in each training class. In this way, we can strengthen the comprehensive management of all the students in Colleges and universities or training classes [3], and understand the real-time information of the students in time. The functions of student information management include adding students, editing students, querying students and deleting students. Figure 4 shows the student information management use case diagram.

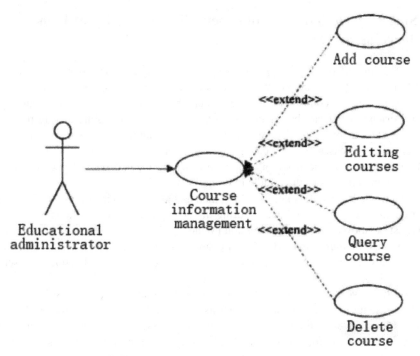

Fig. 3. Course information management chart

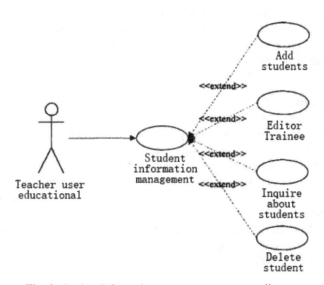

Fig. 4. Student information management use case diagram

4 Structure Design and Implementation of Intelligent Piano Teaching System

In the implementation of piano teaching management system, this paper mainly uses SSH Framework (i.e. Struts.Spring And Hibernate). Through this framework, not only the view, processing controller and database can be separated, but also the logic layer and persistence layer can be separated, so as to reduce the coupling among modules and layers and increase the degree of aggregation among modules. The independence of each layer increases, and the change of one layer has little impact on other layers. If the information in the front-end application layer changes, we only need to make corresponding changes to the middle layer in the model [4].

We have developed the piano teaching management system in B/S mode. The computer environment to be configured during the design is as follows: the operating system must be above Windows XP Version (Windows 7 is recommended), the computer memory must be higher than 1G, the CPU and browser of the computer have no hard requirements (IE browser is recommended), and the browsing mode should be set to 1024 * 768.

SSH framework divides the system into four different levels, the most basic is the system presentation layer, which uses struts framework. The framework used in the business logic layer of the system is spring framework. The persistence layer of the system uses hibernate framework. The last layer of SSH framework is the module layer. In these layers, struts is the basic part of the system. Through struts, the separation of model, view and controller, that is, the separation of MVC, can be completed, and the database can be connected through JDBC, so that the operation of the database will be more persistent. Spring plays a core role in supporting the business logic layer, reducing the coupling degree between the internal modules of the system and increasing the cohesion between the modules of the system.

5 Conclusion

In this paper, combined with the actual project and process of piano teaching management, Using SSH Framework Technology in J2EE technology system, the requirements analysis and system design of piano teaching management system suitable for universities and training institutions are carried out under B/S architecture. After using mature framework technology to determine the system structure framework, the system is implemented with Java language. After deployment and testing, it shows that the design and implementation of the system has basically completed the basic requirements and objectives of the system design.

References

1. Kun, D.: The idea of piano network teaching platform in Normal Universities – the extension of classroom teaching. Sci. Educ. Wenhui **3**(1), 31–36 (2009)
2. Zhou, X., Liu, Y., Wang, S.: Systematic teaching should be strengthened in universal Piano Education. Professional Time Space **8**(7), 43–46 (2011)

3. Qiaohua, Z.: Application research of C/s and B/S hybrid architecture in power management system. Softw. Guide **11**(5), 86–87 (2012)
4. Bingmao, L.: Teaching resource management system based on SSH framework and Ajax technology. Comput. Dev. Appl. **25**(1), 73–76 (2012)

Application and Countermeasure Research of Situational Simulation Teaching Method Under Big Data Analysis in the Teaching of Criminal Law in Colleges and Universities

Fen Li[✉]

Hainan Radio and Television University, Haikou 570000, Hainan, China
blzl2020@sina.com

Abstract. This paper mainly discusses the meaning of big data analysis situational simulation teaching method, expounds the advantages of criminal law situational simulation teaching, points out the requirements of criminal law situational simulation teaching, and puts forward the procedures and methods of organizing and implementing criminal law situational simulation teaching.

Keywords: Big data analysis · Scenario simulation · Teaching methods · Criminal law

1 Introduction

In the new situation, in order to cultivate a large number of high-quality criminal law talents, we must reform the traditional teaching methods of criminal law, adopt some new teaching methods to expand students' knowledge field, shorten the adaptation period of school theoretical study and social practice work, so that students can not only learn theoretical knowledge, but also exercise their legal work skills, So that they can adapt to the needs of their jobs in a short period of time after graduation from university and become a competent socialist legal worker. Based on the teaching purpose and teaching requirements, the author discusses the application of situational simulation teaching method in the teaching of criminal law according to the course practice of criminal law.

2 The Meaning of Situational Simulation Teaching Method

2.1 The Theoretical Basis of Situational Simulation Teaching Method

A Situational simulation teaching method is a new teaching method based on constructivism learning theory [1]. Constructivists believe that knowledge is not acquired by teachers, but by means of meaning construction with the help of other people (including teachers and learning partners) in a certain situation, that is, social and cultural

M. A. Jan and F. Khan (Eds.): BigIoT-EDU 2021, LNICST 391, pp. 420–428, 2021.
https://doi.org/10.1007/978-3-030-87900-6_49

background. From the perspective of learners, it focuses on how individuals construct knowledge based on their original experience, psychological structure and belief. By interacting with the surrounding social environment, learners interact the memory information and information processing strategies stored in the human brain with the current environmental information received, actively select, pay attention to, perceive, organize, store and activate information, and actively construct the meaning of information. This means that learners are not passively stimulated to move knowledge from the outside world to their memory. They should actively select and process the external information through the existing cognitive structure (including the original knowledge experience and cognitive strategies), and actively construct the meaning of information. The meaning of external information is not determined by the information itself, on the contrary, Meaning is formed by learners' repeated and two-way interaction process of new knowledge and experience.

2.2   Characteristics of Situational Simulation Teaching Method

The meaning of knowledge is distributed in all the environments we create. A concept often exists in many different situations. By participating in the activities in the situation, students can get a complete, complex and three-dimensional understanding of a concept from different situations, fully understand the meaning of knowledge, and truly master knowledge. Situation dependence. Through continuous interaction, cooperation and conversation in the whole cultural context, learners use knowledge constantly in different environments, and finally realize meaning construction, and rely on these situational activities to build a rich knowledge system with flesh and blood [2]. The guiding situational simulation of teaching should provide the basis for students to understand the construction documents, guide the students to learn, and at the same time, leave the students with broad construction space, so that students can take appropriate strategies according to the specific situation, form an appropriate cognitive structure, and explore and experience the meaning of knowledge concepts from different angles, And grasp the connotation of knowledge from these situational activities. Situational simulation teachers should adopt "pure natural learning evaluation", that is, according to the students' activities and learning achievements in the learning process, carry out a kind of evaluation which is completely combined with the situation of knowledge, real and natural. S The process of scene simulation teaching is shown in Fig. 1.

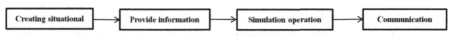

Fig. 1. Teaching system flow

The learning advantage combination evaluation function is as follows

$$good(team1)\begin{cases} 1 & smarllerthanb \\ 0 & therwise \end{cases} \tag{1}$$

3 Advantages of Situational Simulation Teaching Method in the Teaching of Criminal Law

3.1 It is Beneficial to Optimize the Leading Role of Teachers and Students

The highest realm of classroom teaching is the best combination of teachers' leading role and students' main role. Situational simulation teaching method is that teachers and students participate in the activities in the created situation, discuss, analyze, summarize and summarize the cases, so as to master and understand the professional knowledge. Therefore, the application of situational simulation teaching method in the teaching of criminal law can get rid of the general teaching mode of "teachers teach students to take notes". In the situational simulation teaching activities, teachers are in a dominant position. They are responsible for selecting learning topics, creating situations, providing necessary cognitive structures, organizing situational activities, guiding knowledge learning, and evaluating learning results. As an active participant, students carefully study the legal norms, deeply understand the connotation of knowledge, analyze and think about cases independently, actively participate in classroom discussion, and make correct judgments and choices, so as to get rid of the passive acceptance status in traditional teaching.

3.2 It is Helpful to Improve the Teaching Quality and Teaching Effect

On the one hand, situational simulation teaching method puts forward higher requirements for teachers' knowledge structure, teaching ability, work attitude and teaching responsibility than traditional teaching methods. It requires teachers to have profound professional theoretical knowledge, rich practical experience, and integrate theory and practice; it requires teachers to constantly update teaching contents and supplement teaching plans, It also requires teachers to pay more attention to the actual situation of the society, keep highly sensitive to the problems in reality, and constantly seek suitable cases of situational simulation teaching from social practice [3]. This high requirement can mobilize the only polarity of teachers' lesson preparation, better play the leading role of teachers in teaching, so that the curriculum teaching activities are always in a state of living and enterprising, constantly push the old and bring forth the new, and improve the quality of teaching.

3.3 It is Helpful to Improve Students' Comprehensive Ability and Quality

The process of situational simulation teaching in criminal law is actually a demonstration and exercise of students' comprehensive quality. The situational teaching of criminal law often focuses on real cases, so that students can learn to use the basic theories and knowledge of criminal law to analyze and solve practical problems. Experiencing the whole process of reading cases, analyzing questions, classroom discussions, simulating questions and writing analysis reports is not only a test of students' theoretical knowledge and application ability, but also a comprehensive exercise of analysis, judgment, communication, creativity and sound personality. It cultivates the comprehensive ability and quality of students' expression ability, reaction ability and collective cooperation ability, and enhances their adaptability to work in the society in the future.

4 Situational Teaching Method in Criminal Law

Based on the situation created by the simulation, the students are further familiar with the case, fully grasp the data, information and facts provided in the case, identify the key problems according to the needs of the case, analyze the causes of the problems, and seek evidence support. It is the central link of situational simulation teaching to carry out high-quality classroom discussion around questions. The course discussion should focus on the key issues, describe the understanding, analysis, judgment, demonstration and decision-making process of the case, explain the implementation plan to solve the problem, and reanalyze the decision-making plan. The speech should integrate theory with practice, be logical and concise [4]. After a student has spoken, other students can ask questions, put forward different opinions or debate. Through classroom discussion and debate, we can achieve the purpose of brainstorming, sharing views, complementary advantages and correct decision-making, so as to achieve the teaching effect of knowledge construction (see Fig. 2).

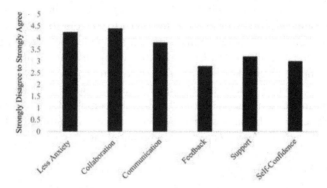

Fig. 2. Simulation of teaching method in criminal law

5 The Concept and Characteristics of Situational Simulation Teaching Method

5.1 The Concept of Simulation Teaching Method

The word "situation" is defined as "situation and environment". Dewey, an American educator, first expounded the concept of "situation" in teaching activities [5]. He believed that situation is composed of conditions that promote or hinder, stimulate or contain the unique activities of a species. In the context of educational significance, Dewey believes that the transmission of beliefs, emotions and knowledge to teenagers must be realized through the media of context. Context allows individuals to participate in the activities of arousing and strengthening some impulses, having some purposes, and requiring them to bear some consequences, so as to shape their spiritual and emotional tendencies in behavior. Dewey's "environment" refers to the situation that can interact with the learning subject. Li Jilin, a child educator, first introduced the concept of "situation" into the field of education and teaching in China. In situational education: a trilogy of main themes, she explains that "the best learning environment" is a "pleasant", "rich", "safe" and "environment in which to live". The situational education advocated by Li Jilin is to enable students to learn knowledge in the interaction with teachers and peers and in connection with the world and life. The "situation" we want to explore in this paper refers to the "real problems" needed by the school law to carry out the rule of law education, which can be used for teachers and students to carry out full simulation. Of course, it also includes the material environment, organizational structure and cultural system of the school rule of law education, It also includes the atmosphere that these organizations and things need to create to carry out the rule of law education activities, as well as various preparatory activities to be carried out and so on [6].

5.2 The Characteristics of Situational Simulation Teaching Method

Simulation is the most significant feature of situational simulation teaching method. "Imitation" refers to simulation and imitation; "truth" refers to real things and situations. In other words, situational simulation teaching method is to create a situation highly similar to the real situation, so that students can carry out simulation behavior in the created simulation situation. "Simulation situation" is based on the real life situation and formed by simple or complex special processing around the teaching objectives. Students should participate in the simulation activities to complete tasks or solve problems, complete a "real behavior" in the "simulation scene", and feel the complex factors that may occur in a certain life scene on the basis of their own experience and learning, and experience their feelings and attitudes towards people, things and things in a certain scene, so as to explore specific strategies to solve problems [7].

Transfer is an important feature of situational simulation teaching method [8]. The theory of knowledge transfer points out that human society should not only use and express its knowledge repeatedly, but also understand it well and solve similar and related problems. Knowledge transfer is mainly affected by situational factors and personal factors. The transfer experience stored in people's mind is in an inert state. Only when people realize that there is a certain relationship between the new situation and the original knowledge, will knowledge transfer take place actively. According to the theory of knowledge transfer, the creation of situations in the process of teaching should focus on the learning content, and should also consider the possibility of future transfer. The "legal knowledge" imparted by the rule of law education has obvious characteristics of application or skill. Learning this kind of knowledge itself is not the goal. The deep purpose of teachers imparting this kind of knowledge to students is to enable them to apply what they have learned and consciously participate in the orderly construction and activities of the rule of law society. The transfer characteristics of situational simulation teaching method can meet this actual demand. Students can exercise in the simulated situation and apply the transfer of legal knowledge to life practice, so as to play a role in the growth of teenagers into qualified legal talents [9, 10].

6 The Application Foundation of Situational Simulation Teaching Method in Teenagers' Legal Education

6.1 The Theoretical Basis of the Application of Situational Simulation Teaching Method

Marx and Engels summed up the experience of human thinking and the rational thought of previous philosophy, and pointed out that the essence of cognition is the active reflection of subject to object on the basis of practice, that is, cognition is the reflection of objective existence. But the cognition activity must take the objective things as the prototype, and has the reflection and the description to the objective things [11]. Therefore, the cognition must contain the content of reflecting or describing some objective things. The Enlightenment of epistemology to educators is that learning belongs to the category of cognitive activities, and its gradual process also conforms to the law of development from perceptual to rational, from concrete to abstract. Therefore, teaching practice should follow the principle of epistemology and enrich students' understanding of the objective world on the basis of practice by creating situations close to the real world. And the simulated teaching situation is to show the real situation that students are not easy to contact in the classroom, but these simulated teaching situations are specially simplified and optimized by teachers, which are more suitable for carrying out legal education. It can be imagined that when students personally promote the development of things in the specially created situation, their understanding develops with the development of things in the situation. The content, atmosphere, character relationship and other specific elements of the situation make students feel the object directly through vision, hearing, smell, etc. in practice, emotional activities can be triggered, exploration interest and learning enthusiasm will rise, and the education effect will naturally be improved. The application of situational simulation teaching method is shown in Fig. 3.

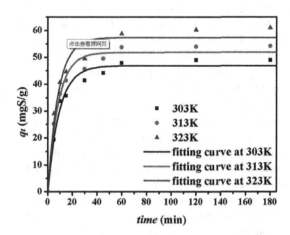

Fig. 3. Application of situational simulation teaching method

6.2 The Practical Basis of the Application of Situational Simulation Teaching Method

"The outline of the rule of law education for young people" is the latest guiding principle for the development of the rule of law education in China [12]. It clearly puts forward the main points of the current rule of law education for young people in China, and cultivates students' concept and consciousness of the rule of law, which puts forward higher requirements for the front-line teachers of the rule of law to carry out teaching. Situational simulation teaching method, as a high simulation, experience oriented and easy to move teaching method, can make up for the shortcomings of traditional teaching methods, realize the gradual progress from "general law popularization" to "real feeling of law", and enable students to deeply transform their feelings of the rule of law from emotion to idea. In addition, in the section of "teaching methods", the syllabus also clearly puts forward the application suggestions of "situational simulation (such as court simulation)" teaching method, and introduces the typical cases into the real situation, so as to provide rich resources and practical support for the rule of law teaching. If the systematic construction of situational simulation teaching can be realized in online teaching, and the whole teaching process can be opened up and improved, then students will be able to plant the seeds of the rule of law in the simulation practice again and again, so that the concept of the rule of law can be rooted in the heart, and the belief in the rule of law can take root [13].

From the perspective of developmental psychology, the period from the age of twelve to the age of eighteen belongs to the period of adolescence, which is mainly concentrated in the senior grade of primary school, junior high school and senior high school. During this period, people's psychological cognition and social development speed will reach a peak [14]. From the point of view of physiological changes, the child's body shape will grow rapidly at this stage, and the brain and nervous system will gradually develop and improve. Due to the change of students' appearance, they have the psychological needs of "adult feeling", and their self-consciousness is gradually formed. At this time, it is "pushing the boat with the current" to carry out legal education through the practice form of situational simulation. However, because the brain and nerves of teenagers are in the period of development from immature to mature, the education in this period should give consideration to learning and activities, and pay attention to the combination of work and rest. To a certain extent, situational simulation is just a kind of teaching activity, which makes students not need to keep nervous in their study, and gradually establish correct values and the concept of rule of law in the cooperative action with their classmates. From the perspective of cognitive characteristics, teenagers can perceive specific things, and their abstract logical thinking is also in a high development period. Logical thinking often needs the direct support of perceptual experience. They can feel emotions and ideas from specific situations, and then make general induction. The experience they get can guide practice, so as to develop and expand knowledge in a circular way. Obviously, the learning path of "refining and summarizing specific cases one by one and guiding practice" followed by situational simulation teaching can make students feel the authority of law, establish the concept of rule of law, and lay the foundation for orderly life in the future [15].

7   The Overall Construction of Situation Simulation Teaching System in the Education of the Rule of Law for Teenagers

Situational simulation teaching needs to rely on specific cases for implementation, so the author thinks that the project of situational simulation teaching design is conducive to teaching application, that is, to design a variety of situational simulation projects from typical cases that meet the content of legal education and have the significance of legal education, and carry out targeted teaching through the design and implementation of the project. This kind of project teaching is not only conducive to improving the operability of practical teaching, but also conducive to the concretization and routinization of innovative teaching mode. Any teaching activity must be based on teaching design, and situational simulation teaching project also needs careful structural design. This kind of structural design refers to the typical form of project design, which should be in line with the goal, cognitive law and operational law of youth legal education, and requires that the absorption of legal knowledge and exercise of practical skills can be scientifically arranged in teaching. Secondly, due to the wide range of legal education content and complex knowledge, we should analyze the legal education content of students at all stages, extract and classify the content suitable for project-based teaching, so as to reasonably design teaching projects and develop teaching guidance in different knowledge objectives. The preparation stage is the main stage of students' autonomous learning in carrying out the situation simulation project. According to the complexity of the situation simulation project, it is necessary to set up "Preparation Class" to provide sufficient time for students to complete the task. "Preparing for class" is divided into two parts, one is "introducing projects and assigning tasks one by one", that is, teachers introduce project types and project cases to students, and issue grouping tasks to prompt and guide the key and difficult points in the tasks. At the same time, they should pay attention to the reasonable assignment of tasks to each student, and should not assign tasks to some students [16]. The "presentation results discussion summary" means that after the students have completed their homework and submitted their learning results, the teachers should arrange class hours for discussion summary. In this part, the students in each group can present the way and process of completing the task, and show the written results of the group. The rest of the students can ask questions to them. After listening to the students' reports, the teachers can comment on their learning results and put forward supplementary and modification opinions. Through the public presentation of achievements and process introduction, students can realize the significance of giving, get a sense of achievement, and stimulate their enthusiasm in the situation simulation project. In addition, in the "Preparation Class", students ask and answer each other's questions, and teachers give comments and guidance. In the atmosphere of communication and discussion, the preparation of the whole scenario simulation project is also improved and promoted, which lays a solid foundation for the next demonstration.

8   Conclusion

The situation simulation teaching method makes the role of teachers and students relocate. From the essence of inquiry learning, it puts forward a sustainable development learning view. It shows the way people know the world and discover the world. This is the revolution of teaching method which is happening around us. With the development of modern education technology, multimedia technology, Internet technology and virtual reality technology are becoming more and more mature, it provides an ideal teaching environment for the creation of situation in situational teaching method, and can realize the teaching purpose and teaching effect of scenario simulation teaching method.

References

1. He, K.: Teaching mode, teaching method and teaching design of Constructivism. J. Beijing Norm. Univ. **51**, 74–81 (1997)
2. Caixia, S.: Application of case teaching in criminal law teaching. J. Hubei Inst. Adult Educ. **12**(5), 58–60 (2006)
3. LiangFang, S.: Teaching Theory: Principles, Strategies and Research of Classroom Teaching. East China Normal University Press, Shanghai (1999)
4. Chen, X., (ed.). Learning and Action in Participation: A Guide to Participatory Approach Training. Education Science Press (2003)
5. Cheng, S., He, Y., Liu, Y.: On the theoretical basis of situational simulation teaching method. Adult Educ. **7,** 43–44 (2011)
6. Ning, D.: Function orientation and Realization of situational simulation teaching mode. Explor. High. Educ. **2**, 45493 (2018)
7. Guo, Q.: Experiential legal education model construction research. Educ. Rev. **6**, 145–147 (2018)
8. Guo, R.: From the perspective of core literacy, "morality and the rule of law" activity oriented curriculum implementation suggestions. Res. Ideol. Political Course **2**, 145–148 (2019)
9. Shubin, H.: Youth Legal Education: target orientation, implementation principle and path. Juvenile Delinquency **2**, 69–75 (2016)
10. Jin, D., Zhang, Y.: Dimensions, standards and implementation of the effect evaluation of the rule of law education for teenagers. Jiangxi Soc. Sci. **3**, 247–253 (2018)
11. Constantina, Z., Thomas, B.: Active citizenship: the contribution of experiential learning and Critical Education. Contemp. Educ. Cult. 11, 1–5 (2019)
12. Peng, L.: On the lack and construction of belief in the rule of law in China. Law Res. **9**, 4 (2018)
13. Li, W.: Enlightenment of scenario simulation teaching method on Management Teaching. Educ. Explor. **7**, 63–64 (2008)
14. Jucai, L., Rucheng, Z., Xingying, G.: Implementation and evaluation of the practical activity curriculum of the rule of law education in primary and secondary schools. Mod. Prim. Second. Educ. **6**, 8–11 (2018)
15. Changshan, M., Jinzhi, L.: Citizenship shaping in the rule of law education for teenagers. J. Shanghai Normal Univ.: Philos. Soc. Sci. **4**, 88–97 (2018)
16. Qin, Y., Dai, Z.: Interpret the rule of law education in American primary and secondary schools. Foreign Prim. Second. Educ. 25–27 (2011)

Application of Cloud Computing Data in Northeast Folk Art Education

Ying Li[(⊠)]

Jilin Normal University, Jilin 136000, China

Abstract. As an important part of traditional culture, northeast folk art reflects the cultural characteristics of different nationalities and integrates rich emotions into it. The combination of modern environmental art design and folk art provides designers with new ideas to improve the efficiency and quality of environmental art design. Based on the clear meaning and content of cloud computing data on folk art, this paper discusses the development process of folk art education, analyzes the contact points between folk art and modern environmental art design, and analyzes its application mode from the innovation, form, modeling mode and region of folk art, so as to improve the application level of folk art in modern environmental art design.

Keywords: Northeast folk art · Folk culture · Cloud computing

1 Introduction

Today's world is in the rapid development of the information age, information technology, digitization has become the trend of the times. In the protection of folk art resources, the traditional way of information collection, recording and preservation has been unable to meet the requirements of a large number of high-quality and efficient protection. Therefore, the transformation from traditional protection mode to modern and digital mode is also the general trend of the development of the times [1].

Folk art is a classification in the field of art. The word "folk" is different from that of the royal court and aristocrats. The scope of "folk art" is very wide, and there are many "unique skills". Elephant skin shadow play, folk paper cutting, embroidery and weaving, dragon dance and lion dance are all very famous folk arts and cultural treasures of our Chinese nation.

2 The Meaning and Development of Traditional Folk Art

Rooted in social life, traditional folk art is a form of literature and art created by the general public. People inject emotion into their works to beautify the living environment and record folk customs. It is the inspiration source in daily art design. Folk art is not only the artistic language and cultural symbol, but also the inheritance of Chinese traditional

M. A. Jan and F. Khan (Eds.): BigIoT-EDU 2021, LNICST 391, pp. 429–437, 2021.
https://doi.org/10.1007/978-3-030-87900-6_50

culture. It contains the plain ideological connotation of people's working life, so it is deeply loved by the people.

With the advancement of globalization, modern art work has been exposed to different cultures from the perspective of globalization, which widens the vision of designers and promotes the development of art to a certain extent. The form of expression of folk art is complex and diverse, and its aesthetic value should break through the limitations of a few representative works. Because of its profound cultural connotation, folk art should shoulder the mission of inheriting Chinese excellent traditional culture. The regional economy, humanities and art reflected in folk art can be reflected in folk art. Folk art in the new era to seek further development, should be combined with other technologies, to find a breakthrough. In the process of environmental art design, folk art factors are added to improve the level of environmental art design.

3   Cloud Computing

The development of cloud computing has made great technological breakthroughs. From the earliest research and development of Google and Amazon to more and more researchers participating in cloud computing research, cloud computing has always been the focus of attention [2]. Cloud computing manages all the network, computing, storage and other resources through the distributed technology. Users can use these services reasonably by purchasing the resources they need. Compared with the traditional enterprises to build these infrastructure, it has significant advantages. Therefore, cloud computing turns resources into services to provide users with massive data processing and storage functions, which is more and more in line with the future development trend. In cloud computing, platform is service, software is service and infrastructure is service. Users only need to use the corresponding basic services according to their needs, and do not need to care about the underlying implementation. At the same time, cloud computing researchers provide database as a service, storage as a service, network as a service, etc. according to the corresponding service requirements.

3.1   Cloud Computing Data Center

Cloud computing is a computing method based on the Internet. Through this way, the software and hardware resources and information shared on the Internet can be provided to computer terminals and other devices on demand. As the infrastructure of supporting cloud computing services, the research of resource allocation and scheduling in data center becomes very important. Next, this section will introduce the evolution process of data center, the technical background of high virtualization of cloud data center and the characteristics of network resources of cloud data center.

3.2   Network Function Virtualization

Middle boxes, also known as network functions (NFS), are ubiquitous in cloud data centers. The data shows that the number of intermediate devices in cloud computing is equivalent to the number of routers and switches. These intermediate devices can perform various deep packet processing functions on the data streams passing through them, such as firewall, IDS, WAN optimization or HTP caching, etc. Not only that, the boundaries between intermediate devices and routers and switches are increasingly blurred, and more and more functions of intermediate devices are integrated into routers and switches. Although intermediate devices have become an indispensable part of the current network, they are often vendor specific hardware devices, which are not only expensive, but also require customized deployment and maintenance. What's worse, it is almost impossible to add new network functions to existing intermediate devices, which makes it difficult for service providers to deploy new services. In most cases, service providers have to purchase new hardware to introduce new network functions.

Calculation of ETT:

Suppose a certain time t, for a certain transmission line e_{ij}, we need to predict the time required for the k + 1 unit task in the task queue to transmit in e_{ij}, and the data volume of the transmission task packet is M. We can obtain the bandwidth (e_{ij}) available on the line e_{ij} at time t by using the assolo algorithm proposed in references. Then, the estimated transmission time ETT of the k + 1 unit task on line e_{ij} can be obtained by the following formula at time t:

$$ETT(e_{ij}) = M/Bandwidth(e_{ij}) \tag{1}$$

Assuming that node a and its descendant node b are connected by n transmission lines, which are $e_0, e_1, \cdots, e_{n-1}$ respectively, the estimated transmission time of the k + 1 unit task from node a to node b is $ATT_{a->b}$:

$$ETT_{a->b} = ETT(e_0) + ETT(e_1) + \cdots + ETT(e_{n-1}) \tag{2}$$

First, we solve a simple two-layer tree structure model, as shown in Fig. 1.

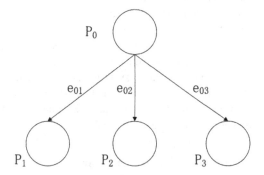

Fig. 1. Tree structure of the second floor

4 Function Design of ICH Cloud Storage Platform

4.1 Manage the Upload And Addition of Folk Art Resources (Hereinafter Referred to as Resources)

The upload function of folk art resources. The uploaded folk art resources are saved according to the classification and rules. When uploading resource files, the file access mode is automatically established according to the file type and category. For some resource files that may depend on the display of the client environment, relevant processing (such as video) is carried out when uploading the file, so as to adapt to the display needs of all possible display platforms [3].

When uploading the files, try to save them in the original format to ensure the effective value of folk art resources. When uploading files, the following methods are proposed:

Using FTP software to upload, the system directly establishes FTP users and allocates the usage directory. After uploading using FTP, the user obtains the upload file address and adds corresponding resource information in the system resource adding function module.

Use flash control or other controls to upload files directly in the system, and file related resource information can also be added at the same time. However, the maximum single upload file of the flash upload control is 1 GB (multiple files less than 1G can be uploaded at the same time, but the total file size is greater than 1 G), and this upload control does not support breakpoint continuous transmission.

Self developed upload controls, while the upload process to achieve file format conversion, into smaller files, but this method can be said to be the core technology of popular video websites, its development costs may be large, beyond the budget, and conversion file format, will not be able to upload files in the original format.

4.2   Format Conversion of Resource File

For more common file formats, such as word processing files, pictures, audio and so on, there are basically no client-side display problems, but there may be some problems for video files. Therefore, it is necessary to convert the formats of some problems after the display of different places, so as to make them more general as possible.

Client conversion, before uploading the file, the file can be directly uploaded by using the client.

In the process of uploading, the file is uploaded at the same time. This method has higher development cost and higher requirements on the server.

After uploading, it is difficult to develop a system service to run the conversion format in the background at a specified time. After uploading, it will be converted manually. After conversion, due to different file formats and additions, it may be necessary to maintain resource management information again (see Fig. 2).

4.3   Auditing, Editing and Sharing of New Resources

In order to better select the value and security of resources, it is necessary to review the newly added resources, which will be displayed in the front desk after passing the audit [4]. At the same time, the value level of resources can be set, corresponding to the security management system, so as to realize the authority control of resource modification and deletion [5].

The deletion and modification of resource files correspond to the security management system, and the operation level of resources is set. Registered users can share their uploaded resources to other users for viewing, which is divided into full sharing and password access (see Fig. 2 and Fig. 3).

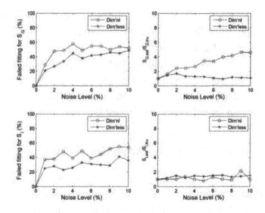

Fig. 2. Simulation for Format conversion of resource file

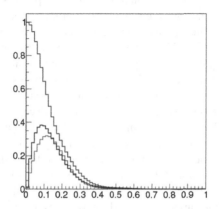

Fig. 3. Simulation for sharing of new resources

5 The Role of Northeast Folk Art in the Development and Utilization of Art Education in Primary and Secondary Schools

5.1 Improving the Comprehensive Quality of Primary and Secondary School Students

The organic integration of Northeast Folk Art into art education plays an important role in promoting the comprehensive quality and personality of primary and secondary school students [6]. "New curriculum standard" requires art education in primary and secondary schools to cultivate modern citizens with humanistic spirit, aesthetic taste and art literacy [7]. Due to the distinct artistic and regional characteristics of Northeast Folk Art, which contains the civilization and wisdom of ethnic minorities accumulated in the long history, the application of these humanistic spirit and cultural connotation in art education in primary and secondary schools can guide primary and secondary school students to establish a correct outlook on life, values and world outlook, and cultivate aesthetic emotion and attitude, Promote the continuous improvement of primary and secondary school students' personality. The northeast national folk art is an important part of China's traditional culture. Learning it can make young people understand different national cultures, deepen their understanding and feelings of the local national folk art, and then make primary and secondary school students understand the broad and profound Chinese civilization in an all-round and multi angle, guide them to continue to learn and explore, and cultivate their broad vision and mind [8].

5.2 Enhance the Aesthetic Ability and Appreciation Ability

National folk art is an art form gradually formed by the working people of all ethnic groups in the process of production practice, which has certain characteristics of natural environment and national development [9]. It has a unique nature and artistic charm, and contains a series of factors such as the mode of production, life attitude, value orientation and religious belief of its nation in the long process of development. The folk arts in different regions have their own characteristics. The northeast is rough and bold, such as shaman clothes, puppets, birch bark crafts, etc., with simple shapes and broad lines; the northwest is bold and passionate, such as shadow play, murals, peasant paintings, etc., with simple shapes, gorgeous colors, enthusiasm and appeal; the central region is moderate and peaceful, such as Zhuxian Town prints, Yellow River Chengni inkstone, Bianjing lanterns, etc., The southwest area is gentle and mysterious, such as Miao silverware, Dai bamboo basket, embroidery, etc., with complex production process, changeable shape, stable color and vitality. In Northeast China, folk arts of different nationalities also have their own artistic characteristics [10]. For example, Ewenki and Oroqen people migrate and hunt all the year round, so their Birch Bark products are small in size and many in variety; Daur people's agriculture and animal husbandry are relatively developed, and their life style is relatively stable, so their Birch Bark products are large in size and few in variety. Most of the Ewenki's hats are decorated with antlers, while most of the Manchu's hats are decorated with feathers and birds. All of these have an important role in promoting the expansion and improvement of students' aesthetic ability and art literacy. It can make students self-study and recognize the shape, color, composition, production technology and cultural connotation of ethnic folk art in other areas, and improve teenagers' art appreciation ability [11].

6   Enhance the Spirit of Innovation and Exploration

Art teachers in primary and secondary schools should have a positive spirit of innovation and exploration. "New curriculum standard" points out in the curriculum design idea that we should strengthen the comprehensiveness and exploration of the curriculum, and give teachers more space while ensuring the stipulation, "so that teachers' teaching activities are flexible, more active and creative." As the fine arts discipline has great flexibility, practicality, innovation and humanity, teachers need to have the spirit of innovation and exploration, in order to cultivate students' innovative thinking and innovation ability in the teaching process [12]. The spirit of innovation and exploration is the prerequisite for the development of curriculum resources, including the development and utilization of school-based curriculum, internal and external curriculum resources and information resources, which requires primary and secondary school art teachers to actively participate in the research of northeast national folk art, Collect, sort out, summarize and summarize the contents and forms that are in line with the development and utilization in primary and secondary school art education, and apply them in art teaching activities in an innovative way to enrich the teaching contents and methods. With the joint efforts of schools, teachers, parents, students and the community, we have developed a variety of school-based curriculum with the characteristics of local folk art, so as to promote the continuous development of art education in primary and secondary schools [13].

6.1 Enrich the Content of Art Teaching in Primary and Secondary Schools

Enrich the basis of art teaching content in primary and secondary schools, so that students can boldly express their feelings and understanding through modeling performance activities. The field of "design and application" emphasizes on training art skills and mastering art materials and tools, showing innovative thinking and creativity, and reflecting the functionality of art works [14]. The field of "appreciation and comment" enables students to feel artistic charm, express their aesthetic feelings, and cultivate positive attitude and values of life through art learning activities. The field of "synthesis and exploration" enables students to master other comprehensive knowledge through the study of art knowledge and skills, and learn to apply them in study and life, so as to cultivate students' comprehensive exploration ability and innovative practice ability. From the historical origin to the natural environment of growth, from the content of art form to religious belief and totem worship, from aesthetic emotion to national spirit and culture, from production process to craft skills, northeast national folk art can be fully developed and utilized in the art education of primary and secondary schools in this region, so as to enrich the art teaching content, So that the four learning areas can be further improved and in-depth research [15].

6.2 Improving the Teaching Methods of Fine Arts in Primary and Secondary Schools

Folk art contains special artistic features and cultural connotations. When it is developed and utilized in art education in primary and secondary schools, flexible and appropriate teaching methods should be adopted to organize teaching activities. First, guide the students to study the national folk art independently. Heuristic teaching is used to stimulate students' interest in learning, encourage students to actively participate in national folk art activities, enhance students' ability of autonomous learning and inquiry learning, and correct their learning attitude towards national folk art. Second, because the northeast national folk art is gradually produced in people's production and labor, most of the works condense the hardworking and wisdom of the working people, and need to cooperate with each other and constantly explore and study. Therefore, the use of cooperative learning teaching methods and learning methods will be more conducive to the study and exploration of national folk art, but also cultivate students' team spirit. Third, the use of vivid and interesting teaching methods for pre class introduction and teaching activities, to create a national folk art learning situation, such as games, visits, interviews, movies, videos, etc., can stimulate students' innovative thinking and imagination, express aesthetic feelings. Fourth, we should strengthen the development and utilization of curriculum resources and information resources of national folk art both inside and outside the school, and actively research and develop school-based curriculum. It is necessary to carry out interdisciplinary exploration, break through the closed state between the original disciplines, improve students' comprehensive exploration ability in the process of comprehensive learning, so that students' art learning is not constrained by textbooks. The development of school-based curriculum needs the joint efforts of schools, teachers, students and communities, which will help students deepen their understanding of local folk art in the process of curriculum research and development. This way is more research and development, cooperative, exploratory and independent.

6.3   Improving the Evaluation of Art Teaching in Primary and Secondary Schools

Art teaching evaluation, teaching goal and teaching behavior constitute a complete teaching activity. Teaching evaluation plays an important role in teaching activities [16]. Due to the particularity of art discipline, its teaching evaluation is more flexible and rich. On the one hand, it can promote the effective use of national folk art in teaching activities and improve the evaluation methods. On the other hand, it can also improve the teaching level of primary and secondary school art teachers and enhance students' learning ability. The northeast national folk art has unique characteristics in shape, line, color, artistic symbol and aesthetic emotion. The national history and culture it contains is also an important part of Chinese civilization [17]. Therefore, when evaluating the teaching of northeast national folk art, we should fully consider its richness, diversity, aesthetics, practicality and humanity. We should not only evaluate the students' homework from various angles, but also involve and pay attention to the students' learning attitude, learning ability, emotion and values of national folk art. In the process of evaluation, various evaluation methods, such as individual, group and so on, are encouraged, such as student self-evaluation, mutual evaluation, teacher evaluation and discussion. Evaluation results can be scores, grades or comments, or the combination of comments and grades.

7   Conclusion

Folk art is an important part of Chinese traditional culture. Its rich and colorful content and diversified forms provide inexhaustible creative inspiration for modern environmental art design. The rich cultural connotation of traditional folk art is still applicable to modern environmental design. The process of integration should not only stay on the surface form, but also pay attention to its internal traditional spiritual and cultural connotation. Modern environmental art design absorbs the essence of form, form, pattern and color from folk art. Modern environmental designers should combine the aesthetic tendency of contemporary people, the integration of tradition and modernity, create new vitality, create excellent art works that conform to the progress of the times, add new artistic charm to modern environmental art design, and promote the development of traditional folk art.

References

1. Zhang, L.: The application of traditional folk art in modern environmental art design. Literary life, Zhongxunpao **8**, 57 (2019)
2. Yajing, Z.: Analysis of the application of traditional folk art in modern environmental art design. Art Lit. **7**, 136–137 (2019)
3. Cao, B., Feng, X., Wang, S.: Research on regional culture cognition of Northeast Folk Art. Art Educ. (16) (2017)
4. New research on folk art heritage in Northeast China. J. Dalian Univ. (2) (2015)
5. Yin, S.: Interpretation of art education. Art Observ. (1) (1999)
6. Yin, S.: Culture, core literacy and art education: reflections on core literacy. Educ. Guide (2015)
7. Qian, C.: New thoughts on art education. China Art Educ. (3) (2003)
8. Qian, C.: Creative art education with "Chinese elements" as the core. J. Aesthetic Educ. (2012)
9. Jia, Y.: On the possibilities of the generation and development of new art learning methods. China Art Educ. (2) (2003)
10. Wang, S. The function of folk art in primary school art education. Teach. Manage. (2014)
11. Ping, W.: General Theory of Chinese Folk Art, p. 9. China University of science and Technology Press, Beijing (2010)
12. Jianjun, S.: Chinese Folk Art. Shanghai pictorial press, Shanghai (2006)
13. Huili, Y.: Chinese National Art. National Publishing House, Beijing (2014)
14. Yin, H.: Collection of National Art Education and Research, vol. 1. Central University for Nationalities Press, Beijing (2010)
15. Li, Z.: Chinese Aesthetics. The Course of Beauty. Shanghai Translation Publishing House, Shanghai (2014)
16. Fuguan, X.: The Spirit of Chinese Art, p. 01. Guangxi Normal University Press, Guilin (2007)
17. Baihua, Z.: Aesthetic Walk, p. 07. Shanghai People's publishing house, Shanghai (2014)

Application of Data Mining Technology in Pedagogy

Xinmei Zhao[1] and Juncheng Duan[2(✉)]

[1] The College of Arts and Sciences, YunNan Normal University, Kunming 653000, China
[2] Yunnan University Secondary School, Kunming 650031, China

Abstract. With the continuous development of the information age, data mining technology is becoming more and more mature to meet the needs of people for a large number of information processing. At present, the application of data mining technology in finance, communication, transportation and other fields is more and more, but the application in the field of education is relatively less. In view of this situation, in the traditional analysis method, data mining algorithm is used to analyze and study the related applications of pedagogy.

Keywords: Data mining · Pedagogy · Association rules · Apriori · Database

1 Introduction

With the gradual maturity of tree database technology and the extensive application of database management system on the Internet, a large number of explosive data have been produced. However, these data are not well analyzed and mined, resulting in the situation of "too much data but forgotten". Therefore, in order to improve the utilization rate of information, data mining technology emerges as the times require and is widely used rapidly. Data mining is a process of extracting potentially useful information and knowledge from a large number of, incomplete, noisy, fuzzy and random data. Here, "data" refers to the collection of facts, records and the original information related to things. "Knowledge" is a more abstract description of the contained information and the process of analyzing a large amount of data, including data preparation, pattern search, knowledge evaluation and repeated modification and refinement [1]. Mining process requirements are extraordinary, that is to require a certain degree of intelligence and automation.

2 Data Mining

Data mining algorithm is a set of calculation methods to create data mining model based on data. The algorithm will first analyze the data proposed by researchers, and look up specific types of models and trends, and then create models according to requirements. The commonly used algorithms in research are association rule mining, decision tree

M. A. Jan and F. Khan (Eds.): BigIoT-EDU 2021, LNICST 391, pp. 438–447, 2021.
https://doi.org/10.1007/978-3-030-87900-6_51

algorithm and clustering mining algorithm. Association rule mining is to discover the association and correlation existing in a large number of data sets, thus describing the rules and patterns of some attributes appearing simultaneously in a thing. It is one of the most mature main technologies in data mining. The most classic association rule algorithm is Apriori algorithm.

Clustering mining is an important human learning behavior. It is a common phenomenon in nature [2–4]. Aggregation analysis is a mathematical analysis method based on this phenomenon. Its purpose is to divide a large number of data points into several categories, so that the larger the gap between the data in each class, the better, the more obvious, The data in different classes should be similar as far as possible. The smaller the difference is, the better l5.6. Dense and sparse data can be found by clustering, so as to find the global data distribution pattern and interesting relationship between data attributes. The data mining process is shown in Fig. 1.

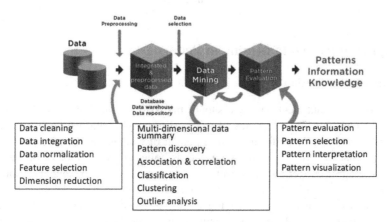

Fig. 1. Data mining process

3   Evolution of Association Rules Mining Algorithm Based on Data Mining Algorithm

The first algorithm of association rules, is the algorithm given by Agrawal and others when they proposed the association rule model. The basic idea is to generate frequency sets by scanning transaction database and count them. If the frequency sets in the previous step appear in the current transaction being scanned, the items in the transaction will be used to expand these itemsets to obtain new candidate sets [5, 6]. However, the major defect of the algorithm is that too many small candidate sets are generated. After that, cumulate and stratify, houstsma and others put forward an association rule algorithm called Setm algorithm, which uses s α L statement to calculate frequency set. The basic idea is to separate the generation and count of candidates, generate candidates by joi operation in SQL, and then save candidate copies and generate T of events in linear structure_ This is a method to transform association rule mining into SQL statement execution.

Suppose that s% of transactions in transaction database T contain xuy, then S% is called the support degree of association rule $X \cup Y$, which is the ratio of the number of transactions containing X and y to the number of all transactions, that is, the probability value $P(X \cup Y)$, which can be recorded as:

$$\sup port(X \cup Y) = P(X \cup Y) = S\% \tag{1}$$

The confidence degree of $X \rightarrow Y$ is the ratio of the support degree including X and y to the support degree containing x, i.e. the probability value $P(Y|X)$, which can be recorded as:

$$confidence(X \rightarrow Y)\frac{\sup port(X \cup Y)}{\sup port(X)} = P(Y|X) \tag{2}$$

4 Application of Data Mining in Pedagogy

4.1 Data Electronization

In order to make data electronic, we should first build a suitable network platform, which is divided into two processes. If we need to collect data, we need to build an object-oriented network platform. In the research of College Students' social system and interpersonal relationship, the scale data is collected automatically on the web. Firstly, the scale is converted into a web page written in assembly language, and then the electronic version of the scale is connected with the table in the database by using aspnet. In this way, only the subjects log in the designated website can complete the scale on the Internet, and the data is directly stored in the database [7, 8]. The database management system uses SQL Server 2000 - and the same method is used in the study of Internet addiction and attention relationship bias.

If we analyze the existing data, we can skip the step of data collection and input the data into the data processing software directly. In the research on the relationship between youth and youth, a data warehouse was created to store the existing data, and sqserver2000 was selected as the construction platform of the data warehouse. Since there are not too many dimensions in the research of adolescent peer relationship and the dimension hierarchy is not complex, in order to consider the query efficiency and whether the user can easily understand, we decided to use star structure to create data warehouse. The star structure of adolescent peer relationship research is shown in Fig. 2.

4.2 Data Mining Simulation Analysis

After transforming the data into the required electronic text format, simple data processing is carried out. After eliminating some missing or obviously wrong data, data mining can be carried out [9]. The common methods of data mining are association rule mining decision tree algorithm and clustering mining algorithm. In this paper, association rule

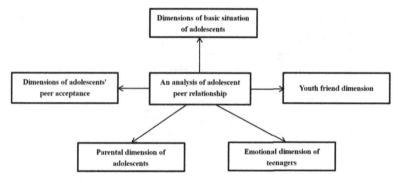

Fig. 2. Star structure of adolescent peer relationship research

mining algorithm is used to explain in detail. In the research of social network and interpersonal relationship of university students, the subjects' satisfaction with interpersonal relationship is selected as an example to mine association rules.

The steps of association rule mining are as follows:

(1) Select data according to the target of association rule mining, select the attributes shown in the above table, select the data through the following sq statement, and connect JE η Xinx table and zongle table through student number. Will you be satisfied with your relationship with your parents, whether you are satisfied with your relationship with your parents, Zongjie b where a student number = B student number.

(2) Save the selected data: first, insert the data selected in the first step into a table. Sq statement is as follows: SERT into guanlianguize1 select gender, whether you are an only child, are you satisfied with your interpersonal relationship, with your parents, with your partner, with your teacher, What kind of evaluation do you think people who know you better will give to your interpersonal relationship.

(3) Construct a transaction database that satisfies the mining of association rules, add an attribute item to the table guanlianguize 'and assign a value to TEM through the following sq statement. Note that the data mining mapping code of each attribute is shown in the above table. New table socia_ guanlian_ 1 as the event database of data mining, import item.

The results show that college students who have a high evaluation of their own interpersonal relationship have higher satisfaction with their own interpersonal relationship [10]. College students who have a low evaluation of their own interpersonal relationship have lower satisfaction with their own interpersonal relationship. Students who pay less attention to interpersonal relationship have lower satisfaction with interpersonal relationship. These data are related to each other, so we call on college students to pay more attention to interpersonal relationship and interpersonal rules, which is conducive to their early recognition of their shortcomings in interpersonal communication, so as to lay a good foundation for entering the society and creating greater social value.

The simulation analysis is shown in Fig. 3 and Fig. 4.

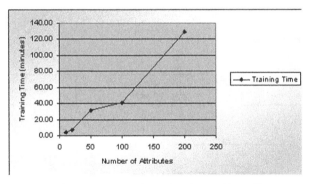

Fig. 3. Data mining simulation for teaching effect

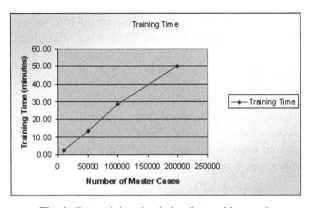

Fig. 4. Data mining simulation for teaching mode

5 Knowledge and Its Subject Attribute

5.1 Subject Attribute

Before discussing the knowledge of pedagogy, it is necessary for us to make a clear distinction between "subjects in the sense of academic research" and "subjects in the sense of teaching subjects". The "subject" mentioned in this paper is obviously not completely different from what we say everyday, such as Chinese, nature, society and other subjects in primary and secondary school curriculum [11, 12]. According to the explanation of Dogan. M. in the International Encyclopedia of social and behavioral sciences, the term "disc upline" refers to both the organizational units in various educational programs and the organizational units in knowledge production, Discipline is basically synonymous with academic classification or teaching subjects. For a long time, although there is little clear demarcation between them in academic circles, "there must be differences in the connotation of academic classification and teaching subjects.". The "discipline in teaching" should be called "teaching subject" in a strict sense, and its knowledge organization aims at promoting the development of teaching objects; while the "discipline in academic research" produces and organizes knowledge in the sense of epistemology.

"As a discipline in a research field, it does not have the meaning of knowledge transfer as teaching.

5.2 Subject Premise

The "discipline" here is based on the emergence of science. "Discipline" is a branch system of scientific knowledge with a fixed research object, while "science and discipline are the relationship between the whole and the part". Science is a branch of all disciplines, and discipline is a branch of local disciplines [13–15]. We can say that since the emergence of science, the classification of knowledge has been inextricably linked with the division of disciplines. From ancient Greece to the middle ages, knowledge has almost always been integrated into the "Virtue" and "wisdom" of philosophy. Aristotle's division of knowledge disciplines is only an attempt of theoretical systematization, which is fundamentally different from what we call "disciplines" today. "With the attention to higher learning, philosophers began to classify knowledge, From the late Middle Ages and the Renaissance, "when universities spread all over Europe, scholars wrote: science has established its own palace. this process of science establishing its own door to build its own house of knowledge, It is a process of knowledge differentiation, classification and reorganization, and the process of separation is based on the difference of knowledge itself. It has internal connection with the classical teaching "seven arts", but it has important differences. "It is worth mentioning that the branches of knowledge in the middle ages, twos and quadriviums, were named after the forks and crossroads in Latin.

5.3 Science Curriculum

In the field of pedagogy, the types of knowledge are very complex, but in many cases, we tend to simply think that the knowledge in the field of education is what we teach students, and that these contents are also the knowledge of academic disciplines, but we lack the understanding of the difference between the knowledge of teaching subjects and that of academic disciplines, It pays little attention to the knowledge of pedagogy itself [16]. The literature search before writing this paper also found that a large number of literatures about knowledge in the field of education mostly refer to the subject knowledge to be taught to students, but the discussion about pedagogy itself is rare, and in many cases, we often confuse "teaching content knowledge" with "subject knowledge". Shulman (L) and others call the subject knowledge as "pedagogic content knowledge", Teaching content knowledge represents the essence of content and teaching method. It exists in the intersection of "content knowledge" and "Pedagogical Knowledge". Learning content knowledge is a kind of special knowledge that distinguishes the understanding of subject content from that of subject experts. We can regard this kind of teaching content knowledge as teachers' reorganization and limited and appropriate transformation of relevant subject knowledge and its presentation form according to the logic of pedagogy knowledge system, so as suitable for teaching. This is also an important knowledge representation to distinguish "physics and physics research" as a middle school teaching subject [17–19]. As a teaching subject, we can organize part of the knowledge of physics into a "physics" course, and we can also organize the knowledge of physics, chemistry and other subjects into a "science" course. This itself also shows that the logic of organizing knowledge of teaching subjects is different from that of "Chinese characters" in the sense of learning.

6   The Subject Characteristics of Pedagogical Knowledge

6.1   The Formation and Development of Education Discipline

In the process of the formation and development of almost all disciplines including mathematics, "differentiation" is a strategy used by disciplines to protect themselves from invasion and self doubt. The establishment of the academic terminology system of this discipline is often one of the results of the discourse practice of this discipline. This process of differentiation is manifested in the division and strengthening of subject boundaries by knowledge classification. In the process of discipline formation, in addition to the academic training and learning organization, the development of bibliography also played a key role. Historically, bibliography played an important role in the efforts of libraries, museums and archives to save the flood [20–22]. This effort was achieved by sorting books, utensils and documents and making them known to the growing community. As shown in Fig. 5. Up to now, the bibliographic arrangement of the library still has an extremely important influence on the classification of knowledge and subjects. In a certain sense, we can say that the classification of knowledge by professional academic training and bibliography is an important force to promote the specialization or differentiation of Chinese characters.

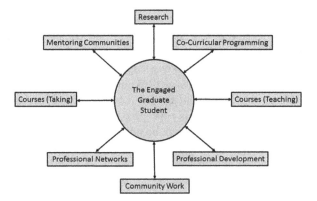

Fig. 5. Development of education discipline

6.2   Subject Classification

The subject classification of knowledge is closely related to knowledge and the social function of the subject producing such knowledge. "Every individual who performs a certain social role is considered by his social circle to have or is confident that he has the necessary knowledge for normal role performance. Pedagogical knowledge is not limited to and sufficient for educators. In other words, teachers must have the knowledge of teaching phonetics, but not all teachers must have the knowledge of teaching phonetics [23]. We can take it as a criterion to judge that a kind of knowledge is teaching knowledge. The fundamental reason why a discipline can produce and exist independently is that it can produce some unique knowledge to meet the needs of society. The existence of teaching phonetics as an independent discipline indicates that there must be some special knowledge only belonging to pedagogy. Therefore, we can establish another criterion to judge the first knowledge of teaching, that is, only teaching is the discipline that mainly produces and provides this kind of knowledge. As the exclusive product of academic discourse practice of a discipline, the knowledge of the discipline is always closely related to the theme of the discipline and serves the main social functions of the discipline. This article can be used as the third criterion for us to determine whether a certain knowledge is pedagogical knowledge.

6.3 Subject Theme of Pedagogy

The subject purport of pedagogy has not been clearly differentiated, which is one of the important reasons why the subject characteristics of pedagogy knowledge are not clear and prominent. The indistinct theme of pedagogy is related to the particularity of pedagogy's own development history. From the pedagogy, which is one of the subjects of normal education and mainly focuses on classroom teaching, to the science of education, which focuses on all kinds of social phenomena in the whole field of education, to the comprehensive, holistic and independent pedagogy, which focuses on all kinds of educational phenomena, The theme of pedagogy has been in subtle changes [24–26]. Anyway, the theme of pedagogy must be about educational phenomena rather than other phenomena. Therefore, pedagogical knowledge must also be about educational phenomena rather than political, economic, legal and other social phenomena. However, it is still difficult for pedagogy to give a clear answer to this fundamental question. However, although there is no clear standard answer in theory, we can clearly distinguish education from experience. For example, when I pay for a shirt, the price of the shirt, the design of the shirt, the idea of guiding me to eliminate my wife, and so on, are obviously not educational phenomena.

7 Conclusion

With the continuous development of the information age, many researchers focus on Pedagogy from different aspects and different fields. In this process, a large amount of scientific data will be accumulated. Therefore, it is urgent to use computer means to conduct systematic data integration, which is conducive to deeper analysis of the data. The application of data mining technology in the field of pedagogy will have a broad prospect and can be further promoted as the research direction of pedagogy in the future.

Acknowledgements. Yunnan Provincial Education Department of the sixth batch of university science and technology innovation team project construction "Yunnan Province university wisdom tourism science and technology innovation team".

References

1. Ming, Z.: Data Mining. China University of science and Technology Press, Hefei (2002)
2. Wang, H., Wu, J.: Research on data mining algorithm based on SQL Server 2000. Comput. Eng. Des. **29**(3), 759–761 (2008)
3. Bai, Y., Gao, Y.: Research on the relationship between Internet addiction and attention bias based on data mining technology and database design. Learning science research center of Southeast University (2009)
4. Wang, X., Yu, L.: Construction of network education resource database based on data mining. J. Southwest Normal Univ. **30**(1), 163–167 (2005)
5. A brief introduction to the master program of adult education in Hebei University. J. College Adult Educ. Hebei Univ. **23**(01), 125 (2021)
6. Ke, L., et al.: Application and effect analysis of mixed teaching mode in quality training of public health talents during epidemic period. Health Voc. Educ. **39**(06), 114–116 (2021)
7. Announcement on the journal being recognized as an academic journal by the State Administration of press, publication, radio, film and television. Road Succ. **09**, 146 (2021)
8. Juan, Z.: Reflections on the discipline development of higher education. Teach. Educ. People (Higher Education Forum) **09**, 10–12 (2021)
9. Li, F., Pang, Y.: Supporting strategic decision with education research and serving reform and development with practice exploration – Summary of the fourth national high end Forum on theory and practice of graduate education discipline construction [J/OL]. Grad. Educ. Res. 1–7 (2021). https://doi.org/10.19834/j.cnki.yjsjy2011.2021.03.01
10. Wu, S.: "Five focuses" to improve the effectiveness of learning and using in Distance Education. Hefei evening news (2021) (A03)
11. Chen, M., Mo, J.: Building a high quality education system to make people satisfied with education. Nanning daily (2021) (005)
12. Yao, S., Gaofeng, L.: Focusing on the cultivation of the sense of Chinese national community, promoting the innovation and development of national ideological and Political Education – Summary of the Forum on "Ideological and political education and casting the sense of Chinese national community." Sch. Party Build. Ideol. Educ. **06**, 96 (2021)
13. Zhao, F., Li, Y., Liu, M., Xue, D., Wang, S.: Propositional guidance and performance support: a Study on the dual knowledge and ability cultivation structure of "future physical education teachers" in Sweden. J. Tianjin Inst. Phys. Educ. **36**(02), 125–133 + 150 (2021)
14. Guangfen, Y., Hui, S., Yuan, Y.: Interdisciplinary research and discipline construction of Vocational Education: context, return and change. China Vocat. Tech. Educ. (09), 11–17 (2021)
15. Qi, J., Gu, Y.: Research on the historical development trend of positivism paradigm from the perspective of Comparative Education. J. Yanbian Univ. (SOCIAL SCIENCE EDITION) **54**(02), 121–127+144 (2021)
16. Xiong, Y., Cheng, L.: Research on discipline development and curriculum construction of family education in the new era. Contemp. Youth Stud. (02), 5–12 (2021)
17. Yaming, Y.: The infiltration of moral education into the education of new music and Art: a review of research methods of music pedagogy. China J. Educ. **46**(03), 163 (2021)
18. Jie, S.: On the change of the category of mutual benefit between teaching and learning and its contemporary value. J. Hebei Normal Univ. (EDUCATION SCIENCE EDITION) **23**(02), 54–63 (2021)
19. Yukun, L.: Research on the innovation path of music education mode in Colleges and Universities under the multicultural background – a review of research methods of music pedagogy. Forestry Ind. **58**(03), 113 (2021)

20. Dong, Q.: Achievements and problems in the development of Ideological and political education since the reform and opening up. Forum High. Educ. **03**, 1–4+15 (2021)
21. Qianli, Y.: Dilemma and reflection of national defense education research in Colleges and universities. Forum High. Educ. **03**, 110–113 (2021)
22. Jianjun, C.: Reflections on Pedagogy Teaching from the perspective of teacher qualification examination. J. Liaoning Vocat. College **23**(03), 83–86 (2021)
23. "Vocational Education Forum" in 2020 National People's Congress reprinted newspapers and periodicals ranked again good results. Vocat. Educ. Forum **37**(03) (2021)
24. Chen, X.: Optimization and innovation of physics classroom teaching method in junior middle school. Math. Phys. Chem. Middle School Students (Teaching and learning) (03) (2021)
25. Introduction to cover characters. Art Educ. (03) (2021)
26. The editorial department of our journal. Continuous contributions in 2021: what kind of history education is needed in the new era. History Reaching Reference in Middle School, vol. 6 (2021)

Construction and Optimization of University Teaching Management System Based on Data Mining Technology

MeiLin Jin[✉]

Wenzhou Vocational College of Science and Technology, Wenzhou 325006, China

Abstract. As an important part of education informatization, the university teaching management system collects a lot of teaching information, but most of them have not been well mined and studied, so the application of data mining in the university teaching management system has practical significance. This paper introduces the basic principle of data mining technology and the method to solve the problem, and discusses a method of combining data mining technology with teaching management system in Colleges and universities, which improves the work efficiency of teaching management in Colleges and universities, realizes the rationality of teaching resource arrangement, and makes a new exploration in the construction of teaching informatization in Colleges and universities.

Keywords: Teaching management · Data mining · Association rules · Decision tree

1 Introduction

In recent years, with the rapid development of computer technology and network technology, the teaching information management system of colleges and universities has been greatly developed and widely used. At present, domestic colleges and universities have been equipped with information-based teaching management systems to varying degrees. Most of these teaching management systems use database technology and network communication technology, and basically include student management, teacher management, curriculum management, performance management and other functional modules [1].

In the teaching management system, a large number of records and data generated in the teaching process are stored and managed in the database, which improves the shortcomings of the traditional paper recording method, such as easy to lose, easy to damage and inconvenient to consult. At the same time, the paper is saved, which can improve the management efficiency and achieve economic and environmental protection. On the other hand, the application of network technology in the teaching management system, So that the transmission, processing and inquiry of teaching information can be completed remotely, and the flexibility of teaching management is improved. The emergence

© ICST Institute for Computer Sciences, Social Informatics and Telecommunications Engineering 2021
Published by Springer Nature Switzerland AG 2021. All Rights Reserved
M. A. Jan and F. Khan (Eds.): BigIoT-EDU 2021, LNICST 391, pp. 448–458, 2021.
https://doi.org/10.1007/978-3-030-87900-6_52

of information-based teaching management system provides great convenience for the teaching management of colleges and universities, improves the operation efficiency of the management of colleges and universities, and reduces the cost of running a school.

However, in the application process of teaching management system, the system will save a large amount of data, such as the basic information of students and teachers, students' scores and so on. If it can't be used effectively and organically, these massive data are simply stored in the database of the management system, which will probably turn the massive data into useless garbage, that is to say, the phenomenon of "data explosion and lack of knowledge" is caused. In fact, there are some potential connections and objective laws between these massive data. Finding and using these connections and laws effectively will be of great help to the analysis and evaluation of teaching quality and the decision support of university management, so as to make the teaching management system play a greater role. Data mining technology is a kind of technology to analyze the relationship and law hidden in massive data, and obtain useful information from it.

2 Overview of Data Mining Technology

2.1 The Concept of Data Mining

With the rapid development and wide application of information technology, database systems in all walks of life save and manage a large amount of data, but most of the database systems can only provide some simple data management and processing functions. On the other hand, with the development of society, the importance of data has become increasingly significant, and people's demand for data analysis and processing has become increasingly strong, which is difficult to achieve by using the traditional, manual data analysis methods and database system. With the explosive growth of data in various industries, the phenomenon of "data explosion and knowledge poverty" is becoming more and more serious. Therefore, in the face of massive data, people are eager to have a scientific and systematic technology that can be used to analyze and process these data, so as to find the valuable information contained in the massive data to serve for decision-making [2].

Data mining refers to the process of analyzing and extracting the knowledge that people are interested in from massive data or database. These knowledge are some potentially valuable information, which can exist in the form of concepts, rules, regulations, patterns, etc. For data mining, another authoritative definition is: data mining refers to the process of extracting hidden, unknown, but potentially useful information and knowledge from a large number of, incomplete, noisy, fuzzy and random practical application data.

Generally speaking, data mining is the process of analyzing massive data and mining knowledge from it. "Mining" vividly represents the process of finding useful and high value data from a large number of unprocessed and low value data. "Knowledge" refers to concepts, rules, rules and patterns, that is, valuable and interesting information extracted from massive and complex data. These "knowledge" can be used to discover data rules, provide decision support, and data mining technology is an effective means to achieve this process.

2.2 Assessment of Students' Academic Performance

In the teaching management of colleges and universities, students' academic performance is also an important index to evaluate the level of running a school and the quality of teaching. However, most of the existing performance evaluation methods are simple manual calculation, which is difficult to make a comprehensive and comprehensive analysis of the performance data. Data mining methods, such as classification based on decision tree, can be used to mine useful information from performance data, so as to provide effective decision support for school managers and improve the level of running a university.

Teacher information management
The staff of educational administration manage the information of teachers through this module, including the addition, modification, deletion, query and so on. When adding information, open a new window to record the teacher's information. When saving, check whether the teacher's number is repeated. If the added teacher's number is repeated, prompt the user. Only when it is not repeated can the information be added. When deleting information, you should first open the prompt window to let the user confirm whether to delete. Only after the user confirms can you delete the information. When modifying the information, you should be able to modify according to the teacher item selected by the user, that is, list all the information of the teacher selected by the user, and modify the teacher information on this basis.

Class information management
Through this module, the educational administration staff manage the information of the class, including the addition, modification, deletion and query of the class information. When adding information, open a new window to input class information. When saving, check whether the class number is repeated. If the added class number is repeated, prompt the user. Only when the information is not repeated, can the information be added. When deleting the information, the user can check whether the class number is repeated, First, pop up a prompt window to let the user confirm whether to delete. Only after the user confirms can the information be deleted. When modifying the information, it should be able to modify according to the class selected by the user, that is, list all the information of the class selected by the user, and modify the class information on this basis (Such as the class management in the fortress).

Student information management
Educational administrators manage student information through student information management module, such as adding, modifying, deleting and querying student information. When adding information, first enter the student information in the new window. When saving, check whether the student number is repeated. If the added student number is repeated, prompt the user. Information can only be added without repetition. When deleting information, you should first open the prompt window to let the user confirm whether to delete. Only when the user confirms can you delete the information. When the information is modified, it should be modified according to the students selected by the user, that is, all the information of the students selected by the user is listed, and the student information is modified on this basis.

Course information management
The educational administration staff manage the basic information of the course through this module, including the addition, modification, deletion of the course information and the setting of the class course. When adding information, open a new window to input information. When saving, check whether the course number is repeated. If the added course number is repeated, prompt the user. Only when it is not repeated can information be added. When you delete information, you should first open a window to let the user confirm whether you want to delete it. You can only delete it after it is confirmed. When the information is modified, it should be modified according to the course selected by the user, that is, the information of the course selected by the user is listed, and the course information is modified on this basis.

Achievement information management
The staff of educational administration manage the students' grades through this module. When adding the students' grades, it can be used to set the curriculum of the class for the students and input the grades directly.

Financial information management
Through this module, educational administration staff manage financial information, including students' payment and arrears. When paying, open a new window to input the payment. When saving, check the database to see whether the students have paid the fees. Payment can only be made without repetition. In the case of students in arrears, you can find out some classes of students in arrears, and you can export Excel to print (Such as the financial payment in the college school connection).

Printing information management
The staff of educational administration can print the student's score information, course selection record table and class table through the printing module. According to the class, student number, course number to print student transcripts, print before you can preview the report to be printed.

Comprehensive information query
Through this module, we can query all kinds of information needed by educational administration. For example: student information query provides information such as student number, name, class, head teacher's name and dormitory, and various query conditions for student information query. Users can query according to a single query condition or their combination. At the same time, it also provides the function of fuzzy query, that is, the module can use the reader's input incomplete query conditions to query, which is more convenient for the user's query management. The comprehensive query module includes student information query, teacher information query, class information query, department information query, course information query and score query.

System management
The module can manage the login users. In this module, educational administrators can add the list of persons allowed to log in and the corresponding password, and modify or delete the password of existing users.

2.3 ID3 Algorithm

ID3 algorithm was put forward in 1986, the core idea of the algorithm is: using information gain as the selection criteria of attributes, selecting attributes for all levels of
nodes in the decision tree, so that the maximum category information can be obtained
at all levels of nodes [3]. The specific process of the algorithm is as follows: first, all the
attributes of the data item are traversed by width first, and the attribute with the largest
information gain is selected as the node of the decision tree; then, starting from the node,
the branches of the node are established according to the different values of the attributes;
then, the branches of each branch are established by recursive method; finally, when all
the subsets only contain the same type of data, the, At the end of the algorithm, the
decision tree is obtained. The information gain of the attribute is calculated as follows:
Then the entropy of a given sample classification is as follows:

$$I = \sum_{i=1}^{m} p_i \log_2 p_i \tag{1}$$

So the entropy of a subset:

$$IYA = a_j Y = \sum_{i=1}^{m} p_{ij} \log_2 p_{ij} \tag{2}$$

ID3 algorithm has the advantages of simple principle, easy implementation and
strong training ability: it is sensitive to noise, and the result is stable only when the
data set is small; when the data set is large, the result of decision tree obtained by ID3
algorithm is not stable.

3 Methods of Data Mining in Teaching Management

3.1 Clarify Management and Decision Making Issues

This paper summarizes and identifies the management and decision-making problems of
education and teaching, determines the management and decision-making objectives to
be achieved, and then transforms the management and decision-making objectives into
data mining objectives, and defines them. The data mining process is shown in Fig. 1.

3.2 Extraction, Analysis and Preprocessing of Original Data

After the data mining task is customized according to the requirements of management
and decision-making objectives, the data is extracted from the teaching management
information system and other related functional management databases to eliminate the
interference of noise data, vacancy data and inconsistent data, and the obtained data is
cleaned up, integrated and transformed [4].

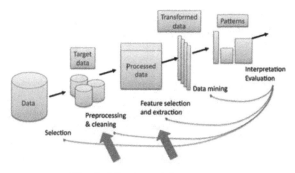

Fig. 1. The data mining process

3.3 Design and Use Data Mining Algorithm

According to different predetermined goals and data mining tasks, design a variety of data algorithms to determine effective data processing models and patterns [5].

The main problem of university teaching management data mining is to apply the new computer data mining technology to university teaching management through research, exploration and practice, and promote the university teaching management information to a higher level. Through the micro, meso and macro statistical analysis, synthesis and reasoning of teaching management data, we can find the relevance, change trend and general knowledge among all kinds of teaching activity data. With the knowledge obtained from the re development of these information to guide the teaching management and decision-making activities in Colleges and universities, we can manage and make decisions more scientifically and reasonably, It is conducive to the orderly and normal teaching activities [6].

3.4 Refine Data and Mining Results

The data of teaching management database is huge. The data obtained after preprocessing and value measurement screening operation and the corresponding mining mode designed based on this data should be adjusted circularly according to the needs of teaching management, and the data processing mode with the most practical application value should be determined, In the form of data analysis report, it provides decision support knowledge for the teaching management departments and school leaders [7].

3.5 Data Mining Results Simulation

We use the data mining structure in Fig. 2. Each structure contains different functions, that is, each structure contains different function nodes [8]. The specific simulation is shown in Fig. 3.

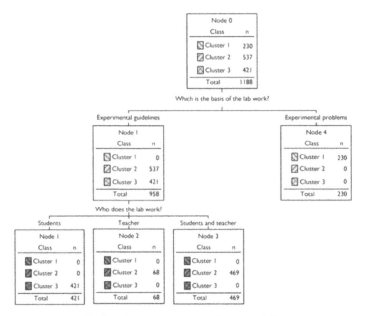

Fig. 2. Simulation structure for data mining

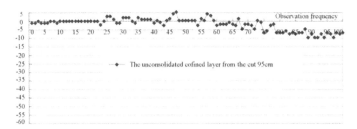

Fig. 3. Results of simulation

4   Application of Data Mining in Teaching Quality Monitoring and Evaluation System in Colleges and Universities

4.1   Determination of Data Mining Target

In order to meet the long-term development of the country, the enrollment scale of colleges and universities is expanding year by year, and the education methods are flexible and diverse. Most colleges and universities are facing the contradiction between the sharp increase in the number of students and the increasing tension of teaching resources. At the same time, some institutions of colleges and universities are constantly reforming and changing, which have brought unprecedented development and challenges to the teaching management of colleges and universities. In such an environment, how to get the maximum development at the minimum cost has become a new problem to be solved. Generally, teachers will accumulate a lot of data in the process of teaching implementation, but now the processing method of these data is still in the primary stage of data backup, inquiry and simple statistics, so it is not able to deeply tap the potential value of these data. So how to excavate the value of these data, and how to use these data to rationally evaluate some aspects of teaching objectively, will be the focus of our research. Based on the above needs, this paper conducts data mining through the data of teaching evaluation and related data, and finds out the results of teachers' teaching quality evaluation, the factors of these factors and the quality problems of improving teaching methods [9].

4.2 Establishment of Data Mining Model

This project is based on data mining, teaching quality evaluation system, teacher management information system and comprehensive education system database data structure analysis goal, you can focus on two aspects of teachers' personal factors and teachers' attributes, classroom, establish mining model (1) teachers' personal factors mining model, teachers' gender, age, professional title, educational background and other personal factors, The relationship between teaching quality may exist [10]. In order to find out the related factors that affect the quality of teaching, this paper establishes the personal factors of teachers and mining model to analyze the relationship between these factors and the evaluation results of teaching quality. (2) In addition to the influence of teachers' personal factors, the evaluation results of teaching quality, the length of course time, the property of elective students in the teaching plan, and the number of elective students in the classroom, many other factors may also have a certain impact on the evaluation results. Therefore, this paper establishes a mining model of teachers' teaching attributes, analyzes the class attributes and teaching quality evaluation results between links, and finds out the related factors that affect the teaching quality.

4.3 Technical Platform of Data Warehouse

For the data warehouse in Colleges and universities, because of its large scale, it can meet the needs of customers by separating the storage management part, application processing and client application of the data warehouse. Therefore, it is particularly important to adopt the three-tier structure of CS. This three-tier structure mainly includes: the client layer based on workstation, the middle layer based on server and the third layer based on host; the host layer is mainly responsible for managing data sources and converting optional data sources; the service layer realizes the operation of data warehouse and data mart software, and stores the data in the data warehouse; The workstation of client layer will run the application program of query and report generation, and also store the partial data dumped from data mart or data warehouse [11].

5 Analysis, Design and Implementation of Teaching Quality Monitoring and Evaluation System

5.1 The Design Idea of the System

The prosperity of the country lies in education, talent training is the fundamental task of colleges and universities, and the quality of education is the lifeline of higher education institutions. Teaching quality evaluation is an important means to strengthen education management, and the promotion of improving teaching quality and methods is an important part of teaching quality monitoring system. Through the evaluation of teachers' teaching, we can provide effective feedback information for teachers' teaching, find out the shortcomings, increase pressure and motivation, promote teachers to improve their teaching level and professional quality, make teaching managers scientifically and comprehensively understand teachers' teaching situation, strengthen teaching monitoring and management, and make students play the main body consciousness [12].

In 2004, the Ministry of education started undergraduate teaching evaluation, and the evaluation of teaching quality is often held in universities [13]. In the past, the work of school teaching evaluation generally focused on the macro or meso level evaluation, for teachers and teachers' personal teaching quality evaluation. The research on evaluation methods is relatively less, most of them are manual operation mode, and completely adopt the manual data collection evaluation and processing, such as the display or academic staff in all levels of research. Evaluation methods and means, not only a heavy workload, low efficiency, evaluation results are not satisfactory reliability and effectiveness. In the face of more evaluation objects and large sample statistics, it is difficult to achieve the expected goal, and a small amount of data processing can still be carried out; it is particularly urgent and important to develop a simple and efficient teaching evaluation tool, and it is of great significance to establish an online teaching quality evaluation system based on campus network. Teachers' teaching quality evaluation system "in the process of classroom teaching quality evaluation of campus network, in the classroom teaching of students' evaluation of teachers' quality, teachers and teaching staff can not only improve the efficiency of teaching management, but also continue to accumulate evaluation data, providing data guarantee for future data analysis. Such a system can not only achieve paperless data acquisition process, but also be able to deal with large data [14, 15].

5.2 Design Principle of Evaluation Index

Student evaluation of teaching is a very complex educational practice, involving a wide range of content, with a strong interdisciplinary, combined with pedagogy, education management, curriculum and teaching theory, educational psychology, statistics, system science and other theoretical knowledge, and guided by these theories, a scientific model of student evaluation of teaching is formed in practice. Therefore, the planning and design of an excellent teaching quality monitoring and evaluation system must follow the following principles: scientific and objective, level oriented, simple [16, 17]. The system must be constructed under the guidance of theory, and the mode, method and means must be the needs of scientific higher education evaluation, so as to ensure the balance of the rights of evaluation subject and object, and realize objective and fair evaluation. The fairness index system should have a level, which should focus on the instructors who care about the quality of teaching, increase investment in teaching, and improve the function of their teaching evaluation system, so as to be concise, Practical for users to understand and operate and system administrator management [18, 19].

6 Conclusion

As an important part of education informatization, a large amount of teaching information is collected in university teaching management system, but most of them have not been well mined and studied, so the application of data mining technology in university teaching management system has practical significance. In this paper, the association rule analysis and decision tree method of data mining technology are applied to evaluate and mine the data of teachers' teaching quality and students' academic performance in the teaching management system of colleges and universities, and some valuable rules are found, which provides decision support for the teaching management of colleges and universities, and makes a new exploration in the teaching reform and information construction of colleges and universities.

References

1. Chang, T.: Application of data mining technology in the research of American universities. Fudan Educ. Forum (2), 74 (2009)
2. Zhu, Q.. On the application of data mining technology in higher education management. Silicon Valley (4), 59 (2009)
3. Li, Y.: Research on the application of data mining technology in university financial management informatization. Accountant (1), 34 (2009)
4. Jiang, H.: Research on the application of data mining technologyty Teaching. China Sci. Technol. Fort. (2), 98 (2009)
5. Chen, Q.: Research on the application of decision tree algorithm in university teaching quality evaluation system. Southwest Jiaotong University (2010)
6. Zhang, C.: Research on the application of data mining based on association rules in university teaching evaluation. Anhui University (2011)
7. Li, X.: Research on the application of data mining in university teaching quality evaluation system. North China Electric Power University (2010)
8. Chen, A., Chen, N.: Data Mining Technology and Application. Science Press, Beijing (2008)
9. Zhang, J., Zhang, X.: Data Mining Algorithm and its Engineering Application. China Machine Press, Beijing (2006)
10. Xie, B.: Data Mining Clementine Application Practice. China Machine Press, Beijing (2008)
11. Huang, D.: Data mining of user information and consumption behavior of mobile intelligent network. Huazhong University of science and technology (2006)
12. Zeng, C.: Research on data mining technology based on clustering algorithm. Central South University (2010)
13. Li, Y.: Application of data warehouse and data mining in college performance analysis. Dalian Dalian University of technology (2009)
14. Zhu, D.: SQL Server 2005 Data Mining and Business Intelligence Complete Solution, vol. 007, issue 10. Electronic Industry Press (20105)

15. Left branch. Research on incremental association rule updating algorithm. Chongqing University (2009)
16. Zheng, Y.: Research and application of data mining in teaching evaluation, vol. 6. Beijing University of chemical technology, Beijing (2011)
17. Fu, L.: Application of data mining in teaching evaluation, vol. 9. Nanjing University of technology, Nanjing (2007)
18. Wu, H.: Research on computer forensics technology. Xi'an University of Posts and telecommunications (2007)
19. Wang, Q.: Design and implementation of university teaching quality evaluation and analysis system, vol. 3. Xi'an University of technology (2008)

Construction of University Education Teaching and Evaluation System Based on Data Mining Algorithm

Juan Li[✉]

Kunming Metallurgical College, Kunming 650033, Yunnan, China

Abstract. This paper discusses the selection of teaching evaluation index, establishes and solves the decision tree model of teaching evaluation, and carries out the concrete application of mining conclusions. The evaluation of teachers' teaching quality is an effective measure to improve teaching quality and regulate teaching behavior. In this paper, we set up a data mining system for teaching evaluation, hoping to find out the information and knowledge that is helpful to improve teaching quality from a large number of teaching data, and apply it to practice. The construction of index system is the basis and basis of teaching evaluation. This paper uses AHP method to analyze the model of teaching evaluation system, and finally defines the evaluation indicators: teaching attitude, teaching content and teaching method as the basis for selecting and mining the teaching information attributes in the database, so as to reduce the mining library attributes; on the one hand, it improves the mining efficiency, On the other hand, it can avoid the phenomenon that the decision tree is too large because of too many mining fields, which leads to the phenomenon of over fitting mining objects.

Keywords: Data mining · Teaching evaluation · Decision tree algorithm · Analytic hierarchy process

1 Introduction

In recent years, with the expansion of enrollment in Colleges and universities, the quality of students declines, which puts forward higher requirements for teachers' teaching quality. Therefore, it is very important to strengthen the construction of teaching staff and the evaluation of teaching quality [1]. The current teaching evaluation methods are almost used to evaluate whether a teacher's teaching quality is "good" or "bad", but it is difficult to explain what factors are related to the level of teaching level, that is, it is difficult to find out the law of teaching quality from the original data collected. This paper adopts the research idea of interdisciplinary integration. Through the comprehensive application of teaching, management science, information theory, computer science and other basic theories, this paper gives the teaching evaluation model based on data mining, and realizes the model solution through programming, and reaches the mining conclusion. These conclusions can reveal the key factors affecting the teaching quality, And the

M. A. Jan and F. Khan (Eds.): BigIoT-EDU 2021, LNICST 391, pp. 459–468, 2021.
https://doi.org/10.1007/978-3-030-87900-6_53

characteristics of teachers with high teaching level should have, so as to effectively help teachers improve the quality of teaching.

2   Common Algorithms in Data Mining

2.1   Decision Tree Algorithm

Classification analysis method is to analyze the data in the training set, make accurate description for each category or establish analysis model or dig out classification rules, so as to use the classification rules to classify the records in other databases in the future.

Decision tree is an algorithm commonly used in classification and prediction model. It can find some valuable and potential information by classifying a large number of data purposefully. Its main advantages are simple description, fast classification speed, especially suitable for large-scale data processing. The most influential and earliest decision tree method is the famous ID3 algorithm based on information entropy proposed by Quinlan. Its main problems are: ID3 is a non incremental learning algorithm; ID3 decision tree is a single variable decision tree, it is difficult to express complex concepts; the relationship between the same sex is not emphasized enough; the anti noise ability is poor. In view of the above problems, there are many better improved algorithms CA.5 (the successor version of 1d3 algorithm) to make the training samples estimate the accuracy of each rule. Since this will lead to an optimistic estimate of the accuracy of the rule, C5 uses a pessimistic estimate to compensate for the bias. As an alternative, a set of test samples independent of the training samples can also be used to assess accuracy.

2.2   Clustering Algorithm

Clustering analysis is different from classification. The class of data objects processed by cluster analysis is unknown. Clustering analysis is the process of grouping objects into clusters composed of similar objects.

Given a database of n objects or tuples, one partition method constructs K partitions of data, each partition represents a cluster, and kqn specifies. The classical algorithms include K-mean and k-medoids, and these algorithms have been added to many statistical analysis software packages or systems, such as SAS and SPSS.

Partition algorithms generally require all data to be loaded into memory, which limits their application on large-scale data; they also require users to specify the number of clusters in advance, but in most practical applications, the final number of clusters is unknown [2]. In addition, the partition algorithm only uses a certain fixed principle to determine the clustering, which makes the clustering results unsatisfactory when the shape of the clustering is irregular or the size of the cluster is very different.

All grid clustering algorithms have the problem of quantization scale. Generally speaking, the possibility of different clustering objects being divided into the same unit is increased due to too rough partition (insufficient quantization); on the contrary, if the partition is too detailed, many small clusters will be obtained.

3   Teaching Evaluation Data Mining System Model

3.1   Overview of dmote Model

Dote (data mining on teaching evaluation) model is a model that applies data mining technology to teaching evaluation. This model combines with the actual teaching evaluation work and builds a decision tree about teaching evaluation information by using decision tree algorithm of mining technology, The non leaf node in the tree represents the key attribute of teaching evaluation, the leaf node represents the judgment of the attribute value of teaching evaluation, its branch represents a partition of tree node attribute value or region, and a path from root node to leaf node represents a rule [3].

The purpose of dhote model is to classify teachers by using decision tree method in data mining, that is, the characteristics of teachers with good or poor teaching quality are mined out and divided into one class; each classification has n rules, which indicates that teachers with good or poor teaching quality have n different types of characteristics; Each rule also shows several key attributes that affect the teaching quality of teachers.

3.2   Theoretical Basis of dmote Model Information Theory

Information theory is a theory established by C.E. Shannon to solve the problem of information transmission (Communication), also known as statistical communication theory. A system for transmitting information is composed of sender (source) and receiver (sink) and the channel (channel) connecting them. Information theory regards communication process as a process of transmitting information in random interference environment. In this communication model, information source and interference (noise) are understood as some kind of random process or random sequence. Therefore, before the actual communication, it is impossible for the receiver (sink) to know exactly what kind of specific information the source will send out, and it is impossible to judge what kind of state the source will be in. In this case, the source state of the destination has uncertainty, and this uncertainty exists before communication, so it is also called prior uncertainty.

(1)   Channel model

       The channel model of information theory is shown in Fig. 1.

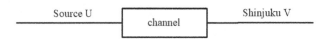

Fig. 1. Channel pattern

The following mathematical formula is obtained:

$$\sum P(v_j \backslash u_l) = 1, \ i = 1, \ 2, \cdots, \ r \tag{1}$$

$P(v_j \backslash u_l)$ is the transition probability of input and output signal letters, that is, when the input signal letter is u_i, the output signal letter is v_j.

(2) Information entropy

The probability of occurrence $P(u_i)$ of message (symbol) u_i constitutes the source mathematical model.

$$\begin{bmatrix} U \\ P \end{bmatrix} = \begin{bmatrix} u_1 \ u_2 \ \cdots \ u_r \\ P(u_1) \ P(u_2) \ \cdots \ P(u_r) \end{bmatrix} \tag{2}$$

3.3 Simulation for ID3 Algorithm with Evaluation System

At present, the most influential example learning method in the world is i03 of J.R. Quinlan. Its predecessor is CS (concept learning system). The working process of CLS is to find out the most discriminating factors first, then divide the data into several subsets, and each subset selects the most discriminative factor to divide until all subsets contain only the same type of data. Finally, a decision tree is obtained, which can be used to classify the new samples.

In the entity world, each entity is described by multiple features. Each feature is limited to take mutually exclusive values in a high scatter set. Each entity belongs to a different category in the world. For simplicity, suppose there are only two categories, P and n. In these two kinds of inductive tasks, the entities of class P and class n are called the positive and negative examples of concepts respectively. Some known positive and negative examples are put together to get the training set.

The leaf of decision tree is a class name, i.e. P or n. Each feature is composed of a different feature. If we want to classify an entity, we test it from the root of the tree. According to the value branch of the feature, we enter the lower level node and test the node [4]. The process goes on to the leaf node, and the entity is judged to belong to the category marked by the leaf node (see Fig. 2).

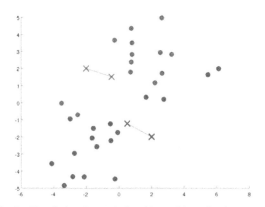

Fig. 2. Simulation for ID3 algorithm with evaluation system

The research of this system is to dig the data of teaching evaluation content. Every school has to evaluate the teaching situation of teachers every half a year [5]. Because of the large number of teachers, and each teacher teaches several courses, the data generated is very amazing. If the school department wants to extract some useful information from it, its workload can be imagined. The development goal of the system is to extract some useful information from the large amount of data, so that the school leaders can be free from the task of studying a large number of data, improve the work efficiency of the school, so as to achieve the purpose of improving the teaching level (see Fig. 3) [6].

The mining system prunes a complete decision tree and adopts post pruning strategy. In the post pruning process, the sub tree replacement operation should be considered. This operation is processed from the leaf node to the tree root. First, access and calculate the error rate of all leaf nodes of a certain subtree, and then calculate the error rate of the subtree by combining the weight of each leaf node (i.e. the number of samples covered); then calculate the error rate after replacing the subtree with a leaf node of the subtree; if the error rate decreases after replacement, the subtree is replaced with this leaf node, otherwise the subtree is retained [7]. Then, consider whether the remaining subtree can be replaced, if so, replace it, otherwise keep it; finally, prune the previously generated decision tree into the simplest decision tree, so as to improve the correctness of the decision tree.

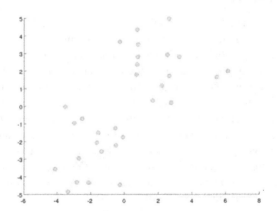

Fig. 3. Simulation for ID3 algorithm with teaching level

4   Demand Analysis of Teaching Evaluation Management System

Before the design and development of the system, we need to analyze the task and function of the system, understand the problems to be solved, the tasks to be completed, and the performance to be achieved. Therefore, the requirement analysis of the system is the basis to ensure the smooth completion of the system and achieve the desired goal. This chapter will analyze the requirements of the teaching quality evaluation system, and provide the basis for the design and implementation of the system [8].

4.1 The Overall Task of Teaching Evaluation System

The teaching evaluation system designed in this paper is to solve the problems of low efficiency of manual operation and poor timeliness in the current school teaching evaluation, ensure the openness and fairness of teaching evaluation, and make teachers and students more convenient to participate in the process of teaching evaluation. Therefore, according to the requirements of school teaching evaluation, there are mainly three links: teacher evaluation, expert evaluation and student evaluation, and the evaluation results should be analyzed and counted to form the final evaluation results. Therefore, combined with all aspects of the evaluation, the system should first be able to manage the basic information of each role. In addition, the most important thing is the evaluation results, that is, the evaluation project, the evaluation algorithm and the evaluation results, which is also the core task of the system. Therefore, around the above tasks, we should first make clear the whole business process of the evaluation, and then complete the demand analysis of the system [9].

4.2 Business Process Analysis

Through in-depth school investigation and discussion, understanding the overall business process of teaching evaluation is the premise of developing this system [10]. Through the interview, we know that the school's teaching quality evaluation is mainly composed of three parts: teacher mutual evaluation, expert evaluation and student evaluation. The specific evaluation process needs to run through the whole semester [11]. The specific business process is that at the beginning of the semester, the school will organize all teachers to give lectures and evaluation activities, that is, all teachers will give Demonstration Courses in their departments, and then the teachers of the same teaching and research department will give their evaluation on the demonstration courses, and this part of the score is the score of teacher evaluation. In the middle of the semester, the school will regularly invite experts from other schools to the school to check the teaching work. In the process of checking, the school will carry out the activities of pushing the door to listen to the class. According to the requirements, every teacher should be attended. If there is no class during the expert inspection, the secondary college will organize the activities to ensure that every teacher should be attended at least once a semester. At the end of the semester, after the students complete the course, the teacher of the course will be evaluated before the final exam, and the evaluation score is the teacher's student evaluation score [12].

5 Analysis of Non Functional Requirements of Teaching Evaluation System

The non functional requirements of the system mainly consider the system function and business, so the following analysis and requirements are from the perspective of performance, database portability and operation [13].

(1) Whether high performance can meet the needs of current teaching quality evaluation is the primary consideration of system performance analysis. First of all, it is

necessary to ensure that a large number of users log in and operate at the same time. It is necessary for the system to investigate the scale of existing teachers and students in Colleges and universities on the spot, reserve space for the above personnel to control the evaluation period and other factors by distinguishing departments and administrators, so as to meet the processing ability of at least 500 people accessing data at the same time. When concurrent access occurs, the system data query is busy, and 3 s is the longest response time or less [14].

(2) There are many drawbacks or defects in database migration ability software system. All kinds of reasons may cause the database used by the software to migrate. Therefore, the migration ability of the system database should be improved, so that it has a variety of database compatibility.

(3) Easy to use, the ease of use of the system should enable users to have a high degree of ease of operation, system design should be based on reference, respect and analysis of customer's operating habits [15].

6   Design and Implementation of Teaching Evaluation Management System

6.1   Design of System Logic Architecture

As the enrollment scale of the school is gradually expanding, the number of students in the school is increasing, the amount of information of students is very huge, and the evaluation mode and emphasis are constantly adjusting, so the system should be well designed for scalability at the beginning of development. As far as the actual situation is concerned, the client of the system mainly includes two parts of the campus LAN and the off campus Internet. In the actual design, due to the huge amount of information of students and teachers, and the student evaluation is the largest data group in the role of using the system, it is mainly for teaching evaluation after logging into the system, so it is necessary to configure a special data server to store the corresponding data, and then realize the operation of reading and writing data through the interface between the functional logic layer and the database, The interaction between system and user is realized through browser. To sum up, the overall architecture design of the system is mainly divided into three layers, namely the presentation layer, business layer and data layer. The performance layer is the front end of the system, which mainly completes the interaction between users and the system; the business layer is the logic layer of the system, which is mainly to realize the function logic of the system: the last layer is the data layer, which is used to store all the data of the system [16].

6.2   System Functional Architecture Design

In the process of comprehensive teaching evaluation, it is found that in the whole evaluation process, users such as teachers, students and experts mainly participate in the evaluation process [17, 18]. Therefore, first of all, it is necessary to manage the basic information data of these users. Secondly, it is the evaluation function of each user role, that is, teacher evaluation, expert evaluation and student evaluation. Finally, it is necessary to conduct comprehensive statistics on the evaluation results [19]. The system is mainly divided into five main functions: basic data management, teacher evaluation, expert evaluation, student evaluation and comprehensive statistical analysis. In addition, in order to ensure the security of the system, the login module should be designed to prevent illegal users from logging in and ensure the security of the system. In addition, in order to ensure that the evaluation among teachers, experts and students is independent of each other in the whole evaluation process, it is necessary to set corresponding authority to evaluate within the scope of its own authority, and it is not allowed to interfere and check the evaluation results of other roles. In addition, the user's password and organizational structure should also be managed, so the corresponding system management module should be designed for the management of basic data such as data, organization, password, etc. in addition to the management of the above basic parameters, the evaluation index can also be managed in the system management, which mainly involves the setting of evaluation index and weight [20].

7   Testing of Teaching Evaluation System

System testing is to find the existing problems and hidden dangers in the operation of the software, and modify and correct them in time to ensure that the computer software is consistent with the initial goal. The main task of this system is to complete the test of the system function. In the process of testing, we don't need to investigate the program structure and algorithm in the system, just need to regard the system as a closed black box, and ignore its internal structure, Only the corresponding output result after the input instruction is tested. Therefore, the black box test is relatively simple, which is often used in the current software testing. Through the design of functional test cases, the various functions of the system are tested by enumeration method.

8   Conclusion

The evaluation of teachers' teaching quality is an effective measure taken by the school to comprehensively improve the teaching quality, effectively regulate the teaching behavior, optimize the structure of the teaching staff, promote the improvement of the teaching level of the teachers, and make the management of the teaching staff systematic and scientific. Especially in recent years, with the expansion of enrollment in Colleges and universities, the quality of students declines, which puts forward higher requirements for teachers' teaching quality. Therefore, it is very important to strengthen the construction of teaching staff and the evaluation of teaching quality. Teachers' teaching quality evaluation is a practical work, which needs a certain scientific theoretical basis and method as the basis. The index system is the basis and basis of evaluation, and the selection of teaching methods directly affects the scientificity of evaluation results. This paper points out the disadvantages of traditional teaching evaluation methods, which are almost used to evaluate a teacher's teaching quality. However, it is difficult to explain what factors are related to the level of teaching level, It is more difficult to tell us what characteristics of teachers' teaching factors, the teaching quality and teaching level will be higher. However, with today's cutting-edge technology data mining, we can break through the limitations of the original method, so as to solve the problem. Based on the B/S structure, this paper develops a teacher teaching evaluation management system, which solves the problems of low efficiency and long time in the traditional manual evaluation operation. Different from the previous way, it adds the functions of fast browsing, statistics and analysis, which has high technical content. At the same time, we should pay attention to solve some problems in the process of system development. In order to achieve the maximum efficiency of the system and the smooth progress of the evaluation work, we have to consider the network speed and the response sensitivity of the website. If we can't solve the problem of user access caused by busy web pages, the best system, the most beautiful interface and the best user experience design will be greatly reduced. Therefore, the powerful, rapid and large capacity of the system must be considered.

References

1. Liu, K.: Modern Teaching Theory. Southwest Normal University Press, Chongqing (1993)
2. Zhu, J.: Statistical Methods and Practice of Data Mining. China Statistics Press, Beijing (2005)
3. Zhang, Y., Gong, L.: Principle and Technology of Data Mining. Electronic Industry Press, Beijing (2004)
4. Zhu, M.: Data Mining. China University of Science and Technology Press, Beijing (2002)
5. Sun, C., Zhang, Y.: Design and implementation of online teaching evaluation system based on B/S structure. Comput. Appl. Softw. (2012)
6. Qi, F.: Design and implementation of teaching quality evaluation system based on B/S structure. Comput. Knowl. Technol. (22) (2012)
7. Huang, X.: Design and implementation of secondary vocational teaching evaluation system based on B/S mode. Hunan University (2014)
8. Cui, X.: Design and implementation of University Teachers' teaching evaluation management system. Jilin University (2014)
9. Deng, Z., Liu, Y.: Design and implementation of university teaching supervision and evaluation system based on mobile terminal. Modern Electronic Technology (2015)
10. Wu, R., Chen, B.: Design scheme of web based classroom teaching quality evaluation system. J. Inner Mongolia Agric. Univ. (Soc. Sci. Ed.) (2) (2013)
11. Yan, Q., Han, J., Xia, Y.: Modeling and implementation of university teaching daily management system based on UML. Comput. Technol. Dev. (4) (2014)
12. Tang, H.: Design and implementation of university teaching process evaluation system. University of Electronic Science and Technology (2015)
13. Wang, Q.: Design and implementation of university teaching quality evaluation and analysis system. Xi'an University of Technology (2008)
14. Yan, Y.: Research on modular teaching design of College Students' career development and Employment Guidance Course. Southwest University (2015)
15. Zhao, Y.: Design and implementation of college teaching evaluation system based on net. Tianjin University (2015)
16. Wang, F.: Design and implementation of comprehensive evaluation system for College Teachers' Teaching. Shandong University (2014)
17. Eagle, M.: Object to Relational Mapping and Relationship with Hibernate. Wiley Computer Publishing, Hoboken (2004)

18. Wang, X., Liu, Z., Shi, L., Liu, C., Wang, F.: Design and implementation of university teaching evaluation system. Agric. Netw. Inf. (05), 158–160 (2016)
19. China Educational Technology and equipment, 2014 contents. China Educ. Technol. Equip. (01), 120–142 (2015)
20. Feng, F., Qi, G., Jia, S., Zhang, H., Li, X.: Construction of innovative mode of university teaching evaluation based on the perspective of system theory. J. Hebei Agric. Univ. (Agric. Forest. Educ. Ed.) **19**(03), 15–21 (2017)

Design of Personalized Recommended English Assisted Teaching System in Big Data Environment

Xuxuan Huang(✉)

Guangzhou University Sontan College, Zhucun Road, Zengcheng District, Guangzhou 511370, China

Abstract. According to the information needs of English learning and the problems existing in current English teaching, this paper proposes an English teaching system based on personalized recommendation. In order to realize the system, the business process of the system is analyzed to provide a reference for the follow-up function design; then, combined with the above requirements, the function, physical architecture, technical architecture of the system are designed, and the login module and personalized recommendation module of the system are designed, and the interface implementation code is given. The above-mentioned auxiliary learning interface not only provides a better idea for the promotion and improvement of current English information teaching, but also provides a reference for the application of Intelligent Recommendation Algorithm in English teaching.

Keywords: Collaborative filtering algorithm · English assisted instruction · MVC architecture · B/S mode · Physical structure

1 Introduction

With the application of computer information technology in teaching, all kinds of English assistant teaching system emerge as the times require. These assistant teaching management systems not only promote the application of information technology in teaching, but also promote the sharing of English teaching resources. Relying on the campus network and adopting the idea of network layering, this paper builds an auxiliary teaching system which can be used for English learning, so that college students can complete their English learning through the campus network; designs and constructs an English auxiliary teaching system with C++ development language, which has the characteristics of simple and practical; takes English writing as the breakthrough point, This paper constructs a special English teaching software for writing, which greatly improves students' English writing ability; Li Feng and others introduce big data inverted index technology into the writing assistant teaching system, whose purpose is to improve the efficiency and accuracy of writing model search [1].

© ICST Institute for Computer Sciences, Social Informatics and Telecommunications Engineering 2021
Published by Springer Nature Switzerland AG 2021. All Rights Reserved
M. A. Jan and F. Khan (Eds.): BigIoT-EDU 2021, LNICST 391, pp. 469–474, 2021.
https://doi.org/10.1007/978-3-030-87900-6_54

2 System Requirement Analysis

The main requirements of the system focus on the following aspects: first, as a system, the basic information of the system should be maintained and managed, which is the basis; second, as an English auxiliary teaching system, various English teaching resources can be managed and stored, so as to facilitate the majority of users to download and consult resources; third, real-time online English examination can be carried out, It includes daily basic English knowledge, CET-4 and CET-6 question bank, final exam, etc., and the backstage administrator can manage and intelligently generate test papers; fourthly, through the system, in order to stimulate the learning initiative, it also provides an interactive discussion area, so as to facilitate the communication between teachers and students; fifthly, through the system, it actively provides learning recommendation content for the majority of students, In order to improve the intelligence of the system. In this paper, intelligent recommendation is a highlight of this paper.

3 System Design

3.1 System Function Design

In the system function module, the whole module function is divided into six parts [2].

(1) User login and registration. This part is mainly for users to log in to the system with their own user name and password. After the login comparison is passed, they can directly enter into different user function interfaces. For users who are not registered, they can log in to the corresponding function interfaces after registration and audit.

(2) System management. This part of the module is mainly to manage the password, and divide the function permissions of different users of the system.

(3) Students learn. This part is mainly to improve the learning interface for English learning students, including the learning of materials, courseware, etc. at the same time, it also includes the test of different knowledge points, chapters and professional public English grades through this module, and the communication with teachers.

(4) Teachers teach. This part is mainly for teachers to manage the examination questions, evaluate the students' examinations online, and answer questions online.

(5) Personalized recommendation module. This module is mainly combined with the database system to complete the personalized recommendation of students' different knowledge points and writing model articles, so as to provide reference learning content according to students' interests.

3.2 System Architecture Design

Combined with the actual situation of the English auxiliary teaching system, this paper decided to rely on the traditional campus network to build the network topology of the system. In this regard, from the logical structure, the whole system is divided into three parts: client, server and transmission. Among them, the transmission of teaching resources relies on the campus network, which aims to maximize the security and transmission efficiency of English resources transmission, and prevent the invasion of viruses outside the school; at the same time, the construction of virtual teaching platform is based on offline technology, that is, teachers can upload their teaching content to the system server by recording videos, And students can view the teaching content through virtual teaching classroom to make up for the lack of learning in class.

3.3 System Technology Architecture Design

For the construction of the system, the quality of its architecture is directly related to the operation of the system. Considering the current system development technology, this paper chooses B/SMVC + Dao development mode. In the aspect of system layering, the system is divided into three layers: page display layer, business layer and data management layer. The page display layer mainly provides interactive interface for users through. ASPX web page. In the business layer, it includes server and business module. In order to improve the logic of the whole system, this paper adopts the mode of model + view + controller, When the user clicks the page, the script embedded in the page triggers the response, that is, the view interface. The view interface interacts with the controller, and then the controller allocates different business functions to different applications. Finally, through the Dao interface, the interaction with the data is completed, and the results are directly transmitted to the view interface and displayed to the user. Through this way of deployment, it has two advantages: one is convenient access, users only need to click the page to complete the access to the system, without updating and installing; the other is the stable operation of the system. Through the logic processing of MVC, the whole auxiliary learning system runs more stably. The specific architecture is shown in Fig. 1 [3].

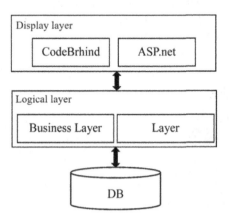

Fig. 1. Overall architecture design of the system

3.4 Design of Intelligent Recommendation Module

For English learning, the most important part is to combine the user's interest, to give students relevant recommendations, in order to expand the students' knowledge, but also progress and improve the intelligence of the system. In this regard, combined with the current intelligent recommendation algorithm, this paper proposes a collaborative filtering of English learning content.

Calculate the similarity, as shown in formula (1).

$$sim(x, y) = \frac{\sum\limits_{m \in m_{xy}} (g_{x,m} - g_x)(g_{y,m} - g_y)}{\sqrt{\sum\limits_{m \in m_{xy}} (g_{x,m} - g_x)^2 \sum\limits_{m \in m_{xy}} (g_{y,m} - g_y)^2}} \tag{1}$$

Where $x \in L$, $y \in L$.

Then, the score value of the non scored video m by the learner x is predicted, which is described as formula (2).

$$g_{x,m} = g_x + \frac{\sum\limits_{a=1}^{k} (g_{a,i} - g_a)sim(x, a)}{\sum\limits_{a=1}^{k} sim(x, a)} \tag{2}$$

Where, denotes the number of nearest neighbors of learner x.

4   Environment Development and System Simulation

This system takes. Net system as the development foundation, and uses ASP.NET The database is developed by SQL Server 2012. In terms of hardware, the memory size is 4 GB, the hard disk size is 512gb, and the processor is core 5; in terms of software, the server adopts iis7.0 version [4] (see Fig. 2).

Old version   New version

Fig. 2. Critical thinking: from theory to teaching

The idea and method of mathematical modeling require students to solve the practical engineering problems by using the mathematical knowledge they have mastered. Students need to simplify and assume the practical problems through positive thinking, seek a reasonable mathematical model to solve, analyze and evaluate the results, and then use a variety of mathematical software, such as MOSEK APS MOSEK, to create a suitable mathematical model, And to improve and optimize the mathematical model, simple understanding is to use computer to transform engineering problems into learning problems. When using mathematical modeling to solve problems, students not only need to actively use the required professional knowledge, but also need to use mathematical thinking, creative ability and problem-solving ability. Mathematical modeling can overcome the defects of traditional higher mathematics teaching, stimulate students' interest in learning mathematics, improve students' mathematical literacy, improve students' ability to use and operate mathematical software, and help students improve the speed and efficiency of solving problems through computers (see Fig. 3).

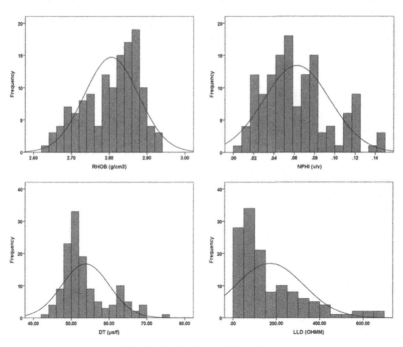

Fig. 3. Study time with students

5 Conclusion

Through the above design, we can see that this system and recommendation algorithm can provide more scientific and intelligent English learning recommendation for the majority of students. Through the design of this paper, we can see that in terms of system construction, B/S + MVC + Dao technology architecture has good advantages in terms of system stability; in terms of intelligent recommendation, collaborative filtering algorithm is widely used. Test or trial run can verify the feasibility of the design. The above two technologies also provide reference for the application of other courses.

References

1. Zhu, Y.: Design and implementation of Higher Vocational English assistant teaching system based on campus network. Electron. Des. Eng. **25**(11), 54–56 (2017)
2. Cao, L.: Computer aided English teaching based on C++ and windows design. Autom. Instrum. **v3**(5), 206–207 (2016)
3. Kang, G.: Design of computer aided English writing teaching system in Higher Vocational Colleges. Vocat. Educ. News **v14**(9), 45–46 (2015)
4. Li, F., Wei, N.: Research and implementation of foreign language writing teaching assistant system based on big data inverted index technology. Audio Vis. Foreign Lang. Teach. **v8**(3), 31–37 (2015)

Digital Teaching Resources of College Physical Education with Cloud Computing

Chen Li[⊠], Mingyuan Zhao, and Yiyuan Yang

School of Physical Education and Health, Zhaoqing University, Zhaoqing 526061, Guangdong, China

Abstract. This paper analyzes the problems faced by the construction of sports information resources in Colleges and universities, probes into the influence of cloud computing on the construction of sports information resources in Colleges and universities and the new opportunities it brings, and puts forward some strategies for the construction of sports information resources in Colleges and Universities under the environment of cloud computing.

Keywords: Cloud computing · Colleges and universities · Sports information resources

1 Introduction

With the development of society, the degree of informatization is higher and higher, people have a new understanding of information resources. University sports information resource is an important part of the information resource database, covering the new direction of the development of sports science at home and abroad, new achievements of sports research, new technology of training and competition and other aspects [1]. In addition, the comprehensive level of college sports is closely related to the collection and management of sports information resources to a certain extent. The rapid development of information technology has brought new opportunities and challenges to the construction of sports information resources in Colleges and universities. The emergence of cloud computing technology has opened up a new way for the management and utilization of sports information resources. With the improvement of cloud computing application, with the help of cloud computing technology, we can use less investment to solve the current problems, further improve the ability of resource construction and information resource service, and enhance the service ability for sports teaching, sports promotion, sports research and other activities. This paper analyzes the current situation of the construction of college sports information resources, and puts forward a new idea of the construction of college sports information resources in the cloud computing environment.

M. A. Jan and F. Khan (Eds.): BigIoT-EDU 2021, LNICST 391, pp. 475–484, 2021.
https://doi.org/10.1007/978-3-030-87900-6_55

2 Current Situation of Sports Information Resources Construction in Colleges and Universities in China

The construction of information resources mainly refers to the use of modern information technology means to process, transfer, develop and utilize the content of information. At this stage, the focus is on the development and utilization of new resources such as electronic literature, database and network resources. In recent years, colleges and universities attach great importance to the equipment of information network equipment, and continue to increase investment, but they do not pay enough attention to the construction of information resources, so the construction of sports information resources in Colleges and universities has not been well developed, especially weak compared with other disciplines. China is a big sports country, leading the world in sports education, scientific research and sports journals, book publishing, but the development and utilization of sports information resources is far from enough, there is a big gap compared with other countries. Even if some colleges and universities have certain advantages in sports literature resources, they are facing the crisis of aging resources, loss, backward equipment and lack of funds to supplement new resources due to insufficient attention and development. Although colleges and universities such as Beijing Sport University have begun to build some Chinese and foreign books and periodicals database of sports major, generally speaking, the construction of professional sports information resources in Colleges and universities in China is still in its infancy, and there is a big gap compared with foreign universities, Among all the databases, there are no professional sports databases, only 19% of which contain sports information resources. As a professional college, Tianjin Institute of physical education has only one non online professional database besides dissertation database.

3 Intelligent Data Desensitization Technology for Cloud Computing

3.1 Long Term and Short Term Memory Network LSTM

LSTM (long short term memory) network is a variant of RNN [2]. By adding gate control, LSTM network can fuse long-term and short-term memory, which solves the problem of only short-term memory due to RNN gradient disappearance to a certain extent. LSTM uses a "Gates" network structure: a method to let information selectively pass through, including SIGMOD function and dot multiplication operation. The "gate" structure can be used to add and delete information to the cell state. The calculation formula is as follows:

$$f_t = \sigma\left(W_f\left[h_{t-1}, x_t\right] + b_f\right) \tag{1}$$

The input gate first defines which information can be stored, and then creates a new candidate value vector based on tanh function. The calculation formula is as follows:

$$i_t = \sigma\left(W_i\left[h_{t-1}, x_t\right] + b_i\right) \tag{2}$$

$$\widehat{C}_t = \tanh\left(W_C\left[h_{t-1,x_t} + b_C\right]\right) \tag{3}$$

The output gate determines which part of the cell state will be output based on the cell state information, and then multiplies the output of the output layer through the tanh layer [3].

According to the current research and application of cloud computing, cloud computing has four main characteristics: network centric, dynamic resource allocation, demand service self-service, resource pooling and transparency. Cloud computing architecture is divided into three layers: user access interface, core services and service management. The core services of cloud computing include software as a service, platform as a service and infrastructure as a service, as shown in Fig. 1. All kinds of services in the core service layer can meet the diverse needs of users. The user access interface layer provides the interface for cloud users to access the services of the core service layer, and the service management layer provides support for the core service layer, which provides a favorable guarantee for the security, reliability and availability of the core service layer (see Figs. 1 and 2).

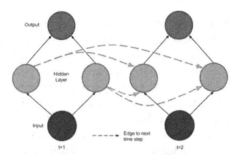

Fig. 1. LSTM structure

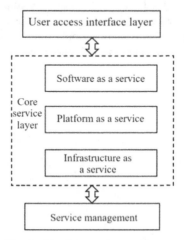

Fig. 2. Cloud computing architecture

4   Construction Strategy of College Sports Information Resources Under Cloud Computing Environment

4.1   Strengthen the Collection and Digitization of Sports Books and Periodicals

University libraries should give full play to their ability to collect various forms of sports information as much as possible, including primary literature and secondary literature, including various sports joint index, encyclopedia, national sports dictionary, Yearbook, etc. The collation of sports materials should not be limited to the surface text, but should be deeply integrated. At the same time, we should also establish some special sports information resource databases, such as the "National Traditional Sports bibliographic database" compiled by the library of Shanghai Institute of physical education and the "table tennis special database" compiled by the library of Beijing Sport University [4].

4.2   Strengthen the Construction of Sports Characteristic Database

The State General Administration of sports has built a variety of databases, including competitive training, management, industry and other aspects [5]. On the one hand, university libraries can make full use of these databases, on the other hand, they need to develop their own databases. They can develop characteristic sports information resource databases based on the existing cloud technology service platform, such as teaching video database, self-study self-evaluation database, exercise prescription database, etc., which are closely related to students' physical education [6]. On this basis, we can establish the evaluation system of students' and teachers' self exercise fitness effect, which not only enables students and teachers to learn the theory and method of physical fitness in the information data, but also can directly test the actual effect of learning and exercise in the database, and more intuitively feed back the problems existing in the process of learning and exercise, It plays a very good role in promoting the improvement of learning and exercise methods in the next step. At the same time, the development of sports characteristic database in Colleges and universities should fully consider the characteristics of local sports, leisure sports, local stadiums and other aspects. Through the construction

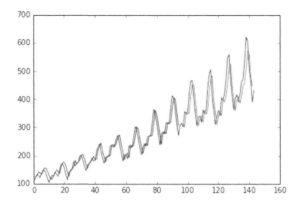

Fig. 3. Simulation for sports characteristic database

of characteristic database, not only can our information resources be expanded, but also colleges and universities have accumulated certain resources to enhance their software strength, which is convenient for teachers and students to quickly inquire the information they need, and then enjoy the teaching resources well (see Fig. 3).

5 The Design of "Physical Education Cloud"

5.1 The Basic Framework of "Physical Education Cloud"

Because the users of "physical education cloud" are only for the students in Colleges and universities for the time being, using the large capacity storage device in the university computer room as the server or renting a small network server can meet the hardware requirements of "physical education cloud" [7]. The software runs the system by several modules. The first is the database management software to manage the data of students and teachers, which is embedded in the server terminal; the second is the client authorized to teachers, which gives teachers corresponding operation authority; the last is the client authorized to students, which also gives corresponding operation authority. Customer end includes mobile software client, tablet software client, web client and computer software client. Students and teachers only need to download the system software on the corresponding intelligent devices, and can log in to the system with the given user name and password. The survey shows that among the 500 college students who fill in the questionnaire, the popularity rate of smart phones has reached 100%, and 93% of them are willing to app the teaching management system [8].

5.2 Operation Mode Design of "Physical Education Cloud"

After the enrollment of new students, the information of each new student will be entered into the database, including the basic information of enrollment, such as name, student number, etc. [9]. After the beginning of the school, the freshmen are given a complete physique test. The content of the physique test is in accordance with the "College Students' physique test standard" issued by the state. After the test, the teacher checks the students' scores and enters them into the database as the "basic data" of the students. After the teacher enters the data, the system will automatically group the students according to their test scores, so as to ensure that the students with similar physical fitness are in a group. Physical education will be carried out according to the groups, and different teaching contents and load and intensity of physical education will be arranged for different groups of students. Students can view and check their basic data through the student's client. If they find any problems with the data, they can contact the teacher for review and modification [10].

5.3 Curriculum Model

At the beginning of the semester, according to the grouping of students by the system and the number of students in each group, the course selection questionnaire is issued to the students in each group. The questionnaire includes all the elective courses pre opened by the school, as well as the skill level of the relevant courses that the students already have [11, 12]. The system analyzes and arranges the required courses and elective courses for each group according to the big data of the questionnaire results. Students can log in to the system to select elective courses in their respective groups [13]. After the completion of course selection, the cloud system automatically generates classes and publicizes them to teachers and students. Students can query their class time, place and teachers through the system; meanwhile, teachers can obtain the data permissions of students in their class. Each class automatically forms a class group, in which teachers can release course information, homework and emergency notice to students. The information released by teachers will be quickly transmitted to students by mobile client push. Students can also leave messages and ask questions to teachers through the system. In the process of class, the smart mobile terminal (including smart phones and tablets) installed in the teacher's hand can replace the roster for attendance, record and score. The situation of students in the classroom can be synchronized with the cloud at any time through the teacher's client and entered into the database [14].

In terms of extracurricular activities, the cloud system will assign different exercise tasks to students according to their basic data, mainly to strengthen the weaknesses of each student in the basic data. The task of extracurricular activities will be completed within the specified time of extracurricular activities, which will be supervised and confirmed by the teachers on duty and entered into the database. For example, some students in group C who are lack of aerobic exercise ability in the previous article will have more than 20 min of fast walking, jogging, riding, swimming and other sports that are of great help to aerobic ability. If conditions permit, the monitoring of extracurricular activities can be separated from the real-time monitoring of teachers under the "physical education cloud" platform [15]. The monitoring means are the GPS data uploaded by the intelligent terminal in the hands of students and the corresponding heart rate (the heart rate can be accurately measured by the camera and flash of mobile phone). The two indicators are combined to determine whether the task of extracurricular activities of students is completed. Reduce the workload of physical education teachers at the same time, the students' extracurricular activities time, intensity and amount of data. This will enable teachers to evaluate students' extracurricular activities more accurately.

5.4   Inter School League

Many foreign college sports associations and inter school leagues have made great achievements. For example, Stanford University in California holds a rugby match with Berkeley University before Thanksgiving every year [16]. This traditional game, which started in 1892, has a very loud name big game, which means the "gratitude and resent-ment" between the two universities spanning a generation, We have to fight each other through such an annual rugby match. A month before the competition, the students began to publicize. On the day of the competition, most local residents were attracted to watch the competition. The results after the competition will be talked about by local residents and students for about a week. This kind of competition between two famous universi-ties, from Harvard University and Yale University on the east coast of the United States to Oxford University and Cambridge University in the United Kingdom, is the same. The football match between Stanford and Berkeley is not only a sports competition, but also a competition in spirit between the two schools, which promotes the development of both sides in academic and scientific research [17].

Various associations and departments can carry out inter school league matches on some popular competitive sports. The league matches are organized and operated by the association president or the sports minister (student) of each department. A relevant special sports teacher is invited to control and supervise as the referee president, and train the student referees. Leagues can be launched through cloud computing platform, and more than a certain number of teams can respond to it. Leagues can also be launched in the name of a challenge from one community or department to another, and the other party can respond to it. In the process of the league, the outstanding athletes, referees and competition organization staff will be nominated by the referee of the league and uploaded to the cloud, which is also one of the evaluation criteria of physical education performance. In addition, the winning League Association or department will receive a series of honors and awards. For example, the first League Association can add a star on the community badge of the cloud platform (refer to the world cup). While inheriting the honor, it can attract more students to join, and encourage other associations to promote the sense of competition in sports competitions and form a virtuous circle of catching up.

6 Comparative Analysis of "Physical Education Cloud" and Traditional Mode

6.1 Sports Cognition

Under the traditional sports mode, students can not easily learn the theoretical knowledge of sports science and lack of awareness of sports participation [18]. In the current college physical education system, because the communication channel between teachers and students is not perfect, there is no good feedback channel, teachers do not fully understand the students, and the feedback is only the feedback of classroom teaching content. Students' interest in sports, students' sports habits, students' specific physical quality can not be well and effectively fed back to PE teachers. Therefore, physical education teachers can not teach students in accordance with their aptitude, only according to the appropriate subjects. At the same time, the traditional physical education curriculum largely ignores the students' Physical Education cognitive education, which can not well stimulate the students' exercise motivation, nor can it teach the students some basic sports science knowledge similar to the basic sports physiology and sports injury prevention and timely treatment. "Physical education cloud" provides an efficient and fast feedback channel between teachers and students. Teachers can understand students' physical condition through students' data, and students can also understand teachers' professional fields through the system. Cloud system provides instant messaging function for communication between teachers and students, so that teachers can adjust the teaching content and methods according to the status of students at any time, and improve the pertinence of teaching. On the other hand, teachers can instill advanced physical education concepts and exercise methods into students through "physical education cloud", improve students' cognition of physical education, stimulate students' internal motivation to participate in physical exercise, and improve students' sports scientific literacy and appreciation level.

6.2 Physical Education Curriculum Management

Teaching students in accordance with their aptitude is one of the principles of pedagogy, but in the current implementation of physical education, in order to facilitate the unified management, colleges and universities generally use administrative classes for teaching, or in the form of elective courses for teaching. From the perspective of teaching, this kind of teaching division ignores the difference of students' physical quality, resulting in the situation that some students can easily complete the learning tasks assigned by teachers, while some students can't, so it's difficult to achieve very ideal teaching effect. "Physical education cloud" carries out class grouping teaching for students according to their physical quality, implements the principle of differential treatment in physical education, and divides students with similar physical quality into a class for teaching, which can facilitate teachers to arrange teaching content and load intensity, strengthen classroom pertinence and improve the efficiency of Physical Education under the condition of constant workload of physical education teachers.

6.3 Extracurricular Activities

"Like physical education, do not like physical education" is a common phenomenon among college students, as physical education workers, it is very worthy of our reflection. At present, the physical education curriculum in Colleges and universities is mainly based on the classroom, in addition to the classroom, there is little communication between teachers and students. Extracurricular sports activities are also organized by students spontaneously, and are not well combined with the classroom. Therefore, students who love sports will consciously participate in extracurricular activities, while students who do not like sports activities will no longer do extracurricular exercises after completing the tasks in the physical education class. The mobilization of students' subjective initiative in the physical education class is not enough to stimulate students' awareness of sports participation, It is not enough to cultivate the awareness of lifelong physical education. "Physical education cloud" will also incorporate extracurricular sports activities into the content of physical education curriculum and serve as a reference for the results of physical education, which can make extracurricular activities closely linked with the classroom, stimulate students' awareness of sports participation, and cultivate students' sports habits. Students can register teams through the system for sports league matches to activate the school sports atmosphere; they can also establish sports interest groups to exercise in extracurricular sports activities and obtain pleasant emotional experience at the same time.

7 Conclusion

As today's hot it technology, cloud computing can process massive amounts of information in an instant and achieve the same powerful performance as supercomputers. At the same time, users can flexibly use these resources and services on demand, so as to realize the dream of providing computing as a public facility. At present, the application of cloud computing in the construction of information resources is still in the primary stage, there are still many problems, but with the maturity of cloud computing technology, the unique advantages of cloud computing can make the construction of sports information resources in a wider range of cooperation, co construction and sharing, so as to provide better services for users. Colleges and universities can hand over the complicated and tedious work to the cloud computing service providers, which can save a lot of money and human resources, and put more energy on improving the quality of teaching. As an effective way to integrate educational information resources, cloud computing has its unique advantages. Colleges and universities should fully tap its advantages and apply it to teaching and scientific research. Cloud computing will have a broader development space in Colleges and universities and education network.

References

1. Peng, G., Zhou, G.: Research on hierarchical architecture of cloud computing. Mob. Commun. (16), 54–58 (2010)
2. Li, Q., Zheng, X.: Overview of cloud computing research. Comput. Sci. (4), 32–33 (2011)
3. Wu, H.: Discussion on the construction of library information resources under the "cloud computing" environment. Sci. Tech. Inf. (25), 644 (2010)
4. Sun, J.: Future computing in the cloud: cloud computing and mobile learning. Mod. Educ. Technol. 12(7), 60–67 (2010)
5. Pan, L.: Discussion on physical education teaching mode. Central China Normal University (2002)
6. Ge, B.: Research on the overall optimization of physical education teaching mode. Northeast Normal University (2007)
7. Lei, J., Jia, J.: Current situation and development trend of physical education teaching mode in Colleges and universities in China. J. Xi'an Inst. Phys. Educ. 03, 109-111 + 130 (2006)
8. Xu, J.: Systematic analysis of the concept of physical education teaching mode – also on the ternary operation mechanism of the concept of physical education teaching mode. Phys. Educ. Sci. 03, 75–78 (2006)
9. Shao, W., Shang, Z.: On the current situation and future development of physical education teaching mode research. J. Beijing Sport Univ. 01, 85–87 (2005)
10. Nie, D., Lin, H., Hang, L., Dong, L., Gou, D.: Analysis on current situation and trend of research on physical education teaching mode in Colleges and universities. J. Xi'an Inst. Phys. Educ. 02, 101-103 +107 (2005)
11. Zhang, Z., Dou, X.: Comparative study on physical education teaching mode between China and America. J. Nanjing Inst. Phys. Educ. (Soc. Sci. Ed.) 05, 86–88 (2007)
12. Yang, J., Liu, H.: Physical education teaching mode under the background of new curriculum. J. Phys. Educ. 06, 66–69 (2008)
13. Mao, Z.: Research on physical education teaching mode. J. Guangzhou Inst. Phys. Educ. 04, 41–48 (2000)
14. Mao, Z., Wu, J., Ma, Z.: On physical education teaching mode. Phys. Educ. Sci. 06, 5–8 (1998)
15. Cao, W.: Research on the current situation of physical education teaching mode of junior middle school in Yantai under the background of new curriculum standard. Ludong University (2014)

16. Wei, Y.: Research and analysis on physical education teaching mode in Colleges and universities. J. Shandong Inst. Phys. Educ. **02**, 75–78 (2010)
17. Chen, K., Zheng, W.: Cloud computing: system examples and research status. Acta Softw. Sinica **05**, 1337–1348 (2009)
18. Peng, G.: Analysis of the relationship between the current physical education teaching concept and the physical education teaching mode in Colleges and universities. J. Guangzhou Inst. Phys. Educ. **03**, 122–125 (2009)

Music Education Online System with Cloud Computing

Macuo Zhuo(✉)

Qinghai Higher Vocational and Technical College, Haidong 810799, Qinghai, China

Abstract. The educational goal of our country is to ensure the all-round development of learning, sports, beauty and labor. The quality of students is comprehensive. We should pay attention to the topics that were originally despised. The happiness of quality education embodies the important position of aesthetic education in education. Our country's ancient grape saw the beautiful, fast, beautiful, healthy moral education music. It can influence people's ideological and moral imperceptibly and promote the improvement of students' moral quality. Therefore, Zhai should attach importance to music education. At present, cloud computing is trying to improve the effect of music education worldwide.

Keywords: Cloud computing · Music · Teaching · Quality education

1 Introduction

Cloud computing is a commercial implementation based on distributed storage and processing, parallel processing and grid computing. Cloud computing can provide at least seven kinds of business services, such as super computing power, secure data storage and software as a service [1]. In other words, cloud computing stores data in the cloud, and puts software and services in the cloud. The services provided by cloud computing are based on various standards and protocols, and can access and process cloud data through various device terminals.

1.1 Cloud Computing has Stronger Security

Many people worry that the data security of cloud computing is not guaranteed, but in fact, cloud data is more secure than ordinary storage devices. Cloud computing operators have a professional team to save, maintain and disaster backup the user's data, so users don't have to worry about data loss and damage. Because the cloud appears as a server cluster, the cloud can provide very powerful data computing capabilities through grid computing. As a result, users do not have to stick to the hardware configuration of terminal devices. Cloud devices can easily handle large-scale data calculation, and then send the results back to the terminal.

© ICST Institute for Computer Sciences, Social Informatics and Telecommunications Engineering 2021
Published by Springer Nature Switzerland AG 2021. All Rights Reserved
M. A. Jan and F. Khan (Eds.): BigIoT-EDU 2021, LNICST 391, pp. 485–493, 2021.
https://doi.org/10.1007/978-3-030-87900-6_56

1.2 Optimization Model of Cloud Computing

Given the cloud workflow task set t and mobile cloud resource set R, the goal of cloud task scheduling is to generate scheduling solution s to minimize the total execution time, total execution cost and total execution energy consumption of tasks [2]. Let time (T_i) denote the execution time of task T; cost (T_i) denotes the execution cost of task T; energy (T_i) represents the execution energy consumption of task T_i; D represents the deadline constraint of task completion; If B is the budget constraint for completing the task, C is the energy constraint of mobile cloud resources, then the multi-objective task scheduling problem can be formalized as

$$\min Time(S) = \max time(T_i) = AFT(T_{exit}) \tag{1}$$

$$\min Cost(S) = \sum_{T_i \in T} \cos t(T_i) \tag{2}$$

$$\min Energy(S) = \sum_{T_i \in T} Energy(T_i) \tag{3}$$

The resource structure is shown in Fig. 1.

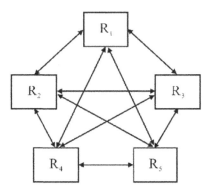

Fig. 1. Electronic resource structure

2   Problems Existing in Music Education in Schools

2.1   Improper Methods of Active Classroom

The new music curriculum standard of our country clearly stipulates that "according to the law of students' physical and mental development and aesthetic psychological characteristics, we should stimulate and cultivate students' interest in learning with rich and colorful teaching contents and lively teaching forms.". In the general music teaching, with the help of the former party's performance method, arranging students to perform part of the role in music teaching can let students live in the scene, better feel the atmosphere described by music, so that students can get closer to music, and then have a pleasant feeling from the aesthetic of music. Many teachers pursue the classroom atmosphere one sidedly, and the teaching plan designed does not match the students' age and psychological characteristics. The performance arranged for students can not help students to deepen their understanding of music, so although the classroom atmosphere is active, it can not bring a little help to classroom teaching.

2.2 Blind Subject Synthesis, Ignoring the Characteristics of Music Itself

According to the requirements of the new curriculum standard, compared with the old teaching materials, the new teaching materials, both the integrity of teaching materials and the integration of subjects, should be significantly improved. However, if everything is to be measured, there must be a limit to synthesis. Synthesis is not abuse, nor is it a divergent and aimless explanation [3]. If it is too chaotic, it will only make students totally unable to accept the teaching content and make them self defeating.

2.3 Excessive Use of Multimedia Technology Teaching, Putting the Cart Before the Horse

As a means of modern teaching, multimedia through a variety of sensory stimulation can be more vivid and three-dimensional display of teaching process and content, and since a few years ago, multimedia teaching as an advanced teaching method has been widely used in students' music classroom teaching. In teaching, teachers use multimedia teaching methods to make sound and color coexist, help students feel and understand well, and let students form good sentiment and sound personality. However, these are only technology after all, and the content of teaching is the most fundamental thing. We need to grasp a certain degree, not putting the cart before the horse. At present, many teachers do not say a word from the beginning to the end, and there is no blackboard writing. They just display the content through the mouse and projector, and a music class becomes a PPT display. This is a very wrong behavior.

3   Application of Cloud Computing in Music Teaching

3.1   Building a Large Scale Shared Music Education Resource Library

At present, there are many problems in the music teaching resource library in China, such as uneven distribution of resources, lack of shared teaching resources, isolated island of teaching resources, and lack of cooperation between different schools. To deal with this problem, we can establish a cloud resource library for music teaching in China through cloud computing. With the powerful data sharing ability of cloud computing, we can summarize all teaching resources and store them in the data center with huge capacity which is shown in Fig. 2.

Fig. 2. The interface with music teaching platform

3.2 Construction of Network Teaching Platform for Music Course with the Help of Cloud Computing

The music classroom teaching is called appreciation class failure due to the wrong use of multimedia in music class. The music class network teaching platform constructed by cloud computing can take advantage of the characteristics of low terminal hardware requirements [3]. Music lessons can be conducted without having to be in the same classroom. Video and voice interaction can be used, and cloud computing platform can be used as the processing center of interactive data, The terminals of teachers and students only provide data input and output functions. This is mainly aimed at ensuring the overall development of students' quality and taking into account the increasingly heavy academic work. Therefore, students can learn music in front of terminals such as computers, tablets and mobile phones at home on weekends, which not only ensures the cultivation of quality, but also promotes the combination of work and rest of students, killing two birds with one stone.

3.3 Construction of Cloud Computing Music Library

Aiming at the problem that many students' music foundation is too poor, we can build a music library in the cloud, which mainly explains some music knowledge, and stores it in the cloud in the form of electronic journals for data sharing, allowing students to access materials anytime and anywhere through various terminals, In addition, the corresponding audio or video works are linked next to the names of different musicians' works [4]. So that students can understand and learn music through the two senses of watching and listening [5].

4   Cloud Online Simulation

Based on the online music assistant system proposed in the third section, in this section, we further optimize its system simulation system in the cloud environment, as shown in Fig. 2. From Fig. 3, we can see that the optimized system is richer in the interface, and has the function of automatically arranging tracks. The advantage of this online assistant system is that it does not occupy any resources of users, except broadband.

Fig. 3. Online assistant system with cloud environment

5   Problems in the Process of Training Self Playing and Self Singing Skills

With the continuous development of music education in Colleges and universities, as well as the improvement of basic music teaching requirements, the course of self playing and self singing has attracted more and more attention of music educators. Most colleges and universities in China have also formulated a set of effective teaching programs on self playing and self singing according to the actual situation of their own schools. However, it is just because the teaching of self playing and self singing has been gradually valued by more and more colleges and universities in recent years, so compared with the traditional conventional courses such as piano and vocal music, it is still not complete and systematic in terms of curriculum setting and teaching methods. It is still in the state of continuous improvement and exploration, and there are many problems in the teaching process [6].

Self playing and self singing is a comprehensive skill which is composed of piano playing, vocal music, improvisation accompaniment, harmony, musical form analysis and other skills. Then, by interviewing the students and searching the undergraduate music education programs of major colleges and universities on the Internet, the author also understands that during the first and second year of the undergraduate course, students majoring in music education usually learn a series of core degree courses, such as basic piano performance, vocal music, basic music theory, harmony, musical form analysis, improvisation accompaniment, etc. Until the third year of undergraduate course, most colleges will open the whole academic year's big class of self playing and self singing [7].

For the final assessment form of self playing and self singing class, each school is different. According to the data from the questionnaire survey, colleges and universities mainly carry out the assessment in two ways: 1. 2. At the end of the semester, we will hold a teaching performance of playing and singing by ourselves. There is also a small part of the paper, classroom practice and competition in the form of assessment. To sum up, the main problems in the teaching of self playing and self singing are as follows: first, in the teaching of "self playing and self singing" at this stage, the teaching materials used are relatively messy, such as the use of vocal art songs and impromptu accompaniment as the teaching materials of self playing and self singing, which will lead to students' lack of scientific and systematic training. Second, the final assessment form of the course is not comprehensive enough. For example, in the form of papers as the final assessment criteria [8].

6 Training Strategies of Self Playing and Self Singing Skills

With the deepening of education reform, it has become the demand of the times to comprehensively promote "aesthetic education" teaching and improve the comprehensive practical ability of music education students. According to the promulgation and implementation of music curriculum standards for compulsory education (2011 Edition), music teachers' skills of "playing and singing by themselves" are playing an increasingly important role in primary and secondary school music classes. The level of a music teacher's self playing and self singing skills can directly affect the quality of teaching. Since 2010, the role of the cultivation of self playing and self singing skills in improving the comprehensive practical ability of students majoring in music education has been recognized by colleges and universities and teachers, and has been valued ideologically. At present, according to the current situation of this course in several colleges and universities involved in the questionnaire survey, except for a few colleges and universities which have not yet opened the course of self playing and self singing, the vast majority of colleges and universities with music education major have opened this course. In terms of curriculum, some colleges and universities set up the course of self playing and self singing as a compulsory course, that is, every student must study it; some colleges and universities set it as an elective course, after the end of the second year of undergraduate students to choose courses, students who choose the course of self playing and self singing learn the course [9].

6.1 Optimize the Curriculum

In the dictionary of education, it is mentioned that "the education content selected for the educational goal of the school is called curriculum setting". Curriculum setting is the arrangement of each specific subject in the whole curriculum system. It is also formulated according to the characteristics of different majors and their teaching objectives. As far as music education major is concerned, its goal is to cultivate qualified music educators with comprehensive music literacy. Therefore, the curriculum should be more teacher oriented [10]. By observing the current curriculum of music education major in Colleges and universities in China, it can be roughly divided into the following three categories: general compulsory courses, professional compulsory courses and professional elective courses.

(1) General compulsory courses: that is, public compulsory courses, including: English; physical education; Chinese modern history, ideological and moral foundation and legal cultivation, introduction to basic principles of Marxism and other political courses; pedagogy, psychology, teachers' oral English, educational psychology and other educational courses.

(2) Professional required course: the course that students must study during their study. Including: Piano, vocal music, impromptu accompaniment and other basic professional courses; and acoustics, musical form analysis, Chinese and foreign music history and other basic theoretical courses; world music, art introduction and other music appreciation courses.

(3) Professional elective courses: some courses that students choose to study during their study, which can develop students' personality and highlight the characteristics of the school. Including: drama appreciation, art appreciation, dance appreciation and other sister disciplines.

6.2 Optimize Teaching Methods

The evaluation standard and the final assessment form of the course are quite different in Colleges and universities. Some take the form of papers as the final assessment; some take the form of concerts as the final assessment; others take the form of random draw for the final assessment. The author analyzes the advantages and disadvantages of these assessment forms for reference [11, 12].

1. Thesis: it is relatively one-sided to take the form of submitting thesis as the final assessment. Because playing and singing is a professional and practical comprehensive skill, so for such a subject, the final assessment form must be practical. The advantage is that playing and singing also has a certain theoretical basis, and all skills training is based on a certain theoretical basis. Through the way of writing papers, it is more conducive for students to have a deeper grasp of the theoretical knowledge of self playing and self singing, so that they can realize the importance of self playing and self singing on the theoretical level, so that they can attach importance to self playing and self singing.

2. Concert: in the form of concert assessment standards, relatively speaking, practice is very strong. But as far as the scope of the examination is concerned, if the time of a concert is counted as one hour, then the playing and singing time allocated to each student will have certain limitations. Basically, each student plays and sings a self playing and self singing song. When preparing for this concert, each student must only focus on practicing a piece of playing and singing repertoire that needs to be performed. In this way, the assessment will lose its significance and cannot check the students' learning effect. But the advantage of the examination in the form of concert is that it can exercise students' comprehensive ability and enrich their stage performance experience.

3. Draw lots: that is, teachers choose several songs to play and sing by themselves, number them, and students randomly choose one of them to improvise. There are two kinds of lottery playing and singing, one is that teachers choose songs they have learned in class to number and draw lots, the other is that teachers choose songs they haven't learned in class to number and draw lots. This method is relatively scientific and effective. The first way of drawing lots can make students have an overall review of the self playing and self singing songs learned in a semester, which plays a role in assessing the learning situation; the second way of drawing lots is more perfect and scientific than the first one. In the "Pearl River Piano" national

music education teachers' basic skills competition, the competition mode is that the contestants randomly select songs to perform impromptu self playing and self singing, with only 10 min to prepare. Some of the songs in this competition are even specially created for the competition, which are songs that we have never heard before, This competition mode can test a player's music comprehensive quality, and the competition results are more referential. However, in the school, such a form of assessment for students' own requirements are very high, it needs students' piano, vocal music, improvisation and other basic professional skills balanced development. As far as the actual situation is concerned, it is still relatively difficult to implement [13].

6.3 Optimizing Training Methods

Playing and singing by oneself is a kind of performing art form in which one can perform independently and simultaneously. In the actual operation, it needs to be multi-functional and coordinated. In the above survey, we found that many students think that when they learn to play and sing by themselves, what makes them feel very difficult is that they can not give good consideration to "singing and playing" at the same time. In view of this problem, the author understands that in cognitive psychology, such behavior of "playing while singing" is called attention distribution [14].

The ability of distribution of attention can not only make students give consideration to and coordinate "playing and singing", but also produce rich expressive force, so that students can have spare power to consider problems in various aspects while "playing and singing", so that the completion of self playing and self singing is higher. Playing and singing by oneself is an extremely complex psychological and physical movement, which requires that attention be always distributed throughout the process of playing and singing by oneself. However, sometimes subjective and objective factors will change, such as the difficulty of the repertoire, the change of the state of mind and so on, which requires the students to shift their attention, so as to ensure that the self playing and self singing repertoire has a high degree of completion. However, the difficulty of the selected music and the change of teaching environment are sometimes unpredictable objective factors, which can directly affect the students' on-the-spot performance. For example, in the class of playing and singing by oneself, the teacher chose one of the students to return the class, and the rest of the students watched from their seats. At this time, if the student is confident about the homework assigned by the teacher in the last class and goes smoothly in the middle of returning the class, he will naturally get praise from the teacher and his classmates [15]. Therefore, the student does not need to allocate his attention to some factors other than the songs, instead, he can concentrate his attention on the songs he needs to return the class, The class will be returned successfully. On the contrary, if the student does not have enough practice after class, then when he is called by the teacher to return the class, his attention will not only be part of the songs, but also be distributed in the evaluation of the teachers and students, which will lead to the unsatisfactory effect of the final return of the class.

7 Conclusion

Cloud computing is the product of the continuous development of the Internet. As a new computing method and new resource use mode, its originality determines the vigorous vitality of cloud computing and the universality of its promotion. At present, cloud computing has gradually entered a better situation in the commercial field, and is promoting the earth shaking changes in the business operation mode. Although in the current situation, cloud computing has not made much achievements in the field of education in China, but with the deployment speed and quality of cloud computing for applications, as well as its incomparable advantages compared with traditional teaching, it can be proved that cloud computing will surely shine in the future education field.

References

1. Deng, Q., Li, J.: Enlightenment of the successful case of "cloud service" on China's educational technology. Educ. Teach. **22**(4), 77–82 (2009)
2. Gu, L.: Cloud computing: future network trend technology. Comput. Knowl. Technol. **12**(2), 596–603 (2008)
3. Xu, H.: Xiangyun computing's impact on Education. Comput. Teach. Educ. Inform. **5**(4), 188–196 (2009)
4. High culture. Problems existing in music class and suggestions for implementation. Lit. Educ. **17**(2), (11), 261–275 (2011)
5. Wang, X.: How to improve the ability of music education students to play and sing by themselves. Qingdao University (2015)
6. Zhou, Y.: Self playing and self singing course. Southwest Normal University Press, Chongqing (2012)
7. Wang, N.: Innovation and development of "playing and singing by oneself" characteristic curriculum system. Northern Music **35**(14), 131 (2015)
8. Wang, W.: The existing value of "playing and singing by oneself" course in Musicology Major of colleges and universities and its implementation countermeasures. Voice Yellow River **12**(14), 12–13 (2017)
9. Zhang, C.: Teaching analysis of self playing and self singing course for music education major in Colleges and universities. Northern Music **21**, 199–210 (2016)
10. Ren, X.: Exploration on teaching material application of self playing and self singing course for music education major. Northern Music **36**(20), 65–66 (2016)
11. Liu Hongling's "aesthetic oriented" teaching of self playing and self singing in normal universities. Northern Music **36**, 59–72 (2016)
12. Liu, C.: Thinking about the teaching of "namely Xinghua" by playing and singing by oneself. Popular literature and art (2017)
13. Ma, M.: Teaching practice on improving vocal music students' ability of playing and singing by themselves. Voice Yellow River **56**(05), 71–81 (2018)
14. Ma, Y.: Cultivation and improvement of the ability of "playing and singing by oneself" of musicology majors in normal universities. Voice Yellow River **7**(07), 104 (2018)
15. Xiong, Y.: Teaching approaches to improve the self playing and self singing ability of vocal music students. Art Eval. **18**(17), 8990 (2018)

Research on College Students' English Online Autonomous Learning Based on Big Data Analysis

Jie Wu[✉]

English Department, School of Foreign Languages,
Dalian Polytechnic University, Dalian 116033, Liaoning, China
wujie@dlpu.edu.cn

Abstract. This paper analyzes some problems existing in the process of College Students' English autonomous learning, and improves the ID3 algorithm in the field of data mining, and applies the traditional ID3 algorithm and the improved ID3 algorithm to the research of College Students' English autonomous learning respesctively. This paper holds that only when college students have a certain degree of autonomous learning ability, can they effectively carry out Network-based College English learning. The key to improve autonomous learning ability is students' self-monitoring. Therefore, after improving the theory and awareness of self-learning, College English teachers should actively strengthen students' self-learning awareness, cultivate students' self-monitoring ability, help students complete the transformation from other control to self-control, from conscious to automatic, from local to overall, so as to improve their autonomous learning ability and realize the goal of College English online teaching, That is to achieve the best learning effect of students through personalized learning.

Keywords: College Students' English autonomous learning · Data mining · ID3 algorithm

1 Introduction

The new model of College Students' English Autonomous Learning Based on ID3 algorithm is favored by colleges and universities because of its strong interactivity, more choices, less restrictions, wide information and high efficiency, and most of them have mastered more mature theoretical methods and practical skills. However, from the current situation of the learning mode in Colleges and universities, there are still some problems, such as the lag of school hardware and software facilities, the lack of teachers' auxiliary effect, the limited ability of students' autonomous learning, etc., which directly limit the advantages of the learning mode. Therefore, it is necessary to study the Network-based English autonomous learning of college students in order to promote the further improvement of the learning mode, provide help for the improvement

© ICST Institute for Computer Sciences, Social Informatics and Telecommunications Engineering 2021
Published by Springer Nature Switzerland AG 2021. All Rights Reserved
M. A. Jan and F. Khan (Eds.): BigIoT-EDU 2021, LNICST 391, pp. 494–505, 2021.
https://doi.org/10.1007/978-3-030-87900-6_57

of College Students' Comprehensive English application ability, and lay a foundation for the lifelong learning of college students [1–5].

In nearly 10 years of English teaching career, I have been exploring, creating and researching to make English class more interesting, more wonderful and more delicious, so that more students can enjoy English class, so that they can gradually fall in love with English. In teaching, teachers should gradually improve the guidance plan of each semester and make exquisite courseware for each class; Often tell students English stories, sing English songs, guess English riddles, tell English jokes, talk about English life, put funny English short films to show their unique problem-solving thinking [6–8].

Modern teachers use computer-aided instruction more and more widely, although teachers spend a lot of effort, and students like and recognize it, but in fact, students are still less active in learning, and students are still in a passive state of acceptance. So how to use the advantages of information technology to give full play to students' active participation and learning ability? It's a good way to let computer network into English class [9–12]. At present, the online "English Paradise" which is suitable for students' autonomous learning is deeply liked by students and has received good results. It makes English more interesting and operational, and cultivates students' ability to use their brains and hands to learn English.

English online "Le Xue Yuan" mainly consists of three parts [13–19], one is "knowledge in mind", the other is "testing I can do", the third is "learning I break through". Learning in the English online "Le Xue Yuan" can be said to be playing in learning and learning by playing. This kind of emotional learning makes English learning no longer boring and boring. Now the specific contents, main functions and operation of the three plates are introduced as follows.

(1) Knowledge is in the heart

It mainly includes pre class, in class and after class learning content, which is compiled into preview case, communication case and test case for students to use. The key and difficult problems are recorded in the "micro class" so that students can learn repeatedly and understand the problems thoroughly. It is necessary to upload students' current typical problems, such as students' homework, test papers, etc., and of course, it also shows the excellent students' test papers, homework, test papers, etc. Methods of solving problems. In this way, comparative learning, mutual learning, can promote learning.

For some classroom experiments, whether they are demonstration experiments or students' experiments, they are more or less confused after learning, and students want to do experiments again to solve their doubts. There is a very good software "junior high school English NB laboratory", which can complete all the experiments of the whole junior high school. Students can operate freely in the "Le Xue Yuan" and complete the experimental exploration, so that they can have a deep understanding of the problems and promote the smooth completion of learning. In the study of electricity, drawing circuit diagram and connecting physical diagram is the basis of learning electricity well. In order to let students have a better understanding, judge the circuit, analyze the circuit, circuit fault, ammeter, voltmeter, the use of sliding rheostat and other electrical problems, we can do it in the "electrical virtual laboratory" on the online "Le Xue Yuan". Teachers often use the software in teaching, which is convenient for teaching and makes the problems intuitive and clear. If students encounter some problems in electricity, they can solve them by using their hands in "Le Xue Yuan" "Knowledge in mind" column, can help students to complete the problems difficult to solve in the classroom, let students free, participate more, experience more, students in real learning, to achieve flexible use of knowledge, they learn more confidence, more fun.

(2) I can do it

As long as it is training and hands-on operation, there will be a special evaluation, which can reflect the students' achievements in time. When assigning homework at the weekend, you can set the time to complete the homework. If it exceeds, the system will stop and you need to do it again. Teachers can know when each student does it, how much time it takes to do it, which questions are wrong, whether to modify it, whether to retest, etc. all these are recorded. Parents can be informed of the unfinished or completed situation in time to understand the children's learning status and learning effect. Of course, parents can log in to the english paradise on the parents' side, and see the homework done by their children on the Internet, so as to better communicate with their children. The whole class has homework feedback form, the highest score, the lowest score, the average score, the number of people in each section, etc. there are comparisons between classes. Very good analysis of homework or examination, easy to teach. Online homework, students can complete more seriously, dare not lazy, dare not careless, also can let students correct their mistakes in time, the system will remind, and the system will automatically put each wrong question together, generate the wrong question book, convenient for students to review. This plate has powerful detection function, thorough analysis, very direct and fast understanding of students' homework and detection situation, better discovery of problems, targeted communication with students, and also reduce the burden of teachers in performance analysis.

2 Introduction of Data Mining and Decision Tree

The platform subverts the previous classroom teaching based course teaching form. Students can easily log on to the learning platform anytime and anywhere to learn a course through modern network means. The process is to evaluate and analyze students from logging on the network learning platform $\rightarrow$ learning course knowledge points $\rightarrow$ completing homework $\rightarrow$ course test and comprehensive test $\rightarrow$ ending course learning.

Auxiliary

The use of autonomous learning platform should be used as the auxiliary and extension of conventional classroom teaching, and can not completely replace classroom learning. Teachers upload the relevant information to the teaching platform, which can help students preview before class and consolidate their learning after class, expand the course content and complement the traditional teaching.

Autonomy

Autonomous learning platform learning lacks effective learning process control mechanism for students. It is difficult to monitor students' learning time and learning effect in a short period of time. Cultivating students' autonomous learning ability is the key to bring the effect of e-learning platform into full play.

Repeatability

Traditional classroom teaching requires students to be highly focused in class, which is often difficult to achieve, and the difficulties of classroom content are difficult to master at one time through classroom teaching. The online autonomous learning platform provides technical support for students' repeated learning. Teachers can record course videos, organize course related materials and upload them to the online learning platform, which can make the classroom reappear and provide students with the opportunity of repeated learning for two or more times.

Asynchronous

Traditional teaching is the synchronization of classroom teaching and learning, students and teachers must be synchronized in time, ideas, in order to achieve better learning effect, and autonomous learning platform can achieve asynchronous teaching and learning, as long as teachers arrange learning tasks and carry out appropriate training, students can reasonably arrange their own time to complete learning within a given period.

Open

The traditional teaching mainly focuses on teaching materials. At the same time, due to the constraints of classroom time, the teaching content is greatly limited. The online learning platform can provide students with an open learning environment. Through the guidance of teachers, the curriculum content can be effectively expanded and extended, especially in combination with the real world. The content is no longer abstract and dogmatic, Let students realize the usefulness of the course, stimulate students' interest in learning.

Interaction

The communication and communication in traditional classroom teaching is very limited. Autonomous learning platform can use various communication tools to improve the space and time of communication, so that teachers can fully grasp students' learning state and effect, better grasp the difficulties of teaching, and promote students' autonomous learning ability, And anonymous interaction can greatly reduce the psychological pressure of students in communication.

Online lesson preparation and online teaching

Autonomous learning platform through the course content management, resource management, learning plan management, work management, question and answer management and learning monitoring management and other functional modules to complete online lesson preparation, online teaching, learning control and a series of teaching activities.

Online learning

Students can carry out autonomous learning, cooperative learning and research-based learning through online courses, topic discussion, friend exchange, question and answer interaction, work mutual evaluation and other functional modules.

Intelligent comprehensive evaluation

In the process of practice evaluation such as classroom practice and synchronous homework, and inspection evaluation such as mid-term test, final test and simulation test, the self-learning platform adopts the latest technologies such as intelligent test paper generation and intelligent evaluation to provide a complete set of solutions for each evaluation stage.

Perfect evaluation management

All the data of teaching and learning process are automatically recorded in the whole process, through which the evaluation scheme is made, and the system generates process evaluation data according to the evaluation scheme, so as to ensure the objectivity and fairness of the evaluation.

Improve teaching efficiency and reduce the burden of lesson preparation

In the process of teaching, teachers can focus on the teaching according to the learning situation monitored by the system and the relevant data recorded, so as to improve the teaching efficiency; In addition, the subject teaching plan and course content are uniformly allocated by the lesson preparation team leader, and teachers can set them according to their own needs, so as to reduce the burden of lesson preparation.

Resource CoConstruction and sharing

The self-learning platform system has the functions of uploading teaching resources, adding test questions, making works and voting evaluation. Test questions, resources and works can be recommended and reviewed level by level, realizing the co construction and sharing of excellent teaching resources.

SNS concept

The system aggregates resources, students and teachers through tags, wikis and other technologies, so as to form the knowledge network and crowd network for autonomous learning and cooperative learning, and provide a good tool and open platform for students' autonomous inquiry learning.

The comprehensiveness, openness and timeliness of evaluation

The system has the process evaluation of students' online learning and the summative evaluation of online unified examination, and supports the open evaluation of works. The relevant examination data is managed uniformly to form students' comprehensive evaluation files.

Student portfolio

The platform automatically records the whole process of students' learning and growth, and finally forms a personal growth portfolio.

Data mining is a process of selecting, exploring and modeling a large number of data in order to discover unknown rules and relationships in advance. The purpose of data mining is to obtain clear and useful results for the owner of data. Data mining is the core technology of discovering knowledge from database. It is developed from machine learning of artificial intelligence. Combined with traditional statistical analysis method, fuzzy mathematics method and visualization technology of scientific calculation, data mining method and technology are formed by taking database as research object.

Data mining methods include decision tree method, set theory method, neural network method, genetic algorithm and so on. The decision tree method uses the principle of information theory to establish a decision tree. This method has good effect and great influence. The representation form of knowledge obtained by this method is decision tree.

The decision tree is a tree structure with the attributes of samples as nodes and the values of attributes as branches. The root node is the most informative attribute among all the samples, the middle node of the tree is the attribute with the largest amount of information in the sample subset contained by the subtree with the node as the root, and the leaf node is the category value of the sample(shown in Fig. 1).

2.1 ID3 Algorithm

ID algorithm is the earliest and most influential decision tree method in the world. Its basic algorithm is greedy algorithm. It constructs decision tree by top-down recursion. The information gain measure is used to select test attributes on each node of the tree. Select the attribute with the highest information gain as the test attribute of the current node.

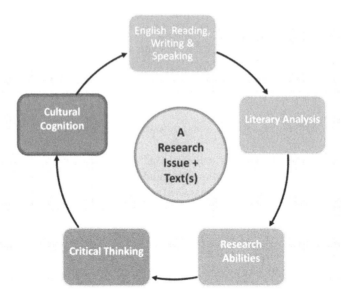

Fig. 1. English online autonomous learning

Let S be the set of s data samples. Suppose that the class label attribute has m different values, define m different Ci (I = 1,2, ..., m) If Si is the number of samples in class Ci and Pi is the probability that any sample belongs to Ci, then the expected information for a given sample classification is as follows:

$$I(s_1, s_2, \cdots s_m) = -\sum_{i=1}^{m} P_i \log_2(P_i) \tag{1}$$

Let attribute A have v different values, We can divide s into v subsets {S1, S2,... Sv}, where Sj contains some samples in S that have a on A. If a is selected as the test attribute, these subsets correspond to the branches growing from the nodes containing the set S. Let Sij be the sample number of class Ci in the subset Sj, then the entropy or expected information divided into subsets according to attribute a is as follows:

$$E(A) = \sum_{i=1}^{v} \frac{S_{ij} + \cdots + S_{mj}}{S} I(S_{ij}, \cdots, S_{mj}) \tag{2}$$

The smaller the entropy, the higher the degree of subset division. Then, the information gain of branch A is as follows:

$$G(A) = I(s_1, s_2, \cdots, s_m) - E(A) \tag{3}$$

This kind of ID3 algorithm tends to choose the attribute with more values, because the weighted sum method makes the classification of instance set tend to abandon the data tuples with small amount of data. However, the attribute with more values is not always the optimal attribute. In other words, according to the principle of minimizing entropy and maximizing information gain, ID3 algorithm lists the attributes that should be selected by ID3 algorithm, and testing it will not provide too much information.

2.2 Improved ID3 Algorithm

Let A be the selection attribute, A has five attribute values, and the corresponding weight is $\omega_1, \omega_2, \cdots, \omega_v$. According to the algorithm of ID3, attribute a is extended, and the corresponding information entropy. Then the weighted entropy is defined as:

$$E(A)^* = \sum_{i=1}^{v} \omega_i \times E(B_i) \tag{4}$$

Among them (B1, B2, Bv) is the attribute selected for v nodes, and ω_i refers to the weight of the subset. The weight ω_i is calculated by the proportion of the subset Bi in the whole set, and then the weighted entropy is calculated, and the value of the attribute is selected by comparing the weight entropy.

In addition, the improvement of ID3 algorithm is used to simplify the complexity of information calculation.

Firstly, the basic properties of logP function are studied. Through the research, it can be proved that the information calculation formula is a kind of convex function, so we can use the unique properties of the convex function to improve the calculation formula of information quantity.

2.3 Functional Modules of Autonomous Learning System

(1) Management interface: teachers log in to the system through the management interface module, use the management interface to make and arrange educational materials, convert educational materials into appropriate learning objectives, and store them in the learning objectives database. These learning objectives form the basis of students' personalized learning content; The processing interface also outputs the learning objectives in the database to the textbook generation engine module to generate the textbook database.

(2) Textbook generation engine: the primary function is to check whether the input learning objectives meet the SCORM standard, and arrange the learning objectives that meet the scrom standard to generate textbooks and store them in the textbook database.

(3) Curriculum architecture engine: the primary function is to build personalized learning content adaptively according to the personal information and learning records of learners in the student file database and student record database, and combined with the learning content in the textbook database, and output the results to the curriculum visualization engine to show to learners.

(4) Course visualization engine: it is mainly used for the emergence of personalized learning content suitable for different learners. Different learners will see different learning content and arrangement forms, which reflects the adaptability and personalization of the system.

(5) Evaluation Center: it is mainly used to evaluate the learning effect of learners. According to the preset test questions, the learners are evaluated. The evaluation results, as the evaluation of the learners' learning ability and common sense, are also the important basis for the dynamic arrangement of learning objectives, and the corresponding learning content, personalized learning environment and learning strategy guidance appear.

3   Research on College Students' Autonomous English Learning by Using Decision Tree Method

How to transfer inquiry learning and extended learning to the Internet to develop students' scientific literacy, humanistic literacy and information literacy?

Online inquiry learning and extended learning is an exploratory research, which needs to be formed and developed in the process of curriculum development and implementation. We have tried novel coronavirus pneumonia online learning course, online learning course "harmony between humans and animal", online English appreciation course, and the online learning mode of "curriculum resource package + learning guidance".

(1) The theme resource package based on network resources is constructed by acquisition, screening, reorganization and a small amount of creation.
(2) Design program: background - knowledge learning - deep learning - interactive learning based on network learning space.
(3) Use learning guide (learning task book) to guide learning.
(4) Extensive reading (text and non text reading) is the basis of extended learning.
(5) Resources should be integrated into the process of students' autonomous learning to guide problems, stimulate thinking and active discussion.

By selecting the five attributes in the process of College Students' English autonomous learning, which are the longest login time, the cumulative online time, the number of visits to the learning resources network, the situation of questions and posts, and the progress of autonomous learning as candidate attributes, and the results of autonomous learning as class label attributes, this paper analyzes the autonomous learning of graduate students. The data record is from the College English learning database, which keeps the College English learning records of the College of foreign languages in recent two years.

Through the decision tree generated by ID3 algorithm, it can be found that if the number of questions and posts of a student reaches or exceeds 5, it indicates that the communication between the student and the teacher is relatively active, and the number of visits to the learning resource network reaches or exceeds 20 times, the autonomous learning progress is normal or ahead, and the accumulated online time reaches or exceeds 28 h, then the student's English autonomous learning result is qualified, The student can be upgraded and qualified for the next College English course.

Using ID3 algorithm and improved ID3 algorithm respectively, we can find that the decision tree generated by the improved I3 algorithm is relatively simple with fewer branch nodes. The simpler the decision tree is, the less the cost of storing the decision tree, Moreover, the cost of transferring information between two entities is smaller. Moreover, the correct classification rate of the improved algorithm is 71.20%, which is higher than that of the improved algorithm (65.23%). Therefore, compared with the traditional ID3 algorithm, the improved ID3 algorithm has more advantages in the field of College Students' English autonomous learning.

The quality of learning materials is the premise of improving learning efficiency in college students' Online Autonomous Learning. Therefore, it is necessary to improve students' information literacy ability in order to obtain high-quality learning resources. Information literacy ability mainly includes four aspects: information acquisition ability, information immunity ability, information integration ability and information transformation ability. Information acquisition is the premise of using information. Students should know how to use various search technologies to find English learning materials that meet their own needs, including quickly and effectively finding useful learning resources in the network learning platform. In addition, there is no lack of negative and junk information in the massive network information, so students need to cultivate immunity to bad learning materials. The ability of information integration refers to the classification of English learning materials obtained by students according to the principle of "removing the rough and reserving the essence, eliminating the false and retaining the true", so as to ensure the practicability, correctness and value of the resources, so as to absorb and digest them, and integrate them into their own English knowledge structure system by using transformation ability. The above four abilities are progressive and indispensable, and these abilities are also the necessary skills for students' lifelong learning after graduation.

The concept of learning community was first proposed by the famous Japanese educator Sato, which is an efficient classroom teaching mode focusing on the interaction between teachers and students. "Changing a school requires teachers to open the door to the classroom," he said In the new era, with the development and driving of technology, the availability of education related resources is getting higher and higher. The unprecedented richness of resources and technology provides great convenience for teachers' classroom teaching, students' learning and parents' education and support for students. At the same time, the complexity of the impact on classroom teaching is also greatly improved. This kind of classroom breaks the original classroom boundary only constructed by teachers and students, expands into a star network topology composed of student-centered, teachers, parents, technology and resources, activates the connection between nodes, and straightens out the relationship between nodes, which has become an important goal to improve classroom efficiency and learning effectiveness. With the increase of community building elements, the number of connections between the elements will increase geometrically. How to help students actively activate the connection with each node, help students learn, and promote students' life growth will be the focus of our research.

According to this model, the elements interact, interconnect and promote each other. The development and drive of technology provide a convenient channel for teachers' teaching, students' learning and parents' support. The influx of resources also brings great trouble for teachers and parents to choose resources suitable for students or students to choose their own resources, In this kind of classroom, which takes students' learning and growth as the core, independent choice becomes the key to improve classroom efficiency. According to the learning situation and their own teaching methods, teachers can choose the appropriate resources independently, and parents can choose the way that conforms to the children's learning habits according to their own ability and children's situation. More importantly, students should actively choose the learning resources suitable for themselves from the resources provided by teachers, given by parents and contacted by their own immediately related technologies.

4 Conclusion

Through the application of ID3 algorithm and improved ID3 algorithm to the research of College Students' English autonomous learning, the root nodes of the two decision trees generated are "questions and posts". It can be seen that in the process of College Students' English autonomous learning, the network communication between college students and College English teachers is very important, Therefore, it is necessary to ensure that college students have a relatively superior network infrastructure environment in the process of English autonomous learning, and the teaching role of College English teachers should not be ignored because it is autonomous learning, but should be paid more attention and applied, so as to better guide college students' English autonomous learning, monitor and master the situation of College Students' English autonomous learning, To improve the efficiency of College Students' English autonomous learning, achieve the expected effect of College Students' English autonomous learning, and ensure the normal progress of College English autonomous learning, so as to improve college English teaching activities.

Autonomous learning system is a kind of learning support channel. The channel takes learners as the main body, dynamically adjusts learning content and learning progress according to learners' cognitive ability and common sense level, and provides learning content, environment and strategy support for learners' individual needs. After personalized evaluation, the system actively adjusts personalized learning plans, Self control the whole learning process.

The main characteristics of autonomous learning system are as follows.

(1) According to the test results of learners' cognitive level, cognitive style and learning style, combined with the characteristics of the learning content, the system actively presents the most suitable learning content for learners.

(2) Autonomy, autonomous learning system can make learning as the main body to participate in learning, and can choose the corresponding learning ways and learning strategies according to their own learning network.

(3) The purpose of developing autonomous learning system is to let learners fully grasp the subject common sense system, which requires the system to comprehensively integrate teaching resources to get used to learners' autonomous selection and arrangement.

References

1. Xu, C., Hou, T., Huang, X., et al. Analysis of network teaching strategy structure. Distance Education in China (Comprehensive Edition), 10 (2006)
2. Sun, Y., Huang, H.: Research on network teaching strategy based on data mining technology. Teaching Method Research of Education and Occupation, 12 (2009)
3. Yuan, F.: Practical Data Mining. Electronic Industry Press, Beijing (2004)
4. Chen, X., Liu, J.: Construction of evaluation index system with decision tree method. Comput. Appl. 2 (2006)
5. Chen, L.: On the activation and improvement of students' autonomous learning system in TVU open and distance education. Mod. Dist. Educ. Res. **04**, 32–35 (2002)
6. Fang, L., Wang, K.: Personalized knowledge push service in network autonomous learning system. Res. High. Eng. Educ. **5**, 145–148 (2008)
7. Yi, H., Yang, J.: Design and development of Internet dynamic autonomous learning system. Comput. Eng. Des. **023**(007), 60–62 (2002)
8. Cao, W.: Design of personalized autonomous learning system based on e-learning. Vocat. Tech. Educ. **26**, 85–87 (2009)
9. Chen, L.: On the activation and improvement of students' autonomous learning system in open and distance education. China's Distance Education (Comprehensive Edition) (2002)
10. Chen, L.: On the activation and improvement of students' autonomous learning system in open and distance education. China Distance Education (2002)
11. Zhang, C.: Research and Design of Network Autonomous Learning System Based on Concept Map. Central China Normal University (2007)
12. Wang, J.: English autonomous learning system for postgraduates. Audio Visual Foreign Lang. Teach. 5, 56–58
13. Cai, J., Ruan, X.: OCPA bionic autonomous learning system and its application in robot posture balance control. Pattern Recogn. Artif. Intell. **024**(001), 138–146 (2011)
14. Gu, J.: Construction and application of English audio visual network autonomous learning system. Research on Higher Education of Science and Technology (2006)
15. Wang, H., Wang, Y., Jiao, Y., et al.: Design and implementation of web based personalized autonomous learning system. In: 13th Annual Conference of Computer Aided Education Professional Committee of Chinese Society for artificial intelligence (National CBE Society) (2008)
16. Li, J., Hu, Z.: On the improvement of online autonomous learning system – based on the research of online autonomous learning system of international accounting. Second Half of Entrepreneur World (Theoretical Edition) (2007)
17. Chi, S.: Development and implementation of web based online autonomous learning system. Value Eng. **34**, 183 (2010)
18. Wang, C.: An AI autonomous learning system and method based on quantum theory. cn110969255a (2020)
19. Zhang, S., Que, H., Yu, W.: A flexible riveting autonomous learning system based on visual guidance. cn108480546a (2018)

Research on English Teaching Ability Evaluation Algorithm Based on Big Data Fuzzy k-means Clustering

Ying Xu[✉]

Faculty of Foreign Languages of Guangdong Ocean University, No. 1 Haida Road, Zhanjiang 524088, China

Abstract. Aiming at the problem of inaccurate classification of big data information in traditional English teaching ability evaluation algorithms, an English teaching ability evaluation algorithm based on big data fuzzy k-means clustering and information fusion is proposed. Firstly, the constraint parameter index analysis model is established; secondly, the quantitative recursive analysis method is used to evaluate the ability of big data information model, and the entropy feature extraction of the ability constraint feature information is realized; finally, the big data information fusion and K-means clustering algorithm are integrated to realize the index parameter clustering and integration of English teaching ability, and the corresponding teaching resource allocation plan is compiled, To realize the evaluation of English teaching ability. The experimental results show that this method has better ability of information fusion and analysis, and improves the accuracy of teaching ability evaluation and the efficiency of teaching resource application.

Keywords: Big data · English teaching · Teaching ability evaluation · Information fusion · Data clustering

1 Introduction

Using information processing technology and big data analysis technology for teaching evaluation and resource information scheduling is of great significance to improve the quantitative management and planning ability of teaching process. Therefore, this paper studies the evaluation of English teaching ability based on big data analysis. Because there are many restrictive factors in English teaching ability evaluation, it is necessary to test and analyze English teaching level, construct parameter model and big data analysis model that restrict English teaching level, adopt big data information fusion and clustering processing method to evaluate English teaching ability, and construct objective function and statistical analysis model of teaching ability evaluation, Improve the quantitative prediction ability of English teaching ability evaluation. This paper proposes a method of English teaching ability estimation based on big data fuzzy k-means clustering and information fusion, which realizes the clustering and integration of index parameters of English teaching ability, compiles the corresponding teaching

© ICST Institute for Computer Sciences, Social Informatics and Telecommunications Engineering 2021
Published by Springer Nature Switzerland AG 2021. All Rights Reserved
M. A. Jan and F. Khan (Eds.): BigIoT-EDU 2021, LNICST 391, pp. 506–516, 2021.
https://doi.org/10.1007/978-3-030-87900-6_58

resource allocation plan, realizes the quantitative planning of English teaching ability evaluation, and realizes the accurate evaluation of English teaching ability.

The evaluation of young teachers' teaching ability is an important part of teachers' management and training. Evaluation needs to start from the qualification, ability and performance of teachers. The growth of young teachers often needs to go through such stages as "adaptation stage", "formation stage of basic teaching skills", "accumulation of experience and skills", and the growth process has a certain ladder. Our school covers a variety of disciplines, such as science, engineering, business and art, and the requirements of each discipline for teachers are different. Therefore, the evaluation standards of young teachers' teaching ability listed here should pay attention to the stages of young teachers' growth and the differences of disciplines in the specific implementation.

In order to play a guiding role and facilitate quantitative evaluation, the indicators are divided into guiding indicators and evaluation indicators.

Guiding indicators

(1) Teaching design ability
1. Be able to determine the teaching objectives properly

    The goal should be clear and meet the requirements of the curriculum; The goal should be comprehensive, giving consideration to knowledge, ability and emotion, and giving consideration to achievement and development; The goal should be moderate, in line with the reality of the school, and pay attention to the requirements of stratification; The goal should be specific and show the observable learning effect of students.
2. Be able to arrange the teaching content properly

    Highlight the characteristics, key points, difficulties and key points of the teaching content; To be able to properly handle the relationship between in class teaching content and out of class teaching content; Be able to deal with teaching materials according to students' learning situation; Be able to select teaching reference materials correctly.
3. Be able to arrange teaching activities reasonably

    To achieve the teaching goal effectively; It can fully mobilize students' learning enthusiasm; It can be full of variety and flexibility.
4. Be able to write teaching plans in a standardized way

    The teaching plan accords with the teaching practice and is practical; Can correctly express the teaching purpose and teaching process.

(2) Teaching organization and expression ability
1. Be able to attract students' attention in the teaching process

    The lectures are in line with the characteristics of students and the actual situation of the prerequisite courses; Can create a good teaching situation.
2. Keep the tense and orderly rhythm of classroom teaching

    Carry out the classroom behavior standard consistently; Have a certain ability of teaching adaptability; Be able to attend class on time.
3. Be able to use standard teaching language

    Teaching with standard Putonghua; The volume, tone and speed of speech should be coordinated with the teaching environment and content; The language is accurate and concise, and body language should be used appropriately.

4. Be able to cooperate with blackboard writing reasonably

The characters on the blackboard are neat, moderate in size and reasonable in layout; The content of writing on the blackboard is concise, which matches the teaching content.

5. Be able to use teaching methods properly

Teaching methods should be conducive to achieving teaching objectives; It is conducive to imparting knowledge and cultivating ability; Be able to use multimedia (PPT) properly, with moderate font size, reasonable layout and appropriate tone; The pictures are clear; The video animation is vivid.

6. It can effectively stimulate students' interest in learning

To infect students with full enthusiasm and rich feelings; Stimulate students' curiosity through interaction; Give students the necessary encouragement.

(3) Teaching research ability

1. Be able to analyze and evaluate teaching behavior correctly

According to the teaching practice to evaluate their own teaching situation; Timely check their own teaching gains and losses.

2. Be able to conduct teaching test effectively

Be able to design stage test papers reasonably; Improve the teaching according to the test results.

3. Teaching and research ability

It can absorb the cutting-edge scientific research achievements in time; Be able to summarize the rules and let students master the frontier of discipline development; Be able to learn and apply the theories of pedagogy and psychology; Learn from the advanced experience of other teachers; Be able to conduct teaching research, write teaching papers, surveys and research reports.

Evaluation index

(1) Teaching design ability.

Check content: syllabus, teaching materials, lesson preparation Notes (teaching plan), courseware, teaching calendar

1. Clear guiding ideology, moderate and specific teaching objectives, and reasonable schedule of teaching calendar (20%)
2. Lesson preparation Notes (teaching plan) and courseware can highlight the key points, difficulties and key points of teaching content; The assignment arrangement is closely related to the teaching content in class and the quantity is reasonable; The selection of teaching reference materials is correct (40%)
3. The prepared cases, examples, classroom discussion questions and thinking questions are conducive to the realization of teaching objectives; It can arouse students' learning enthusiasm (40%)

(2)   Teaching organization and expression ability

Inspection content: classroom lectures, student seminars

1.   Teaching attitude: prepare lessons well and give lectures seriously; To be a teacher and energetic; The teaching stick and other instruments are in place, and the volume and other equipment are adjusted well (20%)
2.   Teaching content: the basic concepts, principles and terms are explained accurately, linked with the prerequisite courses, and easy to understand; The key points are highlighted and the difficulties are analyzed in place; The content is well organized; The combination of theory and practice can be combined with the development of the discipline (20%)
3.   Expression ability: Putonghua is more standard; Speak clearly; The volume, tone and speaking speed are appropriate; Clear thinking, fluent language, infectious; Accurate and concise language, appropriate use of body language; Blackboard writing has neat font, moderate size, reasonable layout and concise content (20%)
4.   Teaching methods: teach students in accordance with their aptitude, the rhythm of the classroom is tense and orderly, have a certain ability to deal with emergencies, and be able to control the classroom; The classroom teaching is detailed and appropriate, highlighting the key points and difficulties, and combining with the teaching content to create a situation, the effect is obvious; The coordination of blackboard writing is moderate; Pay attention to heuristic, interactive and discussion teaching, and pay attention to students' feedback information; Pay attention to the teaching of knowledge and the cultivation of ability; Can use multimedia (PPT) properly, font size is moderate, layout is reasonable, tone is appropriate; The pictures are clear; The video animation is vivid (20%)
5.   Teaching effect: Students' teaching order is good; Focus on learning and have a strong interest in learning; Students' enthusiasm was 3; Students have high recognition of teachers (20%)

(3)   Teaching research ability

Inspection contents: Young Teachers' teaching experience, written summary, forum, test paper, teaching research paper

1.   Self evaluation: self evaluation of teaching situation; Timely check the teaching gains and losses (30%)
2.   Teaching test: reasonable design of students' stage test papers; Adjust the teaching strategies according to the test results (30%)
3.   Teaching research: combining scientific research achievements in teaching; Learn from the advanced experience of other teachers; Write teaching papers, surveys and research reports (40%)

2   The Stander of Teaching Ability Evaluation

Based on teaching research projects, teachers' teaching reform should be promoted. We should strengthen the management of educational scientific research projects, and do a good job in organizing the declaration, process management, and conclusion appraisal of various projects at the national, provincial, and school levels. Implement the "Teacher Excellence Project", encourage and support teachers to carry out theoretical and practical research around education and teaching, talent training, teacher development and other issues, and create a good atmosphere of paying attention to teaching and researching teaching.

To improve teaching ability as the goal, organize teacher training seminars. Organize the induction training for new teachers, and promote the new teachers to change their roles and adapt to the post needs as soon as possible through various forms of teaching training such as "micro teaching world" and "induction teaching world". Focusing on the cultivation of key teachers, we should organize and implement the "training plan for the best teaching key teachers" in a planned and step-by-step way, so as to create a backbone of teachers who play an exemplary role in the practice of education and teaching. For all teachers in the school, a series of training and promotion activities such as "excellent forum", "excellent exhibition forum", "teaching Salon" and "Teaching Workshop" are carried out to promote the renewal of teachers' teaching ideas and the improvement of teaching level.

In order to solve teaching problems, we should carry out teaching diagnosis consultation. According to the needs of teachers, we provide targeted cooperative research and consulting services to help summarize teaching experience and break through teaching bottlenecks. Organize the implementation of "potential teachers' teaching improvement plan", track and guide through classroom evaluation, teaching consultation, teaching investigation, etc., stimulate teachers' teaching potential, and constantly improve teachers' teaching ability. We should carry out consultation on teaching theory, teaching research, teaching methods, modern educational technology and teachers' professional development, so as to meet the needs of school characteristic talent training and teachers' personalized professional development.

With teaching demonstration as the starting point, build a teaching exchange platform. We should actively organize exchanges and cooperation between teachers at home and abroad to promote teaching experience sharing and teaching reform and innovation. Actively expand external contacts, participate in domestic and foreign teachers' teaching development conferences, learn advanced education and teaching concepts, and actively integrate into the process of modern education. We will further improve the "excellent teaching think tank" and give full play to the leading role of our excellent teachers in teaching. Use the network platform to gather high-quality courses inside and outside the school, and form the digital teaching resources co construction and sharing.

Focus on the implementation of teaching evaluation to provide teaching quality assurance. Speed up the construction of teaching quality assurance system, establish the basic status database of undergraduate teaching and professional teaching, organize and carry out teaching evaluation including professional evaluation, curriculum evaluation and practical teaching evaluation, and explore the promotion of social third-party evaluation and international evaluation. We should establish a database of teachers' teaching quality assessment and evaluation, strengthen the assessment, inspection and evaluation of teachers' moral cultivation, professional level, teaching ability and teaching effect, attach great importance to students' teaching evaluation and result feedback, and ensure effective teaching reform and continuous improvement of teaching quality.

Based on the construction of teaching system, we should construct the excellent teaching culture. Establish and improve a series of policies, including project management, teacher training, teaching evaluation, resource construction, etc., to provide action guidance for teachers' teaching development. Improve the teaching incentive system, organize excellent teaching award selection, young teachers' teaching talks, micro class teaching competition and other activities to stimulate teachers' enthusiasm, initiative and creativity in teaching. To promote the advanced teaching culture, we should compile teaching cases, research results of teaching projects and teachers' works.

3   Big Data Analysis Model of English Teaching Ability Evaluation

3.1   Big Data Analysis of Constraint Parameters in English Teaching Ability Evaluation

In order to realize the accurate evaluation of English teaching ability, it is necessary to construct the information sampling model of English teaching ability. Combined with nonlinear information fusion method and time series analysis method, the statistical analysis of English teaching ability is carried out. The index parameter of English teaching ability constraint is a group of nonlinear time series. This paper constructs a high-dimensional feature distribution space to express the parameter index distribution model of English teaching ability evaluation [1]. The main index parameters of English teaching ability include the level of teachers, the investment of teaching facilities, the level of policy relevance, etc. An information flow model is constructed to express the constraint parameters of English teaching ability.

$$x_n = x(t_o + n\Delta t) = h[z(t_0 + n\Delta t)] + \varpi_m \tag{1}$$

The gray model is used to evaluate the level of English teaching ability quantitatively and recursively. Assuming that the historical data of the distribution of English teaching ability is expressed as, the probability density functional of the prediction estimation of English teaching ability is obtained when the initial value of the disturbance characteristic is fixed:

$$u_c(t) = Kx_c(t) \tag{2}$$

By using the method of surrogate data to randomize the amplitude of English teaching ability, we can get x (k). By using the perturbation functional to the empirical distribution data of class k, we can get the subclass set of class K. from this, we can get the utilization ratio of English teaching resources distribution, which can be expressed as follows:

$$U_{unitl} = \gamma \overline{X} \tag{3}$$

3.2   An Assessment Model of English Teaching Ability

Based on the analysis of the big data information model of English teaching ability evaluation by using the fixed recursive analysis method, in order to improve the evaluation ability of English teaching, this paper proposes an English teaching ability estimation method based on big data fuzzy k-means clustering and information fusion, The problem of English teaching ability evaluation is transformed into the problem of solving K-means clustering objective function as least square estimation. As shown in Fig. 1. The least square problem is to find the Consistency Estimation of resource constraints in English teaching ability assessment, which makes the remaining YX β B reach the most F-norm in the European norm, and obtains the feature extraction value of the feature information of English teaching ability constraint.

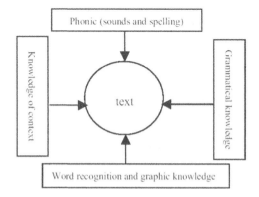

Fig. 1. Model of English teaching ability

4   The Significance of Multidimensional Interactive Teaching Mode in College English Teaching

4.1   Help to Enrich the Teaching Form

In the process of College English teaching, in order to avoid the problem of "indoctrination teaching", teachers blindly guide students to carry out autonomous learning. Although this teaching method can improve students' interest in learning for a period of time, in the long-term learning process, students will be unable to learn deeply because of the problem of learning ability, Eventually lead to serious polarization in the class [2]. Therefore, in the process of teaching, College English teachers need to change the concept of College English teaching, guide students through diversified teaching methods, and then improve students' English learning ability. Different from other teaching stages, College English teaching generally attaches importance to students' English application ability. In more cases, teachers should cultivate students' oral English ability, so as to improve students' ability to master the knowledge. Therefore, in the process of multi-dimensional interactive teaching, teachers can use the multi-dimensional interactive way to organize some communication activities for students, and set aside a lot of time for students to practice English application ability, so as to enrich the teaching form in College English classroom.

4.2   The Concept of Curriculum Ideological and Political Education

Based on the concept of "curriculum thinking and politics", the paper aims to define the training objectives of talents in combination with the characteristics of English subjects and the rules of students' cognitive development. It involves the top-level design of curriculum standards, selection of teaching materials, deep exploration of teaching content, design of classroom teaching, teaching methods, teaching evaluation, and improvement of teachers' team curriculum awareness and ability, This paper studies the teaching practice of cultivating students' critical thinking and innovation ability, taking the advanced course of new generation English published by foreign language teaching and Research Press as an example. Money matter is the reading lesson of unit 4. The teaching content highlights the elements of Ideological and political education, and integrates the elements of Ideological and political education while learning language knowledge. With the help of online and offline blended teaching, through cooperative learning and autonomous learning, students can master the language knowledge points, understand the purpose of reasonably controlling their own money, clarify the overall framework and context, and learn to distinguish rational consumption, avoid money worship and hedonism, so as to help students form a correct outlook on life and values (Fig. 2).

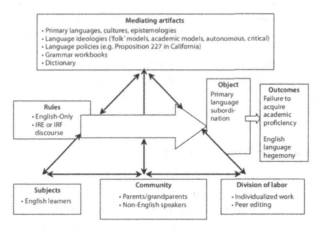

Fig. 2. Main introduction of the course idea

4.3   Help to Stimulate Students' Interest in Learning

Interest in learning is of great significance to students at each stage of learning, and stimulating students' interest in learning is also something that the education department has repeatedly put forward and explicitly requested. However, in the process of College

English teaching, students' interest in learning English course is very low. Many teachers only pay attention to whether students have mastered the knowledge, but ignore whether students can use the knowledge flexibly [3]. As a result, students' English application ability is very weak in the learning process, which makes students unable to raise their interest in learning English course. Therefore, in the process of teaching, teachers should organize corresponding teaching activities for students to stimulate students' interest in learning. At the same time, they should improve the interaction with students, and use effective multi-dimensional interaction to improve students' interest in learning. For example, organize English drama performance or English Movie Dubbing activities for students to ensure that students can master English application ability in the course learning process, so as to improve students' interest in learning, so that students can deeply understand the charm of English course, and improve students' Comprehensive English learning ability.

5   The Application of Multidimensional Interactive Teaching Mode in College English Teaching

5.1   Fully Respect the Subject Status of Students

In the current development process of the times, the society and enterprises have an increasing demand for diversified talents, and the demand for talents with strong English application ability is growing day by day. Therefore, in the current era, College English teachers begin to change their teaching methods in the process of teaching, through the multi-dimensional interactive teaching method to guide students, and show students' dominant position in the classroom. To ensure that students can learn and communicate according to their own understanding of the course in the process of learning, for example, when they encounter some articles with strong communication, teachers can give the classroom to students, and organize dialogue and exchange activities for students, so that students can speak freely in the activities, so that students feel the importance of teachers, and then enhance the dominant position of students in College English classroom.

5.2   Actively Carry Out Group Activities

In College English teaching, the communication between students is very scarce, but the communication between students is the best teaching method. Therefore, when teachers use multi-dimensional interaction to teach students, they should pay attention to this problem and set up learning groups for students, so as to improve students' communication ability and make students find common topics in the process of mutual communication, so as to solve the problem that students dare not speak English aloud. Therefore, teachers can set up some flexible classroom questions for students, or carry out classroom debate activities for students, so as to improve the cooperation ability of students' learning groups through these teaching guidance methods.

5.2.1 Make Clear the Goal of Talent Training

The traditional goal of talent training in Higher Vocational English teaching is to emphasize the training of knowledge and skills, but neglect the training of thinking ability. Proficient in foreign languages, with solid basic skills, master the skills of listening, speaking, reading, writing and translation. But it is easy to lead to the "island effect" that English curriculum and ideological and political education are isolated from each other. Therefore, we need to change our ideas. The direction of Higher Vocational English Curriculum Education Based on "curriculum ideological and political education" must be accurate, otherwise it will backfire. We should think about what kind of people to cultivate and how to cultivate them. We should take students as the center, guide students to transform the knowledge and skills they have learned into their inner morality and accomplishment while imparting knowledge and skills, continuously improve students' Ideological and political awareness, cultural cultivation and moral quality, and lead the ideological and political goal of the course with the combination of morality, intelligence, sports and beauty.

5.2.2 Enhance the Ideological and Political Awareness and Ability of Teachers

Teachers are the key to make good use of the main channel of classroom teaching, the implementer of curriculum education, and the basic requirement of being a teacher and learning high school as an educator. Xi Jinping's qualified teacher should first be a moral qualified person, and a good teacher should first be an example of Naruse Nori and Germany. Teachers are the mirror of students' moral cultivation. Teachers' awareness and ability of Ideological and political education are directly related to the effect of curriculum ideological and political education and the standards for good teachers in the new era are ideal and belief, moral sentiment, solid knowledge and benevolence [4]. The work of teaching and educating people includes not only spreading knowledge, truth, culture and thought, but also shaping peaceful personality and cultivating correct world outlook, outlook on life and values. Teachers identify with the ideological and political leaders of the curriculum, strive to improve the level and pattern of ideological awareness, adhere to socialist ideals and beliefs, and strengthen cultural confidence, so as to realize classroom learning.

5.3 Integrating and Optimizing Teaching Resources

In the process of teaching, College English teachers should pay more attention to the integration of teaching resources. Many college teachers often use the content of teaching materials to teach students, but the content of teaching materials is relatively limited. Therefore, if teachers want to reasonably carry out multi-dimensional interactive teaching, they should use modern teaching tools to teach students, such as using multimedia teaching equipment to play foreign film clips for students, so as to help students understand the western culture and the way of communication with westerners. At the same time, teachers can also guide students to communicate with movie clips, so that college English teaching content can be effectively expanded, and at the same time, students' English application ability can be improved, so as to promote the modernization of College English curriculum.

6 Conclusion

Through the above summary, we can see what problems exist in the teaching process of College English teachers, and also understand the help of multi-dimensional interactive teaching method for teachers and students. Therefore, in the process of teaching, College English teachers should make rational use of the multi-dimensional interactive teaching mode, so as to improve students' English application ability and further improve the comprehensive ability of students. Not only that, teachers should also carry out teaching activities for students in a reasonable way, so as to ensure that students can firmly grasp the knowledge of Chinese characters in teaching activities, Further improve students' English application ability. The application of multi-dimensional interactive teaching mode not only improves students' learning ability, but also helps teachers to make clear the direction of education development, so that teachers can constantly reflect in teaching practice, so as to effectively improve the quality of College English teaching.

Acknowledgements. This paper is an empirical study on the autonomy of business English teachers in the context of information technology (project number: GD17XWW26).

References

1. Lu, J.: Analysis of College English reading ability evaluation model. J. Shanxi Young Manage. Cadre Coll. **22**(2), 105–107 (2009)
2. Zhang, M.F.: Principles and Methods of Intercultural Communicative Competence Assessment in College English Teaching. Hebei Normal University (2008)
3. Zhang, J.: The development trend of English learning strategy research. J. Northeast Agric. Univ. (Soc. Sci. Ed.) **2**, 71–73 (2007)
4. Xie, X.L.: Algorithm and implementation of College English teaching comprehensive ability evaluation system. J. Guilin Inst. Technol. **3**, 360–364 (2004)

System Design Analysis of Economics Teaching in Western Colleges and Universities Under the Background of Big Data

Ping Wang[(⊠)]

School of Yunnan Technology and Business University, Yunnan 651701, China

Abstract. In order to improve the teaching quality of western economics, teachers should carefully compile and select teaching materials, and teachers should play a positive guiding role in enhancing students' subjective learning, so as to realize the significance of teaching reform.

Keywords: Western economics teaching · Innovation · Personnel training

1 Introduction

As the main core course of talent training program in Colleges and universities, western economics is highly valued in most colleges and universities. It is not only a professional compulsory course, but also has a lot of class hours. In addition, there are practical teaching and tutorial teaching. However, in the process of teaching, there are some common problems, such as outdated teaching methods of economics and students low interest in learning. At present, the teaching method and talent training mode of western economics in Colleges and universities need to be adjusted and reformed in combination with the national talent training strategic planning and students learning needs, so as to meet the needs of the development of the times [1].

2 An Analysis of the Problems in the Teaching of Western Economics in Chinese Universities

According to the survey of the actual situation of Western Economics Teaching in most colleges and universities in China, there are several problems in the teaching of western economics in Colleges and universities.

(1) As a discipline, microeconomics and macroeconomics have a history of more than 200 years, while I have only 20 years of education and teaching history. It is difficult to guarantee that western economics education has enough time accumulation. There is not only a lack of excellent teachers in the teaching front line, but also a lack of experience summary in the teaching reform of western economics, and a lack

M. A. Jan and F. Khan (Eds.): BigIoT-EDU 2021, LNICST 391, pp. 517–522, 2021.
https://doi.org/10.1007/978-3-030-87900-6_59

of excellent students engaged in Research-based Learning of economics. According to the survey, students who are engaged in economics, after simple self-study, stand on the platform of western economics according to their own understanding of economics. From a nationwide perspective, although all colleges and universities have basically set up economics courses, the teaching of western economics is still in its infancy, and a complete, scientific and suitable teaching system of western economics needs to be improved.

(2) The teaching mode is old, and the teaching mode is still teacher centered. It adopts indoctrination teaching methods such as classroom teaching theory, homework arrangement after class and final closed book examination. The teaching methods of teachers are old, and the classroom teaching process is chalk writing and oral teaching. Moreover, economics has been set as an elective course in many colleges and universities, the teaching content is scripted, emphasizing theory over practice, basic knowledge is not popularized in all majors, students lack the basic understanding of economic theory, which not only does not reflect the requirements of multimedia teaching mode in the new era, but also is difficult to mobilize students enthusiasm in learning economics [2].

(3) The main problems in the teaching materials of western economics are as follows: (1) at present, the teaching materials of western economics are still traditional ones, whose contents are mainly the mainstream micro and macro-economic theories. Its emergence is based on the western industrial production, and its formation is based on the fully competitive market economic system. Many theories are inconsistent with or even contrary to the reality of China economic development. In the process of teaching, both teachers and learners are puzzled by the theory. (2) Most of the teaching materials are specialized for economics and management majors, which are more theoretical, which is helpful for the students to form a perfect knowledge system, but it is not suitable for non economics and management students to learn the knowledge. The lack of the necessary mathematical model and the introduction of the history of economic theory, the history of economic thought and other professional basic knowledge in the teaching materials leads to the students mental confusion and burnout in their study, and the teachers teaching is also difficult. (3) The textbook lacks the introduction of practical life knowledge such as financial management, investment and entrepreneurship education. More and more college students hope to grasp the guidance of economic activities in social life, such as rational consumption, reasonable investment and innovation and entrepreneurship. If the existing western economics textbooks are not compiled under the guidance of practical application and entrepreneurship and employment education concept, they will not be welcomed and valued in the teaching of economics in Colleges and universities, and the teaching goal of western economics to adapt to the development of the times and promote the cultivation of talents in Colleges and Universities will be even more difficult to achieve.

3 Classification Algorithm and Feature Selection

3.1 The Concept of Machine Learning

Machine learning is simply to let the machine learn human intelligence and become more intelligent, which is also the core of artificial intelligence. We study machine learning in the hope that machines can acquire knowledge from reality and use this knowledge to acquire new knowledge and skills. At the same time, it constructs relevant theories and applies them to various fields. Now all walks of life are entering the era of big data, from search engines to recommendation systems, and so on, covering many aspects. Just because big data has the characteristics of complexity and high dimension, we urgently need the theory of machine learning to help us to mine interesting knowledge from the irregular original big data information. Studies have shown that the effect of machine learning model is directly proportional to the size of data, so the academia generally believes that big data is the driving force of machine learning. In the field of data mining, because of its powerful ability to process all kinds of data and huge commercial application potential, it can better capture the correlation of continuously accumulated data, greatly saving the time and energy of artificial modeling: it meets the needs of the era of big data, and is suitable for the data situation caused by the unstable economic cycle and complex financial environment, So machine learning has been paid more and more attention by academia and industry scholars.

3.2 Common Models of Machine Learning

Support vector machine (SVM) is an algorithm with simple theoretical background and easy to understand. It can be used in machine learning technology related to pattern recognition (classification), and has been widely used in machine tilt and data mining tasks. In order to achieve the effect of classification, SVM develops a hyperplane, namely decision boundary, which separates two classes in data classification and divides them into data points. We know that the data points near the boundary of support vector machine are more important and more difficult to divide. However, in order to construct the decision boundary, SVM realizes the separation boundary between the two data in the data space to the maximum extent and minimizes the classification error. In addition, many experiments show that SVM has better performance and higher generalization ability than other machine learning methods [3].

In binary classification, if there is a sample set X:

$$X = \{(x_i, y_i), i = 1, 2, \ldots, n\} \tag{1}$$

Similarly, we can construct the objective function in the training set

$$min\frac{1}{2}\|w\|^2 + C\sum_{i=1}^{n} x_i \tag{2}$$

Where C is the penalty constant.

Use iris data and R language program example analysis. First, install the function package (el071) loaded with SVM, and then you can analyze and model the data directly. The results are shown in Fig. 1.

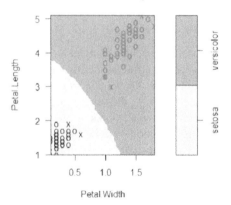

Fig. 1. Classification results of support vector machine

4   Economic Theory and Model

4.1   CRM Analysis Mode

Customer Relationship Management (CRM) is an information intensive process, including all the activities within the company. It is mainly to establish a customer-oriented corporate culture and establish a strategy for acquiring, improving profitability and retaining customers. CRM process is divided into three stages, namely delivery process (sales related activities), support process (what type of customers are the activities oriented to the market) and analysis process (value analysis based on the information collected by the activities). These processes may affect the quality and duration of customer relationship. Especially in the banking sector, making good use of the data related to customer behavior and demand can realize the identification of important customers and develop the relationship with potential customers, which can not only assess the income that these customers may bring to the bank in advance, but also predict the probability that they may participate in bank investment in the future. In customer relationship management, every enterprise must think about three problems: how to find target customers, how to maintain customer loyalty after finding customers, and whether the value created by customers can be maximized on these basis. In many customer relationship management systems, the analysis of relevant indicators can have a preliminary understanding of customers, also can understand the value of customers to the enterprise, and then take different marketing means for different customers [4].

4.2   RFM Model

RFM analysis is a very famous and powerful tool in marketing. It is widely used because it can measure the value of consumers according to their purchasing history. It is an important means and method to know whether customers can bring profits to the company and how much. In CRM analysis mode, this model is also mentioned very much. The main idea of RFM model is to know the customer's value by collecting three kinds of indicators of "customer purchase" behavior: "recency", "frequency" and "monetary". "Recent purchase behavior" refers to the time since the customer last consumed, such as when he last came to the supermarket for shopping. Generally speaking, the shorter the time from the last consumption to the present, the better the customer is, and the greater the response to the instant goods or services provided by the enterprise. "Overall purchasing frequency" refers to the frequency of customers' consumption in the enterprise, such as how many times a customer purchases in the supermarket in a year. Usually, the more times, that is, the higher the frequency, the higher the customer's loyalty and the greater the value to the enterprise. "Purchase amount" refers to the total amount of money that customers spend in the company in a certain period of time. For example, how much money consumers spend in the supermarket in a year, and the higher the amount of consumption, the higher the customer value. By default, accounting calculates the customer's RFM score. The higher the score, the higher the customer's loyalty and satisfaction, and the greater the customer's value. Then build a consumption pyramid according to the customer score, the closer to the top, the greater the customer value, and then formulate different marketing strategies and carry out corresponding marketing activities for customers of different value levels. At the same time, find the lost customers and explore the reasons, and make effective countermeasures to regain these customers.

Based on the idea of RFM model, the factors selected by RFM model are applied to the analysis of bank loan customers, that is, according to the characteristics of bank data, RFM is given new meanings respectively. They are: R refers to the amount of the latest repayment, the more the repayment, the higher the credit rating of the customer; F refers to the frequency of default within a period of time, using the repayment behavior of the customer in a certain period of time to make a general detection of its credit; m refers to the account situation of the customer in a certain period of time, the more the balance of the account, the higher the ability and possibility of the customer's repayment. Through this redefinition, the selected features are applied to the analysis of bank loan customers again.

5 Conclusion

This paper first analyzes the current situation of the credit risk in the banking industry, the means adopted by banks to reduce this risk, and the research and achievements of scholars at home and abroad with various methods on this issue. Then it introduces various classification algorithms in Statistics (including support vector machine, neural network, Bayesian and decision tree), principal component analysis in feature selection and some concepts of theoretical models in economics. Secondly, an example is analyzed. The main work is to apply some algorithms of data mining to economic problems and integrate them with economic theories. It includes applying random forest and principal component analysis in statistics to a group of bank data. Through comparison, it is found that the performance of random forest is better than other algorithms in dealing with this problem; and using principal component analysis to find out the most relevant factor of loan default, and STP analysis on this factor, so as to achieve the purpose of reducing default events.

References

1. Shao, X.: Research on customer credit risk management of commercial banks in the era of big data. Times Finance **20**, 99–101 (2016)
2. Li, J.: Research on credit risk evaluation of individual customers in Internet banking. China Market **14**, 91–92 (2016)
3. Su, J.S.: On the credit rating and realization of banking system. Sci. Technol. Outlook **26**(13), 255–257 (2016)
4. Tang, H.K., Wen, T., Zou, F.L.: Research on perceived credit evaluation system from the perspective of game theory. Soft Sci. **30**(5), 125–129 (2016)

The Feasibility Study Model Design and Development of College English EGP to ESP Transformation Education in the Context of Big Data

Lu Liu and Nan Peng[(⊠)]

East University of HeiLongjiang, HeiLongjiang, Harbin 150001, China

Abstract. Under the background of English reform in China, it is inevitable for EGP teachers to transform into ESP teachers. Based on the examination and reflection of the current situation of English Teaching in higher vocational colleges, this paper analyzes the difficulties faced by the transformation, puts forward the strategies for EGP teachers to transform into ESP teachers, and points out that the transformation can be completed by determining the direction of transformation, self-learning and promotion, and cooperating with professional teachers.

Keywords: Higher vocational education · EGP teachers · ESP teachers · Transformation

1 Introduction

EGP (English for general purpose), also known as general English, refers to the basic English knowledge taught at school. It emphasizes that students understand the basic language structure of English, including vocabulary and grammar. General purpose English focuses on the cultivation of students' language ability, and its main purpose is to help language learners master various language skills. ESP (English for specific purposes) refers to the English related to a specific occupation or subject, which is an English course based on the specific purpose and needs of learners. The purpose of ESP course is to cultivate students' ability to work in English in a certain working environment. In the ESP teaching stage, through professional learning, improve students' English language application ability in a certain industry or discipline.

2 The Present Situation of English Teaching in Higher Vocational Education

According to the author's investigation, the parallel mode of "EGP and ESP" is widely used in Higher Vocational Colleges in China, but the scale of the two kinds of English teaching is quite different. Due to the influence of the traditional teaching mode for a

M. A. Jan and F. Khan (Eds.): BigIoT-EDU 2021, LNICST 391, pp. 523–529, 2021.
https://doi.org/10.1007/978-3-030-87900-6_60

long time, higher vocational colleges in China are used to taking CET-4 and CET-6 and College English proficiency test as the standard to test the effect of English teaching [1]. Therefore, EGP course is very common, and students of almost all departments and majors are required to participate in the above-mentioned test. In contrast, there are great differences in ESP courses offered in various vocational colleges. As shown in Fig. 1. Taking Henan Vocational College of economics and trade as an example, there are 11 departments in our college, including 3 departments with ESP courses, 44 specialties, and 8 specialties with ESP courses. There are 9 ESP courses in our college, with 2–4 classes per week and different semesters. It is not difficult to see that the teaching and management of EGP in China is relatively systematic and standardized, and the teaching materials, class hours, semester settings, teaching software and hardware are very stable. However, ESP teaching is not optimistic, which is mainly manifested in the randomness of curriculum setting, uneven teaching conditions and imperfect teaching equipment, resulting in students' insufficient understanding of FSP course and low enthusiasm for professional English learning, It pays attention to the students' English language foundation and the cultivation of language application ability, and basically conforms to the guiding ideology of the trial implementation of the basic requirements for English Teaching in Higher Vocational Education (hereinafter referred to as the "basic requirements") promulgated by the Department of higher education of the Ministry of education in 2000, but it deviates from the concept of employment oriented and ability oriented higher vocational education.

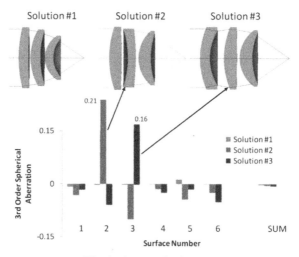

Fig. 1. Current distribution

3 The Inevitability of the Transformation from EGP Teachers to ESP Teachers in Higher Vocational Colleges

3.1 Characteristics of Higher Vocational Education

With the rapid development of China's economy and economic globalization in the 21st century, the society's demand for foreign language ability has shown a trend of diversification and specialization. Higher vocational education is positioned as "training technology, management and skill talents in production and service", and its teaching core is "ability standard". For higher vocational college graduates, the purpose of learning English is to obtain professional information through English, and to express professional ideas by using English as a communication tool. In a certain sense, the teaching of Higher Vocational English is ESP teaching. At present, the teaching of EGP and ESP in Higher Vocational Colleges in China is still difficult to meet the comprehensive skills that students must master in professional communication [2]. If higher vocational English teaching only focuses on EGP and ignores ESP, it will not conform to the development of the times and the needs of the industry. It can not reflect the characteristics of higher vocational teaching itself, and the efficiency of teaching practice will be very low. In view of the current situation of teaching in higher vocational colleges, the reform of Higher Vocational English teaching is imperative. Although the EGP course will exist for a long time in most schools, almost all colleges and universities realize the current situation, esp should be the main direction of Higher Vocational English Teaching in China, so the transformation of Higher Vocational EGP teachers to ESP teachers will become inevitable.

$$\begin{cases} \left(\frac{\partial w}{\partial t} + Fw \right) = 0 \\ w|_{t=0} = w_0^{\circ} \end{cases} \tag{1}$$

$$u(T) = M_T(w_0 + u_0) - (M_T w_0) \tag{2}$$

$$Ju_0 = \|M_T(w_0 + u_0) - (M_T \cdot w_0)\| \tag{3}$$

3.2 The Difficulties Faced by the Transformation of EGP Teachers to ESP Teachers in Higher Vocational Colleges

ESP teachers are language teachers first, and they should have the language teaching quality of foreign language teachers; secondly, professional teachers should have professional knowledge quality of professional teachers. Only when they are combined can ESP teachers be qualified for ESP teaching tasks. The author believes that ESP teaching is in line with the actual situation, but the most basic requirement is to have good English language ability, strong teaching ability and necessary professional knowledge to be qualified ESP teachers. At present, the EGP teachers in higher vocational colleges are composed of English teachers from domestic English majors, non English majors and relevant professional teachers of "returnees" non English majors. They will face three difficulties in the process of transformation. First, EGP teachers in English major mainly study language origin and lack of professional knowledge; secondly, non English majors tend to be professional and solid, but their English language level, especially oral English is poor; third, relevant professional teachers of "returnees" who are not English majors, although language and specialty are close to teaching requirements, However, they do not know or adapt to the current situation and background of Vocational Education in China, and neither of them can meet the needs of ESP teaching.

4   Strategies for the Transformation of EGP Teachers to ESP Teachers in Higher Vocational Colleges

In view of the fact that there is no special teacher training team for ESP teachers in China, a large number of EGP teachers need to turn to ESP teaching. Therefore, EGP English teachers should prepare for this change ideologically and psychologically, and enhance their cognition of ESP.

4.1   Determine the Direction of Transformation

There are many kinds of ESP courses in higher vocational colleges, such as business English, tourism English, Exhibition English, hotel English, Secretary English, financial English, art English, etc. As shown in Fig. 2. All ESP courses are closely related to related professional content, so EGP teachers should first determine their own transformation direction. For the above three types of EGP teachers, the transformation direction can be determined according to their own interests, original majors, second degree and other aspects, so as to achieve targeted.

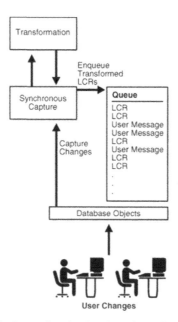

Fig. 2. Determine the direction of transformation

4.2 Self Learning and Improvement

According to he Wenxian's basic model of ESP teacher education, ESP teachers should have knowledge infrastructure (professional knowledge, skills, attitude) and professional practice. EGP teachers should purposefully and directionally add relevant professional basic knowledge to the knowledge structure as the "hardware" for transformation. EGP teachers are mostly "language type" or "combination of English and literature" talents. The problem of single knowledge structure has been mentioned in the survey of many experts. Secondly, EGP teachers can enhance their professional knowledge and practical skills by actively participating in professional training, further study and temporary training in enterprises. At the same time, they can understand the actual needs of students, which is very conducive to the follow-up ESP teaching [3]. Thirdly, get the professional qualification certificate of related major. The examination of qualification certificate is undoubtedly a pass for EGP teachers, which promotes the transformation of EGP teachers and the establishment of self-confidence.

4.3 Cooperation with Professional Teachers

In many higher vocational colleges in China, it is a common phenomenon that language teachers seldom communicate with professional teachers. In order to complete the transformation from EGP teachers to EGP teachers, it is very important to actively communicate and cooperate with professional teachers. EGP teachers are no doubt experts in language teaching, but they are laymen in their profession. EGP teachers can cooperate with professional teachers to optimize ESP teaching. For example, we can audit the courses of relevant professional teachers, assist EGP teachers to analyze students' needs, provide reading bibliography, jointly select textbooks, teaching contents, design teaching links, and even cooperate in the development of ESP courses.

5   An Overview of Teachers' Teaching Skills

At present, teaching skills still occupy a pivotal position, so what is the connotation of teaching skills? In the face of the rapid development of society, what teaching skills should teachers have in the new era? This is the first question we should think about.

5.1 The Meaning of Teaching Skills

There are different views and standpoints on the connotation of teaching skills in academic circles, which can be summarized as follows: (1) art theory. This view holds that teaching skills are not only the key to classroom teaching, but also an important indicator to weigh teachers' teaching art. (2) Experience says. The author thinks that teaching skills are the accumulated experience of educators in teaching activities, and the level of teaching skills is measured by experience. (3) Activity mode. That is to say, teaching skill is a very common way of activity that usually has a certain effect on teaching activities in order to achieve certain purposes required by teaching. In a word, teaching skill appears in the form of operational activity or mental activity. Its essence is a stable operational activity or mental activity mode that can effectively promote students' learning.

5.2 Characteristics of Teaching Skills

(1) Professional. Professional orientation is the primary characteristic of teachers' teaching skills. That is to say, the teaching skills used by teachers in teaching subjects in their respective fields are special and cannot be replaced with each other. For example, Chinese teachers need strong language skills, mathematics teachers need mathematical logic skills, art teachers need space combination skills. These directional teaching skills are different from the general simple imitation, because it contains complex activities such as input, coding and output of the internal and external environment of teaching [4]. It is a kind of creative skills, which can only be produced after special continuous training. (2) Mutual inductance. The mutual inductance of teaching skills shows that in the actual teaching activities, teachers are the leading role of teaching activities, and students are the main body of teaching activities. Emotional communication between teachers and students is also an important way for teachers to carry out emotional teaching activities. For example, the Pygmalion effect refers to the mutual inductance of teaching skills. In other words, the effect of teaching skills is to convey teachers' high teaching enthusiasm to students. Teachers and students inspire each other and collide with creative sparks, so as to promote the efficient teaching activities. (3) situational. The situational nature of teaching skills is determined by the characteristics of teaching objects and the suddenness of teaching activities. On the one hand, students are not only the main body of teaching activities, but also independent individuals. Teaching activities change rapidly without the teacher's will. This requires teachers in the face of different teaching situations, to fully mobilize the existing teaching experience, calm judgment and thinking, take effective methods and strategies, individualized teaching.

5.3 The Significance of Improving Teachers' Teaching Skills

(1) It is helpful to improve the quality of teachers and cultivate their professional ability. Teachers' teaching skills run through the whole process of teaching activities and are an important part of teaching activities. In this process, teachers should pay attention to the development of their own basic teaching skills, such as language expression skills, classroom introduction skills, instructional design skills, and at the same time, they should keep pace with the times, innovate and develop teaching media, extracurricular activities, and independent inquiry skills.

(2) It is conducive to improving learning efficiency and promoting students to learn better. Teaching process is a two-way interactive process between teachers and students. Teachers play a leading role in teaching activities, while students are the main body of learning. Teachers play a key role in improving students' learning efficiency. There is a positive correlation between teachers' teaching skills and students' learning effect. With the improvement of teachers' teaching skills, students' learning efficiency will be improved. It should be noted that since students are the main body of learning, the development of teachers' teaching skills should adapt to students' actual needs and personality characteristics, and organize teaching on this basis, so as to better promote students' learning.

6 Epilogue

Under the background of China's English teaching reform, it is feasible for EGP teachers to transform into EGP teachers through self positioning and promotion and teaching cooperation with professional teachers. Teachers, as an important aspect of the basic ability of vocational education, directly affect the quality of teaching and the cultivation of compound talents. How to solve the reasonable transformation from EGP teachers to ESP teachers in higher vocational education has important practical significance for the development of higher vocational education.

References

1. Gao, Z.R.: ESP teacher: the inevitable turn of College English teachers. China Sci. Educ Innov. Guide (2007)
2. He, W.X.: Economic attributes of language and practice of ESP teaching mode. Foreign Lang. Foreign Lang. Teach. **2** (2006)
3. Guo, J.H.: Research on the mode of Ge teacher's transformation to ESP teacher. Acad. Circles **6** (2008)
4. Ji, C.F.: Teaching cooperation mode between ESP teachers and general English teachers. J. Changchun Univ. Technol. (Soc. Sci. Ed.) (2010)

Research on the Platform Construction of Multimedia Technology Education Curriculum System in Film and Television

Yuelin Hu$^{(\boxtimes)}$

Shanghai Publishing and Printing College, Shanghai 200093, China

Abstract. People often use "film and television media" as the carrier of audio-visual programs, but there is no clear theoretical definition of multimedia technology course teaching and teaching resources construction experience. This paper analyzes the definition, category and development of multimedia film and television technology, summarizes and expounds the construction method and main content of film and television multimedia curriculum system.

Keywords: Film and television multimedia technology · System construction

1 Introduction

In the era of simulation technology, film and television production adopts the traditional video technology, and the production process of shooting, recording and editing cannot be separated from the single storage media of video tape. Since the 1990s, the traditional film and television production technology has been gradually replaced by multimedia film and television production technology. The maturity of computer non-linear editing technology, multimedia three-dimensional animation design and virtual studio technology has completely changed the traditional production process, transmission and reception mode of film and television media shooting, recording and editing.

In order to adapt to the new requirements of technology development on the knowledge structure of talents, broadcasting and television director, multimedia animation production, advertising design and other communication majors have set up new multimedia technology courses. Because the teaching material of this course adopts the general multimedia technology teaching material of electronic information, it is very difficult for teachers to teach and students to learn. At present, the domestic research on film and television multimedia technology is only limited to professional papers, and there is no teaching material that combines the content of film and television production and the dissemination of film and television programs, and there is no more complete auxiliary teaching resources. Therefore, the film and television multimedia technology curriculum system needs to be constructed.

© ICST Institute for Computer Sciences, Social Informatics and Telecommunications Engineering 2021
Published by Springer Nature Switzerland AG 2021. All Rights Reserved
M. A. Jan and F. Khan (Eds.): BigIoT-EDU 2021, LNICST 391, pp. 530–536, 2021.
https://doi.org/10.1007/978-3-030-87900-6_61

2 Definition and Characteristics of Film and Television Media

Under the promotion of the digital process, the traditional film and television media have been greatly impacted, digital coding has become the main media, people will be in the form of digital transmission of film and television media also known as digital film and television media.

2.1 Various Types

Film and television media include many forms. The same information type has different requirements in terms of rate, delay and error code. Therefore, the transmission system must adopt a variety of encoders, a variety of transmission media interfaces and a variety of display modes, and can exchange information with a variety of storage media. Recommendation 374 of ITU-T defines six kinds of media: sense media, presentation media, display media, storage media, transmission media and exchange media. But in different situations, the definition of media is different. For example, when we study the relationship between media representation and time, we define discrete media and continuous media [1]. In the field of mass media, people often use film and television media as the carrier of audio-visual programs. In my opinion, film and television media should also include information representation, storage, transmission technology and means related to hearing and vision. In the era of analog electronic technology, audio tape or video tape is the main storage media of film and television media, open circuit transmission or cable transmission is the transmission media, television and tape recorder is the display media, and analog signal is the representation media.

2.2 Variable Bit Rate

Multiple information transmission requires multiple transmission rates. The transmission rate required by various information media is shown in the Table 1.

Table 1. Transmission rate of various information bodies.

Media	Transmission rate	Compressed bit rate	Sudden peak/average peak
Data, text, still image	155 bps–1 bPs	< 1.2 Gbps	3–1000
Voice, audio	64 kbps1–536 MBPS	16–384 kbps	1–3
Video, motion picture	3–166 MBPS	56 kbps–35 MBPS	1–10
HDTV	1 Gbps	20 Mbps	-

The delay is variable. The time delay of the compressed voice signal is small, but the time delay of the compressed image signal is large, which leads to the problem of different steps between different types of media. Continuity and suddenness. The transmission system is burst, discrete and non real-time when transmitting data information, while the voice signal and dynamic image are real-time, continuous and non burst with high data rate. There is a large amount of data. The transmission system transmits a large amount of dynamic image data. For example, the amount of data generated by studio quality digital video signal is 200 Mbps per second, and the transmission rate of uncompressed HDTV signal is as high as 1 Gbps.

Firstly, the distance between the source node and each neighbor is calculated. The first forwarding node is the farthest node, expressed as N, and the other two nodes are selected according to the location of n. The source node is the origin, the abscissa is the line sn0, and the coordinate system is established. By dividing the source node into three sectors with M/3 transmission range, each neighbor node n defines an angle function and a position function of the formula respectively:

$$f_n = \cos 3\alpha/2 \tag{1}$$

$$g_n = f_n \cdot d_{sn} \tag{2}$$

$$Q_w = (\omega) = \frac{\sum_{pug}(W_{pg})}{p \times q} \tag{3}$$

The main function of network transmission processing module is to carry out user server P2P direct connection transmission, signaling transmission, terminal P2P penetration, transfer and so on. When most wireless network terminals connect to the network, they are in a NAT local area network, and their ports and IP are private to the local area network, so they can't directly connect to two terminals in the local area network. The UDP penetration module of P2P network is mainly based on NAT penetration technology. Both sides get the p address based on the public network, promote the port mapping, and finally complete the direct connection process, And the transmission of multimedia data, if NAT successful penetration.

3 Characteristics and Category of Film and Television Multimedia Technology

3.1 Main Advantages

In addition, it is necessary to construct a home multimedia terminal with digital technology, compression coding technology and network technology, which integrates the fidelity of film and television image, the interaction of computer and the distribution of network. Interactivity. Interactivity is an important feature of film and television multimedia technology. It enables users to control and use the film and television media more effectively, and increase the attention, understanding, planning and production of the media. In a sense, not only the film and television media, but also all forms of media require interaction. The interactivity of film and television multimedia technology is mainly manifested in the realization of two-way interactive services, such as video on demand (VOD), network interactive television and so on. Intelligence. Video multimedia digital equipment is the integration of computer, radio and television and communication functions. The nonlinear editing system, virtual studio, hard disk broadcasting system, etc., which are put into use at present, give full play to the intelligent functions of the control system of the grate [2]. Video multimedia technology is based on digital audio, video technology and computer technology, This paper studies the application of multimedia technology in the production, transmission and reception of digital radio and television system.

3.2 Storage Technology

As one of the important storage devices of computer, hard disk drive (HDD) has become an important storage medium in film and television production system. The hard disk of professional broadcasting system adopts rad technology, and the disk array rad is a fast and super large capacity external memory subsystem composed of many disks. At present, it is widely used in hard disk broadcast system and video on demand system. It has become a necessary equipment with high reliability, fast response and large capacity storage. At the same time, the development of CD storage technology is also very fast. DVD adopts MPEG-2 image compression technology, audio adopts MPEG-2 audio or AC-3 standard 51 channel surround sound technology, audio sampling frequency is 48 kHz. There are four kinds of recording density: single-sided single density, single-sided double density, double-sided single density and double-sided double density. The single-sided single density has a capacity of 4.7 GB (DVD-5) and double-sided double density can reach 17 GB (dvd-17). It has replaced CD as the storage medium of mainstream film and television programs. In addition, there are two kinds of distributed storage technologies that will be gradually promoted.

4 The Development Direction of Film and Television Multimedia Technology

From the perspective of digital process, communication system, computer system and mass communication system are all developing towards digital direction. However, due to the different purposes and technical standards of these systems, there has always been a big gap for end users, which is difficult to integrate, However, they have already penetrated into each other. At present, they have the conditions to realize the "three electric integration" (telephone, television and computer) of information presentation and display media and the "three networks in one" (telephone network, cable television network and computer network) of transmission media. This kind of "integration and unification" is not a simple combination in form, but a combination of the development of multimedia technology in technology, so as to form a unified multimedia information system (MMS), which provides a new opportunity for the development of film and television technology. The combination of the content and style of film and television media and the interactive ability of Web will produce broadband interactive film and television forms, such as webt. Film and television media will enter a new era of interactive media [3]. In the future, radio and television will gradually transfer to broadband IP. The information appliances produced by the integration of Internet TV and computer will become home information terminals (including set-top boxes). Interactive digital video technology based on network will become the development trend of communication technology in the future.

5 Construction Method of Film and Television Multimedia Technology Course

5.1 Multimedia Technology

Establishing the characteristics and technical category of film and television multimedia technology is the basis of determining the teaching objectives of film and television multimedia technology course. However, film and television multimedia technology is a highly comprehensive technology, and its disciplines are competitive, It involves computer technology, network technology, digital audio-visual processing technology and plug-in television technology, and many of the contents are new concepts, new theories and new technologies put forward in recent years. How to organize the teaching content to achieve the teaching objectives and build the curriculum system, the author thinks that we should first study the professional background and the pre curriculum setting of the teaching objects, and find out the advantages of the communication students Secondly, take part in the graduation defense and work report of students to understand what multimedia technology knowledge students have and the existing deficiencies.

5.2 Main Role

On this basis, the teaching plan, course handout and teaching plan are drawn up, and the test feedback method of teaching feedback technology is used in the teaching course to evaluate the teaching effect. Finally, through the analysis and research of the test paper after the mid term and final examination, the difficulties of students in mastering multimedia technology are found out, and the adaptability and pertinence of the teaching scheme (handout) are studied and constantly modified. Practice shows that the combination of theory and practice can achieve good teaching effect. For example, after teaching the theory of compression coding, students are asked to use compression tools (winzip, WinRAR) to compress various media; after teaching digital audio technology, students are required to use coot software to edit and synthesize audio signals, etc. all these have obviously improved students' interest in learning and learning effect.

6 Teaching Requirements of Film and Television Multimedia Technology Course

6.1 Course Teaching Requirements

According to the characteristics of film and television multimedia technology and professional characteristics of technology category integration, through teaching practice, the teaching requirements of this course are determined as follows:

Master the concept of media and the definition of film and television media, understand the six media concepts defined by tu-t, understand the development of film and television technology, and master the four characteristics and technical categories of multimedia digital film and television technology. To master the basic characteristics of visual system (VS) and auditory system (has); to master the basic principles of audio image digitization; to master the physical characteristics and components of image and sound media; to understand the basic characteristics of video signal.

Master the basic theorem and method of audio digitization; master the system structure and working principle of DPCM coding; understand the characteristics of subband coding and ADPCM coding; understand the performance and characteristics of MPEG-1, MPEG2, mpeg-2acc and MPEG-4 audio standards.

Master the basic concepts of data compression; master the methods of Huffman coding, run length coding and arithmetic coding; understand the physical meaning of prediction coding and transform coding to achieve data compression; master the three coding algorithms of JPEG compression standard of still image compression standard; understand the characteristics of h261.

6.2 Main Application Scenarios

Master the main format and characteristics of video tape recorder, master the main technical index and storage principle of CD-ROM memory, master the types and main characteristics of CD-R disc, master the format and application of DD disc, and master the characteristics, mode and application of rad technology, Understand the application of storage area network technology and network attached Technology master the characteristics and basic principles of SCSI, USB, IEEE1394 and SD interface; master the format and characteristics of common video camera; master the main performance indicators and working principles of audio card and video card; master the composition and main functions of Multimedia production platform; understand the classification of multimedia production software; master the application of storage area network technology and network attached technology [4]. Master the basic principle, main functions and classification of nonlinear editing system; master the software configuration and technical indicators of nonlinear editing system. Master the essentials of non-linear editing system steps and steps; master the basic principles of multimedia animation technology.

7 Summary

Working process oriented professional curriculum system construction is a curriculum system model with vocational education characteristics, which enables students to learn and master professional knowledge and skills in the process of completing specific tasks, and is conducive to cultivating students' comprehensive professional ability. It has become the main trend of vocational education curriculum reform. master the goal of MPE frequency compression standard; master the basic concepts of data compression; master the basic concepts of Huffman coding, run length coding and arithmetic coding; Master the application of MPEG-2 in the field of radio and television, understand the main application of MPEG4, MPEG-7, mpeg21 standards and M-JPEG and DV formats.

References

1. Zhao, M.: Application of multimedia technology in film and Television Animation Teaching. J. Tianjin Vocat. Coll. (05), 110–111 (2006)
2. Cao, H., Wang, X.: Analysis of the role of film and television multimedia technology in promoting the development of culture and education. Film Rev. (18), 64 + 58 (2006)
3. Chunlei, H.: On the practical application of multimedia technology. J. Xuzhou Inst. Technol. **09**, 25–26 (2006)
4. Qing, Z.: On the application of multimedia technology in English Teaching. Film Rev. **10**, 80 (2006)

Strategy and Media Construction of Education Platform in the Internet Age

Yixin Gan[✉]

West Anhui University, Hefei 237000, China

Abstract. There are two different modes of competition and game between traditional media industry and new media industry. Platform strategy + era is the most basic growth strategy of Internet media enterprises, which has just been established and developed. In the period of coal resources restructuring, platform strategy is a representative business model of emerging coal industry. Platform media is an online social information dissemination system based on platform strategy. This article will mainly discuss platform strategy and platform media system design strategy in Internet plus era, hoping to provide some inspiration for future research.

Keywords: Internet plus · Platform strategy · Platform media

1 Introduction

China's media industry is gradually carrying out a "radical change" along the evolution path from "emerging", "approaching" to "coexistence" and "domination". In the recent "coexistence" stage, the new and old media industry models are experiencing the most fierce game and competition. According to the Internet thinking and logic, the media industry reorganizes and comprehensively changes the media products, media platforms, the relationship between media and users, and the media industry model. The implementation of platform strategy and the construction of new platform media have become the main axis of media industry resources reorganization [1]. Platform strategy is the basic growth strategy of a group of dynamic Internet media enterprises. It is the representative business model of the new media industry in the process of media resources reorganization. The key points to implement the platform strategy are to build an Internet connected nuclear island (massive user group), build an Internet Ecosystem with independent evolution, dig deep into the profit pool, and open the platform boundary. Platform media is a self-organizing online social information dissemination system based on platform strategy. Using platform strategy to build platform media, we need to take targeted "construction" measures from the Internet nuclear island, social information dissemination and sharing system ecosystem, value network and profit pool, innovative enterprise partners and business model, flat modular network organizational structure and other aspects. The media education platform is shown in Fig. 1.

M. A. Jan and F. Khan (Eds.): BigIoT-EDU 2021, LNICST 391, pp. 537–546, 2021.
https://doi.org/10.1007/978-3-030-87900-6_62

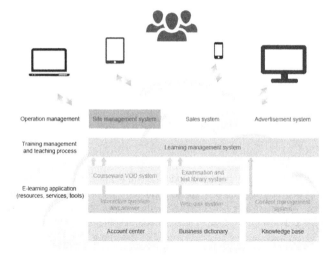

Fig. 1. The media education platform

2   Mathematical Formula Analysis for Latex

Formula symbols include: basic characters, relation characters, operators, case Greek letters and logic symbols. A formula template is defined as the organizational structure of laying out the relationship between symbols and elements in a certain logical order, which includes summation, integral, fraction and root [2–4]. There are non-linear relations between the symbols of formulas, such as up and down, left and right, nested.

$$\frac{\sqrt{a^2 + b^2}}{x} \tag{1}$$

a, b, 2 and x are all basic characters. Fraction represents the logical relationship between the basic elements in the formula, which is the template of the formula.

Each element in the final set Q is an index item, as shown in Fig. 2.

$$\frac{b}{2a} + \sqrt[2]{b^2 - 4ac} \tag{2}$$

3   The Role and Significance of we Media Development in the New Media era

3.1   Internet Advantage

The meaning of the media is the use of the advantages of the Internet, digital technology and information technology, and the birth of various media such as micro-blog, WeChat official account, network community and short video. This kind of media has many characteristics, such as low threshold of media practitioners, high speed of information transmission, wide range of content and so on. Compared with traditional media, it is more convenient and random in communication. It is a new thing in the new media era, which conforms to the development trend of the media industry. Every social individual can participate in the media communication. The impact on social information reform is unprecedented [5]. The expansion of the overall audience of information also reduces the access caliber of information. Using various media platforms, white media shortens the communication radius between social individuals and improves the interaction ability between individuals.

3.2 Audience Group

The audience does not get news information through a single traditional media. It is also through we media to realize the transformation of the relationship between information owners and communicators. Therefore, the new media for the development of the times has far-reaching significance, with a high degree of openness, but also has the timeliness of information collection and transmission. At the same time, with the continuous development of mobile network, mobile electronic society has become more intelligent and convenient, and mobile phones have gradually replaced computer terminals as an information interaction platform. The efficiency and interactivity of we media are improved. However, there are still incomparable characteristics between we media and professional media. Most of US media practitioners do not have professional media knowledge learning and related content training. The performance style of we media with strong personal color and the lack of strict regulations are easy to expose all kinds of obstacles.

4   Obstacles in the Development of we Media

4.1   False Rumors Abound

In the current development of we media, the distinctive personalized style enables the public to express their views and emotions through we media. However, the censorship threshold of information has been lowered, and the ability of professional media to filter some rumor information is also something that most we media practitioners do not have. All of these make the information of we media change in randomness and space-time limitation [6–8]. A lot of we media information is not authentic. Most of the false information begins to spread through we media. Many information that is easy to cause social panic, especially the false information deliberately spread by lawless personnel, has become a relatively bad influence in the development of we media. Some unconfirmed information was deliberately spread. It is very easy to cause the spread of the audience in a short period of time and endanger the security and stability of society.

4.2   Advertising is in Vogue

The development of we media has brought a higher audience. Some businesses have taken a fancy to we media platform and started to invest a lot of advertising. Audience groups will touch many advertisements when they contact all kinds of we media. For example, some short video we media, a lot of goods appear in the form of advertising in the video, such as online game advertising, drug advertising, cosmetics advertising and so on, which all appear in a large number in we media in various forms. In particular, some advertisements prohibited by SARFT from appearing in traditional media TV are constantly flooding in we media [9]. The chaotic situation of advertising agencies makes the management of we media, especially the management of advertising promotion more difficult.

4.3 Vulgarization Content is Forbidden Repeatedly

When many we media were born in the early days, they began to attract a lot of attention from the audience through the low-speed action of attracting attention in a short time. With the development of we media, many we media have vulgar or unhealthy content. Such as Kwai Tai platform, micro-blog and so on are punished by relevant management departments on vulgar content. As shown in Fig. 2.However, the current law of our country is still not mature enough for the management of vulgar content in we media, many management systems are not established in time, and it cannot be prohibited only by self-discipline of we media industry.

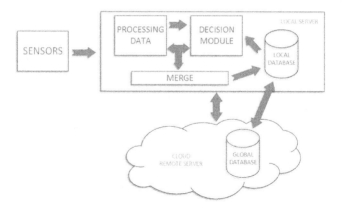

Fig. 2. Improve the operation mechanism of we media

5 Solutions to the Obstacles in the Development of we Media

5.1 We Media Subject Moral Consciousness Needs to be Improved

We media subject is all social audience users, need to effectively improve their own moral consciousness and news literacy, to conduct a high degree of self-consciousness of moral norms and moral consciousness. Only by improving their moral consciousness, can the audience really put an end to the false and obscene contents in we media information [10]. We should face the complex social information with the instinct of thinking, analyze and screen the social information, and correctly edit and process the objective information, so that it can be presented in the correct or advanced form. Even if the correct formula of the rational subject overflows with the sea information in the Internet space, most of them are coated with entertainment, We should correctly enhance the overall moral quality of the media players, change the vulgar publicity atmosphere, strive to promote social progress in all aspects, establish a sense of mission from the media, and do well in the media. We should protect the media from the standard and bottom line of the media. We need the media supervision department as the leading body and the whole society to participate in the network environment. We media operators should establish a good moral outlook and stick to the self-discipline of the media industry.

5.2 The Influence of we Media on the Network Platform cannot be Underestimated

Bad information can quickly spread to the audience through we media in a short time. Therefore, we media practitioners need to sort out the correct values, and pay attention to the extent of their own dissemination of information to guide public opinion. The network operators of their own media also need to set an example, establish the correct values of the website, and resist the erosion of wrong and unhealthy ideas. We media network operators also need to strengthen their own supervision and management functions, the management of the website cannot relax the system management audit mode, strict production of information products [11]. We should also supervise the server operators from the source, increase investment in information censorship institutions, timely delete unhealthy information on the network, and resist the behavior of wanton destruction of the network environment. The Internet world is the whole society, and every netizen and audience has the obligation to maintain a clean network space. Not only do information publishers need to have a basic sense of social responsibility, as the audience, they need to establish a large number of network propaganda and public opinion to guide volunteers. They should take the initiative to attack, supervise, dare to light the sword in the Internet world, dare to fight with negative information with correct public opinion, present all the truth to the society, and guide the correct development of society.

5.3 Improve the Operation Mechanism of we Media

We media information release and management is relatively loose, with a high degree of freedom and randomness. Therefore, we need to improve the operation mechanism of the media, establish an effective registration user management system, clean up the unregistered "waistcoat", improve the real name system, realize an ID number corresponding to a mobile phone number, register only the unique account nickname, and provide a more consistent technical guarantee for the user's network security, so we must adopt strict management mode for the audit information. All Internet security level protection must be seamlessly linked with public security organs and communication institutions to achieve "big data". Personal information should be encrypted to prevent information from being stolen and used. Network recovery should be done without omission. Through continuous research, the legislature should legislate on Internet Security and increase the punishment of Internet crimes. To sum up, we media has achieved unprecedented development in the new media era. Pay attention to the development trend of we media and effectively solve the problems existing in the development of we media [12–14]. In view of the bad false information, we should resolutely crack down on and eliminate it, purify the network environment, ensure that we media can obtain the benign and effective development, and reasonably play the real value of we media in the new media era.

5.4 Strengthen the Supervision and Management of we Media

The supervision and management of we media cannot be carried out only through the improvement of the moral level of the employees of we media. But we should strengthen it in many aspects, especially the function and effect of the gatekeeper. Tiktok and the social bottom line "gatekeeper" are introduced into the media era. We have handled the main media from micro-blog, WeChat, jogyin, post bar and other media, and played the role of the general valve that the society has transmitted the latest and credible information. The operators in the new era, the network information regulatory authorities need to have unhealthy content in the Internet platform of the media. It is necessary to introduce effective technical means to strictly manage the information dissemination of we media network platform, Improve the intensity of information review, standardize the internal management level of operators, and crack down on organizations and individuals disturbing the network security environment through legal means.

6   Radical Change and Reorganization of Media Industry Resources

From the perspective of the overall evolution of the media industry in recent decades, we can see that the new and old industrial models are undergoing a long period of radical change. Generally speaking, the changing track of this process can be described as gradually unfolding along the path from "emerging", "approaching" to "coexistence" and "domination".

The "emerging" stage of radical transformation of China's media industry was in the past ten years from 1987 to 2004. Meanwhile, the important characteristics of the Internet in China's "emerging" stage from scratch and from small to large are: changes from new technologies and customers, and the "threat" of the media industry emerging and growing in those smaller and strategically important market segments. It is in the "new stage" that the Internet has achieved innovation and diffusion along the path of "science and technology institutions, one university and one society" [15, 16]. It has gone through the "four step" development in Chinese mainland: in 1987–1994 years, the application scope of the Internet was limited to scientific research institutions and university campuses. In the 1995–1998 years, the Internet gradually opened to the public, and the traditional media started to build the network version; during the 1999-2001 years, The rise of national news websites such as people's net and Xinhuanet, and commercial portals such as Sina, Sohu and Netease; from 2002 to 2004, with the continuous development of blog, online community and online video, the Internet has entered the Web2.0 era of large-scale, diversified and personalized development. At that time, although the traditional media did not necessarily feel the threat directly, the "threat" itself was growing vigorously, and it constantly brought the elimination pressure to the core business activities and core assets of the traditional media industry, including the newspaper industry and the radio and television industry [3].

At present, we are experiencing the "coexistence" stage of the evolution of China's media industry. 2014 may be the first year of "coexistence". Not only the collapse of traditional media business model is obvious, but also media policy resources, social resources and human resources are inclined to the Internet platform. The period of "coexistence" lasts only four to five years. The so-called "coexistence" is not the long-term development stage of "peaceful coexistence and mutual promotion" of the new and old industrial models, but a special stage of fierce competition and game between the new and old industrial models. It is at this stage that the old industrial model is becoming more and more fragile, and the new industrial model gradually subverts the old industrial model and finally gains a dominant position. In the game process of media industry mode, the vigorous vitality of the new industry mode leads to the decline or collapse of the old industry mode. The way of creating value in the new industry has gradually become the dominant way of the media market [17]. The traditional newspapers have withdrawn from the market, and the traditional radio and television have begun to withdraw from the market, or turn to completely operate the new mode. This is an important characterization of the "coexistence" stage. ① The "domination" stage is the fourth stage of the media industry radical transformation evolution. This stage is not far away. The typical feature of the "domination" stage is that the new media model that creates value for media users is absolutely dominant, and the new industry must create value according to the new model; most media users stop using the old media system and replace it with a new one. At this stage, traditional media may still exist, but it no longer has the possibility of profit. In the dominant stage, new market leaders or new mainstream media platforms will emerge under the new industrial model. What follows is the completion of the whole industrial evolution cycle and the beginning of another new evolution cycle.

7 Implementing Platform Strategy with Internet Logic

Platform strategy is the basic growth strategy of a group of dynamic Internet media enterprises, and it is the business strategy representing the new industrial model in the process of media resources reorganization. The so-called platform strategy emphasizes that the products or services of an enterprise connect two or more specific user groups, provide them with an interactive mechanism, meet the needs of all groups, build an Internet Ecosystem, and form a market strategy of the same side or multilateral network effect. The Internet Ecosystem constructed in this way is actually a "multilateral self-organization management system" [18]. The implementation of the platform strategy is to build a perfect "multilateral self-organization management system" with strong growth potential. It has a unique precise specification and mechanism system, which can effectively stimulate the interaction between multi groups and achieve the vision of platform enterprises.

In the era of "Internet plus", such a self-organizing business system must be developed in accordance with the logic of the Internet. According to Professor Yu Guoming's definition, the Internet is a kind of "high dimensional media", which will greatly activate and release individual energy. ① There are two key words to understand and grasp the logic of the Internet: one is connection. Connection is the essence of Internet. Internet is the connection and integration of all social elements, market elements and all possible value elements. The changes and great possibilities it has brought and will bring to the world are all derived from the connection and connection of all things and human beings as a whole [19]. It is unimaginable that the interconnection among "content network", "interpersonal network" and "Internet of things" and the huge value added space created by the social synergy based on this connection. Without connection, there will be no Internet; without connection, there will be no Internet plus and the future development of the Internet. Second, opening up. As a basic law of survival and development under the logic of interconnection, opening up oneself is the first important thing. The mode of existence in the Internet age is "network existence", and every institution and individual is an end of the network relationship. The decisive factor in the Internet age is the relationship rather than the entity. The relationship determines the entity, the entity obeys the relationship, and the relationship determines the new rules of the game. Therefore, Internet logic requires network actors to realize self opening.

Build an Internet Ecosystem with independent evolution. The core here is to fully release the data energy of the Internet nuclear island, activate online and offline resources, reconstruct supply and demand, cross-border integration, connect everything, build a multilateral market platform ontology, and "build" the specific strategies of the Internet Ecosystem, which are various. It can be "purchased", and the formation of initial products and initial users of the platform is realized by the strategy of purchase and imitation; it can be "entered", and in order to overcome the market entry barriers, the new platform providers must be able to provide revolutionary services and functions; it can be "built", and large-scale social collaboration can be formed to form a bilateral network, and play the same side and cross side network effects; it can be "evolved", With the increasing complementarity, functional diversity, compatibility and interoperability of products, the platform is also evolving and upgrading, from the internal platform of enterprises to the supply chain platform, industry platform and multilateral market platform. As

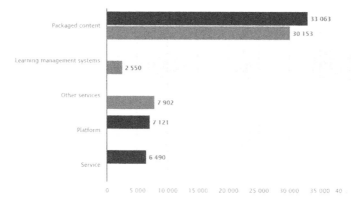

Fig. 3. The platform service people number

shown in Fig. 3.The platform can be "surrounded" and integrated based on the complementary relationship, weak substitution relationship, or completely unrelated functions [20]. Through the way of multi platform binding, we can use and share platform user resources; we can "innovate", implement product platform innovation and ecosystem innovation, expand and upgrade the platform.

8 Conclusion

The new mainstream media is a self-organized social information dissemination platform system with "net generation" as the main user group: it is a new Internet ecosystem that realizes cognitive surplus and user driven, Renren online and global coverage, and influence aggregation. It is a self-organized social information dissemination platform system with "net generation" as the core user. The so-called "new type" is reflected in three aspects: first, facing the new mainstream social groups. To realize the effective link between social information dissemination products and the "Internet generation" after "85", 90 ", and even after" 00 ", so as to solve the pain, difficulty and excitement of the social information needs of Internet aborigines and mobile Internet aborigines. Second, the new business model. Apply platform strategy to build platform media. Third, a new organizational structure. Flat, modular and network organization structure is the inevitable choice of the new mainstream media organization structure. In the traditional pyramid organizational structure, it is impossible to grow a new type of mainstream media.

References

1. Wang, Q., Cong, J.: Literature information retrieval course. Electronic Industry Press, 21–25 (2011)
2. Ma, F.: Fundamentals of Information Management. Wuhan University Press, 6–12 (2002)
3. Zhang, C., Dou, T., Wu, B., et al.: Collection, organization and retrieval of mathematical formulas. J. Univ. Libr. **5**, 57-62 (2005)
4. Baoshui, H.: Research on mathematical formula retrieval and matching technology. Popular Sci Technol. **5**, 46–47 (2011)
5. Jin, X., Liu, J.: Platform strategy: the road of traditional media convergence [a]. Radio and television research center of Communication University of China. 2015 China Communication Forum: "construction of modern communication system: integration and order" paper collection [C], 8 (2015)
6. Yang, W.: On the influence of new media on literary form and competition mechanism. News Commun. (18), 26 + 28 (2015)
7. Yang, J.B.: Platform strategy for controlling the media. Media, Mobile Internet Plus and Media Integration, (14), 49–50 (2015)
8. The editorial department of our Journal: The popular website of "open fun vision and gather the future" officially released the open platform strategy. Sound screen world · advertiser (01), 151–152 + 150 (2015)
9. Gu, H.: Platform strategy for integrated development of radio and television industry and emerging media. J. Jinan (Philos. Soc. Sci.) **36**(09), 153–159 + 164 (2014)

10. Tang, Y.: Understanding the mode of mobile Internet media communication platform from wechat [a] China Federation of journalists and technologists, Guizhou daily press group, Guizhou Radio and television station, Xinhua news agency, Guizhou branch. In: Proceedings of the Sixth Congress of the Federation of journalists and technologists, 2014 annual conference and the seventh WangXuan news science and Technology Award and excellent thesis award awarding Conference (third prize) [C] Guizhou daily news group, Guizhou Radio and television station, Xinhua news agency, Guizhou branch: China Federation of journalists and technicians, 4 (2014)

11. Interaction.: Automobile Accessories **76**(32) (2014)

12. Shuicai, S.: Thinking on the construction of new media technology platform. China Media Sci. Technol. **15**, 16–17 (2014)

13. Zhen, W.: Going into the "reading meeting" – Exploring informal learning. Mod. Enterprise Educ. **07**, 35–37 (2014)

14. Chengyuan, W.: Research on platform strategy under new media environment – taking Shanda network as an example. News World **11**, 146–148 (2013)

15. Xiaowen Q.:The necessity and feasibility of media platform strategy. Young reporter (09), 9-10 (2013)

16. Jialin, Z.: Integration, platform and value chain – analysis of BBC new media strategy. Southeast Commun. **09**, 21–23 (2012)

17. Zhengrong, H.: Challenges and opportunities brought by the trend of media convergence. TV Res. **08**, 13 (2011)

18. Alcatel lucent launched velocix digital media distribution platform Strategic Alliance Plan. Telecom Netw. Technol. (11), 54 (2010)

19. A comprehensive attempt to develop new media publishing era, publishing and Xinhua media reach a "digital reading platform" strategic cooperation. Publishing Reference (31), 18 (2010)

20. Renhai, W.: Platform strategy of TV media integrated marketing. Contemporary TV **10**, 16–17 (2004)

Application of Network Teaching Platform in Higher Vocational Nursing Teaching System

Xiaoqi Miao[✉], Jia Chen, and Yanping Jiang

Gansu Health Vocational College, Lanzhou 730207, China

Abstract. Objective to explore the effect of network teaching platform in Five-year Higher Vocational Basic nursing teaching. After the implementation of the teaching, the final theoretical examination and skill operation examination results of the two groups were compared. Results: after the implementation of the teaching, the test group students' skill operation examination scores were higher than the control group, the difference was statistically significant; there was no significant difference between the two groups of students' final theoretical examination scores; the total score and each subscale score of the test group students' autonomous learning ability were higher than the control group, the difference was statistically significant. Conclusion: the application of network teaching platform improves the skills operation level and autonomous learning ability of five-year higher vocational nursing students.

Keywords: Network teaching platform · Teaching methods · Basic nursing

1 Introduction

In 2010, the national medium and long term education reform and development program (2010–2020) pointed out that colleges and universities should actively innovate the network teaching mode, improve teaching methods, improve classroom teaching effect, and cultivate students' Extracurricular Autonomous learning ability. The network teaching platform provides a relatively complete supporting environment, which can fully and effectively support the teachers' teaching and students' learning under the network environment. It is the basis and core of the implementation of network teaching practice. Research shows that learning burnout is common among nursing students. As the core course of nursing specialty, the teaching method of basic nursing is relatively old, and it is urgent to change the teaching mode. According to the literature review, the research on network teaching of basic nursing at this stage mainly focuses on undergraduate nursing students, while the research on five-year higher vocational nursing students is less. The purpose of this study is to apply the network teaching platform to the five-year higher vocational basic nursing teaching and evaluate its effect [1].

M. A. Jan and F. Khan (Eds.): BigIoT-EDU 2021, LNICST 391, pp. 547–556, 2021.
https://doi.org/10.1007/978-3-030-87900-6_63

2 Method

2.1 Construction of Network Teaching Platform for Basic Nursing

Based on superstar teaching platform, the network teaching platform of basic nursing was constructed. Superstar teaching platform, developed by Beijing superstar Erya Education Technology Co., Ltd., is divided into PC terminal and mobile terminal, which are called "Fanya" and "Xuetong" respectively. "Fanya" is a network teaching platform, and "Xuetong" is a mobile teaching tool. Teachers build courses, edit courses, and count learning tests on PC, while students learn courses on EC or mobile, and complete assignments, tests, and exchanges. Upload teaching resources before teaching, including learning objectives of each chapter, teaching difficulties, teaching courseware, clinical cases, exercises, skill operation flow sheet, video, scoring standard, micro lesson shooting for teaching difficulties and related literature, etc. [2].

Given the input, the input of each neuron in the hidden layer is as follows:

$$u_j = \sum_{i=1}^{n} w_{ij}x_i - \theta_j \quad j = 1, 2, \cdots, m \tag{1}$$

The output of neurons in the hidden layer was as follows:

$$O_j = f(u_j) \quad j = 1, 2, \cdots, m \tag{2}$$

The output of the output layer, that is, the output of the network, is as follows:

$$y = f(\sum_{j=1}^{m} v_j O_j) \tag{3}$$

2.2 Teaching Method

(1) The experimental group adopted the method of combining network teaching with traditional teaching. Before class, teachers release learning notices and requirements on the teaching platform, and assign pre class learning tasks. According to the requirements, students use the course network resources to preview before class, and complete the homework together after group communication. In class, students report and show their homework in groups, and teachers comment and explain the important and difficult points, guide students to discuss and answer students' questions. After class, students are required to upload homework to the network platform in the form of documents, pictures, videos, etc., and expand learning by using literature, website and other resources. Teachers review assignments, guide students to discuss what they have learned on the platform, and organize students to have a stage test once a month on the platform. (2) In the control group, the traditional classroom teaching was used, the teachers orally arranged the learning tasks before and after class, and the class was taught according to the syllabus. Students listen to class, discuss and answer questions, finish homework and stage test after class. (3) In the operation practice class, the two groups are in accordance with the process of teacher's teaching, student's group practice, reverse teaching and summary.

3 Discuss

3.1 The Application of Network Teaching Platform can Improve the Skill Operation Level of Nursing Students

Research shows that the combination of network platform and traditional classroom teaching can improve the performance of undergraduate and three-year higher vocational nursing students. The results of this study show that the application of network teaching platform is conducive to improve the performance of five-year higher vocational nursing students. Before class, students can watch the video preview operation on the network platform, and the video can be watched repeatedly. Some of the video operators are competitors of our school participating in the national, provincial and municipal operation competition [3]. The exquisite video and familiar operators fully mobilize students' learning enthusiasm. In class, students show the operation process in groups, According to the problems in the display and students' questions, teachers focus on analyzing the key and difficult points of operation, so as to make teaching more targeted; after class, students need to upload their own operation video to the teaching platform, which requires more efforts to practice operation, full communication and cooperation. By watching their own video, students can intuitively find shortcomings and promote correction. In addition, the operation assessment scoring standard is issued on the platform before class, which is convenient for students to grasp the operation details from the beginning to the end. All these are conducive to enhancing the teaching effect and improving the skill operation level of nursing students.

3.2 The Application of Network Teaching Platform can Enhance the Self-Learning Ability of Nursing Students

The self-learning ability of nursing students refers to the ability to acquire and master the necessary knowledge and skills of nursing service by using meta cognition and objective human and material resources, including self-management ability, information ability and learning cooperation ability. The results showed that the total score of self-learning ability and the subscale scores of self-management ability, information ability and learning cooperation ability of the experimental group were higher than those of the control group, which indicated that the application of network teaching platform could improve the self-learning ability of five-year higher vocational nursing students. The research of Yin Haiyan also shows that the application of network teaching platform can improve the self-learning ability of nursing students. In this study, the learning task is issued on the platform in the form of notice on time to guide and urge students to study on time; when completing the task, the active students in the group will drive the backward students and improve students' self-management ability to a certain extent. Group work promotes the communication and cooperation among students; platform discussion module provides conditions for the communication between teachers and students, cultivates the sense of cooperation and improves the communication ability. The teaching platform provides students with rich learning resources, so that students can learn to use network resources for autonomous learning, and improve the ability of information analysis.

3.3 Improve Teachers' Teaching Ability

The network teaching method also puts forward higher requirements for our teachers' teaching ability, because the traditional teaching mode does not have high requirements for teachers, and it is centered on teachers and teaching materials, and the information display form is monotonous, which is not conducive to improving teachers' comprehensive ability and broadening students' horizons. After applying the network teaching platform, especially the mobile network platform to carry out teaching activities, teachers can understand the students' pre class learning situation through the mobile app, and explain the knowledge points according to the students' Preview situation. In the teaching process, the software is used for group discussion, data access and in-depth study. Because the platform is open, it is sometimes unpredictable for students to ask some questions on the platform, so teachers need to have more professional knowledge reserves, carefully design teaching, and extensively involve in some related professional knowledge inside and outside the class, so as to improve teachers' teaching level and teaching ability. At the same time, teachers should also increase the investment of extra-curricular time, understand and master the learning state of students at any time, and enhance teachers' sense of professional responsibility and enthusiasm for teaching.

3.4 Improve the Students' Learning Initiative

The application of Hybrid Teaching Based on Pan Ya Network Platform in higher vocational nursing teaching is feasible, especially the development of mobile terminal of Pan Ya platform, which adds motivation to students' learning. Because the knowledge of internal medicine nursing is relatively more, and more boring, students will not be interested for a long time, coupled with the poor self-learning ability of higher vocational nursing students, in addition to learning the classroom knowledge, but also to learn the related subjects of self-study, students' performance will be relatively poor. In the process of self-taught examination guidance, students need to complete the study of professional courses and undergraduate courses in a limited time. For most higher vocational students, the pressure is greater, and there is a problem that teachers do not grasp the classroom knowledge firmly [4]. In the process of tutoring for self-taught examination, students need to complete both professional courses and undergraduate courses in limited time. Most vocational students are under great pressure. There are some problems, such as weak mastery of teachers' classroom knowledge and low effect of review after class [5] Fig. 1.

4 The Problems and Causes of Clinical Practice Teaching in Nursing Major of Higher Vocational Colleges

4.1 The Concept of Clinical Practice Teaching Lags Behind

With the continuous progress of the times, people's requirements for nursing are higher and higher, and modern nursing science is also developing and progressing [6]. At the initial stage, nursing focuses on patients' diseases, mainly assisting doctors, carrying out medical orders, and carrying out simple nursing operations for patients. People lack

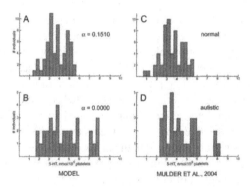

Fig. 1. Simulation result with teaching effect

attention to patients' physical and mental health. At the development stage, people's requirements for nursing are improved, Nursing began to take patients as the focus of work, began to pay attention to the physical and mental health of patients, and adopted a scientific way of holistic nursing for patients. In the third stage, nursing began to expand, and the nursing objects were not only limited to patients, but also extended to all people. The focus of nursing work was human health and disease prevention [7]. The concept of clinical practice teaching lags behind, as shown in Fig. 2.

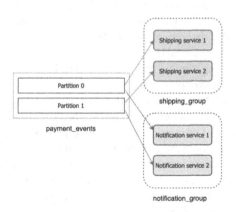

Fig. 2. The concept of clinical practice teaching lags behind

4.2 The Curriculum of Clinical Practice is Unreasonable

Through the interview with the teachers, the author found that the practice curriculum arrangement was unreasonable in the process of nursing practice teaching in higher vocational colleges. First of all, we should pay attention to theoretical study and neglect technical operation. During the period of study in school, nursing students mainly learn professional theoretical knowledge about nursing, while the mastery of operation skills is obtained through clinical practice. In the traditional teaching, students learn professional theoretical knowledge first, and then clinical practice. The time interval is easy to cause students to forget a lot of relevant theoretical knowledge in clinical practice. In practice, it is difficult to establish a relationship with the learned theory, and it is more difficult to use theory to guide practice. In addition, most of the nursing students in Higher Vocational Colleges Experience exam oriented education, only the score pleasure brought by theoretical knowledge. Naturally, they pay more attention to the study of nursing theoretical knowledge, and despise the technical operation of nursing. Moreover, clinical practice is mainly arranged in the last academic year, which often conflicts with the time when students are looking for a job and entering a higher school, which aggravates the students' neglect of clinical practice teaching [8].

Secondly, in the process of practical teaching, the training time is less. In 2015, the Ministry of Education issued several opinions on deepening the teaching reform of vocational education and comprehensively improving the quality of personnel training, which clearly requires that the practical teaching time in vocational education should, in principle, account for more than half of the total school hours. Compared with other majors, nursing specialty is more professional, so it puts forward higher requirements for nursing students' practical operation. Therefore, reasonable setting of training time can enable students to master nursing operation technology during school, and provide great help for students' future nursing work, which is conducive to the cultivation of nursing talents. In the process of practical teaching of nursing specialty in higher vocational colleges, the teacher mentioned in the interview that the school generally only arranges students to carry out practical operation when setting up "basic nursing", and other courses usually only offer theoretical courses [9]. Moreover, when setting up practical training courses, students' practical training time is short, and some nursing students have not fully adapted to nursing clinical practice, This will have a bad impact on students' nursing career. In the process of practical teaching, there are two main reasons for the lack of training time. First, in the construction of training bases, higher vocational colleges lack of capital investment on the one hand, and on the other hand, the school land area is limited, so the number of training bases is relatively small. Due to the limitations of these objective conditions, only the time of students' training courses can be shortened, In terms of curriculum assessment, higher vocational colleges generally only focus on professional theoretical courses, so the teaching teachers focus on the teaching of nursing theoretical knowledge in the aspect of teaching design, so the arrangement of practical training courses is relatively simple [10].

4.3 Clinical Practice Sheet

In the process of clinical practice teaching, some teachers still adopt the classroom teaching mode, teaching knowledge to students by the bedside in the whole process, and the proportion of group discussion is very small, which leads to students' passive acceptance of knowledge and unable to actively participate in the diagnosis and treatment activities [11]. The communication between teachers and nursing students deprives the language communication opportunities between nursing students and patients, and the lack of interaction between students and patients leads to low learning efficiency and lack of experience. In addition, the number of nursing case discussion and clinical lectures is less, some teachers often lack of preparation before class, do not make reasonable planning, clinical teaching is random, just repeat their usual examination process, teaching purpose is not clear, lack of organization or step by step. In this way, it is difficult for nursing students who only have basic knowledge to combine theoretical knowledge with practical operation in a short period of time. They often have little knowledge, and then they lack enthusiasm for class. At the same time, with the development of high and new technology, there are some advanced diagnosis and treatment methods, which make some teaching teachers less enthusiastic in the process of clinical practice, rely too much on advanced science and technology, rely on auxiliary examination, and then despise the teaching of teaching system, resulting in the rigid teaching model of teaching system [12]. The clinical practice chart is shown in Fig. 3.

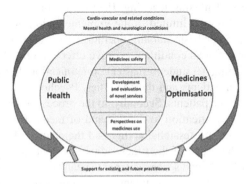

Fig. 3. Clinical practice map

5 Improvement Strategy of Clinical Practice Teaching in Higher Vocational Nursing Specialty

5.1 Changing the Concept of Practical Teaching

The main task of higher vocational nursing specialty is to cultivate technical nursing talents needed by the society [13]. Therefore, in order to cultivate qualified nursing talents, we must always pay attention to the demand of hospitals and relevant medical institutions for the professional ability of higher vocational nursing talents. At the same time, we should also pay enough attention to the relevant policies of the national medical and health industry, Renew the concept of practice teaching. Medical and health care is related to people's health, the country has invested a lot of energy and financial resources in this area. During the 12th Five Year Plan period, its development has been put in an important position. With people's continuous attention to the medical and health industry, the development of the nursing industry has also entered a new turning point. At present, with the continuous improvement of people's living standards and the continuous improvement of the medical security system, nursing education should also conform to the trend of the times [14]. On the one hand, it should broaden the service objects, so that the service population is not limited to patients, it should be extended to all people, on the other hand, broaden the scope of service, from the hospital to the place where people live. On this basis, we should also ensure the quality and level of nursing, so that it can keep up with the trend of the times. On October 25, 2016, the "healthy China 2030" planning outline was issued by the CPC Central Committee and the State Council. The Fifth Plenary Session of the 18th CPC Central Committee put forward the strategic goal of promoting healthy China and improving people's health. The "healthy China 2030" program is an action program to promote the construction of a healthy China in the 15 years from 2015 to 2030. The outline proposes to establish a mature and perfect medical and health service system [15].

With the continuous development and progress of the times, nursing education should also conform to the trend of the times, and constantly update the concept of practical teaching in the process of nursing teaching. First of all, in the teaching process, the teaching content should not be limited to the implementation of medical orders, dispensing, injection and other basic nursing operations, but also should teach students how to understand the patient's condition, curative effect and psychological state, and through situational teaching, let students master communication skills, and apply it to the communication between patients and their families, Psychological nursing and health education were given to the patients. Secondly, in the process of teaching, higher vocational colleges should pay attention to the demand of medical institutions for higher vocational nursing talents' professional ability and the change of policy environment, constantly conform to the trend of the times, adjust the content of nursing education, change the nursing service from disease-centered to health-centered, and change the attitude towards diseases from passive treatment to active prevention, To expand the nursing service population from patients to healthy people, constantly improve the teaching standards, and cultivate nursing talents needed by the society [16].

5.2   Reasonable Arrangement of Practical Courses

Nursing industry is a highly professional industry, which requires nursing graduates not only to master solid nursing professional and psychological knowledge, but also to have skilled nursing operation skills, the ability to solve practical problems in clinical nursing, and the ability to deal with things calmly. In view of the problems existing in the clinical practice teaching of higher vocational nursing specialty, the construction of reasonable practice curriculum system is the foundation.

In view of the problems existing in the practical curriculum arrangement of higher vocational nursing specialty, we can learn from the experience of more mature countries in nursing education. For example, in the United States, the relevant theoretical courses of nursing specialty should be less and more precise, the practical courses should be rich and compact, and the practical teaching should be paid attention to, so as to provide students with experience opportunities in real situations as much as possible. In view of the malpractice of the disconnection between theory and practice of the three-stage course for higher vocational nursing students, the practice course should run through the whole three years, provide students with the opportunity to experience nursing work as soon as possible, gradually acquire clinical nursing skills and accumulate clinical experience. In the process of clinical practice, teaching teachers should provide more opportunities for students to participate in clinical practice, increase students' mobile phone meeting, and let them master operation skills in the process of continuous practice. Not only that, in the teaching process, teaching teachers should cultivate students' ability to find, analyze and solve clinical problems, and combine nursing theoretical knowledge with practice, to better improve the students' nursing skills. In the process of practice, the hospital should also take some measures. First of all, in the process of making the internship plan, we should formulate the specific content of nursing teaching ward inspection in each ward, organize the students to make a ward inspection once a week, and let the students manage the ward. Each student is assigned a ward to act as a small responsible nurse, responsible for admission and discharge, etc., so as to mobilize their internship autonomy and improve their independent practice ability. Secondly, the hospital should develop quantitative indicators of basic nursing technology operation, increase students' specialized nursing operation opportunities, and exercise their hands-on operation ability. In order to achieve the practice effect, the teaching teachers should strengthen the guidance. If some students are not proficient in nursing operation, the teaching teachers should be able to patiently explain and demonstrate the deficiencies of nursing students, and help them to check and fill the gaps.

6 Conclusion

Network teaching platform creates a modern teaching environment and provides students with high-quality learning resources. In this study, the application of network teaching platform in Five-year Higher Vocational Basic nursing teaching has achieved good results, improved the students' skill operation ability and enhanced the ability of autonomous learning. However, the theoretical assessment results of nursing students did not significantly improve, which may be related to the theory course resources are not rich enough, the form is relatively single and lack of pertinence. In the future, we should strengthen the resource construction of the theoretical course of the network teaching platform of basic nursing, strengthen the theoretical course teaching, and promote the mastery of theoretical knowledge.

References

1. Xie Xiaolin, Y., Shengquan, C.G., et al.: New development of network teaching platform. Open Educ. Res. **13**(5), 12–25 (2007)
2. Feng, Z.: Design and development of micro course based on wechat public platform (2019)
3. Jianxin, F.: Architecture and design of distance learning micro course resource construction system. J. Jiangsu Radio TV Univ. **4**, 5–8 (2013)
4. Wu, H., Shi, Y.: The current situation, problems and Countermeasures of the development of micro lecture in China. J. Shijiazhuang Railway Univ., Soc. Sci. Ed. **9**(003), 103–106 (2015)
5. Anli, J.: Nursing education. People's Health Publishing House, Beijing (2012)
6. Deng, J., Wang, J., Pi, H.: Implementation and effect of clinical nursing teacher qualification access system. J. Nurs. Manage. (12), 870–871 (2010)
7. Yujie, P., Lanshu, Z., Yiwen, Z., et al.: Effects of teacher support, personal stress and personal coping style on physical and mental health of nursing students in early clinical practice. China Nurs. Manage. **1**, 47–51 (2013)

8. Lifang, B., Wei, W., Liming, C.: Research on competency model of clinical nursing teachers. Chin. J. Nurs. **10**, 912–915 (2012)
9. Song, C., Shen, N.: Preliminary development of evaluation scale for clinical nursing teachers. Chin. J. Nurs. (12), 888–890] (2004)
10. Huihua, Y.: Research on the education standard of nursing specialty in China. Second Mil. Med. Univ., Shanghai (2011)
11. Ping, Z., Cong, Z., Song, C.: Design and application of evaluation criteria for clinical nursing teachers. China Nurs. Educ. **11**, 12–15 (2013)
12. Wang, Z., Feng, C., Lou, F.: Development and reliability and validity test of teaching ability questionnaire for clinical teaching teachers of undergraduate nursing students. Chinese J. Nurs. (3), 16–20 (2011)
13. Li, H., Wang, H.Z., Shi, L.: Construction of comprehensive evaluation system for clinical teaching teachers of undergraduate nursing. J. Nurs. (5), 68–71 (2012)
14. Xia, C.: Comparison and Reflection on nursing clinical practice between China and the United States. J. Nurs. Educ. (1), 65–67 (2004)
15. Li, C.: Nursing status in Korea. Foreign Med. Nurs. **41**, 44–50 (2000)
16. Mingfang, Z.: Introduction of nursing education in Shengli Christopher University of Japan. J. Nurs. Manag. **9**, 59–60 (2005)

Research on Teaching Mode of College English Ecological Education with Big Data Informatization

Wentao Meng[1,2(✉)]

[1] University of Perpetual Help System DALTA, Las Pina, Philippines
[2] Guilin University of Electronic Technology, Guilin 541004, Guangxi, China

Abstract. In the information age, the impact of big data application on English teaching is gradually increasing, and the traditional education ecosystem has changed. In this case, how to use big data technology to improve the ecological environment of English education and promote the development of College English education and teaching in China has become a problem that must be concerned. Referring to the relevant theories of educational ecology, this paper studies the construction of ecological teaching mode of College English under the background of big data, hoping to provide reference for the improvement of College English teaching environment and the development of English education and teaching.

Keywords: Big data · College English · Ecological education · Teaching mode

1 Introduction

As a new generation of information technology, cloud computing has penetrated into all aspects of production and life in just a few years from the concept proposed to the rapid application and popularization, changing people's traditional life and thinking mode. The so-called cloud computing is simply a super computing service mode based on virtualization technology, network as the carrier, users as the main body, and providing infrastructure, platform, software and other services as the form to integrate large-scale and scalable distributed computing resources such as computing, storage, data, application to work together [1]. On the whole, the application of cloud computing technology in English Teaching in China is still in its infancy, and there is still a long way to go in theoretical exploration and practice. However, the important application value of cloud computing technology in English teaching is gradually highlighted with its advantages of openness, convenience and sharing.

2 The Application Value of Cloud Computing Technology in English Teaching

The application of cloud computing in English teaching will bring about a revolution in English teaching. Its advanced technology, advanced resources, sharing and flexibility

© ICST Institute for Computer Sciences, Social Informatics and Telecommunications Engineering 2021
Published by Springer Nature Switzerland AG 2021. All Rights Reserved
M. A. Jan and F. Khan (Eds.): BigIoT-EDU 2021, LNICST 391, pp. 557–565, 2021.
https://doi.org/10.1007/978-3-030-87900-6_64

will restructure English teaching methods and learning methods to achieve the comprehensive integration of English teaching resources and promote the overall improvement of English teaching quality and learning effect. First, the advanced whenever technology is applied. Cloud computing breaks the limitation of English teaching through technology. It makes English teaching completely meet the requirement of teaching in the space. The English teaching is no longer restricted by the school and classroom. Teachers and students can interact online and offline whenever and wherever possible. Teaching will be truly student-centered, with sufficient teaching resources and flexible teaching methods, teachers will have more time to spend on students, teachers can make personalized teaching programs according to the characteristics and needs of students. Secondly, the resource sharing of the whole school will be greatly improved through the resource sharing of the whole school, which will be greatly improved by the resource sharing of the whole school. The application of cloud computing technology in English teaching can not only break the limitation of time and space, but also develop a variety of more flexible learning tools. For example, the construction of cloud classroom and cloud database, students can flexibly access English learning resources through computers, mobile phones, tablets and other media, as well as installing a variety of applications. While English teaching resources are very rich, students can obtain the same massive resources as teachers to a certain extent [2]. Teachers can easily manage students' learning process and set learning objectives according to their own characteristics and needs. With the help of teachers, they can formulate reasonable and efficient learning plans. Through targeted and targeted learning and training, English learning will become more efficient, More emphasis on interest and application.

3   Application of cloud computing in English Education

Cloud computing is the extension of the Internet, with the network, personalized, low-cost, high-performance and other functional characteristics, the promotion and application of cloud computing technology makes the characteristics of Internet resource sharing play more incisively and vividly, and rapidly expand to various industries and fields with the fastest speed. The application of cloud computing technology in the field of English education mainly focuses on theoretical exploration. Constructivism theory, cooperative learning theory, second language acquisition theory and other language learning theories are the theoretical support for the application of cloud computing technology in English teaching. Constructivism emphasizes that language learning is not a passive absorption of knowledge, but a process in which learners actively construct their own knowledge system. The construction of knowledge system depends on the guidance of teachers, the interaction between learners and the environment, and the interaction between individuals and others, so that learners can establish appropriate connection between the old knowledge and the new knowledge, and integrate the old and new knowledge, so as to develop the knowledge system. The construction of cloud computing English education platform enables learners to interact with language learning environment anytime, anywhere, and gradually improve their knowledge system in the flexible detection of old and new knowledge. Collaborative learning theory attaches importance to collaborative learning among groups or team members through competition, cooperation, interaction and other ways to achieve their common goals. Cloud computing platform provides a variety of interactive platforms and learning communities to achieve a wide range of interaction between learners from different regions, among which anonymous communication can help learners overcome various psychological barriers and achieve free and equal communication with teachers and learners. Although the specific theoretical interpretations of universal grammar theory, monitoring theory and environment theory are different, they all emphasize the importance of language learning environment and emotional factors to language learners. Through the establishment of a standard English language environment and its relaxed online and offline interaction, English cloud platform will play a positive role in promoting language learners' second language acquisition. The practice of cloud computing technology in English education is still in the exploratory stage [3]. English teaching researchers have made a preliminary exploration on the application of cloud computing in College English, business English and other specific English courses. The application of cloud computing technology in English teaching has changed the original English teaching concept. New teaching concepts based on cloud computing, such as English ubiquitous learning mode, personalized teaching, spatial teaching mode and mobile learning, have emerged as the times require. At the practical level, there are also cloud computing technology software such as juku correction network and Moodle cloud platform, which provide more convenience for English teaching and learning. Universities, scientific research institutions and computer enterprises have gradually carried out school enterprise cooperative development to promote the practical application of cloud computing in English teaching. The application of cloud computing in English teaching conforms to the law of English learning, and will play a positive role in the improvement of English teaching methods and learning effect. However, the application of cloud computing in English teaching is still in its infancy. At present, there are still some problems, such as the lack of compound talents in English and cloud computing technology, and the development of English teaching resources based on cloud computing.

4   Fuzzy algorithm in English Teaching

Classroom teaching quality evaluation belongs to the category of fuzzy evaluation, because different people may have different or even completely opposite evaluation results on the same class teaching activities, and the appearance of these evaluation results is not purely random. "On the contrary, it appears similar fuzzy and has no rules to seek. For this kind of evaluation which is mixed with personal subjective consciousness, it is not appropriate to use the traditional one-time quantitative or weighted average method of 21. Therefore, this paper puts forward a fuzzy evaluation model of classroom teaching quality to realize the teaching quality evaluation and improve the scientificity of classroom teaching quality evaluation. Classroom teaching quality evaluation uses the fuzzy algorithm in fuzzy mathematics [4]. Fuzzy algorithm is a valuable method for the evaluation problem which is difficult to quantify directly with accurate numbers. This method is to use a series of mathematical processing to make the factors with fuzzy and non quantitative characteristics have a certain form of quantitative expression, so as to provide a basis for comparison and discrimination of decision-making, and improve the scientificity and correctness of decision-making.

Given three sets: ① evaluation factor set

$$U = \{u_1, u_2, \cdots, u_m\} \tag{1}$$

② A collection of comments

$$V = \{v_1, v_2, \cdots, v_n\} \tag{2}$$

③ Weighted fuzzy subset

$$A = \{a_1, a_2, \cdots, a_m\} \tag{3}$$

and $\sum_{i=1}^{M} a_i = 1$, the weight of the i-th factor is shown.

Constructing membership fuzzy subsets R_i,

$$R_i = \{r_{i1}, r_{i2}, \cdots, r_{in}\} \tag{4}$$

An M × n fuzzy evaluation matrix R is constructed in U × V domain,

$$R = \left\{ \begin{matrix} r_{11} & r_{12} & \cdots & r_{1n} \\ r_{21} & r_{22} & \cdots & r_{2n} \\ \vdots & \vdots & \cdots & \vdots \\ r_{m1} & r_{m2} & \cdots & r_{mn} \end{matrix} \right\} \tag{5}$$

Calculation of fuzzy comprehensive evaluation value

$$S = A \bullet R = (a_1, a_2 \cdots a_m) = \left\{ \begin{matrix} r_{11} & r_{12} & \cdots & r_{1n} \\ r_{21} & r_{22} & \cdots & r_{2n} \\ \vdots & \vdots & \cdots & \vdots \\ r_{m1} & r_{m2} & \cdots & r_{mn} \end{matrix} \right\} \tag{6}$$

In the application of fuzzy algorithm, the key is to determine the membership degree, which reflects the position of the i-th evaluation in the comprehensive evaluation. The multi-level index system is commonly used in the teaching evaluation of teachers. According to the weight of all levels of indicators, the comprehensive evaluation S.

5 Suggestions on Promoting the Application of Cloud Computing in English Teaching

5.1 Creating a Team of Compound Teachers

For non computer major English subject managers and teachers, cloud computing belongs to interdisciplinary technology, and its software and hardware environment construction and application deployment are highly professional. As the demand and user of platform and application, English education practitioners do not have to understand its underlying technical architecture from a deep level, we should be familiar with and apply the basic principles of business. Only in this way can the demander participate in the whole process of platform requirement analysis, implementation and deployment, testing and tuning to business application [5]. English education practitioners can define the cloud computing application standards of this discipline together with cloud computing technicians, so as to ensure that the cloud platform is demand-oriented from the development stage, and make the platform and application based on cloud computing meet English teaching the characteristics of learning meet the requirements of English teaching. It can be seen that the key to promote the application of cloud computing technology in English is to cultivate a team of interdisciplinary teachers. To promote the application of cloud computing in English teaching, the construction of teachers' team is the fundamental element. To cultivate a compound teaching team of English subject and cloud computing technology, efforts should be made in three aspects: - to strengthen professional knowledge training, and to strengthen the understanding of the basic knowledge and concept of cloud computing by means of centralized organization and self-study [6–8]. The second is to actively participate in the project construction of cloud computing in the field of English education, practitioners must actively participate in it, so that the project results can meet the actual needs of English teaching, and practitioners can greatly improve the knowledge level of cloud computing. Third, to strengthen the practical application of English education, practitioners should not only understand and support the application of cloud computing technology from the concept, but also strengthen the practice and application level in the actual teaching work, and constantly put forward higher requirements and standards according to the actual teaching, so as to promote the mutual promotion and common development of teaching and technology (see Fig. 1).

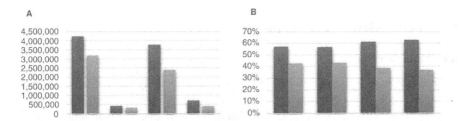

Fig. 1. Teaching and technology for students

5.2 Construction of Space Teaching Mode with Students as the Main Body

Through the construction of resource pool and cloud classroom, cloud computing breaks the space-time limitation of teaching from the technical level. Students can obtain the best learning resources anytime and anywhere, and the mode of teaching and learning will change fundamentally. Students can participate in the classroom learning of well-known schools at home and abroad in real time through computers, mobile phones, tablets and other media at home. In the future, they may interact with teachers and students in the classroom through virtual reality technology; Students can arrange and control their study time more freely. They don't have to worry about missing a certain course or lecture. They can learn the audio and video content of yesterday or even a few years ago through the resource pool. They can also leave messages and interact with teachers for certain knowledge points and doubts. The teaching mode of English has also changed. It is only a link in the process of English teaching to maximize the use of students' learning time and truly make the teaching take students as the main body. In English teaching, the space teaching mode should recommend and share the resources in the teaching resource pool to students according to the characteristics of the students [5, 6, 9]. In the cloud classroom, homework should be arranged, interactive communication and evaluation should be carried out to guide students to carry out self-learning after class, anytime, anywhere and pertinently(see Fig. 2).

Fig. 2. Simulation for space teaching mode

6   An Overview of Ecolinguistics

6.1   Main Overview

In recent decades, it has developed into a discipline to study the interaction between language and its living environment. There are two most famous models in the circle of ecological Linguistics: the Haogen model (dangerous metaphor) and the Halliday model (non dangerous metaphor). In fact, it is linguists and anthropologists such as Walgreen who first put forward the term of ecological linguistics, not Haogen or Halliday. But these two models are the most well-known in ecolinguistics, representing two research approaches. In the 1970s, Professor Hogan of Stanford University proposed the concept of eco linguistics. He believed that eco linguistics studies the interaction between any specific language and environment, and compares the relationship between language and environment to that between animals, plants and natural environment. Halliday's model emphasizes the influence of language on the living environment of human beings and believes that the language used by human beings will have a direct impact on the ecology of human society. From the perspective of eco linguistics, College English teaching mainly studies the process of the interaction between various ecological factors in teaching, including teachers, learners, teaching environment and teaching methods.

6.2 Domestic Main Research

In recent years, there are many and novel researches on Eco linguistics in China, such as the rise and development of Huang Guowen's eco linguistics, He Wei's eco discourse analysis model construction, Hu Gengshen's "applied translation studies from several eco translatological perspectives", etc. There are also many researches on College English teaching from the perspective of eco linguistics, such as song Tiehua's exploration of ecological College English classroom teaching in local colleges, Wang Yanping's reform of College English under the guidance of eco linguistics, etc. However, these studies mainly focus on the level of College English Teaching in universities. Relatively speaking, there are few studies on College English Teaching in Independent Colleges from the perspective of eco linguistics. Over the years, the state has vigorously supported the development of independent colleges, requiring local independent colleges to adapt to local conditions and develop their own characteristics [6, 7, 10]. College English Teaching in independent colleges is also an important part of higher education. Therefore, analyzing and solving the problems existing in College English Teaching in Independent Colleges from the perspective of eco linguistics will help to improve the teaching efficiency of teachers and the learning efficiency of students, and promote the sustainable development of College English teaching.

7 Problems in College English Teaching in Independent Colleges from the perspective of Eco Linguistics

7.1 Teachers are Lack of Quality

College English teaching from the perspective of eco linguistics is a micro ecosystem, which includes many ecological factors, the most important of which are teachers and students. Relatively speaking, due to the short running time of independent colleges, the main body of teachers is young postgraduates and lecturers. Among the five independent colleges in Gansu Province, 67% are lecturers in Longqiao xuexiao Foreign Language Department of Lanzhou University of Finance and economics, 83.3% are lecturers in Changqing College of Lanzhou University of Finance and economics, 72.5% are lecturers in Bowen xuexiao Foreign Language Department of Lanzhou Jiaotong University, and 70% are teachers with sub senior titles or below in Zhixing College of Northwest Normal University, There are 7 teachers in the school of foreign languages, School of technology and engineering, Lanzhou University of technology with the title of deputy senior or above. Most public institutions of higher learning mainly have the title of associate professor or above, or the proportion of associate professor or above is larger than that of independent colleges, such as Lanzhou University in Gansu Province, Northwest Normal University, Lanzhou University of science and technology, Lanzhou University of Finance and economics, Lanzhou University of Arts and Sciences, etc. Therefore, the independent college teachers are lack of professional quality compared with the first two universities [11, 12]. In the College English Teaching of Longqiao College of Lanzhou University of Finance and economics, some teachers, due to the lack of professional quality, are limited to the text itself, unable to effectively explain the culture, politics, history and other aspects involved in the text, so as to expand students' knowledge.

7.2 Imbalance of Teaching Environment

A good teaching environment is the basis of creating a good atmosphere for College English learning. First of all, the financial funds of independent colleges are mainly raised by social organizations and individuals. Compared with the public colleges, the teaching funds are relatively insufficient, which leads to the loss of teaching environment for students to read. Even some of them are relatively old and cannot meet the needs of students. Independent college teaching equipment is relatively lacking and old, College English learning is inseparable from multimedia equipment, especially listening learning. Some colleges and universities equipped with listening multimedia resources sometimes have problems in the process of class, and even the phenomenon of listening equipment in short supply, these problems need teachers to spend a certain amount of time to deal with, delay the progress of teaching. The teacher resources of independent colleges are also out of balance. Most of the teachers have large class hours, and there are many classes and classes, which cannot create a good teaching environment. Secondly, independent colleges belong to private colleges, so the competition pressure is relatively large. In order to enhance competitiveness, independent colleges focus on the completion of various indicators, such as CET-4 and CET-6 indicators [9]. The selected college English textbooks are close to the content of CET-4, and tend to be scientific and technological articles. As shown in Fig. 3. The content is relatively boring, teaching is full of pressure and obstacles, and cannot provide students with a relaxed and interesting teaching environment.

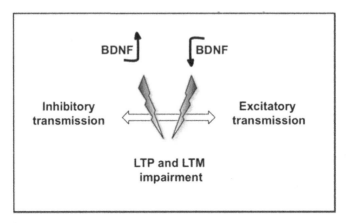

Fig. 3. Imbalance of teaching environment

8 Conclusions

The application of cloud computing in the field of education has very important value and significance, and will also provide strong support for the development of education. The application value of cloud computing in English discipline is also highlighted. At present, the construction and application of cloud computing are still in its infancy.

English educators should improve their understanding, actively strengthen their study and research, and accelerate the promotion of practice and application. Combined with the characteristics of cloud computing technology and the characteristics of English discipline, further deepen the application of cloud computing, so as to continuously improve the level of English teaching.

References

1. Liu D.: Research on English learning mode based on cloud computing and constructivism: taking the learning mode under Edmono platform as an example. J. Hubei Radio Telev. Univ. (9) (2014)
2. Peng, Y.: Research on the integration of space teaching mode and College English Teaching. English Teachers (20) (2015)
3. Baoqing, H.: Basis of fuzzy theory. Wuhan University Press, Wuhan (2004)
4. Lei, P.: Research and development of comprehensive evaluation system of teaching quality in secondary vocational schools. Master's Thesis of South China University of Technology (2007)
5. Ministry of education of the people's Republic of China
6. Fang, W., Ruhai, H.E.: Research on teaching management based on the characteristics of independent college students. J. Anhui Agric. Univ. (Soc. Sci. Ed.) (2), 92–95 (2009)
7. Jinjun, W.: Ecolinguistics: a new perspective of linguistic research. J. Tianjin Univ. Foreign Lang. 1, 53–57 (2007)
8. Han, J.: Review of Ecolinguistics in China. Lang. Teach. Res. (4), 107–112 (2013)
9. Ruijuan, M.: Research on English teaching mode of eco linguistics and dynamic system theory. Educ. Theory Pract. 27, 47–49 (2013)
10. Haugen, E.: The Ecology of Language. Palo Alto: Stanford University Press (1972)
11. Jun, H.: Review of Ecolinguistics in China. Lang. Teach. Res. 4, 107–112 (2013)
12. Xiaojuan, W.: An analysis of improving the timeliness of College English classroom teaching from the perspective of eco linguistics. J. Beijing Jiaotong Univ. (Soc. Sci. Ed.) 02, 122–128 (2013)

Statistical Application of Mental Health Data of College Students Under the Background of Informationization

Yanan Li[✉]

Hubei College of Chinese Medicine, Hubei 434020, China

Abstract. Mental health is an important basic condition for college students to become adults. Educators gradually attach importance to strengthening the mental health education of college students. Traditional colleges and universities on mental health data only stay in the operation of adding, deleting and checking, and do not effectively analyze the potential psychological information of the data. This paper proposes a kind of psychological management system based on K-means clustering analysis method, which uses the idea of data mining to make secondary use of students' psychological data on the basis of traditional system functions. By optimizing the iterative process of K-means algorithm, the valuable part of a large number of precipitation students' psychological data is extracted, and the data model is established to provide decision-making guidance for managers, Scientific management of students' mental health process can not only effectively improve the overall efficiency of psychological counseling, but also play an early warning role in the prevention of risk factors.

Keywords: Data mining · Psychological management system · K-means algorithm

1 Introduction

College students are in the most important stage of life, they have high cultural knowledge and wonderful life experience. But in the face of social pressure and difficulties in life and employment, there are often psychological problems such as inferiority, autism, radicalism, seclusion, depression and so on. Many fields of society have carried out research on the psychology of contemporary college students. The research results show that the proportion of college students in China who need mental health treatment is gradually increasing. More and more college students' mental health problems have been paid attention to by many people in the society. Therefore, it is an inevitable trend to use data mining technology to analyze the mental health data of college students and get the corresponding solutions [1].

Influencing factors of College Students' psychological problems.

(1) Family factors. The behavior and performance of family members have a subtle impact on the growth of children. Children who grow up in a harmonious, friendly,

M. A. Jan and F. Khan (Eds.): BigIoT-EDU 2021, LNICST 391, pp. 566–571, 2021.
https://doi.org/10.1007/978-3-030-87900-6_65

positive and cheerful family atmosphere will have less psychological problems, and even if they have psychological problems, they will be easier to solve. But if there are some disharmonious factors in the family, such as parents' divorce, domestic violence, family disharmony and so on, children are prone to have psychological problems.

(2) Personal factors. University is a semi open society, students in this circle not only contact with students, teachers, but also with all kinds of people in society. Compared with the optimistic students, the introverted students are more likely to have inferiority complex in the process of communicating with others, and they are not confident in anything, which leads to a sense of frustration.

(3) Professional satisfaction. Some students are not satisfied with their major, even have the feeling of boredom and disgust, and have no clear goal for future development, they just study for the exam. But in this process, there will be a huge psychological gap. When reality and ideal contradict each other and cannot be solved, there will be huge psychological pressure, leading to the emergence of psychological problems.

(4) The interpersonal relationship is not harmonious. Bu Ren university means to live with other students. However, some students don't know how to get along with others better, which leads to two extreme phenomena: some students are generous and popular with others; some students don't know how to get along with others; Some students dare not communicate with others, resulting in inferiority, timidity, and further develop autism; What's more, they often have conflicts with their classmates because they can't deal with the relationship between them well, and then they are isolated by their classmates, causing psychological problems.

(5) Love problems caused by emotional distress. Emotional distress and emotional instability caused by love problems will also bring mental health problems to college students. College students are in adolescence, eager to get the attention of the opposite sex in the process of communication. However, due to the immaturity of psychology and the lack of scientific cognition, there are many unavoidable problems in the interaction between boys and girls.

(6) The psychological anxiety caused by the difficulty of employment. At present, there are millions of college graduates in China every year. In 2017, for example, the number of college graduates reached 7.95 million. In addition, college students who have graduated but not been employed in the past few years have joined the new round of employment. At the same time, in the process of choosing a job, we will encounter a variety of problems, such as dissatisfaction with the work unit and lack of experience, which will bring great psychological pressure to college students.

With the continuous innovation of information technology, all levels of society are facing the direction of comprehensive information development, including college mental health management. In the mental health management of colleges and universities, most schools only simply add, delete and modify the data of students' mental health, and obtain the surface information of data through simple statistical functions, but do not analyze and mine the students' mental health data substantially, so it is difficult to extract the hidden and valuable information from these massive data sets. In order to improve the efficiency of school mental health education, it is necessary to organize and analyze students' mental health data.

2 Overview of Data Mining and Clustering Analysis

2.1 Definition of Data Mining

At present, the society is in the stage of rapid development of information. People store different kinds of data. These data have increased at an unimaginable speed with the continuous accumulation of time. How to extract effective information from these massive data and make effective solutions to meet the future needs, The process of discovering potential value information from massive and complex data sets is called data mining. Mathematical methods are used to derive patterns and implied trends in the data. Because of the complexity of data processing and the huge amount of data to be processed, it is difficult to find the patterns in the data using the traditional data processing methods. So we try to establish the corresponding data mining model, using the data model to analyze and predict other data, we can find the information hidden in the mass of information; different ways of data mining, the results are not the same.

2.2 Related Definitions of Clustering

Clustering algorithm is an important branch of machine learning, which generally adopts unsupervised learning. Using clustering analysis algorithm, the data in the database can be divided into several categories. The distance between individuals in the same category is small, so the similarity of objects in the cluster is high; while the distance between individuals in different categories is large, which has great differences [2].

In clustering methods, the commonly used quantitative methods are as follows: absolute distance:

$$D(X, Y) = \left\{ \sum_{i=1}^{k} |X_i - Y_i| \right\} \tag{1}$$

Euclidean distance:

$$D(X, Y) = \left\{ \sum_{i=1}^{k} |X_i - Y_i|^2 \right\}^{\frac{1}{2}} \tag{2}$$

Chebyshev distance:

$$D(x, Y) = \left\{ \sum_{i=1}^{k} |X_i - Y_i|^{\infty} \right\}^{\frac{1}{\infty}} \tag{3}$$

2.3 Steps of Cluster Analysis

(1) Feature extraction: in order to divide the pattern set into different categories, the attributes of the pattern set are very important, and the similarity measure must be defined. The clustering algorithm is to classify the samples with similar characteristics into one

category according to the similarity measure between samples. Therefore, the results of clustering can reflect the inherent characteristics of samples. The related attributes are extracted from the samples as the attribute items of clustering. Another part of the clustering results have nothing to do with the class can not be used as a reference. This will improve the accuracy and robustness of clustering results.

(2) The choice of algorithm: no general clustering technology can explain the implied meaning of multidimensional data set. The choice of clustering algorithm will directly affect the results of clustering. According to the characteristics of data samples and the rules of class accumulation, we can choose different clustering methods.

(3) Parameter setting: select the algorithm to be used by parameter setting according to different applications. In the usual clustering analysis, the classification model needs to be initialized continuously. This will improve the accuracy of the classification model.

3   K-means Clustering Algorithm

3.1   Brief Introduction of K-means Clustering Algorithm

K-means algorithm, also known as k-means or K-means, is a classical clustering algorithm used by many clustering tasks. It is the distance from the data point to the prototype as the objective function of optimization. In this algorithm, the data set is divided into different categories through the iterative operation of function limit, which makes the evaluation index J minimum and the generated class distance close.

3.2   Algorithm Examples

The partition clustering method includes the following three points when clustering data sets:

(1) Selecting a certain distance as the measure between samples, the search process of K-means clustering algorithm is limited to a part of all possible partition space. If the sample similarity between each class is very low, K-means algorithm can often achieve good results. However, if the similarity between the samples is high, further clustering may occur. Therefore, it is possible to obtain the local rather than global minimum solution of the scoring function because of the convergence of the algorithm [3].

(2) Select the criterion function. K-means clustering algorithm will be affected by the selected similarity measurement method. The commonly used similarity measurement method uses the sum of squared error criterion function to improve the clustering performance.

(3) The k-means algorithm is used to measure a certain point in the sample. When facing the clustering problem, the algorithm is more efficient to complete the task. Even in the face of large data sets, the algorithm has high scalability and efficiency.

4   Application of K-means Algorithm in College Students' Mental Health Management

Macro definition of mental health is: refers to a continuous, efficient and able to meet self needs of the psychological state. On the other hand, the definition of mental health is further strengthened on the micro level: it means that people can effectively coordinate cognition, emotion, thought, behavior and personality in the process of complete psychological activities, so as to adapt to society and keep pace with society. To judge whether the students have the basic mental health qualities are: social adaptability, personality quality, self-control, the ability to distinguish right from wrong, calm and so on. These are the basic criteria to judge the students' mental health [4].

The mental state of college students can often reflect their mental state. These factors are often very important to college students. In essence, students' knowledge acquisition and self-development is also a continuous process of psychological activities and psychological development. In the process of receiving education, students constantly choose and absorb the knowledge they provide, so that their psychology gradually becomes mature from childish. Meanwhile, their psychological quality is constantly improved in this process. Colleges and universities vigorously promote mental health education to improve students' psychological quality, which is one of the effective ways to improve students' comprehensive quality.

The level of students' psychological quality is related to their mental health education environment. From the perspective of students, in the process of education, constantly affected by moral norms, social environment and family expectations and other factors, and improve their personality. From an objective point of view, students in contact with different values, constantly measure, evaluate and regulate the development of their own personality, when certain conditions are met, they will produce personality with personal characteristics,. However, mental health education not only has this kind of passive personality transformation, but also actively guides students in the process of transformation. There is no big deviation in the overall direction, so that students can understand themselves and further understand their own behavior, so as to achieve the purpose of psychological sublimation and personality improvement.

5   Conclusion

It absorbs the advantages of student information management system and integrates it into mental health management. It adopts BS architecture and JavaEE platform as support. Write based on SSH framework, use MySQL database to store data, Tomcat as container. It realizes the unified management of College Students' mental health. The use of MySQL and Java makes the system run well in all major operating systems and servers. At the same time, the B/S architecture ensures the convenience of system access, which can be operated by opening the browser. However, the introduction of SSH framework and Tomcat makes the system lightweight enough to ensure the access speed and system security.

References

1. Jiang, T.: Approaches and methods of College Students' mental health education. J. Ideol. Theor. Educ. **05**, 85–87 (2012)
2. Jiang, Q.: Construction of network mental health education system in Colleges and universities. Central South University (2012)

3. Dai, X.: On the mental health education of contemporary college students and the way of implementation. Jilin University (2005)
4. Mengxue, W.: Summary of data mining. Softw. Guide **10**, 135–137 (2013)

Author Index

Printed in the United States
by Baker & Taylor Publisher Services